Hypostyle hall of Temple of Amon, El Karnak, Egypt, the greatest Egyptian temple. The hall has dozens of columns, some 69 ft. high and almost 12 ft. in diameter, bearing incised inscriptions.

FUNK & WAGNALLS NEW ENCYCLO- PEDIA

VOLUME 8

DICTATING MACHINES

to EMBRYOLOGY

LEON L. BRAM
Editorial Director

ROBERT S. PHILLIPS
Editor

NORMA H. DICKEY
Executive Editor

FUNK & WAGNALLS, INC., NEW YORK

FUNK &
WAGNALLS
NEW
ENCYCLO-
PEDIA

LIST OF ABBREVIATIONS USED IN THE TEXT *

abbr.	abbreviated	fr.	from	OHG.	Old High German
AC; a-c	alternating current	Fr.	French	ON.	Old Norse
A.D.	*anno Domini*	ft.	foot	ONF.	Old Norman French
	(Lat., in the year	g	gram	O.T.	Old Testament
	of the Lord)	Gael.	Gaelic	oz.	ounce
alt.	altitude	gal.	gallon	P.M.	*post meridiem*
A.M.	*ante meridiem*	Ger.	German		(Lat., after noon)
	(Lat., before noon)	Gr.	Greek	Pol.	Polish
AM	amplitude modulation	Heb.	Hebrew	pop.	population
amu *or*	atomic mass unit	Hind.	Hindustani	Port.	Portuguese
AMU		h.p.	horsepower	prelim.	preliminary
anc.	ancient	hr.	hour	pron.	pronounced
Ar.	Arabic	Hung.	Hungarian	q.v.	*quod vide*
AS.	Anglo-Saxon	Hz	hertz or cycles		(Lat., which see)**
A.S.S.R.	Autonomous Soviet		per second	r.	reigned
	Socialist Republic	I.	Island	R.	River
at.no.	atomic number	i.e.	*id est* (Lat., that is)	rev.	revised; revision
at.wt.	atomic weight	in.	inch	R.R.	railroad
b.	born	Ind.	Indian	Rum.	Rumanian
bbl	barrel	Ir.	Irish	Russ.	Russian
B.C.	before Christ	It.	Italian	Ry.	railway
bd.ft.	board feet	K.	Kelvin	S.	south; southern
bev *or*	billion electron	kg	kilogram	sec.	second
BeV	volts	kHz	kilohertz	S.F.S.R.	Soviet Federated
b.p.	boiling point	km	kilometer		Socialist Republic
B.T.U.	British Thermal Unit	kw	kilowatt	Skr.	Sanskrit
bu.	bushel	kw hour	kilowatt hour	Sp.	Spanish
Bulg.	Bulgarian	lat.	latitude	sp.gr.	specific gravity
C.	centigrade	Lat.	Latin	sq.	square
cent.	century	lb.	pound	sq.mi.	square mile
Chin.	Chinese	long.	longitude	S.S.R.	Soviet Socialist
cm	centimeter	m	meter		Republic
Co.	County	M.	Middle	St.; Ste.	Saint
colloq.	colloquial	mev *or*	million electron	Sum.	Sumerian
cu.	cubic	MEV	volts	Sw.	Swedish
Czech.	Czechoslovakian	mg	milligram	temp.	temperature
d.	died	MHz	megahertz	trans.	translation
Dan.	Danish	mi.	mile	Turk.	Turkish
DC; d-c	direct current	min.	minute	U.K.	United Kingdom
Du.	Dutch	M.L.	Medieval Latin	U.N.	United Nations
E.	east; eastern	mm	millimeter	U.S.	United States
ed.	edition; editor	mod.	modern	U.S.A.	United States of
Egypt.	Egyptian	m.p.	melting point		America
Eng.	English	m.p.h.	miles per hour	U.S.S.R.	Union of Soviet
est.	estimated	Mt(s).	Mount, Mountain		Socialist Republics
ev *or*	electron volt	N.	north; northern	var.	variant
EV		Norw.	Norwegian	vol.	volume
F.	Fahrenheit	N.T.	New Testament	vs.	versus or against
fl.	flourished	OE.	Old English	W.	west; western
FM	frequency modulation	OF.	Old French	yd.	yard

FUNK & WAGNALLS
NEW ENCYCLOPEDIA

DICTATING MACHINES. *See* OFFICE MACHINES: *Oral Communications: Dictating Machines.*

DICTATOR, title of a magistrate in ancient Rome, appointed by the Senate in times of emergency, and ratified by the *comitia curiata*; (*see* COMITIA). The first such appointment, according to Roman historians, was made in 501 B.C.; the last responsible dictator was appointed during the Second Punic War, in 216 B.C. *See* PUNIC WARS. The dictator held office usually for six months, and during his term he was the chief magistrate of the state, with limited power over life and death. The civil jurisdiction was retained by the regular magistrates, who were subordinate to him, and his military jurisdiction was limited to Italian territory. According to the Roman orator, statesman, and philosopher Marcus Tullius Cicero (q.v.), the office was originally created to cope with civil disturbances. In the last years of the Republic, Roman politicians occasionally assumed the office of dictator with extralegal powers; notable among these were the general and statesman Lucius Cornelius Sulla (q.v.), whose dictatorship lasted from 82 to 79 B.C., and the statesman, soldier, and author Gaius Julius Caesar (q.v.), who became dictator for life in 45 B.C. The office was abolished after Caesar's death in 44 B.C.

In modern times men who have assumed sole power over the state have been called dictators; notable among these have been Porfirio Díaz of Mexico, Miguel Primo de Rivera and Francisco Franco of Spain, Kemal Atatürk of Turkey, Józef Pilsudski of Poland, Antonio de Oliveira Salazar of Portugal, Benito Mussolini of Italy, Adolf Hitler of Germany, and Joseph Stalin of the Soviet Union. Dictators have also come to prominence in Latin America, among them Juan Perón in Argentina, Fulgencio Batista in Cuba, and Rafael Trujillo in the Dominican Republic.

See FASCISM; TOTALITARIANISM. See also separate articles on the dictators mentioned and the *His-*

tory section of each of the countries named.

DICTIONARY, alphabetical compilation of the words of a language, or part of a language, giving their meanings, spellings, derivation, pronunciation, and syllabication; in a more general sense, the term "dictionary" is also applied to any alphabetically arranged compendium in which special terms or subjects are defined. Thus in recent times dictionaries have been devoted to science, biography, geography, mathematics, history, philosophy, slang, and other topics and terminologies.

History. The earliest-known dictionaries were found in the library of the Assyrian king Ashurbanipal (q.v.) at Nineveh. Dating from the 7th century B.C. and consisting of clay tablets inscribed in columns of the system of writing known as cuneiform (q.v.), they remain the chief key to a knowledge of Mesopotamian culture; *see* MESOPOTAMIA. Dictionaries appeared as early as the 5th century B.C. and were for the most part collections of rare words and meanings. Later dictionaries, most of them written after the 5th century A.D., were invariably written in verse and may be grouped in two general classes, lexicons of synonyms and of homonyms. Sanskrit works also include special dictionaries on botany, medicine, and astronomy, as well as Buddhistic glossaries in Pali, and polyglot lexicons in Sanskrit, Tibetan, Mongolian, and Chinese. The first attempt to gather the entire Arabic vocabulary into one work was made probably by Khalil ibn Ahmed of Oman (d. 791), who adopted an arrangement not alphabetical but based on certain phonetic and philological principles. The compilation of Hebrew dictionaries began about the 10th century (although some scholars place the beginnings of Hebrew lexicography between the 6th and 8th centuries), originating from, and being stimulated by, the study of Arabic.

The Greeks and Romans did not conceive of

Noah Webster at work on his dictionary.
Bettmann Archive

as Geoffrey the Grammarian, in Norfolk, England, and printed in 1449 by Wynkyn de Worde (q.v.), may be regarded as the first English dictionary; it consisted of Latin definitions of 10,000 English words and remained a leading wordbook for several generations. It was followed by the *Bibliotheca* (1538) of Sir Thomas Elyot (1490?–1546), another English-Latin dictionary, and by the *Dictionary in Englyshe and Welshe* (1547) compiled by William Salesbury (about 1520–1600). Robert Cawdrey (fl. 1604), in *The Table Alphabetical of Hard Words* (1604), produced the first dictionary giving definitions in English of English words. The word "dictionary" was first used by Henry Cockeram (fl. 1650) in *The English Dictionary* (1623). In 1656 Thomas Blount (1618–79) issued his *Glossographia,* also entirely in English with ". . . hard words together with Divinity Terms, Law, Physick, Mathematicks and other Arts and Sciences explicated". These early works characteristically confined themselves to "hard words" and phrases not generally understood, because the daily vocabulary of the language was not expected to require elucidation. The first attempt at a comprehensive inventory of the English language was the *Universal Dictionary of the English Language* (1721) by Nathaniel Bailey (d. 1742), reissued in 1731 as the *Dictionarium Brittanicum: A More Compleat Universal Etymological Dictionary Than Any Extant.* This work, which used quotations from established literary works to confirm and supplement definitions, served as the basis for the two-volume lexicon *A Dictionary of the English Language* (1755), by the lexicographer, essayist, and literary critic Samuel Johnson (q.v.), who extended the practice of using quotations. Johnson's dictionary remained the model of English lexicography for over a century. Dictionaries with guides to pronunciation were compiled by the British publisher David Buchanan (1745–1812). The actor Thomas Sheridan (1719–88) later compiled a *General Dictionary of the English Language* (1780) with the object of establishing a permanent standard of pronunciation. The most influential of the dictionaries concerned with pronunciation was the *Critical Pronouncing Dictionary and Expositor of the English Language* (1791) by the actor John Walker (1732–1807).

The most comprehensive lexicographic work in the English language, *A New English Dictionary on Historical Principles,* popularly known as *The Oxford English Dictionary,* was begun under the auspices of the English Philological Society in 1857. Sir James Augustus Henry Murray (q.v.) undertook editorship of the work in

a work containing all the words of their own or a foreign language, and their early dictionaries were merely glossaries of unusual words or phrases. The first Greek lexicon, a collection of terms used by the Greek poet Homer (q.v.), was compiled by the philosopher Apollonius during the 1st century B.C. One of the earliest works in Latin lexicography, by Verrius Flaccus (fl. 1st century A.D.), is *De Verborum Significatu,* which survives as part of the compilation of Pompeius Festus entitled *De Significatione Verborum*; this work, in which the words are arranged alphabetically, has furnished much information on antiquities and grammar. The earliest polyglot dictionary (1502) was the work of the Augustine monk Calepino (1435–1511). Originally compiled as a Latin-Greek lexicon, it was extended to include Italian, French, and Spanish; the 1590 Basel edition included eleven languages.

English Dictionaries. The precursors of English dictionaries appeared very early in the Old English period (*see* ENGLISH LANGUAGE: *History*) in the form of lists of relatively difficult Latin terms, chiefly Scriptural, with Anglo-Saxon explanations, or glosses. Around 1400, many such glosses were collected into the so-called *Medulla Grammatica.* The *Promptorium Parvulorum* ("Storehouse for Little Ones"), a redaction of the latter, compiled in 1440 by the Dominican monk Galfridus Grammaticus, also known

1879; the first ten volumes were published between 1884 and 1928, and the last three volumes were added in 1933. *The Compact Edition of the Oxford English Dictionary*, a two-volume micrographically reduced version of the thirteen-volume set, was published in 1971. The *Shorter Oxford Dictionary*, a two-volume abridgment with some revisions in pronunciation, was published in 1933. In 1936 Sir William A. Craigie (q.v.), who had collaborated on the editing of *The Oxford English Dictionary*, began a companion work, *A Dictionary of American English on Historical Principles*, which was completed in 1944.

American Dictionaries. The first historically important contribution to American lexicography was the volume *A New and Accurate Standard of Pronunciation* (1783), popularly known as *Webster's Spelling Book*. This work was issued by the educator and lexicographer Noah Webster (q.v.) as the first part of his *Grammatical Institute of the English Language* (1783–85). Although not a true dictionary, the *Spelling Book*, because of its American origin and emphasis and its simplification of English, became a household reference wordbook throughout the country. Its success led Webster to compile his first American lexicon, *A Compendious Dictionary of the English Language* (1806), an unpretentious enlargement of Entick's *Spelling Dictionary* (London, 1764). Webster's work also contained supplementary encyclopedic material on American life. Webster's major contribution to lexicography, *An American Dictionary of the English Language*, begun in 1807 and published in 1828, included typically American usage as distinguished from the British idiom, as well as 12,000 more words and 40,000 more definitions than had ever appeared in any dictionary of the English language. This work was never popular, however. It was soon followed by the *Comprehensive Pronouncing and Explanatory Dictionary of the English Language* (1830) by Joseph Emerson Worcester (q.v.). Worcester's dictionary, technically superior to and essentially a highly intelligent abridgment of Webster's, paved the way for modern collegiate dictionaries. Webster brought out a revised edition of his dictionary in 1841; since that time the *American Dictionary* has undergone various revisions and editions, including the contemporary *Webster's New International Dictionary of the English Language*, for which it provided the basis. In 1860 Worcester published *A Dictionary of the English Language* with the intention of displacing Webster's *American Dictionary*, which he considered frequently vulgar in vocabulary and pronunciation, but his work enjoyed little suc-

cess, partly because of the lethargy of its publisher. In 1891 *The Century Dictionary*, an American dictionary containing encyclopedic information, and edited by William Dwight Whitney (q.v.), the first great American linguist, was published in six volumes; it was a notable example in English of the French tradition of the combined dictionary-encyclopedia established by the French grammarian, lexicographer, and encyclopedist Pierre Athanase Larousse (q.v.). The *Standard Dictionary of the English Language*, published in one volume in 1895, rivaled Webster's *American Dictionary* in popularity for a time. Both the *Century* and the *Standard* have been frequently revised, editions of the former appearing in a two-volume abridgment called *The New Century Dictionary* and the latter as the Funk & Wagnalls *New Standard Dictionary of the English Language*.

With the publication of *Webster's Third New International Dictionary* in 1961 American lexicographers increasingly attempted to reflect contemporary usage. Many slang words and technical terms were included, and pronunciation schemes were adjusted to indicate regional speech patterns. New comprehensive dictionaries include *The Random House Dictionary of the English Language* (1966) and *The American Heritage Dictionary of the English Language* (1969). These works feature numerous pictorial illustrations, extensive etymologies, and definitions of contemporary sociological and political terms. Abridgments of the larger works include *Webster's Seventh New Collegiate Dictionary* (1967) and a shorter version of the Random House dictionary. Among the intermediate desk-size dictionaries are the *Webster's New World Dictionary of the American Language*; the *Standard College Dictionary*, published by Funk & Wagnalls; the *World Book Dictionary*; the *Random House College Dictionary*; and the Thorndike-Barnhart series of school dictionaries (*see* THORNDIKE, EDWARD LEE).

See also ENCYCLOPEDIA; ETYMOLOGY.

DIDACHE (Gr., "teaching"), *or* TEACHING OF THE TWELVE APOSTLES, ancient Christian document written in Greek and dealing with the organization, belief, and forms of worship of the early Christian Church. It probably originated in Syria in the 1st century, though some critics have estimated that it may have been written as late as the 3rd century. It was discovered in Constantinople (now İstanbul, Turkey) in 1873 by Bryennios (1833–1914), Metropolitan of Nicomedia, in an 11th-century manuscript; ten years later Bryennios published his find in the form of a small book, in Greek, and it has since been widely published in various translations.

The *Didache* contains a description of the Two Ways, one of life, the other of death, and instructions concerning the rites of baptism and of the Lord's Supper (qq.v.). *See also* APOSTOLIC CONSTITUTIONS.

DIDEROT, Denis (1713–84), French philosopher, born in Langres, and educated in Jesuit schools. He went to Paris in 1734, and spent ten years as an ill-paid tutor and hack writer. His reputation, which grew throughout the Age of Enlightenment (*see* ENLIGHTENMENT, AGE OF), began with the publication in 1746 of his *Pensées Philosophiques* ("Philosophical Thoughts"). In the same year he was invited to edit a French translation of the English *Cyclopedia* of Ephraim Chambers (d. 1740). Diderot, collaborating with the French mathematician Jean Le Rond d'Alembert (q.v.), converted the project into a vast, new, and controversial 35-volume work, *Encylopédie ou Dictionnaire Raisonné des Sciences, des Arts et des Métiers* ("Encyclopedia or Systematic Dictionary of Sciences, Arts and Trades"), usually called "The Encyclopedia". Aided by the most celebrated French writers of the day, including Voltaire and Baron de la Brède et de Montesquieu (qq.v.), Diderot used "The Encyclopedia" as a massive propaganda weapon against ecclesiastical authority and the semifeudal intellectual and social forms of French society. All editors and contributors of "The Encyclopedia", Diderot especially, became the object of clerical and royalist antagonism.

Such opposition delayed publication of "The Encyclopedia". Twice, in 1752 and in 1757, Diderot's opponents succeeded in revoking the royal decree granting permission for the work to proceed. In 1759, the Conseil du Roi formally suppressed the first ten volumes of "The Encyclopedia" published from 1751 onward and forbade further publication. Nevertheless, Diderot continued preparation of the remaining ten volumes and had them secretly printed. The work finally appeared in 1765, and miscellaneous supplements continued to be published until 1780. *See* ENCYCLOPEDIA.

Diderot's voluminous writings include the stories *Jacques le Fataliste* (1796) and *La Religieuse,* the latter an attack on conventual life. He wrote two plays, *Le Fils Naturel* (1757, "The Bastard Son") and *Le Pére de Famille* (1758, "The Father of the Family"), but they were unsuccessful. He was a pioneer in aesthetic criticism; he founded *Les Salons,* a journal for which, from 1759 to 1779, he wrote criticisms of the annual

Denis Diderot

exhibitions of paintings in Paris. His correspondence was practically unexcelled in an age of famous letter writers, and he was the author of numerous essays. His espousal of skepticism and rationalism (qq.v.) brought him the patronage of the "enlightened monarch" Catherine II (*see under* CATHERINE), Empress of Russia.

DIDO, in Greek mythology, legendary founder and queen of Carthage, and daughter of Belus, King of Tyre. When Dido's husband was killed by her brother Pygmalion, King of Tyre, Dido fled with her followers to North Africa. She purchased the site of Carthage from a native ruler, Larbus, who, when the new city began to prosper, threatened Dido with war unless she married him. Rather than subject either herself or her followers to these alternatives, Dido stabbed herself.

According to the Roman poet Vergil, the Trojan prince Aeneas (qq.v.), who later founded Rome, was shipwrecked at Carthage. He remained there with Dido, who had fallen in love with him, until commanded by the god Jupiter (q.v.) to abandon her and continue his journey. In despair at his departure, Dido killed herself on a funeral pyre. *See* AENEID.

DIDOT, name of a family of French printers and publishers. Its prominent members were: **François Didot** (1689–1757), born in Paris, the first notable member of the family. In 1713 he went into business as a publisher. Most famous of his publications is an edition (20 vol., 1747) of a collection of travels by his friend the French novelist Abbé Prévost (see PRÉVOST D'EXILES, ANTOINE FRANÇOIS).

François Ambroise Didot (1730–1804), son of François. He improved typefounding by championing the point system of type and was the first to print on vellum paper (1780).

Pierre François Didot (1732–93), son of François, he added improvements to the art of printing, and is noted for a folio edition (1788) of *The Imitation of Christ* by the German Catholic ecclesiastic Thomas a Kempis (q.v.).

Pierre Didot (1761–1853), eldest son of François Ambroise, he printed highly ornate versions of the classics, which came to be known as the Louvre editions.

Firmin Didot (1764–1836), son of François Ambroise, he invented the term and process of stereotyping, translated several Greek and Latin poets, and wrote the tragedies *The Death of Hannibal* (1817) and *The Queen of Portugal* (1824).

Henri Didot (1765–1852), son of Pierre François, he printed minute editions of many standard works, which he engraved in microscopic type.

DIDRIKSON, Babe. See ZAHARIAS, BABE DIDRIKSON.

DIE, any of several types of tools used for the shaping of solid materials, especially those employed in the pressworking of cold metals.

In presswork, dies are used in pairs. The smaller die, or punch, fits inside the larger die, called matrix or, simply, die. The metal to be formed, usually a sheet or precut blank, is placed over the matrix, which is mounted on the press bed. The punch is mounted on the press ram and is forced down by hydraulic or mechanical pressure.

A number of different forms of dies are employed for different operations. The simplest are piercing dies, used for punching holes in the blank. Blanking dies are employed to stamp out special shapes of sheet metal for later operations. Bending and folding dies are designed to make single or compound bends in the blank. Hollow, cupped shapes are formed by drawing dies; if the hollow is deep, redrawing dies are often employed in a second operation after the hollow shape has been partially formed. To produce a reduced section on a hollow part, such as the neck of a rifle cartridge, special reducing dies are used. When a finished part must have a bulge at the bottom or in the middle, hydraulic dies are usually employed; in these the punch is

replaced by a ram that forces oil or water into the part under pressure, thus forcing the metal outward against the matrix. Curling dies form a curved edge or flange on a hollow part; a special form of curling die called a wiring die is used to form a wired edge in which the outside edges of the metal are tightly wound around a wire inserted for strength.

In manufacturing it is common practice to combine several dies in one combination die or progressive die. A combination die is designed to perform more than one of the above operations in one stroke of the press, whereas a progressive die permits successive forming operations with the same die.

In coining, metal is forced to flow into two matching dies, each of which bears a reverse or intaglio of the relief pattern to be formed on the finished coin or part. See MINT.

Wire-Drawing Dies. In the manufacture of wire, a drawplate is usually employed. This tool is a metal plate containing a number of tapered or bell-shaped openings, successively finer in diameter; the openings are known as wire dies. In use, a piece of metal is pulled through the largest die to make a coarse wire. This wire is then drawn through the next smaller opening, and then through the next, until the wire is reduced to the desired measurement. Wire-drawing dies are subject to extreme wear and are commonly made from very hard materials, such as tungsten carbide or diamonds. See WIRE.

Thread-Cutting Dies. For cutting threads on bolts or on the outside of pipe, a special form of die is used. A thread-cutting die is usually made of hardened steel in the form of a round plate with a hole in the center. The hole is threaded in the appropriate form and pitch, and the threads are cut away for part of their circumference, leaving longitudinal grooves in the die. These grooves give clearance for the chips of metal formed when a thread is being cut. To cut an outside, or male, thread, the die, heavily lubricated with cutting oil, is simply screwed onto an unthreaded bolt or piece of pipe in the same way in which a nut is screwed onto a bolt. The corresponding tool for cutting a female thread, as inside a nut, is called a tap.

See DIE-CASTING; FORGING.

DIE-CASTING, method of producing castings of nonferrous metals in which the molten metal is forced into a steel mold or die (q.v.) under pressure. Zinc alloys are most widely used today, followed by brass and aluminum alloys and other nonferrous metals. The advantage of die-casting over the older method of casting with sand molds (see FOUNDING) is that castings

can be produced quickly and economically on automatic machines. By the use of multiple dies a number of similar parts can be cast in one operation. Die castings can be produced with finer finish and detail than ordinary sand castings and are often used for precision parts.

DIEFENBAKER, John G(eorge) (1895–   ), Canadian statesman, prime minister from 1957 to 1963.

Diefenbaker was born in Grey Co., Ontario, on Sept. 18, 1895, and educated at the University of Saskatchewan. A noted trial lawyer, he was elected to the Federal Parliament as a Conservative in 1940. Known as a maverick inside his own Progressive Conservative Party, he was finally elected its leader in 1956. In the 1957 general election, Diefenbaker defeated the Liberal Party, in power for 22 years, and became prime minister of a minority government. In 1958 new elections gave his party an overwhelming parliamentary majority.

It was Diefenbaker's misfortune to govern Canada during a period of high unemployment and economic recession. Despite a successful farm policy and the passage of a Canadian Bill of Rights, his government lost its parliamentary majority in the elections of June, 1962. It lost the general elections of 1963 on the issue of Canadian acquisition of nuclear weapons from the United States, which the Liberals desired and Diefenbaker opposed. He remained leader of the Progressive Conservatives until deposed by a party convention in 1967.   R.Bo.

DIÉGO-SUAREZ, town in Madagascar, and capital of Diégo-Suarez Province, on Diégo-Suarez Bay, an inlet of the Indian Ocean, 300 miles N.E. of Majunga and 470 miles N.E. of Antananarivo. The town, which possesses one of the finest harbors in the world, is a naval base and fueling station and the third largest port of the republic. It exports cattle, corn, coffee, vanilla, pepper, sugar, peanuts, and cloves. Important industries of the area are shipbuilding, meat processing, tuna fishing, salt extraction, and the manufacture of oxygen. The bay was the site of a French pirate colony, Libertalia, at the end of the 17th century; the modern town was not founded until the 1800's. From 1885 to 1895 it was the capital of the French colony of Diégo-Suarez. The town is also called Antsirane or Antsirana. Pop. (1970 est.) 46,886.

DIELECTRIC, substance that is a nonconductor of electricity and that will sustain the force of an electric field passing through it. This property is not exhibited by conducting substances. Two oppositely charged bodies placed on either side of a piece of glass (a dielectric) will attract each other, but if a sheet of copper is interposed between the two bodies, there will be no attraction.

In most instances the properties of a dielectric are caused by the polarization of the substance. When the dielectric is placed in an electric field, the electrons and protons of its constituent atoms reorient themselves, and in some cases molecules become similarly polarized. As a result of this polarization, the dielectric is under stress, and it stores energy which becomes available when the electric field is removed. The polarization of a dielectric resembles the polarization that takes place when a piece of iron is magnetized. As in the case of a magnet, a certain amount of it remains when the polarizing force is removed. A dielectric composed of a wax disk that has hardened while under electric stress will retain its polari-

zation for years. Such semipermanently polarized dielectrics are known as electrets.

The effectiveness of dielectrics is measured by their relative ability, compared to a vacuum, to store energy, and is expressed in terms of a dielectric constant, with the value for a vacuum taken as unity. The values of this constant for usable dielectrics vary from slightly more than 1 for air up to 100 or more for certain ceramics containing titanium oxide. Glass, mica, porcelain, and mineral oils, often used as dielectrics, have constants ranging from about 2 to 9. The ability of a dielectric to withstand electric fields without losing its insulating properties is known as its dielectric strength. A good dielectric must return a large percentage of the energy stored in it when the field is reversed. The fraction lost through so-called electric friction is called the power factor of the dielectric. Dielectrics, particularly those with high dielectric constants, are used extensively in all branches of electrical engineering, where they are employed to increase the electrical capacity of condensers. *See* CONDENSER, ELECTRICAL; ELECTRICITY; INSULATION: *Electric Insulation.*

DIELS, Otto Paul Hermann (1876–1954), German chemist, born in Hamburg, and educated at the Royal Joachimsthalsches Gymnasium and at the University of Berlin. He joined the staff of the Chemical Institute of the University of Berlin in 1899, rose to the rank of titular professor in 1906, and became associate professor in 1914. Diels served as professor of chemistry and director of the Chemical Institute at the University of Kiel from 1916 until 1945, when he became professor emeritus. In 1950, he was awarded, together with his former pupil, the German chemist Kurt Alder (q.v.), the Nobel Prize in chemistry. The award was presented for their joint development of diene synthesis, the chemical process by which complex organic compounds are artificially formed. Diene synthesis, known also as the Diels-Alder reaction, was processed from 1927 to 1928 and still has important applications in present-day technology, especially in the manufacture of synthetic rubber and plastics. Diels also discovered the highly reactive substance carbon suboxide (C_3O_2) in 1906.

DIEM, Ngo Dinh. *See* VIETNAM: *History.*

DIEN BIEN PHU. *See* INDOCHINA: *History: The Indochinese War, 1946–54;* VIETNAM, WAR IN.

DIEPPE, city and seaport of France, in Seine-Maritime Department, on the English Channel, about 33 miles N. of Rouen. Dieppe is on the W. shore of the mouth of the Arques R., at the foot of the steep slopes of a range of chalk hills. The harbor is protected by jetties, and an inner har-

John G. Diefenbaker UPI

bor is equipped with several tidal basins that are accessible at flood tide to vessels drawing up to 20 ft. of water. Regular steamship service is maintained with the town of Newhaven, in Sussex, England. Dieppe also has railway connections with the interior of France. Leading imports are iron, coal, cement, timber, textiles, and machinery. Exports consist chiefly of wines, brandies, potatoes, fruits, and local manufactures. Among the principal manufactures are rope, lace, porcelain, tobacco products, lumber, and horn, bone, and ivory products. Dieppe is one of the most popular summer resorts in France. Outstanding points of interest are a beach promenade, the 14th-century Saint Jacques Church, a castle dating from 1435, and the 16th-century church of Notre-Dame de Bon Secours.

Dieppe has figured prominently in the maritime history of France since the 12th century. The English sacked the town in 1339, occupied it from 1420 to 1435, and laid unsuccessful siege to it in 1442. During the 16th century, Dieppe was a prosperous commercial center, frequented by merchants and pirates, and was a center of the Reformation (q.v.) in France. After the revocation in 1685 of the Edict of Nantes (q.v.), the Catholics took severe reprisals against the town. In 1694, during the war against the Grand Alliance (q.v.), Dieppe was virtually destroyed by the English and the Dutch. The city was rebuilt after the Peace of Ryswick; see RYSWICK, PEACE OF. The Germans occupied Dieppe during the Franco-German War (q.v.) and again, in June, 1940, during World War II (q.v.). On Aug. 19, 1942, the port, transformed by the Germans into one of the most strongly fortified points on the English Channel, was raided by an Allied commando force of about 5000 Canadians, 2000 British, and small detachments of American Rangers and Free French. The purpose of the raid was to obtain data for the subsequent invasion of Europe. Casualties were heavy, especially among the Canadians. The Germans were expelled from Dieppe in September, 1944. Pop. (1968) 29,873.

DIES, Martin, Jr. (1900–72), American legislator, born in Colorado (now Colorado City), Texas, and educated at the former Wesley College, the University of Texas, and the former National University, Washington, D.C. Admitted to the bar in 1920, Dies served in the United States House of Representatives from 1931 to 1945 and from 1953 to 1959. A member of the Democratic Party, he was instrumental in the establishment of a special committee of the House of Representatives to investigate un-American activi-

ties (a standing committee of the House, it became the Committee on Internal Security in 1969 and was dissolved in 1975); Dies was the first chairman. From its inception in 1938, the committee investigated activities such as those of the German-American bunds and their connection with the National Socialist Party of Germany, and Communist activities in the entertainment industry and in labor unions. After his retirement from Congress, Dies resumed the practice of law in Lufkin, Texas. His father, Martin Dies (1870–1922), was a member of the U.S. House of Representatives from 1909 to 1919.

DIESEL, Rudolf Christian Karl (1858–1913), German inventor, born in Paris, France. After studying in England, he attended the Polytech-

Rudolf Diesel   Science Museum, London

nic School in Munich, where he settled in 1893. In 1892 he patented an internal-combustion engine employing autoignition of fuel. Additional research led him to the construction of the first successful diesel engine, an engine utilizing low-cost fuel, which he built while associated with the Krupp (q.v.) firm in Essen. In 1913, while on a voyage to England, he was drowned in the English Channel. See INTERNAL-COMBUSTION ENGINE: *Diesel Engines*.

DIESEL ENGINE. See INTERNAL-COMBUSTION ENGINE: *Diesel Engines*.

DIET. See NUTRITION, HUMAN; VITAMIN.

DIET, term applied to the legislature (q.v.) of certain states or nations. The term is commonly used as the English name for the legislatures of several foreign countries.

The first governmental body to be called a diet originated in the Frankish tribal councils (*see* Franks). The princes and nobles, both clerical and secular, of the Holy Roman Empire (q.v.) met in an imperial diet called the *Reichstag.* By 1300 this body had acquired three principal components: the electors (who elected the king), the princes and nobles, and the town delegates. Among the most important sessions of the Reichstag were the diets of Worms (1521), Spires (1529), and Augsburg (1530), all of which had the primary aim of suppressing the Protestant Reformation. By the Treaty of Westphalia (1648), the diet became merely an assembly of ambassadors of the German princely states, with very little power. The national assembly of Japan, established in 1889, is also called the diet.

DIETRICH, Marlene (1904–), American actress, born Maria Magdalene Dietrich in Berlin, Germany, and trained for the stage at the Berlin school of the German theatrical director Max Reinhardt (q.v.). During the 1920's she became an important performer in the Berlin theater and in silent films. In 1924 she married the German motion-picture casting director Rudolf Sieber. The American motion-picture director Josef von Sternberg (1894–1969) cast her in the leading female role of *The Blue Angel,* filmed in Berlin during 1929–30, with both German and English versions being made at the same time. Her haunting and sensuous singing and acting in this film created a sensation. As a result, Miss Dietrich was brought to the United States, where she starred in a series of films under von Sternberg's direction, including *Morocco* (1930) and *The Devil Is a Woman* (1935). For other directors she appeared in *Desire* (1936) and *Destry Rides Again* (1939). She early denounced the nationalistic tendencies prevailing in post-World War I Germany and became an American citizen in 1937. During World War II she made more than 500 appearances before American troops overseas. Her postwar films include *Witness for the Prosecution* (1958) and *Judgment at Nuremberg* (1961). In 1953 she made her American cabaret debut in Las Vegas, Nev., and in 1967 she made her New-York-City theatrical debut playing a six-week engagement of her internationally-acclaimed song recital.

DIFFERENCE, in arithmetic and ordinary mathematics, the amount by which one quantity is larger or smaller in magnitude than another of the same kind (*see* Subtraction). When the term difference is used with reference to series or sequences (*see* Sequence and Series), or in such expressions as difference function or difference equation, it takes on a specialized meaning. In a sequence, such as the sequence of the squares of the whole numbers:

$$1, 4, 9, 16, 25, 36, \ldots .$$

the differences between consecutive terms yields a new sequence:

$$3, 5, 7, 9, 11, \ldots \ldots$$

called a sequence of first differences. Taking the differences between the consecutive terms of this sequence results in a sequence of first differences of first differences, called a sequence of second differences:

$$2, 2, 2, 2, \ldots \ldots \ldots$$

In a similar manner, sequences of third, fourth, or nth differences might be formed, depending upon the original sequence. Sequences of differences may be used to find the nth term, or the sum of the first n terms, of the original sequence.

The study of sequences of differences and their implications and uses is called the calculus of finite differences. Certain calculating machines, particularly difference engines, are based upon the principle of differences. *See* Arithmetic Progressions; Geometric Progression.

DIFFERENTIAL. *See* Automobile: *Construction: Power Transmission.*

DIFFERENTIAL CALCULUS. *See* Calculus.

DIFFRACTION, in physics, phenomenon of wave motion (q.v.) in which a wave of any type spreads after passing the edge of a solid object, or after passing through a narrow slit, instead of continuing to travel in a straight line. As the waves spread, they tend to cancel out or reinforce each other in different directions, and cause the characteristic rippled patterns readily visible in water waves or light waves, and detectable in radio or sound waves; *see* Interference; Interferometer; Light; Radio; Sound.

The spreading out and blurring of light by diffraction limits the useful magnification of a microscope or telescope (qq.v.), so that details smaller than about a half wavelength of light, or ten millionths of an inch, cannot be seen in a microscope. Diffraction is also the process by which light is sorted out in a diffraction grating (q.v.), reflecting different colors of the spectrum in different directions. *See also* Color; Electromagnetic Radiations; Optics; Spectrum.

DIFFRACTION GRATING, optical device used to determine the different wavelengths or colors contained in a beam of light (q.v.); *see* Color; Diffraction; Optics. The device usually consists of a reflecting surface on which many thousands of very narrow parallel grooves have been made close together. A beam of light directed at such a surface is scattered or diffracted in all directions at each groove, the light waves reinforcing each other in certain directions and canceling out in other directions. The direction of diffraction is different for each different wavelength.

Typical diffraction gratings are 3 or 4 in. wide and have 15,000 grooves per in. A high-quality grating is difficult to make, but similar effects of a simple nature can be observed on butterfly wings, fish scales, phonograph records, and other surfaces with fine scratches. The first crude diffraction gratings were made by the German physicist Joseph von Fraunhofer (q.v.) by winding fine wires on two identical parallel screws. Toward the end of the 19th century, the American physicist Henry Augustus Rowland (q.v.) produced very accurate diffraction gratings containing from 14,000 to 20,000 lines per inch. Today it is possible to control the grooves on diffraction gratings with the aid of optical interferometers, thus increasing the accuracy of the device; the invention of the laser (q.v.) has been useful in the construction of these interferometers; see INTERFERENCE; INTERFEROMETER. See also SPECTRUM.

DIFFUSION, in physical science, the smooth and even flow of energy or matter from a position of high concentration to a position of lower concentration, resulting in a homogeneous distribution. If one end of a rod is heated or electrically charged, the heat or electricity will diffuse from the hot or charged portion to the cool or uncharged portion. If the bar is made of metal, this diffusion will be rapid for heat and almost instantaneous for electricity; if the bar is made of asbestos, the diffusion will be slow for heat and extremely slow for electricity. Diffusion of matter is in general even slower. If a lump of sugar is placed in the bottom of a cup of water, the sugar will dissolve and slowly diffuse through the water; but if the water is not stirred it may be weeks before the solution approaches homogeneity. Even diffusion of one solid into another is possible. For example, if gold is plated on copper, the gold will diffuse slowly into the surface of the copper; however, diffusion of an appreciable amount of gold more than a microscopic distance normally requires thousands of years.

All of these types of diffusion follow the same laws. In all cases, the rate of diffusion is proportional to the cross-sectional area and to the gradient of concentration, temperature, or charge. Thus, heat will travel four times as fast through a rod 2 in. in diameter as through a rod 1 in. in diameter; and when the temperature gradient is 10° per in., heat will diffuse twice as fast as

when the gradient is only 5° per in. The rate of diffusion is also proportional to a specific property of the substance, which in the case of heat or electricity is called conductivity; in the case of matter, this property is called diffusivity or diffusion coefficient; see CONDUCTOR, ELECTRICAL; HEAT: *Transfer of Heat*; RESISTANCE. The amount of material that diffuses in a certain time, or the distance it traverses, is proportional to the square root of the time; thus, if it takes sugar one week to diffuse through water 1 in. from its starting point, it will take four weeks to diffuse through 2 in.

As distinguished from stirring, which is a process of mixing masses of material, diffusion is a molecular process, depending solely on the random motions of individual molecules. The rate of diffusion of matter is therefore directly proportional to the average velocity of the molecules. In the case of gases, this average speed is greater for smaller molecules, in proportion to the square root of the molecular weight, and is greatly increased by rise of temperature. Metallic thorium, for example, diffuses rapidly through metallic tungsten at temperatures in the neighborhood of 2000° C. (3632° F.); the operation of certain vacuum tubes is based on this diffusion.

If one molecule is four times as heavy as another, it will, in the case of gases, move half as fast, and its rate of diffusion will be half as great. Advantage can be taken of this difference to separate substances of different molecular weights, and in particular to separate different isotopes (see ISOTOPE) of the same substance. If a gas containing two isotopes is forced through a fine porous barrier, the lighter isotopes, which have a higher average speed, will pass through the barrier faster than the heavier ones. The gas with the greater concentration of lighter isotopes is then diffused through a series of such barriers for large-scale separation. This technique, known as the gaseous-diffusion process, is widely used in the separation of the fissionable uranium isotope U-235 from the nonfissionable U-238; see NUCLEAR ENERGY; ATOMIC WEAPONS. In another isotope-separation technique, called the thermal-diffusion process, the separation depends upon thermal effects exhibited by some gases; if such gases are enclosed in a chamber subjected to a temperature gradient, the heavy isotopes tend to concentrate in the cool region.

Biological Processes. Diffusion processes are of great biological importance. For example, digestion (q.v.) is essentially a process of chemically changing food so that it will be able to pass, by diffusion, through the intestinal wall into the bloodstream. Shock (q.v.), a condition that frequently follows surgery or injury, is a state in which the blood fluids have diffused excessively through the blood-vessel walls into the body tissues. Treatment of shock consists of injecting into the remaining blood fluid chemicals, usually in the form of blood, plasma, or plasmaexpanders, to compensate for the loss by diffusion and to alter pressure in the blood vessels, thus obviating further loss; see BLOOD: *Blood Transfusion.*

See also COLLOIDAL DISPERSION; OSMOSIS.

DIGESTION, process of changing food chemically for absorption by body tissues. The process varies among vertebrates; it is unique in ruminants, which use intestinal symbiotic organisms to prepare such foodstuffs as cellulose for utilization; see SYMBIOSIS. Digestion involves breaking organic compounds into simple soluble substances absorbable by tissues. This process involves catalytic reactions between ingested food and enzymes (see ENZYMES: *Properties of Enzymes*) secreted into the intestinal tract (see INTESTINE). Digestion of fatty substance appears to involve the assembly of bile salts, phospholipids, fatty acids, and monoglycerides permeable to intestinal cells. Other nutrients such as iron and vitamin B_{12} (see VITAMIN) are absorbed by specific "carrier proteins" that make them transferable by the intestinal cells. The process described here is typical of all vertebrates except ruminants (see RUMINANTIA).

Digestion includes both mechanical and chemical processes. The mechanical processes include chewing to reduce food to small particles; the churning action of the stomach; and intestinal peristaltic action. These forces move the food through the digestive tract and mix it with various secretions. Three chemical reactions take place: conversion of carbohydrate (q.v.) into such simple sugars as glucose (q.v.; see SUGAR; SUGAR, METABOLISM OF); breaking down of proteins into such amino acids (qq.v.) as alanine; and conversion of fats into fatty acids and glycerol; see FATS AND FIXED OILS. These processes are accomplished by specific enzymes.

When food is eaten, the six salivary glands (q.v.) produce secretions that are mixed with the food. The saliva breaks down starches (see STARCH) into dextrin and maltose (qq.v.); dissolves solid food to make it susceptible to the action of later intestinal secretions; stimulates secretion of digestive enzymes; and lubricates the mouth (q.v.) and esophagus for the passage of solids.

Stomach and Intestinal Action. Gastric juice in the stomach (q.v.) contains agents such as hydrochloric acid and some enzymes, including pepsin, rennin, and lipase. Pepsin breaks proteins into peptones and proteoses. Rennin separates milk into liquid and solid portions; lipase acts on fat. Another function of stomach digestion is gradually to release partly digested materials into the upper small intestine, where digestion is completed. Some constituents of gastric juice become active only when exposed to the alkalinity of the small intestine; secretion is stimulated by chewing and swallowing and even by emotion precipitated by seeing or thinking of food; see REFLEX. The presence of food in the stomach also stimulates production of gastric secretions; in turn, these stimulate the production of digestive substances in the small intestine.

The most extensive part of digestion occurs in the small intestine; here most food products are further hydrolyzed and absorbed (see HYDROLYSIS). Predigested material supplied by the stomach is subjected to the action of three powerful digestive fluids: pancreatic fluid, succus entericus, and bile (q.v.).

Pancreatic fluid is introduced into the small intestine through several ducts; see PANCREAS. It contains enzymes that split complex proteins into simpler components that can be absorbed and used in reconstructing body proteins. Steapsin breaks down fat; amylopsin hydrolyzes starches into maltose. Other enzymes then break these into glucose and fructose (q.v.). Secretion of pancreatic juice is stimulated by the ingestion of proteins and fats.

Succus entericus is secreted by the small intestine. It contains a number of enzymes; its function is to complete the process begun by the pancreatic juice. The flow of succus entericus is stimulated by the mechanical pressure of food partly digested in the intestine.

The role of bile in digestion is little understood. Secreted by the liver and stored in the gall bladder (qq.v.), bile flows in response to fat in the stomach and upper intestine. Observation of obstructive jaundice (q.v.) makes it clear that digestion of fat is ineffective in the absence of bile.

Transport of the products of digestion through the wall of the small intestine may be either passive or active. Sodium (q.v.), glucose, and many amino acids are actively transported. The products of digestion are thus assimilated into the body through the intestinal wall, which is able to absorb nutritive substances selectively, rejecting other similar substances. The

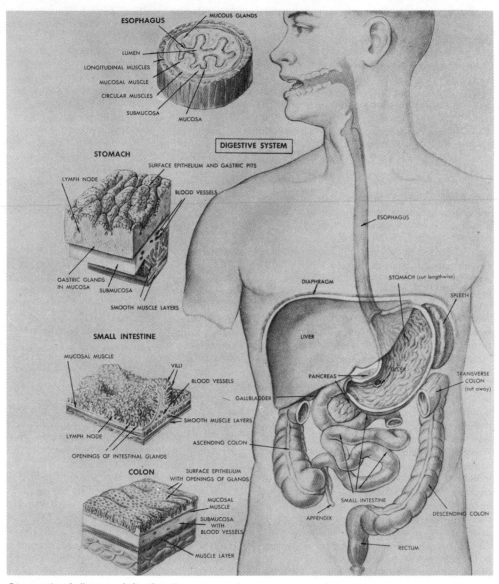

Cross-sectional diagram of the digestive system and the organs that constitute it. In man, digestion is carried on through a continuous tube beginning at the mouth, including the esophagus, the stomach, and the small and large intestines, and ending at the rectum. The liver, the gallbladder, and the pancreas also contribute to the digestive process.

TODAY'S HEALTH, published by the
AMERICAN MEDICAL ASSOCIATION

stomach and the colon or large intestine also have the ability to absorb water, certain salts, alcohol, and some drugs and crystalloids. It is believed that certain whole proteins are also passed through the intestinal barrier. Intestinal absorption has another unique feature. Many nutrients are more efficiently absorbed when the body need is greater. The absorptive surface of the intestine, which is in a sense an external body surface, is large. By extensive convolutions, it amounts to 1500 square feet in an adult.

The water-soluble substances, including minerals, amino acids, and carbohydrates, are transferred into the venous drainage of the intestine and through the portal blood channels (*see* VEIN) directly to the liver. Many of the fats, however, are resynthesized in the wall of the intestine and are picked up by the lymphatic system (*see* LYMPH; LYMPHATICS), which carries them into the systemic blood flow as it returns through the vena caval system (*see* HEART), bypassing an original passage through the liver; *see* CIRCULATION OF THE BLOOD.

Many disorders of absorption are collectively called malabsorptive states. The most profound and difficult is known as sprue. *See* DEFICIENCY DISEASES; FOOD; NUTRITION, HUMAN; TRACE ELEMENTS.   G.V.M.

DIGGERS, during the English Commonwealth (1649–60), members of a communistic movement favoring the abolition of private ownership of land. The Diggers were deeply religious pacifists, and their doctrines were social and economic rather than political. They are often incorrectly identified with the Levellers (q.v.), whose program was chiefly political.

In April, 1649, a band of about forty Diggers, led by Gerrard Winstanley (1609–52) and William Everard, began to dig up uncultivated common land on Saint George's Hill in Cobham, Surrey. They worked for a week and erected tents for dwellings; as they prepared to cultivate a second hill, they were dispersed by government troops. Everard and Winstanley were arrested, tried, and sentenced to pay large fines. Despite government opposition to the experiment, the Cobham colony lasted until 1651. The Diggers founded several other colonies, none of which endured.

Winstanley wrote several pamphlets explaining the principles of the Diggers. Although he was devoutly Christian, he was against organized religion and the clergy, claiming that they supported the class structure of society. His last work, *The Law of Freedom in a Platform* (1652), explains his theory of a social system founded on communistic principles. The Digger movement was one of the influences leading to the development of 19th-century radical thought in Great Britain and of modern socialism.

DIGHTON ROCK, large boulder on the bank of the Taunton R., opposite Dighton, Mass. An ancient inscription on the rock has been the subject of much antiquarian study. Various scholars have attributed Norse, Phoenician, and Scythian origins to the inscription, but the most widely accepted belief today is that it is an American Indian carving.

DIGITALIS, scientific name of a genus of plants of the family Figwort Scrophulariaceae, and of a crude drug obtained from one species, the common foxglove, *D. purpurea.* The foxglove, introduced from Europe, is a self-seeding biennial or perennial herb, widely grown in gardens, and naturalized along roadsides and in meadows or logged-off areas, especially in the

Digitalis, Digitalis purpurea   Joy Spurr–Bruce Coleman, Inc.

western United States. The naturalized plant bears a showy terminal cluster of hanging, tubular, spotted, purple flowers. Cultivated varieties are of various colors and markings. The erect stems are about 3 ft. tall with numerous large, thick leaves at the base.

Digitalis purpurea has been employed by man for medicinal uses. With techniques of modern pharmacology, about a dozen steroid glycosides (q.v.) have been isolated from the leaves. The best known of these exert a twofold action on the heart which results in a more effective heartbeat. These medicines strengthen the force of contraction, and, at the same time, slow the beat so that diastole, the period of relaxation between beats, is lengthened. The heart muscle thus obtains more rest even though working harder.

Man and animals may be poisoned if more than a small amount of the active glycosides enters the system, either through overdose of the drug or by eating the foliage of the plant. Symptoms of poisoning include nausea, diarrhea, abdominal pain, gross disturbances in heartbeat and pulse, and if severe enough, convulsions and death.   J.M.K.

DIHANG. See BRAHMAPUTRA.

DIJON (Lat. *Divonense castrum*), city in France, and capital of Côte-d'Or Department, in the w. part of the Burgundian plain, at the junction of the Ouche and Suzon rivers, about 170 miles S.E. of Paris. It is important as a railroad center and has a port on the Burgundy Canal. Industrial products of Dijon are machinery, automobiles, bicycles, hosiery, leather, tobacco products, flour, bakery products, mustard, soap, and brandy. In addition, the city has large printing establishments, is a center of the wine trade of Burgundy, and has a considerable trade in wool and cereals.

Dijon was the capital of the former duchy and province of Burgundy, created in the 9th century. The city is the site of the 13th-century Cathedral of Saint Bénigne, named for the apostle of Burgundy, Saint Benignus, who, in the 2nd century, was martyred in Dijon. The remains of Philip the Bold (q.v.), Duke of Burgundy, are in the vault of the cathedral. The 13th-century Church of Notre-Dame is of Burgundian-Gothic architecture and other notable churches are Saint Michel, Saint Jean, and Saint Étienne, all dating from the 15th century. The town hall is built on the site of the old ducal palace and includes two towers, the kitchens, and the guardroom of the original structure. The 15th-century Palace of Justice is the former seat of the *parlement* of Burgundy. As capital of the duchy, Dijon was one of the great intellectual centers of France, and it is still an important educational center. The university, founded in 1722, has faculties of law, science, and letters. See BURGUNDY. Pop. (1968) 145,357.

DIKE, in flood prevention, a barrier used to control or confine water. See LEVEE.

DIKE, in geology, wall-like intrusion of igneous rock, cutting across other strata of preexisting rocks, originally formed by a flow of molten rock into a fissure in which it cooled and solidified. A dike may range from an inch to many thousand feet thick, and from a few feet to many miles long. Frequently the rock material of the dike is harder than the surrounding rocks and as a result it may be left standing by itself after the neighboring rock has weathered away. Similar intrusions of igneous rock which lie parallel to the enclosing layers are known as sills.

DILL, common name for an annual or biennial herb, *Anethum graveolens,* of the Parsley family Umbelliferae (qq.v.). It grows wild in grainfields of southern Europe, the British Isles, and the United States, and is also cultivated as an herb.

It has a strong, stimulating, aromatic taste; its leaves are used extensively for flavoring pickles and sauces. The oil and seeds serve to relieve abdominal gas in colic (q.v.).

DiMAGGIO, Joe, in full JOSEPH PAUL DiMAGGIO (1914–), American baseball player, born in Martinez, Calif. From 1932 to 1935 DiMaggio played with the minor-league San Francisco Seals team. In 1936 he began his major-league career as a centerfielder with the New York Yankees team of the American League. He remained with the Yankees until his retirement in 1952, with the exception of three years of service, 1943 to 1946, in the United States Army. During his major-league career he achieved a batting average of .325, and in 1941 established a record by hitting safely in fifty-six consecutive games. He was named most valuable player of the American League in 1939, 1941, and 1947. DiMaggio led the league in batting in 1939, 1940, and 1948. In 1955 he was elected to the Baseball Hall of Fame (*see* BASEBALL HALL OF FAME AND MUSEUM, NATIONAL). In 1967 he was named executive vice-president of the Oakland Athletics team of the American League. Two years later sportswriters and fans, in a national poll, named DiMaggio as the greatest living player in baseball.   B.K.K.

DIMENSION. *See* GEOMETRY: *Four-Dimensional Geometry.*

DIMITROV, Georgi Mihailov (1882–1949), Bulgarian Communist, born near Radomir. A printer by trade, he became a member of the central committee of the Communist Workers' Party in 1909. During an extended visit to Germany, probably undertaken to spread Communist propaganda, he was arrested on the charge of complicity in the burning of the Reichstag in Berlin. During his trial Dimitrov accused the National Socialist Party of deliberately staging the fire and the trial for political ends; (*see* NATIONAL SOCIALISM). He was acquitted and settled in the Soviet Union. From 1935 until 1940 he was secretary of the executive committee of the Communist International, and from 1937 until 1945 he was a member of the Supreme Soviet of the U.S.S.R. During World War II he was a leader in the Bulgarian resistance movement. He became premier of Bulgaria in 1946 and was a founder of the Cominform, successor to the Third International, (q.v.) in 1947.

DINARIC ALPS, mountain group in Yugoslavia, part of the eastern Alpine system, connecting the Julian Alps of N.E. Italy and N.W. Yugoslavia with the Balkan mountain system. The group extends in a S.E. direction to the Drin R. beyond the boundary of Albania, and rises to a height of more than 8000 ft. above sea level (Mt. Durmitor). The Dinaric Alps are characterized by massive limestone areas. The surface soil is thin, and many of the rivers rising in the group at high altitudes soon sink into cavities in the rocks and are lost until the waters reappear at lower levels along the Adriatic Coast. A few rivers, such as the Neretva, flow to the sea in precipitous gorges. The Dinaric Alps have almost no natural passes and constitute a barrier between the Adriatic and the interior of Yugoslavia. Arable lands lie chiefly in scattered depressions and along the seacost.

D'INDY, Paul Marie Théodore Vincent. *See* INDY, VINCENT D'.

DINESEN, Isak, pen name of BARONESS KAREN DINESEN BLIXEN-FINECKE (1885–1962), Danish writer, born in Ringsted. She studied painting in various European cities. In 1914 she married the Danish sportsman Baron Bror Blixen-Finecke and went to live in British East Africa (now Kenya) on a coffee plantation. After her divorce in 1921 she remained in Africa, returning to Denmark in 1931. Her first book of stories, *Seven Gothic Tales* (1934), dealt in highly polished and subtle prose with the world of the supernatural, as did most of her later fiction. *Out of Africa* (1938) was based on her experiences on the plantation. Her only novel, *Gengaeldesens* (1944; Eng. trans., *The Angelic Avengers,* 1947), was published under the pen name Pierre Andrézel; in allegorical terms it described the plight of Denmark during the German occupation in World War II.

Her later works include *Winter's Tales* (1943); *Last Tales* (1957), another collection of stories of the supernatural; and *Shadows on the Grass* (1960), sketches of African life. She wrote both the Danish and English versions of all her works.

Isak Dinesen   UPI

Dingo, Canis dingo   Russ Kinne — National Audubon Society

DINGO, common name for a wild dog, *Canis dingo,* found in Australia. It is about 2½ ft. long and 2 ft. high, with a reddish-brown coat and a bushy tail. The dog has small, erect ears and a sharp muzzle. In the wild state dingos run in packs and frequently raid herds of sheep. They may, however, be domesticated if captured when young. The origin of the dingo is not known. Many authorities believe that marsupials are the only mammals native to the continent and that the dingos were brought to Australia by prehistoric migrants from Asia. However, fossil remains of dingos have been discovered in deposits of the Pleistocene Period in Australia, so that it is possible that the animals are truly indigenous. Dingos are not found in Tasmania, New Zealand, or other surrounding regions.

DINGWALL. *See* ROSS AND CROMARTY.

DINIZ (Eng. *Denis*) (1261–1325), King of Portugal (1279–1325), the son of Alfonso III, King of

21

Portugal (*see under* ALFONSO). The reign of Diniz was notable for the termination of the wars between Portugal and the united kingdoms of Léon and Castile by intermarriage between the family of Diniz and that of Ferdinand IV, King of Léon and Castile (*see under* FERDINAND); and for the encouragement by Diniz of Portuguese agriculture, trade, and arts. He founded schools for the study of agriculture and improved methods of cultivation; because of his interest in agriculture he became known as *ré lavrador* ("farmer king"). A poet himself, he was a patron of artists and musicians and of education, establishing the University of Coimbra (at Lisbon, 1291; moved to Coimbra, 1306). He made a commercial treaty with England (1294) that benefited Portuguese trade, and he established a royal navy (1317). He was succeeded by his son, Alfonso IV, King of Portugal.

DINKA *or* **DENKA,** native people of the Republic of the Sudan, Africa; also, the Nilotic language they speak. The Dinka inhabit both sides of the White Nile R. They are the most important of the Nilotic Negro groups, and are noted for their good physique and valor, and their herds of cattle, sheep, and goats. *See* AFRICAN LANGUAGES: *The Nilo-Saharan Family;* RACES OF MANKIND: *Racial Classification: Negroid Race;* SUDAN, REPUBLIC OF THE: *The People.*

DINOSAUR, common name for Dinosauria, any of the large group of reptiles, now extinct, that flourished in the Mesozoic Era (q.v.). During that period they were the dominant form of land animal life; fossil dinosaur remains have been found throughout the world. The dinosaurs ranged in size from approximately 2 ft. in overall length to 80 ft. In general, the smaller species were the first to appear; the larger forms evolved later. The evolutionary history of the dinosaur lasted throughout the entire Mesozoic Era; the earlier forms made their appearance in the Triassic Period (q.v.), and the more advanced species flourished and finally died off in the Cretaceous Period (q.v.).

Dinosaurs exhibited great variety of form. The carnivorous species generally had short necks and walked on their hind legs. A long, bulky tail served as a counterbalance for their necks and heavy bodies when they stood erect. Their forelegs were small and weak, terminating in talon-like feet adapted for grasping. The herbivorous dinosaurs generally moved on four feet. Many later species were so heavy that some scientists believe they could not have walked for any

Skeleton of the dinosaur Tyrannosaurus rex
American Museum of Natural History

great distance on dry land and therefore spent most of their lives in swamps and shallow lakes, where mud and water gave them buoyancy. A number of the larger species had weak, pencil-like teeth adapted only for browsing on soft plant material. Some of the largest species had brains no larger than that of a dog. For example, the brain of the *Stegosaurus,* an animal the size of a small elephant, was no larger than a walnut. An enlargement of the spinal cord, called the ganglion, near the hip, controlled the movements of the hind limbs and the powerful tail.

Classification. Dinosaurs comprise two orders, the Saurischia and Ornithischia. The earliest saurischians were chiefly two-footed carnivorous animals belonging to the Theropoda, a group that included the largest carnivorous terrestrial animal, the *Tyrannosaurus.* This reptile, which lived toward the end of Mesozoic times, had an overall length of about 50 ft. and stood about 18 ft. high. Its massive head was about 4 ft. in length; its mouth was armed with sharp, daggerlike teeth. The *Tyrannosaurus* had a short neck, a heavy body, and a long tail. Other species of Theropoda included the giant *Allosaurus,* 35 ft. long, and a close relative, the *Gorgosaurus.*

The four-footed herbivorous species of Saurischia are usually classified as Sauropoda. In the Jurassic Period (q.v.) the sauropod dinosaurs reached the culmination of their evolutionary development with such giants as the *Brontosaurus;* the *Brachiosaurus,* the heaviest dinosaur; the *Diplodocus* (qq.v.); the *Cetiosaurus;* and the *Camarasaurus.*

The second order of dinosaurs, the Ornithischia, comprised only herbivorous species. This order included the *Iguanodon* and a number of armored dinosaurs such as the *Stegosaurus* and the *Ankylosaurus.* Some species of ornithischians developed two horns above the eyes and a third at the end of the nose; among these horned dinosaurs was the mighty *Triceratops.* The *Protoceratops,* a horned ancestral species, was a small dinosaur approximately 9 ft. long. Eggs of this reptile have been found in the Gobi desert; they are about 9 in. long.

It is not known why dinosaurs became extinct; no one factor alone could have been responsible. Their extinction was probably the result of a combination of circumstances, including geologic and climatic changes and the inability of such highly specialized animals to adapt themselves to a new environment (*see* ADAPTATION). The dinosaurs were traditionally thought to have no modern descendants, but new evidence has resulted in a theory that birds may have descended from theropod dinosaurs.

DINOSAUR NATIONAL MONUMENT, area in Utah and Colorado, noted for deposits of fossil remains and also for the scenic beauty of the canyons of the Yampa and Green rivers. The fossil remains discovered chiefly in the shale and sandstone of the area are of great scientific interest and include those of Dinosaurs, *Brontosaurs, Allosaurs,* flying reptiles, and other forms of prehistoric animal life; *see* DINOSAUR. Fossil remains were uncovered in the region from 1909 to 1923 by an expedition of the Carnegie Museum of Pittsburgh. A skeleton of a *Brontosaurus* unearthed in the area, 75½ ft. long and 20 ft. high, may be seen in that museum's Hall of Vertebrate Paleontology. The Smithsonian Institution and the University of Utah have also sponsored expeditions to the region. The monument, covering 48,143.21 acres in Utah and 149,121.92 acres in Colorado, was established in 1915. It is administered by the National Park Service (q.v.).

DINWIDDIE, Robert (1693–1770), colonial lieutenant governor of Virginia (1751–58), born near Glasgow, Scotland. In 1754 he dispatched a force under the command of Colonel George Washington (q.v.) to the Ohio R. valley to prevent the French from taking possession of that region. Subsequently the French attack on Washington's detachment at Fort Necessity, on the present site of Pittsburgh, marked the beginning of the French and Indian War (q.v.). Dinwiddie played an active part in the early campaigns of the war. In 1758 he resigned because of ill health and returned to England.

DIO CASSIUS or DION CASSIUS, surnamed COCCEIANUS (155?–235? A.D.), Roman historian and politician, born in Nicaea, in Bithynia. His maternal grandfather was the Stoic philosopher, Dion Chrysostomus (about 40–about 112 A.D.). Dio Cassius held office in Rome under the emperors Lucius Aelius Aurelius Commodus (q.v.), Publius Helvius Pertinax (126–193), Lucius Septimius Severus (q.v.), and Marcus Aurelius Alexander Severus (208?–235). Dio Cassius twice attained (220 and 229) the consulship. He is best known as the author of a history of Rome in eighty books, written in Greek. Only eighteen of these books are extant in their entirety, but fragments of some of the others and epitomes by later writers have been preserved. All are valued by modern historians as source material, especially for the history of the last years of the Roman Republic and the first years of the Roman Empire.

DIOCESE (Gr. *dioikesis,* "administration"), in the Christian Church, the territory over which a bishop (q.v.) exercises ecclesiastical jurisdiction.

The term was used as early as the time of the Greek orator Demosthenes (q.v.) to signify the treasury or department of finance. But in the organization of the Roman Empire introduced by Emperor Diocletian (q.v.), the designation "diocese" was applied to the larger political divisions, which were subdivided into provinces, or eparchies. About the middle of the 5th century, the dioceses of the Empire were Asia, Pontus, the East, Thrace, Macedonia, Dacia, Illyria, Italy, Africa, Gaul, Spain, and Britain. The government of the Christian Church, as established by Constantine I (q.v.), Emperor of Rome, adopted this division, and "diocese", as well as other terms borrowed from the government of the Roman Empire, passed over into ecclesiastical usage. The term was first applied in an ecclesiastical context to a collection of metropolitan churches, or provinces (parishes), each under the charge of an archbishop (q.v.). Later applied to a single metropolitanate, or province, it finally came to signify the local jurisdiction of any bishop of any rank.

DIOCLETIAN, in full GAIUS AURELIUS VALERIUS DIOCLETIANUS (245–313), Emperor of Rome (284–305). He was born of humble parents in Dalmatia, and became an officer in the Roman army. When Marcus Aurelius Numeri-

Roman bust of Diocletian at the Capitoline Museum in Rome.   Bettmann Archive

anus, Emperor of Rome, died in 284, Diocletian's troops proclaimed him emperor. Carinus, the brother of Numerianus, contested his claim and defeated the forces of Diocletian in battle in Moesia in 285, but was killed by one of his own officers, and Diocletian's rule was assured. He was immediately faced with uprisings in many parts of the vast empire and selected as his colleague a Pannonian officer, Marcus Aurelius Valerius Maximianus, better known as Maximian (q.v.), first giving him the title of Caesar (q.v.) in 285, and the title Augustus in 286. In order to obtain more assistance in defending and administering the empire, and also in order to assure a peaceful succession to the throne, Diocletian selected two more colleagues in 293, each with the title of Caesar. He adopted one of them, Gaius Galerius Valerius Maximianus, better known as Galerius (d. 311) as his son; Maximian adopted the other, Constantius I (*see under* CONSTANTIUS). The empire was divided into 101 provinces, grouped into twelve larger divisions, each called a diocese (q.v.), and into four major parts, over each of which a Caesar or Augustus was placed. All edicts were signed jointly by the four rulers, but the superior rank of the Augusti and the supremacy of Diocletian over the others were retained.

The fourfold division facilitated the maintenance of order; victories over enemies of Rome in Africa and in Persia extended the boundaries of the empire, which subsequently were strengthened and fortified. The administrative reorganization of the empire resulted in the centralization of control, on an equal basis, over all its vast territories, and correspondingly ended forever the primacy of Italy. Rome was replaced as capital city of the empire by Mediolanum (Milan) in Italy, the headquarters of Maximian; Nicomedia in N.W. Asia Minor, the capital of Diocletian; Augusta Trevirorum (Trier) in Germany, where the rule of Constantius was based; and Sirmium (Mitrovica) in Pannonia, the administrative center of Galerius. In spite of the fourfold division, organization became increasingly autocratic. Diocletian introduced Eastern ceremonies into his court, and adopted the appellation of Jovius (a form of the name Jupiter), assigning to Maximian that of Heraclius (from Hercules). His regulations were rigid and oppressive, especially the so-called Edict of Diocletian (301), which fixed the maximum prices of commodities and wages throughout the empire. However, the edict proved unenforceable and was soon abandoned. Harsh changes in the system of collecting taxes, however, proved to be more lasting. They made civil officials responsible for payment of fixed sums, leaving officeholding in the hands of the most rapacious citizens and laying the basis for peonage and serfdom. Diocletian's reign is especially remembered, however, for the renewed persecution of Christians, which he authorized beginning in 302. Three years later he abdicated his power, and forced Maximian to follow suit, leaving the succession, as he had planned, to Galerius and Constantius. Diocletian retired to his country estate at Salona, in Dalmatia. *See* ROME, HISTORY OF: *Decline and Fall.*

DIODE. *See* ELECTRONICS: *Diode.*

DIODORUS SICULUS (fl. 1st cent. B.C.), Greek historian, born in Agyrium, Sicily. He lived in the times of the Roman emperors Gaius Julius Caesar and Augustus (qq.v.), traveled in Asia and Europe, and lived a long time in Rome, collecting the material for his great work, *Historical Library,* a history of the world in forty books, from the Creation to the Gallic Wars of Julius Caesar. Of this great work, the first five books are extant in their entirety, the next five are wholly lost, the next ten complete, and of the remainder of the work, considerable fragments have been preserved.

DIOECISM (Gr. *di,* "two"; *oikos,* "house"), condition in which the male and female reproductive organs of a species of plant are borne on different individual plants. In certain species of ferns and mosses, for example, one gametophyte bears the antheridium, or male reproductive organ, and the female organ, the archegonium, is borne on another. In dioecious seed plants, such as the willows, the stamens and pistils occur on separate plants. In monoecious (*see* MONOECISM) plants, such as the oaks, the staminate (male) and pistillate (female) flowers are borne on different branches of the same plant. Where both these organs occur in a single flower (as is usually the case), the plant is said to be monoclinous. *See* PLANT MORPHOLOGY; POLLINATION.

DIOGENES (412?–323 B.C.), Greek philosopher, born in Sinope, in Pontus. His father, Icesias, a banker, was convicted of debasing the coinage, and Diogenes, being implicated in the matter, was obliged to leave Sinope. He traveled to Athens, where he convinced the Cynic philosopher Antisthenes (q.v.) to take him as a disciple. Diogenes then plunged into a life of austerity and self-mortification. He wore coarse clothing, ate the plainest food, and accepted relief from the Athenians. He slept on the bare ground, in the open streets, or under porticoes. His eccentric life did not, however, lose him the respect of the Athenians, who admired his contempt of

comfort. Practical good was the chief aim of his philosophy; and he did not conceal his disdain for literature and the fine arts. He laughed at men of letters for reading the sufferings of Odysseus (*see* ODYSSEY) while neglecting their own, and at orators who studied how to enforce truth but not how to practice it. On a voyage to Aegina he was seized by pirates and carried to Crete, where he was sold as a slave. When asked what business he was proficient in, he answered, "In commanding." He was purchased by a certain Xeniades of Corinth, who recognized his worth, set him free, and made him tutor to his children. According to a popular story, on one occasion Diogenes had an interview with Alexander III, King of Macedonia. The king opened the conversation with "I am Alexander the Great," and the philosopher answered, "And I am Diogenes the Cynic." Alexander then asked him in what way he could serve him. "You can stand out of the sunshine," the philosopher replied. Alexander is said to have been so struck with the Cynic's self-possession that he went away remarking, "If I were not Alexander, I should wish to be Diogenes." Diogenes died at Corinth, according to tradition, on the same day as Alexander. Diogenes was wholly concerned with practical wisdom and established no system of philosophy. (*See* CYNICISM.) Certain literary works were early attributed to Diogenes, but they were recognized even in ancient times as spurious.

DIOMEDE ISLANDS, two rocky islands in the Bering Strait, about halfway between Alaska and Siberia. They were discovered about 1728 by the Danish explorer Vitus Bering (q.v.). Little Diomede (2.4 sq.mi.) belongs to the United States, and Big Diomede or Ratmanov (11.3 sq.mi.), to the Soviet Union. The islands are about 2 mi. apart and lack harbor facilities. Between them runs the international date line (q.v.), part of which forms the boundary between the U.S.S.R. and the U.S. Fewer than one hundred Eskimos are said to inhabit the islands.

DIOMEDES, in Greek mythology, king of Argos, and the son of Tydeus, one of the warriors known as the Seven Against Thebes (q.v.). Diomedes was one of the outstanding Greek heroes of the Trojan War (q.v.). He killed several of the outstanding Trojan warriors, and, with the assistance of the goddess Athena, he wounded Aphrodite, goddess of love, and Ares (qq.v.), god of war, both of whom were aiding the Trojans. When he returned from the war and discovered that his wife had been unfaithful, Diomedes went to Apulia, where he remarried.

DION CASSIUS. *See* DIO CASSIUS.

DIONNE QUINTUPLETS (b. 1934), five Canadian girls, Cécile, Yvonne, Annette, Émilie, and Marie, born in Callander, Ontario, to Oliva Dionne and his wife Elzire, then the parents of six other children. Born prematurely, the infants collectively weighed 11½ lb. after 6 days. The successful multiple birth (q.v.) of identical quintuplets was unique at that period, and the infants' survival made medical history. Dr. Allan Roy Dafoe (1883–1943), the Canadian physician who delivered the quintuplets and kept them alive, won great acclaim for his skill. From the moment of birth, the girls attracted worldwide attention. In an attempt to prevent exploitation of the Dionne family, the Ontario government in 1935 designated the quintuplets wards of the state and placed them in a separate nursery. By 1938 a trust fund totaling $600,000 had accumulated for the girls from gifts donated by people all over the world. After an extensive court battle, the Dionne girls returned to live with their parents. The quints' solidarity was broken in August, 1954, when Émilie died while residing in a Roman Catholic convent in Québec. The youngest, Marie (Dionne) Houle, died in 1970. *See also* MULTIPLE BIRTHS.

DIONYSIA. *See* DIONYSUS.

DIONYSIUS, Saint (d. 268), pope from 259 until 268. After the persecutions of Decius (q.v.), Emperor of Rome, 250–51, Dionysius reorganized the Christian Church.

DIONYSIUS, name of two tyrants of Syracuse, in Sicily.

Dionysius the Elder (about 430–367 B.C.), tyrant (Gr. *tyrannos,* applied to one who usurps power) (405–367 B.C.). He was of humble birth, and worked as a government clerk before he seized power. Until 398 B.C. he maintained peace with the Carthaginians, who ruled a large part of the island of Sicily, but thereafter he conducted wars against them and against the Greek cities of S. Italy. His first campaigns (until 392 B.C.) against the Carthaginians were victorious. He made Syracuse the strongest power in Greek Italy, capturing the city of Rhegium in 386 B.C. His later wars with Carthage were unsuccessful, and he lost the territory west of the Halycus R. previously won by the Syracusans and their allies. He made use of mercenaries both as colonists and as fighters. Dionysius was also a patron of the arts and a playwright. He often competed in the dramatic festivals at Athens.

Dionysius the Younger (fl. 4th cent. B.C.), tyrant (367–56 B.C.; 347–44 B.C.), son of Dionysius the Elder. He ruled at first under the supervision of his uncle, the Syracusan philosopher Dion

(408?–355 B.C.), who served as regent. During this period, at Dion's request, the Greek philosopher Plato (q.v.) visited Syracuse, attempting unsuccessfully to educate Dionysius to his ideals of kingship. At the behest of an envious courtier, the Greek historian Philistus (d. 356 B.C.), Dionysius banished Dion in 357 B.C. Dion raised an army, defeated Dionysius in battle, and drove him into exile. Dionysius returned to Syracuse in 346 B.C., nine years after Dion had been assassinated. His second period of rule was arbitrary and unpopular, and the people of Syracuse welcomed the intervention of the Corinthian general Timoleon (d. 337 B.C.?), who captured Dionysius about 344 B.C. and sent him into exile.
See SICILY: *History;* SYRACUSE.

DIONYSIUS OF ALEXANDRIA, Saint, often known as DIONYSIUS THE GREAT (fl. 3rd cent.), Christian theologian. A pupil of the great churchman Origen (q.v.), he was placed in charge of the catechetical school in Alexandria, Egypt, in 231. Sixteen years later he was made bishop of Alexandria. Under the persecutions of Decius (q.v.), Emperor of Rome, beginning in 251, he sought refuge in the desert. He was banished six years later when Valerian (q.v.) was emperor. In 260 Dionysius returned to Alexandria. He participated in the controversies of his period, particularly in that concerning the status of those, known as *lapsi* (Lat., "fallen ones"), who had foresworn their faith during persecution; Dionysius advocated that the *lapsi* be treated with leniency.

DIONYSIUS OF HALICARNASSUS (fl. 1st cent. B.C.), Greek historian and critic. Many of his critical works are extant, including *The Arrangement of Words, On Imitation,* and *Commentaries on the Attic Orators.* He is best known as the author of *Roman Antiquities,* a history of his adopted city to the year 264 B.C. Nine of the twenty books have been preserved in their entirety; portions of the rest are extant or have been epitomized by later writers. While not authoritative by modern standards, his history is valued as a source dealing with a period about which little written material survives.

DIONYSIUS THE AREOPAGITE (fl. 1st cent. A.D.), member of the Areopagus (q.v.) in Athens and convert to Christianity through the preaching of Saint Paul (q.v.), the Apostle, as related in Acts 17:34. Nothing more is definitely known about him. He is reputed to have been the first bishop of Athens and to have been martyred there in the reign of Domitian (q.v.), Emperor of Rome. Another tradition confuses him with the apostle to France, Saint Denis (q.v.).

Throughout the Middle Ages a body of Greek writings that modern scholars identify as the work of a 6th-century Neoplatonist (*see* NEOPLATONISM) was ascribed to Dionysius. These writings include *The Celestial Hierarchy* and *The Ecclesiastical Hierarchy*, works dealing respectively with the three triads of orders of angelic beings and with their earthly counterparts; *The Divine Names,* a treatise on what Biblical appellations of the Deity can teach respecting His nature and attributes; and *Mystic Theology,* in which the author expounds a form of intuitive mysticism.

These pseudo-Dionysiac writings, which may have been written in Syria or Egypt, were first cited in 553 at the second Council of Constantinople (*see* CONSTANTINOPLE, COUNCILS OF). Their influence is apparent in the theological system of the 8th-century doctor of the Eastern Church, John of Damascus (q.v.). In the West they were unknown until early in the 7th century, but later they exerted a vast influence upon the thought of Christian Europe. In the 9th century they were translated into Latin by the Scottish theologian Johannes Scotus Erigena (q.v.), and in this more accessible form they furnished inspiration to the Scholastic theologians, notably Saint Thomas Aquinas (q.v.), and to the English humanists John Colet (q.v.) and William Grocyn (1446?–1519). From them, theologians and artists derived a conception of angels and were introduced to the ideas of Neoplatonism. The influence of these writings is plainly discernible in *The Divine Comedy* (q.v.) of the Italian poet Dante Alighieri (q.v.) and in the works of the English poet John Milton (q.v.). The Dutch humanist Desiderius Erasmus (q.v.) was among those who first cast doubt upon the assumption that Dionysius was the author of these writings.

DIONYSUS, in Greek mythology, god of wine and vegetation, who showed mankind how to cultivate grapevines and make wine. He was good and gentle to those who honored him, but he brought madness and destruction upon those who spurned him or the orgiastic rituals of his cult. According to tradition Dionysus died each winter and was reborn in the spring. To his followers, this cyclical revival, accompanied by the seasonal renewal of the fruits of the earth, embodied the promise of the resurrection of the dead. The yearly rites in honor of the resurrection of Dionysus gradually evolved into the structured form of the Greek drama (*see* DRAMA: *Greek Drama*), and important festivals were held in honor of the god, during which great dramatic competitions were conducted. The most important festival, the Greater Dionysia,

A statue of Bacchus, or Dionysus, by the Italian Renaissance artist Michelangelo.

was held in Athens for five days each spring. It was for this celebration that the Greek dramatists Aeschylus, Sophocles, and Euripides (qq.v.) wrote their great tragedies. After the 5th century B.C. Dionysus was known to the Greeks as Bacchus. For myths relating to Dionysus, *see* BACCHUS.

DIOPHANTINE ANALYSIS, in mathematics, branch of number theory concerned with determining the solutions in integers of algebraic equations in two or more unknowns. Such problems were treated by the ancient Greek mathematicians Pythagoras, Diophantus (qq.v.), and others.

Typical problems in Diophantine analysis would be to find two integers such that the sum of their squares is a square (3 and 4, or 5 and 12); or to find two integers such that the sum of their cubes is a square (1 and 2); or three integers such that their squares are in arithmetic progression (1, 5, and 7). In algebraic terms, the three examples call for integers x, y, z, . . . , such that $x^2 + y^2 = z^2$; $x^3 + y^3 = z^2$; and $x^2 + z^2 = 2y^2$, respectively. Usually an attempt is made to determine if a problem has infinitely many or a finite number of solutions, or none. Recent approaches to problems of this sort involve the use of high-speed computers to find solutions or to establish counter-examples to the conjectured theory.

See also FERMAT'S LAST THEOREM; INDETERMINATE EQUATION. J.Si. & J.D.M.

DIOPHANTUS (fl. 3rd cent. A.D.), Greek mathematician. He lived in Alexandria, Egypt, where he occupied himself chiefly with Diophantine analysis, earning the title "Father of Algebra". He wrote the Arithmetica, of which only six of thirteen books have survived.

DIOPSIDE, mineral of the pyroxenes (q.v.) group, which crystallizes in the monoclinic system. It is essentially a calcium magnesium silicate, with a hardness of 5 to 6, and a sp.gr. of 3.2. It is usually white, gray, yellow, or light green in color, but sometimes, owing to the presence of iron, it is dark green or nearly black. Diallage, a laminated variety of diopside, is usually of the darker shades. Diopside is a common mineral, often occurring in limestone and dolomite. Transparent, oily, green crystals, especially those occurring in Saint Lawrence County, N.Y., have been found sufficiently large and clear to be cut as gems.

DIOR, Christian (1905–57), French couturier, born in Granville, and educated for the diplomatic service at the École des Sciences Politiques. He began working in the fashion industry in the 1930's and opened his own salon in Paris in 1946. The so-called new look, featuring a long, full-cut skirt, was introduced by Dior in 1947. It revolutionized women's dress and reestablished Paris as the center of the fashion world, and his designs continued to hold a leading role in international fashion. At the time of his death Dior salons had been opened in twenty-four countries.

Dior was succeeded by his protégé, the French couturier Yves-Mathieu St. Laurent (1936–), who headed the Dior empire for three years; he in turn was followed in 1960 by the French couturier Marc Bohan (1926–). Under their direction the Dior name remained associated with fashion leadership.

DIORITE, name given to several closely related igneous rocks, usually gray or dark gray in color. The rocks are crystalline, coarsely granular, and composed mostly of silica and alumina, with some iron oxides, lime, and magnesia. The most common species of diorite contain plagioclase feldspar and hornblende. Other diorites contain biotite, quartz, or various ferromagnesian silicates. See separate articles on most substances mentioned; compare GABBRO.

DIOSCOREACEAE, or YAM, family of monocotyledonous herbs in the order Liliales. Plants in this family have dioecious flowers, twining stems, and leaves with a network of small veins. Some varieties are poisonous. Among the important genera are Dioscorea and Tamus. See YAM; compare SWEET POTATO.

DIOSCORIDES, Pedanius (fl. 1st cent. A.D.), Greek physician, born in Anazarbus, in Cilicia. He accompanied the Roman armies as physician through many countries and collected information on plants. He wrote De Materia Medica ("On Medical Matters"), a book that was long considered authoritative on both botany and medicine.

DIOSCURI. See CASTOR AND POLLUX.

DIPHTHERIA, acute and highly infectious disease, affecting children particularly, characterized by the formation of a false membrane in the passages of the upper respiratory system. The cause of the disease is an organism, Corynebacterium diphtheriae, called the Klebs-Löffler bacillus after the German pathologist Edwin Klebs (1834–1913), who discovered it in 1883, and the German bacteriologist Friedrich August Johannes Löffler (1852–1915), who isolated it in the following year.

The diphtheria bacilli enter the body through the mouth and nose and attack the mucous membranes, where they multiply and secrete a powerful toxin. Beginning about five days after exposure, a gray-white exudate is formed where the bacteria attack the walls of the nose and throat. This exudate increases in size and thickness, becoming a grayish false membrane that adheres to the mucous membrane and may block the air passages, causing asphyxiation. When such a blockage occurs, it is necessary to pass a metal-lined vulcanite tube through the mouth and into the trachea to permit the passage of air, a surgical procedure known as intubation. Even when the false membrane does not grow to this extent, victims of the disease sometimes die from the effects of the toxin absorbed from the bacilli. In nonfatal cases of diphtheria there is often an aftermath of paralysis of the eyes, legs, or one side of the body. Paralytic symptoms, however, are usually not permanent.

Before the development of diphtheria antitoxin in 1894 by Pierre Paul Émile Roux (1853–1933) and Emil Adolph von Behring (q.v.), the mortality rate from the disease averaged 35 percent and was as high as 90 percent in cases of diphtheria of the larynx. The universal use of antitoxin in treatment has cut the mortality rate to approximately 5 percent. Inactive toxin-antitoxins and toxoids have also been developed and have greatly reduced the incidence of the disease by making possible the immunization of children. Another weapon against diphtheria is the Schick test for determining whether an individual is susceptible to the disease; see SCHICK, BÉLA. By a program of testing, immunizing, and treatment with antitoxin, diphtheria has been brought under control in the United States and most other parts of the world.

DIPLODOCUS, extinct reptile, one of the largest of the dinosaurs, of the suborder Sauropoda. It lived during the Jurassic Period, inhabiting the western part of what is now the United States. Fossil specimens indicate that the reptile attained lengths up to 87 ft., which made it one of the longest of the known terrestrial animals. It was relatively slender, however, and somewhat less bulky than the related *Brontosaurus* (q.v.). The *Diplodocus* was a quadruped with a long neck, a low body, and a long tail. A vegetarian, it had a small head with slender teeth and probably grazed in marshes and shallow water where buoyancy would support part of the weight of its great body. See DINOSAUR.

DIPLOMACY, art of managing relations with other nations and of adjusting differences by negotiation, with the aim of protecting the national interest of the home country. Foreign policy, which is based on the national interest at any given time, is carried out through diplomacy. When diplomacy fails, war may result.

Every nation has had to arrange to gather information about and negotiate with the sovereign groups around it; evidence of ancient diplomacy appears in writings on Assyrian tablets, for example, and in the epics of the ancient Greek poet Homer (q.v.). The practical rules and methods of modern diplomacy, however, took shape beginning in the 15th century as the great nations of Europe were developing.

Changes in the language diplomatic agents use for interviews, negotiations, and treaties mirror changes in the prevailing balance of power. In the feudal period when the Church was the unifying force, Latin was used. By the 17th century when France was the leading power, French had become the universal diplomatic language. It remained so through the 19th century, although English gained in importance with the power of Great Britain and then of the United States. After World War I English was officially put on a par with French in diplomatic practice by agreement of the Paris Peace Conference. In the United Nations (q.v.), French, Russian, Chinese, English, and Spanish are the official languages.

The practical rules of diplomacy, which include the titles, ranking, and special immunities of diplomatic agents, and the forms of communication and ceremonies, as well as the official language, have grown through usage and conventions. See INTERNATIONAL LAW. Relations between sovereigns during the Renaissance were unstable and highly ceremonious, and every detail of diplomatic practice reflected the standing and the attitude of the participant.

An important aspect of diplomatic practice is the written communication. The dispatch is the written report sent by the diplomatic agent stationed abroad to his secretary of state or minister of foreign affairs. It carries out a most important function of the diplomatic agent, which is to report and interpret conditions in the foreign country. The home government also sends dispatches to instruct the diplomatic agent on policy and procedure.

The notes the ambassador sends to a foreign government vary in formality. Each has a prescribed style and carries unspoken meanings depending on who sends it to whom in what situation. The most formal is the note collective, or joint note. It is sent by more than one government to another government. The senders must be closely allied to state a joint policy, and this note can and may be used to offend. It is rarely used. Next in formality is the note diplomatique, or first-person note, which expresses the policy of one government. The note verbale, now usually called third-person note, is the most used and middling in formality. A circular is a note sent in identical form to more than one government. The pro memoria is a formal record of a topic discussed by representatives of different nations. For an informal review of the facts or line of discussion in such a conversation, the diplomat uses the aide-mémoire.

Permanent Missions. Prior to the 15th century the ruler himself, or else an envoy picked for a particular negotiation, conducted diplomacy. In the 15th century Venice, at the height of her power and threatened by the Ottoman Empire, established the first permanent resident missions, in France, Spain, London, and in other cities of the Italian peninsula. By the 16th century other states (Spain, France) had established resident missions, and the permanent envoy began to be known as "ambassador" rather than "orator", the older term.

The establishment of the permanent mission was the core of modern diplomacy. An envoy resident in a foreign country can observe and report on the men, opinions, and policies of the foreign country and can get to know both the government leaders of the country and the ambassadors from other nations, who keep him in touch with the policies of their governments. The pressing need for news of foreign intentions, to aid in forming national policy, was the primary reason the use of these resident envoys spread.

The practice of diplomacy by the developing nation-states rapidly assumed importance in European politics. From the 15th to the 18th century, when the national interest was based on personal and dynastic interests, and when statecraft was another name for intrigue, the ambassador was second in importance in foreign affairs only to his sovereign, in whose name he acted and whose prestige he defended. Laws against natives speaking to foreign ambassadors, however, show how dangerous the ambassador was thought to be. He was also feared in his own country as a man who could have gone na-

tive; he lived in a foreign country and might forget the ways of his own nation.

Because the ambassador was regarded as a spy, and because he had to pay his own expenses, which were great, kings sometimes had to use pressure to get someone to accept the post of ambassador. The first permanent ambassadors were not nobles. Louis XI (q.v.), King of France from 1461 to 1483, sent a barber to represent him in Burgundy; in the same century the city of Florence sent a chemist as envoy to Naples. Some ambassadors were not natives of the country they represented, but professionals who worked first for one country, then for another. The Church Curia, however, began to insist that ambassadors be of the upper class. By the 17th century ambassadors were of noble birth, the upper clergy, and the upper bourgeoisie official class, sometimes men of special knowledge.

France was the dominant power in European diplomacy and the model in diplomatic method in the 17th and 18th centuries. The ambassadors Louis XVI (q.v.), King of France, appointed to what were considered the major capitals, Rome, Madrid, Vienna, and London, were nobles. His ambassadors to other capitals were more often of the official class, men who were not nobly born but had already held an administrative

U.S. President Richard M. Nixon and Chinese Premier Chou En-lai review troops in Peking shortly after Nixon's arrival, in February, 1972, for an eight-day visit—one of the most spectacular undertakings in modern summit diplomacy.

Wally McNamee–Woodfin Camp & Assoc.

post which conferred nobility on them (such diplomatic representatives were known as the *noblesse de robe*). Embassy staffs were chosen and paid by the ambassador himself, and the staff was large and expensive.

In the 19th century when the national interest was less and less dependent on the interest of the monarch and more and more dependent on the expansion of trade, commerce, and colonial holdings of republican governments, diplomacy by trained professionals slowly became established. Men began to be appointed not for political or personal influence but on merit, judged by examination, and as they gained experience were promoted to greater responsibilities. This movement toward professionalization took place both in the foreign staffs in the home capitals and in the staffs of the missions abroad. In France in 1661 the foreign office in Paris consisted of the secretary of state plus five staff members (translators, cipher clerks, and clerks) who were appointed by the secretary of state and lost their jobs if he died or was dismissed by the king. But early in the 19th century both France and Austria had permanent professional staffs in the foreign office. The function of these home staffs also began to change from clerical to expert advisory work, drafting messages for example. Great Britain was slow in the change from clerks to expert advisers, which did not fully take place until after World War I.

In 1898, when the Spanish-American War ended and the United States emerged as a world power, the U.S. State Department had only eighty-two employees. Great Britain had an income qualification for diplomatic agents that was not abolished until after World War I. The U.S. had no income qualification, but diplomats abroad had to pay their own entertainment expenses, which were often enormous.

In the U.S. the spoils system (q.v.), which did not take into account the fitness of an appointee for a position, long dominated selection for diplomatic posts, although this political appointment did not mean that some able men were not appointed. In 1895 appointment by examination, excluding political influence, was first used in the U.S. It applied to candidates for the consular service. It was gradually extended to all Department of State appointments below the secretary, undersecretaries, and deputy undersecretaries of state. These appointees, like ambassadors and ministers, are subject to Senate approval whether or not they are career officers. More than two thirds of all U.S. ambassadors today are career officers who have come up through the ranks of the foreign service.

Throughout the 19th century commerce and trade grew in importance and the work of consular officers multiplied. Consuls were originally merchants or the representatives of merchants in foreign countries. They were not the social equals of the diplomatic corps, and often had their offices not in the capital cities but in cities that were trading, mining, or manufacturing centers. Only in the 20th century were the consular services and diplomatic corps combined in most countries. The U.S. combined the two in 1924; Great Britain, not until 1943; Germany, under the Weimar Republic; France, in 1945, although joint examinations for diplomatic and consular posts began there in 1880.

Diplomatic Agents. In crises the head of state, who is always ultimately responsible for the conduct of diplomacy and foreign policy, tends to take over negotiations. His secretary of state or foreign minister is both his political adviser on foreign policy and the head and administrator of the diplomatic machinery, and is usually chosen for compatibility in political views and aims. In the 20th century the complications of the international scene make reliance by the head of state on his foreign minister a necessity. Permanent ambassadors-at-large have been appointed by the U.S. President to be available for assignment anywhere in the world to investigate or negotiate for him; he also uses special ambassadors on occasion. Ambassadors, ministers, and the other regular and appointed representatives serving in permanent missions abroad are the traditional agents of diplomatic action. By far the greater part of the routine international business of the modern world is conducted through the resident embassies. In the U.S. the Senate has broad powers to review foreign policy prior to State Department action through its Committee on Foreign Relations, which can request the appearance of the secretary of state, as well as in the exercise of its constitutional function of approving treaties with foreign states and approving ambassadorial appointments. (For questions raised by the Vietnam war on Senatorial-Presidential control of foreign policy, *see* UNITED STATES OF AMERICA, THE: *History: Administrations of the 50's and 60's.*) The Foreign Affairs Committee of the House of Representatives also reviews policy but in practice never matched the Senate committee in importance. The Congress also controls diplomacy and foreign policy in its function of allocating the spending of government funds.

In 1815 the Congress of Vienna, and in 1818 the Congress of Aix-la-Chapelle, agreed to rank diplomatic agents as (1) ambassadors plenipotentiary ("of full power and authority"), legates, and papal nuncios; (2) envoys extraordinary and ministers plenipotentiary; (3) ministers resident; and (4) chargés d'affaires. Ranks (1) and (2) are agents accredited to the sovereign or head of state; ranks (3) and (4), to the secretary of state or minister of foreign affairs.

The U.S. long refused to recognize this classification; its principal diplomatic agents served as ministers plenipotentiary at legations (the term for a mission at which the chief of mission is a minister). In 1893, however, when Congress appropriated funds for the purpose, the President raised the rank of chiefs of mission to equal grade and dignity with those accredited by foreign powers to the U.S. The legation at London was the first to be raised to embassy status. By the 1960's most missions throughout the world had been raised to the rank of embassies.

The distinction of the ambassadorial office as the direct representative of a sovereign power and the importance of the duties entrusted to it have combined to invest it with a peculiar sanctity. This has taken the form of a privileged status attended with certain immunities which a foreign minister enjoys in the country to which he is accredited. These immunities, included in the legal principle known as extraterritoriality (q.v.), include (1) exemption of the minister and qualified exemption of his family from local, civil, and criminal jurisdiction; (2) inviolability of his house, papers, and goods from search and seizure; (3) exemption of his personal effects from imposts and taxation. The U.N. enjoys the right of extraterritoriality, and both delegates and members of the Secretariat (see SECRETARIAT OF THE UNITED NATIONS) have the rights of diplomatic immunity in their exercise of official duties in member states.

The Setting of Diplomacy. In the 16th century the Austrian Empire and France, and in the 17th century these two powers plus England, Russia, and Prussia, constituted the great powers. The doctrine of balancing powers, avoiding domination by any one of the strongest nations, was and still is the classic method of diplomacy. This doctrine has sometimes meant keeping a balance of justice for all nations, and sometimes meant sharing the spoils of power among the great powers. (See BALANCE OF POWER.) Before the time of U.S. President Woodrow Wilson (q.v.) the small powers were seen as important only in relation to the concerns of the great powers. When World War I started, the U.S., Great Britain, and France were each permanently represented in only ten countries. Some experts in diplomacy and foreign policy describe the

international scene since World War II in terms of shifts in the balance of power among the U.S., the Soviet Union, and (after the Korean War) Communist China, with the once-great powers (Great Britain, France) and the new Afro-Asian nations aiming at the creation of a "third force", or "neutralist", weight in the balance.

Since the advent of nuclear weapons, first in the hands of the U.S. (atomic, 1945; hydrogen, 1952), and then also in the hands of the Soviet Union (atomic, 1949; hydrogen, 1953), Communist China (atomic, 1964; hydrogen, 1967), and other nations (Britain, France), the "nuclear deterrent" (the probability that if any nation uses nuclear weapons the result will be its own destruction by retaliation) has dominated international relations. (For information on the content of foreign policies, see articles on individual countries.)

METHODS OF DIPLOMACY

The methods of diplomatic action vary according to the magnitude of the interests involved, the nature of the circumstance which calls them into play, and the talents and inclinations of the persons responsible.

For the settlement of questions vitally affecting several states, or involving the peace of a continent, or the general policy of the great powers, an international congress or conference may be summoned to negotiate a treaty (q.v.). These international conferences are meetings not of all nations, but of the great powers of the time plus whatever smaller nations are concerned. (For some specific agreements, see DISARMAMENT; GENEVA CONVENTION; HAGUE CONFERENCES; INDOCHINA: *History*.)

Treaties to settle territorial arrangements and other questions following a war are negotiated in congresses of victors and vanquished. Long-range political effects on the power of the negotiating nations, and the creation of new nations, have resulted from such congresses; see VERSAILLES, TREATY OF; VIENNA, CONGRESS OF; WESTPHALIA, PEACE OF. After World War II no international congress was held to set peace terms. Instead, separate treaties were signed after lengthy occupations (of Germany and Japan) and extended negotiations.

In the crisis-ridden state of international affairs since World War II treaties have been supplemented by much less formal, ad hoc agreements that may be supplanted in later years by further or different agreements to suit changed circumstances.

Diplomacy by Permanent Conference. In the 15th and 16th centuries "diplomacy by conference" meant the face-to-face meeting of rulers, usually on a bridge with a wooden lattice put up for the occasion to prevent either one from kidnapping the other. Napoleon, Emperor of France, in 1807 met Alexander I (qq.v.), Emperor of Russia, on a boat in the middle of the Memel R. in Prussia. Although kidnapping is no longer a problem in such "summit" conferences, security from violence is. The careful balancing of prestige when heads of state meet is also still important. When U.S. President Lyndon Baines Johnson (q.v.) met U.S.S.R. Premier Aleksei Kosygin (q.v.) in 1967, the site was Glassboro, N.J., roughly midway between New York City, where Premier Kosygin was attending a U.N. session, and Washington, D.C.

The French statesman and cardinal Duc de Richelieu (q.v.), from 1624 to 1642 "first minister" to the French king and potent builder of French power, spoke of diplomacy as continuous negotiation. Not until the League of Nations was established in 1919, however, was this idea extended to include permanent multilateral negotiation and translated into the practical form of a specific location and buildings and a permanent staff. The League established "permanent diplomacy" by continuous multilateral negotiations to encourage cooperation among nations on the vast range of political, economic, and social problems important to all peoples.

The old machinery of diplomacy, centered on bilateral relations, continued to function side by side first with the League of Nations and later with the U.N. But the multilateral diplomacy or diplomacy by permanent conference carried on through the U.N. and through regional organizations, such as the Organization of American States and the Organization for African Unity; regional economic organizations, such as the Common Market; and organizations for collective security, such as North Atlantic Treaty Organization, ANZUS, and Southeast Asia Treaty Organization, has somewhat reduced the importance of traditional bilateral relations. (See separate articles on some of the organizations mentioned.)

Public Control over Diplomacy. The Treaty of Versailles (q.v.) terminating World War I, was signed by U.S. President Woodrow Wilson (qq.v.), but never ratified by the U.S. Senate. This disagreement between the President, who was one of the principal negotiators of the treaty, and the Congress highlighted the problem of reconciling the classic diplomatic principle that an ambassador speaks for and has the complete confidence of his government in negotiations with the democratic principle of par-

liamentary control over the policies of the head of state.

The first of Wilson's Fourteen Points (q.v.), which he introduced at the Paris Peace Conference, a declaration for "open covenants of peace openly arrived at", fixed attention on the need for accountability to the citizen in the conduct of foreign affairs by democratic countries. Although the "open covenants" point was popularly interpreted to mean that negotiations for treaties should be public, Wilson himself negotiated secretly at the peace conference with the French premier Georges Clemenceau and with David Lloyd George (qq.v.), the British prime minister. Moreover, the course of the negotiations has traditionally been secret in order to promote concessions and compromise by both sides. Wilson himself reinterpreted "open covenants" to mean that any treaty that binds a people to act in a certain way should be divulged to the people who will have to carry out the pledge. With the ever-closer connection between foreign and domestic affairs that the 20th century has brought, with the increasing interdependence of nations, and with the spread of press, radio, and television coverage of foreign affairs, information about foreign affairs and diplomatic activity is much more available than it once was. One effect of this coverage has been called "diplomacy by loudspeaker" or "diplomacy by insult", that is, oratory for propaganda, rather than serious discussion. The problem of keeping the public informed on the genuine issues in diplomatic negotiations is a continuing one. So too is that of the public's controlling the conduct of foreign affairs through the congress or parliament.

In the 1920's and 1930's the League of Nations engendered hopes for a "new diplomacy" based on cooperation for common interests in the advancing of the public welfare of the peoples of the world: the "old diplomacy" based on protecting national interests against inevitably opposing rival interests, whether defensive or aggressive, was to disappear. No longer was the aphorism "war is the continuation of diplomacy by other means" to be true; war would disappear. World War II effectively shattered this optimism; after the war the U.N. Secretariat and specialized agencies institutionalized and carried forward hope for a diplomacy of cooperation, but the once-widespread belief in the eradication of separate national interests seems to have disappeared.

In fact, nationalism and its corollary, anticolonialism, increased the number of sovereign states in the world from more than 50 in 1945 to more than 130 in the 1960's. From the breakup of empires have emerged the new countries of Africa, Asia, South America, and the Caribbean, which have special interests as underdeveloped or developing nations. Through regional organizations and through bloc policy-making and voting in the U.N. these small powers have a weight in world diplomacy that the small powers of another day did not.

Military assistance is a traditional method of supporting the national interest by increasing the military strength of an ally against an actual or potential enemy, and has long been a tool in diplomacy. Increasing the economic well-being of another country by economic and technical aid in the form of grants, credits, loans, and training programs emerged as an extension of the classic tool in 1948 with the creation of the European Recovery Program (q.v.), and since that year has become an established method of diplomacy. In the U.S., such economic aid is currently administered by the State Department through the Agency for International Development, the Alliance for Progress (the Latin American arm of AID), the Food-for-Peace Program, the Peace Corps, U.N. and other international aid programs, and through international financial organizations. Other departments, such as the Department of Agriculture, carry out parts of these and related programs.

The chief of state since World War II has been more than ever in command of the foreign policy of his country. The speedup of communication, beginning in the 19th century but fantastically accelerated since 1945 (by the telegraph, the telephone, radio, and television) has greatly reduced the need for the once-wide discretion of his ambassadors. The chief of state can receive instantaneous reports and give instantaneous new instructions to his embassies, always excepting those missions that are badly equipped. The speed of the jet airplane allows presidents and premiers to travel to foreign capitals without sacrificing much time needed for other responsibilities. The 20th century has been an era of accelerated crises, some of them in areas of the world hitherto nearly ignored by the public and of minor concern to the great powers. The chief of state must in crises assume ultimate responsibility and act quickly.

Unlike the 18th-century monarch the 20th-century head of state has available and must use the knowledge and experience of many different experts to form and carry out the national policy through diplomacy. Although negotiating treaties, which is one traditional function of the ambassador, may be done in summit conference or by special envoys, the traditional function of the ambassador, to report on and interpret conditions in the country in which he lives is still important. He remains also the administrator of the embassy he heads. Attachés for science, labor, and culture, as well as the longer-established attachés for army, navy, and air force, now serve under him. Commerce and other consular officers and information experts also are on his staff. These officers of the embassy remain, with the ambassador, an important communications link between the home capital and the foreign government.

DIPLOMATICS. *See* PALEOGRAPHY.

DIPNOI. *See* LUNGFISH.

DIPPER, common name for birds of the genus *Cinclus,* found in much of the western world and especially *C. mexicanus,* a small, gray, thrushlike bird inhabiting North America. Sometimes called ouzel or water ouzel, it has short wings, a short, stout bill, and a very small tail. It frequents clear, pebbly streams and lakes, feeding chiefly on mollusks and aquatic insects. The dipper usually builds a domed nest of interwoven moss on a bank of a stream, and sometimes near or under a cascade. It is capable of diving under water and moving about under the surface by means of its legs and wings. The name dipper is also given to several unrelated birds

Dipper, Cinclus mexicanus

Ed Cesar — National Audubon Society

that are excellent divers, especially the blather-skite and the grebe (q.v.).

DIPPER, BIG, common name applied to a conspicuous constellation in the northern celestial hemisphere, situated near the North Pole. It was known to the ancient Greeks as the Bear and the Wagon and to the Romans as *Ursa Major* (the Great Bear) and *Septentriones* (seven plowing oxen). The seven brightest stars of the constellation form the easily identified outline of a giant dipper. In Europe, the pattern is known as the Plow, Charles's (Charlemagne's) Wain, and the Wagon; among the Hindus, it represents the seven rishis, or holy ancient sages.

Of the seven stars constituting the Big Dipper, six are of the second magnitude and one is of the third magnitude. Two of the second-magnitude stars, alpha (α) and beta (β) Ursae Majoris, which form the outer edge of the bowl, point directly to the North Star (q.v.), or Polaris, and hence are called the Pointers. At the bend of the handle of the Big Dipper is the readily visible double star known as Mizar, or zeta (ζ) Ursae Majoris. Mizar, the first visual double star discovered, consists of two components having magnitudes of 2.4 and 4 respectively. The brighter component was itself found in spectroscopic studies (1889) to be a double star; subsequently, in 1908, it was discovered that the other component also is a spectroscopic double; see DOUBLE STARS.

DIPPER, LITTLE, common name applied to a constellation in the northern sky, situated close to the Big Dipper; see DIPPER, BIG. Known to the Romans as *Ursa Minor,* or Little Bear, the Little Dipper may be found on winter evenings to the left of and above the Big Dipper, with its handle pointed upward. Polaris, or α Ursae Minoris, known commonly as the North Star (q.v.), or pole star, marks the end of the handle of the Little Dipper; presently the pole star is situated slightly less than 1° from the North Pole. The North Star is a second-magnitude star, the brightest in the constellation.

DIPROTODON, genus of extinct, giant marsupials (q.v.) of the suborder Diprotodontia, related to the kangaroo (q.v.). Fossils of these animals occur in Australia among Pleistocene deposits. Like the kangaroo, they were herbivorous, but unlike the former, they used all four legs for walking. The skull of the diprotodon was heavy and about 3 ft. long; the entire animal was about the size of a rhinoceros. The only known species of this genus is *D. australis.* A related genus, *Nototherium,* the bones of which are often found with those of the diprotodon, was also a giant marsupial.

DIPSOMANIA. See INTOXICATION, ALCOHOLIC.

DIPTERA, one of the largest orders of insects, containing 50,000 or more known species, including the mosquito, the midge, the gnat, and the fly (qq.v.). Most species have a single pair of wings, but some are wingless. Members of the order are characterized by the possession of sucking, and sometimes piercing, mouth parts. Behind the wings most species are equipped with a pair of vestigial wings called halteres, which take the form of small stalks with knobs on their ends. The halteres are vibrated back and forth with great rapidity when the insect is in flight and by their motion act as stabilizers. All species of diptera undergo complete metamorphosis. The eggs of many species of diptera are known as nits, while the larvae are called maggots, bots, or wrigglers. The life habits of the various species of diptera vary widely. Some feed on nectar, some are scavengers, and some are bloodsuckers. Others live as internal or external parasites, while still others prey on other insects.

DIRAC, Paul Adrien Maurice (1902–), British mathematician and theoretical physicist, born in Bristol, England, and educated at the universities of Bristol and Cambridge. In 1932 he was appointed professor of mathematics at Cambridge. He was made a Fellow of the Royal Society (1930) and in 1933 shared the Nobel Prize in physics with the Austrian physicist Erwin Schrödinger (q.v.). Dirac is well known for his researches in atomic structure and in quantum mechanics (q.v.), and particularly for his development of the theory of the positron (q.v.). During World War II he conducted theoretical investigations of chain reactions. He was a member of the Institute for Advanced Study (q.v.) periodically between 1934 and 1959. His writings include *Principles of Quantum Mechanics* (1930).

See ATOM AND ATOMIC THEORY; ELECTRON; ELECTRONICS.

DIRECTION FINDER. See NAVIGATION: *Electronic Navigation.*

DIRECTOIRE, style of furniture and clothing popular in France during the period of the Directory (q.v.). See COSTUME: *Clothing from Medieval Times to the 19th Century;* FURNITURE: *Louis XVI.*

DIRECTORY (Fr. *Directoire*), executive branch of the republican government of France, established in 1795 in accordance with the constitution promulgated by the National Convention (q.v.). The Directory, consisting of five members elected by both houses of the legislature, was in power from October, 1795, to November, 1799.

In rotation, each of the directors held the presidency for a three-month interval, and one director was replaced each year. Among those who served on the Directory were Vicomte de Barras, Lazare Carnot, Joseph Fouché, and Comte Emmanuel Sieyès (qq.v.). As a result of incompetence and corruption within the Directory, the finances of the government became so strained that early in 1796 a proclamation of bankruptcy was issued. The Directory thereupon sought to restore financial security by means of military conquest abroad, and appointed Napoléon Bonaparte, later Napoleon I (q.v.), Emperor of France, to command the French armies in Italy. Napoléon subsequently won a series of victories that augmented his own power and prestige, while the Directory itself was waning in influence at home. In 1799 a combination of military reverses abroad and the increasing number of counterrevolutionary uprisings at home weakened the power of the Directory so greatly that, on November 9, Napoléon was able to seize power with little opposition. This action, which brought the Directory to an end, is known as the "coup d'état of the 18th Brumaire", the date according to the republican calendar proclaimed in 1792. See COMMITTEE OF PUBLIC SAFETY; CONSULATE; FRENCH REVOLUTION.

DIRE DAWA, city of Ethiopia, in Harar Province, about 210 miles N.E. of Addis Ababa. Located midway between Addis Ababa and the port of Djibouti at the Red Sea, Dire Dawa is important commercially. The city has plants producing cement and textiles. Pop. (1970 est.) 60,925.

DIRKSEN, Everett McKinley (1896–1969), American political leader, born in Pekin, Ill. Dirksen left the law school of the University of Minnesota in 1917 to join the United States Army. After his discharge from the army in 1919, he returned to Pekin and entered business. In 1932 he was elected as a Republican to the United States House of Representatives, the first of his eight terms in the House. As a Congressman Dirksen frequently opposed New Deal (q.v.) monetary and fiscal programs and maintained a generally isolationist stance in foreign affairs up to 1941, when the U.S. entered World War II. After a two-year period out of public office Dirksen was elected to the United States Senate in 1950. In 1959 he became Republican minority leader. As party leader in the Senate, Dirksen was most noted for his sudden dramatic shifts from opposition to support of various measures, including the Nuclear Test-Ban Treaty of 1963 and the Civil-Rights Act of 1964. His talent for compromise was responsible for the passage of much legislation that might otherwise have been defeated in the Senate.

DISABILITY, in law, incapability of performing an act or of exercising a right because of a lack of legal competence. Disabilities are classified in several ways. General disabilities relate to incapacity to perform all legal acts of a certain class, whereas specific disabilities relate to only a single act. Physical disabilities result from physical or mental injuries or illnesses. Civil or legal disabilities result from legal disqualifications. In the United States, insane persons are said to be under general disability in that they have no legal capacity to make valid contracts or to enter into any other legal obligations. Minors are similarly affected for the very reason that they have the option of voiding most contracts. In most States, citizens under twenty-one years of age are under specific disability of being ineligible to vote; and foreign-born citizens are legally ineligible for the Presidency, under the specific provisions of the Constitution of the U.S. See also WORKMEN'S COMPENSATION.

DISARMAMENT, regulation, limitation, control, or balanced reduction of all armed forces and all armaments. In the years after World War II, the United Nations (U.N.) has attempted with some success to achieve partial disarmament and prohibition of nuclear and thermonuclear weapons, and other weapons of mass destruction through the negotiation of international treaties. See BIOLOGICAL WARFARE; CHEMICAL WARFARE; INTERNATIONAL CONTROL OF ATOMIC ENERGY; NUCLEAR WEAPONS; WARFARE.

Approaches to Disarmament. The ultimate form of disarmament, often referred to as general and complete disarmament, involves the elimination by every nation of all armaments and armed forces capable of waging offensive wars. Under general and complete disarmament as it is now conceived, each nation would retain only those forces deemed necessary to protect the internal security of its citizens, such as the civil police, and would support and provide agreed manpower for an international police force. The possession of nuclear weapons would be absolutely prohibited.

Present-day efforts toward disarmament generally are aimed at more modest measures, such as partial limitations on armed forces, armaments, and military expenditures, and restrictions on the use or deployment of weapons and forces. The extent of military armament of a country undoubtedly depends on various circumstances. In general, countries in an area of continued political crisis, such as the Middle

East (q.v.) or Southeast Asia, have far greater arms outlays in relation to their gross national product than the countries in Latin America, for example, where regional understanding has promoted relative stability. Also countries such as India and Pakistan, which face conflicts over their border areas, nonetheless voluntarily curb their military expenditures, being greatly dependent upon external economic assistance.

Many different plans for partial disarmament and arms control have come under consideration by diplomats. Among them are proposals for regional disarmament, for limiting or reducing forces and weapons in specified geographic areas, as for example, the so-called nuclear-free zones. Other plans are based on a quantitative approach; one such plan would assign approved levels of military strength on a nation-by-nation basis. In this case, such factors as international political position, industrial capacity, geographical size, or population might influence the level of final strength assigned to a particular nation. Another quantitative basis for arms control might be current military strength. Thus the weapons and forces of a nation might be reduced from current levels on a percentage basis, a method sometimes referred to as proportional disarmament.

In contrast to the quantitative approach, the qualitative approach to disarmament takes into account the nature, purpose, and destructive capacity of particular types of weapons and means of making war. Distinctions are made between strategic and tactical weapons, between offensive and defensive weapons, or between nuclear and conventional weapons.

Methods of Inspection. Governments generally agree that it would be necessary to verify the fact that a state is living up to its disarmament agreements. According to United States authorities in the field of arms control, a verification system should include an intelligence component and an inspection component operating separately. All nations collect intelligence information about other nations through their diplomatic staffs and other official sources, and from secret sources such as espionage. Inspection, because it normally requires the cooperation of the nation being investigated, must take a form acceptable to that nation. Among the types of inspection that have been proposed is so-called bonfire inspection, in which the inspecting party observes the destruction or conversion of matériel or the disbandment of military forces as it takes place. Fiscal inspection involves examination of accounting, statistical, and other forms of documentation. On-site inspection entails examination of an area or installation where a violation may be suspected. Zonal inspection is restricted to specified areas within a country. Technical inspection, involving use of elaborate apparatus on the ground, under the sea, in the air, or in outer space, is for the purpose of seeing or sensing sound, heat, radio waves, radioactivity, and other manifestations that may indicate use or testing of weapons. Inspection may be conducted by another party to the disarmament agreement, so-called adversary inspection, by mixed teams including personnel of the nation under inspection and the adversary nation, or by neutral parties. Plans also have been put forth for progressive inspection or graduated access inspection, which are systems involving a gradual expansion of the intensity and scope of inspection as disarmament proceeds.

AGREEMENTS IN FORCE

Currently the major vehicle for discussion and treaty agreements on disarmament is the Conference of the Committee on Disarmament (known previously as the Eighteen Nation Committee on Disarmament or E.N.C.D.), consisting of the U.S. and its seven allies, and the Soviet Union and seven allies; twelve members from other countries complete the committee, which meets in Geneva, Switzerland. This committee was established by American-Soviet bilateral agreement and was endorsed by a U.N. General Assembly resolution of Dec. 20, 1961. The U.S. body with main responsibility for disarmament information and negotiations is the U.S. Arms Control and Disarmament Agency, which was also established in 1961.

Bans on Nuclear Weapons. Nuclear weapons are banned by international treaty from Antarctica, Latin America, and outer space. The testing of nuclear weapons is banned in outer space, the atmosphere, and underseas as a result of the partial nuclear test ban agreement between the U.S., Soviet Union, and Great Britain in July, 1963. Although 113 nations have signed the treaty, however, China and France have not agreed to it. In 1964 the U.S. and the Soviet Union both agreed to decrease the production of fissionable materials for weapons purposes, and Great Britain announced that it would no longer produce plutonium for military use.

The nuclear nonproliferation treaty, which was signed in 1968 and went into effect in March, 1970, was an important step designed to limit the number of nuclear powers to five, although it was not signed by France and China. The most notable clauses in this treaty committed the signatory nuclear powers (1) not to

President Richard M. Nixon of the U.S. and Leonid I. Brezhnev, Soviet Communist Party leader, sign the Nuclear Arms Limitation Treaty at Vladimir Hall, in the Kremlin, Moscow, in May, 1972. UPI

supply nuclear weapons or weapons-oriented nuclear materials and technology to the nonnuclear nations; (2) to seek agreements between themselves leading to the slowing down of the arms race and toward nuclear and general disarmament; and (3) to make the benefits of peaceful applications of nuclear research available to the nonnuclear states without discrimination. The treaty also was remarkable in that it meant that nations such as Japan, Sweden, and West Germany, which are capable of producing nuclear weapons, would voluntarily refrain from doing so in return for guarantees of protection by the major powers in case of nuclear attack. The treaty also had a clause whereby any signatory party could withdraw from the treaty commitments if it felt its national security threatened for any reason.

A treaty banning nuclear weapons and launching and testing installations from the ocean floor was signed by more than sixty nations in Washington, D.C., Moscow, and London in February, 1971. It went into effect on May 18, 1972, after ratification by twenty-eight nations. The treaty was not signed by France or Communist China.

The most important steps toward stopping the nuclear-arms race, however, were long frustrated for many reasons. Efforts to reach agreement on banning underground nuclear-weapon tests, for example, ended in failure because the nuclear powers wanted to perfect the nuclear warheads for the defensive anti-ballistic missiles (ABM); also, the distant seismic devices were not adequate to identify with certainty an un-

derground nuclear test, and agreement could not be reached on the number of on-site inspections to be permitted. Similar problems have precluded any limitations on long-range bombers and multiple-warhead delivery vehicles, some of the most costly and threatening components of the arms race.

Salt. A step toward fulfilling one of the most important commitments in the nonproliferation treaty, however, was taken when the strategic arms limitation talks (SALT) between the U.S. and the Soviet Union began in Helsinki, Finland, in November, 1969. The agenda at these talks specifically included the discussion of a curb on strategic nuclear-delivery vehicles, but not on the warheads. The talks may foreshadow an era of arms limitation through "negotiated inequalities". For example, should the Soviet Union proceed with the deployment of the ABM, the U.S. would develop its offensive capability with a multiple independently targetable reentry vehicle (see MIRV) system instead of building a heavy defensive ABM shield in place of the planned light Safeguard ABM system. The multiple reentry vehicle system consists of missiles that each carry a number of warheads aimed at different targets; the Safeguard system consists of missiles that would intercept approaching enemy missiles before they reach the target area.

During a summit meeting held in Moscow, U.S.S.R., by President Richard M. Nixon of the U.S. and Leonid Ilyich Brezhnev, Alexsei Nikolayevich Kosygin (qq.v.), and other Soviet leaders, a strategic arms limitation treaty was signed on May 26, 1972. Generally considered as a first step toward a mutual reduction of strategic nuclear weapons, the agreement covered both defensive and offensive delivery vehicles.

Limiting defensive nuclear arms, the U.S. and the Soviet Union agreed, for an unlimited time, to build only two ABM sites, each consisting of only 100 missiles. One site would protect the national capitals (Washington, D.C., and Moscow); and the other site would protect a retaliatory intercontinental ballistic missile (ICBM) installation to guard against surprise attack. See GUIDED MISSILES: Surface-to-Surface Missiles.

An interim offensive weapons agreement of five years' duration limited the installation of ICBM's to those already deployed or being built at the time of the signing of the treaty. Consequently, the U.S. was limited to 1054 ground-base missiles and the Soviet Union to 1618. The treaty also froze for five years the installation of submarine-launched ballistic missiles (SLBM) in nuclear submarines at the numbers deployed or under construction on the date of the agreement; that is, 656 for the U.S. and 740 for the Soviet Union.

The agreement, however, did not cover the possession of nuclear warheads, about 5700 in the U.S. arsenal and 2500 in the Soviet Union. It also did not prohibit the improvement and increased sophistication of the missile systems already installed by the two powers.

In August, 1973, the U.S. announced that the Soviet Union had tested MIRV warheads and was expected to deploy them by about 1975. The Soviet success added impetus to American efforts to reach a permanent offensive weapons agreement based on the 1972 agreement.

Bans on Chemical and Biological Warfare.
The 1925 Protocol for the Prohibition of the Use in War of Asphyxiating, Poisonous, or Other Gases, and of Bacteriological Methods of Warfare is still in effect, although interpretation of this document is controversial. It does not curtail or prohibit the manufacture of weapons. A 1966 resolution of the U.N. General Assembly, to which sixty-four nations assented, called for observing the protocol in principles and objectives. Great Britain and the Soviet Union, among other ratifying nations, declared themselves ready to use gas or bacteriological weapons against nonsigners or against nations that use such weapons in the field.

In July, 1969, however, Great Britain introduced a draft agreement to the Disarmament Committee to prohibit the development, production, and use of biological weapons in any circumstances, leading to the eventual destruction of the existing stocks, or their diversion to peaceful uses. The proposal received Canadian support, but the Soviet Union wished to include

chemical weapons as well in the ban. The U.S. signed the 1925 protocol, but had never ratified it; the United States Senate had failed to vote on the protocol in 1926. In November, 1969, President Nixon renounced the use of biological weapons and ordered the destruction of the existing U.S. stocks. He also announced that the 1925 protocol would be resubmitted to the Senate for ratification and that the U.S. would associate itself with the British proposals before the Disarmament Committee. In February, 1970, President Nixon extended the unilateral U.S. ban to the production and use of military toxins, used as chemical warfare agents.

Economic and Social Consequences. In order to gauge the probable effects of disarmament on the American economy, it is useful to recall the national economic adjustment following World War II. At the end of the war, military expenditures represented more than 40 percent of the gross national product of the U.S. Nevertheless, conversion to a peacetime economy was accomplished without a major economic crisis. Considering that defense expenditures throughout most of the 1960's remained under 10 percent of the gross national product, it might be deduced that disarmament need not create more than a temporary dislocation in the economy. This deduction is in accord with the findings of a study made by the U.S. Arms Control and Disarmament Agency.

In the early 1960's the U.N. conducted a study of the possible worldwide social and economic consequences of disarmament. The report of this study distinguished between the impact of disarmament on highly industrialized nations, where it would affect production and employment in industries that manufacture military equipment, and on the less industrialized countries that import their armaments. In less industrialized countries the greatest impacts of disarmament would be in the release of men from military service and in the release of foreign exchange which would otherwise be spent to import arms. The report concluded that appropriate national and international measures could meet all the problems of transition and that "diversion to peaceful uses of the resources now in military use could be accomplished to the benefit of all countries . . .".

Historical Background. One of the earliest recorded efforts to limit warfare was made by the Amphictyonic League (q.v.), a religious federation of Greek city-states that worshiped Apollo, the sun god. Its members swore an oath to refrain from certain extreme acts of war against other members.

The naval demilitarization of the U.S.-Canadian border on the Great Lakes, established by the Rush-Bagot Treaty of 1817, is an example of effective bilateral disarmament. This demilitarized region is only one of the many buffer zones that have been established at various times and places.

Neutralized states, which unlike buffer zones are multilaterally recognized and may be armed, also have been maintained for varying periods of time; for example, Switzerland has been neutralized since 1815; Belgium was neutralized from 1839 until it was invaded by Germany in World War I; and Luxembourg was neutralized from 1867 until after World War II. Neutralized areas have included the Congo basin and the Suez and Panama canals, and the neutrality of Austria since the signing of the Austrian State Treaty in May, 1955, is another notable example of regional agreement between the great powers; see AUSTRIA: *Restoration of Austrian Sovereignty.*

In the period preceding World War I, the Hague Conferences (q.v.) of 1899 and 1907 attempted to limit armaments and also established a Permanent Court of Arbitration to settle international disputes peacefully. These efforts failed to prevent World War I. After the war the Treaty of Versailles and the covenant of the League of Nations committed signers of these documents to disarmament. All of the Allied powers except the U.S. signed them, but only the defeated nations were pressed to comply with disarmament commitments.

Probably the most significant treaty relating to disarmament during the 1920's was the Washington Naval Limitation Agreement of 1922 (*see* WASHINGTON CONFERENCE), which limited, on a tonnage basis, the capital ships and aircraft carriers that each of the Pacific naval powers (Great Britain, Japan, Italy, France, U.S., China, Netherlands, Portugal, and Belgium) could have. Later, the London Naval Treaty of 1930 established tonnage quotas on cruisers, destroyers, and submarines for Japan, Great Britain, and the U.S., but France and Italy, who were also expected to be parties to the treaty, could not reach agreement on the terms. Both the 1922 and the 1930 treaties expired in 1936.

In 1932 a general world disarmament conference attended by League of Nations members, as well as the U.S. and the U.S.S.R., met at Geneva and drafted an agreement that limited military spending, military forces, and periods of military service. After France opposed the draft and proposed an alternative plan involving an international police force, the meeting was deadlocked. It adjourned early in 1933 and when it reconvened later the same year Germany, which had been demanding the right to rearm unless other countries disarmed to the German level, withdrew both from the conference and the League of Nations. Although the conference met sporadically thereafter, it had no influence over events as the world moved toward World War II.

Post-World War II Attitudes. Since the end of World War II attitudes toward disarmament have been markedly cautious and skeptical compared to the hopes of the interwar period. Since 1945, nations have relied on the arms control approach. At the end of the 1960's self-restraint had remained effective in one vital area: although about fifty-three significant armed conflicts had occurred since World War II, strategic nuclear weapons were not used in any of them. *See* UNITED NATIONS: *Arms Control and Peacekeeping Operations.*

Two draft treaties for general and complete disarmament embodying the differences between the U.S. and the U.S.S.R. on disarmament were presented in 1962 to the Eighteen-Nation Disarmament Committee. These plans remain on the agenda of the committee, but little progress has been made toward resolving differences between the two great powers. The U.S. proposal is for balanced disarmament by percentages (30 percent in the first stage, 50 percent in the second, the remainder in the third) of all arms and armed forces. Reduction is to be accompanied by inspection and verification of all facilities, not simply those publicly declared, and inspection must be considered workable before the next stage is entered. Nuclear arms and foreign bases would not be eliminated until the third stage is reached. The Soviet proposal also calls for three stages. It limits inspection to declared facilities and arms. Inspectors would be allowed to verify destruction of arms but not to determine how many were retained. In the first stage nuclear delivery vehicles and foreign bases would be eliminated, except for a so-called nuclear umbrella to be maintained by both the U.S. and the Soviet Union until the end of the third stage. This cover would include intercontinental ballistic missiles, antiballistic missiles, and antiaircraft missiles on the territory of the two countries. Inspection would be confined to declared launching pads and missiles. Both plans suggest an international disarmament organization associated with the U.N.

The nonproliferation treaty assigned to the International Atomic Energy Agency (q.v.) the responsibility for making sure that nonnuclear powers do not divert fissionable materials for weapons. This decision was believed to indicate that the I.A.E.A. might become the inspection agency for any future agreements.

W.W. & W.W.R.

DISCHARGE, in the United States armed forces, document presented to each soldier, sailor, airman, and marine on leaving the service. Enlisted men cannot be discharged from the armed services until they have completed their terms of enlistment, except by order of the President, by sentence of a general court-martial, by certificate of disability, or by writ of habeas corpus. Enlistments may occasionally be terminated prematurely, however, "at own convenience" or "at convenience of the government".

The armed forces of the United States issue several kinds of discharges. The honorable discharge is most frequently issued and is presented to those soldiers whose service records are good or excellent. The general discharge, a type of honorable discharge, is given to those whose records are not sufficiently meritorious to warrant an honorable discharge. Undesirable discharges are given to those who have demonstrated unfitness or misconduct while in the service. Discharges without honor or bad conduct discharges, which may operate to deprive the recipient of some civil rights, are given for more serious offenses only by an approved sentence of a special or general court-martial. Dishonorable discharge is given only by an approved sentence of a general court-martial to those who commit grave crimes such as mutiny, desertion, murder, and rape. Depriving the recipient of many civil rights and Federal benefits, it is similar in effect to conviction for a felony.

DISCIPLES OF CHRIST CHURCH. See CHRISTIAN CHURCH (DISCIPLES OF CHRIST).

DISCOBOLUS or **DISCOBOLOS,** in Greek antiquity, term meaning a discus thrower. In Greek sculpture, the term is applied to a specific bronze statue—reputedly by the Greek sculptor Myron (q.v.)—of a man in the act of throwing a discus. Three copies of the lost original statue exist today, one in the Vatican Museum, Rome, one in the British Museum, London, and one in the Palazzo Lancelotti, Rome. The last is considered the finest of the copies. See GREEK ART AND ARCHITECTURE: *Classical Period: Middle Classical Period.*

DISCOUNT, in commerce, deduction from the price of a commodity. Discounts are usually made in consideration of payment on delivery of merchandise, or of payment within a specified time limit. Quantity discounts are special ones given to purchasers of large quantities of merchandise. Trade discounts are given to wholesalers and other trade groups to cover the cost of performing specific functions, such as warehousing and merchandising.

In the United States, the Robinson-Patman Act of 1936, amending the anti-monopoly Clayton Antitrust Act (q.v.) of 1914, makes unlawful in interstate trade special discriminatory discounts. The principal objective of this provision is to protect smaller concerns from price discrimination in favor of larger competitors.

In finance, discounts are premiums or considerations given on the purchase of promissory notes, bills of exchange, or other forms of negotiable commercial paper in advance of their maturity dates. Such discounts comprise deductions from the face value of the discounted paper and are made at the time of purchase. The principal agencies engaged in discounting commercial paper are commercial banks and, in a few countries, financial institutions which specialize in that practice. When discounted paper is again put into circulation by a bank or discount house and is discounted again, it is said to be rediscounted.

Because the holders of discounted bills and notes, at the time they mature, receive the full face value of the commercial paper they present for payment, the practice of discounting bills and notes is, in effect, a means of extending credit in the form of loans; the discounts are regarded as advance collections of interest on the loans. Rates for discounting and rediscounting commercial paper are established by commercial banks and discount houses in accordance with the relative supply of money available for commercial loans. In countries in which the banking system is organized on a centralized basis (*see* BANKS AND BANKING), discount and rediscount rates are determined in large part by the central banks; in the United States, these rates are established in part by the Federal Reserve System (q.v.) to control the volume of credit and thus stimulate or slow the economy.

DISCOUNT STORES or **DISCOUNT HOUSES,** in retailing, establishments that sell consumer merchandise mainly on a self-service basis and at the most competitively low margins. The term "discount" (q.v.) relates to the practice of selling at a percentage off the list price, the basic retail price set by the manufacturer and published in a manufacturer's catalog, price list, or advertisement.

Originally discount houses were comparatively small firms with low maintenance expenses. Early houses frequently specialized in certain products and claimed to limit their clientele to particular customer groups that were given special admission cards. In the 1930's, although the position of department stores (q.v.) in the retail community had become firmly fixed, the serious economic depression throughout the United States acted as a strong impetus to discount stores as declining sales forced many manufacturers and wholesalers to dispose of their inventories. Subsequently, State and Federal fair-trade laws (q.v.) were passed, prohibiting the sale of merchandise below a specific price contracted by manufacturer and retailer; this was called the fixed price. The early fair-trade laws, with their many loopholes, were not strenuously enforced.

After World War II, discount stores continued to operate, meeting the demand for products that had been scarce during the war as well as satisfying the market created by expanded consumer income. Although various manufacturers filed suits to prevent discounting of their fixed prices, discount stores offered selections of goods, with and without brand-name labels, which had not been price-fixed by the manufacturer. They usually offered limited service or self-service, operated on low profit margins, and were located in less expensive areas. Because of the population shift to the suburbs commencing in the 1950's, established urban retail outlets faced loss of patronage. The public, having become accustomed to self-service as supermarkets (q.v.) grew in popularity, flocked to the discount stores, which adopted similar techniques of streamlining, convenience, and buying and selling in mass volume.

In the 1960's, chain discount-store firms began to dominate the field; see CHAIN STORES. As expansion accelerated, discount stores became the leading outlet among general merchandise retailers. Traditional retailers, particularly the chain organizations in other fields (department stores, drug stores, variety stores, and supermarkets), came into the discount business by building or acquiring discount stores of their own.

By the late 1960's many States had revoked their fair-trade laws. Selling at discount prices had become an accepted practice, and discount stores were a financially stable element in the retail structure. By 1971 discount-store sales had grown to $28,150,000,000 annually, and were also successful in Canada and Western Europe.

DISCRIMINATION, in common law (q.v.), improper distinction made in serving patrons by one engaged in a public or common calling, such as a common carrier. It is the legal duty of everyone engaged in such a calling to serve all persons in the order in which they present themselves. Further than this, however, the common-law duty does not extend.

Under the common law, a common carrier is not permitted to transport the goods of one man in preference to those of another, but is not forbidden to carry for favored individuals at an unreasonably low rate, or even gratis. The earliest statute on this subject is a British law, known as the Railway Clauses Consolidation Act of 1845. Its main purpose was to prohibit a common carrier from charging more to one person for the carriage of freight than was charged at the same time to others for the same service.

This legislation has served as a model for various Federal and State statutes in the United States. The most important legislation on the matter is that known as the Interstate Commerce Act (q.v.), created in 1887 and subsequently amended. Under its provisions, common carriers are required to make just and reasonable charges for transportation and are forbidden to exercise undue and unreasonable preferences or discrimination. The Interstate Commerce Commission (q.v.) has charge of the enforcement of the provisions of this act.

The enactment of the Robinson-Patman Act in 1936 by Congress was another step taken to eliminate discrimination in commerce. Under its provisions, no seller of commodities in interstate commerce is permitted to discriminate in price between different purchasers of goods of like grade and quality, where such goods are sold for use, consumption, or resale within the U.S. or any of its territories.

Federal and State Enactments. Although civil rights and civil liberties (q.v.) are established in the Constitution of the United States (q.v.), Federal and State governments have enacted laws to combat discrimination against minority groups. Such discrimination has been particularly serious for Negroes, who have been restricted in their use of public facilities, in job opportunities, in education, in choice of residence, and in exercising voting rights, and much of the civil-rights legislation in the U.S. has been inspired by the plight of this group; see NEGROES IN THE UNITED STATES. Thus, during the period of Reconstruction (q.v.) after the Civil War, several laws were passed to assure equality for Negroes. The most sweeping of these was the Civil Rights Act of 1875, which guaranteed the right of Negroes to equal accommodations in public facilities. In 1883, however, most of the provisions of this law were declared unconstitutional by the Supreme Court of the United States (q.v.), which ruled that Congress could be concerned only with State action, not individual action, against the rights of citizens.

Thereafter discriminatory practices remained largely unchallenged until 1941, when President Franklin Delano Roosevelt (q.v.) issued an Executive Order forbidding discrimination in employment by a company working under government defense contract. States began to legislate against discrimination in 1945; by 1964, twenty-five States had legal prohibitions against discrimination in employment, and thirty-one had laws against discrimination in public accommodations. In addition, some banned discrimination in the sale and rental of private housing, and some prohibited discrimination in college admissions. Provisions for enforcing such laws varied from State to State.

On the national level, a major blow against discrimination was the unanimous decision of the Supreme Court of May, 1954, declaring that the segregation of Negro children in separate public schools was a violation of the Fourteenth Amendment to the Constitution. Over bitter opposition, Congress passed the Civil Rights Act of 1957, but the only civil right expressly guaranteed by the law was voting; other provisions of the act established a new civil-rights division in the Department of Justice and a fact-finding Civil Rights Commission. Additional legislation in 1960 strengthened sanctions against racially inspired violence and obstructionism to evade integration of schools and registration of Negro voters. (The desegregation of public schools in the U.S. continued to be a matter of major legislative and judicial concern in the 1960's and 1970's.) See CIVIL RIGHTS AND CIVIL LIBERTIES: *Civil Rights in the United States.*

Subsequent legislation strengthened enforcement of anti-discriminatory practices in other areas. The Civil Rights Act of 1964 outlawed racial discrimination in most hotels, restaurants, and other public facilities; private employers and unions were prohibited from racial discrimination; and registrars were prohibited from applying different standards to white and black voting applicants, provisions that were strengthened by the Voting Rights Act of 1965 and its amendments in 1970. The 1964 law also authorized the U.S. attorney general to file an action where there was a "pattern or practice" of widespread discrimination in violation of the act, and Federal financial aid could henceforth be withdrawn from programs in which racial discrimination was allowed to persist.

In 1968 Congress passed the Fair Housing Act, barring racial discrimination in the sale, rental, or financing of all housing in which Federal monies are involved by way of loans, mortgages, or redevelopment grants.

In 1972 the Civil Rights Act of 1964 was amended: Racial discrimination in employment by any State government agency was banned; U.S. attorneys were given authority to sue State agencies; a limitation on the conciliation power of the Equal Employment Opportunity Commission (the E.E.O.C., established in 1964) was removed; and the commission was given authority to file suit. Aggrieved employees retained the right to intervene in E.E.O.C. suits and to file suit even if the commission elected not to.

Other groups who have been subjected to discrimination throughout U.S. history include such minority groups as American Indians (q.v.), Orientals, and Jews; the aged, who have suffered from discrimination in employment; consumers harmed by fraudulent business practices; urban voters, who have been improperly represented by a system of election districts that do not accurately reflect population density; and the poor, discriminated against in legal representation, voting and running for office, educational opportunities, and welfare benefits (if they have moved). Spanish-speaking Americans or those of Latin American descent—especially Puerto Ricans in the urban East and Mexican Americans in California and the Southwest—have also suffered discrimination. Organizations such as the Mexican American Legal Defense and Educational Fund, Inc., founded in 1968, have participated in hundreds of legal actions aimed at ending this discrimination. Areas of litigation include land and water rights, employment, voting rights, prison reform, issues involving the communications media, bilingual education, and prison reform. American women, who in most States did not receive the right to vote until 1920 (see WOMAN SUFFRAGE), began in the 1960's to make specific demands for legal equality with men. Among the groups known collectively as the women's liberation movement there has been concern not only with discriminatory practices and laws but with outmoded attitudes toward the role of women in society; see WOMEN'S RIGHTS. Homosexuals, too, have begun to take an active role in promoting the reform of legal inequities affecting them and the traditional sexual prejudices and stereotypes.

See also SOCIAL LEGISLATION.   L.D.C.

DISEASE, state of ill health or, conversely, an absence of a state of good health. The word is formed of the prefix *dis-,* meaning absence of, and *-ease,* the combination implying a state of discomfort. However, disease or illness may afflict a person without causing immediate discomfort or feelings of ill health.

History. Man has known disease and grappled with it since the dawn of civilization and has regarded it with awe and superstition. Early man conceived of illness as a consequence of witchcraft or as the work of evil spirits or a vengeful god. He believed in hexes, enchantments, spells, and curses. He sought relief through magic, supplication, and penance. He turned to complex rites, rituals, dances, and celebrations and looked to his spiritual leaders and his wise men for healing and relief.

In time, healers assumed the roles of medicine men and witch doctors. They used a variety of potions, herbs, roots, seeds, leaves, and other natural substances, not knowing to what to attribute the occasional efficacy of their prescriptions, but accepting the fact that they often alleviated symptoms and promoted healing. Many of these potions have since been found to contain medicinal ingredients, which have been purified and used in modern medicine, for instance, digitalis and morphine (qq.v.).

As the sciences developed, certain men

Spraying insecticides in streams, swamps, and other breeding places of insects helps to prevent the spread of malaria and other diseases. WHO

began to be curious about illness and its causes and treatment, and this new attitude toward disease heralded the modern age of medicine (q.v.). Anatomists dissected the human body and described it. Pathologists examined diseased tissue and characterized it. Physiologists described the normal functions of the organs of the body in health and their malfunctions in illness. Microbiologists studied and identified the organisms that cause disease. Pharmacologists studied drugs and their actions on the body. Thus, as knowledge of disease progressed, medicine developed into a scientific discipline as a result of study, experimentation, and research. *See* ANATOMY; PATHOLOGY; PHARMACY; PHYSIOLOGY.

Diagnosis. Disease may cause no symptoms and may then be detected purely by a routine examination or by laboratory or X-ray procedures. In most cases, however, diseases create symptoms that make a person feel ill. The most common manifestation of disease is pain, which may be generalized or localized, mild or severe, constant or remitting, of brief or long duration. The physician may deduce a patient's disease from the character of the pain it causes. Other general symptoms commonly encountered include alterations in body temperature, most often fever (q.v.); fatigue; weakness; loss or gain of weight; changes in appetite; development of swellings or lumps; and symptoms related to alterations in the function of parts of the body. Although the symptoms of many illnesses may mimic each other, the diseases of many organs exhibit characteristic signs peculiar to that disability; *see, for example,* HEART: *Heart Diseases;* LIVER: *Disease of the Liver.*

Classification. Disease may be classified in several ways. A simple method of classification is based on the natural history of the disease, such as whether it is acute or chronic. Another method classifies diseases as organic disorders caused by pathological changes in organs or tissues and functional disorders. The two most widely used classifications, however, are by organ systems and by types of disease.

In the organ system method, diseases are classified in terms of a special body system, such as the respiratory system (*see* RESPIRATION), or in terms of the organs involved, such as diseases of the eye or blood vessels. In this encyclopedia, such subjects are covered under such respective headings as NERVOUS SYSTEM: *Disorders of the Nervous System;* SKIN: *Skin Diseases.*

Classification by types of disease considers their basic nature, including, for example, those caused by congenital or hereditary disturbances

Disease. Plate 1. In Somalia a mother soothes her apprehensive child as a World Health Organization worker takes a blood sample to test it for the presence of malaria-causing parasites. The organization, a branch of the United Nations, has accomplished notable work in the checking of disease around the world.

United Nations

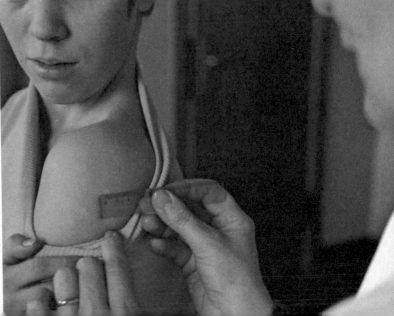

Measuring a child's reaction to tuberculin. One of the tests used to detect tuberculosis is performed by introducing tuberculin, a liquid derived from tuberculosis germs, into the skin. If the reaction is positive, as here, it means the patient has had a tuberculosis infection at some time and other tests may be needed to determine whether it is still active.

WHO

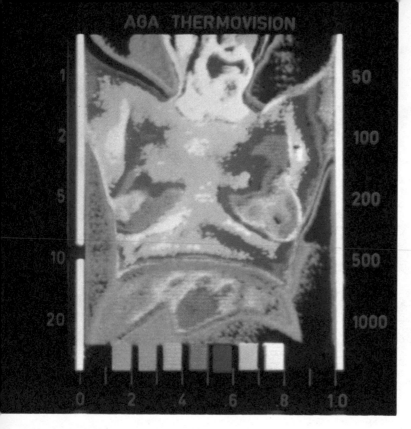

AGA THERMOVISION

A thermogram of the breast. Thermography is a new diagnostic technique which utilizes infrared rays emanating from the breast to record its heat pattern in a photograph. Each color represents a different degree of heat. Certain characteristic heat patterns alert the physician to the possibility of cancer. Thermography, which is generally done in black and white, is also used on parts of the body other than the breast.

Philip Strax, M.D., Medical Director–
Guttman Breast Diagnostic Institute, New York City

(see HEREDITY); by infectious agents (see BACTERIA; FUNGI; VIRUS); by a parasite (q.v.); by nutritional disturbances (see DEFICIENCY DISEASES; NUTRITION, HUMAN); by hormonal abnormality or glandular malfunction (see GLAND; HORMONES); by congenital errors of metabolism (q.v.); by allergy (q.v.); by cancer and tumor (qq.v.); and by aging processes (see GERONTOLOGY). Another group comprises disorders in which disturbances of body functions result from emotional stress; see PSYCHOSOMATIC MEDICINE. A final group embraces diseases of unknown cause.

Modern Developments. As medicine advances and makes new discoveries, certain diseases become less frequent or even disappear. Thus, with an understanding of proper nutrition, many nutritional diseases such as scurvy and pellagra (qq.v.) have become rare where people have access to a balanced diet. The use of antibiotics has controlled many dangerous infectious diseases, notably tuberculosis, syphilis, and pneumonia (qq.v.). Vaccines and sanitation have greatly reduced the incidence of epidemic and endemic diseases; see ANTIBIOTIC; INFECTION; VACCINATION.

A corollary, however, to the victory over many diseases that formerly tended to cause premature death is the appearance of others that affect middle-aged and elderly people. Currently, heart and vascular diseases and cancer seemingly claim more lives than they did several generations ago, when people died earlier of illnesses that are now less formidable. The history of medicine indicates, also, that advances in the treatment, control, or prevention of one group of diseases are followed by the emergence of others that come forward to command the attention of researchers and scientists.

See also HEALTH; PUBLIC HEALTH.   L.J.V.

DISEASES OF ANIMALS, disorders affecting animals, mainly farm and pet animals, but including laboratory animals, zoo animals, and wildlife. These diseases are of concern to man because of their importance economically and as regards public health (q.v.).

Animal diseases may be classified, according to causative agent, as bacterial diseases, fungous diseases, viral diseases, parasitic diseases, hereditary diseases, and diseases caused by environmental factors. Often diseases may be of multiple causation. A relatively mild viral infection, for example, if favored by hereditary susceptibility, may weaken body resistance to bacterial invasion.

Bacterial Diseases. Bacteria (q.v.) cause disease in several ways. Some produce powerful

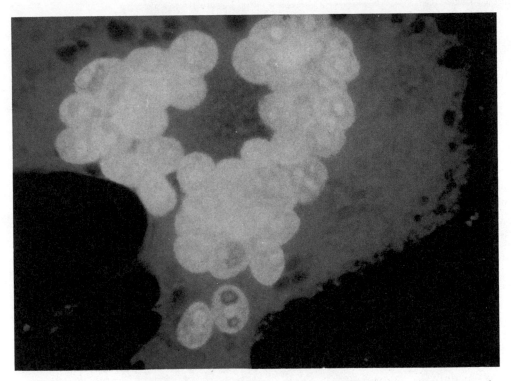

Disease. Plate 2. *Invasion of cells by disease organisms. Above: The photomicrograph shows the response of a group of living cells under attack by measles virus, which will eventually kill them. In an effort to resist, all the cytoplasm of the cells, or all the cellular substance except the nuclei, is fused into one syncytial, or giant, cell. The nuclei, in the center of the picture, cluster together in the same way. Below: Normal liver tissue of a mouse (left) is contrasted with tissue that has been invaded by leukemic cancer (right), both magnified ten times.* Pfizer Inc.

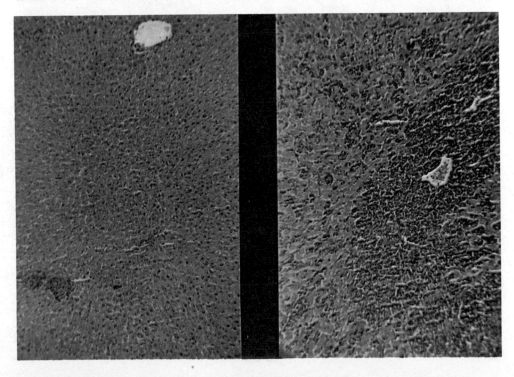

Complex electrical apparatus in use today have simplified the processes of observation and diagnosis. The polygraph (in the background) amplifies, measures, and at the same time records a number of body functions, including heartbeat, respiration, and muscle contraction.
Sterling Drug Inc.

Disease. Plate 3.

The study of viruses and other aspects of disease is facilitated by new high-speed electronic analyzers such as this spectrophotometer. The instrument performs clinical tests on a large number of samples with great speed and precision. Union Carbide

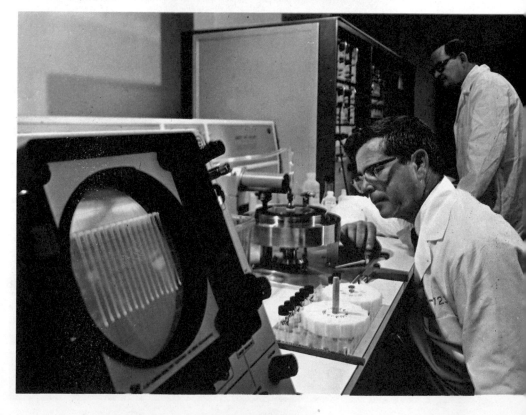

poisons (see POISON) or toxins (q.v.), for example, the botulinus bacillus, the tetanus bacillus, and the gas gangrene bacillus. Other bacteria cause local or general death of body tissues, block the flow of blood, or cause severe irritation. Salmonelloses, or any disease caused by *Salmonella* bacteria, is widespread. Pullorum disease, caused by *S. pullorum*, threatened the chicken and turkey industry until brought under control by elimination of infected birds through blood-testing; see BLOOD: *Blood Diseases*. Almost 2000 other *Salmonella* serotypes are known, each of which may cause disease in man and animals. The bacterium *S. typhimurium* is responsible for about half the so-called food poisoning cases in man, and for many losses of poultry and other animals.

Leptospirosis, due to spiral bacteria of the genus *Leptospira*, causes losses in cattle, dogs, and man. Ponds, lakes, and other bodies of water are common sources of leptospirosis, and infected rodents may carry the infection.

Tuberculosis may be caused by bacteria of the genus *Mycobacterium*. Monkeys and other primates in zoos must be protected by glass walls from tubercular human beings. Human beings must likewise be protected from tubercular cattle, by periodic testing of milk cows and by examination of meat animals at slaughter; see DAIRYING; MEAT.

Anthrax, caused by *Bacillus anthracis*, affects man and domestic animals. Extremely resistant spores carried in hair, hides, or flood waters explain sudden appearances of the bacterial disease.

Pasteurellosis, or any infection caused by bacterium of the genus *Pasteurella*, such as fowl cholera caused by *P. multocida*, is troublesome, affecting wildlife, domestic poultry, rabbits, and other animals.

Tiny, soft-walled bacteria of the genus *Mycoplasma* cause a variety of diseases in animals and man, including pleuropneumonia of cattle, infectious sinusitis of turkeys, and chronic respiratory disease of chickens.

Diseases traditionally thought to be viral in nature, such as psittacosis, or parrot fever, are now believed by some to be caused by bacteria of the genus *Chlamydia*. A number of serious diseases which occur both in man and animals are in this group.

Fungous Diseases. Fungi (q.v.) cause many serious diseases of animals. *Aspergillus* fungi may cause necrosis of the lungs, the nervous system, and other organs. These fungi may also produce toxic products in feed components, causing mycotoxicosis in the animal ingesting such feed. A yeastlike fungus, *Candida albicans*, may cause death in turkeys, ptarmigan, hummingbirds, and other animals. Dermatophytic fungi affect the skin of animals and man. Dust-borne fungi, such as *Coccidioides immitis* and *Histoplasma capsulatum*, produce lung disease or generalized disease in animals and man.

Viral Diseases. Viral agents are multitudinous, causing equine infectious anemia, Newcastle disease, hog cholera, fowl pox, rabies, canine distemper, encephalitis, and a host of other diseases. Several viral agents cause tumor formation in poultry, known as the leukosis complex, resulting in serious economic loss. Influenza viruses cause serious problems in swine, horses, and birds. See VIRUS.

Some viruses spread from mother to offspring through the placenta or through the egg, and some have very resistant forms that can survive in dust. Other viruses require intimate contact to be contagious. Still others are spread by biting arthropods.

Viruses are not always limited to one species of animal, nor to one kind of tissue or organ. On the other hand, severity of diseases may be much greater in one species or kind of tissue.

Parasitic Diseases. Parasites, which attack all animals, range in size from tiny protozoa to yard-long kidney worms; see PARASITE.

Protozoan diseases include the coccidioses, of great economic importance and generally intestinal, although rabbits are susceptible to liver coccidiosis and geese to kidney coccidiosis; the malarias, arthropod-borne infections with *Plasmodium*, *Leukocytozoon*, or *Haemoproteus* protozoa, all of which afflict zoo and wild animals; flagellate infections, such as trichomoniasis, caused by *Trichomonas gallinae* in birds, or by *T. fetus* in cattle; and trypanosomiasis, also known by the names nagana, surra, and dourine, caused by flagellates (q.v.) related to the agent of African sleeping sickness.

Worms called helminths comprise a large, heterogeneous group of parasites, including roundworms, nematodes, flukes, trematodes; tapeworms, cestodes; thorny-headed worms, acanthocephala; and tongue-worms, linguatulids.

Migrating larval roundworms cause considerable damage to lungs and other organs in some animals. *Capillaria* worms may attack the lining of the digestive tract. Adults of the heartworm, *Dirofilaria immitis*, live in the heart of dogs and produce microscopic larval stages which swim in the blood. Larvae of *Strongylus vulgaris* cause arterial obstruction, with resultant digestive troubles and even lameness.

Tapeworms, adults of which are commonly found in the intestines of animals, often have very damaging larval stages in body tissues of secondary hosts. Larval dog tapeworms form large cysts in liver, lungs, and other organs of man and other animals; the disease is called echinococcosis.

Flukes, with several hosts in a complex life cycle, may be very damaging in themselves, for example, the liver flukes affecting cattle, sheep, and goats; or they may act as carriers of other disease agents, as in the case of flukes carrying the salmon poisoning agent of dogs, which is contracted from infested salmon or trout. Swimmer's itch in man is caused by developmental stages of waterfowl flukes.

Thorny-headed worms embed their heads, armed with many stout hooks, in the intestinal wall. They are common in the robin, as well as in other birds.

Tongueworms have a complex life history, passing through stages, one of which has legs, in the internal organs of one host; they then develop into adulthood in the respiratory passages of another species of host. Arthropods, generally external parasites, have some species with some or all stages inside the body of the host. They damage animals by feeding on body tissues, by producing toxic substances, by producing sensitizing substances, and by transmitting disease agents.

Insects, among the arthropods, include those that are bloodsuckers as adults, for example, mosquitoes, gnats, some flies, fleas, and some lice; those that are bloodsuckers in larval stages, such as ear-maggots, *Protocalliphora,* of hawk nestlings; and those that eat tissue, including some larval flies and some lice. Great damage to meat and hides of cattle is caused by larval flies such as ox warbles, which migrate through the tissues and, after boring breathing holes through the skin, finally leave the body to pupate. Bloodsucking *Diptera* often transmit blood protozoa and arboviruses. A wingless fly, the sheep ked, is often mistakenly called a sheep tick.

Lice are of two types, those with chewing mouthparts, and those with sucking mouthparts. Lice cause irritation, carry disease agents, and may cause anemia.

Fleas are all bloodsuckers. They may carry larval tapeworms, may transmit filarial worms, and may carry other disease agents. The sticktight flea may kill young birds by excessive bloodsucking.

Acarine parasites include the mites and the ticks. Mites may be external bloodsuckers, such as the red mite of birds, which can also affect man and other animals; or they may be internal parasites, such as the *Sternostoma* mites of the lungs and air passages of canaries and other birds. Ticks, larger than mites, suck blood and transmit disease agents in the forms of protozoa, viruses, and bacteria. Ticks may have several hosts during their life cycle.

Hereditary Diseases. Heredity (q.v.) plays a large part in animal disease, either in directly causing skeletal, skin, or endocrine defects, or by making the animal more susceptible to other disease agents. Animals have been bred for resistance to specific disease agents. Breeders must be alert, however, for unwanted characteristics that may accompany desirable characteristics in the genetic apparatus.

Environmental Factors. Heat is an important factor environmentally, especially in young animals whose protective coats or physiological mechanisms have not yet developed. Chilling or overheating can cause death, and male sterility may develop from relatively slight overheating. Electricity, in lightning or in feed-intake inhibiting shocks from mechanical feeders, is always a hazard to animals. High-frequency radiations may also cause serious trouble. Poorly pigmented animals may be harmed by ultraviolet light, and even radar waves, at close range, can kill animals. X rays and atomic radiation may damage blood-forming tissues, reproductive cells, and other tissues. *See* RADAR; RADIATION; ULTRAVIOLET RADIATION; X RAY. Ordinary physical injuries, from objects or other animals, are always a matter of concern since they can lead to bacterial infection.

Poisonous plants may cause serious losses, usually in places, such as western ranges, or at times, such as early spring, when nonpoisonous forage plants are not readily available. Some plants are poisonous only at certain times, for example, Sudan grass (q.v.), which is poisonous only when wilted or frozen. Other plants, such as white snakeroot (*see* MILKWORT), are always poisonous. *See* PLANTS, POISONOUS.

Pesticides, insecticides, herbicides, fungicides, and rodenticides cause sickness and death if improperly used. Pesticides are often wrongly blamed for animal losses actually due to undetected viral or bacterial disease. *See* AGRICULTURAL CHEMISTRY; INSECTICIDE.

Drugs (q.v.) used excessively or otherwise improperly kill many animals. Broad-spectrum antibiotics (*see* ANTIBIOTIC) in guinea-pig feeds are often lethal, and excess salt may kill pigs and chickens.

Water is essential to most body functions. If it

is lacking death results. Overeating, especially of unusual feeds, causes digestive disorders. Starvation may result from feed not being visible or from social domination by other animals; see FAMINE.

Nutritional requirements and complexities of animals, despite many years of intensive research, are still imperfectly understood. Each species, as well as each breed or strain within a species, varies in its needs. A Great Dane puppy, for example, will develop rickets on a diet adequate for a terrier pup. Pheasant and turkey young require much more protein than do chickens. Certain feeds may also predispose animals to disease. Thus, hummingbirds develop candidiasis on honey feeding, but not on sucrose syrup. Feeds may contain antivitamins which produce deficiency diseases.

Control of Diseases. The annual toll from animal diseases is extremely high, and the expense in wasted feed, drugs, vaccines (see VACCINATION), and veterinary services, costly. Since public health is a major concern, many Federal agencies exist to deal with diseases of animals. Most important is the Agricultural Research Service (q.v.) of the United States Department of Agriculture, formerly the Bureau of Animal Industry. Wildlife problems are the province of the U.S. Department of the Interior. The U.S. Department of Health, Education, and Welfare is concerned with animal diseases affecting human health, such as rabies, and with the use of drugs in animals that yield human food.

In the past, Federal programs eradicated such devastating diseases as dourine and glanders of horses, and pleuropneumonia and foot-and-mouth disease of cattle, and have brought under control such diseases as brucellosis and hog cholera.

Control measures in present-day programs include quarantine (q.v.) of imported animals, despite serious gaps in legal authority to impose quarantine; cooperation of Federal and State agencies in the study and control of animal diseases; inspection of red meat and poultry to minimize the danger of spread of animal disease to human beings; and the inspection and evaluation of vaccines and other pharmaceutical and Biological products as to purity, efficacy, and safety. Universities and other research institutions conduct research on the many disease problems that affect animals of all kinds.

See CONSERVATION: *Wildlife Conservation*; VETERINARY MEDICINE. See also separate articles on most of the animals and on the more well-known diseases, or types of diseases, mentioned above.   W.J.M.

DISEASES OF PLANTS, deviations from the normal growth and development of plants incited by microorganisms, parasitic flowering plants, nematodes, viruses, or adverse environmental conditions. In the United States alone known plant diseases attributable to these causes are estimated to number more than 25,000; the estimated annual losses therefrom approximate $3,000,000,000. Injuries to plant life due primarily to insects, mites, or animals other than nematodes are not regarded as plant diseases.

Bacteria-Induced Diseases. Bacterial diseases are marked by various symptoms, including soft rot, leaf spot, wilt of leaves and stems, canker, leaf and twig blight, and gall formation. Fire blight, a disease of apple and pear trees, is historically interesting because it was the first plant disease in which a bacterium was shown to be the inciting agent. Infected trees exhibit a blackening of the flowers, leaves, and twigs, and the disease finally may involve the entire tree, causing serious damage and even death. Citrus canker, an Asian disease of the orange tree and its relatives, is characterized by corky growths on the fruit, leaves, and twigs. Common scab of potato, bacterial canker of tomato, angular leaf spot of cotton, and black rot of crucifers are a few of the bacterial plant diseases prevalent in the U.S. Crowngall, or plant cancer, which occurs in a wide range of woody plants and some herbaceous groups, is a striking example of bacteria-induced disease. See BACTERIA.

Destructive Fungi. The majority of plant diseases are incited by fungi (q.v.). Fungus diseases have been observed and commented on since ancient times. Biblical records mention blights and mildews on the cereal and vine crops of the ancient Hebrews. Fungus diseases were responsible for several major catastrophes in various parts of the world. Prominent among these fungus diseases was the late blight, a disease of the potato which invaded Europe after 1845, with particularly devastating results in Ireland. Powdery mildew of the grape, native to America, became established in France and nearly wrecked the French wine industry. A parasitic rust fungus called the *Hemileia* destroyed the coffee plantations of Ceylon and other Oriental countries. In the U.S. the chestnut, a most important timber, nut, and tannin-producing tree, has been eliminated by an introduced Oriental fungus. Over 1400 species of rust fungi, all parasitic, and several hundred species of smut fungi occur in North America. Equally large numbers of fungi in other groups produce a bewildering array of diseases characterized by leaf spots, ulcerous le-

The contrast between diseased and healthy fruit. The shriveled pears (left) died of a bacterial disease called fire blight before they were ripe. The ripe fruit (right) from the same orchard was treated with a spray containing the antibiotics streptomycin and Terramycin.
Chas. Pfizer & Co., Inc.

sions, blights, powdery and downy mildews, cankers, wood rots and stains, root rots, wilts, club root, and various other symptoms.

Viral Infections. The viruses cause as wide a range of host reactions as do the bacteria and the fungi. The number of recognized virus diseases of plants has increased rapidly in recent years. Typical symptoms of viral infections include mosaic patterns, yellowing of foliage, vein-clearing, ring spots, stunting and premature death, malformations, and overgrowth. Under some conditions the symptoms may be masked. Such virus diseases as peach yellows, tobacco mosaic, potato-leaf roll, and curly top of beets have been studied intensively because of heavy losses to U.S. crops affected with these diseases. All economic plants suffer from one or more of these obscure but potentially dangerous entities. Virus diseases are infectious and are transmitted largely by insects. Control of these insects is the best means of reducing the disease incidence. Virus infections also may be transmitted in the process of budding or graft-

ing, by contamination of the soil, and less commonly by means of seed or parasitic flowering plants. Among the flowering plants or so-called higher plants are a few true parasites that cause injury or death to their hosts. The mistletoes, dodders, and root parasites of the genera *Striga* and *Orobanche* (broomrape) are the more common of these parasitic plants. *See* VIRUS.

Nematodes. Nematodes (q.v.), or roundworms, are an important cause of disease in plants. For many years attention was focused on the root-knot nematodes, which cause fleshy root knots or galls on plants. More recent investigations were concerned with other species, including the stem or bulb nematodes, which live in the leaves, stems, bulbs, and roots of narcissus, phlox, and many other plants, and the leaf nematodes, growing in such herbaceous plants as begonia and chrysanthemum. The golden nematode of the potato and related plants and the soybean cyst nematode are recent introductions into America that are causing much concern.

Environmental Enemies. Nonparasitic diseases attributable to adverse environmental conditions are numerous and include many of economic importance. Major factors involved in these diseases are excessively high or low temperatures, soil-moisture disturbances, atmospheric impurities, lightning, and nutritional disorders. Low temperatures, for example, are responsible for winter injury to fruit trees and potatoes, and high temperatures produce such disturbances as water core of apple and heat canker of flax. Excessive or irregular water supplies cause a variety of troubles, such as blossom-end rot of tomatoes. Among atmospheric impurities may be mentioned escaping illuminating gas and smelter fumes. The latter in particular may be responsible for widespread killing of crops and forests. An adverse environmental factor not often recognized is lightning, which frequently causes injuries to plantings of cotton, bananas, sugar cane, potatoes, and many other field crops. Excessive soil acidity adversely affects many plants. On the other hand, high alkalinity may be deleterious. An excess of nitrogen or any other substance required for normal growth may cause abnormalities in plant development. Mineral deficiencies also cause diseases, and the characteristic symptoms produced by lack of each of many minerals are well established; see TRACE ELEMENTS.

For diseases of specific plants, see articles on the individual plants.   J.A.S.

DISINFECTANTS. *See* ANTISEPTICS.

DISLOCATION, in medicine, displacement of the bones forming a joint (*see* JOINTS). A partial or incomplete dislocation is called a subluxation. It is possible to dislocate almost any articulated joint in the human skeleton, but certain dislocations, such as those of the jaw, knee, shoulder, and finger bones, are more frequent than others. The ease of dislocation from a wrench or twist depends on the shape of the bones involved and on the amount of strength in the ligaments that hold the joints in place. Dislocations of the wrist and the ankle are comparatively rare in the absence of fracture, since the wrist joint is held firmly in place by ligaments, and the shape of the bones of the ankle makes displacement difficult. These joints, are however, subject to sprain (q.v.) or strain. The treatment for all types of dislocation is to move the bones back into proper relation with each other, a process known as reduction. Dislocations should be reduced as quickly as possible to avoid impairment of muscle and tendon function. The contraction of muscles sometimes makes reduction difficult unless the patient is anesthetized.

DISMAL SWAMP, former name of GREAT DISMAL SWAMP, marshy region of S.E. Virginia and N.E. North Carolina, extending from near Portsmouth, Va., to the vicinity of Albemarle Sound and covering about 1940 sq.km (750 sq.mi.). Through it runs the Dismal Swamp Canal, which connects Chesapeake Bay with Albemarle Sound. Lake Drummond (11 km/7 mi. long), in the midst of the swamp, is the setting for "The Lake of the Dismal Swamp" by the Irish poet Thomas Moore (q.v.). A large part of the swamp is heavily wooded and is noted for hunting and fishing. The Great Dismal Swamp was surveyed (1763) by George Washington (q.v.), who helped organize a company to drain it.

DISNEY, Walt, in full WALTER ELIAS DISNEY (1901–66), American cartoonist and motion-picture producer, born in Chicago. He left school at the age of sixteen; later he studied briefly at art schools in Chicago, Ill., and Kansas City, Mo. In 1923 he began to produce animated motion pictures in Hollywood, Calif., in partnership with his brother Roy O. Disney (1893–1971). Their first productions, a series called "Alice in Cartoonland" (1923–26), combined animated cartoon figures with a living actress. Disney produced (1926–28) a cartoon series, "Oswald the Rabbit", for Universal Pictures. *Steamboat Willie* (1928), produced by his own company, introduced Disney's most popular and enduring cartoon character, Mickey Mouse. This film also utilized sound for the first time in an animated cartoon. His "Silly Symphony" series was inaugurated with *Skeleton Dance* (1929); his first use of color occurred in one of the short films of

Walt Disney is photographed with a sketch of his most famous cartoon character, Mickey Mouse.

this series, *Flowers and Trees* (1932). Disney originated the feature-length cartoon with *Snow White and the Seven Dwarfs* (1937) and followed it with other feature-length films, such as *Pinocchio* (1940), *Fantasia* (1941), and *Bambi* (1942).

In the 1950's and 1960's, his company, Walt Disney Productions, Ltd., with Disney as executive producer, was one of the major producers of films for motion-picture theaters and television. As the scope of his enterprises expanded, Disney retained as much artistic control as possible. The company was involved in the publication of books for children and the syndication of comic strips, most of them featuring characters from the Disney cartoons, including Donald Duck and Pluto, the dog. In 1955 Walt Disney Productions, Ltd., opened a huge amusement park called Disneyland in Anaheim, Calif. Featuring historical reconstructions, displays, and rides, it became one of the most famous tourist attractions in the world. Meanwhile, in addition to cartoons, the company made several documentary films as part of the "True-Life Adventure" and "People and Places" series; these included *The Living Desert* (1953) and *Secrets of Life* (1956). Beginning in 1950 the company released a long series of adventure, comedy, and musical films; among these were *Treasure Island* (1950), *Robin Hood* (1951), *The Shaggy Dog* (1959), *The Absent-Minded Professor* (1961), and *Mary Poppins* (1964). Animated features of this period included *Peter Pan* (1953) and *The Sword in the Stone* (1963). Disney's company was also responsible for several popular television series, including "Davy Crockett", "The Mickey Mouse Club", and "Walt Disney's Wonderful World of Color".

Disney received a total of thirty-nine awards from the Academy of Motion Picture Arts and Sciences for the theatrical films produced by him or under his supervision.

DISNEYLAND. See CALIFORNIA: *Parks, Forests, and Other Places of Interest;* DISNEY, WALT.

DISPERSION. See OPTICS: *Physical Optics.*

DISPLACED PERSON, or D.P., term used during the World War II era to designate an individual forced to live outside the borders of his home country. See REFUGEE.

DISRAELI or **D'ISRAELI,** name of a British father and son distinguished for their achievements in letters and politics.

Isaac D'Israeli or **Isaac Disraeli** (1766–1848), writer, born in Enfield, England. He was the son of Benjamin D'Israeli, a Jewish refugee who came to England in 1748 from Venice, and who amassed a fortune as a merchant. Benjamin D'Israeli planned a business career for his son, but was persuaded to allow Isaac to follow literary and scholarly pursuits. Isaac spent the remainder of his life in quiet study. He wrote several novels, but his popularity as a writer was due mainly to such books of research and criticism as *Curiosities of Literature* (6 vol., 1791–1834), which in spite of inaccuracies contains many interesting literary and historical anecdotes. In 1802 he married Maria Basevi, and had four sons, one of whom was Benjamin Disraeli, 1st Earl of Beaconsfield. In 1817 Isaac D'Israeli had his children baptized in the Anglican Church. His writings include *Calamities of Authors* (1812–13), *Quarrels of Authors* (1814), *Genius of Judaism* (1833), and *Amenities of Literature* (3 vol., 1841).

Benjamin Disraeli, 1st Earl of Beaconsfield (1804–81), statesman and novelist, born in London, England, and educated at private schools in Blackheath and Walthamstow. Between the ages of seventeen and twenty, Disraeli was a law apprentice in a London office. During the same period he speculated in stocks and suffered heavy financial losses. Primarily in order to pay off his debts, he began writing novels, the first of which, *Vivian Grey,* appeared in 1826 with some success. Continuing to write novels in a fanciful, romantic vein, he frequented fashionable salons and dressed in an eccentric manner. In 1830 he traveled in Spain, the Balkans, Turkey, and the Levant. Upon his return he decided to enter politics; from 1832 to 1835 he ran unsuccessfully for Parliament, first as a Radical and then three times as a Tory.

Despite these defeats, he became well known through a series of pamphlets, tracts, and letters to the London *Times,* in which he set forth the foundation of his conservative philosophy. In the elections of 1837, after Victoria (q.v.), Queen of Great Britain, came to the throne, he finally won a seat in the House of Commons. With his maiden speech, however, he nearly ruined his career because his extravagant phraseology and eccentric clothing provoked derisive laughter from his fellow members. He slowly acquired a reputation in Parliament, but in 1841 was refused a cabinet post in the Conservative ministry of Sir Robert Peel (q.v.). Disraeli labored to win support for his policies, which included championing factory workers against the rich Whig manufacturers and regarding the queen, the aristocracy, and the church the custodians of civil liberties. His novels *Coningsby, or the Younger Generation* (1844) and *Sybil, or the Two Nations* (1845) expressed his views and increased his prestige in Parliament, expecially

Benjamin Disraeli　　　　Bettmann Archive

with the so-called Young England group, which opposed Peel's conservatism. When Peel was engaged in his successful effort to repeal the Corn Laws (q.v.) in 1846, Disraeli's eloquent attacks on his party's chief won him leadership of the protectionists (*see* FREE TRADE AND PROTECTION); the divided Conservative Party, however, was defeated by the Liberal Party in the national election of that year. Disraeli supported the Liberal prime minister Lord John Russell (q.v.) in 1847, when his government lifted the ban excluding adherents of the Jewish faith from Parliament. In 1852 Disraeli became chancellor of the exchequer under Edward George Geoffrey Smith Stanley, 14th Earl of Derby (1799–1869), and he held the same office in the Derby ministries of 1858–59 and 1866–68.

In 1859, as Conservative leader in the House of Commons, Disraeli introduced a reform bill extending the franchise to all taxpayers. The bill failed to carry, but later Disraeli succeeded in the passage of the much more democratic Reform Act of 1867. When Derby retired the next year, Disraeli became prime minister, but his government was defeated in 1868, and he spent six years in bitter parliamentary opposition to Prime Minister William Ewart Gladstone (q.v.). After the elections of 1874 Disraeli was able to form a strong majority government backed by the partisan sympathy of Victoria, whose close friend he became. His prime ministership was marked by many notable events. He promoted legislation in 1874 against Roman Catholic tendencies in Church of England ritual. In 1875, to protect the "lifeline" of the empire, he took a personal responsibility for borrowing £4,000,000 to purchase for the government the shares in the Suez Canal (q.v.) that were owned by the khedive of Egypt. Disraeli further emphasized his imperial policy by creating for Queen Victoria in 1876 the title of Empress of India. In that year Queen Victoria created him earl of Beaconsfield in recognition of his services to the empire.

Disraeli's most spectacular triumph in external affairs came in 1878 as British plenipotentiary to the Congress of Berlin (*see* BERLIN, CONGRESS OF) which redrew the boundaries of southeastern Europe after the defeat of Turkey in the Russo-Turkish War of 1877–78. During the war Disraeli had been concerned with preventing Russia from gaining strategic advantages in the Mediterranean and had sent the British fleet to the Dardanelles in February, 1878. At the Congress of Berlin, by brilliant diplomatic maneuvers, he deprived Russia of many of the advantages of victory and returned to England claiming to have won "peace with honor". The queen offered to reward him with a dukedom, which he refused. The Primrose League, so called after Disraeli's favorite flower and dedicated to his political ideas, was founded in 1883, two years after his death. Members of the league pledged themselves to the "maintenance of religion, of the estates of the realm, and the imperial ascendancy of Great Britain".

Disraeli's writings include *Vindication of the British Constitution* (1835) and the novels *The Young Duke* (1831), *Henrietta Temple* (1837), *Tancred, or the New Crusade* (1847), and *Endymion* (1880).

Despite the fact that he exerted a profound influence on the course of British politics and left an enduring stamp on the Conservative Party (q.v.), Disraeli is still regarded as an enigma. His multitude of enemies characterized him as an opportunist and a seeker of power; his legions of followers regarded him as a man of high principle. These opposing views probably resulted from the contradictions inherent in his public acts. He was both a conservative and a radical and perhaps embodied the best of both traditions.

DISSECTION. *See* ANATOMY.

DISSENTERS, *or* DISSIDENTS, persons who refuse to accept the authority of, or conform to, the laws of an established church. "Dissenters" was commonly used in 17th-century England, especially after passage of the Toleration Act in

1689, to denote groups who separated from the Church of England (q.v.). English Roman Catholics were called "recusants". After the middle of the 19th century, "Dissenters" and "Dissidents" were largely replaced by "Nonconformists" (q.v.) and "Free Churchmen".

DISSOCIATION, in chemistry, breaking up of compounds into simpler constituents, especially under the influence of heat and pressure. The term is usually applied only to those reactions that are reversible, that is, to those reactions in which the final products are capable of reforming the original substance by changing the equilibrium of the reaction. Dissociation therefore is different from decomposition, in which no implications as to the behavior of the final products are assumed.

By heating phosphorus pentachloride in a glass vessel, dissociation into phosphorus trichloride and chlorine gas can be readily observed, because of the green color of the chlorine:

$$PCl_5 = PCl_3 + Cl_2$$

Even more striking is the dissociation by the application of heat of nitrogen tetroxide, N_2O_4, a faintly colored gas, into the brownish-red oxide of nitrogen, NO_2:

$$N_2O_4 = 2NO_2$$

In the case of both phosphorus pentachloride and nitrogen tetroxide, a lowering of the temperature causes a recombination of the products of dissociation into their original forms, and a consequent disappearance of the colors.

The extent to which a compound may be dissociated is strongly influenced by the temperature of the reaction and by the pressure exerted upon the reactants. In the case of nitrogen tetroxide, the application of a moderate degree of heat causes only a small fraction of the original amount to change. As the temperature is raised, however, the dissociation fraction increases. This is plainly shown by the darkening of the gas. Increased pressure causes the dissociation fraction to diminish, as indicated by the gradual disappearance of the color. Careful experiments, carried out at a temperature of 50° C. (122° F.), have shown that, at that temperature, nitrogen tetroxide is almost completely dissociated if the pressure is very low. When subjected to a pressure of about 500 mm of mercury, only half of the tetroxide is changed. *See also* ELECTROCHEMISTRY; IONIZATION.

DISTEMPER, acute and dangerous disease of dogs, analogous to influenza in human beings. In general it attacks animals between the ages of two months and one year, although it sometimes occurs in older dogs. The disease frequently ends in death; even if the victim recovers from distemper, chorea, a disease marked by uncontrolled muscular twitching, and other nervous diseases, often follow.

The primary cause of distemper is a filtrable virus (q.v.), but often the disease is complicated by secondary bacterial infections. Distemper is extremely contagious and it is believed that the infecting virus is transmitted by airborne water droplets inhaled by the animal. The first symptoms of the disease are a rise in temperature, shivering, sneezing, lassitude, and discharges from the mouth and nose. As the attack continues, pneumonia, convulsions, chorea, and paralysis may occur. The course of distemper is normally about four weeks, if the animal lives, and in the later stages the victim may be extremely weak. The sick dog should be kept warm, dry, and quiet, and should be fed small amounts of such easily digested foods as milk, raw egg yolks, and beef broth. During convalescence, overeating and overexercise should be avoided. No known medication will cure distemper, but serums and antibiotics administered by a veterinarian offer protection against secondary infections.

To prevent attacks of distemper, the American Veterinary Medical Association recommends annual vaccination of all young dogs except pregnant females. Multiple doses of attenuated live virus vaccine are believed to be more effective than passive immunizing agents of killed virus. In 1954 several new strains of distemper virus were discovered; authorities now believe that vaccine should be modified periodically to include the viral types currently infecting dogs. A young puppy may be given temporary immunity by an injection of serum from a highly immune animal. The serum injections, however, must be repeated at intervals.

DISTHENE. *See* CYANITE.

DISTILLATION, process of heating a liquid until its more volatile constituents pass into the vapor phase, and then cooling the vapor to recover such constituents in liquid form by condensation. The main purpose of distillation is to separate a mixture of several components by taking advantage of their different volatilities, or the separation of volatile materials from nonvolatile materials. In evaporation and in drying, the purpose usually is to obtain the less volatile constituent, and the more volatile constituent, in most cases water, is discarded; in distillation on the other hand, the principal object of the operation is to obtain the more volatile constituent in pure form. The removal of water from glycerin by vaporizing the water, for example, is called evaporation, but the removal of water from alcohol by vaporizing the alcohol is called distillation, although similar apparatus is employed in both cases; see EVAPORATION.

If the difference in volatility (and hence in boiling point) between the two constituents is great, complete separation may be easily accomplished by a single distillation; see BOILING POINT. Sea water, for example, which contains about 4 percent dissolved solids (principally common salt), may be readily purified by vaporizing the water, condensing the steam thus formed, and collecting the product, distilled water. This product is, for most purposes, equivalent to pure water, although actually it contains some impurities in the form of dissolved gases, the most important of which is carbon dioxide.

If the boiling points of the constituents of a mixture differ only slightly, complete separation cannot be achieved in a single distillation. An important example is the separation of water, which boils at 212° F. (100° C.), and alcohol, which boils at 173° F. (78.5° C.). If a mixture of these two liquids is boiled, the vapor which rises is richer in alcohol and poorer in water than the liquid from which it came, but it is not pure alcohol. If one desires to concentrate a 10 percent solution of alcohol (such as might be obtained by fermentation) to obtain a 50 percent solution (a common strength for whiskey),

it is necessary to redistill the distillate once or twice, and if industrial (95 percent) alcohol is desired, many redistillations are required.

Distillation Apparatus. Technically, the term "still" is applied only to the vessel in which liquids are boiled during distillation, but the term is sometimes applied to the entire apparatus, including the fractionating column, the condenser, and the receiver in which the distillate is collected. The term still is also extended to cover apparatus for destructive distillation or cracking (q.v.). The term "retort" is sometimes used for a still, and historically, the term "alembic" was used for the same apparatus in the days of alchemy (q.v.). Stills for laboratory work are usually made of glass, but industrial stills are generally made of iron or steel. In cases in which iron would contaminate the product, copper is often employed, and small stills for the distillation of whiskey are frequently made of glass and copper.

Fractional Distillation. If a portion of the distillate is returned from the condenser and made to drip down through a long column onto a series of plates, and if the vapor as it rises on its

A forced circulation, vapor-compression distillation process is used to convert saline water to one million gallons of fresh water daily at the Office of Saline Water Demonstration Plant at Roswell, New Mexico.
Office of Saline Water

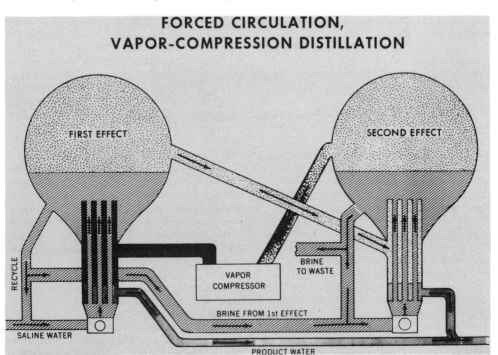

FORCED CIRCULATION, VAPOR-COMPRESSION DISTILLATION

FIRST EFFECT   SECOND EFFECT

RECYCLE

VAPOR COMPRESSOR

BRINE TO WASTE

BRINE FROM 1st EFFECT

SALINE WATER

PRODUCT WATER

way to the condenser is made to bubble through this liquid at each plate, the vapor and liquid will interact so that some of the water in the vapor condenses and some of the alcohol in the liquid vaporizes. The interaction at each plate is thus equivalent to a redistillation, and by building a column with a sufficient number of plates, 95 percent alcohol can be obtained in a single operation. Moreover, by feeding the original 10 percent alcohol solution gradually at a point in the middle of the column, virtually all of the alcohol may be stripped from the water as it descends to the lowest plate, so that no alcohol need be wasted.

This process is known as rectification, fractionation, or fractional distillation, and is very common in industrial usage, not only for simple mixtures of two components, such as alcohol and water in fermentation products or oxygen and nitrogen in liquid air, but for highly complex mixtures, such as those found in coal tar and petroleum; see PETROLEUM: *Refining*. The fractionating column most often used is the so-called bubble tower, in which the plates are arranged horizontally a few inches apart and the ascending vapors are forced to rise through bubble caps in each plate and then bubble through the liquid. The plates are baffled so that the liquid flows from left to right on one plate, then overflows onto the plate below, and there flows from right to left. If the interaction between liquid and vapor is incomplete, or if frothing and entrainment occur so that some of the liquid is carried up by the vapor to the plate above, five actual plates might be required to do the work of four theoretical plates, producing four redistillations. An inexpensive equivalent of a bubble tower is the so-called packed column, in which the liquid flows down over a packing of earthenware rings or bits of glass tubing.

The only disadvantage of fractional distillation is that a large fraction (which may be as much as one half) of the condensed distillate must be refluxed, or returned to the top of the tower and eventually boiled over again, and more heat must therefore be supplied. On the other hand, the continuous operation made possible by fractionation allows great heating economies, for the outgoing distillate may be used to preheat the incoming feed.

When the mixture consists of many components, they are drawn off at different points along the tower. Industrial distillation towers for petroleum often have over 100 plates, with as many as ten different fractions being drawn off at suitable points. Although it is not possible,

with a mixture as complex as petroleum, to obtain pure components with a tower of practical size, the fractions produced, such as kerosene and gasoline (q.v.), are pure enough for practical purposes. Towers with more than 500 plates have been used for the separation of isotopes (q.v.) by distillation.

Theory of Distillation. In the simplest mixture of two mutually soluble liquids, the volatility of each is undisturbed by the presence of the other. In such a case, the boiling point of a 50–50 mixture, for example, would be halfway between the boiling points of the pure substances, and the degree of separation produced by a single distillation would depend only on the vapor pressure, or the volatility, of the separate components at this temperature. This simple relationship was first stated by the French chemist François Marie Raoult (1830–1901) and is called Raoult's law. Raoult's law applies only to mixtures of liquids that are very similar in chemical structure, such as benzene and toluene. In most cases wide deviations occur from this law, and these deviations must be determined experimentally. Thus, the volatility of alcohol in dilute aqueous solution is several times as great as predicted by Raoult's law. In extremely concentrated alcohol solutions, the deviation is even more striking: the distillation of 99 percent alcohol produces vapor that has *less* than 99 percent alcohol. For this reason, alcohol cannot be concentrated by distillation beyond 97 percent, even by an infinite number of distillations; see ALCOHOL.

If one component is only slightly soluble in the other, its volatility is abnormally increased. Fusel oil, for example, which consists mainly of amyl alcohol, is a common impurity in freshly fermented alcohol; it is slightly soluble in water, and is normally less volatile than water. In aqueous solution, however, it is extremely volatile, and for this reason it rises above the lowest plates of an alcohol distillation tower, but condenses at the level where fairly pure alcohol is being formed. It thus collects near the middle of the tower, and may be drawn off in comparatively pure form for further purification as a valuable by-product.

Steam Distillation. If two insoluble liquids are heated, each is unaffected by the presence of the other (so long as they are agitated so that the lighter liquid does not form an impenetrable layer over the heavier), and vaporizes to an extent determined only by its own volatility. Such a mixture, therefore, always boils at a temperature lower than that of either constituent; and the percentage of each constituent in the vapor depends only on its vapor pressure at this temperature. This principle may be applied to distill, at temperatures below their normal boiling points, substances that would be damaged by overheating if distilled in the usual fashion. The normal boiling point of pure aniline, for example, is about 184° C. (363° F.), and of impure aniline somewhat higher. A mixture of water and aniline, however, boils at 98° C. (208 ° F.), and the vapor rising from this mixture contains about one aniline molecule to every fifteen water molecules, or about one third aniline by weight. It is thus possible to purify aniline by distillation at a low temperature simply by blowing steam through it.

Vacuum Distillation. Another method of distilling substances at temperatures below their normal boiling points is by partially evacuating the still. Thus aniline may be distilled at 100° C. by removing 93 percent of the air from the still. This method is as effective as steam distillation, but somewhat more expensive. The greater the degree of vacuum, the lower is the distillation temperature. If the distillation is carried on in a practically perfect vacuum, the process is called molecular distillation. This process, which is now regularly used industrially for the purification of vitamins and certain other unstable products, was perfected during World War II. The substance is placed on a plate in an evacuated space, and heated. The condenser is a cold plate, placed as close to the first as possible. Most of the material passes across the space between the two plates, and very little is lost.

Centrifugal Molecular Distillation. If a tall column of mixed gases is sealed and placed upright, there will be a partial separation of the gases as a result of gravity (*see* GRAVITATION) pulling the heavier components to the bottom, the lighter gases moving to the top of the column. In a high-speed centrifuge (q.v.), the forces separating the lighter and heavier components from each other are thousands of times greater than gravity, making the separation more efficient. A newly developed instrument, the vortex, may be employed for separations of gases. Separation of uranium hexafluoride, UF_6, in the gaseous state, may be effected by means of centrifugal molecular distillation so that two kinds of molecules result: $U^{235}F_6$ and $U^{238}F_6$. The uranium atoms in these formulas differ from each other in that the number, 235, shows a lighter-weight mass than the one followed by 238; *see* ATOM AND ATOMIC THEORY: *Atomic Weight;* MOLECULE.

Sublimation. If a solid substance is distilled, passing directly into the vapor phase and back into the solid state without a liquid being formed at any time, the process is called sublimation. Sublimation does not differ from distillation in any important respect, except that special care must be taken to prevent the solid from clogging the apparatus. Rectification of such materials is impossible. Iodine (q.v.) is regularly purified by sublimation.

Destructive Distillation. If a substance is heated to a high temperature and decomposed into several valuable products, and these products are separated by fractionation in the same operation, the process is called destructive distillation. The important applications of this process are the destructive distillation of coal for coke, tar, gas, and ammonia, and the destructive distillation of wood for charcoal, acetic acid, acetone, and wood alcohol. The latter process has been largely displaced by synthetic processes for making the various by-products. The cracking of petroleum is essentially identical with destructive distillation.   T.W.D.

DISTILLED LIQUORS, beverages of high alcoholic content, produced by distillation, formerly called ardent spirits or aqua vitae. They may be made from other beverages of lower alcoholic content, such as brandy from wine or applejack from hard cider, or from fermented mixtures originally containing large proportions of carbohydrates, such as rum from molasses or whiskey from grain mash. The earliest alcoholic beverages were products of simple fermentation which, at most, yielded about 12 percent alcohol.

The first mention of distillation on record was made by Abul Kasim, a 10th-century Arabian physician. At first only wine was distilled, but soon afterward other fermented products were employed. The process of distillation not only concentrates the alcohol, but also removes from the beverage a large portion of the unpleasant-tasting impurities. If rectification (purification by repeated or by fractional distillation) is carried too far, however, all of the flavoring elements are removed with the impurities, and pure alcohol is produced. Consequently, in the distillation of potable liquors, the process is only partially completed, and the remaining impurities are removed by filtration of the liquors through charcoal and by aging in charred wooden barrels. During aging, the impurities, which consist mostly of a mixture of higher alcohols, are in part oxidized to acids which react with the remaining alcohols to form pleasantly flavored esters. The amount of flavoring material remaining in the finished beverage is less than one half of 1 percent; the remainder consists of water, and alcohol ranging from 80 proof (about 40 percent) for mild whiskies to 150 proof or more for strong brandies and rums. Many cordials and liqueurs are made by distilling mixtures of alcohol and flavoring agents. See ABSINTHE; ALCOHOL: *Ethyl Alcohol*; BRANDY; DISTILLATION; FERMENTATION; GIN; LIQUEUR; LIQUORS, FERMENTED AND DISTILLED; RUM; WHISKEY.

DISTILLED WATER. *See* DISTILLATION; WATER: *Purification.*

DISTRIBUTION, in economics, term applied to two different, but related, processes: (1) the division among the members of society, as individuals, of the national income and wealth; and (2) the apportionment of the value of the output of goods among the factors or agents of production, namely, labor, land, capital (qq.v.), and management. The division or apportionment of this value takes the form of monetary payments, consisting of wages and salaries, rent, interest (qq.v.), and profit. Wages and salaries are paid to workers and managers; rent is paid for the use of land and for certain kinds of physical objects; interest is paid for the use of capital; and profit is realized by the owners of business enterprises as a reward for risk-taking; *see* NATIONAL INCOME.

Recipients of these payments do not receive equal parts of the total. The formulation of the economic laws governing the division of the total of these payments into their various forms and relative portions constitutes the central problem of economic theory in the sphere of distribution.

Economists have not agreed in formulating these economic laws. Different schools of economists have defined them differently at various times; *see* ECONOMICS: *History.* A large body of authoritative opinion maintains that inequalities in income result, in great part, from the operation of the law of supply and demand (q.v.). In this view, for example, an overproduction of cotton will result, through a consequent fall in the price of cotton, in a decrease in the income of cotton growers. It will also tend to result in an increase in the real income, or purchasing power, of the purchasers of cotton, who can buy it more cheaply than would otherwise be possible. Similarly, when capital is abundant and the demand for it is low, interest rates tend to fall. As a result, the relative share of the national income of creditors tends to decrease, while the share of borrowers tends to rise. Variations in the relative share of the national income of workers are also explained in terms of the operation of the law of supply and demand: when labor is plentiful, wage rates tend to fall;

when labor is scarce, as in wartime, wages tend to rise. And, finally, inequalities in income among workers are explained by the relative abundance or scarcity of their skills: skilled workers, less numerous than unskilled workers, receive higher wage rates; and workers with rare skills are paid at a higher rate than workers with skills found in abundance.

Economists recognize, however, that the distribution of the national income is influenced by a number of factors in addition to the operation of supply and demand. These factors include the practice by some monopolies and cartels of creating artificial scarcities and fixing prices; collective bargaining by unions and management; and social-reform legislation, such as social-security and minimum-wage and maximum-hour laws. Such factors tend to increase the income of one group or another above the level it would reach through the unimpeded operation of the law of supply and demand. Taxation (q.v.) is also an important factor effecting income distribution; *see* INCOME TAX.

In commerce, distribution refers to the physical movement of commodities into the channels of trade and industry; *see* MARKETING.

See also WEALTH.

DISTRIBUTION OF ANIMALS. See ANIMALS, GEOGRAPHIC DISTRIBUTION OF.

DISTRIBUTION OF PLANTS. See PLANTS, GEOGRAPHIC DISTRIBUTION OF.

DISTRIBUTOR. See AUTOMOBILE: *Ignition.*

DISTRICT ATTORNEY, in the legal system of the United States, the public prosecuting officer within a defined district. In some States, he is called county or state's attorney or county solicitor. The office of district attorney is one of great importance in the administration of the criminal law (q.v.), including the investigation of charges of crime, the gathering of evidence against alleged criminals, the submission of criminal charges to the grand jury (q.v.), and the drawing of indictments, as well as the supervision of the several stages of the criminal prosecution through the actual trial of the accused; *see* INDICTMENT; TRIAL.

Jurisdiction over crimes is divided in the U.S. between Federal and State courts; thus, the Federal government has one set of district attorneys, and each State has an entirely different set. The former, appointed by the President, are deputies of the Attorney General of the U.S., to whom they are required to make report of their official acts. They are appointed for the several judicial districts into which the U.S. is divided, and are charged with prosecuting offenses against the Federal government, as well as with

Japanese cherry blossoms near the Washington Monument. U.S. Dept. of Agriculture

conducting government civil actions. *See* COURTS IN THE UNITED STATES.

In most of the States, a district attorney is elected in each county. His most important duties are discharged in prosecuting criminals in the State courts, but he also serves as the prosecuting officer in the county court of the county in which he was elected.

Under the common law (q.v.), the prosecution of criminal offenses was left to the initiative of the persons injured or other private persons representing them, and in Great Britain it was not until 1879 that the state undertook that duty in any effective or systematic way. By act of Parliament in that year, and in 1882, a new department was created under a director of public prosecutions, with functions and powers like those of the district attorney in the United States. *See* CRIME; CRIMINAL PROCEDURE.

DISTRICT OF COLUMBIA, Federal District of the United States, coextensive with the city of Washington (q.v.), the national capital. The District is situated about 30 miles S.W. of the center of Baltimore, Md., on the E. bank of the Potomac R., which separates the District from Virginia. The District of Columbia forms a rectangular enclave in the State of Maryland, with one irregular side along the river. The greatest width, measured along the S.E. boundary, is about 9 mi.

The length of the N.E. boundary is approximately 10 mi. Except for a number of swampy areas contiguous to the river, the terrain is hilly and gently rolling, with an extreme elevation of about 420 ft. above sea level. The Anacostia R., a tributary of the Potomac, traverses the S.E. portion of the District. Rock Creek, a smaller tributary of the Potomac, flows across the north-central portion.

The District of Columbia contains, in addition to the urban areas surrounding the Capitol, numerous suburban communities. Georgetown, the best-known suburb, is the site of Georgetown University (q.v.), one of several outstanding institutions of higher learning in the District. Other prominent schools include The American University, The Catholic University of America, The George Washington University, and Howard University (qq.v.). The District has a free public-school system, comprising elementary and junior and senior high schools. Public schools number about 185, and in 1972 total enrollment was about 143,400. College and university enrollment totaled about 80,500.

The District of Columbia is the seat of the Federal government, and the chief activity of the District is the execution of the work of a multitude of governmental departments and agencies. A large tourist and convention trade is carried on in the District, which is also the site of several scientific development firms that manufacture technical equipment. Transit facilities of the District include an extensive bus system and a network of highways. The District is served by a number of railway systems; most domestic airlines operate at National Airport near the center of the city; overseas air service is provided at neighboring Dulles International Airport in Virginia and Friendship International Airport in Baltimore, Md.

By the terms of Article I of the Constitution of the United States (q.v.), executive and legislative authority in the District of Columbia is vested in the Congress of the United States. The purpose of this provision was to prevent the District from gaining undue local influence in the affairs of the Federal government. Residents of the District were therefore unable to vote in national elections and were not represented in the United States Congress. In 1802, the Congress authorized a city council, to be elected by District residents. Subsequent legislation, passed in 1878, abolished the right of suffrage in the District, which became a municipal corporation under the administrative control of three commissioners appointed by the President. In 1961, the Twenty-third Amendment to the U.S. Constitution gave residents of the District the right to vote in Presidential elections and to be represented by three members in the Electoral College (q.v.). In September, 1970, Congress passed a bill allowing the District to elect, for the first time since 1875, a delegate to the House of Representatives. In March, 1971, the clergyman Walter E. Fauntroy (1933–) was elected; although a nonvoting delegate to the House, he is a member of, and entitled to vote in, committees dealing with District affairs.

Government. The form of government of the District, approved by Congress in 1967, is modeled after an elected city government (see MUNICIPAL GOVERNMENT). The District is governed by a commissioner (mayor), an assistant commissioner, and a nine-man council, all appointed by the President and confirmed by the United States Senate. The Congress has delegated to the commissioner various executive and administrative responsibilities, and the council exercises certain ordinance-making and regulatory powers. The ruling body has less authority than that vested in the governing authorities of large American cities; it cannot, for example, levy taxes on real estate and personal property. Local taxes are levied by Congress and are payable directly to the U.S. Department of the Treasury. Income from taxation is usually sufficient to defray a large percentage of local expenses; the balance is appropriated by Congress. The judicial system of the District includes a U.S. court of appeals, a U.S. district court, a municipal court of appeals, and several municipal and juvenile courts.

History. Bills passed by Congress in 1790 and 1791 created the District on a 10-sq.mi. tract of land ceded by Maryland and Virginia. The enclave contained the corporations of Georgetown, Alexandria, and Washington. In 1846, Alexandria and the remainder of the District on the w. side of the Potomac were returned to the State of Virginia by an act of Congress. Georgetown retained the status of a separate corporation within the District until 1895, when the town was merged with Washington. A territorial form of government for the remaining area was adopted in 1871.

Area of the District of Columbia, 67 sq.mi. (land, 61 sq.mi.; water, 6 sq.mi.). Pop. (1960) 763,956; (1970) 756,510.

DITHYRAMB, in ancient Greece, originally an orgiastic hymn sung in honor of the god of wine Dionysus (q.v.) by revelers attired as satyrs, as they danced about his altar to the accompaniment of music on an *aulos* or flute. Later, the dithyramb was composed in honor of other gods, including Apollo and Athena (qq.v.), and sung at festivals in their honor. At Athens there were annual contests at the Greater Dionysia, Lesser Dionysia, Panathenaea, Thargelia, and Lenaea (see FESTIVALS AND FEASTS: *Ancient Greek Festivals*) between choruses of singers of dithyrambs. In the earliest period (6th century B.C.), the prize for the best performance was an ox; in later periods, the prize was a tripod.

The subject of the dithyramb was the birth and life of the god celebrated. The semilegendary 7th-century B.C. Lesbian poet Arion wrote dithyrambs of a tragic rather than a laudatory nature, and about 536 B.C. the Greek poet Thespis (q.v.) wrote dithyrambs to be sung by a chorus and a leader, and also introduced passages to be sung by one person alone. Out of this practice the Greek tragedy reputedly arose (see DRAMA: *Greek Drama*). After the development of tragedy, the dithyramb was still composed independently by important Greek poets, including Bacchylides and Pindar (qq.v.); only fragments of the dithyrambs written by these poets have been preserved. In modern times, the term serves to designate poetry of a wild, impassioned nature, as well as speeches delivered in an ardent and unrestrained manner.

DITMARS, Raymond Lee (1876–1942), American naturalist, born in Newark, N.J., and educated at Barnard Military Academy, New York City. During his lifetime he was considered the world's outstanding herpetologist. After serving for five years as assistant curator of entomology at the American Museum of Natural History, he was appointed curator of reptiles at the New York Zoological Park in 1899 and curator of mammals in 1910. He was a corresponding member of the Zoological Society of London and a fellow of the New York Zoological Society. He wrote *The Reptile Book* (1907), *Strange Animals I Have Known* (1931), *Reptiles of North America* (1936), *The Book of Living Reptiles* (1936), and *The Making of a Scientist* (1937).

DIU. See PORTUGUESE INDIA.

DIURETICS, chemical compounds that increase the flow of urine and thus eliminate accumulations of water in cells, tissues, blood, and organs. The retention of excess water may occur following injury, as when water accumulates in the knee; in congestive heart failure, when the heart pumps insufficient blood to eliminate a normal volume of fluid; and in a variety of other disabilities, including hypertension, cirrhosis of the liver, and kidney diseases. Heart stimulants, such as digitalis (q.v.), produce a diuretic effect by increasing blood pressure and thus increasing the flow of blood through the kidneys. Certain alkaloids found in coffee and tea (caffeine, theobromine, and theophylline, in increasing order of strength) increase urine output by counteracting the tendency of blood proteins to prevent the removal of water from the blood by the kidneys. Some diuretics, such as calcium chloride, increase the ability of the blood to carry water, causing the kidneys to remove the excess. Others exert their effect directly on the kidney; examples are the xanthines and the powerful organic mercurials such as meralluride, which must be injected. Less effective diuretics, such as acetazolamide, may be taken by mouth. The new thiazide diuretics, such as chlorothiazide and hydrochlorothiazide, are extremely effective when taken orally. Diuretics are especially useful in cases of organic poisoning, as by barbiturates; since the body breaks down these poisons slowly, they may be rapidly eliminated through the kidneys. All diuretics may have severe side effects, may cause abnormal excretion of sodium, potassium, and chloride, and may become ineffective after repeated use.

See also EXCRETION; KIDNEY; URINE AND THE URINARY SYSTEM.

DIVER'S DISEASE. See BENDS.

DIVIDE, in geography, term usually applied to the watershed ridge between two or more river-drainage systems; see RIVER.

DIVIDEND, in corporation finance, a fund appropriated out of the profits of a corporation and distributed among its stockholders; also the share of the fund received by a stockholder. Dividends are usually declared periodically—quarterly, semiannually, or annually—by the directors of a corporation. The action of a board of directors with respect to the declaration or nondeclaration of dividends is usually final and conclusive upon the stockholders and is subject to review by the courts only in the event that the action is arbitrary or capricious.

Dividends are distributed on a proportional basis; the fractional share of the total dividend received by a stockholder is equal to the proportional share of the stock owned by him. Holders of the preferred stock of a company have generally a prior right to the payment of dividends over holders of common stock, and, if their stock so provides, are paid at a fixed periodic rate; see STOCK. Preferred dividends may be cumulative or noncumulative: cumulative dividends are those which, if not paid for one or more periods, constitute charges on the profits of succeeding periods and must be paid at a future date before dividends may be distributed on common stock; noncumulative dividends, if omitted, do not constitute charges on future profits. Dividends may take the form of additional shares of stock or of the right to purchase stock for a fixed sum per share; such dividends are called stock dividends and rights, respectively.

The term dividend is applied also to the assets of a bankrupt or insolvent business which are distributed among its creditors during the course of its liquidation. The term is used in insurance to signify the sum appropriated out of profits for distribution among policyholders whose policies so provide; such dividends may be used to reduce the next premium.

In arithmetic, the dividend is a number divided by another, called the divisor; see ARITHMETIC; DIVISION.

DIVINATION, practice of attempting to acquire hidden knowledge and insight into events, past, present, and future, through the direct or indirect contact of human intelligence with the supernatural. The practice was formerly closely allied with religion among pagan, Hebrew, and early Christian peoples.

Contact with the supernatural is usually sought through a psychic medium, that is, a person supposedly endowed with supernormal receptivity. In direct divination, the medium acquires knowledge through direct contact with the unknown. The oracle (q.v.), a medium or diviner, who figured prominently in the beliefs of a number of ancient peoples, including those of Babylonia and Greece, typified the mediumistic method. Oracles employed various techniques in establishing contact with divinity. Some, like the oracle at Delphi (q.v.), passed into a trance and, in this condition, uttered divine messages. Others practiced oneiromancy, or divination by dreams, and necromancy, the art of conjuring up revelations from the souls of the dead. The direct method of divination is closely approximated in much of modern spiritualism (q.v.).

The accomplishment of indirect or artificial contact with the supernatural depends on the interpretation by a medium of the behavior of animals and natural phenomena, which might convey messages from the supernatural. In antiquity, common artificial or inductive means of divination were the casting of lots; haruspication, the inspection of animal entrails; and ornithomancy, the study of the activity of birds. In ancient Rome, augurs or priests performed their divination in elaborate ceremonies, called auguries, by reading auspices or omens. To determine the will of the gods, they utilized such forms of divination as haruspication, ornithomancy, and the interpretation of dreams and visions. These augurs, members of a college that existed in Rome from the founding of the city until late in the 4th century A.D., exercised enormous power. No Roman would embark upon a major undertaking unless the augurs decided the auspices were favorable. The forms of inductive divination best known today include astrology (q.v.); crystallomancy, or crystal gazing; bibliomancy, the interpretation of secret messages from books, especially from the Bible (q.v.); numerology, the study of numbers; and the reading of palms, tea leaves, and cards.

Divination in China followed a different course. In the Shang dynasty, shoulder blades of oxen and the bottom shells of tortoises were inscribed and heated. A message was derived from the pattern of cracks formed across the inscription after heat was applied. The founder of the Chou dynasty is said to have established the traditional patterns of lines and added the judgments of their significance. His son, the duke of Chou, is said to have composed the commentaries. The collected judgments are known as T'uan and the commentaries as Yao.

In the time of Confucius (q.v.) additional texts, the Wings, were appended. The result was the text known as I Ching, or "Classic of Changes". The interpretations found in the Wings are sometimes attributed to scholars of the Han dynasty. See CHINA, PEOPLE'S REPUBLIC OF: History.

The cosmological principle behind the I Ching is simply that of change. Change is the movement between the cosmic forces of yin and yang, as represented by the divided and undivided lines of the traditional patterns, the eight trigrams, and the sixty-four hexagrams formed from them by casting lots. Three divided yin lines signify earth; three undivided yang lines signify heaven. The sixty-four hexagrams, therefore, represent all possible situations or changes in creation. Examination of the hexagrams will furnish a description of the universe at that particular moment in its endless process of change and will provide hints of its future course of development.

See also CLAIRVOYANCE; FORTUNE-TELLING.

DIVINE, Father, also known as REVEREND MAJOR J. DIVINE (1882?–1965), American religious cult leader, born probably near Savannah, Ga.; his original name was probably George Baker. In 1915 he began to preach in the Harlem neighborhood of New York City as Major J. Divine. His Peace Mission Movement, in which he became known as Father Divine, evolved gradually, and in 1919 he established the first of his communal dwellings, originally called Heavens, in Sayville, N.Y. The movement grew rapidly during the 1930's and is estimated to have about 500,000 adherents. Members of the movement are known as Rosebuds, Lily-Buds, and Crusaders. The followers of Father Divine live strictly according to his International Modest Code. During the economic depression of the 1930's, many of the members operated low-cost restaurants in major cities in the eastern section of the United States.

Currently, the Peace Mission Movement supervises six churches in New Jersey, New York, and Pennsylvania. A trustee board administers church affairs in cooperation with the executive branch of the movement; these, in turn, work with the operators of various cooperative enterprises of the movement.

DIVINE COMEDY, THE, or (It.) LA DIVINA COMMEDIA, epic poem by the Italian poet Dante Alighieri (q.v.) and one of the greatest of all works of literature. It was probably begun about 1307 and finished about 1321, the year of Dante's death. The Divine Comedy is an account of Dante's imaginary journey through hell, purgatory, and heaven. Its three main sections are correspondingly named l'Inferno, il Purgatorio, and il Paradiso. Dante is guided

An illustration for The Divine Comedy *by the 19th-century French painter Gustave Doré.*

through hell and purgatory by the Roman poet Vergil (q.v.), who is, to Dante, the symbol of reason. The woman he loved, Beatrice (*see* BEATRICE PORTINARI), whom he regards as both a manifestation and an instrument of the divine will, is his guide through heaven.

Each section contains thirty-three cantos, or divisions, except for the first section, which has, in addition, a canto serving as a general introduction. The poem is written in terza rima (q.v.) and was the first composition of high artistic merit in this popular verse form. Dante intended the poem to be a popular work for his contemporaries and wrote it in Italian rather than Latin, the language in which medieval works of literature were often composed. He named the poem *La Commedia* ("The Comedy") because it ends happily, in heaven; the adjective *divina* ("divine") was first added to the title in an edition of the poem that appeared in 1555.

The narrative action of *The Divine Comedy* forms part of the philosophical and theological arguments expounded by the poem. The incidents that occur during the course of the journey provide vivid illustrations of the working of divine justice as it affects all aspects of human experience. In addition, the work provides a summary of the political, scientific, and philosophical thought of the time.

The Divine Comedy may be interpreted in many ways. Dante himself states, in a letter to the Veronese nobleman Can Grande della Scala (1291–1329), that it has four levels of meaning, the literal, allegorical, moral, and anagogical, or mystical. Indeed, the greatness of this work rests on its multiplicity of meaning even more than on its masterfully poetic and dramatic qualities. It is supreme as a dramatization of medieval Christian theology; but even beyond that framework, Dante's imaginary voyage can be understood as an allegory of the purification of man's soul and of his achievement of inner peace through the guidance of reason and love.

By the 15th century many Italian cities had established professorships for the study of the work; in the centuries following the invention of printing, almost four hundred Italian editions were published; some of the editions were illustrated by such artists as Sandro Botticelli, Michelangelo, John Flaxman, and Gustave Doré (qq.v.). The Italian composer Gioacchino Antonio Rossini and the German composer Robert Schumann (qq.v.) set parts of the poem to music, and it formed the subject of a symphonic poem (q.v.) by the Hungarian composer Franz Liszt (q.v.). It has been translated into more than twenty-five languages. A notable English translation of *The Divine Comedy* was made in 1867 by the American poet Henry Wadsworth Longfellow (q.v.). The work has been translated in the 20th century wholly or in part by the British poet Laurence Binyon (1869–1943), the British writer Dorothy Leigh Sayers (1893–1957), the American poet John Ciardi (1916–), and others.

DIVINE OFFICE, public prayer service of the Roman Catholic Church (q.v.). It is made up of psalms, hymns, readings, and prayers and is intended to sanctify certain parts of the day. The various elements of the service for these parts, known as the canonical hours (q.v.), are contained in the breviary (q.v.). *See* LITURGY.

DIVINE RIGHT *or* **DIVINE RIGHT OF KINGS,** ancient doctrine that sovereigns are representatives of God and derive their right to rule directly from Him. The concept was derived from the theocracies of the East. Before the Reformation (q.v.), the king was considered God's representative in all secular matters. After the Reformation, in Protestant countries, the king filled this function in religious matters also. According to the doctrine, a ruler's power is not subject to secular limitation. He is responsible only to God, and not to his subjects. In the 17th century the doctrine was supported by the English Royalists against the Parliamentarians, who maintained that the exercise of political power springs from the will of the people. The opponents of divine right included the Englishmen, poet and prose writer John Milton, Republican leader Algernon Sidney (qq.v.), and political theorist James Harrington (1611–77). The chief supporters of the doctrine were the English philosopher Thomas Hobbes (q.v.), the French classical scholar Claudius Salmasius (1588–1653), and the English political writer Sir Robert Filmer (d. 1653), whose *Patriarcha, or The Natural Power of Kings Asserted* (1680) contains a complete exposition of the theory. The controversy terminated in 1689, following the Glorious Revolution when William III and Mary II (qq.v.) were crowned after William had agreed to accept the Act of Toleration and the Declaration of Rights (*see* BILL OF RIGHTS).

The doctrine was perhaps best epitomized by Louis XIV (q.v.), King of France, and was one of the elements contributing to the French Revolution (q.v.).

DIVING, act of plunging into water head foremost, usually as a preliminary to swimming (q.v.), or other aquatic sport. Surface diving,

used in lifesaving, is the act of plunging under the water, while swimming, by lowering the head, at the same time kicking the legs and making an upward stroke with the arms. Fancy diving is the performance of dives involving a takeoff, usually from a springboard, a maneuver in the air, and an entry either feet or head foremost into the water.

Fancy dives are classified into three types: the layout, in which the body must not be bent, and the arms are kept straight and the feet together; the pike, in which the body is bent at the hips, and the knees are kept rigid; and the tuck, in which the body is compactly bunched, while the diver clasps his ankles with his hands. The swan dive, or swallow dive, is a layout dive executed with the head bent backward, the back slightly hollowed, and the feet held together so that they form a straight line from the hips to toes. As the diver springs upward, he spreads his arms to the sides at shoulder height and holds them there until he is near the water. Then he swings them forward over his head, maneuvering his hands so that they break the water before the rest of his body. In the jackknife, a pike dive, the diver bends at the hips, generally at the highest point of the dive, clasps or touches his ankles, and then straightens before he enters the water. Somersault dives, in which the diver executes a somersault before entering the water feet first, are usually pike dives; when more than one full revolution is made, the dive is more easily done as a tuck. The full gainer, or Mollberg, is a back somersault that begins from a front takeoff; after completing the maneuver, the diver enters the water feet first. The half gainer, or Isander, begins from a front takeoff, but at the highest point of the dive the diver turns in a back half-somersault and straightens to enter the water head first. Either the full or half gainer may include a jackknife. All fancy diving is based on combinations or variations of these types, which may be modified by twists or other intricate movements in the air.

Fancy diving was first made a competitive sport in Great Britain in 1905. Since then, international diving contests have become subject to regulations made by the International Amateur Swimming Federation; in the United States, the Amateur Athletic Union regulates competitive diving. The following heights are international standards for diving boards used in contests: for springboards, 1 m (3 ft., 3 in.) or 3 m (9 ft., 9 in.); for firm boards or platforms, 3–5 m (9 ft., 9 in.–16 ft., 3 in.), 5–8 m (16 ft., 3 in.–26 ft.), or 8–12 m (26 ft.–39 ft.). Boards higher than 10 m (32 ft., 6 in.) are rarely used in actual practice. In principle, the height of the board should be no more than twice the depth of the water, which should be at least 6 ft. Water need be no more than 15 ft. deep for any height of diving board.

DIVING, or DEEP-SEA DIVING, act of entering water and remaining below the surface for such purposes as working or exploring. Diving without mechanical aids has been practiced since ancient times in the harvesting of pearls and sponges. Various devices to supply the diver with air and thus permit him to prolong his stay under water have been tried since at least the 4th century B.C. Alexander III (q.v.), King of Macedonia, supposedly made a descent in a machine that was probably a primitive form of diving bell; and the Greek philosopher Aristotle (q.v.) mentions devices that enabled divers to breathe under water. Practical apparatus was not developed, however, until the 18th century.

Diving Bells. In 1717 the British astronomer Edmund Halley (q.v.) devised one of the first practical diving bells, an open-bottomed wooden chamber with glass windows in the top to admit light. Air was supplied to men inside the bell through leather tubes connected to air casks that could be lowered into the water as needed. As water entered the casks the air in them was forced through the tubes into the upper part of the diving bell, which was kept clear of water by the pressure of the air. A modern steel version of this device, supplied with compressed air pumped through a hose, is used for underwater work involved in building bridges, piers, and jetties.

In underwater stations, developed in the 20th century from the diving-bell principle, men live and work for extended periods at depths of up to several hundred feet. Inside air pressure is equalized with outside sea pressure; thus, the station walls, although relatively thin, do not cave in, and water does not enter. A trapdoor permits access to the sea. While living in such stations and breathing compressed air (mixed with light gases to ease lung strain), men become temporarily acclimated to water pressures well beyond normal human endurance. Such systems are not feasible for deep seas where water pressure is enormous. The deepest diving is performed in watertight vessels that maintain normal atmospheric pressure inside and rely on structural strength to withstand the deep-sea pressure. Notable examples of such vessels are the bathysphere (q.v.), invented in the 1930's by the American scientist Charles William Beebe (q.v.), and the bathyscaphe (q.v.), invented by the Swiss physicist Auguste Piccard (q.v.).

Diving Suits. From the 17th century on, efforts

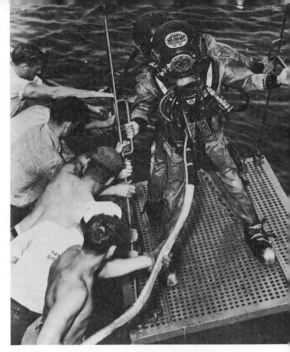

Two U.S. Navy deep-sea divers prepare for an ocean descent to keep in training for a salvage or rescue call.
U.S. Navy

were made to perfect a helmet or suit to give divers maximum protection and freedom of movement. One of the first such successful devices was created in 1819 by the Anglo-German inventor Augustus Siebe (1788–1872). Based on the principle of the diving bell, it consisted of a leather jacket fitted to a metal helmet into which air was pumped from the surface through a flexible hose. The helmet was not watertight, but air pressure kept water below the diver's chin. The modern closed diving suit, essentially the same as one introduced by Siebe in 1830, is made of rubberized fabric. It covers the diver completely and is airtight. Valves on the helmet allow the diver to regulate air pressure inside the suit and thus to control his buoyancy. Auxiliary equipment of modern diving dress includes weighted shoes to keep the diver upright and leaden plates for weight on back and chest. A rope containing telephone wires connects the diver with the surface and permits conversation; his jerk on the rope signals an emergency or his desire to ascend. For deeper diving than is permissible in the ordinary suit, jointed metal suits heavy enough to withstand great water pressures are used. In these suits air pressure can be kept normal, and the diver experiences less stress than when diving in shallower water with an ordinary suit.

A troublesome feature of ordinary diving dress is the unwieldy lengths of air hose and lifeline a diver must drag with him. This problem has been met by the development of diving suits with a self-contained air supply consisting of a pressure cylinder of mixed oxygen and air and a regeneration chamber filled with caustic soda. Exhaled air is passed through the regeneration chamber, carbon dioxide is removed, and the air is then combined with oxygen and air from the cylinder and rebreathed. The air supply of such units lasts from about 45 min. to 2 hr.

Self-contained underwater breathing apparatus (called "scuba"), independent of diving suits, has been developed for skin diving (q.v.). It differs from the conventional diving suit in that it is designed for swimming, whereas the more cumbersome type is suitable only for walking on ocean floors. One form of this apparatus, a lightweight breathing mask operating on the same principle as the self-contained diving suit, was used during World War II by underwater demolition teams to clear away mines and other obstacles before amphibious landings. At present, the most popular form is the aqualung designed in France during World War II by the French naval officer and underwater explorer Jacques-Yves Cousteau (q.v.). It consists of one, two, or three cylinders (carried on the back) of compressed air fed to the diver's mouthpiece through valves that assure a constant flow at a pressure automatically equalized with outside water pressure. Simple to operate, the aqualung is popular for exploration, salvage, and sport.

Diving Equipment. Because of the difficulty of working under water with ordinary hand tools, divers usually employ pneumatic hammers, drills, wrenches, and other implements. Cutting and welding are carried out with standard torches. Because in many waters daylight penetrates only a few feet beneath the surface, it is necessary to supply artificial light by which divers can work. High-power incandescent electric lights are usually employed.

Depth of Working. For divers without mechanical aids, a depth of about 60 ft. is the practical limit of working. Pearl and sponge divers have been credited with reaching depths of 100 ft. in individual dives, but normally they remain submerged for from 50 to 80 sec. at depths of about 40 ft. With breathing apparatus using conventional mixtures of compressed air and oxygen, divers cannot safely go below 250 ft., but with special light breathing mixtures (such as oxygen with helium or hydrogen to replace nitrogen), dives to below 500 ft. have been made successfully by surface divers. Divers acclimated to undersea pressures, through living

in underwater stations established at a depth of several hundred feet, are expected to dive from a station to a maximum depth of from 1300 to 1500 ft. in flexible suits.

Divers are sometimes afflicted with the bends (q.v.), a disease caused by the rapid decrease of atmospheric pressure.

See also DEEP-SEA EXPLORATION.

DIVING BEETLE. *See* WATER BEETLE.

DIVING, SKIN. *See* SKIN DIVING.

DIVINING ROD, forked stick, usually of hazel or willow, but sometimes of metal, believed to be a means of locating underground water or ore deposits. Rods used to locate water are also called dowsing rods. The rod is held lightly in the hands as the diviner walks about, and supposedly bends downward of its own volition when directly above the source of water or metal. The use of the divining rod dates back to the Middle Ages, and is still common in many parts of the world. Scientific explanations of the action of the rod range from deliberate chicanery on the part of the user to his automatic moving of the rod following a subconscious impression or perception. Despite widespread belief that use of the divining rod is indulgence in superstition, dowsers continue to practice their art and, sometimes, to find water.

DIVISION, in mathematics, process for determining how many times one number is contained in another. Division is related to multiplication in the same way that subtraction is related to addition. An integer, a, is said to divide an integer, b, if an integer c exists such that $b = c \times a$. The sign for division is $\div$ and is read "divided by", as in $b \div a = c$. The dividend, b, is divided by the divisor, a, and the result is the quotient, c.

A theorem of numbers theory (*see* NUMBERS, THEORY OF) asserts that if a and b are any two integers and if a is greater than b, two unique integers q and r exist such that $a = bq + r$ and $0 \leq r < b$. The number q is sometimes called the partial quotient (or the quotient, if $r = 0$), and r is called the remainder. In another definition, division is the process of determining the numbers q and r, the existence of which is asserted by this theorem. These processes are sometimes referred to as short division and long division.

If the divisor is a number less than 10, the process is often called short division, an example of which is considered below. Consider the problem of dividing 453 by 7; that is, let $a = 453$ and $b = 7$. We display the work as follows.

$$7\overline{)453}$$

Note that the first digit in the dividend is

smaller than the divisor. Then consider the first two digits, 45, and note that 45 = 6(7) + 3, and equivalently, 450 = 6(70) + 30. The expressions 6(7) and 6(70) mean 6 times 7 and 6 times 70, respectively. The 6, which is the partial quotient, is placed above the 5 in the dividend.

$$\frac{6}{7\overline{)453}}$$

The remainder, 30, is then added to the 3 in the dividend. Note that

$$33 = 7(4) + 5$$

and take the partial quotient 4 over the 3 in the dividend. The 5, which is the last remainder, is usually written over the divisor as a fraction.

$$\frac{64\ 5/7}{7\overline{)453}}$$

The answer may be written as a mixed fraction (q.v.), 64 5/7. In practice, the application of this short-division algorithm and the carrying of remainders is usually done mentally, and only the quotient and last remainder are actually written down.

If the divisor is a number greater than 10, the process is usually called long division. For example, to divide 2756 by 34, the problem is written and solved as follows:

$$
\begin{array}{r}
81\ 2/34\ \text{(quotient)} \\
34\overline{)2756} \\
\underline{272} \\
36 \\
\underline{34} \\
2
\end{array}
$$

To begin, the divisor, 34, is checked to see if it can be contained in the first two left-hand integers, 27, of the dividend. This partial dividend, 27, is too small. Next, the divisor is checked against the first three integers of the dividend, 275. This partial dividend is large enough, so the operation can proceed. To approximate how many times 34 is contained in 275, the first left-hand integer, 3, of the divisor is divided into the first two left-hand integers, 27, of the partial dividend, 275. Three will go into 27 nine times. This is the reverse of 3 × 9 = 27 and illustrates the relation of division to multiplication. The next step is to test 9 to see if it is truly the first integer of the desired quotient; 9 × 34 = 306, and thus 9 is shown to be too large. Obviously, 34 goes into 275 less than 9 times, so the next figure tried is 8; 8 × 34 = 272. Because 272 is less than 275, 8 is the largest whole number that gives a figure that can be contained in the partial dividend, 275. The 8 is placed over the 5, which is the last integer in the partial dividend. The product, 272, is placed below the partial divi-

dend and is subtracted from it. The difference is 3. The next integer, 6, in the dividend is brought down. No matter how long the dividend, this integer is always the next figure to the right of the previous partial dividend. The 6 is placed alongside the 3, and 36 becomes the next partial dividend. The divisor, 34, will go into this new partial dividend only once. Therefore, 1 is put in the quotient above the 6. The 1 is multiplied by 34, and the product, 34, is subtracted from the second partial dividend, 36. The difference is 2. Because no more integers can be brought down from the dividend, the long division is completed. The 2 that is left over as the last difference is the remainder. Thus, 34, the divisor, is contained in 2756, the dividend, 81 whole times with 2 left over. The answer to the problem may be expressed as a quotient of 81 and 2 parts of 34, or it may be written as a mixed fraction, 81 2/34. If the remainder is zero, the divisor is contained in the dividend an exact number of times, and the division is called exact.

The operation of division as applied to decimal fractions (q.v.) is shown in the following example:

$$
\begin{array}{r}
17.31 \\
243\overline{)4206.93} \\
\underline{243} \\
1776 \\
\underline{1701} \\
75\ 9 \\
\underline{72\ 9} \\
3\ 03 \\
\underline{2\ 43} \\
60
\end{array}
$$

The decimal point in the quotient is placed above the decimal point in the dividend. The remainder is usually not written with the quotient; if additional decimal places are needed for the quotient, zeros may be added to the right of the digits in the dividend and the division process continued. To divide 23.467 by 4.03, move the decimal place two spaces to the right in both the divisor and the dividend and proceed as in the above example. The divisions 23.467 ÷ 4.03; 234.67 ÷ 4.03; 2346.7 ÷ 4.03; and 23.467 ÷ 0.00403 are carried out by performing equivalent divisions: 2346.7 ÷ 403; 23467 ÷ 403; 234670 ÷ 403; and 2346700 ÷ 403.

The method of dividing fractions is shown in the following example (ab means a times b).

$$a/b \div c/d = ad/bc$$

The sign of the quotient is determined by the signs of the dividend and the divisor. If the signs of the dividend and the divisor are not the same, the quotient is negative; if the signs are the same, the quotient is positive. The usual check for the correctness of a division is to multiply the quotient by the divisor; the result should equal the dividend. Division of large numbers, and series of divisions, are easily performed by the use of logarithms (q.v.) or calculating machines (*see* COMPUTER).   J.McP.

DIVISION, in the United States Army (q.v.), a unit comprising from 13,000 to 16,000 troops commanded by a major general. It consists of the division base, the support command that provides supplies, and nine maneuver or combat battalions supported by six artillery battalions. Attached to the division base are reconnaissance forces; combat engineer, signal, and aviation battalions; and a company of military police (q.v.). A division can be organized into two or more brigades (*see* BRIGADE) to meet the demands of a special maneuver or situation. Airborne, armored, infantry, air mobile, and mechanized divisions are organized for special missions. A corps, commanded by a lieutenant general, usually comprises three divisions; three or more corps form into an army under the command of a general (q.v.). In the United States Marine Corps (q.v.), divisions comprise as many as 20,000 men and are divided into landing teams, each with the power of independent action.   U.S. DEPARTMENT OF THE ARMY

DIVISION OF LABOR, in economics, separation of the work involved in production and trade into processes performed by different workers or groups of workers. The separation may occur on several bases, the most frequent being geographical, or territorial, and occupational. Geographical division of labor may develop from the occurrence of raw materials in one part of the world and the establishment of manufactories which use them in another. Crude rubber produced in the Far East is compounded, vulcanized, and manufactured into auto tires and other products in the United States; iron ore mined in the Mesabi Range, Minnesota, is used in the manufacture of steel in Chicago, Detroit, Cleveland, Pittsburgh, and other cities. Geographical division of labor also includes the localization of the manufacture of component parts of a finished product in various places. The window glass and tires made in Pittsburgh and in Akron, respectively, are used in the manufacture of automobiles which are produced chiefly in Detroit.

Separation of the productive process into individual operations, each performed by different groups of workers, is called occupational, or technical, division of labor. For example, the au-tomobile consists of thousands of parts, each requiring a number of distinct manufacturing processes. Many of these parts are manufactured in plants devoted solely to the production of those particular items; within these plants the productive process is divided among many different groups of workers, each of whom has a specialized task to perform. The major advantage of the technical division of labor is greater productivity. In 1971, for instance, 8,585,000 automobiles were produced. Approximately 676,000 workers were employed to produce this number. This production would not have been possible if each worker had performed all of the operations involved in the production of one automobile. Greater productivity results from several factors, among which the most important are a marked increase in individual and collective efficiency due to specialization and the increase in skill specialization provides; economy in training of workers, especially with respect to time; economy resulting from the continuous use of tools which would otherwise remain idle during part of the working time as workers move from process to process; and the development of highly productive, specialized tools, machinery, and equipment.

Division of labor has been a feature of production from the earliest times. In primitive society, men hunted, trapped, fished, and fought; and women managed their households and tended crops. As civilization developed, a division of labor took place on a vocational basis. Different economic activities were performed by separate groups of producers. With the development of tools, utensils, and productive techniques, handicrafts and agriculture were carried on by separate groups. The growth of cities fostered a wider specialization of handcraftsmen and artisans. Vocational division of labor became more widespread during the Middle Ages (q.v.) as a result of the development of the guilds (*see* GUILD).

During the later Middle Ages, technical division of labor appeared for the first time on an important scale, in connection with a widespread increase in the production of articles for sale. The industrial revolution (q.v.) which followed during the latter part of the 18th and the first part of the 19th centuries created the modern factory system of production and gave a tremendous impetus to the development of technical and geographical division of labor. The division of labor in modern industry into many thousands of individual processes and skills created many complex technical, organizational, and personnel problems. To cope with these problems sophisticated and highly specialized industrial management techniques were developed.

DIVORCE, in modern law, dissolution of marriage by public authority at the instance of one of the parties, for a cause arising after marriage. Divorces are usually granted by courts under general laws. A judicial declaration that two persons who have gone through the form of contracting marriage are not husband and wife, as when one of the parties was already married, is not a divorce; nor is the term divorce properly applied to an annulment of marriage for a cause that antedates the marriage, as for impotence or fraud. Again, a judicial separation that merely relieves the parties of some of the duties and suspends some of the rights connected with the connubial relation is not a divorce, for divorce dissolves the connubial bond itself.

Jurisdiction. Because divorce results from a court decree, the first essential is that the court have jurisdiction. In the United States the place of marriage confers no jurisdiction. The location of the marriage status is that of the domicile of the parties. When husband and wife make their home in the same State, that State has jurisdiction. When they live separately the domicile of the husband determines jurisdiction, because, in law, the domicile of a wife is that of her husband. But when a wife is living apart from her husband, in another State, and makes her home there, she is said to have acquired a separate domicile for the purpose of securing a divorce; and the courts of the State in which she resides may take jurisdiction in such a case.

Aside from these general considerations, statutes in many States require residence therein for a definite period of time, usually from six months to a year, with the intention of establishing a permanent domicile, before the courts will take jurisdiction; but no State can, by statute, assume jurisdiction over something outside its boundaries. In some States divorces granted under Mexican law to U.S. citizens are not always recognized as valid. All divorce actions must be begun by the service of process on the other spouse. The method of service, whether personal or by publication, is regulated by statute in each State.

Unlike an action for damages, a divorce is never granted solely upon the default of the defendant. The plaintiff must prove his case; that is, he (or she) must produce legal evidence showing the existence of the necessary facts upon which a divorce is granted under the law of the State in which the action is brought. A divorce trial is usually held before a judge but not before a jury. In many cases, however, it is customary for the court to appoint a referee to take testimony and make a report to the court. Sometimes the court, on its own motion, may direct that certain issues be tried before a jury. The right of either party to demand a jury trial exists in some States.

The marriage relation is dissolved when the final decree is made. According to the laws of many States, the final decree of divorce forbids the defendant to remarry, or to remarry within a certain period. Some States permit the defendant to remarry at once. If a divorced party remarries contrary to a decree forbidding it, he is subject to punishment for contempt of court. Such violation, however, does not affect the validity of the divorce or the remarriage. A divorced person who is forbidden to remarry by the laws of the State that granted his divorce sometimes remarries in another State despite a decree forbidding such remarriage. Whether he is subject to punishment for contempt of court, if he returns to the State that granted the divorce, is a moot question. Some courts have held that he cannot be punished, on the ground that the contempt of court was committed outside of the jurisdiction of the State.

In a divorce action, the court may direct a husband to pay the wife sufficient money for employment of counsel to prosecute or defend the action, and may also grant her alimony (q.v.) temporarily. The final decree of divorce may grant the wife alimony to be paid by the husband at stated periods. Rare instances have occurred in which alimony was awarded to a husband. The final decree may also award the custody of children to either or both parties, and make suitable regulations for visiting and support of the children by either party.

Grounds for Divorce. The grounds for divorce vary from State to State. In South Carolina divorce was not recognized by law until 1949; in New York, prior to 1967, the only ground for divorce was adultery. Adultery is a ground for divorce in practically all the States; some provide that it must be without the connivance of the other party; some that the plaintiff must be innocent; some that it is no ground if forgiven by the injured party. Other grounds for divorce are desertion (q.v.), failure of a husband to support his wife, habitual drunkenness, cruelty, habitual manifestations of violent temper, incurable insanity, confinement in an asylum for a long period of time, pregnancy at the time of marriage which was unknown to the husband, concealment of a loathsome disease at the time of marriage or contraction of one after marriage, membership in a religious society forbidding cohabitation, conviction of a felony, and imprisonment for life.

The U.S. Supreme Court, in a ruling in 1942, ostensibly overruled a long line of previous decisions and held that no State could attack the validity of divorce granted by a State having jurisdiction of the parties. This decision was based on the constitutional doctrine that each State is required to give full faith and credit to the judicial decrees of every other State. In 1945 this general principle was considerably limited by a Supreme Court decision holding that the question as to whether the State granting the divorce had jurisdiction was still subject to review in the courts of any other State. If the reviewing court finds that no proper domicile was established by the party obtaining the divorce, the decree does not have to be recognized by a State under the full faith and credit clause of the Constitution, because the State granting the divorce is assumed never to have had proper jurisdiction.

Statistics. The first divorce census in 1887 showed 27,919 divorces, or 0.5 divorces per 1000 persons. In 1910 the number of divorces stood at 83,045, or 0.9 per 1000 persons. Divorces in 1915 numbered 104,298, or 1.0 divorces per 1000 persons. By 1920 this figure had risen to 170,505 (1.6 per 1000 population). The increase in the next five years was not so great, and the figure in 1925 was 175,449 (1.5 per 1000 population). The 1930 figure, 191,591 (1.6 per 1000 persons) showed a slight decrease from the 1929 figure, 201,468 recorded divorces.

By 1934 the figure was 204,000 divorces (1.6 per 1000 population), and in 1940, 264,000 divorces occurred, or 2.0 per 1000. A record number of divorces, about 610,000, was reported in 1946, the year after the end of World War II. By 1950 the number of divorces was about 385,000, or 2.6 per 1000 population, a rate that remained fairly constant, with slight variation, through the 1960's. In 1971 about 768,000 divorces, or 3.7 per 1000 population, were reported.

Divorce in Other Countries. The status of divorce in countries where Protestantism is the prevailing religion is the result of a long evolutionary development. This development began about the 16th century, during the Reformation (q.v.). Although marriage maintained its religious sentiment, the Roman Catholic doctrine that marriage is indissoluble was rejected. The changing attitude toward divorce also results from philosophical and political theories that marriage is preeminently a civil contract and therefore subject to dissolution for sufficient cause. These views were strongly emphasized by the leaders of the French Revolution (q.v.) of 1789, and became increasingly popular throughout the world in the 19th and 20th centuries. An extreme application of these theories, in the view of some historians, took place in the Soviet Union, following the revolution of 1917 and the disestablishment of the Orthodox Church (q.v.). Marriage and divorce were easily arranged and consisted primarily of an official recording of the essential facts for purposes of vital statistics and for the establishment of legal responsibility with respect to children. In 1944, however, the Soviet government made it necessary for citizens seeking divorce to have recourse to the courts.

In countries where Roman Catholicism is the dominant religion and canon law (q.v.) prevails, as in Spain and Italy, and among Catholics the world over, the traditional attitude toward divorce is that a true marriage (one entered into as a religious sacrament) is indissoluble by legal means. The Roman Catholic Church, however, does permit separation of one spouse from the other because of unnatural sexual congress, cruelty, infidelity, and the taking of vows in connection with entry into a religious order. Among grounds for the annulment of marriages between Roman Catholics are impotence prior to marriage, and consanguinity (in any degree of direct line, and in some degrees of collateral line of kinship). Notwithstanding the strict interdiction of divorce by Roman Catholicism, and the provisions established by the Church for separation of married couples and the annulment of marriages, large numbers of Roman Catholics in the U.S. and other countries procure divorces in the courts. These divorces are often obtained with the approbation of Church authorities in order to protect the civil rights of the injured party. In the eyes of the Roman Catholic Church, however, such divorces are viewed as merely a form of legal separation, and remarriage is not permitted.

Divorce on various grounds is recognized among peoples of the Buddhist and Islamic faiths (see BUDDHISM; ISLAM). Prior to 1898 the Japanese attitude toward divorce was derived from a code of law formulated by the Chinese sage Confucius (q.v.); the Confucian code permitted men to divorce women because of barrenness or lasciviousness, among other reasons. A new code, adopted in 1898 and amended in 1914, modernized the Japanese attitude toward divorce, making it essentially similar to that in the U.S. Since about 1913 the Chinese attitude has also been essentially modern. In general, it may be said that the tendency in the world today is toward viewing marriage and divorce as primarily civil relationships.

See ANNULMENT OF MARRIAGE; FAMILY; MARRIAGE; SEPARATION.

DIX, Dorothea Lynde (1802–87), American philanthropist and reformer, born in Hampden, Maine. About 1820 she established a school for girls in Boston and served as its head during the ensuing fifteen years. She became interested in conditions in almshouses and prisons in 1841 after visiting such institutions in Massachusetts. Subsequently, she set about securing legislation for their improvement. Through her activities, institutions for the insane and destitute were founded in twenty States and in Canada. Her efforts also resulted in drastic reforms in prison and almshouse conditions in European countries. During the American Civil War she served with the Union army as superintendent of women nurses. Her writings include *The Garland of Flora* (1829) and *Prisons and Prison Discipline* (1845).

DIX, Dorothy. *See* GILMER, ELIZABETH MERIWETHER.

DIX, John Adams (1798–1879), American statesman and soldier, born in Boscawen, N.H., and educated at the College of Montréal. He served in the War of 1812, remaining in the army until 1828. He was secretary of state of New York from 1833 to 1839; a United States senator from 1845 to 1849, and in 1861 was appointed secretary of the treasury by President James Buchanan (q.v.). During the American Civil War, Dix served in the Union army with the rank of major general, and in 1863 he was given command of the military Department of the East. From 1866 to 1869 he was U.S. minister to France. He was, during his later years, president of the Union Pacific and of the Erie railroads. In 1872 he was elected governor of New York State and served for one term. Dix wrote *Resources of the City of New York* (1827), *A Winter in Madeira and A Summer in Spain and Florence* (1850), and *Speeches and Occasional Addresses* (2 vol., 1864).

DIXIE, name of a song composed in 1859 by the American minstrel and song writer Daniel Decatur Emmett (q.v.). The words of the song touch on life in the Southern States, popularly known as Dixie (q.v.). The song was sung for the first time at a performance of Bryant's Minstrels, at Mechanics' Hall, New York City, in 1859. It speedily became popular, especially in the South. It was sung at the inauguration of Jefferson Davis (q.v.) as President of the Confederate States of America, at Montgomery, Ala., in February, 1861. During the American Civil War it

was the principal war song and marching tune of the Confederate soldiers. The song is often played and sung today throughout the United States. Two alternative sets of words for it were written during the Civil War period. One, written in 1861 by the Confederate General Albert Pike (1809–91), favored the cause of the South; the other, written by T. M. Cooley, favored the cause of the North.

DIXIE, *or* DIXIE LAND, name given collectively to the Southern States of the United States. The origin of the term is obscure. It is supposed by some to be derived from the French *dix* ("ten") inscribed on the back of $10 bills issued by the Citizens' Bank of Louisiana before the American Civil War. Others believe that the term originated among Negroes from memory of a kindhearted slaveholder of New York during the late 18th century, named Dixie. Slaves transported to the South supposedly sang of "Dixie's," their old home, until finally, the use of the term becoming widespread, the original meaning was lost and it was applied to the entire South. Mason and Dixon's Line (q.v.), which once divided the free States from the slave States is also credited with giving rise to the name. In 1859, a song entitled "Dixie" (q.v.) was composed by the American composer Daniel Decatur Emmett (q.v.), and later became the distinctive song of the Confederacy.

DIXON, city in Illinois, and county seat of Lee Co., about 32 miles S.E. of Freeport. The city is in a rich agricultural area and manufactures farm machinery, metal products, shoes, caskets, and cement. It is the site of Sauk Valley College, established in 1965. Pop. (1970) 18,147.

DIYARBAKIR (anc. *Amida*), city in Turkey and capital of Diyarbakir Province, on the left bank of the Dicle R., about 415 miles S.E. of Ankara. A commerical and manufacturing center, the city trades in livestock, skins and furs, wine, and wool; it also contains flour and rice mills. The city is surrounded by black basalt walls, which mainly date from the 4th century A.D. Originally a Roman colony, Diyarbakir had a series of rulers until, in 1515, it was taken by the Ottoman Turks. Pop. (1970) 138,657.

DJAJAPURA, town in Indonesia, and capital of West Irian, at the foot of the Cyclops Mts., on Humboldt Bay, on the N. coast of New Guinea, about 675 miles N.W. of Port Moresby, Papua, and almost 2400 miles N.E. of Djakarta. A port, shipping chiefly copra, it lies in a coastal belt raising coconuts, cacao, fruit, vegetables, and cattle. Founded in 1910 by the Dutch as an administrative center, the town was called Hollandia until 1963. It was a Japanese base in World

Residents of Djakarta bathe and wash clothing in the
city canals.   Standard Oil Co. (N.J.)

War II until captured by Allied forces in 1944,
and it was capital of Netherlands New Guinea
colony from 1949 to 1962. Reverting to United
Nations control, it was placed under Indonesian
administration in 1963. At first called Kotabaru,
it was renamed Sukarnapura in 1963 in honor of
the Indonesian statesman Sukarno (q.v.). The
town received its present name in 1969. Pop.
(latest census) 14,100.

DJAKARTA *or* **JAKARTA,** formerly BATAVIA,
capital, most populous city, and chief seaport of
the Republic of Indonesia, on the N.W. coast of
the island of Java, on both sides of the estuary
of the Tji Liwung R., about 75 miles N.W. of
Bandung. Besides shipping, the leading industries of Djakarta are printing, iron founding,
automobile assembling, tanning, and the manu-

facture of textiles, chemicals, leather products,
soap, and margarine. The city consists of three
well-defined sections: Tandjung Priok, which is
the port area; the Old City, about 6 mi. to the w.;
and the Upper City, known also as "Weltev-
reden", adjoining the Old City on the s.w. In the
relatively modern Upper City are the principal
hotels, theaters, government buildings, parks,
and shopping and residential districts. Industrial
and commercial enterprises are concentrated in
the Old City, which closely resembles a typical
Dutch town, with narrow streets, old buildings,
and a network of canals. Points of interest in
Djakarta include an archeological museum, a
meteorological observatory, and Willemschurch
(1835). The city is also the site of the University
of Indonesia.

In 1610 the Dutch East India Company (*see*
EAST INDIA COMPANY) established a trading post in

Jacatra, a native settlement on the site of the present-day Old City. In 1618 the company constructed a fort nearby, and the next year seized control of Jacatra, which was renamed Batavia. The town became company headquarters and, subsequently, capital of the Netherlands Indies (q.v.). In 1699 Batavia was devastated by an earthquake. French forces took the city in 1811, during the Napoleonic Wars (q.v.), but were expelled later that year by the British, who restored it to the Dutch in 1814. Japanese forces occupied the city from March, 1942, to August, 1945, during World War II (q.v.). Indonesian independence was proclaimed in Batavia on Aug. 17, 1945. The city was renamed and made the capital of the year-old Indonesian republic in 1950. See INDONESIA, REPUBLIC OF. Pop. (1971) 4,576,009.

DJAMBI, city in Indonesia, and capital of Djambi Province, in S.E. Sumatra, on the Hari R. (Batang Hari or Djambi R.), about 400 miles N.W. of Djakarta. Djambi is an ocean port, although it is 55 mi. upriver from Berhala Strait, an arm of the South China Sea. The city, a road hub and trade center, is in an important oil region that also produces rubber, rice, timber, and rattan. The area was originally settled by Hindus from Java; later, Muslims established a sultanate that was one of the last areas of the island to come under Dutch control. An informal protectorate was created after 1858; the sultanate was abolished in 1901. The name was formerly spelled Jambi. Pop. (1971) 158,559.

DJERBA or **JERBA** (anc. *Meninx*), island of Tunisia, in the Gulf of Gabès, an arm of the Mediterranean Sea. The terrain is flat and arid, but the soil is arable; artesian wells are the principal source of water. Olives, dates, and figs are the chief crops. Besides farming, occupations include sponge and oyster fishing, pottery and jewelry making, and the manufacture of cloth and olive oil. Houmt-Souk on the N. side of the island is the administrative and trade center. In ancient Greek and Roman legend the island is the home of the lotus-eaters. As *Meninx*, it was a Roman possession, and during the Middle Ages it was taken successively by the Normans of Sicily, the Spanish, and the Turks. In 1881 Djerba, together with the mainland of Tunisia, was occupied by the French. Area, 197 sq.mi.; pop. (latest census) 65,533.

DJIBOUTI, republic of N.E. Africa. See AFARS AND ISSAS, FRENCH TERRITORY OF THE.

DJIBOUTI, or JIBUTI, city, capital of Djibouti, N.E. Africa. The city is a port on an inlet of the Gulf of Aden and is the terminus of a railroad to Addis Ababa, Ethiopia. Its principal exports are coffee, hides, and salt. Djibouti became the capital of French Somaliland in 1892. Pop. (1976 est.) 120,000.

DJILAS, Milovan. See YUGOSLAVIA: *The People: Culture: Literature; History.*

DJOKJAKARTA or **JOGJAKARTA,** city of the Republic of Indonesia, in S. central Java, about 275 miles S.E. of Djakarta, and about 20 mi. inland from the Indian Ocean. It is serviced by the Djakarta-Surabaya railway line and by a branch line to Semarang. The region surrounding the city is one of the most fertile areas of Java. Sugarcane, rice, and tobacco are the leading crops. Points of interest include Mt. Merapi, a quiescent volcano that overlooks the city; an imposing palace of the sultan of the former principality of Djokjakarta; the municipal botanical gardens; and a bazaar. The city of Barabudur, famed for the ruins of a magnificent 8th-century Buddhist temple, is easily accessible from Djokjakarta. Before the Japanese occupation of Java during World War II (q.v.), the principality of Djokjakarta was a Dutch protectorate. After the establishment of the Republic of Indonesia in August, 1945, the principality was merged with the republic. The city served as the provisional national capital until 1950 when it was replaced by Djakarta. Pop. (1971) 342,267.

DNA. See NUCLEIC ACIDS.

DNEPRODZERZHINSK, city and port in the Soviet Union, of the Ukrainian S.S.R., in the Dnepropetrovsk Oblast, on the Dnieper R., about 20 miles N.W. of Dnepropetrovsk. The city is in a district rich in mineral resources, notably coal and iron ore, and is an important center of the metallurgical industry of the Soviet Union. It contains large iron and steel works, engineering works, plants for the manufacture of machinery and railway rolling stock, and chemical works. Pop. (1970) 226,998.

DNEPROPETROVSK, city of the Soviet Union, in the Ukrainian S.S.R., and capital of Dnepropetrovsk Oblast, situated about 120 miles S.W. of Khar'kov on the Dnieper R. at the point where the river turns from a southeasterly to a southerly direction. Dnepropetrovsk is in a region rich in minerals. An important rail and water hub, it has access to iron ore from Krivoi Rog, manganese from Nikopol, and coal from the Donets Basin. Industrialization of the city began in the 1880's when rail connections were established with other parts of Russia. Since completion in 1932 of the Dnieper hydroelectric plant, about 50 mi. downstream at Zaporozh'ye, Dnepropetrovsk has become one of the most important industrial cities in the U.S.S.R. It has large steel mills and metal fabricating plants; important manufactured products include construction materials, mining and metallurgical equipment, electric locomotives, and other heavy machinery. Industries include railway equipment repair shops, food processing, chemical, and concrete plants. The city is the site of a state university (founded 1918), several institutes of higher education, and a state art museum.

Founded in 1787 by the Russian statesman Prince Grigori Aleksandrovich Potëmkin (q.v.), the city was originally named Ekaterinoslav in honor of Catherine II (*see under* CATHERINE), Empress of Russia. During World War II Dnepropetrovsk was occupied (1941–43) by the Germans. Pop. (1972 est.) 903,000.

DNIEPER (Russ. *Dnepr*; anc. *Borysthenes*), river and important traffic artery of the Soviet Union, about 1420 mi. long. The Dnieper is the third-longest river of Europe, exceeded in length only by the Volga and Danube rivers. The Dnieper rises about 140 miles s.w. of Moscow in the Valday Hills (q.v.) and flows in a general southerly direction to empty into the Black Sea, about 12 mi. beyond the city of Kherson, in the Ukrainian S.S.R. The Dnieper is navigable throughout its entire course, and is entirely free of ice for eight months of the year.

The Dnieper drains an area of about 200,000 sq.mi. The upper course of the river lies partly through hilly country and skirts the E. end of the Pripet Marshes. The middle and lower reaches pass through the fertile agricultural and highly industrialized areas of the Ukrainian S.S.R., where the river attains its greatest breadth— about 1 mi. The chief tributaries of the Dnieper are the Berezina, Desna, and Pripyat' rivers. Kiev is the principal city on the Dnieper. Other im-

portant cities on the river include, from s. to N., Kherson, Zaporozh'ye, Dnepropetrovsk, Dneprodzerzhinsk, Mogilev, and Smolensk. A large hydroelectric power station above Zaporozh'ye, with a capacity of up to 650,600 kw per hr., supplies power to the cities along the s. reaches of the river. Grain, lumber, and metals are transported on the Dnieper in great quantities.

In ancient times, the Dnieper was an important commercial artery between the northern and southern parts of eastern Europe. As the size of ships increased, the commercial importance of the Dnieper lessened, principally because of the impossibility of navigating the rapids above Zaporozh'ye. The problem of making the entire river navigable was solved in 1932, when the great Dneproges Dam and hydroelectric station above Zaporozh'ye was completed. The dam sufficiently raised the water level above the rapids to allow vessels to pass safely. Construction of a canal linking the Dnieper with the Bug R. in the south, and the construction of canals in the north linking the Berezina and Pripyat' rivers with the Western Dvina and Niemen rivers, respectively, made the Dnieper the principal link in a continuous waterway from the Black to the Baltic seas.

DNIESTER (Russ. *Dnestr*, Rum. *Nistru*, anc. *Tyras* or *Danastris*), river of the Soviet Union, about 850 mi. long. It rises in the Carpathian Mts., about 5 miles w. of Drogobych in the Ukrainian S.S.R., and flows in a generally s.E. direction, partly along the E. boundary of the Moldavian A.S.S.R., and empties into the Black Sea, about 20 miles w. of Odessa. The broad estuary of the river comprises several arms that form a marshy lagoon, called the Dniester Liman. The average width of the river is 500 to 750 ft.; the maximum width is about 1400 ft. For about seventy days during the winter, a large part of the Dniester is frozen.

The Dniester drains an area of about 30,000 sq.mi., and is an important traffic artery for the shipment of grain, vegetables, sunflower seeds, cattle and cattle products, and lumber, all of which are produced in the Dniester basin. The most important city on the river is Tiraspol.

Before World War II the Dniester formed part of the boundary between Rumania and the Soviet Union. During the war large-scale battles were fought on the banks of the river between the German and Rumanian invaders and the Soviet defenders.

DOBERMAN PINSCHER, working dog that originated at Apolda, Thuringia, Germany, where it was first bred about 1890 from the German shepherd dog, the Rottweiler, the black

Doberman pinscher   Walter Chandoha

and tan terrier, and the German pinscher. The Doberman pinscher derives its name from its first breeder, Louis Dobermann, a German watchman who developed the dog to help him with his guard duties. It was employed at first as a watchdog and later was trained to act as a police dog and a war dog. Characteristics of the breed are a wedge-shaped head; dark eyes ranging from brown to black in color and having an alert, courageous expression; a well-muscled neck; and a smooth, hard, close-lying coat that is black, brown, or blue in color. Males are from about 25 to 28 in. high at the shoulders; bitches, from about 24 to 26 in. The male weighs from about 65 to 75 lb. The Doberman pinscher is obedient, loyal, and especially fond of children. The breed became popular in the United States about 1921.

DOBROGEA, region of N.E. Bulgaria and S.E. Rumania, fronting the Black Sea and bounded on the N. and W. by the Danube R. The Dobrogea region is generally fertile; major crops are cereal grains, beets, grapes, mulberries, fodder plants, and tobacco. Rumania acquired northern Dobrogea from Bulgaria in 1878 by the terms of the Treaty of Berlin following the Russo-Turkish War of 1877–78; see RUSSO-TURKISH WARS. Southern Dobrogea was ceded to Rumania under the terms of the Treaty of Bucharest following the Balkan Wars (q.v.) of 1912–13. The latter acquisition was upheld by the Treaty of Neuilly in 1919; see NEUILLY, TREATY OF. Southern Dobrogea, comprising about one third of the area of the region, was returned to Bulgaria in September, 1940, by the Treaty of Craiova. After 1949 Bulgarian Dobrogea was included within the Bulgarian provinces of Ruse and Stalin. Rumanian Dobrogea constituted a Rumanian province until 1952. Area of region, 8969 sq.mi.

DOBSON, (Henry) Austin (1840–1921), born in Plymouth, England. In 1856 he became a clerk in the marine department of the British Board of Trade; from 1884 to 1901 he was principal clerk. In 1873 a collection of his poems that had previously appeared in periodicals was published in book form under the title *Vignettes in Rhyme.* He was one of the leaders of the movement that introduced such French verse forms as the rondeau (q.v.), the triolet, and the ballade into English poetry; see POETRY. Among his works, which include both poetry and prose, are *Proverbs in Porcelain* (1877), *At the Sign of the Lyre* (1885), *Eighteenth Century Vignettes* (1892–96), and *A Paladin of Philanthropy* (1899); and the biographies *Fielding* (1883), *Steele* (1886), *Goldsmith* (1888), and *Samuel Richardson* (1902).

DOBSON FLY. See CORYDALUS.

DOBZHANSKY, Theodosius (1900–75), American geneticist and zoologist, born in Nemirov, Russia, and educated at the University of Kiev. In 1927 he came to the United States because of political interference with genetic studies in the Soviet Union. He joined Thomas Hunt Morgan (q.v.) at Columbia University and moved with him in 1928 to the California Institute of Technology, where he became a professor of zoology in 1936. Dobzhansky returned to Columbia in 1940, worked at Rockefeller University from 1962 to 1971, and spent his last years as adjunct professor at the University of California at Davis.

Dobzhansky's studies in population genetics, performed mainly with the fruit fly (see DROSOPHILA), served as a basis for his explanation of how the evolution of races and species may have come about through adaptation. He held that human culture is conditioned by heredity but warned that exaggerating genetic over environmental factors in human affairs could lead to distorted theories of racism and class prejudice. In addition to his classic text, *Genetics and the Origin of Species* (1937), his books include *Evolution, Genetics, and Man* (1955) and *Mankind Evolving* (1962).

DOCK, common name for several plants of the genus *Rumex* of the Buckwheat family.

Curly dock, Rumex crispus
John H. Gerard – National Audubon Society

A view of the Brooklyn-Port Authority Marine Terminal in New York Harbor, extending 2 mi. from Brooklyn Bridge to Atlantic Basin. The $100,000,000 redevelopment of the waterfront area, begun in 1961 by the Port of New York Authority, had replaced 25 obsolete piers with 12 new ones by 1968. The 2000-ft. pier at right is the longest in the series; others average between 750 ft. and 1000 ft. in length. The tip of Governors Island and a ventilation building for the Brooklyn-Battery Tunnel are visible at left.   Port of New York Authority

Other plants in this genus are called sorrel (q.v.), slightly different in form of leaf and flower. Sorrel generally includes low-growing plants in the subgenus *Acetosa* which have a sour herbage. Dock generally includes plants of the subgenus *Lapathum*, which are taller and have herbage that is not acid, or is only slightly so. Plants of this genus include about a hundred species of biennial and perennial herbs. Of the thirty or more species found in North America, about one third have been introduced from Europe. They have stout taproots, or running rootstocks, and their tapered leaves, with smooth and sometimes wavy margins, are placed alternately on the stems. The greenish flowers, which have no petals, are arranged in circular clusters. The fruits are red or brown triangular nuts enclosed in leathery sepals (*see* FLOWER: PARTS OF A FLOWER). Most of these plants are troublesome weeds. The great water dock of Europe, *R. hy-* drolapathum, which grows to a height of 6 ft., is used for landscaping; the root extract of *R. conglomeratus* has been used for dyeing. *See also* CANAIGRE.

DOCK, type of harbor structure used for the loading, unloading, or repair of ships. In accurate usage the term applies either to the water channel in which a ship is berthed beside a pier, or to a so-called dry dock in which a ship is placed for repairs. In common American usage the term signifies a pier or a quay.

In harbors that have a large tidal range, ships are usually berthed in wet docks. These are basins, able to accommodate a large number of vessels, which can be shut off from the rest of the harbor by movable gates that hold the water in the dock at the high-tide level. Wet docks are a necessity in most ports of the British Isles and in other localities where the height of the tide is more than about 10 ft. Among great ports of the world equipped with wet docks are London, Liverpool, Cardiff, and Aberdeen in the British Isles; Le Havre, France; Bremerhaven, West Germany; Antwerp, Belgium; and Bombay and Calcutta in India. The London wet-dock system is the largest in the world; the combined length of the quays and piers in London amounts to about 45 mi.

In most United States seaports the rise and fall of the tide is sufficiently small to permit the use of tidal docks. Such docks, almost universally used in this country, consist of a series of rectangular water spaces between projecting piers. In some ports, ships are berthed around the edge of open tidal basins, where they are also subject to the rise and fall of the tide.

The advent of container freight, whereby shipments are delivered at dockside in the trailer components of tractor-trailer truck rigs, has led to the development of containership docks. These are quay-type berths with wide aprons to provide easy shipside access for tractors delivering or picking up containers. Containership docks can handle 500,000 tons of freight per berth a year, compared to about 100,000 tons per berth a year for the newest conventional docks. The biggest containership docks in the U.S. are at Newark and Elizabeth, N.J.

For the repair of ships, dry docks are universally employed. These are structures into which the ship can be floated and which are then closed and pumped free of water, leaving the ship resting on props and shores at the bottom of the dock. Dry docks are of two types: graving docks, fixed basins of masonry and timber; and floating dry docks, usually made of steel. Floating dry docks have certain advantages over graving docks in that they can be built more quickly and economically than fixed docks, and can also be built at a distance from their final location and then towed into place. The largest commercial floating dock in the world is at Southampton, England. It is 860 ft. in length, 130 ft. in breadth, and can accommodate ships with a draft of 38 ft. The largest commercial graving dock in the world, at Malmö, Sweden, is 1330 ft. long, 246 ft. wide, and 30 ft. deep.

See BREAKWATER; HARBOR.

DOCTORS OF THE CHURCH, eminent Christian teachers, proclaimed by the Church to be worthy of the title, which is taken from the Latin *doctor ecclesiae.* In according the title, the Church recognizes the cited theologian's contribution to doctrine and the understanding of the faith. The person so named must be a canonized saint; *see* CANONIZATION; SAINT. He must also be of great sanctity and of renowned learning. The proclamation must be made by a pope or by an ecumenical council; *see* COUNCIL. The original doctors of the Church were the Western theologians Saints Ambrose, Augustine, Jerome (qq.v.), and Pope Gregory I (*see under* GREGORY), who were named in 1298. The corresponding Eastern doctors are Saints Athanasius, Basil, John Chrysostom, and Gregory of Nazianzus (qq.v.). They were named in 1568, in the same year as was Saint Thomas Aquinas (q.v.). The first women doctors of the Church, Saints Catherine of Siena and Theresa of Ávila (qq.v.), were named in 1970.

See also CHRISTIAN CHURCH, HISTORY OF THE; FATHERS OF THE CHURCH; ROMAN CATHOLIC CHURCH.

DOCTRINE. See DOGMA.

DODD, William Edward (1869–1940), American historian, born in Clayton, N.C., and educated at Virginia Polytechnic Institute and the University of Leipzig. He was professor of American history at Randolph-Macon College from 1900 to 1908 and at the University of Chicago from 1908 until 1933. From 1933 to 1937 he was American ambassador to Germany; he subsequently described his experiences in Germany in the book *Ambassador Dodd's Diary, 1933–38* (1941). Among his other writings are *The Life of Jefferson Davis* (1907), *Statesmen of the Old South* (1911), *Expansion and Conflict* (1915), *Woodrow Wilson and His Work* (1920), and *Lincoln or Lee* (1928). With the American writer Ray Stannard Baker (q.v.) he edited *The Public Papers of Woodrow Wilson* (6 vol., 1924–26).

DODDER, common name for plants of the genus *Cuscuta,* family Convolvulaceae. Dodder is also called love vine, strangleweed, goldthread, and hell-bind. It is one of the few higher plants that are parasitic on other plants. It has yellowish or reddish threadlike twining stems and no leaves or chlorophyll. The young plant attaches itself on germination to surrounding vegetation by means of sucking organs, called *haustoria,* through which it takes nourishment from the host. Dodder is especially harmful to clover, alfalfa, and flax, and is also found on ornamental plants. Commercial clover and alfalfa seed is always specially treated to avoid contamination by dodder seed.

Several species of the plant are common in Europe and the United States. Dodders are annuals, with small white, pink, or yellow flowers, which appear from summer to autumn. The plants produce an abundance of seeds from July until frost.

DODDS, Harold Willis (1889–   ), American political scientist and educator, born in Utica, Pa., and educated at Grove City College (Pa.), Princeton University, and the University of Pennsylvania. He taught economics and political science at various universities from 1914 to 1920, except for a period of service with the United States Food Administration during World War I. From 1920 to 1928 he was secretary of the National Municipal League and edited its journal, the *National Municipal Review,* until 1933, at the same time acting as adviser to the government of Nicaragua and to the Plebiscitary Commission in the Tacna-Arica dispute (q.v.). He served as professor of politics at Princeton University from 1927 until 1934, a year after his appointment as president of the institution. During his twenty-four years as president at Princeton, Dodds expanded the university's School of Political and International Affairs and inaugurated a curriculum plan to broaden the teaching of the liberal arts. Among his writings are the collection of essays *Out of This Nettle . . . Danger* (1943), *The Academic President: Educator or Caretaker?* (1962), and numerous articles and reports on political and public administration.

DODECANESE, *or* DODECANESUS, group of about fifty islands and islets belonging to Greece, in the s.e. Aegean Sea, off the coast of Asian Turkey. The group comprises the Southern Sporades (*see* SPORADES). Total land area, 1036 sq.mi.; pop. (1971) 121,017. Only fourteen of the islands are permanently inhabited. Of these, the most important are Rhodes, Kos (qq.v.), and Kárpathos. Rhodes, on which Ródhos or Rhodes, capital of the group, is located, has the largest area and population of the islands. The other inhabited islands (latest census figures) are Kálimnos (area, 41 sq.mi.; pop. 26,032); Léros (21 sq.mi.; pop. 6611); Sími (22 sq.mi.; pop. 3123); Nísiros (16 sq.mi.; pop. 1788); Pátmos (13 sq.mi.; pop. 2564); Kastellorizón (4 sq.mi.; pop. 481); Astipálaia (37 sq.mi.; pop. 1558); Kásos (25 sq.mi.; pop. 1422); Khálki (11 sq.mi.; pop. 501); Tílos (24 sq.mi.; pop. 789); and Lípsos (6 sq.mi.; pop. 724).

Agriculture is the chief occupation of the Dodecanese; the leading crops are tobacco, olives, grapes, oranges, and other fruits and vegetables, with Rhodes and Kos producing the largest yields. Sheep, oxen, horses, mules, and pigs are raised. The sponge-fishing industry is important in several of the islands, particularly in Kálimnos and Sími. Principal manufactures of the group include olive oil, decorative pottery and tiles, carpets, silk, tobacco products, leather goods, and wine.

Greeks constitute the overwhelming majority of the population. Episcopal sees of the Greek Orthodox Church are situated on the islands of Rhodes, Léros, Kásos, and Kos. Administrative authority is vested in a governor-general appointed by the Greek government.

Only twelve islands were included in the Dodecanese group in antiquity, accounting for the name (Gr., "twelve islands"). Several islands of the group, especially Rhodes, were settled by the ancient Greeks and figured prominently in Hellenic civilization for many centuries. The islands subsequently became Roman dominions. Following the division of the Roman Empire, they belonged to the Byzantine Empire. In 1522 the Dodecanese were seized by the Ottoman Turks, who retained control until the successful invasion of Rhodes in 1912 by the armed forces of Italy. The Turkish government formally relinquished control of the group in 1923. During World War II, in 1943, German troops occupied the Dodecanese; in May, 1945, the islands were relinquished to a British force, which remained in a caretaker role. In September, 1947, by the terms of the Italian peace treaty, the island group was ceded to Greece, with formal unification taking place on March 7, 1948.

DODECATHEON, genus of hardy Asian and North American herbs of the Primrose (q.v.) family, growing wild in shaded woodlands and damp mountain meadows. An American species, *D. meadia,* the American cowslip (q.v.) or shooting star, has rose-colored flowers and leaves up to 6 in. long.

DODGE, Mary Elizabeth Mapes (1831–1905), American author and editor, born in New York City. She was editor of *St. Nicholas Magazine* for children from 1873 until her death. Her most successful book was *Hans Brinker, or, the Silver Skates* (1865), which became a juvenile classic soon after publication and for which she received a prize from the French Academy. Among her other works are *Donald and Dorothy* (1883), *The Land of Pluck* (1894), and *Poems and Verses* (1894).

DODGE CITY, city in s.w. Kansas, and county seat of Ford Co., on the Arkansas R., crossed by the line separating Central and Mountain time, about 150 miles w. of Wichita. It is the center of transportation for w. Kansas, and the trade center for a great wheat and livestock region. The city contains flour and feed mills and railroad shops. Dodge City was first settled around 1871 and incorporated in 1875. Located on the old Santa Fe Trail (q.v.) and at one time the outpost of the Santa Fe railroad, Dodge City was a famous frontier town and a shipping point for Texas cattle. The present municipal building is located on Boot Hill, burial ground in frontier days for adventurers who died by gunfire and were hastily buried "with their boots on". Beeson Museum houses pioneer relics and Indian craft. Fort Dodge, built in 1864 for defense against the Indians and now a State home for war veterans, is 5 miles e. of the city. Pop. (1960) 13,520; (1970) 14,127.

DODGSON, Charles Lutwidge, also known as LEWIS CARROLL (1832–98), British author and mathematician, born in Daresbury, Cheshire, England, and educated at Rugby and at Oxford University. From 1855 to 1881 he was a member of the faculty of mathematics at Oxford. He was the author of various mathematical treatises, including *Euclid and His Modern Rivals* (1879). In 1865 under the pen name Lewis Carroll, he wrote *Alice's Adventures in Wonderland* (q.v.); its sequel *Through the Looking Glass and What Alice Found There* appeared in 1871. These were followed by *Phantasmagoria and Other Poems* (1869), *The Hunting of the Snark* (1876), and *Sylvie and Bruno* (1889).

Alice in Wonderland, which has made the name Lewis Carroll famous throughout the world, was originally written for Alice Liddell (d. 1934), a daughter of Henry George Liddell (1811–98), dean of Christ Church College, University of Oxford. On its publication, the work, illustrated by the British cartoonist Sir John Tenniel (q.v.), became immediately popular as a story for children. Its subsequent appeal to adults was based upon the ingenious mixture of fantasy and realism, irony and absurdity. The names of its characters, such as the March Hare, the Mad Hatter, and the Cheshire Cat, have become familiar in everyday speech.

DODO, common name applied to a large, flightless bird, *Raphus cucullatus,* belonging to the order Columbiformes and now extinct. The dodo inhabited the forests of the island of Mauritius. About the size of a turkey, the bird had a large hooked bill, undeveloped wings and tail, and short, thick, yellow legs. It laid a single large egg in a ground nest made of grass. The dodo was first reported in 1598 by Dutch colonizers, who characterized it as a sluggish bird unafraid of man. Dodos were last observed in 1681. The speedy extinction of the species is attributed in part to domestic animals imported to Mauritius by the settlers; animals such as hogs escaped to the woods, multiplied, and destroyed many of the dodo eggs. The name "dodo" is derived from the Portuguese word *doudo,* meaning "silly" or "stupid". In present-day usage the word "dodo" is applied to a simple-minded person unable to adjust to new situations and ideas.

DODONA, most ancient Greek shrine, in the interior of Epirus Region, about 50 miles E. of Kérkira (Corfu). It was sacred to Zeus and his consort Dione. Priests of the temple interpreted as responses from Zeus the rustling of a great oak tree, the activities of doves in its branches, the clanging of brass pots hung from the branches, and the murmurs of a fountain. Both Homer and Hesiod (q.v.), poets of Greek antiquity, mention Dodona. The oracle at Dodona was one of the most respected of ancient times, and it was consulted by Greeks from many cities and by foreigners; Croesus, King of Lydia, was said to have visited the temple. The shrine was destroyed in warfare by the Aetolians in 219 B.C., but was probably restored later. Archeological finds have been made at the site.

DOE. *See* DEER.

DOE, John. *See* JOHN DOE.

DOENITZ, Karl. *See* GERMANY: *History: World War II.*

DOG, name given to members of several species of the family Canidae, particularly the domestic dog, *Canis familiaris.* More than 200 different breeds, or kinds, are distinguished. A dog is a four-footed carnivore that has a compact body and slender legs. Each forefoot bears five nonretractile claws, and each hind foot bears four. A dewclaw, a vestigial digit, is found on the inner aspect of each foot. The head of the dog narrows to form a muzzle. The true dog has forty-two permanent teeth. Each jaw has six incisors, two canines or fangs, and eight premolars. The upper jaw carries two molar teeth on each side, and the lower jaw carries three. Characteristically the bodies, heads, and legs are covered with thick hair.

Although dogs are carnivorous and, when in the wild state, subsist chiefly on red meat, they also eat reptiles, fish, insects, and some forms of vegetable matter. Dogs are gregarious in habit and usually hunt in packs. Most species mature in about eight months to two years, according to size, and have an average life span of ten to twelve years. Some dogs may live to an age of more than twenty years. The normal body temperature of the dog is 101° F., and the heartbeat count ranges from 70 to 120 per minute.

Wild Dogs. The genus *Canis* includes a number of wild species, several of which are known as wild dogs. Among them are the Australian dingo (q.v.), *C. dingo;* the wild dog of Burma, *C. rutilans;* the Siberian wild dog, *C. alpinus;* and the African hunting dog, *C. lycaon.* The coyote (q.v.), *C. latrans,* of the western United States is also sometimes called a wild dog. The wild dogs of India, such as the dhole, belong to a related genus, *Cuon,* and differ from the true dogs in that they have one less molar on either side of the lower jaw. Some other members of the family Canidae are also called dogs, including the fox dog of South America, *Dusicyon gymnocerus,* and the raccoon dog, *Nyctereutes procyonides,* which is found in Japan and China and resembles a small raccoon.

Domestic Dogs. The extraordinary variety shown by the various breeds of *C. familiaris* is strong evidence of the length of time that the dog has been bred selectively as a domestic animal. Neolithic remains indicate that dogs shared human habitations in prehistoric times, and Egyptian monuments of about 3000 B.C. depict several well-defined breeds of dogs. It is impossible to be certain of the ancestry of the domestic dog, but it is extremely likely that the species arose from wolf stock, *C. lupus,* and crossing with other members of the genus.

In the U.S. domestic dogs number about 25,000,000, many breeds of which are grouped into two broad general classes: sporting dogs, or hunting dogs, and nonsporting dogs. The traditional grouping used by the American Kennel Club assigns all domestic dogs to the six divisions described in the following paragraphs. For information concerning each group or breed mentioned, see the individual articles under the name of each group or breed.

SPORTING DOGS. These dogs are also known as gun dogs or field dogs, used in the sport of hunting. The group comprises the following breeds and varieties of breeds: the griffon and the pointer, including the English or American pointer and the German short-haired pointer; the retriever, including the Chesapeake Bay, curly or curly-coated, flat-coated, golden, and Labrador retrievers; the setter, including the English, Gordon, and Irish setters; and the spaniel, including the American water, Brittany, Clumber, cocker, field, Irish water, English springer, Welsh springer, and Sussex spaniels.

Trained dogs, such as the German shorthaired pointer (above, left), retrieve game for hunters. In some U.S. cities dogs work with police on patrol duty; a German shepherd (above, right), scheduled for assignment to a subway beat, demonstrates his obedience to commands. Huskies (below) are used in teams in the Arctic regions to draw transport sleds.

DOG

Sporting Dogs of the Hound Type. These mainly comprise hunting dogs that follow their quarry by scent, but include also a few breeds of hound that follow quarry by sight. The principal breeds of hound are the Afghan hound, basset hound, beagle, bloodhound, borzoi or Russian wolfhound, dachshund, Scottish deerhound, Norwegian elkhound, foxhound, greyhound, otterhound, saluki, whippet, and Irish wolfhound.

Working Dogs. These dogs are useful for such practical tasks as herding, pulling carts or sleds, carrying packs, guarding, and assisting police in pursuing and catching criminals. The principal breeds of working dogs are the Alaskan Malamute, Belgian sheepdog, boxer, Briard, collie, Eskimo dog, German shepherd dog, great Dane, great Pyrenees dog, Komondor, Kuvasz, mastiff, Newfoundland dog, old English sheepdog, Samoyed, Shetland sheepdog, Siberian husky, and Saint Bernard.

Terriers. These are small or medium-sized dogs originally used for hunting small, furred game but now kept chiefly as pets. The terrier group includes the Airedale, Bedlington, bullterrier, Dandie Dinmont, fox, Irish, Kerry blue, Manchester, Norwich, Scottish, Sealyham, Skye, and Welsh terriers, and the Schnauzer.

Toy Dogs. Small dogs, or miniature varieties of larger dogs, kept principally as pets. The group includes the Chihuahua, Italian greyhound, Mexican Hairless, Papillon, miniature pinscher, Pomeranian, pug, toy Manchester terrier, toy poodle, and Yorkshire terrier.

Nonsporting Dogs. These dogs are kept mainly as companions. Among the breeds of nonsporting dogs are the Boston terrier, the English and French bulldog, Chow Chow, Dalmatian, keeshond, poodle, and Schipperke.

Diseases of Dogs. Among the commonest and most noxious of dog diseases are distemper and mange (qq.v.). Hydrophobia, known also as rabies (q.v.), occurs less often, but it is a dangerous disease both to dogs and to man.

Blacktongue, a disease that attacks dogs chiefly in middle or old age, is caused by a deficiency of B vitamins, particularly of nicotinic acid, as in pellagra in man. Blacktongue is characterized by inflammation of the tongue and the inside of the mouth and by similar symptoms in the intestinal tract, accompanied by vomiting and diarrhea. During the course of the disease the tongue frequently becomes blueblack in color. The prevention and treatment of blacktongue depend on diet. Dried yeast is prescribed by veterinarians for animals suffering from the disease. The use of yeast, fresh meat,

Loyal, gentle, and affectionate, most breeds of dogs make excellent pets and playmates for children. UPI

milk, and salmon in the normal diet of a dog, moreover, has been found to be a good preventive measure.

Fits or convulsions in dogs can arise from a number of causes, including foreign bodies or parasites in the intestinal tract, indigestion, violent exercise or excitement, and teething in puppies. In these attacks the dog will usually become rigid, make chewing motions, froth at the mouth, and fall, kicking spasmodically, to the ground. When fits occur, veterinarians recommend that the animal be removed to a quiet place, without being fed, for a day after the attack has passed. Running fits or fright disease, in which the animal runs around, barks wildly, and seemingly exhibits great excitement or fear, is a malady of obscure origin that is sometimes mistaken for rabies. It is believed that diet may play some part in this disease, since it seems to be more common in dogs that have been fed largely on cereals and breadstuffs than in dogs that have had plenty of meat.

Dogs are subject to a number of internal parasites, including protozoa, flukes, and worms. The most destructive of these parasites are hookworms, small roundworms that have sharp, hooklike teeth, with which they fasten themselves to the intestines. These worms draw a large quantity of blood from the host and cause symptoms of anemia, such as loss of weight and pallor of the mucous membranes of the mouth. A number of drugs have been used to control hookworms, of which the most effective are tetrachloroethylene and n-butyl chloride. Dogs are also susceptible to tapeworms. These flattened worms attach themselves to the intestinal walls and in some cases grow to a length of 16 ft. The symptoms caused by tapeworm infestations vary, but usually include diarrhea and other digestive disturbances. The drug used for treatment is arecoline bromide, a strong purgative. Dogs are also subject to heartworms, nematodes that are transmitted by the bites of mosquitoes and fleas and infest the valves of the heart and the pulmonary artery. A dog suffering from heartworms becomes tired easily and may collapse after exercise and exhibit other symptoms of poor circulation. Heartworms have been treated successfully by injections of various antimony compounds. Other types of worms that attack the lungs, kidneys, and eyes are less common among dogs.

Of the external parasites that attack dogs, ticks are the most dangerous, not only for the harm that they do to dogs but because they transmit Rocky Mountain spotted fever and tularemia (qq.v.), which are highly dangerous to humans. Dogs may be kept free of ticks by being dipped twice weekly in a solution of soap and derris powder.

DOGBANE, common name for plants of the genus *Apocynum,* for which the Dogbane family (Apocynaceae) is named. Two species, spreading dogbane *(A. androsaemifolium)* and Indian hemp *(A. cannabinum),* are widely distributed in the United States and Canada on poor soils of waste areas, roadsides, and gravel banks. Both species are perennial herbs, somewhat woody, the former more branched and spreading than the latter. They have opposite leaves, copious milky juice, and pencillike pods hanging in clusters. The pods are filled at maturity with a cottony mass of milkweedlike fuzz and seeds. Indian hemp was used by the American Indians as a source of fiber for making rope. Vegetation of both species contains a number of glycosides (q.v.) which make them toxic when eaten.

Dogbane, Apocynum cannabinum

DOG DAYS. *See* Canis Major.

DOGE, old Venetian word derived from the Latin word *dux* meaning leader, specifically applicable to the chief magistrate of the republic of Venice from 697 to 1797 and, with the exception of a short interval, to the chief magistrate of Genoa from 1339 to 1805. *See* Genoa: *History;* Venice: *History.*

DOGFISH, *or* DOG SHARK, common name loosely applied to some species of small sharks, and formerly applied to two species of bony fish. The two best-known species bearing this name are the spiny dogfish, *Squalus acanthias,* of the dogfish shark family Squalidae and the smooth dogfish, *Mustelus canis,* of the smoothhound family Triakidae. The dogfish sharks are characterized by a hard spine at the base of each of the two dorsal fins. Other species of Squalidae that are called dogfish include the Atlantic black dogfish, *Centroscyllium fabricii*; the Cuban dogfish, *Squalus cubensis*; and the green dogfish, *Etmopterus vivens*, found in deep waters of the Gulf of Mexico. In the cat shark family Scyliorhinidae, at least four species are called dogfish: the chain dogfish, *Scyliorhinus retifer*, found off the Atlantic coast of the United States; two Mediterranean spotted dogfish, *S. stellaris* and *S. caniculus*; and the Malaysian marbled dogfish, *Atelomycterus marmoratus*. Two bony fishes have been called dogfish: the bowfin, *Amia calva*, and the central mudminnow, *Umbra limi*.

The spiny dogfish, first described by Swedish botanist Carolus Linnaeus (q.v.) in 1758, is found on both sides of the North Atlantic Ocean, generally in temperate to subarctic latitudes. The California dogfish, *Squalus acanthias suckleyi*, which ranges in the Pacific Ocean from Alaska to Baja California, is now considered to be a subspecies, called the Pacific spiny dogfish. A closely related form is found off Japan, China, and Hawaii.

The spiny dogfish is usually slate-colored above and pale gray or white below, with an irregular row of small white spots along the sides. The Atlantic subspecies has a maximum length of about 4 ft., a weight of about 20 lb., and an average length 2 to 3½ ft. The Pacific subspecies may reach 5 ft. in length.

The spiny dogfish was formerly valued for its oil, and during the 1940's was caught for the vitamin A (and some vitamin D) content of its liver. It is used as a food in Europe.

DOGGER BANK, extensive flat sandbank near the middle of the North Sea, between England on the w. and Denmark on the e. It has an average breadth of about 40 mi., and stretches N.E. and S.W. for a distance of about 160 mi. The water is generally less than 120 ft. deep, and toward the English coast is little more than 50 ft. deep. The bank has been a commercial fishing ground for centuries; cod, plaice, and herring are especially abundant.

Dogger Bank has been the site of several naval engagements. In 1781, during the American Revolution, a British fleet routed the Dutch here. In 1904, during the Russo-Japanese War, the Russian Baltic squadron, under Admiral Zinovi Petrovich Rozhdestvenski (1848–1909), fired by mistake upon a British fishing fleet and killed two men. The incident was arbitrated by an international commission, and Russia paid damages. In 1915, during World War I, a British fleet under the command of Vice-Admiral Sir David Beatty (q.v.) defeated a German fleet commanded by Rear Admiral Franz von Hipper (1863–1932) in the Battle of the Dogger Bank.

DOGMA, in Christian theology, truth directly proposed by the Church for belief as an article of divine revelation. Originally, in general use, the term designated an opinion or proposition put as a positive assertion, its truth being supposed to have been previously shown. In theology, the term signifies a doctrine defined by the Church and advanced, not for discussion, but for belief.

The first attempt to give a connected view of Christian dogma was made in the 4th century by Saint Augustine (q.v.), who in his *Enchiridion* ("Handbook") and other works compiled and discussed the whole body of doctrine held by the Church, though not according to a scientific scheme. The contributions to doctrinal theology, or dogmatics, made in the 5th, 6th, and 7th centuries were isolated statements rather than organized bodies of doctrine.

In the East, in the 8th century, the dogmas of the Greek Church were gathered and codified by John of Damascus (q.v.), and his work may be considered the first systematically arranged treatise on dogmatics. Many theologians of the Roman Catholic Church have since given exhaustive study to the subject, especially Saint Thomas Aquinas (q.v.), whose works Pope Leo XIII (*see under* Leo) designated as the standard of modern dogmatic theology.

Because the dogmatic method in theology is often thought to sanction groundless opinions, the terms "dogma" and, even more, "dogmatic" have come into frequent use in everyday speech to denote or describe assertion without proof.

DOG RACING, contest in which trained dogs, usually greyhounds, compete against each other by pursuing a swiftly moving, mechanical rabbit around a circular or oval track. The sport is popular internationally, notably in Great Britain, the United States, Australia, France, and Italy. Dog racing is an outgrowth of coursing, a similar sport involving the pursuit of live game, also by sight rather than scent; coursing largely has been eclipsed in popularity by dog racing, but the event is still held in many countries.

Most of the dogs participating in organized competition are male or female greyhounds, although races between whippets and between salukis are held also; see Greyhound; Saluki; Whippet. The racing greyhound, a slender, graceful animal weighing about 65 lbs., is in its prime between the ages of one and five. In action the greyhound covers from 12 to 20 ft. in a stride and attains speeds of more than 35 m.p.h. The price of a trained racing greyhound ranges from $1000 to $50,000, depending on its record in competition. During its racing life an outstanding dog may earn more than $100,000 in purses and breeding fees.

Most dog-racing stadiums are specially designed plants comprising a grandstand, a running track, kennels, accommodations for parimutuel betting, a judges' stand, and a system of floodlights for night racing. The racing area proper is an oval strip of land about 450 yds. long and about 20 ft. wide; its inside or outside circumference is ringed by metal rails along which the lure is propelled by electrical power.

vance of the pack; if any of the dogs catch the rabbit at any point short of the finish line, the race automatically is declared null and void. The first dog to cross the finish line wins the race.

Betting and the prospect of winning large purses are important elements in the appeal of the sport to spectators and greyhound owners, respectively. In the U.S. dog racing is estimated to rank seventh among spectator sports, and betting is legal in Florida, Arkansas, Oregon, South Dakota, Arizona, Colorado, and Massachusetts. In 1972 spectators numbering about 13,666,000 wagered approximately $875,000,000 at forty major dog-racing tracks in the U.S.;

Greyhounds in midstride during a race. UPI

Of the world total of about 250 major dog-racing tracks, some 200 are located in Great Britain and about 30 are in the U.S.

Races are held at distances varying from 330 to 770 yds., but the distance run most frequently is 550 yds. The American 550-yd. record is 30.8 sec. From 6 to 8 dogs compete in each race, and about 10 races are run during a given program. The competing dogs are muzzled as a precaution against fighting and are raced in brightly colored, numbered jackets to facilitate their identification by judges and spectators.

As a prelude to each race the mechanical rabbit is set in motion in full view of the dogs, which are confined in stalls on the starting line; when the rabbit is about 20 ft. beyond the stalls the dogs are released in pursuit of the lure. As the race progresses the speed of the rabbit is so controlled that it remains about 20 ft. in ad-

about $310,000,000 is wagered annually on dog races in England, Scotland, and Wales. The oldest and most famous of the British greyhound stakes is the Waterloo Cup, held since 1776 in Liverpool, England; the richer American stakes include the Flagler Derby, held in Miami, Fla., which offers a purse of $80,000.

Dog racing originated as a sport about 2500 B.C. in Egypt, where the pastime took the form of coursing. Coursing remained popular throughout ancient times and during the Middle Ages, and it was a favorite sport of royalty in 16th-century England. Coursing competition was organized on a formal basis in Great Britain in the 18th century and in the U.S. in the 19th century. In the early 20th century, opposition to the use of live rabbits as lures in coursing led to the development in the U.S. of the mechanical rabbit, which was first demonstrated successfully in Emeryville, Calif., in 1919. Dog racing subsequently replaced coursing in popularity in the U.S. and in Great Britain, where the sport was introduced in 1925. The pastime spread later to the European continent, Australia, China, Mexico, and Central America.

DOG SHOWS AND TRIALS, events in which purebred dogs compete for prizes and titles on the basis of their show qualities or training. Such events usually take one of three forms. Dog shows are exhibitions in which the dogs entered are judged on the basis of the standard of perfection for their particular breeds; obedience trials compare the facility with which trained dogs respond to verbal commands or hand signals; and field trials test the hunting ability of certain breeds of dogs. The main purpose of the events is to exhibit outstanding animals to the dog-loving public and to professional dog breeders and handlers. Dog shows and trials are popular in a number of countries, notably Great Britain, Germany, and the United States. In the U.S. alone there are 30,000,000 dogs, of which more than 1,100,000 were registered with the American Kennel Club in 1975. Each year more than 100,000 of these animals are entered in thousands of exhibitions. Some major dog shows in the U.S. draw several thousand entries each year. All dogs competing in shows, obedience trials, and field trials under American Kennel Club rules must be registered with the American Kennel Club or with some other recognized body.

Dog Shows. Dog shows are divided into so-called benched and unbenched events involving one or more breeds, groups, and classes of pedigreed animals. At benched shows, prior to judging, the dogs, except puppies, are displayed to the public on benches or platforms set up in individual stalls. At unbenched shows the dogs are seen by the public when they are exhibited in the judging rings and around the grounds of the event. In dog shows all of the breeds are divided into six groups, namely sporting, hound, working, terrier, toy, and nonsporting; *see* DOG: *Domestic Dogs.* In every dog show the regular classes within each breed are puppy, novice, bred-by-exhibitor, American bred, and open.

The standards for judging the entries of the various breeds differ with each breed. Typical criteria include shape of head, placement of ears, color, gait, and texture of coat. Dogs entered in a particular class are taken into the judging ring by their owners or handlers. After the dogs have been gaited, or walked at differ-

ent speeds, and examined by the judge, the class is placed 1-2-3-4. The dogs placed first in each of the classes compete for "winners", and the "winners" receive points toward their championship based on the number of dogs in their particular breed that have been in competition at the show. To attain a show championship a dog must have accumulated 15 championship points under different judges, and in the 15 points there must have been two "major" wins, meaning 3, 4, or 5 point wins. Dogs that attain their championships are entitled to have the abbreviation "Ch." carried before the name.

Following the judging of the "winners" classes, dogs that have already won their championships compete, along with the "winners dog" and "winners bitch", for best of breed and best of opposite sex. Each best of breed competes in its respective group, and the dog placed first in each of the six groups competes for the award "best in show", which is the final judging at any all-breed dog show.

Among the shows in the U.S. with entries of more than 2000 dogs are those of the Westminster Kennel Club in New York, the International Kennel Club of Chicago, the Kennel Club of Beverly Hills in Los Angeles, and the Kennel Club of Philadelphia in that city. The Crufts show, held in London, is the largest in England.

Obedience Trials. Obedience trials are competitions that test the ability of dogs to obey a series of verbal or nonverbal commands. Most obedience trials are held in conjunction with dog shows, which they resemble closely in respect to organization and scoring. At obedience trials dogs compete in four progressively difficult test-classes: companion dog, companion dog excellent, utility dog, and utility dog tracker.

Six basic obedience skills are tested at companion dog trials. These skills include heeling on the leash, heeling free, the stand for examination, the recall, the long sit, and the long down. In heeling exercises, the dog paces along beside its handler, keeping its right shoulder even with the handler's left knee. To stand for examination the dog must remain perfectly still on command and allow a judge to examine him closely. To execute the recall the handler orders his dog to sit, withdraws to a distance of 20 ft., and commands the animal to come to him. Finally, the long sit and long down exercises require a dog to sit or lie still for varying periods in the absence of its handler.

The three higher obedience-test trials, known popularly as C.D.X., U.D., and U.D.T., require mastery of more difficult skills. Among these are, variously, retrieving, tracking of scents, jumping over hurdles, and response to hand signals. A dog attaining a prescribed high score in authorized obedience competition receives points toward a title in his competition category.

Field Trials. Field trials are competitions designed to simulate closely the conditions of actual hunting. There are many different types and classes of field trials, of which the most popular are those held for hounds, bird dogs, and retrievers. According to their age and experience, the dogs usually compete in puppy, derby, or all-age classes. Championship points are awarded to those reaching the winner level in open all-age trials conducted or licensed by a recognized parent organization.

Hound trials comprise field tests for beagles, dachshunds, and bassets. Each of the three breeds competes separately under slightly different rules. In hound trials the dogs must run down and corner hares or cottontail rabbits. The hounds are released usually in teams of two, known as braces, and are followed closely by judges mounted on horses. Skills on which scoring is based at hound trials include keenness of scent, willingness to push through punishing thickets or undergrowth, and perseverance and accuracy in the pursuit of game.

Bird-dog trials test the entrants' ability to scent and seek out for the hunter game birds such as the pheasant, partridge, grouse, and quail. Typical bird-dog breeds include the Brittany spaniel, the English, Irish, and Gordon setters, the Weimaraner, and the various breeds of pointer. In competition, as in actual hunting, bird dogs range back and forth in the field until they scent a game bird. The dogs then track the bird to its hiding place in a thicket or other undergrowth and aim, or point, their bodies directly at their prey, standing stock still until the bird is flushed out of its hiding place and is fired at by the hunter. Bird dogs accumulating ten points in trials held under American Kennel Club auspices become field-trial champions.

Retriever trials test the ability of trained hunting dogs to find fallen birds and to fetch them from both land and water locations. This function is known as retrieving. Depending on the type of trial, the dog may or may not be allowed to observe the bird's fall. When the fall is "blind", his handler directs him to the bird's general location by means of various signals. In either case, once in the general area the dog depends on scent to find the bird.

Breeds eligible for retriever trials include Irish water spaniels and Labrador, Golden, and Chesapeake Bay retrievers. One or more of these breeds may compete in the same trials. The prize classes, or stakes, at retriever trials are based on the age and experience of competing dogs. To qualify as champions, retriever-trial competitors must amass a total of ten points under conditions prescribed by the American Kennel Club.

DOG STAR. See CANIS MAJOR; SIRIUS.

DOGWOOD, common name for plants of the genus *Cornus* of the Dogwood family Cornaceae. About twenty-five species of dogwood grow in Europe, Asia, and North America. They are nearly all showy shrubs or small trees. A few species, such as *C. canadensis,* are herbs; some, such as *C. nuttalli,* which grows in the Pacific Northwest, are trees that may grow to a height of 75 ft. or more. The native American flowering dogwood, *C. florida,* is rarely more than 30 ft. tall. In the early spring its "blossoms" are a familiar sight in the Atlantic States. These consist of dense heads of small, inconspicuous greenish flowers, each head surrounded by four prominent, white or pink, blunt-ended bracts. In the fall the leaves turn red, and the tree bears scarlet fruits.

Cornus amomum, the silky dogwood, is a purple-branched shrub found from Massachusetts to Tennessee. It has yellowish inflorescences and blue fruits. The red osier dogwood, *C. stolonifera,* which spreads by means of underground stems, grows from Newfoundland to Virginia. It has dark red branches and white or blue fruits. The panicled dogwood, *C. racemosa,* found from Maine to Georgia, has gray branches and red stems. It produces attractive white inflorescences in early summer and bears white fruits in the fall. The round-leaved dogwood, *C. rugosa,* which is found from Québec to Virginia, has purple branches and bears creamy-white inflorescences. The red or blood-twig dogwood, *C. sanguinea,* is the common European species. It has dark red branches and its leaves turn deep red in the fall. The cornel or cornelian cherry, *C. mas,* is a large European shrub which bears red, edible fruits in late summer. The Tatarian dogwood, *C. alba,* of western Asia, grows to a height of 10 ft. It has blood-red branches, creamy-white inflorescences, and white or bluish fruits.

Oil extracted from the fruit of the blood-twig dogwood is used in France for making soap. The hard, white, fine-grained wood of *C. nuttalli* is used for inlaying and turning.

DOHA, town, port, and capital of the sheikhdom of Qatar, on the eastern coast of the Qatar Peninsula, on Doha Harbor of the Persian Gulf, about 425 miles N.W. of Muscat and 300 miles N.E.

of Riyadh, Saudi Arabia. Doha, linked by road with the oil field at Dukhan, has become a commercial center for the area because of interior and offshore oil developments. It exports fish and tomatoes. The pearl industry, formerly important, has been almost abandoned. The city was ruled by Bahrein until 1872 and by Turkey until 1916. Doha, also spelled Dawhah, Dauha, and Dohah, was formerly called Bida. Pop. (1971 est.) 95,000.

DOHNÁNYI, Ernö (1877–1960), Hungarian composer, pianist, and conductor, born in Pressburg (now Bratislava, Czechoslovakia). From 1885 to 1894 he was a pupil in piano and harmony of Carl Forstner, in Pressburg; later he studied at the Royal Academy of Music, Budapest, and with the British-born German pianist and composer Eugen D'Albert (1864–1932). As a pianist, Dohnányi toured the Continent, Great Britain, and the United States from 1897 to 1908. He was director of the Budapest Conservatory and conductor of the Budapest Philharmonic Orchestra. In 1926 he conducted a number of concerts in New York City. In 1931 he became general director of the Hungarian National Radio. After 1948 Dohnányi lived in the U.S. and taught at Florida State University. Among his compositions are orchestral works, including two symphonies, three piano concertos, and two violin concertos; the opera *The Tower of Voivod* (1922); the comic operas *Tante Simona* (1912) and *The Tenor* (1929); Concertina for Harp and Orchestra (1952); chamber music; music for piano; and songs.

DOISY, Edward Adelbert (1893–), American biochemist, born in Hume, Ill., and educated at the University of Illinois and Harvard University. From 1923 to 1965 he was professor of biochemistry at the Saint Louis University School of Medicine, and in 1924 he became director of the department of biochemistry at Saint Mary's Hospital in St. Louis. He is best known for his research with female sex hormones, blood buffers, antibiotics, and vitamin K. With the Danish biochemist Henrik Dam (q.v.), he received the Nobel Prize in medicine and physiology in 1943 for his discovery of the chemical nature of vitamin K (*see* VITAMIN). He is a coauthor of *Sex and Internal Secretions* (1939) with the American anatomists Edgar Allen (1892-1943) and C(harles) H(askell) Danforth (1883-1969).

DOLDRUMS, region of calms, light variable winds, and thunderstorms, girdling the oceans near the equator and varying in position and extent according to the season. The doldrums lie between the belt of northeasterly trade winds of the Northern Hemisphere and the southeasterly trade winds of the Southern Hemisphere. Air heated at the surface of the earth rises in the doldrum region and flows northeastward and southeastward, at heights from a few thousand feet to 4 mi. to form the "antitrade winds" of the upper air. The doldrums and the horse latitudes (*see* WIND) are sometimes known as the calm latitudes.

DOLE, Sanford Ballard (1844–1926), American statesman and lawyer, born in Honolulu, Hawaii, and educated at Oahu College, Hawaii, and Williams College. He was a member of the Hawaiian legislature from 1884 to 1887, and was active in securing the Constitution of 1887 and the overthrow of Liliuokalani, Queen of the Hawaiian Islands (1838–1917), in 1893. In 1894 he was elected first and only president of the Republic of Hawaii, a position he held until 1900. In 1898 Dole went to Washington, D.C., to use his influence in favor of annexation of Hawaii by the United States. When Hawaii was established as a territory of the U.S. in 1900, President William McKinley appointed Dole its first territorial governor. From 1903 until his retirement in 1915 he was U.S. district court judge in Hawaii.

DOLL, in the modern sense, a child's plaything that resembles a human being, usually of reduced size in three dimensions.

Ancient Dolls. History records the existence of dolls before 3000 B.C. An Egyptian tomb bearing the remains of a child buried in that year also contained a painted doll, carved of wood. Although meant to serve as religious objects, ancient dolls often became the cherished possessions of children. Most ancient dolls were homemade of common clay, rags, wood, or bone; better examples were fashioned of ivory or wax, or of terra-cotta (a baked reddish-brown clay). Then, as now, the objective of dollmakers was to achieve realism. Indeed, some dolls made as early as 600 B.C. had movable limbs and removable garments.

Until the late Middle Ages dolls were intended primarily for religious usage. The religious use of dolls or doll-like figures persists in a few modern observances. The processions featuring representations of patron saints such as Saint Anthony of Padua or Our Lady of Guadalupe are Christian traditional uses. Ceremonies involving the Kachina dolls of the Hopi represent another form of ancient practice.

European Dolls. The first dolls known to have been commercially produced as children's playthings were made in Germany during the 14th century in factories at Nuremberg, Augsburg, Sonneberg, and Judenburg (now in Austria). Production methods were crude, but their "lady" doll products, costumed to represent German women of that period, were impressive. Papier-mâché (a molding material composed of paper and glue) was used in addition to traditional wood, clay, rags, and wax. Manufacturers in other European countries soon began producing dolls dressed in fashions common to their own respective localities. In the 15th century doll factories were established in England, France, Holland, and Italy. By the early 17th century, merchants were showing their ornately dressed "lady" dolls at trade fairs in Venice and Florence, and European competition was keen. In the 1600's basic qualities were improved. Manufacturers began fashioning doll heads out of glazed stoneware; later they used tragacanth (a gum derived from an Asian plant) and alabaster (a soft gypsum that resembles marble). In 1636 a doll with glass eyes that moved was offered in Holland, and in 1675 another firm's dolls wore wigs of human hair.

Early in the 18th century it was discovered that soft leather could be treated to feel like human skin and used to cover dolls' torsos and limbs. Although virtually all dolls had been designed as adults up to 1710, one manufacturer then introduced a wax "baby" doll with movable eyes and a crying voice. In 1737 walking dolls were made in Paris. Dolls had begun to look, feel, and move more like humans, but the popularity of high-fashion "lady" dolls remained paramount. Such dolls were often used to illustrate style trends and were sent from one country to another to show the latest fashions.

The 19th Century. Nineteenth-century progress was extraordinary. One of the major developments before 1850 was the introduction of ball joints, which gave dolls more natural limb flexibility. New materials included gutta-percha (a rubberlike Malayan gum), glazed porcelain, unglazed parian (a soft-bodied china), India rubber, and bisque. Imperfections were covered over with gesso (a mixture of plaster of Paris and glue) before the dolls were painted. Events in the second half of the 19th century altered the course of the industry. In 1851 American-patented vulcanized rubber dolls were introduced by the Goodyear Rubber Co. In 1860 the first "baby" doll that could sit upright was shown in Europe. Manufacturers introduced metal heads in 1861 and celluloid in 1862. In the meantime, they experimented with "composition" (mixtures of varied pastes with other undisclosed ingredients), which could be molded into smooth, practically unbreakable heads and limbs. In 1865 the first American doll-manufacturing enterprise (other than rubber) was founded by E. I. Horsman, and at least ten similar operations were functioning in the United States by 1900. These firms imported French or German bisque and composition heads and limbs for assembly with their own, domestically produced bodies. When the century ended, the overwhelming preference had changed from "lady" dolls to "baby" dolls of either bisque or composition. Dolls then looked but did not quite feel like humans; their movable heads and limbs simulated but did not quite duplicate the movements of humans.

Modern Dolls. In 1905 American manufacturers featured rag dolls with mask faces and in 1906 dolls of pressed felt with celluloid faces. The year 1909 brought European baby dolls with bent legs, as well as the "Billiken", the first American "character dolls" (fashioned after famous personalities and characters). The "Campbell Kids" were introduced in 1911 and Rose O'Neill's charming "Kewpie" in 1913. Johnny Gruelle, a cartoonist, originated "Raggedy Ann" in 1915. World War I curtailed European doll production in 1914, and American doll companies were handicapped. Previous attempts to produce bisque in the U.S. had been unsuccessful, and American composition was only fair. The challenge was met, however, and by 1917 the quality of American bisque was quite good. Americans also created the hot-pressed method for producing composition in 1916, and their composition doll heads were superior to all others. At the end of World War I it was clear that the U.S. had become a leading contender in doll manufacture. Early postwar concepts were marked in 1922 by the "Perfect" life-sized three-day-old infant doll and by the scientifically proportioned "ByLo Baby" from Germany. Multiheaded dolls were featured in 1923, and the first fully jointed dolls ("Hebe-Shebe") were offered in 1925. Noteworthy innovations between 1925 and World War II included sleeping eyes with lashes, dimpled cheeks, open mouths with tiny teeth, fingers with nails, and most importantly, drink-and-wet dolls of latex rubber. After World War II, vinyl plastics provided dollmakers with the kind of basic material they had long been seeking. Late 20th-century dolls of vinyl appear and feel as if alive, and many are equipped with various action features that enable them to behave as if alive. Some of today's dolls have "hearts" that beat and facial expressions that change. Hair can be repeatedly washed, dried, combed, curled, and set because each strand is firmly embedded in the scalp. Certain dolls can cry wet tears, suck their thumbs, bathe, drink and wet, laugh, blow

Dolls from different ages. A doll of the 18th century (left); a French doll of the 19th century (center), with a wax head and arms, kid body, blond wig, and blue inset eyes; Raggedy Ann (right), an American character doll (about 1910), shown with one of the books that made her famous.   Museum of the City of New York

bubbles, flirt, hug, lie down, sleep, sit up, stand, crawl, walk, talk, sing, dance, and write. For teenage boy and girl dolls, large varieties of wardrobe changes and accessories can be procured. The winsome "Sasha" dolls, designed by the Swiss dollmaker Sasha Morgenthaler, have skin tones approximating those of several different ethnic groups and include boy as well as girl dolls.   M.Fr.

DOLLAR, in currency, name of various coins formerly or currently in use in certain parts of Europe, Asia, and the Western Hemisphere, and specifically the standard value, or unit of account, in the monetary systems of Canada and the United States. The word "dollar" is derived from *daler,* Low German form of the German *thaler.* The latter word is an abbreviation of *Joachimsthaler,* the name of a large silver coin bearing an effigy of Saint Joachim, which was struck for the first time about 1518, following the discovery of a rich silver mine in Joachimstal ("Joachim's dale"), Bohemia.

Joachimsthaler were widely used in what is

now Germany and were subsequently called dollars by English-speaking people. Later, Spanish coins, equal in value to eight reales and bearing a representation of the Pillars of Hercules, the rocks flanking the entrance of the Strait of Gibraltar, were called pieces of eight, pillar dollars, and Spanish dollars; a large, milled-edged silver coin, minted in Spain and widely used in the Spanish and English colonies of the New World, was called *peso duro* in Spanish and hard dollar in English. From this usage probably arose the practice of identifying the coins of a number of Latin-American countries, such as the peso of Mexico, as dollars. An Austrian silver coin bearing a likeness of Maria Theresa (q.v.), Archduchess of Austria, and issued since 1780, with the original date, for use in trade in the Middle East and East Africa, is known as the Maria Theresa dollar or Levant dollar. In the latter part of the 19th century the British government began minting silver coins for use in the crown colonies of Hong Kong and the (Malay) Straits Settlements; these coins were called

Hong Kong dollars or British dollars, and Straits dollars, respectively. The Chinese yuan, issued by the central government of China in 1914 and for some years thereafter, is also frequently called a dollar. In the mid-1970's dollars of varying par values were current in various nations, including Australia, Bahamas, Canada, Ethiopia, Guyana, Liberia, Malaysia, New Zealand, Singapore, Trinidad and Tobago, and the West Indies Associated States.

Canada adopted the decimal system of coinage in 1867; dollars, cents, and mills were defined as the denominations of Canadian currency, and a dollar of 2.58 grains of gold was established as the standard of value of its monetary system.

United States Dollar. The Continental Congress, in 1786, after it had adopted the decimal system of coinage, fixed the legal value of the dollar then circulating in the States at 375.64 grains of pure silver. The first dollars minted in the U.S. were issued by the Federal government in Philadelphia in 1794, following passage of the Coinage Act of April 2, 1792. That enactment provided for two standards of value: a silver dollar "of the value of a Spanish milled dollar the same as is now current", containing 371.25 grains of pure silver; and a gold dollar, containing 24.75 grains of pure gold. The ratio between these two standards, called the coinage ratio, was expressed as 15:1. In 1834, Congress increased the coinage ratio to 16.002:1 by decreasing the gold content of the gold dollar. In 1837, Congress increased the metallic content of the gold dollar and decreased the content of the silver dollar, making the coinage ratio about 15.98:1. The gold dollar itself, a very small coin, was minted only from 1849 to 1889; most U.S. gold coins were in denominations of $2.50, $5, $10 (eagles), and $20.

In revising the coinage law in 1873, Congress authorized the minting of dollars of 420 grains of silver, 900 fine; these coins, issued for use in trade with the Far East and known as trade dollars, were last minted in 1885. In the revision of 1873, Congress omitted authorization for the continued minting of the silver dollars provided for in the legislation of 1837. Thereafter, no silver dollars of this type were issued until 1878, when passage of the Bland-Allison Act provided for resumption of their coinage. A Congressional enactment in 1900 established the gold dollar as the monetary standard of value in the U.S., thereby fixing the legal value of legal-tender paper money in terms of the metallic gold dollar. Following passage of the Gold Reserve Act of 1934, the gold content of the dollar was reduced to 59.06 percent of its former content, all gold coins and paper-money gold certificates except those in the hands of coin dealers and private collectors were called in by the Federal government and exchanged for other forms of the national currency of equal face value, and the coining of gold pieces was officially discontinued; see DEVALUATION. At that time, about 311,000,000 dollars in gold pieces were in circulation in the U.S. Silver dollars continued in circulation until 1965, when they almost disappeared because the value of their silver content exceeded their face value. The U.S. dollar was officially devalued from 0.888671 gram of fine gold to 0.81513 gram of fine gold in 1972 and to 0.736662 gram in 1973. Beginning in 1975, U.S. citizens were allowed to own, buy, and sell gold as a commodity, but gold coins could not circulate as money.

See BIMETALLISM; FOREIGN EXCHANGE; GOLD STANDARD; MINT; MONEY; NUMISMATICS.

DOLLFUSS, Engelbert (1892–1934), Austrian statesman, born in Texing, Lower Austria. He was educated at the universities of Vienna and Berlin, receiving a degree in political economy from the latter institution. During the 1920's, as secretary of the Peasant Federation of Lower Austria and director of the Lower Austrian chamber of agriculture, he became a leading member of the Christian Socialist Party. In 1930 he became president of the Federal Railways, and the following year, minister of agriculture and forestry. In 1932 he was appointed chancellor of Austria. To resist National Socialist (Nazi) efforts to undermine the independence of Austria and forcibly incorporate it into Germany, Dollfuss made an alliance with the Heimwehr (Home Guard), a private fascist army led by Prince Ernst Rüdiger von Starhamberg (1899–1956) and supported with arms and money by the Italian dictator Benito Mussolini (q.v.). In March, 1933, shortly after the dictator Adolf Hitler (q.v.) came to power in Germany, President Wilhelm Miklas (1872–1956) of Austria invested Dollfuss with extraordinary powers. Dollfuss immediately dissolved the parliament, abolished freedom of speech, the press, and assembly, and dissolved the Communist Party and the Schutzbund (the armed defense body of the Social Democratic Party). In June he outlawed the National Socialist Party. In February of the following year, in protest against Heimwehr raids on their centers and press, the workers of Vienna, led by the Social Democrats, declared a general strike. Civil war broke out. Dollfuss, using the Heimwehr, crushed the strike after several days of fighting that resulted in more than 1000 casualties. He then dissolved the Social Democratic Party and called a rump parliament which voted a new constitution establishing a "Christian German Federal State on a corporative basis". During the unsuccessful National Socialist putsch of July 25, 1934, Dollfuss was assassinated.

See AUSTRIA: *History: Anschluss.*

DÖLLINGER, Johann Joseph Ignaz von (1799–1890), German Roman Catholic theologian and historian, born in Bamberg, Bavaria, and educated at the lyceum for philosophy and Roman Catholic theology in that city. He was ordained a priest in 1822 and four years later became professor of theology at the University of Munich. In 1844, he represented his university in the second chamber of the Bavarian legislature. In *Die Reformation* (1848) and *Luther* (1850; Eng. trans., 1853) he vehemently attacked the Reformers and their work. Döllinger delivered two addresses in Munich in 1861 that were regarded as hostile to the temporal sovereignty of the pope; he attempted to justify his position in *Kirche und Kirchen, Papstthum und Kirchenstaat: Historischpolitische Betrachtungen* (1861; *The Church and the Churches, or, The Papacy and the Temporal Power*, 1862).

When Vatican Council I (see VATICAN COUNCILS) issued a decree affirming the doctrine of papal infallibility (see INFALLIBILITY) in 1870, Döllinger refused to accede to the doctrine. In the following year he organized a meeting of theologians in Nuremberg that publicly repudiated the doctrine, and he later was a principal organizer of the Old Catholic Movement; see OLD CATHOLICS. In 1871, Döllinger was excommunicated by the archbishop of Munich. In 1874 and 1875 in Bonn, he presided over joint conferences of theologians of the Old Catholic, Orthodox, and Anglican churches that were convened to formulate plans for church unity. Among his other writings is *Die Universtäten sonst und jetzt* (1867; Eng. trans., *Universities Past and Present*, 1867).

DOLLY VARDEN TROUT, common name of the *Salvelinus malma,* a char (q.v.) of the Salmonidae family, named for the Dolly Varden, a gaily printed muslin dress popular from 1865 to 1870. These trout are olive green with orange or red spots; they are 2 to 3 ft. long and weigh from 5 to 12 lb. They are native to the streams of the Pacific northwest of the United States, Canada, and Alaska. See also TROUT.

DOLMEN, type of prehistoric chamber consisting of two or more huge unhewn stone slabs, or megaliths, set edgewide in the earth and supporting a flat capstone that serves as a roof. Dolmens were sometimes covered with immense artificial hillocks or tumuli, but at times the covering of earth reached only the capstone. Many dolmens are surrounded by a circle of megaliths collectively called a cromlech. Archeologists believe that dolmens were burial chambers. They are known to have served as altars, as on the island of Guernsey (q.v.), where they were used by the Druids (see DRUIDISM) in their religious rites. Dolmens are particularly numerous in Ireland and Wales and in the English counties of Devon and Cornwall; and in N.W. France, especially in Brittany, and in Spain. They are also

The Lanyon dolmen, the remains of a Stone Age burial chamber in Cornwall, England. British Information Services

Dolphins and porpoises are playful and friendly. Easily trained, a dolphin here catches a ball in the Seaquarium in Miami. UPI

found in N. Africa, in Syria, and in other countries ranging as far east as Japan. Sometimes the mound enclosing the dolmen was of great size, like that of Sidbury Hill, Wiltshire, which was 170 ft. high and 316 ft. along the slope.

See also MEGALITHIC MONUMENTS.

DOLOMITE, common mineral with the formula $CaMg(CO_3)_2$, found chiefly in rock masses as dolomitic limestone, but occurring sometimes in veins. It has a hardness of 3½ to 4, and sp.gr. 2.85. It is usually colorless, white, pink, or flesh-colored but may be brown, black, or green, depending on the impurities present. In the United States it is found at many localities in Vermont, Rhode Island, New York, and New Jersey. Good crystals of dolomite have been obtained from deposits at Joplin, Mo. When treated with sulfuric acid, dolomite yields calcium sulfate (gypsum) and magnesium sulfate (Epsom salts). Calcined dolomite is extensively employed as a lining for Bessemer converters in the production of steel from pig iron.

Some varieties of dolomite are called bitter spar or pearlspar. The name dolomite is sometimes given to any rock composed chiefly of massive dolomite, or of any combination of magnesium and calcium carbonates. Compare CALCITE; LIMESTONE; MAGNESITE.

DOLOMITE ALPS *or* **DOLOMITES,** subdivision of the Eastern Alps mountains and part of the South Tirolese Alps, located in N. Italy, E. of the Adige R. Some peaks in the group are formed of dolomite (q.v.), and are marked with unusual colors. The Dolomites reach their greatest height in Mt. Marmolada, 10,964 ft. above sea level. Many of the sharp peaks of the range were first ascended in the latter part of the 19th century by British mountain climbers.

DOLPHIN, common name for aquatic mammals belonging to the family Delphinidae in the order Cetacea (q.v.), which includes the whales. Dolphins are similar to the porpoise (q.v.), but are distinguished by their beaklike snouts. Found in all seas and some large rivers, they travel in schools and are graceful swimmers and divers. Dolphins feed on small fish and have many small, sharp teeth. The snout of the dolphin is a distinct flattened beak about 6 in. long to which the skull drops sharply. The top of the head has a single, crescent-shaped blowhole. Most species have a conspicuous triangular back fin. Most dolphins are less than 10 ft. long.

The common dolphin, *Delphinus delphis,* sometimes called porpoise, is found in the Mediterranean Sea and in the North Atlantic Ocean. It is about 7 ft. long, black on top and white underneath. This dolphin has about 200 sharp teeth, and its dorsal fin is about 9 in. high. A pure white dolphin, *D. sinensis,* occurs in the China Sea, and an allied species, *D. seronii,* is native to the South Seas. In the waters off the eastern coast of North America, the bottlenose, or bottle-nosed dolphin, *Tursiops truncatus,* is often seen. Among other dolphins are the bouto, an inhabitant of South American coastal waters; the tucuxi, which is found in the rivers of the Amazon valley; and the beluga (q.v.).

The name "dolphin" is applied also to food fishes of the genus *Coryphaena*.

See also ANIMAL COMMUNICATION.

DOLTON, village of Illinois, in Cook Co., about 12 miles s. of Chicago. Dolton is in a truck-farming area and its industries include glass and metal products. Settled in 1832, Dolton was incorporated in 1892. Pop. (1960) 18,746; (1970) 25,937.

DOMAGK, Gerhard (1895–1964), German chemist, born in Lagow and educated at the University of Kiel. He was a professor of chemistry at the University of Münster, and in 1925 he became a member of its Pathological Institute. In 1927 he was made director of the research institute of the I.G. Farbenindustrie in Wuppertal. Domagk discovered the drug prontosil, the forerunner of sulfanilamide, the "wonder drug" used in combating infectious diseases; *see* SULFA DRUGS. For this discovery he was awarded the Nobel Prize in medicine and physiology in 1939. The government of the German dictator Adolf Hitler (q.v.) angered in 1935 by the award of the Nobel Peace Prize to the imprisoned German journalist and pacifist Carl von Ossietzky (1889–1938), forbade Domagk to accept the award. In 1947 Domagk received his Nobel gold medal, in a belated tribute.

DOME, in architecture, roof usually with a spherical surface, like that formed by slicing off a section of a hollow sphere; *see* ARCHITECTURE. The term "dome" is also applied to structures having other doubly curved surfaces with rotational symmetry, such as ellipsoidal or paraboloidal surfaces; *see* ELLIPSE; PARABOLA. Domes today are constructed in a variety of materials, including steel, aluminum, reinforced concrete (poured in place over formwork or precast in segments), glued laminated wood, or plastics. These materials, however, have only become available since the end of the 19th century, and prior to that time, most domes were constructed of masonry, wood, or masonry reinforced with steel chains or wooden ties. *See* ALUMINUM; BUILDING CONSTRUCTION; CONCRETE; IRON AND STEEL MANUFACTURE; PLASTICS; WOOD: *Plywood.*

The structural efficiency of the dome is illustrated by various notable large-span dome roofs constructed in recent years. In Houston, Texas, approximately 9 acres of playing field used for

The Astrodome, Houston, Texas, a sports stadium built in large prefabricated-steel sections with translucent plastic roof panels, has the largest circular dome in the world.

baseball and other sporting events is enclosed by the Astrodome, the largest circular-dome roof in the world. The huge steel structure, arranged as a gridwork of curved trusses in a radically symmetric so-called lamella pattern of pipe-shaped segments, spans 642 ft. across its base diameter and rises to a height of 202 ft. above the center of the field. Prefabrication of the dome in large sections permitted safe and economical erection with a minimum of false work, or temporary supporting framework. The United States Pavilion at Expo 67, in Montréal, Canada, which was a three-quarter sphere rising 200 ft. above its lowest base and spanning 250 ft. at its widest point, enclosed a vast open space utilized for hanging space vehicles and other exhibits. Designed by the American engineer R(ichard) Buckminster Fuller (q.v.), the pavilion utilized a new system for construction of large steel domes; it was assembled from about 24,000 sections of steel pipe and 6000 cast-steel hubs connecting the pipe, arranged in a repeating geodesic pattern. Structural economy was derived by the geodesic geometry of the framework, which provided members of similar length and design and facilitated erection in circumferential rings without any falsework. A unique feature of this large dome, which is still standing on its original site, is its transparent acrylic plastic skin that is made up of molded sub-domes supported on the hexagonal inner framework of the primary structural frame. The auditorium of the Hawaiian Village Hotel in Honolulu, Hawaii, is covered by another type of geodesic dome in which the enclosure skin and the structural frame are combined by utilizing folded aluminum sheets that are arranged to obtain a triangular pattern of fold lines. The resulting structure, spanning 145 ft., is made up of repeating patterns of a few identical folded-sheet units with a shimmering-faceted exterior surface. The 415-ft. diameter dome over the Civic Auditorium in Pittsburgh, Pa., may be opened by sliding pie-shaped steel-framed panels over each other on motorized tracks. In the fully open position, all roof panels stack in a single location with their apexes supported by a large exterior steel-trussed arm extending from one side of the building. The 192-ft. diameter Palazzetto dello Sport and the much larger Palazzo dello Sport in Rome, Italy, designed by the Italian architect-engineer Pier Luigi Nervi (q.v.) for the 1960 Olympic Games, express the flow of dome stresses in uniquely beautiful interior patterns formed by units of precast reinforced concrete. In structures such as these the precast units are tied together by poured-in-place concrete ribs. The oblique pressures at the edge of the dome shells are transferred to the foundations by splayed buttresses that complement the graceful interior pattern of the ribbed domes. The field house at the University of Montana with a base diameter of 300 ft. and a rise of 50 ft. is the largest wooden dome in the world. Glued laminated-wood members, fabricated in a factory by gluing together thin wood planks, and connected to each other by bolted-steel fittings, are utilized for curved meridional ribs and for straight beams arranged in circumferential rings.

Lightweight domes have been constructed with sandwich panels made with fiber glass-reinforced plastic facings bonded to phenolic-impregnated paper honeycomb or foam-plastic cores. The largest such domes are the 140-ft. diameter three-quarter spheres that enclose the large radar antennas of the Ballistic Missile Early Warning System (BMEWS) in the Arctic regions of North America (see COAST DEFENSE). Other plastic domes have been used for exhibition structures and to provide the basic structures for vacation homes. Lightweight domes are also made with flexible vinyl-coated nylon fabrics inflated to a rigid state by internal air pressure. These structures are used to enclose radar antennas, exhibitions, and warehouses, and have been constructed up to a maximum diameter of about 120 ft.

In structural engineering today, the dome is widely used as a cover for utilitarian structures such as water and oil storage tanks, sewage digestion tanks, grain silos, and other circular structures; see SEWAGE DISPOSAL. Steel-plate shells with meridional and circumferential stiffening ribs, or reinforced-concrete shells 3 to 4 in. thick and poured in place over formwork, are the most common type of domes for sizes up to about 200 ft. in diameter. Newer systems utilizing tubular or folded sheet-metal members arranged in geodesic patterns, precast concrete elements, or laminated wood members sometimes offer lighter, more beautiful and economical structures. Such domes find widespread application for roofs of school auditoriums, exhibition and convention halls, swimming pools, restaurants, libraries, factories, warehouses, and fluid-storage tanks.

Early Domes. The dome was first developed as roofing for circular huts in ancient Mesopotamia. Representations of such dwellings and domes are also found in Assyrian bas-reliefs dating from the 8th and 7th centuries B.C. The domes of the Assyrians and Persians, on palaces as well as on ordinary dwellings, were sometimes of low hemispherical and sometimes of

Above: The Renaissance drum-and-lantern dome of Saint Peter's Basilica, designed by Michelangelo, was finished after his death in 1564. Below: The Dome of the Rock, in Jerusalem, is in the Islamic style of architecture.   **UPI**

high ovoidal form; they were usually constructed of brick and were supported by solid walls. The shape of the dome was characteristic of Mycenaean beehive tombs, the domical shape being supported by corbel construction, the corbel being a member that projects upward from a vertical surface and supports a weight. The Romans learned the construction of the dome from the Etruscans, and developed it into a form that exerted great influence on the architecture of succeeding periods. The most noteworthy of the Roman domes is that of the Pantheon (q.v.), built between 110 and 125 A.D. by order of Hadrian (q.v.), Emperor of Rome. The largest masonry dome in the world, the Pantheon is hemispherical in shape, measures 144 ft. in diameter, and rests upon a continuous wall; light is admitted by means of a great circular opening in the top of the dome, the *oculus* or "eye". The Roman hemispherical dome was used in early Christian times for roofing mausoleums and baptisteries. The dome (built about 325 A.D.) of the mausoleum of the Church of Santa Constanza, Rome, is notable because it was the first dome not supported by a continuous wall, but by a series of twelve arches borne on a double circle of columns; see ARCH; COLUMN. The dome of the church of Saint Sophia (q.v.) or Hagia Sophia (built 532–538 A.D.) in Constantinople, now İstanbul, is supported, not by a circular wall as is the dome of the Pantheon, but by four piers, one in each corner of the square area covered by the dome. From the upper part of each pier extends a triangular segment of masonry called a pendentive; the pendentives join and form four round arches which span the sides of the square. The dome is supported on the arches, its weight being transferred to the piers through the pendentives. By the use of pendentives, domes could be constructed, not only over square areas, but over areas of any shape; one additional advantage with the Church of St. Sophia was that the floor space beneath the dome was unenclosed. The dome of St. Sophia was imitated in Italy, France, and in the lands conquered by the Muslims, including India, Persia, Turkey, Egypt, North Africa, Sicily, and Spain. Notable examples of the Byzantine type of dome are the dome of Saint Mark (1063), Venice, and that of Saint Front (1120), Périgueux, France.

Islamic Domes. Muslim builders did not use the circular form of dome but developed the pointed dome, the ovoid dome, and (in Persia, about the 15th century) the swelling or bulbous dome; see ISLAMIC ART AND ARCHITECTURE. The Muslim domes of India are particularly notable,

and include those of structures in Delhi and Bijapur, dating from the 16th and 17th centuries, and the famous alabaster dome of the mausoleum Taj Mahal (q.v.), at Agra.

Renaissance Domes. A major structural problem with large masonry domes is that they have great weight and inherently tend to have great radial lateral thrust at their base due to the circumferential tension in this area. During the Renaissance many large domes were built with their bases reinforced by wooden beams held together with a chain, and sometimes two separate shells were constructed with the smaller inner shell supporting a heavy lantern often placed at the apex. The dome designed by the Italian sculptor, painter, architect, and poet Michelangelo (q.v.) for Saint Peter's Basilica in Rome (completed in 1590), is 137 ft. in interior diameter and has two shells of brick, the inner supporting the lantern.

A departure both from the traditional Byzantine and the Western European dome styles is seen in the Russian bulbous cupolas, the so-called onion domes. Two good examples of this style, which is probably the result of the Oriental influence on native Russian architecture, are the Cathedral of the Annunciation (built 1482–90), and the church of Saint Basil the Blessed (1555–60), both in Moscow, U.S.S.R. The former building is built on a square plane and is covered with bulbous domes that have corbeled arches leading up to them.

Among the many notable masonry domes constructed in Western Europe during and after the Renaissance are Santa Maria della Salute, Venice (1631), with two shells, the inner an 80-ft. diameter masonry dome, the outer made of timber; Saint Paul's Cathedral, London (1675–1710), 102-ft. interior diameter; the Church of Les Invalides, Paris (1706), 92-ft. interior diameter, and the Panthéon, Paris (1764), 74-ft. interior diameter.

The dome has been widely used in the United States for State capitols, beginning with the construction (completed 1798) of the dome for the capitol of Massachusetts, designed by the American architect Charles Bulfinch (*see under* BULFINCH). The dome of the Capitol at Washington, D.C., 90 ft. in interior diameter, is made of cast iron and was designed and completed (1865) by the American architect Thomas Ustick Walter (q.v.). Large libraries are often built with domes. The dome of the Library of Columbia University, New York City, is 80 ft. in diameter, and that of the public library of Melbourne, Australia, is 124 ft. Domes of glass and steel are often used for the buildings of expositions and for large conservatories. The Hayden Planetarium, in New York City, has an outer dome 81 ft. in diameter and an inner dome 75 ft. in diameter. The outer dome holds the weight of the inner, upon the surface of which images of the celestial bodies are projected by stereoscope lanterns.

DOMENICHINO, IL (1581–1641), Italian painter, born Domenico Zampieri in Bologna. He studied under the painter Agostino Carracci (*see under* CARRACCI) at the Accademia degli Incamminati in Bologna, and later with Agostino's brother Annibale in Rome. Il Domenichino is considered, after Guido Reni (q.v.), the most distinguished pupil of the Carracci and one of the best painters of the Eclectic or Bolognese School. Among his works are the paintings "Diana at the Chase" (1614–18, Borghese Gallery, Rome), and "Communion of St. Jerome" (1614, the Vatican); the fresco "Death of Adonis" (Loggia of the Giardino Farnese, Rome); and frescoes in the abbey of Grotta Ferrata (1609–10), Rome. The Louvre, in Paris, has a large number of his works.

DOME OF THE ROCK, first domical mosque. *See* JERUSALEM; TEMPLE.

DOMESDAY BOOK, or DOMESDAY, document embodying the results of a statistical survey of England carried out by order of William I (q.v.), King of England. The survey, made in 1086, was an attempt to register the landed wealth of the country in a systematic fashion, with a view to determining the revenues due to the king. The previous system of taxation was of ancient origin and had become obsolete. By listing all feudal estates, both lay and ecclesiastical, the Domesday Book enabled William to strengthen further his authority by exacting oaths of allegiance from all tenants on the land, as well as from the nobles and churchmen on whose land the tenants lived. The survey was executed by groups of officers called *legati,* who visited each county and conducted a public inquiry. The set of questions which these officers asked of the town and county representatives comprised the *Inquisitio Eliensis*; the answers to these questions supplied the information from which the Domesday Book was compiled. The term Domesday is a corruption of Doomsday (the day of the final judgment), and the work was so named because its judgments as to levies and assessments were final and irrevocable.

Of the two volumes in the original manuscript, the first and larger one, sometimes called the Great Domesday, included information on all of England with the exception of three eastern counties (Essex, Suffolk, and Norfolk), several northern counties, London, and some other towns. The surveys of the three eastern counties made up the second volume, which was known as the Little Domesday. These manuscripts were frequently used in the medieval law courts, and in their published form they are occasionally used today in cases involving questions of topography or genealogy. The two volumes were first published in 1783; an index was published in a separate volume in 1811; and an additional volume, containing the *Inquisitio Eliensis* with various surveys of the lands of Ely (q.v.) was published in 1816.

DOMESTIC ECONOMY. *See* HOME ECONOMICS.

DOMICILE, in United States law, legal residence of a person. Although generally understood as synonymous with home or place of abode, in the strict legal sense the term "domicile" denotes the place that the law will hold to be a man's residence. This may or may not coincide with the place where he usually or habitually resides. Modern law requires that every person have a definite location in some jurisdiction to which his legal rights and obligations may be referred and by which his legal status, public and private, is determined.

Three kinds of domicile are now generally recognized: domicile by birth, by choice, and by operation of the law. The first is determined by place of birth. The second is acquired by individual volition; it excludes mental incompetents because it requires intent to make the selected place one's domicile. An illustration of the third is the domicile of a wife, which is acquired at the time of marriage and is that of her husband for as long as she lives with him. A child has the domicile of his parents (or, if he is illegitimate, generally that of his mother) and is considered incapable of changing his domicile of his own accord. When the father of a family dies, the domicile of his children and widow continues to be that of the husband's last residence until a new residence is acquired. In relation to private rights and obligations, the general rule holds that the law of the place of domicile governs in contracts relating to personal property and in wills and bankruptcy (q.v.); in matters relating to real estate the law of the place of its situation (*lex rei situs*) prevails. *See* CITIZEN.

DOMINIC, Saint, original name DOMINGO DE GUZMÁN (1170–1221), Spanish theologian, born in Caleruega, Castile. According to legend, even in his childhood he revealed extreme asceticism and Christian devotion. At the age of seventeen he entered the University of Palencia, where he studied theology and philosophy. He was known for his acts of piety and renunciation, on one occasion offering to become a slave to the Moors in exchange for the liberation of a widow's only son. About 1196 he became canon of the cathedral of Osma, in Castile, and was soon actively engaged in local ecclesiastical reforms. He accompanied his superior, Didacus of Acebes, Bishop of Osma (d. 1207), on a religious mission to Rome in 1203; on his way back to Spain he was overwhelmed by the clerical abuses and the prevalence of the Albigensian heresy (see ALBIGENSES) that he observed in the Languedoc region of southern France. In Montpellier he encountered three papal legates (see PAPAL LEGATE) who had been sent out by Rome to suppress the heretics; at the sight of their pomp and sybaritism, he recommended setting an example of humility and self-denial as the most efficient means of defeating the Albigenses. Thereupon he and Didacus set out to preach against the heretics throughout the Languedoc, and in 1206 he founded at Prouille, near Toulouse, his first institution, an asylum for women converts from Albigensianism. Dominic continued his campaign against the heretics for ten years, but failed to suppress them; he is said to have brought about a number of miracles on his tours through the Languedoc. Pope Innocent III (see under INNOCENT) finally launched a crusade of extermination against the Albigenses under the leadership of Simon de Montfort (q.v.), who conducted the war with a ruthlessness equal to his military skill. Dominic's part in this war was limited to prayer for the success of Catholic arms and diligent work for the conversion of the people. In 1215 he founded in Toulouse the first house of the Dominican Order (see DOMINICANS), to which he thereafter devoted his life. He is credited with numerous miracles and was canonized by Pope Gregory IX (1147?–1241) in 1234. His feast day is Aug. 7.

DOMINICA, island of the West Indies, one of the Windward Islands, politically a member of the West Indies Associated States. The island is approximately midway between the French islands of Martinique and Guadeloupe. Dominica is about 29 mi. long and has a maximum width of 16 mi. The terrain is mountainous, with a number of elevations higher than 4000 ft. above sea level. Morne Diablotin (5314 ft.) is the highest peak. The island exhibits numerous volcanic phenomena, notably hot springs, and Boiling Lake, from which subterranean gases and fumes frequently arise. The vegetation is luxuriant and includes valuable stands of timber on the mountain slopes. The soil is fertile and well watered, yielding a wide variety of crops, including bananas, coconuts, citrus fruits, cocoa beans, and vanilla. The annual rainfall is more than 160 in. in some parts of the island, but the climate is generally healthful. Temperatures range between a maximum of 86° F. in the hot season from August to October, and a minimum of 72° F. in the cool season. The population consists mainly of Negroes, with a few people of French and English origin and a small group of Carib Indians. The capital and chief town is Roseau (pop. about 12,200). Chief manufactured products are rum, lime juice and oil, bay oil, and copra.

Dominica was discovered and named by the Genoese-born navigator Christopher Columbus (q.v.) on Nov. 3, 1493, during his second voyage to the New World. In 1632 it was colonized by the French, who were expelled by the British in 1756; a French patois is still the language of the countryside. Under British rule the island became a presidency of the Leeward Islands colony in 1833, was assigned to the Windward Islands group as a colony in 1940, and was a member of the Federation of the West Indies from 1958 to 1962. On March 1, 1967, Dominica became an internally self-governing state associated with Great Britain, which retained responsibility for the foreign affairs and defense of the island. Area, 304 sq.mi.; pop. (1970) 70,-300. See also WEST INDIES, THE.

DOMINICAN REPUBLIC, republic of the West Indies, comprising the E. portion (about two thirds) of the island of Hispaniola (q.v.). The country is bounded on the N. by the Atlantic Ocean; on the E. by the Mona Passage, which separates it from Puerto Rico; on the S. by the Caribbean Sea; and on the W. by Haiti. Situated between about lat. 17°36' N. and lat. 19°56' N. and long. 68°19' W. and long. 72°48' W., the Dominican Republic has an extreme length in an east-to-west direction of about 235 mi., and a maximum width, in the W., of about 165 mi. The frontier with Haiti is 193 mi. long. The area of the country is 19,129 sq.mi. A number of adjacent islands, notably Beata and Saona, are possessions of the Dominican Republic.

THE LAND

The Dominican Republic is a fertile, well-watered, mountainous country. About 80 percent of the country is covered with a series of massive mountain ranges, extending in a N.W. to S.E. direction. Pico Duarte, 10,417 ft., is the highest mountain in the country. Between the Cordillera Central and the Cordillera Septentrional, a

DOMINICAN REPUBLIC

parallel range to the N., is the Valley of Cibao, one of the most fertile and best-watered areas of the country. The coastal plain in the S.E. is another fertile region. Among the numerous streams of the Dominican Republic are the Yaque del Norte, Yasica, and Nagua rivers in the N., and the San Juan, Jalina, Ozama, and Yuna rivers in the S.

The principal lake is the saltwater Lake Enriquillo, about 27 mi. long and 8 mi. wide, situated approximately 30 mi. inland from the S.W. coast. The coastline of the Dominican Republic, about 1015 mi. in length, is irregular and indented by many bays forming natural harbors, notably Calderas Bay in the S.W. and the Bay of Samaná in the N.E.

Climate. The country has a semitropical climate, tempered by the prevailing easterly winds. Temperatures above 74° F. are registered in the lowlands throughout the year. During the summer months; temperatures range between 80° and 95° F. in these regions. The highlands are considerably cooler. Annual precipitation averages 120 in., and the heaviest rainfalls occur N. of the Cordillera Central. The wet season is from June to November. Tropical hurricanes occur occasionally.

Natural Resources. The main resources of the Dominican Republic are agricultural. The fertile soil in the valleys is conducive to farming, and many of the mountain slopes are covered with forests. The country also has some valuable mineral deposits.

Plants and Animals. The vegetation of the Dominican Republic, like that of the other islands of the West Indies, is extremely varied and luxuriant. Among the species of indigenous trees are mahogany, rosewood, satinwood, cypress, pine, oak, and cacao. Many species of useful plants and fruits are common, including rice, tobacco, cotton, sugarcane, yam, banana, pineapple, mango, fig, grape, and breadfruit.

The most noteworthy mammal among the indigenous animals is the agouti (q.v.). Wild dogs, hogs, and cattle are abundant, as are numerous reptiles, notably snakes, lizards, and caymans. Waterfowl and pigeons are the predominant birds.

THE PEOPLE

Most of the population is of mixed Spanish, African, and Indian origin. The society is primarily rural.

Population. The population of the Dominican Republic (census 1970) was 4,006,405. The overall population density is about 231 per sq.mi. (U.N. est. 1970). The population increases by approximately 33.8 per 1000 population annually, one of the highest rates among Latin-American countries.

Political Divisions and Principal Cities. The country is divided into twenty-six provinces, including the Distrito Nacional (National District), which encompasses Santo Domingo, the capi-

The Cathedral of Santa María la Menor in Santo Domingo, built between 1514 and 1540.
Dominican Republic Information Center

In the Cathedral of Santa María la Menor, remains thought to be those of Christopher Columbus are entombed behind the wrought-iron gate.
Dominican Republic Information Center

tal. The provinces are subdivided into seventy-six municipalities and about 1600 townships.

Santo Domingo, the capital, is the leading port and had a population of about 671,402 (1970 prelim.). Other important cities include the agricultural centers Santiago (pop. 155,151), in the N. part of the country, and San Cristóbal (pop. 25,829).

Language and Religion. Spanish is the official language. English is also spoken by many in the capital, and the French dialect, Creole, is heard along the Haitian frontier. The state religion is Roman Catholicism. The government guarantees freedom to all faiths.

Education. The Dominican Republic provides free, compulsory education to children between the ages of seven and fourteen. Only about 35 percent of the population is literate, however.

In the early 1970's approximately 727,500 pupils were attending primary schools. Students in secondary schools numbered about 105,000, including those attending vocational schools and institutions for teacher-training.

The University of Santo Domingo, founded in 1538, is the oldest in the Western Hemisphere. Some 18,000 students were attending institutions of higher learning in the early 1970's.

Culture. The first permanent New World colony of Europeans was established in the Domin-ican Republic, where Western traditions have thrived ever since. Some of the old colonial buildings are still standing; fine examples may be seen in Santo Domingo. Art, music, and literature are mainly developed on Western patterns. Almost equally strong is the African cultural strain. The great majority of the citizens are of mixed European and African descent. In the folk culture, especially the music, the African heritage is most noticeable. These two traditions blend in the popular national song and dance, the *merengue*.

THE ECONOMY

Agriculture accounts for 80 percent of all economic activity. The government provides a variety of incentives to break this dependency and to promote the development and diversification of industry. Revitalization of the sugar industry and plans to diversify agriculture also are under way. Efforts to establish investment programs have been only partially successful because of

The Dominican Republic is the natural habitat of the common flamingo, Phoenicopterus ruber, *which breed in Barahona Province.*
Arthur Ambler –
National Audubon Society

frequent political disorders. The country depends largely on thermal plants for electricity; about 1.63 billion kw hours are produced annually. In the mid-1970's the budget was balanced at about $610,000,000 per year.

Agriculture. About 3700 sq.mi. of the total arable land (9900 sq.mi.) are cultivated. Sugarcane is the main crop; the largest plantations are in the s.e. In the mid-1970's some 9,337,000 metric tons of sugar were produced annually. Other important crops were rice (218,600 metric tons), coffee (103,700 metric tons), cocoa (33,200 metric tons), and tobacco (16,800,000 metric tons). Cattle and hogs are raised primarily for local consumption.

Forest and Fishing Industries. About 18 percent of the land is forested. The government fosters conservation and has regulated the forest industry since the early 1960's. The main woods are mahogany, satinwood, pine, and cedar. About 2,470,000 cu.yd. of lumber are produced annually. The fishing industry is underdeveloped, mainly because of a lack of deep-sea fishing equipment and refrigeration facilities. The annual catch, which includes mackerel, tuna, bonito, and snapper, totaled about 8392 metric tons in the mid-1970's.

Mining. Production of bauxite in the mid-1970's was about 1,196,000 tons per year; in addition, some 40,000 metric tons of rock salt and 32,000 metric tons of nickel were produced. Deposits of gold, silver, platinum, and copper have been found.

Manufacturing. Sugar refining is the main industrial activity in the Dominican Republic; annual output of raw sugar in the mid-1970's was about 1,245,000 metric tons. Also produced were textiles, cement, cigars, and cigarettes.

Commerce and Trade. The unit of currency is the peso (1 peso equals U.S.$1; 1977). The republic has several commercial banks; one, the Banco de Reservas, is government-controlled. The Central Bank of the Dominican Republic is the sole bank of issue.

The principal exports of the country in the mid-1970's were sugar, nickel, coffee, cocoa, bauxite, and bananas. Sugar and sugar products made up about 75 percent of all export earnings. Machinery, iron and steel, foodstuffs, and chemicals were the leading imports. The total value of exports was about $878,000,000 per year, and of imports $716,000,000.

Transportation. The highway system totals about 6880 mi.; one main highway connects all of the major cities. Most of the nearly 900 mi. of railroad in use are privately owned and serve the sugar plantations. Aside from the Santo Domingo port, other large ports are located at Puerto Plata in the n.e. and Barahona in the s.w. The country is served by several international and local airlines.

Communications. The Dominican Republic has about 45 radio stations and some 185,000 radio receivers, 2 television stations and about 156,000 television sets. Ten daily newspapers, with a total circulation in excess of 197,000, are published. Some 108,000 telephones are in use.

Labor. The labor force comprised some 1,300,-000 workers in the mid-1970's. The majority were engaged in agriculture; manufacturing accounted for slightly over 10 percent. The remainder were engaged in services, commerce, construction, and the professions. The Confederación Nacional de Trabajadores Libres, with about 188,000 members, is the most important labor union.

GOVERNMENT

The Dominican Republic reinstituted a constitutional form of government with the election held in June, 1966.

Central Government. Executive power is vested in the president, who is popularly elected for a term of four years. The president appoints the cabinet; he may also introduce bills in congress.

Health and Welfare. In 1964 the government inaugurated a program aimed at raising health standards. Drainage systems, garbage disposal plants, and aqueducts were built in all of the larger cities. Several government agencies were established for the purpose of increasing water facilities in rural and urban areas.

Government programs provide some health services, but the republic has no comprehensive system for welfare.

Legislature. The bicameral congress is composed of an upper chamber (*Senado*), which has twenty-seven members, and a lower chamber (*Camara de Diputados*), with seventy-four deputies. All legislative members are popularly elected for terms of four years.

Political Parties. The Dominican Party was the only legal party between 1930 and 1961, when it was dissolved and new parties were established. Thirteen political organizations participated in the election of 1966. The principal parties are the Partido Reformista (P.R.), led by President Joaquín Balaguer (1906–), and the Partido Revolucionario Dominicano (P.R.D.), of which Juan D. Bosch (1909–), a former president, is the head. The P.R. draws support from the peasant and middle classes, whereas the P.R.D. is composed largely of landless peasants and urban workers.

Local Government. The provinces are ruled by governors who are appointed by the president. Each municipality and the Distrito Nacional elects a mayor and a municipal council as the administrative body.

Judiciary. The Supreme Court is composed of a president and eight judges, all of whom are appointed by the *Senado,* and a procurator-general, appointed by the president. Lesser courts include courts of first instance, courts of appeal, and communal and tribunal courts.

Defense. The armed forces comprise an army, navy, and an air force; personnel numbers about 12,000, 4000, and 3500, respectively. Two-year terms of service are compulsory for all males of eighteen years and over.

HISTORY

The Dominican Republic first achieved independence in 1844; until that time the region was ruled by several sovereignties for varying periods of time (*see* HISPANIOLA).

A Period of Strife. The first president was Pedro Santana (1801–64), who served for three terms (1844–48; 1853–56; 1858–61). Both his administration and subsequent ones were characterized by popular unrest and frequent boundary disputes with Haiti. The internal strife was most clearly discernible in the two political groups that took root within the republic: one faction advocated return to Spanish rule, and the other, annexation to the United States. For a brief period, from 1861 to 1863, the country, led by former President Santana, did return to Spanish rule, but a popular revolt in 1863 through 1864, and subsequent military reverses and U.S. intervention, forced the Spanish government to withdraw its forces and to annul the annexation. The second Dominican Republic was proclaimed in February, 1865. Political turmoil continued, however, throughout the remainder of the 19th century.

Because of Dominican indebtedness to a number of European nations, some of which threatened intervention, the Dominican government signed a fifty-year treaty with the U.S., in 1906, turning over to the U.S. the administration and control of its customs department. In exchange the U.S. undertook to adjust the foreign financial obligations of the Dominican government. Internal disorders during the ensuing decade finally culminated in the establishment of a military government by the U.S. Marines, who occupied the country on Nov. 29, 1916. Control of the Dominican Republic was gradually restored to the people; and by March, 1924, a constitutional government assumed control. Later that year the American occupation ended.

The Trujillo Era. The outstanding political development of the subsequent period was the dictatorship established by General Rafael Leonidas Trujillo Molina (q.v.), head of the Dominican Party. Elected to the presidency in 1930, Trujillo forcibly eliminated all opposition, thereby acquiring absolute control of the nation. In 1935 the government settled with Haiti the ninety-one-year-old boundary dispute. Border incidents occurred during 1937, in which thousands of Haitians living in the Dominican Republic were massacred. The matter was settled in 1938, and Trujillo agreed to pay a large indemnity to Haiti.

In 1941 the U.S. government terminated the administration of the Dominican customs. In December, shortly after the U.S. entered World War II, the Dominican Republic declared war on Japan, Germany, and Italy. It subsequently became a charter member of the United Nations.

Resumption of the multiple-party system in Dominican politics was announced by President Trujillo in 1945. Despite the formation of two oppositionist and several pro-government parties, Trujillo was reelected in 1947, by an overwhelming majority, and the Dominican Party won all but two seats in the congress.

At the 9th Inter-American Conference, held in Bogotá, Colombia, in April, 1948, the republic became a signatory of the charter of the Organization of American States (O.A.S.).

During the ensuing years, the Dominican Republic was frequently involved in local conflicts. In 1949, after a small party of revolutionaries invaded Puerto Plata Province, the government accused Cuba, Guatemala, and Costa Rica of encouraging anti-Trujillo activities. Early in 1950 the O.A.S. found the Dominican Republic guilty of interfering in the internal affairs of Haiti, but Trujillo and the Haitian president settled most of their differences the following year. A diplomatic crisis developed between the Dominican Republic and Cuba in February, 1956. Each nation charged that the other was planning an attack. A commission of the O.A.S. studied the incident but declined to arbitrate. Four years later, when Venezuela asked the O.A.S. to investigate mass arrests in the Dominican Republic, the Trujillo regime was accused of "flagrant and widespread violations of human rights".

General Héctor Bienvenido Trujillo Molina (1908–   ), president of the republic since 1952, when his older brother had resigned, relinquished the post on Aug. 3, 1960, and was succeeded by Vice-President Joaquín Balaguer.

Royal palms, typical of the climate, line a road in the Santo Domingo Zoological Park.
Dominican Republic Information Center

Dictatorial power, however, was still exercised by Gen. Rafael Trujillo. During the year the Dominican Republic was implicated in several plots to overthrow the Venezuelan government and in August was condemned by a resolution of the O.A.S. that called upon member states to sever relations with the republic. The U.S. did so on Aug. 26.

The Growing Threat of Civil War. On May 30, 1961, Rafael Trujillo was assassinated; on June 1, Rafael Trujillo, Jr. (1929–   ), replaced his father as head of the armed forces and, in effect, ruler of the country. During the thirty-one years of the dictatorship Trujillo was responsible for an increase in the number of hospitals and housing projects, a pension plan, and improved public health facilities, harbors, and roads. After the assassination pressures mounted, both inside and outside the country, against the continued political dominance of the Trujillo family. Numerous exiles began to return ·to the Dominican Republic, and political parties reestablished themselves. In October the two brothers of the late dictator left the country, but returned in November, apparently with the intention of seizing governmental power. President Balaguer reacted to the threat by assuming control of the armed forces. To demonstrate support of Balaguer, the U.S. stationed warships and planes off the Dominican coast. The show of force speedily induced all members of the Trujillo family to leave the country. Later in November opposition groups rallied against President Balaguer; after a wave of strikes and demonstrations, he and his opponents agreed on a plan whereby Balaguer would retain the presidency until sanctions, imposed by the O.A.S. since 1960, were lifted. The sanctions were revoked on Jan. 4, 1962, and on Jan. 16 Balaguer resigned. Two days later Rafael Bonnelly (1905–   ), an opponent of Balaguer, and a member of the newly formed National Civic Union (N.C.U.) Party, was designated president to serve until elections.

In December, 1962, the Dominican Republic held its first free election in nearly four decades. Juan Bosch won by a wide margin and was inaugurated on Feb. 27, 1963. Almost immediately opposition to his regime began to develop. Bosch was criticized as being too tolerant of pro-Castro and Communist groups; and the business community felt threatened by changes in economic policy. On Sept. 25 Bosch was deposed by a military coup. The leaders suspended the 1963 constitution, and installed a

107

Vast government-sponsored irrigation projects make cultivation feasible on much of the arable but still unused land of the Dominican Republic.

Dominican Republic Information Center

three-man civilian junta. To indicate disapproval of the coup, the U.S., Costa Rica, Honduras, and Venezuela broke relations with the Dominican Republic; and the U.S. withdrew foreign aid. The new government received recognition from the U.S. in December, after promising to hold elections in 1965.

The United States Intervenes. Throughout 1964 restlessness within the country was manifested by strikes and sabotage; and conflicts within the junta resulted in replacement of the original members. On April 24, 1965, a group within the army rebelled against the government with the avowed purpose of restoring Bosch as president. Air force and navy elements opposed the insurgents and Santo Domingo became the battleground of a civil war. On April 28 a contingent of U.S. Marines was landed in Santo Domingo to protect and to help evacuate U.S. citizens. In the succeeding days U.S. President Lyndon B. Johnson (q.v.), reacting to reports that the rebellion was falling under Communist control, reinforced the Marine contingent in order "to prevent another Cuba". The U.S. forces took up positions in the so-called international zone, which was established as a safety area for foreign nationals and which also served as a barrier between the rebel-occupied area of the city and the sections occupied by the junta

loyalists. From his exile in Puerto Rico, Bosch accused rightists of provoking intervention by the U.S., which, he said, had prevented a rebel victory. He denied charges by the U.S. of Communist takeover of the rebel cause. A peace commission of the O.A.S. arranged a cease-fire on May 5. On May 6 the O.A.S. approved a resolution by the U.S. to establish an inter-American military force for peacekeeping duties. The O.A.S. forces began arriving in mid-May, and in June U.S. Marines were withdrawn from the country; 12,500 other U.S. troops remained.

The Balaguer Government. During the summer fighting continued sporadically while the O.A.S. tried to arrange a settlement between the loyalists and the rebels (who called themselves "constitutionalists" to indicate their desire to restore the constitutionally elected government of Bosch). On Aug. 31 the two factions agreed to establish a provisional government, and on Sept. 3 Hector García-Godoy (1921–70), former foreign minister under Bosch, assumed the presidency. In succeeding months former President Bosch (who returned from exile on Sept. 25), Balaguer, and Bonnelly announced their candidacies in the presidential election scheduled for June, 1966. In the election, Balaguer, a conservative, won with 56 percent of the vote. Diplomatic relations between Haiti and the Dominican Republic, severed in 1963, were resumed in 1967. The Dominican economy received financial and technological aid from the U.S.

Balaguer was easily reelected to a second four-year term on May 16, 1970. The Dominican Revolutionary Party (P.R.D.), led by Bosch, boycotted the election, charging that its campaign activities had been restricted.

The Dominican economy showed strength in the early and mid-1970's, aided by high sugar prices, foreign investment, and increased tourism. Land reform measures were adopted in 1972. In 1973 the O.A.S. granted an $11,000,000 loan for development of the northwestern part of the country.

Terrorist activities by leftist guerrillas and student rioting, however, continued throughout Balaguer's second term. He was reelected to a third term in 1974, with the P.R.D. again boycotting the elections. In the mid-1970's a sharp decline in world sugar prices adversely affected the country's economy. In 1978 Antonio Guzmán (1911–), the candidate of the P.R.D., defeated Balaguer in the presidential elections, apparently ending his twelve-year regime.

DOMINICANS or **FRIARS PREACHERS,** Roman Catholic order (see ORDERS, RELIGIOUS) founded in 1214; two years later it adopted, with certain modifications, the rule of the Latin Father and doctor of the Church Saint Augustine (q.v.); see AUGUSTINIANS. Saint Dominic (q.v.) and sixteen disciples founded the order, at Toulouse, France, for the purpose of counteracting, by means of preaching, teaching, and the example of austerity, the heresies prevalent at the time. The order was formally recognized by the Apostolic See in 1216, when Pope Honorius III (d. 1227) granted the Dominicans the necessary papal confirmation and various special privileges, including the right to preach and hear confessions anywhere without obtaining local authorization. The necessity for such an order had become apparent to Dominic during his early attempts, about 1205, to convert the Albigenses (q.v.), and he had resolved to devote his life to the organized salvation of the souls of the heretical and the ignorant.

Preachers and Upholders of Orthodoxy. The Dominicans insisted on absolute poverty, rejecting the possession of community property and becoming, like the Franciscans (q.v.), a mendicant order (see MENDICANT FRIARS). The first house of the order was at the church of Saint Romain, in Toulouse, from which, in 1217, Dominic sent some of his disciples to spread the movement elsewhere in France as well as to Spain. Within six years the order was introduced into England, also, a house having been founded in Oxford. In England the Dominicans acquired the name of "Black Friars" from the habit they wore outside the convent when preaching and hearing confessions, a black coat and hood over a white woolen garment. By the end of the century fifty friaries were functioning in England, and the order had houses in Scotland, Ireland, Italy, Bohemia (now in Czechoslovakia), Russia, Greece, and Greenland.

In accordance with the declared purpose of their foundation, the Dominicans have always been known as dedicated preachers and as combatants against any departure from the teaching of the Roman Catholic Church. In the latter capacity they were entrusted with the conduct of the Inquisition (q.v.) as an ecclesiastical enterprise, and even in Spain, after the Inquisition became virtually a department of civil government, a Dominican was usually at its head. The office of master of the sacred palace, created for Saint Dominic in 1218 and subsequently endowed with great privileges by Pope Leo X (see under LEO), has always been held by a member of the order, and since 1620 the censorship of books has been one of its functions. In 1425 permission to hold property was granted to certain houses by Pope Martin V (see under MARTIN); it was extended to the entire order by Pope Sixtus IV (see under SIXTUS) in 1477.

Contributions to the Church and the Arts. Dominicans have held many high church offices; four popes, Innocent V (d. 1276), Benedict XI (1240–1304), Pius V (see under PIUS), and Benedict XIII (see under BENEDICT), and more than sixty cardinals have belonged to the order. Apart from their specific work, the Dominicans have done much to aid and foster the development of art. Their cloisters have produced such distinguished painters as Fra Angelico and Fra Bartolommeo (qq.v.). Their contributions to literature have been chiefly in the fields of theology and Scholasticism (q.v.), in which they produced such important writers as Saint Thomas Aquinas (q.v.), author of the standard work on dogmatic theology; Saint Albertus Magnus (q.v.), the "father" of Scholastic philosophy; and Raymond of Peñafort (1176?–1275), the codifier of the canon law. The important medieval encyclopedia *Speculum Majus* (see ENCYCLOPEDIA) was the work of a Dominican, Vincent of Beauvais (d. before 1264). Also Dominicans were the German mystics Johannes (Meister) Eckhart (1260?–1327), Johannes Tauler (1300?–61), and Heinrich Suso (1300?–66) as well as the Italian preacher and religious reformer Savonarola (q.v.). In the later Middle Ages (q.v.) the order was equaled in influence only by the Franciscans, the two brotherhoods sharing much power in the church and often in the Catholic states and arousing frequent hostility on the part of the parochial clergy, whose rights had been invaded by the friars. The Dominicans played the leading part in the evangelization of South America; the first American saint, Rose of Lima (q.v.), was a nun of the Third Order of Dominicans. In 1805 the Dominicans introduced their order into the United States. Missionary work still remains one of the important Dominican functions. The head of the entire order is the master general, whose term of office is twelve years; the residence of the master general is at the convent of San Sabina, in Rome. The order is organized into forty geographic provinces, each with a provincial at its head, and two vice-provinces.

Auxiliary Orders. The Dominican nuns were founded by Dominic, for women in danger of being converted to Albigensianism, in 1205, before the male branch of the order was established. They nevertheless called themselves the "Second Order of Saint Dominic". In 1220, to provide a constant supply of lay defenders of the Church against the assaults of the Albigenses and other militant innovators, Dominic established the "Militia of Jesus Christ" and pledged its members to defend the Church with their arms and possessions. In the late 13th century it joined with the "Brothers and Sisters of the Penance of St. Dominic", another lay group vowed to piety, which was under the direction of the First Order. The new body became known as the "Third Order of Saint Dominic".

DOMINION, term formerly applied to a self-governing member of the Commonwealth of Nations (q.v.) that recognized the British monarch as head of state. *See* Australia; Canada; New Zealand; South Africa, Republic of; Westminster, Statute of.

DOMINION DAY. *See* Canada: *History: British Rule to Confederation.*

DOMINOES, game played by two or more persons, with twenty-eight oblong blocks made of ivory, bone, plastic, or wood, called dominoes. Although the game originated in China in ancient times, it was not introduced in Europe until the middle of the 18th century. The first European pieces had ivory faces backed by ebony; they are thought to have been named because of their resemblance to the hooded cloak called a domino. Each domino, also called a piece or a man, is divided in half by a line or ridge, with a combination of spots, or pips, at each end. One man is blank; the remainder are numbered downward from double six, that is, 6–6, 6–5, 6–4, 6–3, 6–2, 6–1, 6–0; 5–5, 5–4, 5–3, 5–2, 5–1, 5–0, and so on through all the other numbers. Before the game starts, the twenty-eight pieces are turned face downward and intermixed, and each player draws a domino. The player who draws the highest domino is the first to play. Then, according to the particular variation of the game about to be played, either the entire number or a certain portion of the dominoes is selected alternately, one piece at a time, by the players. Each player sets his dominoes up on edge so that they cannot be seen by his opponents. The dominoes that are not drawn make up the reserve, called the stock or boneyard.

The first player poses (places) one man from his hand face up on the table. Against it at either end of the piece the second player must place a match; that is, one end of the piece he plays must have the same number of pips as one end of the piece already laid down. The next player in turn must play from his hand a domino with an end that matches one of the two ends of the dominoes on the table. Doubles, or dominoes with the same number of pips at both ends, are posed *à cheval* (crosswise) in the line of dominoes, rather than lengthwise. In certain variations of the game, the play of a double provides additional branches for matching. If a player has no piece to match either end, he passes, and the next player takes his turn. In a draw game (a game in which less than the whole number of dominoes is dealt) a player, in his turn to play, may draw on the stock up to, but never including, the last two dominoes. He may thus nearly exhaust the stock even when he has a match; this practice is occasionally good strategy, especially when the opponent is blocked. The game proceeds until one of the players wins by setting out the last of his dominoes, or until no player can match at either end. In the latter case, the winner is the player with the smallest number of pips on his remaining dominoes, or, in the case of an equal number of pips, the player with the fewest dominoes.

DOMITIAN, in full TITUS FLAVIUS DOMITIANUS AUGUSTUS (51–96 A.D.), Emperor of Rome (81–96 A.D.), second son of Emperor Vespasian, and brother of Emperor Titus (qq.v.), whom he succeeded. In the early years of his rule he was a conscientious and capable administrator, but he was unable to maintain peace on the borders of his empire and suffered a humiliating defeat at the hands of the Dacians under their king, Decebalus. In 84 A.D., probably acting out of resentment and envy, he recalled Gnaeus Julius Agricola (q.v.), his general in Britain, who was in the midst of a successful military campaign. Four years later Domitian ruthlessly crushed a revolt led by Antonius Saturninus, his general in Germany. Following these incidents his reign was characterized by terror, especially against members of the Roman Senate. He was murdered by a former slave, who had been encouraged by court officials and Domitian's wife, Domitia.

DOMRÉMY-LA-PUCELLE, village in France, in Vosges Department, on the Meuse R., 7 miles N. of Neufchâteau. It is the birthplace of Joan of Arc (q.v.), from whom its name (Fr. *La Pucelle,* "the Maid") is derived. The cottage where Joan was born still remains. A number of memorials throughout the town are dedicated to the French national heroine, the most important of which is the modern basilica of Le Bois Chenu, on the hill where she is supposed to have received, in a holy visitation, the spiritual mission to deliver her country from the English. The village was freed from all taxes by Charles VII (q.v.), King of France, in honor of Joan of Arc, and it enjoyed this privilege until the French Revolution. A yearly pageant representing the life of Joan is given by the people of the village. Pop. (1968) 184.

DON, river of the Soviet Union, about 1220 mi. long. It rises in the Russian S.F.S.R., about 140 miles S.E. of Moscow, flows in a general southeasterly direction to a point about 50 miles W. of Volgograd, and then in a southwesterly direction, emptying into the Sea of Azov, about 25 miles W. of Rostov. The three mouths of the river form a delta with an area of about 130 sq.mi.

The Don drains an area of about 166,000 sq.mi. Most of the land in the Don basin comprises fertile steppes. The Donbas, a region N.W. of the delta, is rich in coal and iron ore and is highly industrialized. The chief tributary of the Don is the Donets R.; other tributaries, from N. to S., include the Voronezh, Khoper, Medveditsa, and Manych rivers. Rostov is the chief port and principal city on the Don; other cities include Voronezh, Shakhty, and Novocherkassk.

The Don varies in breadth from about 500 to 1900 ft. and in depth from about 4 to 70 ft., with numerous shallow reaches. It is navigable for some 800 mi., but during the winter the greater part is frozen; in the spring, melting snow and ice swell the Don, especially its lower reaches. In June the river begins to subside and in August most of it is usually so shallow that navigation is almost halted.

The Don was long an important traffic artery from the Black Sea and Caucasus regions of old Russia to the central part of the country. Following the revolution of 1917 and the inception of national economic planning, the commercial importance of the river was enhanced as a result of its integration with other important waterways. In the N., the Yepifan Canal was constructed to link the Don with the Upa R., a feeder stream of the Oka R. The Oka is a tributary of the Volga, which in turn is connected with Moscow by another canal. In the S.E., the Volga-Don Canal, approximately 60 mi. long, connects the Don with the Volga S. of Volgograd.

Ancient Greek geographers considered the Don, which they called the Tanais, to be part of the boundary between Europe and Asia. Later, Tatar invaders of Europe called the stream the Tuna or Duna. In the Middle Ages, serfs fleeing the oppression of Muscovite princes in the north settled in the Don basin; their descendants became known as the Don Cossacks (*see* COSSACKS). During World War II, major battles were fought on the banks of the Don between the invading Germans and the Soviet forces.

DONATELLO, real name DONATO DI NICCOLO DI BETTO BARDI (1386?–1466), Italian sculptor, born in Florence, the son of a wool comber. Nothing is known of his early life or training in sculpture; but it has been established that when he was seventeen he assisted the noted sculptor Lorenzo Ghiberti (q.v.) in constructing and decorating the famous bronze doors of the baptistery of San Giovanni, Florence; and that Donatello was also an associate of the noted architect Filippo Brunelleschi (q.v.), with whom he reputedly visited Rome in the early years of the 15th century in order to study the monuments of antiquity.

His career may be divided into three periods. The first or formative period comprised the years before 1425, when his work is marked by the influence of Gothic sculpture but also shows classical and realistic tendencies. Among his sculpture of this period are the statues "Saint Mark" (Church of Or San Michele, Florence), "Saint George" (Museo Nazionale, Florence), "John the Evangelist" (Opera del Duomo, Florence), and "Joshua" (campanile of the cathedral, Florence). The second period extended from 1425 to 1443 and is generally characterized by a reliance on the models and principles of the sculpture of antiquity. From 1425 to 1435 Donatello worked together with the Florentine sculptor and architect Michelozzo (q.v.) on a number of projects, including the monument to Bartolomeo Aragazzi (Cathedral of Montepulciano). In their joint work Michelozzo executed the architectural designs and also helped in the making of the bronze castings; Donatello executed most of the statues. From 1433 to 1434

Donatello was in Rome, where he created a number of works, notably the Ciborium in the sacristy of the basilica of Saint Peter, decorated with reliefs of two "Worshiping Angels" and "Burial of Christ". He spent the following nine years in Florence; the most noted work of this period is his bronze statue "David" (Museo Nazionale, Florence), the first nude statue of the Renaissance. In his third and culminating period, Donatello broke away from classical influence and in his work emphasized realism and the portrayal of character and of dramatic action. Notable examples of his sculpture of this period are "Miracles of Saint Anthony" (basilica of Sant' Antonio, Padua); "Gattamelata" (in the square before the basilica of Sant' Antonio, Padua), the first bronze equestrian statue since ancient times; and "Judith and Holofernes" (Loggia dei Lanzi, Florence).

The sculpture of Donatello influenced that of Florence and northern Italy in the 15th century; it was one of the influences that stimulated the development of realism in Italian painting, notably in the work of the great Paduan artist Andrea Mantegna (q.v.). Donatello is generally considered one of the greatest sculptors of all time and the founder of modern sculpture. He had many pupils, the most important of whom was Desiderio da Settignano (q.v.).

DONATI, Giovanni Battista (1826–73), Italian astronomer, born in Pisa. He became professor at the Royal Institute and director of the observatory in Florence. He discovered six comets, one of which bears his name, and determined the gaseous composition of comets by means of the spectroscope. *See* DONATI'S COMET.

DONATI'S COMET, comet (q.v.) discovered by the Italian astronomer Giovanni Battista Donati (q.v.) at Florence on June 2, 1858. When the comet was nearest the earth, its triple tail had an apparent length of 50°, more than half the distance from the horizon to the zenith, and corresponding to the enormous linear figure of 45,000,000 mi. The period was estimated at more than 2000 years, and so it will not return until about the year 4000.

DONATISTS, dissident Christian sect in North Africa during the 4th and 5th centuries. Donatists held that for the sacraments to be valid, the minister must be sinless. The group was formed as a result of the consecration of a bishop of Carthage (now a suburb of Tunis, Tunisia) in 311 A.D. One of the three consecrating bishops was believed to be a *traditor* (Lat., "one who hands over, traitor"), that is, one of the ecclesiastics who had been guilty of betraying their office by handing over their copies of the Bible to the op-

"The David of the Casa Martelli" by Donatello.
National Gallery of Art – Widener Collection

pressive forces of Diocletian (q.v.), Emperor of Rome. An opposition group of seventy bishops, led by the primate of Numidia (approximately coextensive with present-day Algeria), formed itself into a synod at Carthage and declared the consecration of the bishop invalid. They held that the Church must exclude from its membership persons guilty of mortal sin, and that therefore no sacrament could rightly be performed by a *traditor*. The synod excommunicated the Carthaginian bishop when he refused to appear before it and in his place consecrated a *lector* (Lat., "reader"). Four years later, upon the death of this new bishop, the theologian Donatus the Great (d. 355) became bishop of Carthage, and the dissident group took its name from him. As a result of the desire of the Roman Emperor Constantine I (q.v.) to settle the dispute, it was submitted to various ecclesiastical bodies and in 316 to the emperor himself; in each case the consecration of the bishop elected originally, in 311, was upheld. Constantine at first attempted to suppress the Donatists by force, but in 321 adopted a policy of tolerance, a policy reversed, however, by his youngest son, Flavius Julius Constans (323?–50), who, succeeding to the rule of Africa and other portions of the empire upon his father's death, instituted a regime of persecution. In 411 a conference between the Donatist and Catholic bishops was held at Carthage for the purpose of arriving at a final settlement of the dispute. The decision, confirmed by Flavius Honorius, Emperor of the West (384–423), was once again adverse to the Donatists. As a result, they were deprived of all civil rights in 414, and, in the following year, their assemblies were banned under penalty of death. The sect then began to decline; the invasions of the Vandals (q.v.) from Andalusia (now Spain) and of the Saracens (q.v.) in the 5th and 8th centuries, respectively, completed its destruction.

DONATUS, Aelius (fl. about 350 A.D.), Roman grammarian, who numbered Saint Jerome (q.v.) among his pupils. He is best known as the author of *Ars Grammatica* ("The Art of Grammar"). This book was so widely used in the Middle Ages that its author's name, in the form *Donat* or *Donet*, became synonymous with a grammar or any elementary textbook. The *Ars Grammatica* and fragments of other works by Donatus have been preserved.

DONBAS, river of the U.S.S.R. *See* DONETS.

DONCASTER, Great Britain, county borough of West Riding, Yorkshire, England, on the Don R., 32 miles S. of York. It is a coal-mining and railroad center and has a considerable trade in farm produce. Manufactured products include agricultural machinery, chocolate, linen and woolen textiles, locomotives and railway cars, sacking, and wallpaper. The Doncaster horse races have been annual events since 1615; the famous Saint Leger race, which originated in 1776, is run each September. Doncaster was called Danum by the Romans and Dona Ceaster by the Saxons. The town suffered severely during the Danish invasion of England. Doncaster received municipal rights from Richard I (q.v.), King of England, in 1194; from this period date the Doncaster fair of the Annunciation, held in March, and the fair of Saint James the Apostle, held in July. Doncaster was created a county borough in 1927. Pop. (1971) 82,505.

DONEGAL, northernmost county of the Republic of Ireland, in Ulster Province, bounded

The highlands of Donegal, Ireland, with the Derryveagh Mts. in the background. Irish Tourist Board

on the N. and W. by the Atlantic Ocean. It is mountainous and boggy, and has many small lakes and rivers. Numerous islands lie off the long and deeply indented shoreline of the county. The soil is not fertile; small crops of barley and wheat are grown in cultivated areas. About 35 percent of the land is in pasture, and cattle, sheep, and poultry are raised extensively. The chief manufactures are linens, muslins, and woolens, including the well-known Donegal homespun. The county has sandstone and granite quarries and important deep-sea and salmon fisheries.

Donegal in ancient times was called Tyrconnell, and sometimes O'Donnell's country, after the family that ruled much of the area before the 17th century. Along the coast are many ruins of castles, including that of the early northern Irish kings, at the head of Lough Swilly, and Kilbarron Castle, near Ballyshannon. The county seat is Lifford; other towns are Buncrana and Letterkenny. Area 1865 sq.mi.; pop. (1971) 108,000.

DONELSON, FORT. *See* FORT DONELSON NATIONAL MILITARY PARK.

DONETS, river of the Soviet Union, rising in the East European Plain of the Russian S.F.S.R., and flowing in a general southeasterly direction through the Ukrainian S.S.R., joining the Don R. about 60 miles N.E. of Rostov, Russian S.F.S.R. The river is about 670 mi. long and navigable for some 140 mi. above its mouth. The river flows through the Donbas, or Donets Basin, an important coal-mining and industrial center.

DONETSK, formerly STALINO *or* STALIN, city of the Soviet Union in the Ukrainian S.S.R., and capital of Donetsk Oblast, on the Kalmius R., 100 miles N.W. of Rostov. It is the largest city and a major industrial center of the Donbas or Donets R. basin. Among the principal manufactures are chemicals, clothing, food products, iron and steel machinery, and nitrates. The city has several institutions of higher learning, including an industrial school, a medical school, and a teachers college. The city was started in 1870 when a British manufacturer John Hughes received a concession from the Russian government to make iron rails. The community he founded was named Hugheskova in his honor, or, in Russian, Yuzkova. After the Russian Revolution the Bolsheviks changed the name to Stalin. The city expanded rapidly between 1923 and 1926; this period was marked by a twofold increase in population. It was renamed Stalino in 1935. German troops occupied and severely damaged the city during World War II. It received its present name in 1961. Pop. (1972 est.) 905,000.

DON GIOVANNI. *See* DON JUAN.

DONIZETTI, Gaetano (1797–1848), Italian operatic composer, born in Bergamo and educated in music at the Naples Conservatory and at the Liceo Filarmonico, Bologna. He composed sixty-five operas and operettas; his fourth opera, *Enrico di Borgogna,* produced in 1818, was his first work to be staged. He did not become widely known until his thirty-third opera, *Anna Bolena,* was produced in 1830. Donizetti's musical style, considerably influenced by that of the composer Gioacchino Rossini (q.v.), is characterized by brilliant and graceful melodies, designed chiefly for virtuoso singers such as the soprano Giulia Grisi (1811?–69) and the tenor Giovanni Battista Rubini (1798–1865). The most important works of Donizetti are the grand operas *Lucia di Lammermoor* (1835), his most popular work, based on the novel *The Bride of Lammermoor* by the Scottish writer Sir Walter Scott (q.v.); and *Linda di Chamounix* (1842); and the light operas *L'Elisir d'Amore* ("Elixir of Love", 1832); *La Fille du Régiment* (*Daughter of the Regiment,* 1840; revived a century later by the Metropolitan Opera in New York City, with the coloratura soprano Lily Pons (q.v.) in the role of Marie); and *Don Pasquale* (1843).

DON JUAN, legendary hero who originated in a Spanish tale and is found in the folklore and literature of various European lands. The Spanish tale recounts Juan's seduction of the daughter of the military commander of Seville. After killing the commander in a duel, Don Juan ironically invites his statue to a feast. The statue comes to life, seizes the hero, and drags him down to hell. Variations of this story have occurred in the literature of countries throughout the world; the hero is regarded as the prototype of the libertine.

The first formal literary treatment of the story was the play *El Burlador de Sevilla y Convidado de Piedra* ("The Rake of Seville and the Stone Guest"), attributed to the Spanish dramatist Gabriel Téllez, who wrote under the pen name Tirso de Molina (q.v.), and printed in 1630 at Barcelona. About 1657, traveling Italian actors performed the story as a pantomime in France, where it was later dramatized by several French playwrights. These adaptations led the French dramatist Molière (q.v.) to write *Dom Juan ou le Festin de Pierre* ("Don Juan or the Stone Banquet", first acted in 1665), in which he added comic effects to the tale. The theme was treated in 17th-century England in the *Tragedy of Ovid* (1669), by the English poet Sir Aston Cokayne (1608–84), and in *The Libertine* (1676), by the English dramatist Thomas Shadwell (1642?–92).

The story and the character of the hero were greatly changed by later writers, including the British poet George Gordon Byron (q.v.) in his mock epic *Don Juan* (1819–24) and the Anglo-Irish dramatist George Bernard Shaw (q.v.) in his comedy *Man and Superman* (1903). A dramatic treatment of the story in verse, *Don Juan Tenorio* (1844) by the Spanish poetic dramatist José Zorrilla y Moral (q.v.), is frequently produced throughout Spain.

The legend of Don Juan has attracted many composers; foremost, Wolfgang Amadeus Mozart (q.v.) of Austria, who composed the famous opera *Don Giovanni* (1787) to a libretto by the Italian poet Lorenzo da Ponte (1749–1838). The German composer Richard Strauss (q.v.) wrote *Don Juan* (1889), a symphonic poem (q.v.).

DONKEY. *See* Ass.

DONNE, John (1573–1631), English poet, lawyer, and divine, born in London. At the age of eleven, he entered Hart Hall, University of Oxford, where he studied for three years. According to some accounts, he spent the next three

John Donne

years at the University of Cambridge. He began the study of law at Lincoln's Inn, London, in 1592. About two years later, he relinquished the Roman Catholic faith, in which he had been brought up, and joined the Anglican Church. His first book of poems, *Satires,* written during this period of residence in London, is considered one of Donne's most important literary efforts. Although not immediately published, the volume had a fairly wide readership through private circulation of the manuscript, as did his love poems, *Songs and Sonets,* written at about

the same time as the *Satires.* In 1596, possibly as a result of his friendship with the English diplomat and author Henry Wotton (q.v.), whom he had met at Oxford, he joined the naval expedition which Robert Devereux, 2nd Earl of Essex (*see under* DEVEREUX), led against Cádiz, Spain. On his return to England, Donne was appointed private secretary to Sir Thomas Egerton, Keeper of the Great Seal (1540?–1617). Donne's secret marriage in 1601 to Egerton's niece, Anne More (1585–1617), resulted in his dismissal from this position and in a brief imprisonment. A cousin of his wife offered the couple refuge in Pyrford. While there, Donne wrote his longest poem, *Metempsychosis: The Progresse of the Soule* (posthumously published, 1633), which ironically depicts the transmigration of the soul of Eve's apple.

During the next few years, Donne made a meager living as a lawyer, serving chiefly as counsel for Thomas Morton (1564–1659), an anti-Catholic pamphleteer. Donne may have collaborated with Morton in writing pamphlets which appeared under the latter's name from 1604 to 1607. Donne's principal literary accomplishments during this period were *Divine Poems* (1607) and the prose work *Biathanatos* (posthumously published, 1644). In the latter he argues that suicide is not intrinsically sinful. In 1608 a reconciliation was effected between Donne and his father-in-law, and his wife received a much-needed dowry. His next work, *Pseudo-Martyr* (1610), is a prose treatise maintaining that English Catholics could, without breach of their religious loyalty, pledge an oath of allegiance to James I (q.v.), King of England. This work won him the favor of the king, at whose urging Donne became a priest of the Anglican Church in 1615. He was appointed royal chaplain later that year. In 1616 he received livings at Keyston, Huntingdon; became rector of Sevenoaks, Kent; and was appointed divinity reader at Lincoln's Inn. He soon attained eminence as a preacher, delivering sermons that are regarded as the most brilliant and eloquent of his time. He continued to write poems, notably *Holy Sonnets* (1618). In 1621 James I appointed him dean of Saint Paul's Cathedral; he held that post until his death. His friendship with the essayist and poet Izaak Walton (q.v.), who later wrote a moving but inaccurate biography of Donne, began in 1624. While convalescing from a severe illness, Donne wrote *Devotions upon Emergent Occasions* (1623–24), a prose work in which he outlined twenty-three phases of his illness and treated the themes of death and man's relationship to man ("No man is an Iland, intire of it selfe; . . . any man's death diminishes me, because I am involved in Mankinde; and therefore never send to know for whom the bell tolls; It tolls for thee".). It is almost certain that Donne would have become a bishop in 1630 but for his poor health. During his final years he delivered a number of his most notable sermons, including the so-called funeral sermon, *Death's Duell* (1631), delivered less than two months before his death.

The poetry of Donne is characterized by complex imagery and irregularity of form. His intellectuality, introspection, colloquial usages, and striking syntheses of apparently irrelevant ideas make his poetry boldly divergent from the smooth, elegant verse of his day. His diction is seemingly "unpoetic", but is always chosen for its unique precision of meaning and connotation. The content of his love poetry, often cynical and sensuous, represents a reaction against the sentimental Elizabethan sonnet, and influenced the attitudes of the Cavalier school of English poets. The 17th-century religious poets, sometimes referred to as the metaphysical poets and including Richard Crashaw, George Herbert (qq.v.), and Henry Vaughan (1622–95), drew their inspiration from the imagery and spirituality of Donne's religious poetry. Donne was almost forgotten during the 18th century. Renewed interest in his work developed during the 19th century, and his popularity has reached new heights since the 1920's. Such modern poets as T. S. Eliot and W. H. Auden (qq.v.) have been greatly influenced by his style.

Most of the poetry remained unpublished until after the death of Donne, the first collection appearing in 1633. In addition to works already cited, Donne wrote the *Anniversaries,* an elegy in two parts, entitled *An Anatomie of the World* and *The Progresse of the Soule* (1611–12); the collection of essays *Juvenilia, or Paradoxes and Problems* (1633); *Essays in Divinity* (1651); *Letters to Several Persons of Honour* (1651); and six collections of sermons.

DONNER PARTY, group of American emigrants to California in 1846–47. Two families, the Donners and the Reeds, accounted for most of the eighty-seven members of the party, which left Sangamon County, Ill., in 1846, under the leadership of George Donner (1784–1847). After considerable difficulty crossing the Great Salt Lake (q.v.) in Utah, they were trapped by heavy snows in the Sierra Nevada (q.v.) in November. Forced to camp for the winter at a small lake, now named Donner Lake, about 13 mi. N.W. of Lake Tahoe (q.v.), they suffered enormous hardships. Party members resorted to cannibalism (q.v.) in order to survive. Forty-seven of them were eventually brought to California by rescue parties over what is now known as Donner Pass.

DONORA, borough of Pennsylvania, in Washington Co., on the Monongahela R., about 20 miles S.E. of central Pittsburgh. Manufactures include iron, steel, and zinc products. In 1948 a severe smog resulted in several thousand illnesses and twenty-two deaths. Pop. (1970) 8825.

DO NOTHINGS, derisive name for members of the Constitutional Union Party (q.v.).

DONOVAN, William Joseph, known as WILD BILL DONOVAN (1883–1959), American lawyer and soldier, born in Buffalo, N.Y., and educated at Columbia University. He began the practice of law in Buffalo in 1907. During World War I he served as colonel of the 165th Infantry ("the Fighting 69th") and was awarded the Congressional Medal of Honor.

After World War I, Donovan served as an investigative attorney for the United States Department of Justice, the State of New York, and New York City. During World War II he was coordinator of information (1941) and director of the Office of Strategic Services (1942–45), the most important U.S. intelligence agency of the war. Donovan resigned from the army (1945) with the rank of major general. In 1948 he went to Berlin as an unofficial observer during the Soviet and East German blockade of that city. His last public position was ambassador to Thailand (1953–54).

DON QUIXOTE, or in full *THE HISTORY OF DON QUIXOTE DE LA MANCHA,* a satirical novel and one of the masterpieces of world literature, by Miguel de Cervantes Saavedra (q.v.), originally published in two parts (1605 and 1615).

The principal character of the novel is Don Quixote, an elderly village gentleman of modest means. An avid reader of old-fashioned tales of chivalry, he becomes obsessed with the idea of reintroducing the practice of knight-errantry into the world. Don Quixote equips himself with arms and armor and rides forth on Rosinante, a broken-down horse, to challenge evil wherever he may find it. He is accompanied by the loyal and shrewd, but credulous, peasant Sancho Panza, who serves him as squire.

In his deranged state, Don Quixote sets himself the task of defending orphans, protecting maidens and widows, befriending the helpless, serving the causes of truth and beauty, and reestablishing justice. His adventures and skirmishes are often grotesquely inappropriate to the situation at hand; for example, he attacks a windmill, thinking it a giant, and a flock of sheep, thinking it an army. The obstinacy of his illusions never permits him to yield to the warnings of Sancho Panza, whose attitude is as realistic as that of his master is idealistic. The philosophical perception of the novel lies in the suggested balance of their contrasting views.

In Part II the contrast between the romanticism of Don Quixote and the practical wisdom of Sancho Panza is less striking. Don Quixote becomes a trifle more reasonable, and Sancho Panza begins to understand rather dimly the illusions of his master. In the end Don Quixote returns to his village and abandons knighthood. He realizes the error of his ways, declaring that "in the nests of yesteryear there are no birds today", falls ill, and dies. Critics generally agree that Part II of *Don Quixote* is superior because of its more compact organization.

Don Quixote has had a tremendous influence on the development of prose fiction; it has been translated into all modern languages and has appeared in some seven hundred editions. The first publication in English was in a translation by Thomas Shelton (Part I, 1612; Part II, 1620). It has been the subject of a variety of works in other fields of art, including operas by the Italian composer Giovanni Paisiello (1740–1816), the French composer Jules Massenet, and the Spanish composer Manuel de Falla; a tone poem by the German composer Richard Strauss (qq.v.); a German motion picture (1933) and a Soviet film (1957) directed, respectively, by Georg Wilhelm Pabst (1885–1967) and Grigori Kozintzev (1905–); and an American musical, *Man of La Mancha* (1965), by the playwright Dale Wasserman (1917–), with music by Mitch Leigh (1928–) and lyrics by Joe Darion (1917–). The theme was also used by the French artist Honoré Daumier in several of his paintings, and the French artist Gustave Doré (qq.v.) prepared illustrations for *Don Quixote*.
E.F.

DOOLEY, Mr. See DUNNE, FINLEY PETER.

DOOLEY, Thomas Anthony (1927–61), American physician and author, born in Saint Louis, Mo., and educated at the University of Notre Dame and Saint Louis University. In 1953 he received a medical internship with the rank of lieutenant (junior grade) in the medical corps of the United States Naval Reserve. In 1954 he was assigned to a naval hospital in Japan, but he soon volunteered for duty as the lone medical officer aboard a ship transporting refugees from North Vietnam to Saigon in South Vietnam, the newly divided country; see VIETNAM: *History*. Dooley remained at a refugee camp in Haiphong, North Vietnam, for eight months. His ex-

periences in Vietnam were related by Dooley in his first book, *Deliver Us from Evil* (1956). In 1956 he resigned from the navy and built a small hospital at Nam Tha in the jungles of Laos; two years later he built another hospital at Muong Sing, Laos. Meanwhile he had founded MEDICO (the Medical International Committee), an organization dedicated to medical aid for underdeveloped countries. Dooley personally raised nearly $1,000,000 for MEDICO through his television appearances, lecture tours, and books, including *The Edge of Tomorrow* (1958), *The Night They Burned the Mountain* (1960), and *Doctor Tom Dooley, My Story* (1960). Following an operation for chest cancer in 1959, Dooley returned to his work in the jungles, but late in 1960 he was forced to leave; he died in New York City in January, 1961.

DOOLITTLE, Hilda (1886–1961), American poet and author, born in Bethlehem, Pa., and resident in England after 1913. Miss Doolittle, who signed her work with the initials H.D., was identified with the Imagist school, a group led by the American poet Ezra Pound and the British poet Richard Aldington (qq.v.), Miss Doolittle's husband. Their work was characterized by freedom from restrictions in both subject matter and style; see IMAGISM. Among her books of poetry were *Sea Garden* (1916), *Heliodora and Other Poems* (1924), and *Flowering of the Road* (1946). She also wrote novels, including *Palimpsest* (1926) and *Bid Me to Live* (1960).

DOOLITTLE, James H(arold) (1896–), American aviator and army officer, born in Alameda, Calif., and educated at the University of California and the Massachusetts Institute of Technology. He served in World War I as a cadet in the aviation section of the Signal Corps of the United States Army and as a gunnery and flight instructor; after the war he became chief of experimental flying for the United States Army Air Corps at McCook Field, Dayton, Ohio. He became in 1922 the first pilot to fly across the United States in less than a day and in 1929 the first pilot to make a takeoff and landing completely guided by instruments. He resigned from the United States Army in 1930 to join the Shell Oil Company. As manager of the aviation department of the company, he furthered the development of high-octane gasoline. In 1932 he set a world record for speed (252 m.p.h.) in a land plane over a ten-lap, ten-mile course. In 1940 he was recalled to active army duty. On April 18, 1942, in the early stages of World War II, Doolittle led a force of planes in a bombing attack upon Tokyo, the first American air raid upon Japan proper; for this achievement he was awarded the Congressional Medal of Honor and promoted to the rank of brigadier general. During the same year he was placed in command of the U.S. aviation forces taking part in the invasion of North Africa, and in 1944 he was given command of the Eighth Air Force, stationed then in England and later in Okinawa. He became a lieutenant general in 1944. In 1946 he retired from active military duty and returned to the Shell Oil Company, from which he retired in 1959. Among the numerous official boards and commissions concerned with aviation and with military intelligence upon which Doolittle served were the Air Force Science Advisory Board, the Joint Congressional Aviation Policy Board, and the National Advisory Board of the National Air Museum of the Smithsonian Institution.

DOOM PALM or **DOUM PALM,** common name for species of palm (q.v.), *Hyphaene thebaica,* with fan-shaped leaves. It is remarkable among palms for the repeated forking of its stem. A native to the Arabian Peninsula, northern Egypt, and central Africa, the doom palm in some districts forms forests and serves to stabilize desert soils. The edible red fruit, which contains one hard, semitransparent seed, is about the size of an orange. Because the dry, spongy pulp of the fruit tastes like gingerbread, the palm is sometimes called the gingerbread tree. Ropes are made of the fiber of its leaf stalks, and the seed is used for beads and other small ornaments.

DOOMSDAY BOOK. See DOMESDAY BOOK.

DOOR, in architecture, movable barrier, of wood, iron, bronze, or other material, for closing and opening the entranceway or doorway (q.v.) to a building, apartment, or room. A door usually turns on hinges; sometimes it turns on pivots or is moved by sliding. In its commonest form a door consists of a single part or "leaf" hung to one door jamb; if the entranceway is more than four feet wide the door may consist of two leaves which meet at the middle of the entranceway. In a double-swing door the leaves are each hung on separate hinges and swing either in or out. Wide doorways in the interior of buildings and such wide exterior doorways as those of barns and railroad cars may be closed by sliding doors, rolling on metal rails. In some cases, as in garages, doors roll down to close and up to open. Also of a sliding type are creased accordion doors, generally made of a flexible plastic composition and adaptable to a variety of domestic uses, such as room dividers and closet doors. Storm doors are temporary doors, set outside of an entrance doorway, generally during the winter months, to provide added protection against the elements. In place of storm doors, modern buildings use either two sets of permanent entrance doors with a vestibule or lobby between them, or revolving doors, consisting of four leaves placed at right angles to each other and revolving on a pivot in a cylindrical enclosure. Fire-retarding doors may be wholly of metal or of wood covered with sheet iron, tin, or copper.

History. In antiquity, wooden doors in Palestine, Syria, and Mesopotamia were often covered with sheets of metal in which ornamental patterns in relief were worked. A notable example of doors of this type was the double door, or gate, to the palace of Shalmaneser III, King of Assyria (r. 859–825 B.C.) at Balawat, northern Mesopotamia, now Iraq. The door consisted of two leaves, each 27 ft. high and more than 8 ft. wide, adorned with bands of sheet bronze ten inches high and ornamented with reliefs of battle scenes and figures; the British Museum contains many of these bands. The doors of ancient Greece and Rome were generally of wood and were paneled. No examples of the ordinary house doors of the period are extant; but wall paintings and reliefs of the ancient city of Pompeii contain representations of doors which closely resemble the ordinary doors of today. The doors of important edifices of ancient classic times were chiefly of bronze. Among examples of Roman bronze doors are several in the city of Rome, including those of the Pantheon (q.v.), of the Basilica of Saint John Lateran, and of the basilica of Saints Cosmas and Damian. In Italian Romanesque buildings, bronze doors were made of thin metal hammered into low relief and applied to paneled frames of wood. Examples of such doors dating from the 11th and 12th centuries and earlier are to be found in churches in Rome, Pisa, Verona, Amalfi, Ravello, and elsewhere.

The doors of the Gothic cathedrals of the late 12th century were usually made of wood, their sole decoration consisting of their hinge plates of wrought iron. In the late Gothic period the wood door itself was intricately carved; such carving became more and more elaborate in Rennaissance times, as seen in the carved wooden doors (1540) of the Church of Saint Maclou in Rouen, France, attributed to the French sculptor Jean Goujon (q.v.). Bronze doors in simple classic style, cast in solid bronze and then chiseled and finished by hand, came into vogue in Italy with the doors (set up in 1336) for the south side of the baptistery at San Giovanni, Florence, by the Italian sculptor Andrea Pisano (q.v.). Doors of like nature, famous for their workmanship, were constructed during the Renaissance by the Italian sculptor Lorenzo Ghiberti (q.v.) for the north (1424) and the east (1447) doorways of the baptistery in Florence; by the Florentine sculptor and architect Filarete (1400?–70) for the basilica of Saint Peter, Rome; and by the Florentine sculptor Luca della Robbia (*see under* ROBBIA) for the sacristy of the cathedral of Florence. Modern bronze doors often follow the Italian Renaissance models.

DOORWAY, in architecture, opening in a wall designed to give access to, or exit from, a room, enclosure, or building. It may or may not be provided with a door (q.v.) or doors. The vertical sides of the opening are jambs, the beam or stone that spans the top of a square doorway is the lintel, and the undersurface of the lintel is the soffit. The woodwork which surrounds an interior doorway is collectively the door casing, and the portions of this casing that are visible on either side of the wall constitute the trim. It has been customary in all ages to frame or enclose the opening with some form of architectural adornment. The shape of the doorway is determined by the architectural style of the building in which it is placed. In Egypt it was always rectangular, surmounted by a prominently projecting cornice. In Babylonia and Assyria the doorway was arched, made of brick, and often decorated with faience (q.v.) and flanked with protecting colossi. The Persians largely imitated the Egyptians in their style of doorways but surrounded them with banded architraves. The primitive Greeks chiefly used a square doorway constructed of huge, often unwrought stone, with heavy lintels; the Lion Gate of Mycenae is a famous example; *see* MYCENAE. The Hellenic Greeks confined themselves to the rectangular doorway and evolved a type of which the most perfect example is the doorway of the Erechtheum (q.v.) in Athens. The Roman doorways were sometimes arched but more often rectangular, as in the Pantheon (q.v.). In the usual Roman type, the doorway was surrounded by a banded architrave and surmounted by a cornice, the ends of which were brackets. In the early Christian style, doorways were of small artistic importance. Those of Byzantine buildings were, however, often of magnificent proportions and appearance, as in the Church of Saint Sophia (q.v.), İstanbul, and Saint Mark's Cathedral (q.v.), Venice; *see* BYZANTINE ART: *Architecture.*

Romanesque Doorways. In the 11th and 12th centuries an entirely new type of doorway, originating almost simultaneously in Lombardy and

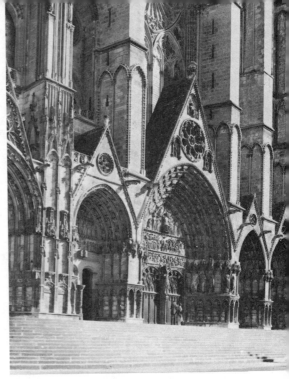

The 13th-century Cathedral of Bourges, France, exemplifies Gothic doorway construction.
French Government Tourist Office

France, became popular throughout Europe. This type of doorway was formed by a series of arches successively diminishing from the exterior face of the walls, the innermost and smallest arch enclosing a rectangular opening under a lintel, above which a lunette or a tympanum was sculptured in relief. Shafts in the angles of the recessed jambs supported the successive arches, which were richly carved. In Italy, elaborate canopies on columns often sheltered the entrance to this type of doorway. In France, figure sculpture was frequently used in the decoration of the doorway, as in the great portals of Saint-Gilles and Saint-Trophime at Arles, in Provence.

Gothic Doorways. About the beginning of the 12th century, French builders began to develop pointed portals, singly or in groups of three, with more stylized and more thoroughly architectural sculpture, as in the cathedrals of Chartres (q.v.) and Bourges and the Abbey of Saint-Denis. From these were developed the magnificent Gothic doorways, of which the 13th-century masterpieces are at Notre Dame (q.v.), Paris, and the cathedrals of Amiens and Reims. To secure sufficient depth for the increased sculptural adornments and to allow the doorway to become in itself a porch in which the worshiper might pray before entering the

The doorway of Ely House in Dublin, Ireland, shows a distinctive feature of 18th-century Western architecture.
Irish Tourist Board

church, these portals were made to form gabled structures projecting beyond the face of the wall. Medieval conceptions of the history of the universe are represented in the sculptures of these cathedral doorways, which thus acquire remarkable importance in the history of art. Only seldom is their value in this respect equaled outside of France. In Italy, there are a few fine examples of such doorways, notably at the cathedrals in Verona, Perugia, and Altamura; and in Germany, in the portals of the cathedrals of Freiburg and Nuremberg.

Renaissance Doorways. During the Renaissance (q.v.), the style of doorways returned to classic simplicity, having three principal types: (1) the arched doorway framed in rusticated masonry, that is, blocks of stone beveled at their edges to emphasize the joints, as in the Pitti Palace in Florence and the Farnese Palace in Rome; (2) square-headed or arched doorway flanked by pilasters or columns bearing an entablature with or without a pediment, as in the San Giobbe in Venice; and (3) the square-headed doorway framed by a banded architrave bearing an entablature or pediment, often with consoles, as in the Massimi Palace in Rome. The French developed monumental variations of these types in the 17th and 18th centuries. The German Renaissance doorways are low and broad, often adorned with fantastic and grotesque sculpture, as in the Heidelberg (q.v.) castle.

Modern Doorways. The historical styles are generally followed today, often with ingenious modifications, as in the French Gothic portals of the Riverside Church in New York City and the Romanesque doorway of the Trinity Church in Boston.

DOPPLER, Christian Johann (1803–53), Austrian physicist and mathematician, born in Salzburg and educated there and in Vienna. He was a professor successively at the Technical Institute at Prague and at the Polytechnicum of Vienna, and became director of the Physical Institute of Vienna University in 1850. He described the law of physics known as Doppler's principle (q.v.) in his monograph on the color effect of double stars, *Über das Farbige Licht der Doppelsterne* (1842).

DOPPLER'S PRINCIPLE, law of physics stating that the apparent frequency of any emitted wave, such as a wave of light or sound, varies as the source approaches or moves away from the observer. The principle takes its name from the Austrian physicist Christian Johann Doppler (q.v.), who first stated it in 1842. Doppler's principle explains why, if a source of sound of a constant pitch is moving toward an observer, the sound seems higher in pitch, whereas if the source is moving away it seems lower. This change in pitch can be heard by an observer listening to the whistle of an express train from a station platform or another train. The lines in the spectrum (q.v.) of a luminous body such as a star are similarly shifted toward the violet if the distance between the star and the earth is decreasing and toward the red if the distance is increasing. By measuring this shift, the relative motion of the earth and the star can be calculated.

DORCHESTER, former unincorporated town of Massachusetts, in Suffolk Co., about 5 miles S. of downtown Boston, of which it is a residential section. Notable landmarks include several houses built during the first half of the 17th century and a graveyard containing some of the oldest marked graves in the United States. Dorchester was settled in 1630 by Puritans (q.v.) from Dorsetshire, England. In 1633 the settlers organized probably the first town-meeting form of government in New England; see MUNICIPAL GOVERNMENT. In 1776, during the American Revolution (q.v.), George Washington (q.v.) fortified Dorchester Heights, a hill S.E. of Boston, and forced the British evacuation of the city. In 1870 Dorchester was made a part of Boston.

DORCHESTER, Great Britain, municipal borough and county town of Dorsetshire, England, on the Frome R., 6 miles N. of the English Chan-

120

nel, and about 115 miles s.w. of London. It is an agricultural trade center and is noted for the brewing of ale. In Roman times, Dorchester was a walled town with a moat, known as Durnovaria. In the vicinity are the Maumburg Rings, the most complete remains of a Roman amphitheater in England; the seats, cut from the native chalk, are capable of holding 13,000 spectators. The town was incorporated in 1610 by James I (q.v.), King of England. In March, 1645, during the Great Rebellion (q.v.), the anti-royalist general Oliver Cromwell (*see under* CROMWELL) held Dorchester with 4000 men. In 1685, Justice George Jeffreys (q.v.) presided in Dorchester over the Bloody Assizes (q.v.), in which 292 persons were sentenced to death for participation in the rebellion led by James Scott, Duke of Monmouth (q.v.).

Dorchester has erected statues to the Dorsetshire poet William Barnes and the novelist Thomas Hardy (qq.v.). Hardy was born near the town, which is the "Casterbridge" of his Wessex novels. Pop. (1971 prelim.) 13,737.

DORCHESTER, Baron. *See* CARLETON, SIR GUY, 1ST BARON DORCHESTER.

DORDOGNE, river of central and s.w. France, rising in the Auvergne mountains s. of Monts Dore. It flows westward for about 300 mi., through the departments of Corrèze, Lot, Dordogne, and Gironde, to Bec d'Ambès, 13 miles N. of Bordeaux. There, along with the Garonne R., it enters the Gironde estuary. The longest tributary of the Dordogne is the Isle R., which joins it at Libourne, Gironde Department, the head of navigation for seagoing ships.

DORDRECHT, or DORT, town of the Netherlands, in Holland Province, on an island in the Merwede R. (the lower Maas), 12 miles s.e. of Rotterdam. Industrial establishments in Dordrecht include gristmills, sawmills, shipyards, and factories producing chocolate, cigars, cordage, glass, and metalware. The town has a good harbor and a considerable trade in wine. It is an import center for lumber from Scandinavia and North America. An architectural feature of Dordrecht is the 14th-century Church of Our Lady (Groote Kerk), which contains mid-16th-century carved stalls depicting Biblical scenes. The Dordrecht Museum contains a number of paintings by famous masters. Founded in 1018, Dordrecht was the commercial center of the region and a member of the Hanseatic League (q.v.). The site of the town was formerly on the mainland but became an island as a consequence of a river flood in 1421. In 1572 the first assembly of the independent States of Holland was held at Dordrecht, and in 1618–19 the city was the meeting

An illustration by Gustave Doré for Don Quixote *by Miguel de Cervantes Saavedra.*   Bettmann Archive

place of the Synod of Dort, which affirmed the doctrines of the French theologian and reformer John Calvin (q.v.) and rejected Arminianism (q.v.). Pop. (1972 est.) 101,576.

DORÉ, (Paul) Gustave (1833–83), French illustrator and painter, born in Strasbourg. He was a precocious artist; at the age of fifteen he was regularly employed as an illustrator for the periodical *Journal pour Rire.* He is best known for his book illustrations, which are characterized by dramatic action against weird and gloomy backgrounds; the drawing, as a result of his insufficient training, is often faulty. Among the books that he illustrated were the Bible; an 1854 edition of the works of François Rabelais; an 1856 edition of *Contes Drolatiques* (Eng. trans., *Droll Stories*), by Honoré de Balzac; an 1861 edition of the *Inferno,* by Dante Alighieri; an 1863 edition of *Don Quixote,* by Miguel de Cervantes Saavedra; an 1866 edition of the *Fables* of Jean de La Fontaine; an 1866 edition of *Paradise Lost,* by John Milton; an 1880 edition of *Orlando Furioso,* by Lodovico Ariosto; and an 1883 edition of *The Raven,* by Edgar Allan Poe (qq.v.). Among Doré's paintings are "The Retreat from Moscow" (1865) and "Don Quixote and Sancho Entertained by Basil and Quiteria" (both in the Metropolitan Museum of Art, New York City).

DORIA, Andrea (1468?–1560), Genoese admiral and statesman, born in Oneglia. During the first half of his long career as one of the last of the great condottieri (q.v.), he fought as a sol-

121

dier of fortune under various princes. When French rule ended in Genoa about 1512, he commanded the Genoese galleys against the Turks and the pirates of North Africa (*see* Barbary Coast). Meanwhile, Genoa fell again to the French, but when it was captured in 1522 by forces of the Holy Roman Empire, Doria entered the service of Francis I (q.v.), King of France, and helped to place the city again under French rule. As French captain general, he inflicted losses on the fleet of Charles V (q.v.), Holy Roman Emperor. In 1528, failing to win concessions for Genoa from King Francis, he changed his allegiance to Charles V. He took all his forces with him, thus destroying French hopes of dominating Italy. He expelled the French again from Genoa and established a republic there under the protection of Charles V, who made him imperial admiral. He refused the lordship of Genoa, but was awarded palaces, important privileges, and the title of "liberator and father of his country". Although involved in a number of murderous feuds and conspiracies, he did much to establish order in the city. As imperial admiral, he captured Pátrai (Patras) and other southern Greek towns from the Turks in 1532, fought beside the emperor when Charles V captured Tunis in 1535, and saved Charles from disaster in the expedition against Algiers in 1541. In his eighty-fourth year Doria fought against the Barbary pirates once more and when nearly ninety spent two years fighting against the French in Corsica.

DORIANS, one of the three principal peoples of ancient Greece, the others being the Aeolians and the Ionians (qq.v.). According to legend, the Dorians took their name from Dorus, the son of Hellen, who settled in Doris, which the Dorians regarded as their mother country. Dorians invaded and occupied Crete, the Dodecanese (qq.v.) and other Aegean islands, and Laconia, Argolis, and Corinth in the Pelopónnesus. The invaders apparently kept themselves separate from the conquered tribes only in Laconia, and consequently the inhabitants of that region were always regarded as the representatives of unmixed Dorian blood. In Greek legend the conquest of the Pelopónnesus, placed about 1104 B.C., was related to the mythical return of the Heraclidae, the descendants of Heracles or Hercules (q.v.). The migrations probably took place during the 12th and 11th centuries B.C. or even earlier. From the Pelopónnesus the Dorians colonized the southwestern corner of Asia Minor and the neighboring islands, and planted settlements in Sicily and southern Italy. For Doric dialect, *see* Greek Language.

DORIC ORDER, in architecture, one of the three major styles of ancient Greek columns and entablatures. *See* Column.

DORMOUSE, common name for any of the small, arboreal rodents of the family Gliridae, or Muscardinidae in the order Rodentia (q.v.). The members of this family, widely distributed through Europe, Asia, and Africa, and distinguished from other rodents by several features of internal structure.

Most dormice are small; the species *Muscardinus avellanarius* of Europe and Asia, called the common dormouse in England, is about the size of the common mouse (*Mus musculus*). The species *Glis glis*, however, found in central and

Dormouse, Glis glis

southern Europe, grows to a length of nearly 7 in., not including the tail. This species, called the edible dormouse, is eaten in Europe in the season just before hibernation, when the animal is very fat. Another large European dormouse is the parti-colored lerot or garden dormouse, *Eliomys quercinus*. African dormice include *Graphiurus ocularis*, a large gray form with a tufted tail. The Chinese *Typhlomys cinereus* is conspicuous because of its feathery tail. The spiny dormouse of India, *Platacanthomys lasiurus*, named for its rough, spiny coat, belongs to the family Platacanthomyidae.

Dormice have large ears and long, usually bushy tails. Their fur is generally soft and fine. A resemblance to squirrels, more or less marked in some genera and species, is heightened by the fact that dormice sit up on their hind legs and hold their food in their forepaws. Unlike squirrels, dormice are nocturnal. Their food includes nuts and acorns, and also such insects as aphids, weevils, and caterpillars. The species living in cool climates hibernate; the name "dormouse" is probably derived in part from *dorm*, an English dialect word for "doze", and indirectly from the French *dormir*, "to sleep". The dormouse is called the sleepiest of the hibernators, for its winter sleep may last six months. During this period, as with all true hibernators, its temperature drops sharply and respiration is slow. The winter nest of the dormouse may be a bird nest refurbished with a soft lining of moss and occasionally with a roof added. During hibernation the dormouse often falls prey to the weasel.

The dormouse builds a nest for its young, which usually number four to the litter. The average female has two litters a year. The young are born blind but soon open their eyes, and mature remarkably quickly.

DORR, Thomas Wilson (1805–54), American lawyer and politician, born in Providence, R.I., and educated at Harvard College. Admitted to the bar in 1827, Dorr was elected to the Rhode Island Assembly in 1834. He became a leader of the movement to reform the colonial charter of 1663 by which the State was still governed and that deprived most of the population of representation in the legislature. Dorr's followers proclaimed a People's Convention in 1841 and held an election in 1842. After both regular and "people's" legislative sessions were convened, Dorr was declared an enemy of the State. In 1844 he was convicted of high treason by the State Supreme Court and sentenced to life imprisonment. He was released by vote of the State assembly in 1845 and in 1851 was restored to full citizenship. *See* RHODE ISLAND: *History*.

DORSETSHIRE *or* **DORSET,** Great Britain, county of s. England, on the English Channel between Devonshire and Hampshire. The surface of the county is irregular, with high chalk hills in the central area. The Dorsetshire coast has many summer resorts, including Lyme Regis, Bridport, Weymouth, Melcombe Regis, West Lulworth, East Lulworth, and Swanage. To the east, south of Poole Bay, is the Isle of Purbeck, which supplies a marble much used for buildings in England and a white pipe clay exported to the potteries of Staffordshire. The Isle of Portland, to the west, supplies a widely used white freestone. The principal industries of Dorsetshire are farming and stock raising. The county is noted for Devon, Hereford, and Shorthorn cattle, and for its butter, cheese, and cream. The chalk downs provide pasturage for many sheep. Dorsetshire has a number of prehistoric ruins of barrows and cromlechs and many evidences of Roman occupation, notably the remains of a huge amphitheater at Dorchester. Among the ruins left from Anglo-Saxon times are those of Corfe Castle, a seat of the Saxon kings of Wessex, on the Isle of Purbeck. Dorsetshire has served as the setting for literary works by Jane Austen, William Wordsworth, William Barnes, and Thomas Hardy (qq.v.). The county town is Dorchester (q.v.). Area, 977 sq.mi.; pop. (1971) 361,213.

DORSEY, name of two American brothers who were musicians famed as orchestra leaders: **James Francis Dorsey,** called Jimmy (1904–57), and **Thomas Francis Dorsey** called Tommy (1905–56).

The Dorsey brothers were both born in Pennsylvania, Jimmy in Shenandoah, and Tommy in Mahanoy Plains. Tommy, a trombonist, and Jimmy, a clarinetist and saxophonist, organized the first of their jazz bands about 1920. During the late 1920's and early 1930's they played together in several famous jazz bands including that of the American orchestra leader Paul Whiteman (q.v.). The brothers formed their own band in 1934. The following year they separated, and for the next eighteen years each had his own orchestra. Tommy's band, which featured so-called sweet jazz, and included many well-known musical personalities, was the better known, and was especially popular in the early 1940's. In 1953 the brothers formed the dance band called the Fabulous Dorseys, which, during 1954–56, enjoyed large audiences on the weekly television program called "Stage Show".

DORT. *See* DORDRECHT.

DORTMUND, city of West Germany, in the State of North Rhine-Westphalia, on the Ems R.,

73 miles N.E. of Cologne. Dortmund is in the heart of the Ruhr coalfields and near extensive iron-ore deposits. It is connected with Emden and the North Sea by the Dortmund-Ems canal, a 170-mi.-long waterway that was opened in 1899. Leading products are iron and steel, mining machinery, railway cars and locomotives, sewing machines, and wire and cables. Many institutions of higher education are located in Dortmund, including branches of the Max Planck Institute and of the University of Münster. Four churches in Dortmund are architecturally noteworthy: the cloistered Dominican Church; Saint Mary, in Romanesque style, dating from about 1150; Saint Peter; and Saint Reinoldi, with fine stained-glass windows. The town hall, built in the 13th century and restored in the 19th, contains a valuable antiquarian collection.

History. The city was first mentioned about 885 A.D. as Throtmannia, and it became a free city of the Holy Roman Empire. About the middle of the 13th century Dortmund joined the Hanseatic League (q.v.). The city enjoyed great prosperity in the succeeding centuries, but by the end of the 18th century it had declined in importance. With the rise of industrialization in the mid-19th century, however, Dortmund again prospered. After World War II, during which it was heavily bombed, Dortmund was included in the British zone of occupation. Pop. (1972) 642,396.

DORY. **1.** Common name for fish of the genus *Zeus,* typifying the family Zeidae of the order Acanthopterygii. These fish have large eyes, and are colored olive-brown with two dark patches on each side. The body is compressed and has numerous spines, particularly along the top. The dory projects its mouth outward to catch the small fish upon which it feeds. Dories are sometimes as long as 22 in. and may weigh up to 18 lb. They are native to the moderately deep waters of tropical and temperate seas. The most common of the dories is the John Dory (q.v.). **2.** Local name in the Great Lakes region for the walleyed pike (*Stizostedion vitreum*), also known as pike perch or pickerel. *See* PERCH.

DOS PASSOS, John Roderigo (1896–1970), American writer, born in Chicago and educated at Harvard University. During World War I he served as an ambulance driver in France. He utilized his wartime experience as background for his first novel, *One Man's Initiation—1917* (1920). Both critical and popular recognition came to Dos Passos with his next bitter antiwar novel, *Three Soldiers* (1921). *Manhattan Transfer* (1925), a panoramic view of life in New York

City between 1890 and 1925, became immensely successful. Containing fragments of the lyrics of popular songs, contemporary news reports and headlines, stream-of-consciousness monologues, and naturalistic fragments from the lives of a horde of unrelated characters, this powerful novel determined the style of the best of the later novels of Dos Passos; it also strongly influenced a generation of American writers. Dos Passos wrote the trilogy *U.S.A.* (collected in 1938) in the same style, expanding his panorama to encompass the entire nation. Comprising *The 42nd Parallel* (1930), *1919* (1932), and *The Big Money* (1936), the trilogy depicts the growth of the materialistic philosophy of America from the 1890's to the great depression of the early 1930's.

After the publication of this trilogy, Dos Passos underwent a change of philosophy; previously expressing a rather radical outlook, he became increasingly conservative. At the same time his writing became less impassioned and his style more direct and simple. He continued to produce a great deal of work, including several novels, books of personal observation, history, biography, and travel. Of the works of his later period, the best-received was *Midcentury* (1961), a novel in which Dos Passos returned to the kaleidoscopic technique of his earlier successes to depict a panoramic view of postwar America. At the time of his death he had completed most of a novel, *The 13th Chronicle.* Posthumously published were *Easter Island* (1971), a travel book, and *The Fourteenth Chronicle* (1973), his diaries and letters.

DOSTOEVSKI, Fëdor Mikhailovich *or* **DOSTOYEVSKY, Fëdor Mikhailovich** (1821–81), Russian novelist, born in Moscow, and educated at the School of Military Engineers, Saint Petersburg (now Leningrad). He was commissioned a sublieutenant in 1841 and in 1843 was appointed to a government post; he resigned the following year to devote himself to literature.

Early Idealism and First Writings. Dostoevski's first novel, *Poor Folk* (1846), was acclaimed by the critic Vissarion Grigorevich Belinski (1811–48), and won him recognition as one of the most promising of the young Russian writers. Despite poverty and incipient epilepsy, he produced another novel, *The Double* (1846), and several short stories. Belinski's reception of these works was hostile, the reigning circle of critics was equally cold, and Dostoevski became alienated from them.

Dostoevski's concern for the poor and downtrodden had led him to become associated with a group of utopian socialists led by Mikhail Pe-

Fëdor Dostoevski   UPI

trasherski. He and other members of the group were arrested in the wave of repression that swept Russia following the revolutions in Europe in 1848. After eight months of imprisonment, they were tried in 1849 and sentenced to death. Moments before the condemned men were to be shot they received a reprieve, which had been signed by the czar three days earlier but had been kept secret on his orders until the time of execution. Dostoevski's sentence was commuted to four years of hard labor in a Siberian penal colony and four years of military service in the ranks. The ordeal before the firing squad greatly aggravated his epilepsy, and for the rest of his life he suffered seizures of disabling intensity.

Dostoevski spent four years in a penal settlement near Omsk and an additional two and a half years as an army private and noncommissioned officer. During the period of his imprisonment he renounced his socialist dreams, becoming devoutly religious and ardently nationalistic. By fusing nationalism and religion, he virtually deified the Russian people, perceiving them as bearers of the truth, destined, through their sufferings, to save mankind.

Marriage and Literary Recognition. Dostoevski married Maria Dmitrievna Isaeva (d. 1864), a widow, but the marriage was unhappy. Through the influence of an old schoolmate who had become a general, his commission was restored in

1856, but he was required to remain in Siberia three more years.

Returning to St. Petersburg in 1859, he resumed his literary career. In 1861 he published *Memoirs from the House of the Dead,* a thinly fictionalized account of his bitter experiences in Siberia. The same year Dostoevski, together with his brother Mikhail Dostoevski started a literary review, *Vremya* ("Time"), in which his novel *The Insulted and Injured* (1862) first appeared. Although its editorial policy was strongly nationalistic, the magazine aroused official suspicion, and in May, 1863, it was suppressed.

Dostoevski meanwhile had become intimately involved with Apollinaria Suslova, an emancipated, emotionally unstable girl twenty years his junior, and toured Europe with her. His passion for gambling caused him to lose both his mistress and his money.

Upon his return to Russia late in 1863, Dostoevski and his brother started a new review, *Epokha* ("Epoch"). Mikhail died shortly thereafter, and *Epokha* failed, leaving Dostoevski overwhelmingly in debt, and compelled to write at great speed to satisfy his creditors. During this period he had also to nurse his wife, who was dying of consumption. In spite of the pressures under which he worked, Dostoevski's genius quickly reached full maturity. In 1864, the year his wife died, the first of his great novels, *Notes from the Underworld,* was published. *Crime and Punishment,* probably his best-known novel, appeared in 1866.

Dostoevski married his 21-year-old secretary, Anna Snitkina, in 1867 and, to escape his creditors, lived in Europe with her until 1871, gambling and writing furiously. The devotion of his wife and her business ability enabled him eventually to put his finances in order.

After returning home from Europe he wrote for a conservative weekly and published a journal of his own, *A Writer's Diary,* which became popular, and towards the end of his life he became fairly affluent. His final triumph came in 1880 when he was selected to deliver the main address at the unveiling of a memorial to the Russian poet Aleksander Sergeevich Pushkin (q.v.). The death of Dostoevski in the following year occasioned a nationwide demonstration of homage and sorrow. His most important novels, in addition to *Notes from the Underworld* and *Crime and Punishment,* are *The Idiot* (1868), *The Possessed* (1871), and *The Brothers Karamazov* (1880), which is generally considered his masterpiece.

Dostoevski ranks with Count Lev Nikolaevich

125

Tolstoi (q.v.) as the greatest of Russian novelists, and most critics regard him as among the three of four greatest of all novelists. He penetrated the minds and hearts of men with exceptional insight, anticipating the scientific findings of the Austrian psychoanalyst Sigmund Freud (q.v.) and other pioneers in the field of abnormal psychology. Dostoevski's main characters, all vividly realized, lead lives of almost unbearable intensity. They ask anguished questions of God about the basic human concerns, about the problems of evil, of responsibility, of guilt, and of freedom. They do not merely discuss ideas, they suffer them, lacerating themselves and each other with the thoughts that possess them. For the sake of their thoughts, they form revolutionary conspiracies, commit horrible crimes, go mad, destroy themselves. Most of Dostoevski's later novels are stories of crime and suspense, but what is most interesting about them is not so much the surface action as the momentous spiritual struggles that go on beneath. A seminal thinker who profoundly influenced the modern intellectual climate, Dostoevski produced in his novels mixture of thought and feeling perhaps more perfect than any achieved in literature.

DOTHAN, city in Alabama, and county seat of Houston Co., about 120 miles S.E. of Montgomery. The city is in a rich farming region. In the city are cotton compresses and cottonseed-oil mills, lumber mills, sash and door factories, and plants producing fertilizer and textiles. Dothan was founded in 1884 and incorporated in 1885. Pop. (1960) 31,440; (1970) 36,733.

DOU, Gerard or **DOW, Gerard** (1613–75), Dutch painter, born at Leiden. He was a pupil of the famous Dutch master Rembrandt (q.v.). Dou's early career was devoted chiefly to portraiture, but he is known principally for his later genre work. His paintings are small and are characterized by minute detail, skillful chiaroscuro, and lifelike effect. Among his paintings are "The Poulterer's Shop" (National Gallery, London), a self-portrait (1653?, Metropolitan Museum of Art, New York City), and "The Young Mother" (The Hague Gallery).

DOUAI, formerly DOUAY, town of France, in Nord Department, about 110 miles N.E. of Paris. The town is a major industrial and commercial center of the surrounding region. Manufacturing establishments include breweries, flax mills, glass and chemical works, ironworks, and sugar and salt refineries. Trade is chiefly in agricultural products and building materials. Douai was held by the counts of Flanders from the 7th century until 1384, when it was taken by the dukes of Burgundy. It then passed to the Hapsburgs,

and was finally awarded to France in 1713 by the Treaty of Utrecht. Several famous seats of learning were established in Douai during the 16th and 17th centuries. Philip II (q.v.), King of Spain, established a university there in 1562, and six years later, the English cardinal William Allen (1532–94) opened a seminary for English Catholics. Allen was one of many Catholic alumni of the University of Oxford who fled to Douai from England following the adoption by the Church of England (q.v.) of The Thirty-nine Articles; see ARTICLES, THE THIRTY-NINE. The Douai-Reims Bible, an English translation of the Vulgate, was begun in the town by members of the seminary; the Old Testament was published in Douai in 1609; see BIBLE, ENGLISH TRANSLATIONS OF THE.

The seminary was suppressed in 1793 during the French Revolution (q.v.). Other seminaries had been established by the English Benedictines and Franciscans during the 16th century. In World War I, the Germans captured Douai, but caused little damage to the large library, scientific and archeological museum, and historical buildings of the town. Pop. (1968 est.) 50,104.

DOUALA or **DUALA,** largest city and principal port of the Republic of Cameroon, about 130 miles W. of Yaoundé. The city is on the bank of the Wouri R. at the point where it enters the Bight of Biafra. The chief commercial center of the country, Douala has an airport and more than a mile of dock space, and is a terminus for two railway lines extending into the interior. Industries include the manufacture of aluminum products, beer, soft drinks, and textiles, and the processing of lumber and cacao beans. The city was named probably for the Duala, a coastal tribe which originally settled the area. Pop. (1970 est.; greater city) 250,000.

DOUAY. See DOUAI.

DOUBLE BASS or **CONTRABASS,** largest and lowest-pitched instrument of the violin family. The modern double bass has four strings, tuned in E_1 (E on the first line below the bass staff), A_1 (first space of the staff), D_1 (third line), and G (fourth space). The notes of the instrument sound an octave lower than written. It has a range of about three octaves extending upward from E_1. Some double basses have a fifth string, adding one below the E string and extending the range downward to the C three full octaves below middle C. The double bass is essentially an orchestral instrument, rarely used for solo performances. The first orchestral use of the double bass on record occurred about 1555; it was then one of the twenty instruments, the others being violins, of the orchestra of the

French ruler Catherine de Médicis (q.v.), led by the Italian violinist Baltazarini (d. about 1587). Virtuosi on the double bass have included the Italians Domenico Dragonetti (1763–1846) and Giovanni Bottesini (1821–89), and the Russian-American Serge Koussevitzky (q.v.).

DOUBLEDAY, Abner (1819–1893), American army officer, born in Ballston Spa, N.Y., and educated at the United States Military Academy. Some authorities credit Doubleday with the creation of the modern game of baseball (q.v.). They assert that in 1839, during a visit to Cooperstown, N.Y., the young man devised the diamond-shaped field and established the present-day playing positions.

Doubleday served in the U.S. Army during the Mexican War (1846–48). He fired the first gun from Fort Sumter in response to the Confederate attack in 1861, at the beginning of the American Civil War. He was appointed a brigadier general of volunteers and placed in command of the defenses of Washington, D.C., in 1862, and was promoted to major general in the same year. He fought in many battles of the Civil War, including the second Bull Run, Antietam, and Fredericksburg. On the first day of the Battle of Gettysburg (July 1, 1863), he commanded the Union troops in the field for several hours after his superior officer, Major General John Fulton Reynolds (1820–63), had been killed. After the war he continued to serve, as a colonel, in the regular U.S. Army until his retirement in 1873. He wrote *Reminiscences of Forts Sumter and Moultrie in 1860–61* (1876) and *Chancellorsville and Gettysburg* (1882). *See* CIVIL WAR, THE AMERICAN; individual articles on battles mentioned.

DOUBLE ENTRY. *See* BOOKKEEPING: *Double Entry.*

DOUBLE JEOPARDY. *See* ACQUITTAL.

DOUBLE STARS. *See* STARS: *Double Stars.*

DOUGHERTY, Paul (1877–1947), American marine painter, born in Brooklyn, N.Y. He studied art in various European cities, including Paris, London, and Florence. Among his works are "Sun and Storm" (National Gallery, Washington, D.C.), "A Freshening Gale" (Albright Art Gallery, Buffalo, N.Y.), "October Seas" (1910, Metropolitan Museum of Art, New York City), and "The Land and the Sea" (Corcoran Gallery, Washington, D.C.). He was a brother of the American actor Walter Hampden (q.v.).

DOUGHTY, Charles Montague (1843–1926), British poet, explorer, and scholar, born in Suffolk, England, and educated at Caius and Downing colleges, University of Cambridge. He studied geology, archeology, and philology in Norway, Greece, Spain, North Africa, and the

Near East until he was thirty-three, and then embarked on a hazardous journey into the interior of Arabia. He left Damascus with a pilgrim caravan in November, 1876, and after many adventures and discoveries he reached Jidda in August, 1878. *Travels in Arabia Deserta* (1888), his account of this journey, contained a mass of scientific observation but was also used as the vehicle for Doughty's theories on the English language. He wrote in a style that he hoped would restore to written English the simplicity of its origins in Anglo-Saxon and in Chaucerian and Elizabethan writers. *Travels in Arabia Deserta* was almost disregarded for fifteen years but Doughty continued his experiments in language, notably in the form of epics and verse drama. His works in verse include *The Dawn in Britain* (6 vol., 1906), *Adam Cast Forth* (drama, 1908), *The Cliffs* (1909), *The Clouds* (1912), and *Mansoul, or the Riddle of the World* (1920).

DOUGHTY, Thomas (1793–1856), American painter, born in Philadelphia, Pa. Self-taught as an artist, Doughty was one of the earliest of the Hudson River school (q.v.) of painting. The subjects of his works are mostly river scenes. Among his paintings are "A View of the Schuylkill" (Edinburgh Museum), and "On the Hudson" and "A River Glimpse" (Metropolitan Museum of Art, New York City).

DOUGLAS, city of Arizona, in Cochise Co., adjoining Agua Prieta, Mexico, and situated in the fertile Sulphur Spring Valley. Hereford cattle are raised in the surrounding region of Arizona. Vast copper smelters in the city are supplied with ore from mines in Arizona and Mexico. Douglas contains hotels, guest ranches, and other accommodations for tourists. It was incorporated in 1905. Pop. (1960) 11,925; (1970) 12,462.

DOUGLAS, Great Britain, seaport and capital of the Isle of Man, on the E. coast of the island, about 75 miles N.W. of Liverpool, England, across the Irish Sea. It is at the common mouth of the Dhoo and the Glass rivers, and is noted as a summer resort and as the principal packet station of the Isle of Man, with daily sailings to and from Liverpool and seasonal connections with Belfast and Dublin, Ireland; with Glasgow, Scotland; and with Fleetwood, Heysham, and Barrow in England. Pop. (1971 prelim.) 20,389.

DOUGLAS, noble Scottish family prominent in the history of Scotland and England for more than 700 years. The historic titles held by the family, those of the Black Douglases (earls and marquises of Douglas) and of the Red Douglases (earls of Angus) were merged and were held in modern times by the marquises and dukes of Hamilton. Other modern titles of the family include the marquis of Queensberry and the earl of Morton.

The origin of the family is lost in legend, part of which attributes the foundation of the Douglases to a chieftain named Sholto Douglas in 770. The rise of the Douglases may be attributed to their part in the incessant wars of medieval Scotland, and to the fact that their principal estates were close to the English border, involving them constantly in warfare between England and Scotland.

Among the most important members of the Douglas family were the following.

William of Douglas (fl. 1200), the first Douglas recorded in authentic history, whose name appears on documents beginning in 1175, in the century after the kingdom of Scotland was founded by the amalgamation of the four original tribal kingdoms of the Scots, Picts, Britons, and Angles. His holding was in Lanark, in the Vale of Douglas (Gaelic *dubh glas,* "dark water"), from which he seems to have derived his name. The estate is now held by the Douglas-Home branch of the family.

Sir Archibald or **Erkenbald** (d. about 1240), son of William, and the first to attain knighthood.

Sir William of Douglas, called "the Hardy" (d. 1298), who first formally assumed the title of Lord of Douglas. William the Hardy twice broke his sworn allegiance to Edward I (q.v.), King of England. He commanded the forces of John de Baliol, King of Scotland (*see under* BALIOL), at Berwick Castle, and was imprisoned when it fell to the English under Edward. William was released and his Scottish estates were restored, but in 1297 he joined the rising of Sir William Wallace (q.v.) and died a prisoner in the Tower of London.

Sir James Douglas, Lord of Douglas (1286–about 1330), called "the Good", and by the English "the Black Douglas", son of the 1st Lord, educated at Paris. His offer of allegiance to Edward I was refused and he joined Robert Bruce (q.v.), King of Scotland, in his coronation at Scone in 1306 and became his greatest captain in the subsequent wars. He fled to the highlands with Bruce after the battle of Methven. Douglas is said to have won fifty-seven of his seventy battles. Three times he destroyed English garrisons in his own castle of Douglas. On one occasion (1307), the butchery was so notorious as to be called "the Douglas Larder". He was knighted by Bruce on the battlefield of Bannockburn (1314). Invading Yorkshire in 1319, Douglas defeated an army raised by the arch-

bishop of York and the bishop of Ely in a battle known as "Chapter of Myton", at a locality in Yorkshire also known as Mitton. Until 1327, his constant raids across the border made "the Black Douglas" dreaded in English homes. After he had laid waste the north of England, he returned to Scotland, and in 1329 the dying Bruce commissioned him to take his heart to the Holy Land. Douglas reached Spain with the embalmed heart but fell fighting the Moors. Since that time, a human heart has been worn on the Douglas coat of arms.

Sir Archibald Douglas (about 1296–1333), half-brother of the Black Douglas. He defeated Edward de Baliol, King of Scotland (*see under* BALIOL) in 1332 and was appointed regent of Scotland during the minority of King David II (q.v.). Douglas was killed shortly afterward when he invaded England and was defeated at Halidon Hill.

James Douglas, 2nd Earl of Douglas and Mar (about 1358–88), conqueror of Hotspur (*see* PERCY, SIR HENRY). In 1373, he married Lady Isabel Stewart, daughter of Robert II (q.v.). In 1385 he made war on England with French assistance. At the battle of Otterburn (1388), the Scots captured Hotspur and his brother but Douglas was killed. The battle is celebrated in the English ballad *Chevy Chase* and the Scottish ballad *The Battle of Otterburn.*

Archibald, 3rd Earl of Douglas, Lord of Galloway (about 1328–1400), called "the Grim", and also "the Black Douglas". He was the illegitimate son of Sir James the Good. In 1389, he invaded England. Between wars with the English, he imposed order on the wild chieftains of the border and the western marches. During his lifetime the power of the Black Douglas house was greater than that of the Scottish crown. Douglas was able to marry his daughter to David Stewart, Duke of Rothesay (1378?–1402), the son and heir of Robert III (q.v.), King of Scotland, and two sons to the king's daughters.

Archibald, 4th Earl of Douglas, 1st Duke of Touraine (1372–1424), called "the Tineman" (loser), son of Archibald the Grim, and son-in-law of Robert III. With the regent of Scotland, Robert Stewart, Duke of Albany (1340?–1420), Douglas was suspected of complicity in the murder of the Duke of Rothesay, but the alleged plotters were exculpated by the Scottish parliament. In 1402, Douglas raided England and was captured by Hotspur. Douglas fought at Shrewsbury (1403) with Hotspur against Henry IV (q.v.), King of England, and was captured in turn by Henry. Later he formed a personal alliance with John the Fearless, Duke of Burgundy (1371–

"The Death of Douglas" (James Douglas, 2nd Earl of Douglas and Mar) by the 19th-century British painter Charles Landseer.   Granger Collection

1419), and led 10,000 Scots against the English in 1423. He was given a French duchy. He died in action in a battle with the English at Verneuil, France.

Archibald, 5th Earl of Douglas and 2nd Duke of Touraine (about 1391–1439), son of the 4th Earl. He fought against the English at Baugé, France (1421), and brought James I (q.v.), King of Scotland, home from captivity in England.

William, 6th Earl of Douglas (about 1423–40), and **David of Douglas,** sons of the 5th Earl. They were taken as boys before the young James II (q.v.), King of Scotland, subjected to a mock trial, and summarily beheaded in the courtyard of Edinburgh Castle. This judicial murder broke the power of the Black Douglases.

William, 8th Earl of Douglas (1425?–52), cousin of the 5th Earl. He formed an alliance against James II and was murdered at the instigation of the king.

James, 9th and last Earl of Douglas (1426–98), brother of the 8th Earl. He raised arms against James II after the murder of his brother but submitted to the king when his allies fell away. He married his brother's widow in order to keep the Black Douglas lands intact. In 1455, he rebelled again, but he and his three brothers, the lords Ormond, Moray, and Balvany, were routed by a kinsman, "the Red Douglas", George, 4th Earl of Angus (1412?–62). Moray was killed and Ormond was captured and executed. Douglas and Balvany escaped to England, where the earl was later employed by Edward IV (q.v.), King of England, to induce the western Scottish highlanders to league themselves against James. Douglas was captured while raiding across the border from England and confined to a monastery, where he died. The Douglas castles were dismantled and the Douglas honors were distributed among their rivals, chiefly to the earls of Angus.

Archibald Douglas, 5th Earl of Angus (about 1450–1514), called "the Great Earl". After he captured Robert Cochrane, Earl of Mar (d. 1482), the hated favorite of James III (q.v.), King of Scotland, Douglas was nicknamed "Bell-the-Cat". He intrigued with the English king Edward IV and rebelled against James III, but became chancellor under James IV (q.v.), King of Scotland. Two of his sons were killed at Flodden Field (1513). Another son, Gawin Douglas (q.v.), was the poet and bishop of Dunkeld.

Archibald Douglas, 6th Earl of Angus (about 1489–1557), grandson of the 5th Earl. In 1514 he married Margaret Tudor (q.v.), the widow of

James IV and sister of Henry VIII (q.v.), King of England. His marriage led to jealousy and civil war, during which the regent of Scotland, John Stewart, 4th Duke of Albany (1481-1536), besieged the queen and seized her young son, James, later King of Scotland as James V (q.v.). Douglas briefly enjoyed supreme power when he defeated James Hamilton, 1st Earl of Arran (1477?-1529), but in 1522 Albany banished Douglas for high treason. Douglas returned to Scotland under the protection of Henry VIII in 1525, and assumed control of his stepson. For three years Douglas was all powerful, but in 1528 Queen Margaret obtained a divorce and roused Albany to opposition. James escaped from Douglas' tutelage and the earl was forced to flee to England. In 1542, on the death of James, Douglas returned and was made lord lieutenant of the south of Scotland, and in 1545 he defeated the English at Ancrum Moor. Lady Margaret Douglas (1515-78), his only surviving legitimate child, was the mother of Henry Stewart, Lord Darnley (q.v.), the second husband of Mary, Queen of Scots (q.v.).

Archibald Douglas, 8th Earl of Angus, 4th Earl of Morton (1555-88), called "the Good Earl", grandson of the 6th Earl. In 1577, he became warden of the western marches and next year was made lieutenant general of the kingdom. He was involved in partisanship of his uncle, James Douglas, 3rd Earl of Morton (d. 1581), who played a part in the assassinations of David Rizzio (q.v.), favorite of Mary, Queen of Scots, in 1566, and of Lord Darnley in 1567. When Morton fell from power, Douglas appealed to England to invade Scotland and rescue his imprisoned uncle, but he was instead declared guilty of high treason. In 1581, when Morton was executed, Douglas fled to England where he was welcomed by Queen Elizabeth I (q.v.). He later returned to Scotland and became reconciled to James VI of Scotland, later King of England as James I (q.v.). However, Douglas was soon banished and he joined the rebellion of John Erskine, 2nd Earl of Mar (1558?-1634). The rebels fled to Newcastle, but with Elizabeth's encouragement they invaded Scotland and secured from James the restoration of their estates.

William Douglas, 11th Earl of Angus, 1st Marquis of Douglas (1589-1660), great-great-great-grandson of the 5th Earl of Angus. He was a Roman Catholic and he fought against the Presbyterian sect, the Covenanters (q.v.), during the Great Rebellion (q.v.). After the Covenanter victory at Philiphaugh in 1645, he was imprisoned in Edinburgh Castle and released only upon signing the Covenant. His son, William

Douglas, 1st Earl of Selkirk (1635-94), became 3rd Duke of Hamilton in 1660, four years after his marriage to Anne, Duchess of Hamilton (about 1632-1716). He and succeeding dukes of Hamilton became male heirs of the main line of the House of Douglas in 1761.

Sir John Sholto Douglas, 8th Marquis of Queensberry (1844-1900), originator of the modern rules of boxing (q.v.). He served in the British navy from 1859 to 1864. In 1865 he and the British athlete John Graham Chambers (1843-83) drafted the so-called Marquis of Queensberry rules that largely govern both amateur and professional boxing today. From 1872 to 1880, Queensberry sat in the House of Lords as a representative peer from Scotland. In 1895 he was acquitted of libel after publicly objecting to the relationship between his son, Lord Alfred Douglas (1870-1945), and the Irish dramatist Oscar Wilde (q.v.). Wilde, in a separate case, was convicted of immoral conduct.

Sir Alec Douglas-Home, Baron Home of the Hirsel (1903-), born in London and educated at Eton College and Christ Church College, University of Oxford. He was a Conservative member of the House of Commons (1931-45; 1950-51; 1963-74) and a member of the House of Lords (1951-63; after 1974); in 1951 he succeeded his father as the 14th Earl of Home. He held several government posts before 1960, when he was appointed foreign secretary by Prime Minister Harold Macmillan (q.v.). Douglas-Home became prime minister on Oct. 19, 1963, and he subsequently renounced his title. The Conservatives were defeated in the elections of Oct. 15, 1964, and he resigned as prime minister. From 1970 to 1974 he was foreign secretary in the Conservative government of Prime Minister Edward Heath (q.v.). In 1974 he was created a baron and a life peer.

DOUGLAS, David (1798-1834), British botanist, born in Scone, Perth, Scotland. After working as a gardener in the Glasgow botanical gardens, he was sent to the Pacific coast of the United States as a collector for the British Royal Horticultural Society. In the course of this expedition and subsequent surveys in California, Oregon, and British Columbia, Douglas discovered more than 150 varieties of native American plants and trees, all of which he introduced into England. The name of the botanist was given to the Douglas fir and to the Douglas squirrel of northern California.

DOUGLAS, Gawin or **DOUGLAS, Gavin** (1474?-1522), Scottish poet and ecclesiastic, the son of Archibald Douglas, 5th Earl of Angus (*see under* DOUGLAS). After being educated for the priesthood at Saint Andrews University, he was made provost of Saint Giles Cathedral, Edinburgh, in 1501. From that time until 1513, he devoted himself to his ecclesiastical duties, to writing poetry, and to translating the classics. After the marriage of his nephew, Archibald Douglas, 6th Earl of Angus (*see under* DOUGLAS) to the widowed Margaret Tudor (q.v.), Queen of Scotland, in 1514, he was appointed archbishop of Saint Andrews. The chapter voted against Douglas, and the prior, who was the poet's enemy, expelled him. Pope Leo X (*see under* LEO) appointed him bishop of Dunkeld in 1515, but Douglas became involved in the political quarrels of the time, and, before he could be consecrated, he was imprisoned for a year by the regent, the Duke of Albany. In 1516 he was consecrated bishop but four years later was deprived of his see after his nephew fell out of favor with the queen. He went to London to ask Henry VIII (q.v.), King of England for aid, and died there of the plague.

The poems by Douglas include the allegories *The Palice of Honour* and *King Hart,* and *Conscience.* He is best known for his translation of the *Aeneid* (q.v.), which was the first translation of a classical work into English.

DOUGLAS, Sir James. *See* BRITISH COLUMBIA: *History.*

DOUGLAS, Lloyd Cassel (1877–1951), American clergyman and novelist, born in Columbia City, Ind., and educated at Wittenberg College, Springfield College, and Hamma Divinity School. In 1903 he was ordained a Lutheran minister and for most of the next thirty years he served as pastor of various congregations in the United States and Canada. After 1933 he devoted all his time to writing. His novels deal with the Christian themes of self-sacrifice, brotherhood, and faith. *The Robe* (1942), based on the life of the Roman soldier who received Christ's robe after the crucifixion, was a popular best seller. Among his other works are *Magnificent Obsession* (1929), *Green Light* (1935), *Disputed Passage* (1939), *The Big Fisherman* (1948), and *Time to Remember* (autobiography, 1951).

DOUGLAS, Norman (1868–1952), British writer, born in Kincardine County, Scotland, and educated in Karlsruhe, Germany. From 1894 to 1896 he served at the British Embassy in Saint Petersburg (now Leningrad), Russia. His literary reputation was established by his novel *South Wind* (1917), a tale of the cosmopolitan and unconventional inhabitants of a Mediterranean island similar to Capri, Italy, where Douglas lived. The novel is characterized by the hedonistic philosophy of the author. Other writings by Douglas include the novel *They Went* (1921); a travel book, *Old Calabria* (1928); and two autobiographical works, *Looking Back* (2 vol., 1933) and *Late Harvest* (1946).

DOUGLAS, Stephen Arnold (1813–61), American politician, born in Brandon, Vt., and educated in schools at Brandon and at Canandaigua, N.Y. He practiced law in Illinois, where he became successively public prosecutor, member of the legislature (1836), State secretary (1840), and judge of the State supreme court (1841–43). He was elected to the United States House of Representatives and served from 1843 until 1847. Douglas became an outstanding spokesman for a policy of national expansion. Because of his small stature but great ability as an orator and legislator, Douglas was soon nicknamed "the Little Giant". He advocated the annexation of Texas, supported the war with Mexico, and opposed compromise with Great Britain in the Oregon dispute (*see* OREGON: *History*). He became chairman of the Committee on Territories in the House, and when elected to the United States Senate in 1847 by the State legislature, Douglas was chosen head of the Senate Committee on Territories. In this capacity he was in charge of legislation by which Minnesota, Oregon, New Mexico, Utah, Washington, Kansas, and Nebraska were constituted as territories; and Texas, Florida, Wisconsin, Iowa, Minnesota, California, and Oregon were admitted to the Union as States. He opposed ratification of the Clayton-Bulwer Treaty (q.v.) and advocated the annexation of Cuba. With Henry Clay (q.v.), Senator from Kentucky, he was mainly responsible for the Compromise Measures of 1850 (q.v.). Douglas, however, brought about the reopening of the entire slavery question in 1854 by incorporating in the bills that established the territories of Kansas and Nebraska the principle of "popular sovereignty", which provided that the inhabitants might decide whether or not slavery should be permitted within their borders.

In 1858, while campaigning for the election of friendly candidates for the State senate to ensure his selection for a third term as U.S. Senator from Illinois, Douglas was opposed by Abraham Lincoln, (q.v.) and the two candidates met in a momentous series of debates on the slavery issue. Douglas was reelected, but the Lincoln candidates gained more popular votes, and Lincoln emerged with a national reputation. In 1860, Douglas and Lincoln were opponents for the Presidential election. Douglas had won the Democratic nomination, but Southern Democratic delegates seceded and nominated the incumbent Vice President, John Cabell Breckinridge (q.v.), for the Presidency, thus splitting the party vote. Douglas lost the election, winning 12 electoral and 1,375,157 popular votes to 180 electoral and 1,866,352 popular votes for Lincoln. When the American Civil War broke out, Douglas gave Lincoln loyal support. Douglas contracted typhoid fever while on a mission in the midwestern and border States to rally popular backing for the Union cause, and died in Chicago on June 3, 1861.

DOUGLAS, William Orville (1898–), American jurist, born in Maine, Minn., and educated at Whitman College and Columbia University. Admitted to the New York State bar in 1926, Douglas taught law at Columbia and Yale universities until 1934. From 1934 to 1939 he served on various Federal regulatory commissions. In 1939 he was nominated by President Franklin Delano Roosevelt (q.v.) to be an associate justice of the Supreme Court of the United States (q.v.). He retired in 1975, having served on the Court longer than any other justice. A liberal on social and economic questions and an internationalist and champion of civil rights, Douglas was drawn into many public controversies.

The Court opinions that show his basic attitudes most explicitly include his supporting (1962) the Supreme Court ban on prayers in public schools; defining (1965) the right of privacy as implied in the Constitution of the United States (q.v.); dissenting (1968) from a majority opinion upholding a Federal statute making the burning of a draft card a crime; and explaining (1970) his lone dissent from an opinion upholding a New York State statute exempting church-owned property from real estate taxes. In 1970 a resolution was offered in the United States House of Representatives calling for an investigation preliminary to impeachment (q.v.) of Douglas, alleging conflict of interest and promoting rebellion through his writings, citing in particular *Points of Rebellion* (1970). The more than thirty books written by Douglas, reflecting his interest in such divergent subjects as world affairs, conservation, and mountain climbing, include *Of Men and Mountains* (1950), *The Bible and the Schools* (1966), and *Towards a Global Federalism* (1968).

DOUGLAS FIR, common name of a species of large coniferous tree, *Pseudotsuga taxifolia* or *menziesii,* belonging to the Pine family Pinaceae and named for David Douglas (q.v.). It is sometimes called Douglas spruce, but is not closely related to either the firs or the spruces. The Douglas fir sometimes reaches a height of 250 ft., and commonly grows to 200 ft. in height

Douglas fir, Pseudotsuga taxifolia   NATURE Magazine

and 6 ft. in diameter. It is the most important timber tree of the western United States and British Columbia, and is particularly abundant in the States of Oregon and Washington. Douglas fir lumber, usually known as Oregon pine or yellow fir, amounts annually to about one fourth of all the lumber produced in the U.S. The saplings are popular as Christmas trees.

DOUGLASS, Frederick, assumed name of FREDERICK AUGUSTUS WASHINGTON BAILEY (1817?–95), American abolitionist orator and writer, born in Tuckahoe, Md. He was the son of a slave, Harriet Bailey (d. 1824?), and was largely self-educated. Poor treatment instilled in him a hatred of slavery; he failed in an attempt to escape in 1836 but two years later he succeeded and reached New Bedford, Mass., where he assumed the name of Douglass.

His career as an abolitionist (*see* ABOLITION-ISTS) began dramatically in 1841 at an antislavery convention in Nantucket, Mass., where his impromptu address to the convention revealed him to be an orator of great eloquence. As "a recent graduate from the institution of slavery with his diploma on his back", he was forthwith engaged as an agent of the Massachusetts Anti-Slavery Society. His speeches in the following years in the northern States and his work for the Underground Railroad (q.v.) did much to further the cause of the abolitionists and made his name a symbol of freedom and achievement among the Whites and Negroes.

In 1845, Douglass, at the urging of his friends, went to England to escape the danger of seizure under the fugitive slave laws. His lectures in the British Isles on the slavery question in the United States aroused sympathy for the abolitionists' cause and prompted his admirers to raise funds to purchase his freedom. After returning to the United States in 1847, Douglass became the "station-master and conductor" of the Underground Railroad in Rochester, N.Y., where he also established the abolitionist newspaper *North Star,* which he edited until 1860.

During these years he became friendly with the American abolitionist John Brown (q.v.), and was given a hint of Brown's strategy of destroying "the money value of slave property" by

Frederick Douglass

training a force of men to help large numbers of slaves escape to freedom in the North via the Underground Railroad. In 1859, however, when Douglass learned, on the eve of the raid on Harpers Ferry, that it was Brown's intention to seize the Federal arsenal there, he objected on the ground that an attack on the arsenal would be tantamount to an assault on the U.S. government and would prove disastrous, and withdrew from further participation.

After the raid, fearing reprisals by the government, Douglass fled to Europe, where he stayed for six months. On his return to the U.S., he campaigned for Abraham Lincoln during the Presidential election of 1860 and, following the outbreak of the American Civil War, helped raise two regiments of Negro soldiers, the Massachusetts 54th and 55th. After the war, Douglass, as a recognized leader of and spokesman for the former Negro slaves, fought for enactment of the 13th, 14th, and 15th Amendments to the Constitution of the United States (q.v.). He became U.S. marshal for the District of Columbia (1877–81), recorder of deeds for the District of Columbia (1881–86), and U.S. minister to the Republic of Haiti (1889–91).

So impressive were Douglass' oratorical and intellectual abilities that opponents refused to believe he had been a slave and alleged that he was an impostor foisted on the public by the Abolitionists. In reply, Douglass wrote *Narrative of the Life of Frederick Douglass, An American Slave* (1845), which he revised in later years; in final form, it appeared in 1882 under the title *Life and Times of Frederick Douglass.* B.Q.

DOUKHOBORS or DUKHOBORS (Russ. *dukhobortsy,* "spirit wrestlers"), name applied to a nonconformist sect of Russian peasantry. They were so called as early as 1785 by the priests of the Russian Orthodox Church (*see* ORTHODOX CHURCH), who gave the sect the name disparagingly as fighters against the spirit of God. The Doukhobors were content for a considerable time to accept the term at its literal significance and use it as their name, but eventually they decided to call themselves "Christians of the Universal Brotherhood". Basing their belief on the premise that all human beings are brothers and equals, they refused to acknowledge any worldly ruler or to participate in military service, and, in consequence, were banished in 1840 to the Caucasus. They built this sterile land into a flourishing community, but in 1887 Alexander III (q.v.), Emperor of Russia, introduced universal conscription into the Caucasus and Doukhobors were subjected to violent persecution. Their sufferings were eventually alleviated through the efforts of the Russian writer Count Lev Mikolaevich Tolstoi (q.v.) and of the Society of Friends (*see* FRIENDS, SOCIETY OF) in England, and in 1898 they were permitted to emigrate to British territory. In the summer of that year, 1126 members of the sect sailed for Cyprus, where the community intended to settle. Sufficient money later became available, however, to take two other parties, totaling over 4000, to Canada in January, 1899; these were eventually joined by the Cyprus party, and by about 2000 other Doukhobors from the Caucasus, totaling in all some 7500 members of the sect. The Canadian government granted them territory in what is now Saskatchewan Province, and in 1902 they were joined by their leader, Peter Vasilivich Verigin (1858–1924), who had just been released from exile in Siberia. Except for some disagreements with the Canadian government, occasioned from time to time by the Doukhobor refusal to accept any authority but that of their leader, or of his son and successor Peter Verigin (d. 1939), the sect has lived peacefully and has developed flourishing communities in Canada. In recent years, Doukhobor colonies have settled in Mexico and in various parts of the Soviet Union.

DOUMA. *See* DUMA.

DOUMERGUE, Gaston (1863–1937), French statesman and twelfth president of the Third French Republic. *See* FRANCE: *History: Post-World War I.*

DOURO (Port. *Douro*; Sp. *Duero*; anc. *Durius*), river of the Iberian Peninsula. It rises in Soria Province, N. central Spain, and empties, after a course of 556 mi., into the Atlantic Ocean 2 miles S. of Oporto, Portugal. The general course is westward to the boundary of Spain and Portugal, then southwestward, delimiting the boundary for about 60 mi., and finally again westward, across Portugal to its mouth. Navigation on the river is possible in Portugal but is hampered by rapids and by occasional floods in the lower reaches; sandbars at the mouth permit only shallow-draft vessels to enter. Of greater economic importance than navigation are the Douro irrigation projects in Spain and the expanding development of the hydroelectric potential of the river in Portugal. At Leixões, the port for Oporto N. of the mouth of the Douro, a harbor accommodating seagoing vessels has been constructed. The river yields fish and serves as a means of transportation to market for the port and other wines of the Paiz do Vinho region of Portugal.

DOVE, common name for any bird of the family Columbidae, usually restricted to the smaller varieties. The turtledove, *Streptopelia turtur*, common to Europe and Asia, but not found in North America, was sacred to the ancient Israelites and most Mediterranean peoples. The dove, which became a Christian symbol of simplicity and gentleness, is now commonly used as a symbol of peace.

Several species of doves are native to North America, and doves are common in all parts of the United States. The mourning dove, *Zenaidura macroura*, the most common variety in the U.S., appears in rural areas and is named for its call, which is low and plaintive. It is about 12 in. long, with a brown body and bluish gray wings. Its white-tipped, short outer tail is banded with black. The Inca dove, *Scardafella inca*, with scaled brown and black plumage and grayish pink breast; the ground dove, *Columbigallina passerina*; and the white-winged dove, *Melopelia asiatica*, are native to the extreme southern States of the U.S. *See* PIGEON.

DOVER, city and capital of the State of Delaware, and county seat of Kent Co., in the central part of the State, on the Saint Jones R., about 50 miles S. of Wilmington. The city is the commercial center of a rich agricultural region noted for its apples, peaches, grapes, strawberries, dairying, and poultry. Dover produces canned and dried fruits, gelatin, flour, rubber products, automobile bodies, mattresses, wood products, hosiery, and plumbing and electrical equipment. The State House, constructed between 1787 and 1793, is the second-oldest State capitol still in use in the United States. Among other noteworthy buildings in Dover are Christ Church, built in 1734; the old Presbyterian Church, erected in 1791 and now housing the Delaware State Museum; and the home of Caesar Rodney (q.v.), a signer of the Declaration of

Mourning dove, Zenaidura macroura
Allan D. Cruikshank — National Audubon Society

Independence. Delaware State College (1891) and Wesley College (junior college, 1873) are located in the city. A World War II air base situated to the E. of Dover became a Military Air Transport Service terminal in 1952. Dover was established, by order of William Penn (q.v.), in 1717. In 1777 Dover became the capital of the State of Delaware, replacing New Castle. Dover was incorporated as a town in 1829 and as a city in 1929. Pop. (1960) 7250; (1970) 17,488.

DOVER, city in New Hampshire, and county seat of Strafford Co., 10 miles N.W. of Portsmouth. Dover is on the Cocheco R., which at that point has a fall of more than 30 ft., furnishing excellent waterpower. The city is the eastern gateway to the White Mts. The chief industries are the manufacture of textiles, boats, motors and blowers, printing presses, cash registers, shoes, and of wood, rubber, leather, steel, chemical, and electronic products. Historical buildings in the city include the county courthouse (1789), Wentworth Manor (1652), and a hand-hewn log fort (1675). The last-named is contained in the Woodman Institute, a museum of history and natural science. The municipal building, dedicated in 1935, is one of the largest in New England, N. of Boston. Durham, 5 miles S.W. of Dover, is the site of the University of New Hampshire.

Dover was one of the first settlements in what is now New Hampshire. Founded in 1623, it was successively called Piscataqua, Bristol, and Northam, receiving its present name in 1639. The early settlers suffered frequently from Indian attacks, the most notable of which was the Cocheco Massacre of 1689. Dover was chartered as a city in 1855. Pop. (1960) 19,131; (1970) 20,850.

DOVER, town of New Jersey, in Morris Co., about 20 miles W. of Paterson. It was settled in 1722 as the center of an iron-mining district. Manufactures include machinery, wood and metal products, and sportswear. Nearby is the Picatinny Arsenal, a rocket-research center. Dover was incorporated as a village in 1826, a town in 1869, and a city in 1896. Pop. (1960) 13,034; (1970) 15,039.

DOVER, Great Britain, seaport and municipal borough of Kent County, England, on the Strait of Dover, at the mouth of the Dour R., about 75 miles S.E. of London. It is the point on the English coast nearest to France, 21 mi. distant. Dover has an excellent harbor, through which passes a great volume of freight and passenger traffic to and from Calais and Dunkirk, France, and Ostend, Belgium. Industries include the manufacture of paper, flour, and iron castings.

On the east height of the Dover chalk cliffs, 375 ft. above sea level, is Dover Castle, one of the largest and most notable examples of medieval fortification in existence as an intact unit. The castle, which has been altered at various times in accordance with changing military requirements, is said to predate the invasion led by the Roman statesman and general Gaius Julius Caesar (q.v.) in 55 B.C. It contains the remains, almost intact, of a Roman lighthouse and of the ancient fortress-church Saint Mary in Castro, a unique specimen of Roman-British architecture. On the citadel heights, north of the castle, is a restored circular church of the Knights Templars. In the High Street of the town are the central hall and other remnants of the Maison Dieu founded in the 13th century by the English statesman Hubert de Burgh (q.v.), as a hospice for pilgrims from all lands. The Dover museum (1849) contains many historical relics. Outside the town hall hangs a bell taken from Antwerp, Belgium, by the Germans during World War I and used as an air-raid warning at Zeebrugge, Belgium; it was later presented to Dover by the Belgians.

History. Dover was an important port in Roman times, when it was called Dubris. During the Middle Ages, it was one of the Cinque Ports (q.v.); and Dover Castle was frequently besieged in civil wars and attempted invasions because the town was regarded as the key to England.

In World War I, Dover was subjected to German attacks by submarines and aircraft in 1914, and was bombed frequently in 1916. In 1917–18, attempts were made by sea and air to damage the harbor, which served as the base for the flotilla known as the Dover Patrol. The patrol not only safeguarded English and Allied traffic in the Strait of Dover but also prevented the passage of German submarines from the North Sea to the English Channel by maintaining a barrier of moored mines across the 21-mi.-wide strait. The monitors and siege-gun units of the patrol provided the main artillery support for the left flank of the British army in Flanders. The patrol also attacked the German submarine base at Zeebrugge, Belgium, on April 23, 1918, and sank ships in the harbor to block German traffic. The exploits of the Dover Patrol are commemorated by memorials at Dover and at Cape Gris-Nez, France; and a memorial, provided by popular subscription in England, has been erected at Fort Hamilton, Brooklyn, overlooking the New York City harbor.

During World War II, Dover was repeatedly subject to German air raids and to shelling by German guns entrenched at Cape Gris-Nez.

More than 1200 buildings were damaged or destroyed. Pop. (1971 prelim.) 34,322.

DOVER, STRAIT OF, strait separating England from France and the European continent, and connecting the English Channel (q.v.) and the Atlantic Ocean with the North Sea. The limits of the strait on the English coast are defined as the promontories of Dungeness and South Foreland; on the French coast, as those of Cape Gris-Nez and Calais. The strait is known to the French as *Pas de Calais*. It is about 21 mi. wide and 6 to 162 ft. deep. Near the center of the strait are the Ridge Shoals, more than 8 mi. long, where the depth is 10 to 24 ft. Both the English and French shores are formed by chalk cliffs; their corresponding strata show that in prehistoric times a land connection existed at that point. The strait is one of the busiest maritime routes in the world. Frequent proposals have been made in the 20th century to construct a tunnel under the strait; preliminary work on a joint Anglo-French tunnel project was begun in 1974, but was discontinued in 1975.

DOW, Gerard. *See* DOU, GERARD.

DOW, Herbert Henry (1866–1930), American chemist, born in Belleville, Ontario Province, Canada, and educated at the Case School of Applied Science (now Case Institute of Technology). In 1889 he founded the Midland Chemical Company in Michigan. Later, he founded the Dow Process Company and the Dow Chemical Company, serving as president and general manager of the latter until his death. He developed more than 100 new chemical processes, including methods of extracting bromine, magnesium, and iodine (qq.v.) from brine. Virtually all of the world supply of metallic magnesium is produced by a Dow process. Dow also developed the lightweight alloy Dowmetal and produced the first synthetic indigo dye in the United States. During World War I, Dow was a member of the advisory committee of the Council of National Defense. In 1930 he was awarded the Perkin Medal by the Society of Chemical Industry.

DOWDEN, Edward (1843–1913), Irish critic, poet, and educator, born in Cork, and educated at Trinity College, Dublin. He was professor of English literature at Trinity from 1868 until his death, but lectured extensively elsewhere, notably at the University of Oxford in 1889, at Trinity College, University of Cambridge, from 1893 to 1896, and at Princeton University in 1896. He is best known for his work as a Shakespearean critic. The publication of his *Shakespeare, His Mind and Art* (1875) gave him a wide academic reputation, and he later became noted as well

for his studies of 19th-century poets. His work includes *Studies in Literature* (1878), *Life of Shelley* (1886), *Introduction to Shakespeare* (1893), and *Essays: Modern and Elizabethan* (1910). His *Collected Poetical Works* (2 vol.) and *Letters* appeared in 1914.

DOWER, in law, the common-law right of a widow to a one-third interest for life in the real estate of her deceased husband. Dower applies only in those cases in which the husband was possessed of an inheritable estate at any time during the marriage, which any issue she might have had could inherit. The law of the place, where the property (q.v.) is located, governs the right of dower. Dower still exists in many States of the United States, usually by statutes that have modified the rules that applied under the old English common law. It has been abolished in New York and in a number of other States.

Dower should not be confused with dowry (q.v.).

DOWIE, John Alexander (1847–1907), religious leader, born in Edinburgh, Scotland, and educated at the University of Edinburgh. He studied for the Congregationalist ministry and, after he was ordained, became pastor of a church in Alma, South Australia. Believing that he could cure disease by prayer, he went to Melbourne and established there the Divine Healing Association of Australia and New Zealand. In 1888 he came to the United States, where he attracted many followers. In 1896 he organized the Christian Catholic Church in Zion. Dowie proclaimed himself Elijah the Restorer in 1901 and, using money contributed by his followers, bought a tract of land in Illinois 42 miles N. of Chicago on the western shore of Lake Michigan. On this land he founded Zion City, later renamed Zion, a town populated entirely by supporters of Dowie, who ruled almost as a dictator. Branches of the Christian Catholic Church in Zion were established in many countries. In 1903 Dowie was ridiculed in New York City when he led his "hosts" there to regenerate the city, and he was attacked by a mob in London a year later. In 1906 the inhabitants of Zion City deposed him on charges of fraud, tyranny, and polygamy.

DOWITCHER, bird, *Limnodromus griseus,* of the Sandpiper (q.v.) family. Although it is not a snipe, it is commonly called the long-billed snipe or red-breasted snipe. Its plumage is gray in the winter and brown in the summer. The bill is from 2 to 2½ in. long, and the overall length of the bird varies from 10 to 12 in. The dowitcher occurs from the Arctic coast of North America to Alaska and northwestern Canada in

A shepherd and his flock cross a rustic stone bridge in hilly County Down, Northern Ireland. British Travel Association

the summer, and from Florida and Mexico to northern South America in the winter.

DOWLAND, John. *See* ENGLISH MUSIC: *Italian Influence.*

DOWN, Great Britain, easternmost county of Northern Ireland. The coastline, on the Irish Sea, is low, rocky, and indented by many bays. The greater part of Down consists of low hills and many bogs, though the Mourne Mts., in the south, rise to 2796 ft. above sea level at the peak Slieve Donard. The county is drained by the Lagan R. in the N. and by the Bann R. and the Newry R. in the W. The principal crops grown in the rocky loam soil are oats, potatoes, and turnips. The growing of flax, once important in the county, has been practically abandoned. Hogs, sheep, and poultry are raised; and the county is noted for the breeding of racehorses. Manufactures in County Down include electrical products, aircraft parts, linens, woolens, raincoats, shoes, thread, and leather goods. The county contains megalithic monuments (q.v.), early Christian ruins associated with Saint Patrick (q.v.), and remains of castles built by Norman invaders between the 12th and 14th centuries. Downpatrick is the county seat and Bangor is the largest town. Area, 951 sq.mi.; pop. (1971 prelim.) 310,617.

DOWNERS GROVE, suburban residential village of Illinois, in Du Page Co., about 25 miles S.W. of Chicago. Downers Grove manufactures tools, typewriters, food products, furniture, chemicals, machinery, industrial and electrical equipment, and metal, rubber, and plastic products. The surrounding area has dairy, poultry, and truck farms and plant nurseries. The Morton Arboretum is nearby. Settled in 1832, the village was incorporated in 1873. Pop. (1970) 32,751.

DOWNEY, industrial suburban city of California, in Los Angeles Co., between the San Gabriel R. and the Rio Hondo Channel of the Los Angeles R., 10 miles S.E. of downtown Los Angeles. Downey is in an area of truck farms and citrus-fruit orchards. Manufactures include aircraft and missiles, machinery, wire, electronic equipment, asbestos, rubber, chemicals, truck bodies, and plastic, metal, glass, and wood products. John Q. Downey, governor of California from 1860 to 1862, subdivided the area in 1864, and his name was given to the community in 1873. The city was incorporated in 1956. Pop. (1960) 82,505; (1970) 88,445.

DOWNING STREET, street in the West End of London, England. It was named in honor of Sir George Downing (1623–84), secretary of the treasury in 1667. The official residence of the British prime minister, where cabinet meetings are often held, is located at No. 10. Also on Downing Street are the residence of the chancellor of the exchequer and both the Foreign Office and the Colonial Office. The term "Downing Street" is frequently used as a synonym for the British government.

DOWNS, term generally applied to hillocks of sand thrown up by the sea or wind along the shore of a sea or other body of water; and also a general name for any undulating tract of upland too light in soil for cultivation but covered with grass fit for grazing sheep. Specifically, the term is applied to the system of undulating chalk hills in England, S. of the Thames R., of which the best known are the North Downs, in Surrey and Kent counties, and the South Downs, in Sussex County. Both ridges extend from a series of hills, the Western Downs, in the chalk area of Dorsetshire and Hampshire. The North Downs, reaching from Farnham to the English Channel between Dover and Folkestone, are 95 mi. long, and are broken by a series of deep gaps made by streams. The South Downs, from Petersfield to the Channel at Beachy Head in E. Sussex, are 65 mi. long and also are breached by the courses of streams. The highest point of the North Downs is Leith Hill, 965 ft. above sea level; that of the South Downs, Butser Hill, 889 ft. above sea level. Smooth, rolling lines are characteristic of the Downs. The sides of the hills are wooded; the uplands are covered with good grazing sod for sheep. The English Downs enclose a once thickly wooded district called the Weald.

The Downs is also the name of a nearby roadstead in S.E. Kent, 9 mi. long and 6 mi. wide, where the Goodwin Sands (q.v.) form a natural breakwater.

DOWN'S SYNDROME. See MONGOLISM.

DOWRY, property (q.v.) which the wife brings to the husband as her marriage portion. Although recognized in common law (q.v.), and often forming an important element in the arrangement known as a marriage settlement in Great Britain, it is almost unknown in the United States. In most countries that have adopted the system of the civil law (q.v.), it constitutes a distinct and important form of property. It is given to the husband, who has exclusive control and administration of it during marriage, to be employed in defraying the expenses of the family. The wife may not deprive the husband of its control, and he, on the other hand, is bound not to alienate real estate which comes to him as dowry. See also DOWER.

DOWSON, Ernest Christopher (1867-1900), British writer, born in Kent, England. He was a prominent member of the Aesthetic Movement, a group of British poets and painters of the 1890's, formed as a reaction against Victorianism. He wrote polished, delicate lyrics, of which the most famous is *"Non sum qualis eram bonæ sub regno Cynaræ"*, better known by its refrain, "I have been faithful to thee, Cynara, in my fashion". Among his other works are two novels written in collaboration with the British novelist Arthur Collin Moore (1866-1952), *A Comedy of Masks* (1893) and *Adrian Rome* (1899).

DOXIADIS, Constantinos A(postolos), (1913-75), innovative Greek architect, urban planner, and engineer who developed the science of ekistics (Gr. *oikos*, "house"), a multidisciplinary study of human habitation that analyzes the present and future needs of the modern city (or other community) to create within it a more humane environment.

Doxiadis was born in Stenimachos, Bulgaria,

on May 14, 1913, but was taken by his family to Greece at the outset of World War I. Raised in Athens, he received a degree in architecture there, at the National Metsovion Technical University in 1935; he later earned a doctorate in civil engineering (1937) at the Berlin-Charlottenburg Technical University in Germany. Returning to Greece, Doxiadis served as chief of regional and town planning (1939-44), and was also active in the antifascist underground. After the war he was named minister of development and helped to formulate United Nations housing policies in Geneva. He handled all American Marshall Plan aid to Greece, supervising the reconstruction of thousands of villages. In 1953 he founded Doxiadis Associates, an engineering firm that undertook large-scale planning and building projects in Pakistan, Iraq, Syria, the Sudan, the United States, and many other countries. Doxiadis died June 28, 1975, in Athens. His writings include *Ekistic Analysis* (1946) and *Urban Renewal and the Future of the American City* (1966).

DOXOLOGY (Gr. *doxa*, "glory, opinion"; *logia*, "logy"), hymn offering praise to God. Doxologies are found in the Bible in Rom. 16:27, Eph. 3:21, and Jude 25; these verses are known as Biblical doxologies. The "lesser" and "greater" doxologies are two responsive forms that originated in the 4th century and are now used in the liturgies of the Roman Catholic Church, the Church of England, and some other churches. The lesser doxology is named *Gloria Patri:* "Glory be to the Father, and to the Son, and to the Holy Ghost; as it was in the beginning, is now, and ever shall be, world without end. Amen". The greater doxology, *Gloria in excelsis Deo,* is an early Church expansion of the song of the angels in Luke 2:14: "Glory to God in the highest, and on earth peace, good will to men". In the Roman Catholic Church, the lesser doxology is recited in all responsories of the breviary (q.v.) and Romans and Anglicans use it at the end of all but two psalms and canticles, the *Te Deum* and the *Benedicite.* It is omitted in seasons of mourning and in requiem Masses. The greater doxology is used in the Roman Catholic Mass, except during Advent and Lent (qq.v.) and in certain Masses throughout the year. In the liturgy of the Church of England, the lesser doxology occurs at the end of psalms and canticles, and the greater doxology is used in certain seasons in the communion service. A special doxology, which is known as the *Trinitarian,* concludes the canon of the Mass by emphasizing Christ's mediatorship: "Through Him, with Him, in Him, in the unity of the Holy Spirit, all glory and honor is yours, almighty Father, for ever and ever". The greater, lesser, and Trinitarian doxologies are called liturgical doxologies.

The last stanza of a hymn by the English bishop Thomas Ken (1637–1711), beginning "Praise God from Whom all blessings flow", is commonly called "The Doxology" in Protestant churches.

See also HYMN; LITURGY.

DOYLE, Sir Arthur Conan (1859–1930), British physician, novelist, and detective-story writer, born in Edinburgh, and educated at Stonyhurst College and the University of Edinburgh. From 1882 to 1890 he practiced medicine in Southsea, England. *A Study in Scarlet,* the first of sixty-eight stories featuring his famous fictional detective, Sherlock Holmes, appeared in 1887. Doyle was so speedily successful in his literary career that about five years later he abandoned his medical practice to devote his entire time to writing.

The Holmes stories, of which some of the best known are *The Sign of Four* (1890), *The Adventures of Sherlock Holmes* (1892), *The Hound of the Baskervilles* (1902), and *His Last Bow* (1917), made Doyle internationally famous; *see* MYSTERY STORY. His remarkable literary versatility brought him almost equal fame for his historical romances, such as *Micah Clarke* (1888), *The White Company* (1890), *Rodney Stone* (1896) and *Sir Nigel* (1906).

He served in the South African War as a physician, and on his return to England wrote *The Great Boer War* (1900) and *The War in South Africa: Its Causes and Conduct* (1902), for which he was knighted in 1902. During World War I (q.v.), he wrote *History of the British Campaign in France and Flanders* (6 vol., 1916–20) as a tribute to British bravery.

After the death of his eldest son in the war, he became an advocate of spiritualism (q.v.) and toured Australia, Africa, and the United States in the interest of his new belief. During the last part of his life, he wrote extensively on spiritualism, including such books as *History of Spiritualism* (2 vols., 1926). Among his other works are poems and plays. His autobiography, *Memories and Adventures,* was published in 1924. *See also* PSYCHICAL RESEARCH.

Another of his sons, Adrian Conan Doyle (1910–70), was renowned as a big game hunter, fisherman, zoologist, and writer. He collected and reprinted original Sherlock Holmes manuscripts written by his father and in 1954 published *The Exploits of Sherlock Holmes,* twelve new Holmes stories drawn from previously published works.

Sir Arthur Conan Doyle

D'OYLY CARTE, Richard (1844–1901), British operatic impresario, born in London, England. At the age of seventeen he left school to enter his father's business of music publishing and the making of musical instruments, and to study music. He opened a concert agency in 1870, acting as manager for singers and for lecturers such as the American explorer Sir Henry Morton Stanley, and the Irish playwright Oscar Fingal O'Flahertie Wills Wilde (qq.v.). In the early 1870's D'Oyly Carte began to produce light operas, introducing into England two productions by French composers, *Whittington* by Jacques Offenbach (q.v.) and *Giroflé-Girofla* by Alexandre Charles Lecocq (1832–1918). D'Oyly Carte soon became interested in promoting English light opera and, in 1875, produced *Trial by Jury,* an operetta with libretto by William Schwenck Gilbert and music by Sir Arthur Seymour Sullivan (qq.v.). In 1879 in New York City, D'Oyly Carte introduced a new comic opera, *The Pirates of Penzance,* also by Gilbert and Sullivan, which was produced in London the following year. From 1881 to 1896 he produced their operettas at the Savoy Theatre, which was built especially for that purpose and was the first theater in the world to be lighted by electricity. The Savoy Theatre under D'Oyly Carte was noted for its high standards of acting and production and D'Oyly Carte is credited with having improved

139

standards of performance in the English theater of his time.

After D'Oyly Carte's death, his second wife, Helen Lenoir D'Oyly Carte (d. 1913), directed the D'Oyly Carte Opera Company; after her death, his son Rupert D'Oyly Carte (1876–1948) managed the company; Rupert was succeeded by D'Oyly Carte's granddaughter, Bridget D'Oyly Carte (1908–   ). The company has made numerous appearances in the United States and has retained the traditional style of performing Gilbert and Sullivan operettas.

DRACO (Lat., "dragon"), circumpolar constellation situated in the northern celestial hemisphere between the Big Dipper and Little Dipper, just below the celestial pole. The star Etamin or γ Draconis, a second-magnitude star and the brightest in the constellation, was the principal object of measurement used by the British astronomer James Bradley (q.v.) in 1729 in discovering the aberration of light.

DRAFT. See CONSCRIPTION; SELECTIVE SERVICE.

DRAFT, written order for the payment of money drawn by one person, directing a second person or financial institution to pay a third person. A draft is called a check when it is drawn on a bank. When a transfer of money is made between institutions in different countries, a draft is called a bill of exchange (q.v.). A draft is payable on sight or on demand; however, in some business transactions drafts are often payable at a stated date in the future.

See also BANKS AND BANKING; NEGOTIABLE INSTRUMENTS.

DRAFTING. See MECHANICAL DRAWING.

DRAFT RIOTS, in United States history, mob violence incited in New York City from July 13 to July 16, 1863, during the Civil War (see CIVIL WAR, THE AMERICAN), by opponents of conscription (q.v.) and individuals sympathetic to the Confederate cause. Because of the traditional hostility of the American people to compulsory military service, the Federal government had relied, during the early stages of the war, on voluntary enlistment to obtain recruits for the Union armies. The pressing need for more soldiers compelled Congress to pass (March 3, 1863) legislation, known as the Enrollment Act, which imposed liability for military duty on virtually all able-bodied males between twenty and forty-five years of age. Opponents of the administration and policies of President Abraham Lincoln (q.v.) vigorously attacked the bill, criticizing with particular emphasis a provision which enabled draftees to obtain exemption from service by supplying a substitute or by the payment of $300. As the date for enforcement of

the act approached, dissatisfaction with this provision, called "The Rich Man's Exemption", became widespread among the poor of New York City, especially those who had emigrated from Ireland.

Although no disturbances occurred on Saturday, July 11, when the draft came into effect, its resumption on the following Monday was marked by the rapid gathering of an unruly crowd, which soon attacked and burned the draft headquarters. The crowd kept fire apparatus from the building, and flames shortly spread to the entire block. Attempts by the New York City police and a small detachment of United States Marines to disperse the rioters provoked the mob to intensified violence. The rioters, joined by additional thousands of sympathizers, roamed freely through the city, destroying property and committing other outrages. These were directed especially against Negro citizens, who, in the opinion of the mob, were responsible for the Civil War. Many were lynched, and on Monday afternoon the rioters sacked and burned the Colored Orphan Asylum, a charitable institution housing nearly 800 Negro children.

The rioting subsided late Monday night but was resumed with even greater violence on Tuesday, July 14. Police, aided by small detachments of troops stationed in and near the city, made vain attempts to disperse the mobs. More Negroes were murdered, Negro neighborhoods were burned, and general pillaging took place. Unrestrained rioting continued until July 15, when military detachments reached the city from Pennsylvania and from West Point, N.Y. Temporary suspension of the draft was announced the same day. By Thursday, July 16, law and order had been restored. Estimated fatalities during the three days of violence totaled more than 1000. More than fifty large buildings were destroyed by fire, and property damage approximated $2,000,000.

DRAGO, Luis María (1859–1921), Argentine jurist, statesman, and writer, born in Buenos Aires. He was trained as a lawyer. In 1902–03, he was foreign minister of Argentina and later became a member of the Permanent Court of Arbitration at The Hague, Netherlands. Drago is famous mainly because of his support of the principle of international law known as the Drago Doctrine. In 1902, Great Britain, Germany, and Italy sent armed naval units to blockade several Venezuelan ports because the government of Venezuela had refused to pay claims arising from international loans. Drago, in a note to the United States Department of State, enunciated the doctrine that public indebted-

Japanese gilded-wood helmet crest in the shape of a dragon, dating from the 19th century.
Metropolitan Museum of Art – Bequest of George C. Stone

ness in the form of bonds, owed by a sovereign American state to citizens of a European state, must not be collected by armed intervention of the European state on American territory. He desired this principle to be accepted as a corollary to the Monroe Doctrine (q.v.).

The Drago Doctrine was proposed to the Hague Conference of 1907 (see HAGUE CONFERENCES), at which the nations represented accepted it in a modified form. They agreed that the government of one nation shall not use armed force to recover debts due from the government of another nation until after the case has been submitted to international arbitration and the debtor nation has obstructed the formulation of a compromise or has failed to implement an adverse decision.

DRAGON, in mythology, a reptilic monster similar in form to a crocodile and usually represented as having wings, huge claws, and a fiery breath. In some folklore of antiquity, the dragon symbolizes destruction and evil. This conception is found, for example, in the creation epic of Babylonia (see CREATION EPIC, BABYLONIAN). One of the central figures of the legend is the goddess Tiamat, a dragonlike personification of the oceans, who headed the hordes of chaos and whose destruction was prerequisite to an orderly universe. In the sacred writings of the ancient Hebrews, the dragon frequently repre-

sents death and evil. Christianity inherited the Hebraic conception of the dragon, which figures in all the important apocalyptic literature of the Bible, notably in Revelation, and appears in later Christian traditions (see GEORGE, SAINT). In Christian art, the dragon is a symbol of sin. It is often represented as crushed under the feet of saints and martyrs, symbolizing the triumph of Christianity over paganism.

In certain mythologies, the dragon is more generally credited with beneficent powers. The ancient Greeks and Romans believed that dragons had the ability to understand and to convey to man the secrets of the earth. Partially as a result of this conception of the monster as a benign, protective influence, and partially because of its fearsome qualities, it was employed as a military emblem. The Roman legions adopted it in the first century A.D., inscribing the figure of a dragon on the standards carried into battle by the cohorts. The folklore of the pagan tribes of northern Europe contained both beneficent and terror-inspiring dragons. In the *Nibelungenlied* (q.v.), Siegfried kills a dragon, and one of the principal episodes of *Beowulf* (q.v.) deals with a similar achievement. The ancient Norsemen adorned the prows of their vessels with carved likenesses of dragons. Among the Celtic conquerors of Britain the dragon was a symbol of sovereignty. The legendary monster was also depicted on the shields of the Teutonic tribes that later invaded Britain, and it appeared on the battle standards of the English kings as late as the 16th century. Beginning in the early 20th century, it was inscribed on the armorial bearings of the Prince of Wales.

The dragon also figures in the mythology of various Oriental countries, notably Japan and China. It is deified in the Taoist religion, and was the national emblem of the Chinese Empire. Among the Chinese people, the dragon is traditionally regarded as a symbol of good fortune.

DRAGONET, common name for marine fish of the genus *Callionymus*, especially *C. draco,* inhabiting the temperate coasts of Europe and the tropical seas of the Orient. Dragonets are usually classified in the same family with the gobies, but some authorities give them separate family rank. Their tiny gill openings are located close together near the back of the head. Dragonets have no air bladder. The sexes vary greatly in appearance: the females are dull in color, and the males are brilliantly colored, especially during the mating season. Dragonets reach a length of 12 in. Small shellfish form the bulk of their diet. The name "dragonfish" is sometimes applied to the dragonet.

DRAGONFISH, fish of the genus *Pterois,* inhabiting Oriental and Australian seas. It is covered with bony plates, movable except near the tail, and has large, fanlike, pectoral fins. It has prominent eyes, and a greatly prolonged, toothless snout. *Pterois volitans,* which grows to a length of 10 in., is frequently seen dried as a curiosity, and is sometimes depicted on ornamental boxes made in China. The dragonet (q.v.) is also sometimes called dragonfish.

DRAGONFLY, common name of any predaceous insect of the order Odonata. This order is usually divided into two principal suborders: the Zygoptera, or damselflies, which hold the wings above the body when resting; and the Anisoptera, the true dragonflies, which hold the wings spread when resting. Members of both suborders have large heads with very large and sensitive compound eyes and relatively short antennae. They have mouths adapted for biting and two nearly equal pairs of elongated membranous wings. The abdomen is relatively very long. The legs are located far forward on the body and are seldom used for walking. The damselflies are generally smaller and weaker in flight than the true dragonflies. Both types are known by a number of popular names such as

darning needle, devil's darning needle, snake feeder, snake doctor, and mosquito hawk.

The dragonflies undergo incomplete metamorphosis during their development. Some species simply drop their eggs into the water or attach them to the stems of aquatic plants, but others, including all the damselflies, make slits in the stems of plants at or below the waterline and there deposit elongated eggs. The eggs of all species hatch into nymphs, which mature in the water, feeding on various forms of aquatic life. Nymphs of some of the larger species will even attack small fish. Dragonfly nymphs have a special extensible lower jaw, called the mask, with which they seize their prey. The length of time which dragonflies spend in nymphal form varies from one to three or more years, during which period the nymph molts ten or more times. When nymphs have fully matured they leave the water and undergo metamorphosis into the adult form.

Approximately 4870 species of Odonata are known, and members of the order are found in all temperate and tropical regions of the world. Species of Zygoptera common in the United States include the ruby-spot, *Hetaerina americana,* which has white wings and a red body in the male, and the black-wing, *Calopteryx maculata,* which has black wings in the male and brown wings in the female. Among the common species of Anisoptera found in the United States are members of the family Gomphinae, with black bodies striped with green or yellow, and *Anax junius,* which has clear wings and a

Dragonfly, Hetaerina americana

green head and thorax. The latter species is one of the most widely distributed of dragonflies. It is found in Asia, in the Pacific islands, and in the Western Hemisphere as far north as Alaska and as far south as Costa Rica.

Most temperate-zone species of dragonflies have wingspreads of 2 to 3 in., but tropical species sometimes reach 7½ in. The largest known dragonfly lived in the Carboniferous Period (q.v.) and had a wingspread of 2 ft.

DRAGONHEAD, common name for plants of the genus *Dracocephalum* of the Mint family. The plants bear blue, purple, or white two-lipped flowers in whorls. They are easily raised from seed or cuttings, but have no great horticultural value because their flowers quickly wither in the sun. *Dracocephalum bullatum,* a perennial herb which bears bright blue flowers, is sometimes grown in shady corners of rock gardens. The plants grow to a height of 1 ft. Most species have flowers with spikes 6 in. long, but some, such as *D. grandiflorum* and *D. nutans,* bear flowers with spikes 3 to 6 in. long.

DRAGON'S BLOOD, oleoresin, usually dark red in color, derived from the coat of the ripe fruit of several species of trees, particularly of the rattan palm *Daemonorops draco.* Other trees which yield dragon's blood include the dragon tree, or *Dracaena draco,* and some species of the genera *Croton* and *Eucalyptus.* Dragon's blood is used extensively in photoengraving and is also sometimes employed for coloring varnishes and lacquers.

DRAINAGE, removal of surface or subsurface water from a given area by natural or artificial means. The term is commonly applied to the removal of excess water by canals, drains, ditches, culverts, or other structures designed to collect and transport water either by gravity or by pumping. A drainage project may involve large-scale reclamation (q.v.) and protection of marshes, underwater lands, or lands subject to frequent flooding. Such a project usually involves a system of drainage ditches and dikes, and often pumps are required to raise the water into the drainage network; *see* CANAL; PUMPS AND PUMPING MACHINERY.

In cases of large-scale drainage where improvement of outlet facilities is essential to the protection of adjacent property, it is customary to improve natural stream channels to provide required discharge capacity and to excavate main and lateral drains as open ditches or canals to convey the effluent from farm drainage systems to these improved channels. Such connecting drains commonly follow the natural surface drainage pattern of the area, intercepting the normal surface runoff which takes place during periods of excessive rainfall.

Small-scale drainage is often practiced by farmers and other land owners who wish to remove surface water from arable fields or to improve water-laden soil. Properly constructed drainage systems can also prevent erosion and gullying of land on slopes by catching the surface water before it reaches the slope. Another important purpose of drainage is to prevent an excessive accumulation in the soil of soluble salts that might be detrimental to plant growth.

The essential principle of any type of land drainage is to provide an open, adequate, and readily accessible channel through which the surface or subsoil water can flow. For this purpose open ditches are sometimes used, but these are not always satisfactory because they may become choked with sediment and vegetation. Underground drains are usually employed, particularly on land that is to be plowed. Different types of closed drains exist, the most efficient being the so-called tile drain, which consists of pipes made of sections of hollow earthenware or concrete tiles buried at a depth of 3 to 6 ft. Excess water in the soil seeps into the pipes through apertures in the tiles.

In draining comparatively flat land, it is common practice to lay along one side of the plot a main drain to which are connected a number of transverse laterals. The laterals are often set parallel to the main drain, coming together to join it at the lower end of the field. Local conditions of soil and terrain govern the spacing of laterals and the depth at which they are placed. Laterals may be from 15 to 300 ft. apart and from 2 to 4 ft. below the surface.

To prevent water from higher ground from reaching lower areas, catchment or interception drains are frequently built. They consist of ditches or underground drains placed across the slope which catch water and carry it away before it reaches the low ground.

The drains discussed above operate by gravity, but in the drainage of low-lying areas it is not always possible to set the outlet of the drain low enough to obtain a natural flow of water. This situation occurs in many areas in the Netherlands and Belgium, in the fen country of England, in large portions of the southern United States and in many small areas throughout the world, such as at some airports in river-bottom areas near large U.S. cities. Where gravity flow is impossible, the water from the drainage system is pumped away into streams or canals, the level of which is often higher than that of the drained land. The difficulty of drainage in low areas is increased by the fact that drained land frequently settles as its moisture content is lowered. In the English fens this sinking has amounted to an average of 18 in. If the soil rests on a water-bearing foundation such as gravel, subsurface drainage may be provided by pumping water from wells, thus lowering the water level in the soil.

Netherlands Information Service

U.S. Bureau of Reclamation

Left: A concrete-pipe section 72 in. in diameter is placed in position for a cross-drainage culvert. Below: A polder dike is constructed in an attempt to reclaim land in the Netherlands.

Drainage in the United States. According to estimates of the U.S. government, there were about 76,000,000 acres of wetlands in the U.S. in the mid-1970's. About 300,000 acres per year were being drained, mostly for conversion to agricultural use. Of the total, about 250,000 acres were in the lower Mississippi R. basin; drainage is also extensively practiced in Florida, the Carolinas, Minnesota, Michigan, and Iowa. Most of the drainage was accomplished by means of group-enterprise projects whereby several property owners joined to install drainage systems extending throughout their individual farms. The various State governments have played an important part in drainage enterprises because in 1850 the Federal government gave the States sovereign rights over swampland. During the late 1930's the Works Progress Administration and the Civilian Conservation Corps, both Federal agencies, undertook many drainage projects. The Soil Conservation Service in many sections assists farmers with on-farm drainage improvements. The Bureau of Reclamation carries out drainage as a part of Federal reclamation projects in the seventeen western States. See CONSERVATION.

Drainage Abroad. The Netherlands has one of the best and most extensive systems of drainage and land reclamation in the world. The greater part of the country is low and flat and must be protected by dikes against inundation by the sea. The soil was originally marshy, and there were many lakes, but owing to drainage and the pumping off of the drained water by windmills the land has been made arable. In 1923 the Netherlands began its largest project, the reclamation of 550,000 acres of land from beneath the waters of the IJsselmeer, formerly known as the Zuider Zee. This project, a little more than half of which had been accomplished in the early 1960's, was scheduled for completion in 1980. The process of reclamation, called poldering, consists of creating large, enclosed lakes by building dikes, and pumping the lakes dry.

Following extensive damage from a North Sea storm in 1953, an equally monumental project was undertaken. Known as the Delta Plan, it encompasses closing off various entrances of the sea southwest of Rotterdam, thus affording protection from storm attack and reclaiming large areas of land; see NETHERLANDS; THE: *Agriculture: Land Reclamation.*

A large area of eastern England between the cities of Cambridge and Lincoln, known as the Fens, has been reclaimed from marshland. The reclamation, which has continued for centuries, has been accomplished by extensive drainage, the building of dikes, and by rechanneling the rivers of the area to prevent silting. In addition, between 60,000 and 70,000 acres have been retrieved from the sea.

Other large drainage and reclamation programs of recent years have been carried out in the Pontine Marshes in Italy and in the Salonika Valley at the mouth of the Vardar River in Greece.

See also SEWAGE DISPOSAL.   T.Sa. & F.La.

DRAKE, Edwin Laurentine. See PETROLEUM: *History.*

DRAKE, Sir Francis (1545?–96), English navigator, born near Tavistock, Devonshire. He served an apprenticeship as a mariner, and in 1567 he was given his first command. His ship, the *Judith,* was one of a squadron of vessels led by a kinsman of Drake, the English navigator Sir John Hawkins (q.v.), on a slave-trading voyage in the Gulf of Mexico. All but two ships of the expedition were lost when attacked by a Spanish squadron. In 1570 and 1571 Drake made two profitable trading voyages to the West Indies. In 1572 he commanded two vessels in a marauding expedition against Spanish ports in the Caribbean Sea. During this voyage, Drake first saw the Pacific Ocean; he captured the port of Nombre de Dios on the Isthmus of Panama and destroyed the nearby town of Portobelo. He returned to England with a cargo of Spanish silver and a reputation as a brilliant privateer. He was sent next to Ireland to help quell the rebellion there from 1573 to 1576.

In 1577 Drake was secretly commissioned by Elizabeth I (q.v.), Queen of England, to undertake an expedition against the Spanish colonies on the Pacific coast of the New World. With five ships and 166 men, Drake set sail from Plymouth, England, on Dec. 13, 1577. After completing the crossing of the Atlantic Ocean, two of the ships had to be abandoned in the Río de la Plata estuary of South America. In August, 1578, the three remaining ships left the Atlantic Ocean and entered the Strait of Magellan at the southern tip of the South American continent. Sixteen days later they sailed into the Pacific Ocean. A series of violent storms, lasting more than fifty days, destroyed one ship. Another sailed back to England. Drake, blown far south, sailed on in his flagship, the *Golden Hind.*

The lone vessel moved northward along the Pacific coast of South America, plundering Valparaíso and other Spanish ports and capturing Spanish ships and making use of their more accurate charts. Seeking an eastward passage back to the Atlantic Ocean, Drake continued to sail north, possibly reaching as far as 48° N. latitude,

145

near the present United States–Canadian border. Unable to find a passage, he came about and headed south. The *Golden Hind* put in for repairs at Drake's Bay, an inlet north of San Francisco. Drake claimed the land for England, naming it New Albion.

On July 23, 1579, Drake set sail again, this time heading westward across the Pacific Ocean. In November he reached the Moluccas, a group of islands in the southwest Pacific. He stopped at Celebes and Java, islands of Indonesia, rounded the Cape of Good Hope at the southern tip of Africa, and reached England in September, 1580. Bearing a rich cargo of spices and captured Spanish treasure, he was hailed as the first Englishman to circumnavigate the world. Seven months later, he was knighted aboard the *Golden Hind* by Queen Elizabeth. He became mayor of Plymouth in 1581 and served as a member of Parliament in 1584 and 1585.

Later in 1585 Drake sailed again with a large fleet for the West Indies. He raided many Spanish settlements, including Saint Augustine (q.v.) in present-day Florida. Before returning, he put in at the first English colony in the New World, on Roanoke Island (q.v.), off the coast of what is now North Carolina, and brought the unsuccessful colonists back to England. Traditionally, Drake introduced tobacco to England as a result of this visit to North America.

In 1587 war with Spain was an accepted fact, and Drake was dispatched by the queen to destroy the fleet being assembled by the Spanish in the harbor of Cádiz. He accomplished most of his purpose, and in the following year served as vice admiral of the English fleet that defeated the rebuilt Armada (q.v.) of Spain. In 1589 Drake was unsuccessful in an expedition designed to destroy the few remaining Spanish ships. He returned to Plymouth and to Parliament. In 1595 the queen sent Drake and Hawkins on an expedition against the Spanish forces in the West Indies. This mission, too, was a failure. Both Drake and Hawkins contracted dysentery in the Caribbean and were buried at sea. *See* ENGLAND: *History: The Elizabethan Age.*

DRAKENSBERG, *or* QUATHLAMBA, mountain range in the Republic of South Africa, paralleling the E. coast N.E. to S.W. for about 700 mi. from the S. Transvaal to Cape of Good Hope Province, and forming the E. boundary of Lesotho and, in part, of the Orange Free State. It is the highest portion of the eastern scarp of the South African plateau. Among its peaks are Thabana Ntlenyana (11,425 ft. above sea level, the highest in South Africa) and Mont-aux-Sources (10,822 ft.), near which the scenic Royal Natal National Park is lo-

cated. The Drakensberg Mts. are crossed by rail at two points, Van Reenan Pass (5400 ft.) and Laing's Nek (4100 ft.).

DRAKE UNIVERSITY, privately controlled coeducational institution of higher learning, founded in Des Moines, Iowa, in 1881. The university comprises colleges of liberal arts, fine arts, business administration, pharmacy, education, journalism, law, and university (evening study). The degrees of bachelor, master, and doctor are granted. In 1972 the university library housed more than 358,600 volumes; it is a depository of United States documents. Student enrollment was 7520, the faculty numbered about 400, and the endowment of the university was about $5,142,280.

DRAMA (Gr. *dran*, "to do"), literary composition, in either verse or prose, that tells a story through action and speech and is usually intended to be performed by actors before an audience. A drama, which may also be called a play, is one of the elements of theater (q.v.). *See also* ACTING.

A conventional drama is divided into acts, which are often further divided into scenes. Traditionally, each act marks a stage in the development of the story, successively introducing the characters and situations, developing the story to its climax, and resolving the conflicts of the plot. Some plays have only one act, some three or four acts; others have many scenes but no formal act divisions.

Three principles of dramatic construction have at various times exercised great influence on the composition of drama. These principles, known as the unities, were set down in the 4th century B.C. by the Greek philosopher Aristotle in his *Poetics.* According to Renaissance interpreters of Aristotle, the unity of time requires that the events of a play occur within a period of a single day; the unity of place requires that these events take place within a single locality; and the unity of action requires that no element be introduced which is inconsistent with the theme or mood of the play. The unities were slavishly observed in periods of classical influence, especially by the tragedians of 17th-century France, but were ignored by romantic or realist playwrights. The English playwright William Shakespeare ignored the unities of time and place, freely covering long time spans and widely separated places within his plays; and he frequently ignored the unity of action by introducing into a tragedy a comic scene. Modern playwrights do not observe the unities.

The two principal branches of the drama are traditionally accepted to be tragedy and comedy, terms which originated in ancient Greek times. A tragedy deals with a serious theme; its hero is brought to a tragic end by some flaw in his character. The hero is otherwise admirable, however, and may, by achieving an understanding of the forces with which he has been contending, experience an inspiring growth of his inner being. A comedy, on the other hand, deals with the light and amusing side of life and has a happy ending. A comedy often depicts the follies and absurdities of human beings and it may have a satiric purpose; see SATIRE. The object of a tragedy is to excite deep feelings of pity and fear; of a comedy, to excite laughter.

Among the various historical types of comedy is the comedy of manners, the purpose of which is to satirize in brilliant language the fashions and modes of a particular segment of society, usually of the period in which it is written; this form had its greatest vogue in the 17th and 18th centuries. The closest contemporary parallel is the satiric sketch as performed on television and in cabarets. Other important types of comedy are the comedy of humors, popular in England in the 17th and 18th centuries, and sentimental comedy, developed in England in the 18th century, which had for its specific purpose the reform of immorality. Other forms of comedy are farce (q.v.), in which a complicated and extravagant plot springs from an unrealistic premise; burlesque (q.v.), which is a broad travesty of a serious work; and the vaudeville (q.v.), in which pantomime (q.v.) or dialogue sketches are combined with singing and dancing.

Many types of drama do not fall precisely into the category of either tragedy or comedy. Among these are the historical drama and the romantic drama. A melodrama is a play in which romance, excitement, a contrived and complicated plot, and exaggerated pathos are stressed at the expense of characterization. Both the opera and the contemporary musical (qq.v.) may contain elements of both tragedy and comedy, while pantomime and ballet (q.v.) are also related to the drama, but tell a story exclusively through action. Modern drama has become increasingly difficult to categorize, as every year hundreds of widely varied new plays are performed, not only in the largest cities and cultural centers, but throughout the world. Hundreds more plays are written and never performed, although some of these may be published.

The following article is a general survey of the recorded dramatic literature of the world, showing how this particular form of human endeavor rose from its classical roots to its present ubiquity. For more detailed information the attention of the reader is directed to individual articles on the literature of the countries or of the languages mentioned, such as ENGLISH LITERATURE; FLEMISH LANGUAGE AND LITERATURE; and the section on *Culture* in an article on a specific country. See also articles on literary forms, movements, and styles; historical epochs; and each of the authors whose birth and death dates are not indicated in this survey.

GREEK DRAMA

Both Greek tragedy and comedy originated in religious ceremonies, probably in honor of the god of wine Dionysus (q.v.). The principal feature of these ceremonies was a dance around the altar of the god by a chorus who sang or recited an ode known as a dithyramb. In 536 B.C. the Greek poet Thespis wrote dithyrambs to be sung or recited by the chorus with responses made to the chorus by its leader, thus creating a primitive form of dramatic dialogue. The playwright Aeschylus added a second actor; the playwright Sophocles added a third. Greek tragedy reached its highest development in the 5th century B.C. in the works of these two men and those of Euripides. Fortunately many of their tragedies are still extant. A Greek tragedy contained a prologue, a number of dramatic episodes separated from one another by lyric choral passages, and an exodos, a dramatic scene following the final choral ode. The works of the Greek playwrights were generally written as tetralogies or groups of four, three tragedies followed by a burlesque in which the chorus dressed as satyrs.

According to Aristotle, tragedy was intended to produce catharsis, a release of the emotions of pity and terror and a resultant mood of serenity. Greek tragedy usually had religious and ethical significance. In the dramas of Aeschylus, divine vengeance is a religious mystery which may not be questioned. The plays of Sophocles emphasize ethical problems. With Euripides, however, Greek tragedy becomes a means of portraying human dilemmas and conflicts, with religious or ethical concepts given a psychological interpretation.

The development of Greek comedy was parallel to that of tragedy; the rude jests with which some Dionysiac festivals were enlivened led to the creation of comedy. The history of Greek comedy is commonly divided into three periods: Old Comedy (5th cent. B.C.); Middle Comedy (4th cent. B.C.); and New Comedy (4th and 3rd cent. B.C.). Many of the Old Comedies of Aristophanes, one of the greatest comedy writers of all time, are extant. Through the medium of satire, Aristophanes attacked the social and political abuses of his time with wit and audacity. Organized in a manner similar to that of tragedy, his comedies also included an ode known as the *parabasis,* in which the audience was directly addressed by the chorus. In Middle Comedy the language was more restrained than in Old Comedy, and the satire, still largely political, was aimed at classes rather than at individuals; in Middle Comedy the chorus disappeared. New Comedy, of which Menander is the best-known writer, found its subject matter no longer in political questions, but in the complications of life in a society which had lost its simplicity and much of its virtue.

The contribution of the ancient Greeks to the history of drama is inestimable. Many of the Greek classics are timeless; the plays of Aeschylus, Sophocles, and Euripides are performed today in Greek and in a variety of translations. Furthermore, the Greek language is the source of much dramatic nomenclature. The word "drama" itself is Greek, and such terms as "theater", "scene", "thespian", and "proscenium" are derived from the Greek.

A performance of Oedipus Rex, *the most famous of the tragedies of Sophocles. Ancient Greek actors also wore masks, which had metallic mouthpieces and fixed expressions.* **National Film Board of Canada**

ROMAN DRAMA

Roman drama was largely an imitation of Greek drama. Two important Roman playwrights of the 3rd and 2nd centuries B.C. were Plautus and Terence, both of whom wrote comedies based on Greek models. The plays of Plautus are marked by rough vigor; those of Terence are more refined. The most important Roman writer of serious drama was Lucius Annaeus Seneca, among whose nine formalized tragedies are *Hercules Furens, Phaedra,* and *Troades,* written in the 1st century A.D. The most important aspect of Roman drama is that it served as a model for Renaissance dramatists.

ORIENTAL DRAMA

Several distinct forms of drama originated in India, China, Japan, and Indonesia. These are noticeably different from what is usually called Western drama; the difference lies primarily in their extensive reliance upon dance and pantomime to tell a story.

India. The drama of India, like that of Greece, originated in the dances and songs of religious festivals. Indian drama, however, stresses romantic love more than does Greek. Indian drama, written mostly in Sanskrit, reached its highest development in the period between the 4th and the 9th centuries A.D. The greatest dramatist of India, Kālidāsa, flourished in the

5th century A.D.; his best-known play is *Sakuntala*, a heroic drama of love. Many classic Indian dramas are based on the Sanskrit epic *Ramayana* (q.v.). Among other notable plays of India are the *Mricchakatika* ("The Little Clay Cart"), a ten-act drama of social life, probably written in the 6th century; and *Ratnavali* ("The Pearl Necklace"), a romantic play from the 7th century. Sanskrit drama, including the 700 plays which exist today, was written well into the Middle Ages, but only unrecorded folk and dance dramas were performed for several centuries thereafter. While contemporary Indian drama has been westernized, it is still often based on the old religious and heroic Sanskrit legends. The most striking feature of this Indian drama is its extensive use of song and dance.

China. As early as 2000 B.C., Chinese temple festivals included dance-and-dialogue portrayals of the lives of deified ancestors. The first classical Chinese dramas were recorded in the 6th century A.D., but no significant theater developed until the 8th century, when an emperor of the T'ang dynasty, Ming Huang, established an acting school known as the Pear Garden. Chinese drama reached its highest development in the classical Yüan period (1280–1368); plays from this period, although extensively revised, are still performed. This classical Chinese drama has as its purpose the glorification of virtue; and dance, acrobatics, and singing are a part of all traditional Chinese plays. Costumes are elaborate, but stage settings are simple, with little attempt at realism; simple properties are used and are placed on the stage during the performance by the property man, in full view of the audience. Early in the 20th century Chinese drama underwent a profound change. With the founding of the Chinese republic, dramatists attempted to make the Chinese theater more democratic by writing in the vernacular and by portraying social emancipation; Western influence was evident. On the mainland, under the Communist regime, Chinese drama after the revolution served as a propaganda instrument.

Japan. The people of Japan have supported a flourishing dramatic literature for more than one thousand years. Several distinct types of traditional Japanese drama exist, including the most ancient form, the *nō*; the melodramatic and highly stylized *kabuki*; the farcical *kyogen*; and the unique puppet theater, the *bunraku*. The modern cities of Japan have also seen a great deal of Western-influenced theater produced during the past half-century, both native Japanese plays and translations of English, French, and German works; but the traditional forms remain sacrosanct.

Indonesia. The classic drama of Indonesia, which flourishes particularly in Java and Bali, is a composite of dialogue in prose, narration in verse, songs, instrumental music, and choreographed movement. The most important native dramatic form is the *wajang kulit* or shadow play, first recorded in the 11th century. From the *wajang kulit,* which is narrated by a solo performer who also manipulates the leather puppets which serve as actors, evolved several complicated ritualized forms of Indonesian drama.

MEDIEVAL EUROPEAN DRAMA

In the early medieval period, the Christian Church condemned dramatic performances of all kinds. But it was within the church itself that a new form of drama developed. Toward the end of the 10th century, during Easter services, priests representing women engaged in a few lines of dialogue about the Resurrection (q.v.) with other priests representing angels. From this primitive beginning came short dramatic scenes in Latin of episodes from the life of Christ, also performed by priests. Later the subject matter was broadened to include tales from the lives of the saints and laymen began to take part. The liturgical drama thus gradually developed into full-fledged miracle and mystery plays performed outdoors on the steps of a church. Eventually these plays were produced by the lay members of the guilds of the various European cities and towns. Another form of medieval drama, the allegorical morality play, was also developed. *Everyman,* first printed about 1529, is a 15th-century English morality play that is still occasionally performed. In these medieval religious dramas and in the secular farces of this period, performed in marketplaces and innyards, are found the roots of modern drama.

NATIONAL DRAMA

The drama of the early Middle Ages was in Latin. During the late Middle Ages, drama began to be written in the vernacular, the particular languages of the people of Europe. National drama, in such languages as French, Italian, and English, grew under the influence of the two traditions then at work, an academic interest in the classical drama of Greece and Rome and a popular interest in the theater of the marketplace and the itinerant entertainer. In each language a dramatic tradition developed, each with its own seminal works; often these works and their authors are important or popular only in their own country. On the other hand, as the countries of Europe became less insular, the drama of one country began to affect the drama of another country. The demand of audiences for theater had often to be met in part by translations of plays from other languages. This tradition still obtains in the theater of today.

Italy. The religious drama of the late Middle Ages attained considerable sophistication in Italy. Its principal form was the *rappresentazione sacra* (It., "sacred play") of the 15th century, produced in the Italian language. A notable example of this type of drama is *Abramo e Isaaco* ("Abraham and Isaac", 1449) by Feo Belcari (1410–84).

The Renaissance gave a new stimulus to drama in Italy. The drama of this period took two principal forms, the popular improvised outdoor farce of the commedia dell'arte and the literary neoclassical drama produced in the courts of the Renaissance princes. Among the plays of this period based on classical models are the tragedy *Sofonisba* (1515) by Giovanni Giorgio Trissino (1478–1550) and the pastoral drama *Il Re Torrismondo* ("King Torrismondo", 1587) by Torquato Tasso. A type of comedy modeled after the plays of Plautus was also written at this time, notably by Lodovico Ariosto and Niccolò Machiavelli. In the 17th century the most prevalent works were pastoral dramas, such as *La Fiera* ("The Fair", 1618) by Michelangelo Buonarroti (1568–1646), nephew of the great artist Michelangelo. In 1594 Ottavio Rinuccini (1562–1621) wrote the words for *Dafne,* a pastoral for which music was composed by Jacopo Peri (1561–1633); *Dafne* was the progenitor of a new art form, the opera. Opera librettos of high literary quality were among the most important products of Italian dramatists during the 18th century. But the foremost names in 18th-century Italian drama are those of playwrights Carlo Goldoni, Carlo Gozzi (1720–1806), and Conte Vittorio Alfieri. Goldoni is considered the greatest writer of Italian comedy; some of his plays, including *La Locandiera* (1753; Eng. trans., *The Mistress of the Inn,* 1856), are still performed. Gozzi's contribution to Italian drama was to give literary form to the formerly improvisational commedia dell'arte. Alfieri wrote neoclassic tragedies, strict in their observance of the unities; his plays are important because of their nationalist fervor.

Among the Italian dramatists of the 19th century Risorgimento, a period of cultural nationalism and political unification, devotion to country was the most frequently recurring theme. Alessandro Manzoni, better known as a novelist, wrote several romantic dramas, including *Il Conte di Carmagnola* ("The Count of Carmagnola", 1820) and *Adelchi* (1822). Later in the century the excesses of Romanticism gave way to a new, more naturalistic style known as *verismo* ("realism"). An example of *verismo* is *Cavalleria Rusticana* ("Rustic Chivalry"), first written as a short story, then dramatized (1884) by the author, Giovanni Verga; it was later the source of a well-known opera.

One of the most popular Italian playwrights of the 20th century was Gabriele D'Annunzio. His melodramas, such as *La Città Morte* (1898; Eng. trans., *The Dead City,* 1902) and *La Figlia di Iorio* (1904; Eng. trans., *The Daughter of Jorio* 1904), provided florid vehicles for international star actresses. Of considerable importance to the development of modern drama is the work of Luigi Pirandello, author of plays that are experimental in form and daring in their examination of established definitions of reality. Two of his plays are *Così È, Se Vi Pare* (1917; Eng. trans., *Right You Are if You Think You Are,* 1922) and *Sei Personnagi in Cerca d'Autore* (1921; Eng. trans., *Six Characters in Search of an Author,* 1922). Of the many other 20th-century Italian dramatists, only two achieved some international reputation. Ugo Betti (1892–1953) wrote dreamlike, poetic dramas such as *Corruzione al Palazzo di Giustizia* (1944; Eng. trans., *Corruption in the Palace of Justice,* 1949). Eduardo De Filippo (1900–   ), on the other hand, is an actor-writer-producer who deals with the lively everyday world of Naples in *Filumena Marturano* (1946; Eng. trans., *The Best House in Naples,* 1956) and his many other plays.

Spain. The late 16th and early 17th centuries constitute the golden age, the most brilliant period of Spanish drama. At this time the novelist Miguel de Cervantes wrote many long plays, including verse tragedies, but made his greatest dramatic contribution with his prose *entremeses* ("interludes"), short satirical farces. Tirso de Molina is notable for his drama *El Burlador de Sevilla y Convidado de Piedra* ("The Deceiver of Seville and the Stone Guest", 1630), in which the character of Don Juan (q.v.) first appeared in literature. Critics agree that the two greatest Spanish dramatists are Lope de Vega and Pedro Calderón de la Barca, both of whom belong to this period. At a time when critics were insisting that playwrights follow the Aristotelian unities, Lope de Vega disregarded nearly all classical principles in writing his more than 1800 vigorous dramas, both secular and religious. Calderón de la Barca gave expression in his philosophical dramas to such ideals as devotion to the king, to the church, and to personal honor. He is also noted for his *autos sacramentales,* one-act religious plays.

During the 18th century, the theater of Spain was devoted to neoclassical tragedies and rewrites of the plays of Lope and Calderón. Early in the 19th century there was a brief Romantic period; several plays from this time provided librettos for Italian composers of opera. The Spanish form of operetta (q.v.), the *zarzuela,* in which there is a great deal of spoken dialogue, also began to be immensely popular. One play from this period, *Don Juan Tenorio* (1844) by José Zorrilla y Moral, is still performed annually throughout the Spanish-speaking world.

Spanish dramatists of the late 19th and early 20th centuries included José Echegaray y Eizaguirre; Gregorio Martínez Sierra (1881–1947), among whose plays is *Canción de Cuna* (1911; Eng. trans., *The Cradle Song,* 1913); and the brothers, Serafín Álvarez Quintero and Joaquín Álvarez Quintero, authors of comedies set in Andalusia. Jacinto Benavente y Martínez, however, was the most influential dramatist of the period, with his nearly 200 simple and charming dramas.

The works of the remarkable poet Federico García Lorca, among which are *Bodas de Sangre* (1933; Eng. trans., *Blood Wedding,* 1939), *Yerma* (1934; Eng. trans., 1939), and *La Casa de Bernarda Alba* (1936; Eng. trans., *The House of Bernarda Alba,* 1939), have been admired, translated, and performed throughout the world.

France. The 17th century in France was notable for both the revival of classical drama and the development of comedy to its highest point. The two most illustrious writers of tragedy in French, both of whom strictly observed the Aristotelian unities, were Pierre Corneille and Jean Baptiste Racine. They were concerned mainly with the subordination of passion to a sense of duty. In Corneille's dramas the protagonists are men; in Racine's, they are women. Among the dramas of Corneille are *Le Cid* (1636 or 1637), *Horace* (1640), and *Polyeucte* (about 1642); among those of Racine are *Phèdre* (1677) and

Molière's Tartuffe, a 17th-century French farce, exemplifies the use of comedy as a vehicle for exposing the foibles of human nature. **Barry Hyams**

Athalie (1691); all have been frequently translated into English, in spite of their complicated formal versification. To this period also belongs Molière, regarded by critics as one of the greatest writers of comedy in the history of the drama. Among his plays, rich in wit and understanding of life, are *Tartuffe* (1664), *Le Misanthrope* (1666), *L'Avare* ("The Miser", 1668), and *Le Bourgeois Gentilhomme* ("The Would-be Gentleman", 1670). In the 18th century the chief writers of French tragedy were Voltaire, who wrote *Zaïre* (1732), and Crébillon, the Elder, author of *Catilina* (1748). The most notable writers of comedy in this period are Pierre de Marivaux, author of the sentimental and ornate *Le Jeu de l'Amour et du Hasard* ("The Game of Love and Chance", 1730), and Pierre Augustin Caron de Beaumarchais, author of *Le Barbier de Seville* ("The Barber of Seville", 1775) and *Le Mariage de Figaro* ("The Marriage of Figaro", 1784), both now famous in operatic adaptations.

The 19th century was a period of rich and varied dramatic production in France. First came Victor Hugo, whose *Hernani* (1830) evoked a storm of protest for its disregard of dramaturgical rules and signaled the arrival of Romanticism. The poet Alfred de Musset wrote several delicate psychological studies, while Comte Alfred Victor de Vigny, author of *Chatterton* (1835), and Alexandre Dumas père, who wrote *Kean* (1836), continued the colorful Romantic tradition. Later in the century, Augustin Eugène Scribe, Alexandre Dumas fils, and Victorien Sardou, reacting to Romanticism, wrote hundreds of contemporary melodramas in the genre known as the well-made play. Two remarkable playwrights of the 1890's were Alfred Jarry (*see The New Drama,* below) and Edmond Rostand, whose *Cyrano de Bergerac* (1898) is probably the supreme example of Romantic drama, although written fifty years after the end of the Romantic era.

An important new literary genre, the naturalistic drama, began with the performance in 1873 of a dramatization by Émile Zola of his novel *Thérèse Raquin*. Most influential of the naturalistic playwrights were Henry Becque and Eugène Brieux, the latter the author of the anti-authoritarian *La Robe Rouge* ("The Red Robe", 1900). Symbolism was represented by the works of the Belgian poet Maurice Maeterlinck, writer of *Pelléas and Mélisande* (1893).

In the 20th century playwrighting in French continued to be enormously vital, producing well-made melodramas, works of photographic naturalism, comedies of manners, poetic and religious fantasies, and avant-garde enigmas, many of which achieved success at home and abroad. Among the important authors of this varied fare are Paul Claudel, Jules Romains, Sacha Guitry, Jean Giraudoux, Jean Cocteau, Jean Anouilh, Jean-Paul Sartre, Eugène Ionesco, and Jean Genet.

Germany. The medieval *fasnachtsspiel* or carnival play, which reached its height in the 16th century, was the only characteristically German drama until the 18th century. Then three of the most important poet-dramatists of Germany, Lessing, Schiller, and Goethe, produced their major works. Gotthold Ephraim Lessing, more critic than playwright, is the author of *Nathan der Weise* ("Nathan the Wise", 1779), which became the standard of German classicism. Johann Christoph Friedrich von Schiller wrote what have been called idea dramas, such as the trilogy *Wallenstein* (1799); his *Mary Stuart* (1800) has frequently been revived in English translation. Among the plays of Johann Wolfgang von Goethe are *Götz von Berlichingen* (1773), which inaugurated the Romantic school of drama in Germany, and his famed *Faust* (1st part, 1808; 2nd part, 1832); see FAUST, JOHANN.

German drama was Romantic in theme and style until about 1880. Among the authors of Romantic dramas of the 19th century were Heinrich von Kleist and the Austrian Franz Grillparzer. The most remarkable German playwright of the 19th century, since he was a precursor of both naturalism and expressionism, was Georg Büchner (1813–37), who wrote *Dantons Tod* (*Danton's Death,* 1835) and *Woyzeck* (1836), both of which were first produced long after the author's death and were not translated into English until 1928.

From 1880 until World War I a new type of play, the naturalistic drama that attempted to achieve an almost photographic reality, dominated the German stage. Gerhart Hauptmann wrote the powerful naturalistic works *Die Weber* (1892; Eng. trans., *The Weavers,* 1899) and *Die Ratten* (1911; Eng. trans., *The Rats,* 1913). Other important playwrights of the period were Hermann Sudermann; Frank Wedekind, also a forerunner of expressionism; and the Austrian Arthur Schnitzler. Another Austrian, Hugo von Hofmannsthal, wrote *Elektra* (1903) and other plays from classical models. With the drama *Der Bettler* ("The Beggar", 1912) by Reinhard Johannes Sorge (1892–1916), expressionist drama became important in Germany. To the expressionist school, which was the leading dramatic movement in Germany from shortly before World War I to about 1933, belong Ernst Toller and Fritz von Unruh. The importance of the German expressionists in the development of world drama lies not in their plays but in the new theatrical techniques they introduced. This influence is particularly strong upon the dramatically vital work of Bertolt Brecht in his plays and librettos, such as *Die Dreigroschenoper* (1928; Eng. trans., *The Threepenny Opera,* 1933) and *Mutter Courage und ihre Kinder* (1940; Eng. trans., *Mother Courage and Her Children,* 1941). The first-named work is based on *The Beggar's Opera* by the 18th-century British author John Gay. The Berliner Ensemble, a theatrical group formed by Brecht in East Germany after World War II, stimulated interest in epic theater, a form of drama advocated by Brecht. Epic theater combines narration and dialogue for didactic purposes, hoping to involve the audience intellectually rather than emotionally.

Among contemporary German playwrights who continue to emphasize the didactic and the polemical are the West German Rolf Hochhuth (1931–), who wrote *Der Stellvertreter* (1963; Eng. trans., *The Deputy,* 1963), and Peter Weiss (1916–). The last-named became a Swedish citizen but continued to write in German such plays as *Die Verfolgung und Emordung des Jean Paul Marats Dargestellt durch die Schauspielgruppe des Hospizes zu Charenton unter Anleitung des Herrn de Sade* (1963; Eng. trans., 1964), which in English production is usually known as *Marat/Sade;* and *Die Ermittlung* (1965; Eng. trans., *The Investigation,* 1965). Two other playwrights, both Swiss, writing in German, achieved international success after World War II: Friedrich Dürrenmatt and Max Frisch (1911–). *Biedermann und die Brandstifter* (1958; Eng. trans., *The Firebugs,* 1959), by Frisch, exemplifies their incisive and original work.

Czechoslovakia. Czechoslovakia, including Bohemia, Moravia, and Slovakia, had no drama of consequence through the Renaissance, but late in the 18th century and early in the 19th a rise in nationalism caused a rise in Czechoslovak drama, both folk and poetic. Following a brief Romantic period, Czech drama advanced through realism and naturalism. The National Theater in Prague opened in 1883. The first Czechoslovak playwrights of international stature were expressionists. These were two brothers, Karel Čapek, author of *R.U.R.* (1921; Eng. trans., 1923), and his brother Josef Čapek, with whom he wrote *Ze Zivota Hmyzu* (1921; Eng. trans., *The Insect Comedy*, 1923).

Hungary. Hungarian drama followed a pattern of development similar to that of Czechoslovakia, although the National Theater in Budapest was founded earlier, in 1831. The first Hungarian dramatist to be known internationally was Ferenc Molnár, who wrote *Liliom* (1909; Eng. trans., 1921) and several other plays popular in translation during the 1920's and 1930's.

The Netherlands. In the Low Countries several 16th- and 17th-century Dutch playwrights, most noteworthy of them Joost van den Vondel (1587–1679), brought about a humanist revival of drama. The later Dutch stage largely imitated the contemporary French drama; few Dutch and Flemish plays have been translated, however. One exception is the work of the journalist and writer Herman Heijermans (1864–1924), who won international acclaim with the naturalistic *Op Hoop von Zegen* (1900; Eng. trans., *The Good Hope*, 1912), written under the pen name Koos Habbema.

Scandinavia. While Denmark, Finland, Norway, and Sweden have deep-rooted dramatic traditions, particularly in folk comedy, the first notable Scandinavian dramatist did not appear until the first half of the 18th century. Ludvig Holberg is a Danish writer whose comedies did much to supplant the trivial plays from the French and German which prevailed upon the Danish stage at that time. In the first half of the 19th century, nationalist movements spurred native Scandinavian theatrical activities. Two of the most influential playwrights in the history of modern drama were Scandinavians. The Norwegian Henrik Ibsen, after writing the poetic and philosophical plays *Brand* (1866) and *Peer Gynt* (1867), turned to realistic drama on contemporary problems. Ibsen further discarded the incredible characters and improbable situations of formula melodrama and thus profoundly influenced the drama of the entire civilized world. Among his many dramas are *Et Dukkehjem* (1879; Eng. trans., *A Doll's House,* 1882) and *Hedda Gabler* (1890). The Swedish writer August Strindberg also strongly influenced drama

outside his native land, particularly the expressionist theater of Germany and the United States. Among Strindberg's plays are the realistic tragedies *Fadren* (1887; Eng. trans., *The Father,* 1907) and *Fröken Julie* (1888; Eng. trans., *Miss Julie,* 1911), which even more than Ibsen's work realistically explored human behavior. His expressionist fantasies, especially *Ett Drömspel* (1902; Eng. trans., *A Dream Play,* 1912), were instrumental in freeing later playwrights to express themselves in poetic and highly individual language and theatrical effects.

Russia. Russian drama, long under the influence of the drama of Germany, France, and Italy, had its own minor beginnings in the 18th century in the work of two men, the prolific Aleksandr Petrovich Sumarokov (1718–77) and Denis Ivanovich Fonvizin (1745–92). *Nederosl'* ("The Minor", 1791) by Fonvizin is a comedy which in its sympathetic portraits of characteristically Russian types has had a lasting influence on the Russian theater.

One play which was an exception to the general European-influenced trends of 19th-century Russian drama was *Gore ot Uma* ("The Misfortune of Being Too Clever", 1824) by Aleksandr Sergeevich Griboedov (1795–1829), a satire in verse on czarist officialdom. Unfortunately, the dramatic works of two important poets of 19th-century Russia, Aleksander Sergeevich Pushkin and Mikhail Yurievich Lermontov, were neither published nor performed until many years after their deaths and thus had no influence on their contemporaries. Three Russian playwrights of the 19th century achieved international success. They were Nikolai Vasilievich Gogol, who wrote *Revizor* ("The Inspector General", 1836), a brilliant satire on Russian bureaucracy; Ivan Sergeevich Turgenev, whose *Mesyats v Derevne* ("A Month in the Country") was written in 1850 and produced in 1872; and Aleksandr Nikolaevich Ostrovski (1823–86), who wrote more than eighty plays in the second half of the century. But the most influential of all Russian dramatists is Anton Pavlovich Chekhov. His plays, characterized by a new combination of poetic atmosphere, emotional tension, and profound psychological understanding, gave rise to a new adjective. In the 20th century, virtually every playwright more interested in the introspective complexity of his characters than in plot or action has been called Chekhovian by the critics. Among the plays of Chekhov are *Chaika* ("The Seagull", 1896), *Tri Sestry* ("The Three Sisters", 1901), and *Vishnevyi Sad* ("The Cherry Orchard", 1904). The famous novelists Maksim Gorki, who wrote *Na Dne* ("The Lower

A scene from the New York Shakespeare Festival's 1977 production of Anton Chekhov's The Cherry Orchard, which was directed by Andrei Serban and starred Irene Worth as Mme. Ranevskaya.   Sy Friedman

Depths'', 1902), and Count Lev Tolstoi, who wrote *Vlast Tmy* (''The Power of Darkness'', 1889), were naturalistic playwrights, but their contemporary Leonid Nikolaevich Andreyev, who wrote *Tot, Kto Poluchaet Po Shchechiny* (''He Who Gets Slapped'', 1915), was an expressionist.

After the Revolution of 1917, Russian dramatic activity increased greatly. The dramatists of the U.S.S.R., however, have come under official pressure to write what has been called socialist realism. Consequently contemporary Russian plays are rarely performed outside the Russian sphere of influence.

England.   English comedy, which originated about the middle of the 16th century, was derived in part from medieval morality plays and, more particularly, from Greek and Roman classical comedy. *Ralph Roister Doister,* written about 1540 by Nicholas Udall (1505–56), is considered the earliest English comedy but is actually an adaptation of the Roman comedy *Miles Gloriosus* by Plautus. In 1561 appeared the first English

tragedy, a play in blank verse, *Gorboduc,* or *Ferrex and Porrex,* by Thomas Norton and Thomas Sackville. *Gammer Gurton's Needle* (1566), the first English farce, is attributed, variously, to the clergymen John Bridges (d. 1618), William Stevenson (d. 1575), and John Still (d. 1608).

English drama developed rapidly in the latter part of the 16th century, known as the Elizabethan era (*see* ELIZABETH I), and was brought to its culmination in the work of William Shakespeare. Among the dramatists who wrote during the vital early Elizabethan years were John Lyly, Thomas Kyd, Thomas Nash, George Peele (1558?–96?), Thomas Lodge, and Robert Greene. The greatest of the early Elizabethans was Christopher Marlowe, second only to Shakespeare in his mastery of dramatic blank verse, as in *Tamburlaine the Great* (produced about 1587) and *The Tragedy of Dr. Faustus* (about 1588).

Generally accepted to be the foremost dramatic genius the world has ever produced, William Shakespeare wrote for a theater which employed only the slightest of scenic accessories. His comedies, historical plays, and tragedies, of which some thirty-nine exist, exemplify the depth, sublimity, refinement, and variety of which the drama is capable. His career lasted through the end of the Elizabethan era and into the Jacobean era that followed.

Among Shakespeare's contemporaries were Ben Jonson and the collaborators Francis Beaumont and John Fletcher. Jonson, like Shakespeare, wrote both comedy and tragedy; his work shows more classic influence than does that of Shakespeare. Jonson was a noted writer of the court masque, which was popular with English royalty and nobility in the 16th and 17th centuries; he also wrote comedies of humors such as *Every Man in His Humour* (1598) and *Volpone* (1605). Beaumont and Fletcher wrote approximately fifty plays, including the comedy *The Knight of the Burning Pestle* (1607) and the tragedy *The Maid's Tragedy* (about 1611). Other important playwrights of the Jacobean era and the following Caroline era were George Chapman, Thomas Dekker, Philip Massinger, John Webster, and John Ford.

In September, 1642, a month after the outbreak of the Great Rebellion (q.v.), the civil war between Parliament and King Charles I (q.v.), when power was in the hands of the Puritans, Parliament passed an ordinance that forbade the performance of any kind of theatrical entertainment. For eighteen years, until the Restoration in 1660, theaters in England were closed. With the Restoration, however, English drama reached a new height in popularity.

The principal writers of neoclassic tragedy after 1660 were John Dryden, Thomas Otway, and Joseph Addison. This period, however, was most notable for comedies of manners that caricatured the life of the upper classes and, in reaction against Puritanism, were often licentious. The most important writer of Restoration comedy was William Congreve, whose graceful and witty dialogue has rarely been equaled in the English theater. Among his plays are *Love for Love* (1695) and *The Way of the World* (1700). Other writers of comedy of the time were Thomas Shadwell, William Wycherley, Sir John Vanbrugh, and George Farquhar. Somewhat later in the 18th century came Colley Cibber and John Gay. Two outstanding writers of the gentler sentimental comedy of the latter part of the 18th century were Oliver Goldsmith and Richard Brinsley Sheridan.

The many British dramatists of the first part of the 19th century wrote mostly Romantic melodramas and tragedies in verse, while the last two decades of the 19th century were marked by the rise of drama dealing with social issues. Important dramatists of the latter school were Arthur Wing Pinero and Henry Arthur Jones. The English comedy of manners was exemplified during this period by the plays of the Irish-born Oscar Wilde, including *Lady Windermere's Fan* (1892).

In the first decade of the 20th century, George Bernard Shaw, also born in Ireland, began to attain international recognition with plays that were characterized by witty dialogue and brilliant satire and that also continued the late 19th-century concern for examination of social and economic conditions. Other dramatists of the time who showed this analytical tendency were Harley Granville-Barker and John Galsworthy. Sir James Matthew Barrie rose to importance as a playwright with works of whimsical comedy and fantasy, such as *Peter Pan* (1904).

British playwrights have continued to write in an almost unlimited variety of dramatic styles. Some important modern authors are W. Somerset Maugham, Noel Coward, J. B. Priestley, T. S. Eliot, Terence Rattigan, Christopher Fry, Peter Ustinov, Peter Schaffer (1926–), author of *Five-Finger Exercise* (1958) and *Equus* (1973), and Robert Bolt (1924–), author of *A Man for All Seasons* (1964). An influential event in the development of contemporary drama in England was the establishment in 1956 of the English Stage Company at the Royal Court Theatre in London. There, and at the Theatre Workshop of producer Joan Littlewood (1914–), a group of new playwrights, including John Osborne, Shelagh Delaney (1939–), John Arden (1930–), and Arnold Wesker (1932–), began to write a series of strong, realistic, and characteristically British plays; at the same time, Harold Pinter was creating a dramatic style in which a realistic surface masked the underlying theme.

Ireland. The Irish theater was an adjunct of the English theater until 1900. No drama written in Gaelic was performed until 1901, and virtually no Gaelic drama written since then has been translated. A few native plays had previously been produced in Dublin, based on English models. But Irish-born playwrights such as Richard Sheridan, Oliver Goldsmith, Dion Boucicault, Oscar Wilde, and George Bernard Shaw inevitably gravitated to London. Not before the early 20th century did national Irish drama come to the fore. A movement for encouraging the writing and producing of plays based on Irish themes, initiated principally by William Butler

Yeats, culminated in the founding of the Irish National Theatre Society in 1899. In 1904 the society acquired the Abbey Theatre (q.v.) in Dublin, which became the center of Irish drama. The most significant of the dramatists whose plays were performed by the Abbey Theatre was John Millington Synge, who wrote *The Playboy of the Western World* (1907). Others were William Butler Yeats; Lady Gregory; Edward Plunkett, 18th Baron Dunsany; St. John Greer Ervine; and Esmé Stuart Lennox Robinson. Significant contemporary playwrights whose works are identifiably Irish are Sean O'Casey, Brendan Behan, and Paul Vincent Carroll (1900–68), author of *Shadow and Substance* (1937) and *The White Steed* (1939).

United States. The first permanent playhouses in the American colonies were the Southwark Theatre, erected in Philadelphia in 1766, and the John Street Theatre, built in New York City in 1767. Most of the plays presented during the colonial era were by British dramatists. The first tragedy by an American was *The Prince of Parthia* by Thomas Godfrey, Jr., produced at the Southwark Theatre in 1767. The first play on an American theme was *The Contrast* by the American jurist Royall Tyler (1757–1826), which appeared at the John Street Theatre in 1787. It was followed by many so-called Yankee plays, dealing with American character types, which soon superseded the British plays in popularity. Other American playwrights of the late-18th and early-19th centuries were William Dunlap, the first American to adopt playwriting as a profession, and the actor John Howard Payne, who wrote several tragedies.

Between 1820 and 1840 a number of British actors visited the United States. Appearing almost exclusively in the plays of Shakespeare, they were led by Edmund Kean, Junius Brutus Booth, and William Charles Macready. But American drama received a more lasting impetus from the American actor Edwin Forrest, who offered prizes for American playwrights and produced several new American plays during the 1830's. The first successful American comedy of manners was *Fashion, or Life in New York* (1845) by the American actress and playwright Anna Cora Mowatt (1819–70). One of the most successful plays in the annals of the American theater was the dramatization by George L. Aiden (1830–76) of the novel *Uncle Tom's Cabin* by Harriet Beecher Stowe. The play, produced in 1852, had a record run then and remained popular well into the 20th century.

Among the other American playwrights of the second half of the 19th century were the Irish-born Dion Boucicault, who wrote between 100 and 150 melodramas; Augustin Daly; Bronson Crocker Howard; and William Gillette, who dramatized stories by Sir Arthur Conan Doyle in *Sherlock Holmes* (1899). David Belasco, both as playwright and producer, strongly influenced the American drama for fifty years, from the late 19th century through the 1920's. Belasco stressed literal and elaborate realism in such productions as *The Girl I Left Behind Me* (1893) and *Laugh, Clown, Laugh* (1923). The work of Augustus Thomas also spanned the two centuries, and among his melodramas *The Copperhead* (1918) is probably most notable.

In the early years of the 20th century some American playwrights became concerned with the economic, social, and ethical problems of the country, but their work had to retain the sentimentality and sensational plots of melodrama in order to obtain popular success. These playwrights included Clyde Fitch, William Vaughn Moody, and Edward Brewster Sheldon (1886–1946), who wrote *Salvation Nell* (1908) and *The Nigger* (1909). George Michael Cohan wrote, produced, and acted in his own very popular comedies and musicals, including *Forty-Five Minutes from Broadway* (1905) and *Get-Rich-Quick Wallingford* (1910). During and immediately following World War I, American drama flourished. This was due in part to several organizations. The 47 Workshop was founded at Harvard University in 1905 by George Pierce Baker for the instruction of young playwrights. The Washington Square Players, founded in New York City in 1916, was the nucleus of the Theatre Guild, producers of plays of artistic merit. The Provincetown Players, established in 1915, were notable for their productions of the early works of Eugene O'Neill, the first American to receive a Nobel Prize in literature for his plays.

Many American dramatists of the 1920's and 1930's, led by O'Neill, Maxwell Anderson, S. N. Behrman, Sidney Howard, Elmer Rice, and Robert Sherwood, developed a realistic style. These dramatists, some of whom were liberal-minded and critical of contemporary society, made the first significant attempts to depict human life as it is actually lived. Thus they paved the way for the playwrights of the 1940's and 1950's, including Clifford Odets, Lillian Hellman, Arthur Miller, William Inge, and Tennessee Williams, who showed an ability to move audiences with what has been called selective or poetic realism. These later playwrights freed the drama from the strictures of formula melodrama and created a sense of life that is evocative of reality but not filled with naturalistic detail. At the same time

DRAMA

the theater faced increasingly intense competition from motion pictures and television for the attention of the public. As a result, commercially successful drama after the late 1950's—with the exception of some examples of poetic realism such as Edward Albee's *Who's Afraid of Virginia Woolf?* (1962) and *That Championship Season* (1972), written by Jason Miller (1940–)—consisted almost entirely of musicals, which became increasingly dramatic, and sophisticated comedies. Among the notable musicals were *West Side Story* (1957), with music by Leonard Bernstein, book by Arthur Laurents (1918–), and lyrics by Stephen Sondheim (1930–), based on Shakespeare's *Romeo and Juliet*; and *Fiddler on the Roof* (1964), with music by Jerry Bock (1928–), book by Joseph Stein (1912–), and lyrics by Sheldon Harnick (1924–), based on stories by Shalom Aleichem.

Both these productions were directed by Jerome Robbins, whose work exemplifies the increasing importance of the director in the creation of contemporary drama. The leading writer of American theatrical comedy in the 1960's and 1970's was the highly prolific Neil Simon (1927–), author of *Barefoot in the Park* (1963) and *The Sunshine Boys* (1972).

One new and intriguing aspect of the theater in America after the mid-20th century was the proliferation of plays by and about Blacks. *Raisin in the Sun* (1959) by Lorraine Hansberry (1930–65), *No Place To Be Somebody* (1969) by Charles Gordone (1926–), and *The River Niger* (1972) by Joseph A. Walker (1935–) exemplify the serious purpose and frequent commercial success achieved in this genre. Although black regional theaters, including Karamu House in Cleveland, Ohio, had been in existence for a

Left: A scene from a recent New York City production of A Moon for the Misbegotten, *starring Colleen Dewhurst and Jason Robards. The play, by the American dramatist Eugene O'Neill, was based upon a tragedy in his personal life. Generally considered to be his country's leading playwright, O'Neill introduced a unique blend of poetic symbolism and psychological realism into American drama.*

Martha Swope

Opposite page: Members of the Polish Laboratory Theater of Wrocław in a scene from The Constant Prince, *directed by Jerzy Grotowski, a major innovator in the production of contemporary drama. Grotowski's methods, which include involvement of the actors with the audience, have had a wide influence on the European and American avant-garde theater during the last decade.*

Polish Laboratory Theater

generation, the truly notable developments of this later period were centered in New York City. There groups such as the Negro Ensemble Company were active in producing meaningful drama. The black musical, too, which traces its lineage to the 1920's, began to achieve both a wider audience and deeper significance in the 1970's with the emergence of such works as *Don't Bother Me, I Can't Cope* (1972) by Micki Grant.

Another development in the second half of the 20th century that affected the course of American drama was the decentralization of the theater. Broadway, as the theatrical district of New York City is known, had been the source of most new American plays for a century. Then, as production costs soared, the emphasis shifted. Small, impromptu, and less expensive New York City theaters, known collectively as Off Broad-

way, took the lead in discovering new authors, such as Jean-Claude Van Itallie (1936–) and Terence McNally (1939–). Plays especially successful in this milieu were occasionally moved to Broadway, but the more unorthodox and experimental productions found their only hope for lasting influence in college or university drama departments.

The academic theater, flourishing since the 1920's, increased in importance, as it attracted or commissioned original works rather than depending on a dwindling number of good plays from Broadway. Another source of new American drama was the professional resident theaters, which began to proliferate across the nation, from New Haven, Conn. (the Long Wharf Theater), to San Francisco, Calif. (the American Conservatory Theater).

Also during these years American playwrights,

Polish Laboratory Theater

like those of the rest of the world, were beginning to investigate new forms of drama, outside the traditional arenas; see *New Drama,* below.
Other National Drama. In every modern language there are examples of dramatic literature. For instance, the first great writer in the Portuguese language was a dramatist, Gil Vicente, who wrote in the early part of the 16th century. Two centuries later, Antonio José de Silva (1705–39) wrote during his brief life seven comedies important for their depiction of Portuguese society; and João de Almeida Garrett (1799–1854) was the leading Romanticist in Portugal.

Polish drama, too, has a long history, beginning in the Renaissance and highlighted by the opening of a National Theater in 1765. Its brisk Romantic period was inspired by a director of the National Theater, Wojciech Bogusławski (1757–1829). The excitement of the nationalist Young Poland period (1890–1914) is represented by the work of Stanisłav Przybyszewski (1868–1927). The surprisingly fruitful theater in spite of Communist domination today is led by such authors as Jerzy Broszkiewicz (1922–).

Modern Greek theater shows the influence of Ibsen and Chekhov as well as a particularly strong effort to explore the Greek character in dramatic terms, as in the works of Alexandros Matsas (1910–) and Alexis Solomos (1918–).

Turkey has several traditional forms of native drama, including the *meddah,* derived from ancient storytelling, and the *karagöz* or shadow theater, utilizing thin leather puppets to act out complex mystical and satiric incidents. The change in Turkish culture, looking away from the Orient to the West, brought a parallel change in Turkish drama in the late 19th century, when authors like Namik Kemal (1840–88) wrote patriotic plays in the European style.

Arab drama, with roots going back to 3000 B.C., was for centuries represented only by serious lyrical narratives, although a lusty tradition of folk puppet or shadow plays also existed. Modern drama in the Arab world, however, is almost entirely written in the style of Western drama. The Egyptian playwright Taufiq al-Hakīm (1898–   ) is probably most representative of contemporary Arab dramatists.

In another language, Yiddish, there is a remarkable body of dramatic literature, unlike any other. In little more than half a century, between 1875 and 1939, Yiddish drama arose, flourished, and virtually disappeared, although since World War II there have been periodic efforts to revive interest in Yiddish drama in such cities as Warsaw, Poland, and New York City.

The Hebrew language was traditionally restricted to prayers and sacred studies, so there is no early dramatic literature in Hebrew. The first professional Hebrew theater, the Habimah, was formed in Moscow in the 1920's but settled permanently in Tel Aviv in 1931. This company continues to perform such classics as *The Dybbuk* (1922), originally written in Yiddish by the Russian-born writer Shloyme Zaynvi Rappaport (1863–1920) under the pen name S. Ansky and translated into Hebrew by the Russian-born Chaim Nachman Bialik. Since the establishment of the State of Israel in 1948, more than 100 original plays in Hebrew have been presented. The flourishing Israeli theater has produced works by the poet Nathan Alterman (1910–) and such younger writers as Nafthali Ne'eman and Israel Eliraz.

In Africa, contemporary authors are employing a variety of languages to produce a body of dramatic literature that presages considerable future theatrical activity. Some Black playwrights utilize the language of their nation, as does Joseph Boakye Danquah of Ghana, who writes in Twi. Others write in French, like Keita Fodeba of the Republic of Guinea, who is also the impresario of the internationally known Ballets Africains. Still others use English, including Wole Soyinka (1934–) of Nigeria, probably the leading dramatist of Africa, whose plays *The Strong Breed* and *The Trial of Brother Jero* were both published in 1963 and have been performed in the United States. *See* AFRICAN LITERATURE.

Latin American literature for the theater has been written in both Portuguese and Spanish. Of Portuguese writers, the Brazilians Jorge Andrade (1922–) and Dias Gomes (1924–) are well-known playwrights; in the past century Martins Pena (1815–48) wrote comedies which are still performed and Gonçalves de Magalhães (1811–82) wrote verse tragedies that are historically important. As early as 1600 there were Spanish-language theaters in Lima, Peru, and Mexico City, Mexico; thus began a tradition still alive in the dramatic works of the Mexican Rodolfo Usigli (1905–), the Argentine Osvaldo Dragún (1929–   ), the Chilean Alberto Heiremans (1928–64), and the Cuban José Triana (1933–   ). *See* BRAZILIAN LITERATURE; SPANISH-AMERICAN LITERATURE.

THE NEW DRAMA

In the mid-20th century a type of drama usually referred to as the theater of the absurd emerged in France. Its roots were in such works as the scatological, mechanistic farce *Ubu Roi* ("King Ubu", 1896) by Alfred Jarry (1873–1907) and a

Bubbling Brown Sugar, *a musical revue that opened on Broadway in 1976, was an all-black testimonial to the music, performers, and style of Harlem from 1910 to 1940. Among the celebrants of the great jazz era were Josephine Premice and Avon Long.* UPI

surrealist play by Guillaume Apollinaire, *Les Mamelles de Tirésias* (1917; Eng. trans., *The Breasts of Tiresias,* 1930). Theater of the absurd embraces various concepts of earlier experimental theater, including surrealism and symbolism, and is also influenced by Brecht's concept of epic theater, by Pirandello's concern with illusion versus reality, by the nightmarish situations created by the Austrian writer Franz Kafka, and particularly by the theater of cruelty, as delineated in the theories of the French director and playwright Antonin Artaud (1895–1948). Artaud regarded the depiction of cruelty and eroticism as necessary to convey the human condition. Important initiators of the theater of the absurd are Irish-born Samuel Beckett, author of *Waiting for Godot* (performed 1952) and *Endgame* (1957), and Rumanian-born Eugène Ionesco, who wrote *La Cantatrice Chauve* (per-

formed 1950; Eng. trans., *The Bald Soprano,* 1958). The world that the theater of the absurd presents is an abstract, cruel, and mechanized world. Frequently rejecting conventional dialogue and plot, the absurdist author creates this world out of incongruities of plot and exaggerations of character. It is, moreover, a timeless world and without national boundaries. It has appealed, therefore, to international playwrights such as the Spanish-born French author Fernando Arrabal (1933–), the Czechoslovak Václav Havel (1936–), the Polish Słavomir Mrożek (1930–), the British Norman Frederick Simpson (1919–) and Joe Orton (1933–67), and the Americans Edward Albee and Arthur Kopit (1937–).

The new ritual drama, as practiced throughout the world in the late 1960's, evolved in part from the theater of the absurd. But the practitioners of this new form of theater also made use of any device deemed necessary for the creation of a desired dramatic effect, including improvisation, music, audience participation, films, and photographic slides. In much of this new theater the author assumed a secondary role compared to the director and performers. The effect of this experimentation on world drama was extensive, as dramatists of the 1970's freely incorporated new theater techniques into their works.

Another field of dramatic activity, attracting increasingly serious critical attention in the mid-20th century, was the motion picture. Films that are frequently classified by critics as important drama are the works of Ingmar Bergman of Sweden, of Michelangelo Antonioni and Federico Fellini of Italy, and of Jean-Luc Godard and François Truffaut of France. This applies also to those dramas that were written for the screen by such Americans as Arthur Miller, Tennessee Williams, and Paddy Chayevsky (1923–) and British authors like Robert Bolt and Harold Pinter. Television, too, has produced some noteworthy drama.

See separate articles for those individuals whose birth and death dates are not given. *See also* MOTION PICTURES; RADIO AND TELEVISION BROADCASTING. B.A.

DRAMATIC ARTS, AMERICAN ACADEMY OF. *See* AMERICAN ACADEMY OF DRAMATIC ARTS.

DRAMMEN, city and seaport in Norway, and capital of Buskerud County, at the junction of the Drammen R. and the Drammen Fjord, about 25 miles S.W. of Oslo. Drammen is a railroad junction and an export center for one of the most productive forest districts of Norway. Important industries are the processing of wood pulp, cellulose, paper, and other lumber by-products; the mining of zinc, nickel, and cobalt; shipbuilding; and salmon fishing. Pop. (1971) 49,847.

DRAUGHTS, or DRAFTS. See CHECKERS.

DRAVA, or DRAVE (Ger. *Drau*), river of Europe, an important affluent of the Danube R. It rises s. of the Hohe Tauern Alps in the s.w. part of the Austrian Tirol and flows through the scenic Pustertal, the longest longitudinal valley of the Alps, toward Lienz, Austria, where it is joined by the Isel R. It then flows eastward through Maribor, a town of Slovenia, Yugoslavia, traversing the N. tip of that country, and is joined by its principal branch, the Mur R., near Kaposvár, a Hungarian town on the Yugoslav border. For about 90 mi., the Drava forms most of the boundary between Hungary and Yugoslavia from a point 25 miles E. of Varaždin, Hungary, to a point 25 miles N.E. of Osijek, Yugoslavia; then, turning S.E., it ends by joining the Danube 11 miles E. of Osijek. In the first part of its 450-mi. course, the Drava is a mountain torrent. From Villach, Austria, to Barcs, Hungary, it is navigable by raft only; from Barcs to its mouth, a distance of 65 mi., it is navigable by small vessels. At its mouth the Drava is 1055 ft. wide and 20 ft. deep.

DRAVIDIAN, name applied to the short, dark peoples indigenous to the southern part of the Indian peninsula prior to the advent of the Aryans (see CASTE). The present-day Dravidians are much intermixed racially; Caucasian and other stocks are strongly represented in the total Dravidian population of more than 110,000,000. Similarly, the culture of the Dravidians is heterogeneous. Totemism, kinship in the female line, and other primitive customs are encountered among some segments of the Dravidians; in contrast, a high state of civilization, embracing a literature and architectural skill, exists among other Dravidian groups. See GOND; INDIAN PEOPLES: *Modern Racial and Cultural Groups.*

Properly, the term "Dravidian" is applied to language rather than to race, because the languages have remained comparatively pure. The Dravidian languages, agglutinative in structure, form an isolated group dominant in southern India and northern Ceylon. In the four Dravidian-speaking Indian States of Andhra Pradesh, Kerala, Tamil Nadu, and Mysore, sometimes violent agitation has been directed against attempts by the government of India to institute Hindi as the national language. Of the many Dravidian languages the principal ones are Tamil, spoken by more than 21,000,000 persons; Telugu, by about 38,000,000; Kanarese, by

about 18,000,000; and Malayalam, by about 17,000,000. Tamil and Malayalam have their own alphabets; those for Telugu and Kanarese are almost identical. See INDIAN LANGUAGES.

Most Dravidian literary works are comparatively modern, despite the antiquity of the Dravidian civilization. Various grammatical treatises in Tamil are attributed to the legendary sage Agastya, who is said to have lived before Christ; but these writings probably date from the 10th century A.D. Of about the same period are the *Kintamani,* a romantic poem of some 15,000 verses, and the *Naladiyar,* a moralistic poem of some 1330 stanzas. Around 1100 the Tamil poet Kamban wrote a version, or adaptation, of the Sanskrit epic *Ramayana,* and in the 16th century a native king of the Pandya dynasty wrote poetic works of merit. In the 18th century, the Tamil poet Tayumanavan flourished, and the Italian Jesuit missionary Joseph Beschi (d. 1742) wrote prose and poetry in the Tamil language. In the Telugu language the oldest extant work is a version of the Sanskrit epic *Mahabharata,* written by the poet Bhatta Narayana perhaps as early as the 9th century A.D. A poet named Kesava wrote in Kanarese in the 12th century, and in the Malayalam language are various works based upon Sanskrit.

DRAWING, delineation of form upon a surface, usually plane, by means of lines and tints or shading. Painting is broadly distinguished from drawing by its use of varied color to represent the original object, whereas in drawing only the form and light and shade ("modeling") are represented. The forms delineated may be visible objects, imagined forms presented as if actually seen, or purely arbitrary or abstract forms. Because the delineation of form lies at the foundation of all the plastic arts, drawing is one of the most important single branches of study in schools of art, architecture, and engineering.

The drawing of visible objects is essentially the graphic recording of mental impressions received through the eye. The draftsman seeks to produce upon the paper, by means of lines and tints, visual images calculated to awaken in the beholder mental images and impressions as nearly as possible like those evoked by the actual objects. Because it is not possible, however, to present all the visible facts and aspects of an object in black and white on a plane surface, the drawing must by suggestion stimulate the imagination of the beholder to supply whatever is lacking in the representation. A drawing of a tree, even though merely an aggregation of black lines and dots on a small piece of white

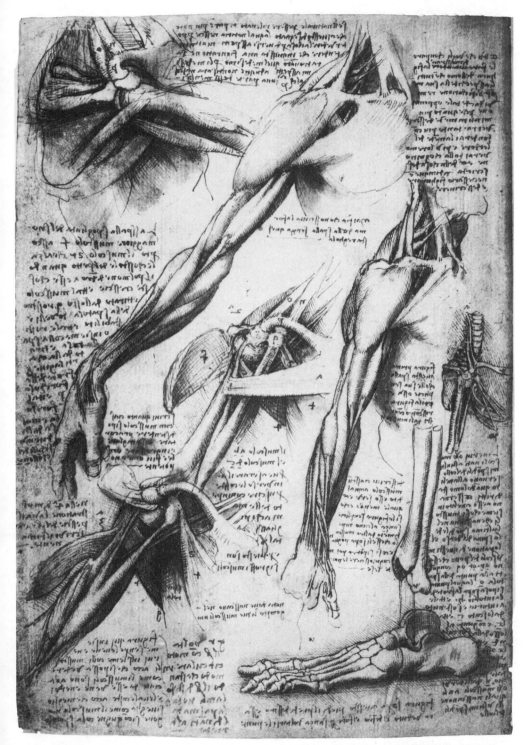

Analysis of the shoulder girdle, an anatomical drawing by the Florentine Renaissance artist Leonardo da Vinci.
Royal Library – Windsor Castle

163

paper, may so strongly suggest the outline, foliage, masses, light, and shade of an actual tree that it evokes the impressions one has in seeing such a tree; imagination supplies the size and distance, usually by perspective (q.v.), and the detail color that the drawing lacks. Artistic power in drawing consists largely in the ability thus to create by suggestion a vivid impression of reality. A sketch is a drawing that attempts to present in a summary way only partial and momentary aspects of the object represented. In an effective sketch, the simplicity and vigor of the personal interpretation of the artist are not sacrificed in the effort to achieve elaborate finish. The judicious choice of what to show and what to omit calls for a highly developed taste and can be mastered only by long experience.

Freehand Drawing. Drawing in which the hand receives no assistance from mechanical appliances is called freehand drawing. It lies at the foundation of all the arts of plastic design, including sculpture, and constitutes an art in itself. The great Italian masters of drawings, such as Raphael, Leonardo da Vinci, and Michelangelo (qq.v.), have been among the geniuses of their times. Even the greatness of such colorists as Titian and Paolo Veronese (qq.v.) depends in large measure upon their consummate draftsmanship.

The different kinds and schools of drawing are distinguished by the ways in which the restrictions imposed by the medium of black and white on a plane surface are evaded or overcome. In outline drawings, and in some sketches, only the outlines and contours or salient edges and markings of an object or scene are shown. The power of pure line, even without color, to suggest the most varied modeling of surfaces and to express the minutest detail is admirably exemplified in Chinese and Japanese art. The European schools, on the other hand, lay great stress upon values, or the rendering of the varied gradations of light and dark. European artists have striven to achieve the desired effects by means of corresponding gradations in the black-and-white tones of the drawing. Even different colors may be suggested, or rather interpreted, in black and white by a careful rendering of their apparent values; a dark red, for example, is indicated by darker shading than a light blue or a yellow. The great artists of the Renaissance (q.v.) stand midway between the Japanese exponents of pure line and the modern European interpreters of values. Their drawings are remarkable for the purity, vigor, and delicacy of their lines, as well as for the skillful though somewhat conventional modeling of the forms as expressed by shading.

TECHNIQUE OF FREEHAND DRAWING. The fundamental principles of the art are the same, whatever the medium employed. In drawing from any object or model, the first step is to observe and sketch in the dominant structural lines, contours, and masses. The more important details are next added and corrected, and the minor details are left to the last. In executing these various stages of the drawing, lightness of touch and sureness of line are important. Experience gives the artist the knowledge of the most effective methods for expressing the facts and aspects he is seeking to record.

The detailed technique of drawing, however, varies greatly with the medium employed. The chief instruments are the pencil, pen, black or red crayon, charcoal, and brush. Of these the pen is the most exacting, since it makes an absolutely black mark on the white paper, and tints must be expressed by dots, closely serried lines, and crosshatching. The masters of pen drawing must be masters of pure line. With charcoal the artist must "paint" on his paper, fine charcoal lines being nearly impossible to draw; this difficulty is also true of the brush, and the artist frequently resorts to sepia and other "wash" drawings. Pencil and crayon require the use of the line but also permit broad, soft strokes and stumped or rubbed-in shading. Very effective drawings are made by using a tinted paper, often either gray or pale blue, on which the highlights are laid on in white with chalk or Chinese white; the darker shades and masses are indicated with the pencil, and the tone of the paper is left to represent the intermediate values. The great masters of the Renaissance, who lacked the familiar graphite "lead" pencil, which is a 16th-century development, sometimes used a lead or a silver point on parchment or heavy paper, giving a pale gray line; more often, they used sanguine or red chalk. In place of the modern steel pen they used the quill, which made a softer and broader stroke.

Mechanical Drawing. For scientific purposes, for the working drawings from which buildings and machinery are to be made and erected, and for all purposes requiring great exactitude of representation, a different sort of delineation is necessary from that of the artist working with a free hand. Freehand drawings are personal interpretations of form. Their value is artistic, not scientific; no two drawings of the same object by different persons, or by the same person at different times, can be absolutely alike. In mechanical, or instrumental, drawing, on the other hand, mathematical exactness of line and dimension is secured by the use of various instruments, the most important of these being the T-square, rule, and triangles for drawing right lines; compasses for drawing circles and arcs of circles; dividers for laying off exact distances; the scale for determining and measuring dimensions; the protractor for laying off angles; the ruling pen for drawing clean and faultless lines in ink; and a considerable number of special instruments. The object of drawings executed by these means is to furnish scientifically correct graphic records of the actual proportions and

Instruction and practice perfect the drawing student's coordination of hand and eye.

Robin Forbes – Ford Foundation

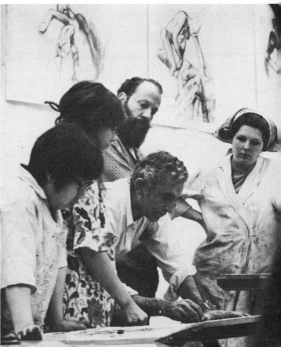

form relations of objects, usually at a much reduced scale. This object is effected by means of projections upon imaginary vertical and horizontal planes, called planes of projection, with two dimensions of the object being shown in each projection. These projections comprise plans, or top views, showing the object as if seen from an infinite height above; elevations, or front, side, and rear views, as if seen from a point infinitely distant horizontally; and sections, which show the object as if sliced in two with the nearer half removed, exposing the interior structure. These projections show the correct geometrical relations of the various dimensions and parts of the structure or object, and the use of two or more projections shows all the dimensional relations. To assist the eye in interpreting these highly conventional drawings, which are really not pictures but diagrams, they are often (especially architectural drawings) drawn with the shadows cast as if sunlight were falling on the object in each projection at an assumed and uniform angle. This angle is usually such that the rays, falling from in front of the vertical plane and downward to the right, are projected at 45 degrees to the ground line.

Instrumental drawing is divided, according to its various applications, into mechanical drawing, a general term for all engineering drafting; machine drawing, or the preparation of the working drawings for the construction of machinery; architectural drawing, ship drafting, and topographical drawing; and the various purely mathematical divisions of descriptive geometry: stereotomy, or the preparation of drawings for cut stonework; crystallography; and the like.

In architectural drawing and in most forms of machine drawing and engineering, the purpose is to furnish diagrams of all parts of a structure or machine to be erected. These diagrams are drawn to exact scale and marked with the proposed dimensions for guidance of those who are to execute the work. They are made up of as many plan views as may be necessary, elevations of the various faces of the structure, and sections showing its internal arrangement. The plans are drawn to a small scale, which may be from $\frac{1}{32}$ in. to the foot to $\frac{1}{4}$ in. or even $\frac{1}{2}$ in. to the foot (with approximately corresponding scales when the metric system is used). Many of the details of construction are shown in drawings to a larger scale, 1 ft. being represented by $\frac{3}{4}$ in., 1 in., or even 2 or 3 in. A large number of full-size drawings of structural details are also prepared. At the mill, stoneyard, or shop where the work is executed, these drawings are supplemented by shop drawings to assist in laying out the work and to serve as exact patterns for its execution. The largest shop drawings are those made in the mold lofts of shipyards, in which every rib of the ship is drawn to its full size on the smooth floor of the loft. The drawing of decorative details of carving, inlay, and other ornament in architectural work is of necessity chiefly freehand work and involves an artistic element not called for in the purely technical drawings described above. See also MECHANICAL DRAWING.

Perspective Drawing. Perspective drawing stands midway between freehand or pictorial drawing and instrumental drawing. It aims to represent the actual aspect of an object from a given point of view, and yet this field of drawing is a matter less of personal and artistic interpretation than of scientific determination. The object is shown with all the angular distortion and foreshortening that it exhibits to the eye placed at the given point of view; but the exact angles, dimensions, distortion, and foreshortening of each part are determined by mathematical processes and not by mere visual impressions. Perspective drawing, therefore, is a type of descriptive geometry (q.v.), characterized by the accurate representation of three-dimensional forms in two-dimensional drawings. In the latter, however, an object is represented as if it were projected by parallel lines on two planes. Perspective drawing represents the object as if it were projected by rays, converging at the eye, upon an assumed picture plane represented by the paper, which intersects the rays. All lines and planes that are not parallel to the picture plane converge at points called vanishing points or traces. A special type of angular projection called isometric projection shows all three dimensions at once, as does a perspective drawing, but with a uniform scale for all parts of the picture; in true perspective the same actual dimension appears of varying size according to its distance from the eye.

A perspective drawing, thus scientifically laid out in outline, may be finished as to line, color, light and shade, and accessories in a pictorial manner, as in freehand drawing; it then emerges from the category of scientific drawing into that of fine art. Indeed, no artist can master the correct portrayal of form, especially of scenery and buildings, without training in perspective; it is accordingly an important branch of study in all schools of art. It is absolutely indispensable to scene painters and forms the basis of the illusory effects of stage settings. The artists of the Renaissance were the first to systematize the principles of perspective. Those of the late Renaissance, notably Michelangelo and Paolo Veronese, employed the resources of perspective with striking effect in their great decorative paintings. Japanese drawings are interesting for their treatment of perspective, the point of view being in almost all cases assumed at a high elevation, giving an effect called "bird's-eye perspective".

Skill in Drawing. The delineation of an object actually seen involves, first, observation, which comprises perception and attention; secondly, the memorizing or mental retention of the visual impression while the eye is momentarily withdrawn from the object to the paper; and, thirdly, the coordination of the movement of the hand with the outlines of the movement of the memorized image. In drawing imaginary forms or designs originating in the mind of the artist, a mental image takes the place of the visible object. Therefore the ability to visualize these mental images clearly and distinctly in the "mind's eye" is an important element in all draftsmanship of the highest order. Skill in drawing is as dependent on intellectual factors as on skill of hand, and no system of teaching drawing which confines itself to the mere discipline of hand and eye can be considered scientifically or philosophically correct. The draftsman draws best what he knows best. Consequently a thorough acquaintance with the widest range of forms is as essential to consummate draftsmanship as is manual skill in portraying them. Constant drawing from life, from nature, and from the object not only gives facility of execution but also, by enlarging knowledge of forms, gives the artist a broader grasp of form in general.   R.B.H.

DRAWING, MECHANICAL. See MECHANICAL DRAWING.

DRAYTON, Michael (1563–1631), English poet, born in Hartshill, Warwickshire. He settled in London in 1590, and a year later wrote his first volume of poems, *The Harmony of the Church,* a rendering of scriptural passages. This work offended the archbishop of Canterbury, and almost the entire edition was publicly burned. Soon thereafter he wrote *Idea, the Shepherd's Garland* (1593), consisting of nine pastoral poems, and *Idea's Mirror* (1594), a collection of love sonnets. Drayton's historical poem *The Barons' Wars* (published in a shorter form as *Mortimeriados* in 1596) was printed in 1603. The ambitious *Polyolbion,* a patriotic description of England, appeared in 1612 and 1622. His *Nymphidia, the Court of Faëry* (1627), a poem of imaginative fancy, and his narrative poem "The

Ballad of Agincourt" (In *Poems Lyric and Pastorall,* 1605) are considered his finest works. Among his other writings are the historical poems *Piers Gaveston* (1593), *Matilda* (1594), and *Robert, Duke of Normandy* (1596).

DREAMING, act of experiencing apparent sensations and events during sleep, trance, or other unconscious states. Dreams may be confined to a single sensation but more often include incidents and whole chains of connected events in which the dreamer seems to take part. Among the most important characteristics of dreams are their seeming reality and their usually fantastic content.

Many hypotheses have been advanced concerning the causes and mechanism of dreaming. Until recently dreams were sometimes believed to represent, either directly or symbolically, events which would take place in the future, or visitations by ghosts or other spirits; see DIVINATION.

One modern explanation of dreams is that of the psychoanalytic school, which holds that dreaming represents the activity of a part of the mind called the unconscious (q.v.). According to psychoanalytic theory, dreams represent the imaginative fulfillment of wishes and desires that are repressed in the conscious mind during periods of wakefulness. In young children the wish fulfillment of dreams is readily apparent; for example, the child will dream that he has been given a box of candy or a new toy. In adults, in whom repressions are stronger and more deeply seated, the wish or desire is clothed in symbols. The interpretation of these dream symbols, which recur again and again, with modifications, in the dreams of different individuals, is one of the techniques of psychoanalysis. See PSYCHOANALYSIS: *Theory of the Unconscious.*

Dreaming usually is accompanied by rapid eye movements that probably represent continuous scanning of the changing scene, in which the sleeper is both actor and spectator. Since these eye movements can be recorded even while the eyes remain closed, they provide an objective method for studying the incidence and duration of dreams. Experiments conducted since the late 1950's have revealed that most dreaming occurs in the later part of the night, and that dreams last anywhere from several minutes to more than an hour. Although many people do not recall dreams in the morning, the evidence from studies of eye movements suggests that everyone dreams. The dreaming state is characterized by a high degree of electrical activity in the brain together with an unusually relaxed state of the musculature. The sleeper is relatively difficult to awaken while he is dreaming. Sleepwalking and sleep talking, although commonly believed to be associated with dreaming, seem to occur in a different stage of sleep altogether and to be unrelated to dreams. *See also* SLEEP. D.Ka.

DREBBEL, Cornelis. *See* SUBMARINE.

DREDGING, work of removing soil or material from the bottom of a river, lake, or ocean harbor. Dredges are the machines used for this purpose and consist of powerful, usually steam-powered hoisting or suction equipment mounted on bargelike floats. Dredges are used to deepen or widen waterways, to reclaim underwater land by filling, to build dikes or foundations, and to mine alluvial deposits of precious metals such as gold and tin (qq.v.).

Various types of dredges are used to recover underwater material, which is called spoil. Dipper or bucket dredges, used in digging the Panama Canal (q.v.), have a bucket on the end of a movable arm. Grab-bucket dredges are similar but use a bucket swung by cables from the end of a boom, and can operate in depths greater than 100 ft. Elevator dredges employ an endless chain of small buckets. Hydraulic dredges suck the spoil into the dredge through a pipe, and are commonly fitted with a floating pipeline through which the spoil is discharged on the shore. Mining dredges usually separate the precious material from the rest of the spoil, which is discarded. Stirring dredges are used to open passages for navigation by agitating soil until the current carries it away. Pneumatic dredges, using compressed air, are used where it is desirable to discharge materials, through a pipe, to a considerable distance or greater height. Barges are also used to receive the spoil from dredges.

The term dredge is also applied to the smaller bucket equipment used by scientists to probe the ocean floor for soil or zoological specimens. *See also* EARTH-MOVING MACHINES.

DRED SCOTT CASE, case that came before the Supreme Court of the United States (q.v.) in 1856–57, and that involved determination of the constitutionality of the Missouri Compromise (q.v.), and of the legal right of a Negro to become a citizen of the United States. Dred Scott (d. 1858) was a slave owned by an army surgeon Dr. John Emerson (d. 1846) of Missouri. In 1836 Scott had been taken by his master to Fort Snelling, in what is now Minnesota, then a territory in which slavery (q.v.) was expressly forbidden according to the terms of the Missouri Compromise. While still on free territory, Scott had been allowed to marry a woman who was also a slave

owned by Dr. Emerson. In 1846, after an attempt at self-purchase, Scott brought suit in the State court on the grounds that residence in a free territory released him from slavery. The Supreme Court of Missouri, however, ruled in 1852 that upon his being brought back to territory where slavery was legal, the status of slavery reattached to him and he had no standing before the court. The case was brought before the Federal Circuit Court, which took jurisdiction but held against Scott. The case was taken on appeal to the Supreme Court of the U.S., where it was argued at length in 1855 and 1856, and finally decided in 1857. The decision handed down by a majority vote of the court was to the effect that there was no power in the existing

Dred Scott Bettmann Archive

form of government to make citizens of Negroes, slave or free, and that at the time of the formation of the Constitution they were not, and could not be, citizens in any of the States. Accordingly, Scott was still a slave and not a citizen of Missouri, from which it followed that he had no right to sue in the Federal courts. The decision of the majority was matched in importance by the views expressed by Chief Justice Roger Brooke Taney (q.v.) as *obiter dicta*. These opinions went beyond the actual point to be settled to the extent of asserting that Scott, having originally been a slave, and therefore a mere chattel, might, according to the law of Missouri, be taken, like any other chattel, anywhere within the jurisdiction of the U.S.; that the Missouri Compromise was in violation of the Constitution; and that slavery could not be prohibited by Congress in the territories of the U.S. The case, and particularly the court's *dicta* aroused intense bitterness among the Abolitionists (q.v.), widened the breach between the North and South, and was among the causes of the American Civil War. B.Q.

DREISER, Theodore (1871–1945), American novelist and journalist, born in Terre Haute, Indiana. He began newspaper work as a reporter on the Chicago *Daily Globe* in 1892, and was dramatic editor and traveling correspondent of the Saint Louis *Globe Democrat* in 1892–93, and traveling correspondent of the St. Louis *Republic* in 1893–94. His career as a novelist began in 1900 with *Sister Carrie,* which he wrote in the intervals between work for various magazines. Public outcry against the novel for its realistic treatment of sexual problems caused the publisher to withdraw it from public sale. Dreiser continued writing, and was managing editor of *Broadway Magazine* from 1906 to 1907, and editor in chief of Butterick publications from 1907 to 1910. By the time his second novel, *Jenny Gerhardt,* was published in 1911, his work had found influential supporters, including the British novelists H. G. Wells and Hugh Seymour Walpole (qq.v.), and he was able to devote himself entirely to literature. His writings continued to excite controversy. In *The Financier* (1912) and *The Titan* (1914), he drew harsh portraits of a type of ruthless businessman. In *The "Genius"* (1915), he presented a study of the artistic temperament in a mercenary society. This novel increased his influence among young American writers, who acclaimed him leader of a new school of social realism. Real fame, however, did not come to Dreiser until 1925, when his *An American Tragedy* had great popular success. The novel was dramatized and was made into a motion picture. Although Dreiser's style was regarded by some critics as clumsy and plodding, he was generally recognized as an American literary pioneer. The American writer Sinclair Lewis (q.v.) hailed *Sister Carrie* as "the first book free of English literary influence". Toward the end of his career Dreiser devoted himself largely to promoting his radical political views. He had visited the Soviet Union and, in *Dreiser Looks at Russia* (1928), declared his sympathy for that country. Six months before his death it was announced that he had become a member of the Communist Party of the United States. His last novels, *The Bulwark* and *The Stoic,* appeared posthumously, in 1946 and 1947. His other work includes *Plays of the Natural and Supernatural* (1916), *A Hoosier Holiday* (1916), *Twelve Men* (1919), *A Book About Myself*

Theodore Dreiser with his wife on his sixty-fourth birthday. Brown Brothers

(1922), *The Color of a Great City* (1923), *Moods* (verse, 1926), *Chains* (1927), *A Gallery of Women* (1929), *Dawn* (1931), *Tragic America* (1932), and *America Is Worth Saving* (1941).

Dreiser's older brother Paul Dresser (1857–1911), composed the popular songs "My Gal Sal" and "On the Banks of the Wabash".

DRESDEN, city in East Germany, and capital of Dresden District, on the Elbe R., about 100 miles s. of Berlin and 65 miles s.e. of Leipzig. The city is composed of several quarters, notably Altstadt and Friedrichstadt, on the s. bank of the Elbe; and Neustadt, Antonstadt, and Albertstadt, on the N. bank. Five bridges, including a railroad bridge, link the N. and s. divisions of the city. Famous squares of Dresden include the Theaterplatz, the Altmarkt, and the Schlossplatz, all in the Altstadt. This quarter is also the site of the Brühl Terrace, a promenade along the Elbe. The principal park of the city is the Grosser Garten.

Dresden has long been known for its churches. Noteworthy among these is the Roman Catholic Hofkirche, a structure in rococo style constructed between 1739 and 1751. The Protestant Sophienkirche, an edifice with twin spires, dates from the 14th century. The Church of Our Lady, dating from early in the 18th century, is surmounted by a stone cupola 311 ft. in height. One of the most prominent

Barges are moored on the River Elbe at Dresden, with the spires of some of the city's historic churches in the background.
Ewing Galloway

secular buildings in Dresden is the former royal palace, the Georgenschloss, built (1530–35) in the German Renaissance style and restored between 1890 and 1902. Other buildings are the Prinzen-Palais, built in 1715; the Hoftheater, a Renaissance-style structure; the Opera House (1878), also in Renaissance style; the Rathaus, or city hall, a huge building in the German Renaissance style, surmounted by a 387-ft. octagonal tower; the Albertinium, formerly the arsenal of Dresden and later a museum of oriental and classical antiquities; and the Zwinger, an incompleted palace. The Zwinger contains the Semper Gallery, one of the foremost institutions of its kind in the world. It has more than 2500 paintings, including works by masters of the Italian, Flemish, and Dutch schools such as Raphael's "Madonna di San Sisto" ("Sistine Madonna"), Correggio's "La Notte", Titian's "Venus", Rembrandt's "Portrait of Himself with Wife Sitting on His Knee", and Rubens' "The Boar Hunt". Among other features of the Zwinger museum are a collection of about 350,000 engravings and drawings, exhibits of works by modern painters, and a collection of casts depicting the development of sculpture from ancient to modern times. The Zwinger also has zoological, mineral-ogical, and other scientific exhibits. The Johanneum Museum contains one of the most complete historical collections in Germany and specimens of porcelain from all parts of the world. The Green Vault, in the Georgenschloss, has collections of precious stones; gold, amber, ivory, and silver art objects; and weapons. Dresden also has extensive educational facilities, including research institutions, an institute of technology, an academy of art, and various schools of higher learning.

Commerce. The city is one of the principal industrial centers of East Germany, and is served by a wide network of railway systems and by waterborne carriers operating on the Elbe. Among the broad variety of light industrial products manufactured in Dresden are precision, surgical and musical instruments, china, perfumes, gold and silver ornaments, cameras, soap, leather goods, paper, beer, distilled liquors, chemicals, straw hats, artificial flowers, and gloves. Dresden porcelain, which is named for the city, is manufactured chiefly in Meissen (q.v.), about 15 miles to the N.W.

History. Founded late in the 12th century, Dresden first attained prominence in 1270, when it became the seat of government of Henry the Illustrious, Margrave of Meissen (1215–88). Wenceslaus II, King of Bohemia (1271–1305), acquired control of the town after

170

the death of Henry. Bohemian rule was superseded by that of the margraves of Brandenburg, but the margraves of Meissen regained Dresden early in the 14th century. In 1485 it was acquired by Albert III, Duke of Saxony (1443–1500), who made it the capital of his dominions. Numerous improvements were accomplished in Dresden during the next few centuries, notably in the reign of Frederick Augustus I, Elector of Saxony, and as Augustus II, King of Poland (1670–1733). The city was severely damaged during the Seven Years' War and the Napoleonic Wars (qq.v.). In 1813 Napoleon I (q.v.), Emperor of France, established headquarters in Dresden. That year he won his last great victory in and around the city.

Dresden expanded considerably during the second half of the 19th century, particularly between 1880 and 1900. In February, 1945, during the final phase of World War II in Europe, three fifths of the city was all but obliterated by American and British air raids. In May, Dresden was shelled and taken by Soviet armed forces. It was later included in the Soviet zone of occupation. The city is being rebuilt on modern planning principles, and much rebuilding had been accomplished by the late 1960's. Pop. (1971 prelim.) 500,051, compared to 630,216 in 1939.

DRESDEN, BATTLE OF, major engagement of the Napoleonic Wars (q.v.) in which the French forces defeated the allied armies of Austria, Prussia, and Russia at Dresden, Saxony (now in East Germany), in August, 1813. *See* MURAT, JOACHIM; NAPOLEON I.

DRESS. *See* COSTUME.

DREW, name of a famous American stage family of British origin. The following are among its most important members.

Louisa Lane Drew (1820–97), born Louisa Lane in London, of a British theatrical family. She traveled to the United States in 1827 and in the same year made her first stage appearance in Philadelphia, Pa. Subsequently, she became celebrated for many roles, especially those of Lady Teazle in *The School for Scandal* and Mrs. Malaprop in *The Rivals,* both plays by the British playwright Richard Brinsley Sheridan (q.v.). She married the Irish-American actor John Drew (see below) in 1850 and with him managed the Arch Street Theater in Philadelphia. After his death in 1862, she was sole manager until 1893. Her son, John Drew, her daughter, Georgiana Drew (1856–93), and her adopted son, Sydney White (1868–1919), all became actors. Georgiana married the Anglo-American actor Maurice Barrymore and was the mother of the American actors Lionel, Ethel, and John Barrymore; *see under* BARRYMORE.

John Drew (1827–62), husband of Louisa Lane, born in Dublin, Ireland. After making his debut in New York City in 1846, he became well known for his portrayals of comic Irish parts, particularly that of Sir Lucius O'Trigger in *The Rivals.* His stock company, which performed in the Arch Street Theater, became one of the most successful theatrical groups in America.

John Drew (1853–1927), son of John and Louisa Drew, born in Philadelphia, Pa. He made his debut with his mother's company in 1873. From 1879 to 1892 he was the leading actor of the New York company formed by the American playwright and manager John Augustin Daly (q.v.). Drew later starred in many productions in which he usually played witty, semi-ironical society roles. His handsome appearance and polished manner made him one of the most enduring of the so-called matinee idols. One of his best-known roles was that of Petruchio in *The Taming of the Shrew,* a comedy by the English dramatist William Shakespeare (q.v.).

DREW, Charles Richard (1904–50), American surgeon, born in Washington, D.C., and educated at Amherst College and McGill University. In 1935 he was appointed assistant in pathology at Howard University and in 1936, assistant in surgery. From 1938 to 1940 he was in New York City as resident in surgery at Columbia-Presbyterian Medical Center and fellow in surgery at the College of Physicians and Surgeons, Columbia University. In 1940 and 1941, during World War II, Drew did pioneering research in the collection and storage of blood plasma (*see* BLOOD: *Blood Transfusion: Transfusion of Plasma*). In 1941 he returned to Howard University as head of the department of surgery.

DREW UNIVERSITY, formerly DREW THEOLOGICAL SEMINARY, coeducational institution of higher learning, founded in 1866. It is located in Madison, N.J., and conducted under the auspices of The United Methodist Church (*see* UNITED METHODIST CHURCH, THE) for the training of its ministers. Although many of its courses are devoted to theology, the university also offers a broad range of secular subjects. The master of sacred theology and master of religious education degrees are conferred, as well as the degrees of bachelor, master, and doctor. In 1968 the university library housed more than 300,000 bound volumes. In 1972 enrollment was 1691; the faculty numbered 157, and the endowment was approximately $13,966,000.

DREXEL, Anthony Joseph (1826–93), American banker and philanthropist, born in Philadelphia, Pa. At the age of thirteen he began to work in the banking house founded three years earlier by his father, the Austrian-born American banker Francis Martin Drexel (1792–1863). In 1847 he was named a member of the firm, Drexel & Co. After the death of his father, Drexel expanded the firm; such branches as Drexel, Harjes & Co., Paris, and Drexel, Morgan, & Co., New York City, were established. As a philanthropist, Drexel made extensive donations to hospitals, churches, and charitable institutions. His gifts to the Drexel Institute of Art, Science, and Industry (now the Drexel Institute of Technology), founded in 1891 in Philadelphia, amounted to more than $3,000,000.

DREXEL UNIVERSITY, privately controlled nonsectarian coeducational institution of higher learning, located in Philadelphia, Pa., and founded in 1891 by the American banker Anthony Joseph Drexel (q.v.) as the Drexel Institute of Art, Science, and Industry. The university consists of colleges of business administration, home economics, engineering, humanities and social science, and science; a graduate school of library science; and an evening college. The degrees of bachelor, master, and doctor are granted. Drexel was one of the first schools to adopt the cooperative plan, whereby students combine academic work with experience as employees in business and industry. The university houses a 200,000-volume library. In 1972 en-

Alfred Dreyfus

rollment was 10,800 students, and the faculty at that time numbered 600. The endowment of the university in 1968 was about $13,200,000.

DREYFUS AFFAIR, in French history, the controversy involving the French army officer Alfred Dreyfus (1859–1935), convicted on a charge of treason in 1894. His conviction precipitated a national conflict that almost resulted in civil war, that advanced the progressive republican wing to a dominant position in French political life, and that eventually led to the separation of church and state in France; see FRANCE: *History: The Third Republic to World War I.*

In 1893 Dreyfus, a captain of artillery of Jewish faith, who was assigned to the general staff in Paris, was charged with treason. He was accused specifically of having written an anonymous *bordereau* (Fr., "schedule") containing a list of secret French military documents that were scheduled for delivery to the German embassy in Paris. In 1894 Dreyfus was found guilty by a court-martial, reduced in rank, and transported to Devil's Island (q.v.), there to be imprisoned for the rest of his life. In 1896, two years after the trial, Lieutenant Colonel George Picquart (1854–1914), then head of French military intelligence, uncovered evidence indicating that a French infantry officer, Major Marie-Charles Ferdinand Walsin Esterhazy (1847–1923), was actually the writer of the treasonous *bordereau* ascribed to Dreyfus. Picquart was silenced by his superiors and dismissed from the service. About the same time similar evidence implicating Esterhazy was uncovered by relatives and friends of Dreyfus. The army, in order to save face, had to court-martial Esterhazy, but early in 1898 he was acquitted. In August, 1898, Lieutenant Colonel Hubert-Joseph Henry (1846–98) confessed that as Picquart's successor as head of intelligence he had forged documents implicating Dreyfus; he was arrested and committed suicide in his cell. Esterhazy was dismissed from the army and left France, settling in England. In 1899 the Dreyfus case was brought before the *cour de cassation,* the highest French court of appeal, which ordered a new trial. The resultant second court-martial again pronounced Dreyfus guilty, but reduced his sentence to ten years imprisonment. Ten days after the trial was completed, a new, more progressive government of France, under Premier Pierre Waldeck-Rousseau (1846–1904) and President Émile Loubet (1838–1929), nullified the verdict and pardoned Dreyfus. Seven years later, in 1906, Dreyfus was fully rehabilitated by a judgment of the *cour de cassation,* restored to the army with the rank of major, and decorated with the legion of honor (q.v.). He served in World War I with the rank of lieutenant colonel. Of the other figures in the case, Esterhazy, remaining in England, confessed late in 1899 to having been the German spy. His accuser Picquart was reinstated, promoted to general, and served from 1906 to 1909 as minister of war in the cabinet of Premier Georges Clemenceau (q.v.).

In the volatile France of the 1890's, the Dreyfus case provided the spark for an inevitable political and social flare-up. Extremists of the right and the left used the affair as an illustration of their disillusionment with the prevailing order. When Dreyfus was found guilty at the first court-martial, a storm of anti-Jewish propaganda was unleashed by the powerful anti-Semitic forces that existed at the time, particularly in the French army; see ANTI-SEMITISM. Liberal Frenchmen, in view of Dreyfus' apparent guilt, had to remain silent at first. They did not remain silent, however, after the discovery of the evidence against Esterhazy, the dismissal of his accuser Picquart, and the eventual acquittal of Esterhazy. These apparent injustices provoked widespread protests and the Dreyfus case soon became the most important public issue in France. Right-wing political elements, the army, and the Roman Catholic Church upheld the courts-martial. Liberals and many intellectuals, led by the authors Anatole France (q.v.) and Charles Péguy (1873–1914) denounced them. The novelist Émile Zola (q.v.) wrote an impassioned letter, printed in the Paris newspaper L'Aurore in January, 1898, under the heading J'accuse (Fr., "I accuse"). Zola's courageous denunciation of both military and civil authorities, whom he accused of lying, resulted in his being tried for libel and sentenced to a fine and a year in prison. He escaped, however, and during his brief self-imposed exile in England, his trial and the ideas he had expressed caused the Dreyfus case to become a subject of worldwide concern. In France, public demand for a retrial of Dreyfus was omnipresent and vociferous. The verdict of the second court-martial proved so unpopular that a liberal-oriented government was voted into power in the national elections of 1899. After 1900 the power and prestige of the military declined in France, and anticlerical legislation was introduced in the assembly, leading in 1905 to the separation of church and state.

DRILL, any of several small carnivorous gastropod mollusks (see MOLLUSCA) which bore through the shells of other mollusks and suck out their juices. A common drill of the waters off the eastern coast of the United States is Uro-salpinx cinerea, which destroys huge numbers of oysters. Drills lay eggs in small vase-shaped capsules which are often found in groups attached to the undersurface of stones. They live in tidal pools and in weedy borders of rocky shallows. See BORER.

DRILL. See BABOON.

DRILL, cutting tool for making round holes in wood, metal, rock, or other hard material. Tools for drilling holes in wood are commonly known as bits, as are certain specialized types of tools used in rock drilling.

The most common tool for drilling wood is the auger bit, which is provided with single or double helical cutting surfaces and is revolved by a cranklike brace. A number of special forms of wood bits are also employed, including the expanding bit, which has a central guide screw and a radial cutting arm that can be adjusted to drill holes of different sizes.

For drilling metal, twist drills are usually employed. A twist drill is a cylindrical rod with two spiral flutes cut around the rod. The flutes meet at the point of the drill in an angle that is usually between 118° and 120°. Twist drills are made in sizes from a few thousandths of an inch in diameter to an inch, and the diameter of the drill governs the size of the hole produced. When a larger hole is required the drilled hole is enlarged by means of a boring tool. Twist drills are rotated either by hand in geared hand drills or breast drills, or by motor-driven drilling devices. The hand drill is operated with one or both hands, and the breast drill is equipped with a plate that is braced against the chest in operation. The simplest form of drilling machine is a small, hand-held electric motor with a chuck that grasps the drill. For precise work and for larger drills a drill press is employed. This machine consists of one or more motor-driven spindles, usually vertical, with chucks at the lower ends for holding drills. The spindle can be raised or lowered by means of a hand wheel or lever. An adjustable metal table below the spindle holds the work to be drilled. Hand-rotated or power-rotated twist drills can also be used for drilling in glass, plastics, and ceramics.

Small, shallow holes in stone, concrete, brick, and similar materials are usually drilled by hand with a star drill, a steel rod with an X-shaped cutting point. In use, the point is held against the object to be drilled and the other end of the rod is struck with a hammer or sledge. The drill is revolved slightly after each stroke. Similar rock drills powered by pneumatic hammers are used to drill holes larger in diameter, such as those used for the placement of explosive charges in mining and quarrying. A rotary drill consists of an augerlike bit fastened to a series of connected steel pipes. It is used in drilling to great depths, as in drilling oil wells, both on land and at the bottom of the ocean; *see* DEEP-SEA DRILLING; PETROLEUM: *Oil Wells*.

DRIN, *or* DRINI (anc. *Drilon*), longest river of Albania. The Drin R., about 95 mi. long, has two headwaters, the White Drin, which rises in the Kosovo Autonomous Province of Yugoslavia and flows S. into Albania, and the Black Drin, an outlet of Lake Ohrid in the Macedonian Republic of Yugoslavia, that flows N.W. into Albania where it joins the White Drin near the town of Kukës. From there the Drin flows W. and S.W. through gorges for about 80 mi. before emptying into the Adriatic Sea near the town of Lezh. The Drin is not navigable.

DRINKWATER, John (1882–1937), British poet, playwright, and critic, born in Leytonstone, Essex, England. Beginning at the age of fifteen, he worked as an insurance clerk for twelve years, during which he also wrote poetry. In 1907 Drinkwater helped to found the Pilgrim Players, which later became the Birmingham Repertory Theatre. He used historical themes for many of his own plays, the most successful of which was *Abraham Lincoln* (1918). He wrote many critical and biographical works, including *William Morris* (1912), *Swinburne* (1913), *Mr. Charles, King of England* (1926), *Oliver Cromwell: A Character Study* (1927), and *Charles James Fox* (1928). Among his plays are *Mary Stuart* (1921), *Oliver Cromwell* (1921), *Robert E. Lee* (1923), and *Robert Burns* (1925). His *Collected Poems* was published in 1923.

DRIVER ANT. *See* ARMY ANT.

DROMEDARY. *See* CAMEL.

DRONE. *See* BAGPIPE; BEE: *Bumblebees.*

DROP FORGING. *See* FORGING: *Machine Forging.*

DROPSY. *See* EDEMA.

DROSERA. *See* CARNIVOROUS PLANTS.

DROSOPHILA, genus of small flies, commonly called fruit flies (*see* FRUIT FLY), belonging to the family Drosophilidae. The most important species is the red-eyed pomace fly, *D. melanogaster,* also called the sour fly or vinegar fly. It has a yellowish body marked with black, and can often be observed on open baskets of fruit in the summer. The larvae of this species feed on overripe fruit, vinegar, stale beer, and similar fermenting substances. Two characteristics of *D. melanogaster* make the species an ideal subject for genetic experiments: it has exceptionally large chromosomes, and it can produce a large new generation of flies in a period of

about two weeks. Much of the most valuable data on heredity is derived from the study of this genus. *See* HEREDITY; MORGAN, THOMAS HUNT.

DROUGHT. *See* DUST BOWL; IRRIGATION; METEOROLOGY: *Weather Forecasting and Modification: Cloud Physics and Weather Modification.*

DRUG ENFORCEMENT ADMINISTRATION, agency of the United States Department of Justice (q.v.) established on July 1, 1973. The agency merged four previously established drug enforcement agencies and their functions: the Bureau of Narcotics and Dangerous Drugs, the Office of Drug Abuse Law Enforcement, the Office of National Narcotics Intelligence, and the Bureau of Customs' enforcement section on narcotics regulations. *See* NARCOTICS AND DANGEROUS DRUGS, BUREAU OF.

DRUGS, chemical agents or mixtures of agents used for the cure or prevention of disease or for alleviation of discomfort, pain, or anxiety. In a more specific sense, the term is used to designate narcotic and sleep-producing agents; *see* NARCOTICS. Drugs enhance, suppress, or alter existing biological functions, exerting their effects through interactions with living systems.

Sources and Synthetic Drugs. Drugs are derived from plant, mineral, or animal products and are also produced synthetically. Many of the early medical preparations were crude mixtures of roots, vines, barks, and herbs. Digitalis, reserpine, quinine, and morphine (qq.v.) are plant products, the active principles of which were isolated and identified by modern chemists. By virtue of their discoveries, these drugs at present often are prepared synthetically. Antibiotics are the products of bacteria, yeasts, molds, and other microorganisms. Mineral drugs in common use include iodine, iron, boric acid, and epsom salt (qq.v.).

Some of the most significant medical advances of the 20th century have been made possible by animal products, including liver (q.v.) for the treatment of pernicious anemia, insulin (q.v.) for diabetes, and cortisone and ACTH (qq.v.) for rheumatoid arthritis and other diseases. Immune serums, which are used in prevention and treatment of infectious diseases, also are of animal (including human) origin; *see* IMMUNITY.

Synthetic drugs, which are pure chemical substances produced in the laboratory, may be imitations of or improvements on compounds found in nature, or may be wholly new compounds such as the barbiturates (q.v.), sulfonamides (*see* SULFA DRUGS), and general anesthetics; *see* ANESTHESIA. Both types of compounds are represented in the newly developed group of psychopharmacologic agents used in the treatment of mental disorders (q.v.); see PSYCHIC ENERGIZERS; TRANQUILIZERS.

Nomenclature. A drug may have several names. Besides the precise chemical designation, based on the formula of the drug, it has a generic name by which it is commonly known. In addition, each manufacturer gives his own preparation of the drug a registered, or trade, name. In those cases in which no patent exists, the same agent may be produced by many pharmaceutical houses under as many different names. A drug patent is legally valid for seventeen years, after which any manufacturer may market the drug. More than 7000 registered medications are marketed in the United States.

Drug Action and Effects. Despite great advances in the treatment of disease in the last century, little is known of the precise mechanisms by which drugs act on living systems. A drug may stimulate or depress certain cells, thus increasing or reducing their normal activity. Such action usually is selective, affecting primarily only one type of tissue. Drugs may act as irritants, producing an effect which is generally nonspecific; mild degrees of irritation increase the blood supply and hence may restore indolent cells to normal activity. Drugs may also be used in replacement therapy, substituting for a deficiency of hormones, vitamins, or minerals. The anti-infective drugs, such as the sulfonamides and the antibiotics, differ from the previously described agents in acting primarily not upon the body cells but upon the invading microorganisms; see CHEMOTHERAPY.

A drug may produce undesirable secondary, or side, effects, which usually vary in intensity with the dosage. Even small doses of a drug, however, may cause unexpected and harmful side effects in some individuals. Such reactions, known as idiosyncrasy or hypersensitivity, include skin eruptions, fever, reduction of blood-cell formation, and hepatitis; see HEPATITIS. A few drugs produce desirable side effects, such as the sedative action of certain antihistamines or the euphoric effect of some recently developed anti-tuberculosis drugs.

With repeated administration of some drugs, there occurs a phenomenon known as tolerance, that is, the progressive reduction in the response produced. Occasionally the development of tolerance to one drug confers crossed tolerance, or resistance, to another, related agent. In the case of bacterial resistance to antibiotics, it was demonstrated that when the drug kills sensitive forms of the disease-causing organism, mutant forms not vulnerable to its effects survive and multiply, producing eventually a disease not responsive to the previously effective agent. Tolerance to depressant drugs acting on the central nervous system (see NERVOUS SYSTEM) may be followed by the state of physiological dependence known as drug addiction. Recent research conducted by scientists at Rockefeller University indicates that addiction to narcotics may be the result of a metabolic disorder; see DRUGS, ADDICTION TO.

Administration of Drugs. The method of administering a drug modifies its action. For local effects, drugs are administered topically, or locally, to the skin in the form of ointments or lotions, or to the mucous membranes of the nose and throat by inhalation or spraying; or, in the case of poorly absorbed agents, orally for direct effects on the intestinal tract. Some drugs, for example, novocaine (q.v.), may be injected under the skin to produce local anesthesia.

General, or systemic, effects are produced after a drug is absorbed by the blood and carried by the circulation to the tissue or organ upon which it acts. The general bodily routes of administration, in decreasing order of effectiveness, are intravenous, intramuscular, subcutaneous, and oral. Drugs may be administered also by inhalation, as in anesthesia, rectally either by enemas or by suppositories, or by injection into the spinal fluid.

The type, extent, and duration of the response to a particular drug may be influenced by the route of its administration. Magnesium sulfate, or epsom salt, for example, acts as a cathartic when taken orally, relieves pain and reduces swelling when applied locally in a warm solution, and causes depression of the central nervous system when injected intravenously.

Government Regulation. A prescription is a written order from a physician to a pharmacist for drugs; see PHARMACY. It contains the names and quantities of the drugs to be used and directions for use by the patient. Prescriptions are required by law for hypnotic (see HYPNOSIS) or habit-forming drugs, as well as for drugs not safe for use except under supervision of a physician.

Legal standards for drugs in the U.S. are available in the United States Pharmacopeia (U.S.P.), which provides a listing of compounds and information on their preparation, dosage, identification, and standards for strength and purity. The first edition of an International Pharmacopeia was published in 1951 by the World Health Organization (q.v.). The Federal Food, Drug, and Cosmetic Act, enforced by the Food and Drug Administration (q.v.), regulates standards for drugs in interstate commerce. Drugs known to produce addiction are controlled by the Harrison Narcotic Act of 1914, supplemented by the Narcotics Control Act of 1956. Jurisdiction of addictive drugs was placed under the U.S. Treasury Department and later transferred to the Department of Justice; see DRUG ENFORCEMENT ADMINISTRATION. See illustrations on opposite and next pages.   H.C. & S.Z.L.

DRUGS, ADDICTION TO, physical and psychological dependence upon substances that affect the mind, behavior, or the senses. The substances include not only narcotics (q.v.), which depress the central nervous system, but also stimulants, sedatives, tranquilizers (q.v.), hallucinogens, alcohol, and tobacco.

Mind-altering drugs have been known since ancient times. Opium and marijuana (qq.v.), or hashish, probably were cultivated by prehistoric man. The first recorded use of opium dates to about 5000 B.C. By the beginning of the Christian era, some segments of the world population probably were addicted to this drug. Hallucinogens were commonly used in religious rites, and hashish was used to fortify soldiers going into battle. Hemp (*Cannabis sativa; see* CANNABIS; HEMP), the source of hashish and marijuana, was described by the Chinese emperor Shen Nung about 2700 B.C. The plant was cultivated in India around 800 B.C.; the Greek historian Herodotus (q.v.) reported its use by the Scythians in 500 B.C. Kat, a drug derived from the plant *Catha edulis,* has been used by Africans for centuries. Alcohol, which is classed as an intoxicant, was also well known in ancient times; a brewery was operating in Egypt about 3700 B.C.

Psychological or emotional dependence upon drugs usually precedes physical dependence, in which body tissues need the drug in order to function normally. A person who feels more at ease in a social situation if he takes an alcoholic drink or a tranquilizer is said to have emotional dependence. Physical dependence develops as the body tissues gradually adjust their metabolism to accept a regular supply of the drug. Physical dependence is a sign of true addiction. When this point has been reached, withdrawal of the drug upsets the metabolic balance of the body, and the patient becomes violently ill. Addiction also is manifested by a need for increasingly larger doses to produce the same euphoric effect in the patient, known as tolerance.

With regard to the antisocial manifestations of narcotics addiction, law-enforcement officials contend that most addicts are criminals or juvenile delinquents before they become addicted. Available statistics, however, may be misleading because they are based solely on the records of narcotics users who have been in conflict with the law. Nevertheless, nearly all addicts eventually resort to crime in order to obtain money to support their addiction. The crimes are primarily robbery, burglary, prostitution, fraud, or other offenses intended to obtain money, rather than crimes against persons, such as rape or murder, in which money is not an objective. It has been estimated that each year 50,000 narcotics addicts in New York City alone steal goods valued at $2,500,000,000 to finance drug purchases.

Drug addicts in the United States are offered treatment and rehabilitation at hospitals operated by the Federal government at Fort Worth, Texas, and Lexington, Ky. State rehabilitation programs have been established in California, Maryland, and New York. Two independent organizations of former addicts, Synanon and Narcotics Anonymous, offer assistance to persons who wish to abandon the use of drugs. Synanon sponsors a residential facility to help return former addicts to normal community life. The British system for rehabilitation of addicts permits a physician to accept a drug user as an inpatient and provide small amounts of drugs as part of a planned pattern of withdrawal. If the patient appears unable to return to normal life, the physician attempts to persuade him to enter an institution for treatment. Some of the medically supervised withdrawal programs in the U.S. provide methadone, a synthetic drug, as a substitute for narcotics during treatment.

The National Institute for Drug Abuse awards grants and contracts to States, localities, and institutions for research, treatment and rehabilitation, and training and education programs for drug addicts, with special emphasis on children and youth. It also collaborates with several countries in Europe and Latin America on drug-abuse research.

Patterns of Behavior. The Expert Committee on Addiction-Producing Drugs of the World Health Organization recommended in 1964 that the term "drug dependence" be substituted for both drug addiction and drug habituation. Drug dependence was defined as "a state of psychic or physical dependence, or both, arising in a person following administration of that drug on a periodic or continuous basis". Previously, habituation was considered as a set of characteristics that included a desire, but not a compulsion, to continue use of a drug for its effects; little or no tendency to increase the dose; and an absence of physical dependence. Addiction characteristics, by contrast, included physical as

Advances in the preparation and preservation of drugs permit one-dose injection of the most complex drug combinations. Etrenol, for example, is used in the treatment of schistosomiasis, or snail fever, a severe endemic disease common in Africa, Asia, and South America. This striking photograph, made by Sterling Drug Inc., contrasts the effective treatment with a number of snails, which normally act as hosts for the disease-causing flukes during their early stages of growth.

Drugs. Plate 1.

Below, left: The development and application of disease-preventing drugs, one of the most promising facets in the fight against serious epidemics; is exemplified in the work of a laboratory technician inoculating chicken eggs in the course of an antivirus research project. Below, right: After thorough testing, drugs are manufactured for general distribution. The output of a machine producing capsules, which are much used in the dispensation of modern drugs, is inspected by trained personnel.

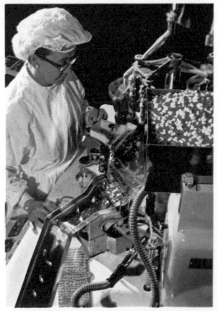

Sterling Drug Inc.

Pfizer Inc.

Left: Various techniques are employed to determine the sensitivity of bacteria to potential new antibacterial agents. The addition of certain dyes, for example, to a culture medium made from agar, a red algae extract, results in specific color changes and patterns if bacterial growth occurs. Above: A symmetrical colony of cultivated green mold Penicillium chrysogenum, a mutant form or strain of which today provides almost all of the world's penicillin.

Drugs. Plate 2.

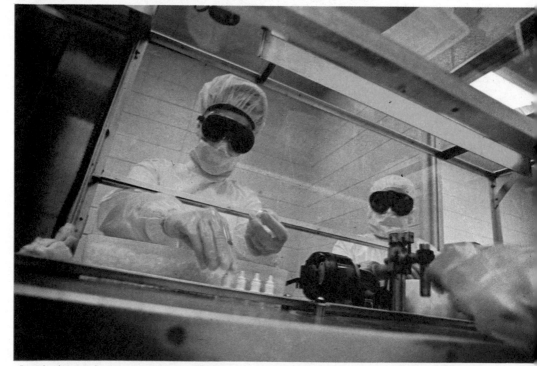

Completely germ-free manufacturing procedures are essential in the production of quality drugs, and the use of sterile chambers is a common practice.

A Thai girl (top, left) makes incisions in the skin of unripe opium-poppy capsules to enable the milky opium resin to escape. Thailand is a major source of opium in Southeast Asia, but in the 1970's Latin America became an important supplier to the North American market. **United Nations**

The sticky white opium paste (top, right) turns reddish-brown as it dries and is then collected and processed to produce codeine or morphine for medical use. The narcotic heroin is processed illicitly from morphine at a later stage. **U.S. Drug Enforcement Administration**

A lush marijuana crop thrives at a U.S. Department of Agriculture research center at the University of Mississippi. Medical opinion about the possible harmful effects of marijuana smoking varies markedly. **U.S.D.E.A.**

well as psychic dependence on the drug and a compulsion to continue use of the drug, employing any means necessary to obtain it.

Types of Drugs Producing Dependency. The drugs producing dependency are classified according to the type of dependency produced. They are morphine (opium), barbiturate, alcohol, cocaine, Cannabis (marijuana), amphetamine, and hallucinogen types.

OPIATES. Raw opium is a dark brown gum extracted from the unripened seed pods of certain poppy plants. The opium poppy is grown in China, India, Turkey, Iran, Yugoslavia, Mexico, and many parts of Southeast Asia. Iran at one time produced enough opium to supply all of

the world's medical needs, about 1200 tons a year. Farmers scratch the seed pods and collect the drops of opium gum that collect around the wounds. One farmer can maintain a large field of opium poppies, selling the raw opium for $350 to $500 per kilogram (2.2 lb.). Resold on the illegal drug market, the same amount of opium may be valued ultimately at nearly $250,000 when divided into tiny packets for distribution to addicts.

Opium is refined to yield two kinds of drugs. One group includes the narcotics: morphine, codeine (qq.v.), and thebaine, which are central-nervous-system depressants. The other drugs, papaverine and narcotine, affect mainly

179

The processing of heroin from opium requires elaborate refining equipment, as shown in the photograph (above) of a crude illicit laboratory in Denver, Colo. Federal narcotics agents (left) examine a haul of heroin confiscated at John F. Kennedy Airport, New York City.

U.S.D.E.A.

the smooth muscles and are not important as addictive substances. Morphine is the principal component of opium; it is about ten times as potent as raw opium and is responsible for most of the effects of opium as eaten, taken in tea, or smoked by addicts, chiefly in the Orient.

In properly controlled doses, morphine is one of the most effective pain relievers known and one of the most valuable drugs available to physicians. It is the standard by which other pain-relieving drugs are measured. Codeine, which was discovered in 1932, resembles morphine in its analgesic effects, but is much weaker.

Heroin (q.v.) is prepared from morphine. It is about four times as powerful, exerts a stronger effect upon the brain, and is more toxic. Just as morphine and codeine were first used to treat opium addiction, heroin was developed in 1898 as a nonaddicting substitute for morphine. This claim soon proved false; the addictive powers of heroin were so great that its use was prohibited in the United States, even in medical prac-

tice. Most of the heroin sold in the U.S. in the mid-1970's is manufactured in small laboratories in southern France and Mexico, and distributed through illicit channels.

STIMULANTS. The dangerous stimulants are cocaine (q.v.) and drugs of the amphetamine family. Cocaine, a white, crystalline powder with a bitter taste, is made from the leaves of the coca bush, which grows in South America. Coca is not to be confused with cacao, the source of chocolate; the plants are not related. Although cocaine was originally valued as a local anesthetic, it has been replaced by such less poisonous drugs as procaine and tetracaine.

Amphetamine was introduced in the 1930's for the treatment of colds and hay fever and later was found to affect the nervous system. It is still used to depress the appetite in the treatment of obesity, to relieve mild depression, and to treat narcolepsy, an ailment in which the patient is unable to remain awake. Amphetamines, commonly known as "pep pills", give the user a sense of well-being. Prolonged or heavy use of these drugs, especially when injected into the veins, can be both physically and psychologically damaging. Since amphetamines depress the appetite, the user may develop malnutrition and digestive disorders. Respiratory and circulatory problems and destruction of brain tissue are also known to result from overdoses of amphetamines.

TRANQUILIZERS. Introduced in the 1950's, tranquilizers comprise a large group of drugs used in medicine to counteract tension and anxiety without producing sleep or seriously hampering normal mental and physical functions. The so-called major tranquilizers are used primarily in the treatment of serious psychotic ailments. An example is chlorpromazine (Thorazine). The major tranquilizers are not known to produce physical dependence. The "minor" tranquilizers, of which meprobamate (Miltown) is an example, are commonly used in the treatment of milder emotional disorders. There is evidence to show that they may cause psychological dependence.

SEDATIVES. Like the true narcotics, the morphine-type depressants, and stimulants, sedative drugs are valuable medical tools, but may be used illegally to produce changes in behavior. The most commonly abused sedatives are the barbiturates (q.v.), sometimes called "goof balls". They are used in medicine primarily for treatment of epilepsy, high blood pressure, insomnia, and mental-health problems. Although more than 2500 barbiturates are known, only 30 are used medi-

cally. These drugs are widely misused; because they create physical dependence, withdrawal is difficult.

HALLUCINOGENS. Marijuana, hashish, mescaline, lysergic acid diethylamide (LSD), dimethyltryptamine (DMT), and psilocybin are among the drugs that distort perception and cause hallucinations. Although used for centuries as drugs of indulgence or in religious rituals, they have limited therapeutic value. LSD has been employed experimentally in the treatment of alcoholism by physicians and in easing the pain and mental conflicts of persons dying of cancer. After twenty years of experiment, however, LSD has not yet found an established medical use. Because of its suspected effects on the chromosomes, persons taking LSD may run the risk of having deformed children. It has been demonstrated in the laboratory that marijuana also may distort the chromosomes (q.v.).

Although marijuana results in psychological rather than physical dependence, it is erroneously classified as an addictive drug by the United States and sixty other nations. Prolonged or heavy doses of marijuana may cause severe emotional reactions and personality changes. The active ingredient in marijuana was first synthesized in 1966 by scientists in Israel for research purposes. The hashish form of marijuana, sold in some parts of the Middle East, is a more potent form of the drug than the American variety of marijuana.

See also BENZEDRINE; MENTAL DISORDERS; PSYCHIC ENERGIZERS. J.L.G.

This striking poster draws attention to the most widely abused drug in the U.S. today, alcohol. In the mid-1970's an estimated 9,000,000 Americans were victims of alcoholism.
National Institute on Alcohol Abuse and Alcoholism

DRUIDISM, religious faith of ancient Celtic inhabitants of Gaul (q.v.) and the British Isles. It flourished from the 2nd century B.C. until the 2nd century A.D., but in parts of Britain that the Romans did not invade, druidism survived until it was supplanted by Christianity two or three centuries later. The tenets of this religion included belief in immortality of the soul, which, upon the death of an individual, was believed to pass into the body of a newborn child. According to the Roman statesman Gaius Julius Caesar (q.v.), who adapted a tendentious account of the cult written by Posidonius, a Stoic philosopher and historian of the early 1st century B.C., the followers of druidism believed that they were descended from a Supreme Being.

The ancient accounts assert that the functions of priests, religious teachers, judges, and civil administrators were performed by druids, with supreme power being vested in an archdruid. Three classes of druids existed: prophets, bards, and priests. They were assisted by prophetesses, or sorceresses, who did not enjoy the powers and privileges of the druids. The druids were well versed in astrology, magic, and the mysterious powers of plants and animals; they held the oak tree and the mistletoe, especially when the

latter grew on oak trees, in great reverence; and they customarily conducted their rituals in oak forests. Archeologists consider it probable that the druids used as altars and temples the stone monuments known as dolmens (*see* DOLMEN), which are found throughout the areas where druidism flourished. Stonehenge (q.v.) in England antedates druidism by many centuries.

The druids led their people in resisting the Roman invasions, but their power was weakened by the rebelliousness of the Gallic warriors, who were envious of their political authority. The superior military strength of the Romans and the subsequent conversion of many followers of druidism to Christianity led to the disappearance of the religion. *See* CELTIC PEOPLES AND LANGUAGES.

DRUM *or* **DRUMFISH,** any of several fishes of the family Sciaenidae, capable of making a noise under water resembling the roll of a muffled or distant drum. *Pogonias cromis,* the saltwater drum of the Atlantic coast of the United States, has been known to exceed 100 lb. in weight, but ordinarily weighs less than 50 lb. It is a heavily built fish, with large scales arranged in diagonal rows and a large number of short barbels hanging from the lower jaw. It frequents

182

Massed bands of infantry parade in London. One of the oldest of musical instruments, the drum has been used in most ages and countries. It is a key instrument in the military band. Mace & Bariff/Bruce Coleman Inc.

bays and shallow coastal waters in search of mollusks, upon which it feeds. It is commonly encountered in the oyster beds, and destroys annually a vast number of cultivated oysters, crushing into fragments far more than it eats.

A South Atlantic variety of drumfish, *Pogonias curbina,* is known by the Brazilians as curbina, meaning "croaker". *Aplodinotus grunniens,* also called thunderpumper, sheepshead, and croaker, is a related fish of the lakes and streams in the Mississippi valley. It is highly prized as a food fish in the southern U.S.

Other species of drums are the channel bass or red drum of the South Atlantic and the Gulf States, *Sciaenops ocellata,* and the black drums, mostly of the Old World, of the same genus.

DRUM, musical instrument of the percussion group, consisting of a hollow cylinder or hemisphere of wood or metal, over one or both ends is stretched a dried animal skin or other membrane, called the head, held taut by mechanical contrivances, such as cords, hoops, and screw rods. The drum is played by beating the head or heads with a stick or sticks or with the hands. The principal modern types of the instrument are the bass drum, a large drum which is held so that its heads are in a vertical position and is played by striking the heads with ball-end sticks; the snide drum, or snare drum; and the kettledrum (qq.v.). The trap drum, used extensively in theater orchestras and dance bands, is a bass drum with a cymbal attached; the two instruments are played by means of separate sticks operated by a foot pedal. With the exception of the kettledrum, drums cannot be perfectly tuned and therefore are used mainly to mark rhythms in music; kettledrums participate in the orchestral harmony.

A wide variety of drums of different shapes, sizes, and degrees of pitch are used in Asian and African music (*see* AFRICAN MUSIC). In India and Egypt, drums have been used since ancient times. Various primitive tribes throughout the world use a small, hand-beaten type of drum, usually called a tom-tom, in religious ceremonies, for transmitting signals, and in war. The bongo drum, tall and with a tunable head, developed as a Cuban tom-tom; it has been adopted for a variety of other types of popular music. The drum was known to the ancient

Greeks and Romans, mainly in the form of the tympanum, which resembled an undersized kettledrum although it could not be exactly tuned. Greek and Roman drums were used chiefly in the worship of the nature goddess Cybele and the god of wine Dionysus or Bacchus. The drum was introduced into Western Europe from the East by the Crusaders.

See also MUSICAL INSTRUMENTS.

DRUMMOND, Henry (1851–97), British theologian, biologist, and lecturer, born in Stirling, Scotland, and educated at the University of Edinburgh. In 1877 he lectured on natural science at the Free Church School, Glasgow, later traveled in Africa and the Orient, and made lecture tours of Australian and American colleges. His works include *Natural Law in the Spiritual World* (1883), an attempt to reconcile the principles of evolution to evangelical Christianity; *Tropical Africa* (1888); *The Ascent of Man* (1894, delivered as the 1893 Lowell Lectures in Boston, Mass.), stressing the altruistic elements of animals in natural selection; and *The Greatest Thing in the World* (1890).

DRUMMOND, William Henry (1854–1907), Canadian poet, born in County Leitrim, Ireland, brought to Canada at the age of eleven, and educated at McGill University and the medical school (now part of McGill University) of Bishop's University, Lenoxville, Québec. He practiced medicine in the villages of southern Québec Province and in Montréal, taught at Bishop's University, and superintended his family's silver mines in the province of Ontario. But his most important contribution is his verse, collected in *The Habitant* (1897), *Johnny Courteau* (1901), *The Voyageur* (1905), and *The Great Fight* (1908), in which he transcribes the colorful patois, a mixture of French and English, spoken by the French habitants of rural Canada.

DRUNKENNESS. See ALCOHOLISM; INTOXICATION, ALCOHOLIC.

DRUPE. See FRUIT: *Types of Fruit.*

DRURY LANE THEATRE, playhouse in London, England, on Russell Street, not far from Drury Lane. The original building, properly known as the Theatre Royal, Drury Lane, was built under a royal patent in 1663 by the English playwright Thomas Killigrew (1612–83) for his company, the King's Servants. Two years later, the English actress Nell Gwyn (see GWYN, ELEANOR), who was later the mistress of Charles II (q.v.), King of England, made her debut at Drury Lane. After the theater was badly damaged by fire in 1672, a new one was built from designs by the English architect Sir Christopher Wren (q.v.) and opened in 1674. Between 1695 and

1746 the theater was involved in a constant struggle against financial difficulties, and its reputation suffered because of the superior offerings of rival playhouses. In 1746 management was assumed by the British actor David Garrick (q.v.); the following thirty years are considered the golden age of Drury Lane. After Garrick retired in 1776, the theater was managed by the British playwright Richard Brinsley Sheridan who presented his own comedies and later brought to stardom the British actress Sarah Siddons (qq.v.). A new theater was built in 1791, and it was replaced by the present structure in 1812. From 1814 to 1820 Drury Lane audiences witnessed the performances of the British actor Edmund Kean (see under KEAN), who appeared in many plays by the English dramatist William Shakespeare (q.v.). Subsequently the theater, which in 1817 became one of the first in London to be lighted by gas, was used for a variety of productions, including operas and pantomimes. Since World War II, Drury Lane has become known as the London home of successful American musical comedies.

DRUSUS, name of a distinguished Roman family, or *gens.* Among its important members were the following.

Marcus Livius Drusus (d. 109 B.C.). As tribune of the people with Gaius Sempronius Gracchus (see under GRACCHUS) in 122 B.C., he undermined the reform program of his colleague. In 112 B.C., Drusus became both Roman consul and governor of the province of Macedonia. At the time of his death he held the office of censor.

Marcus Livius Drusus (d. 91 B.C.), son of the above. He was tribune in 91 B.C., and as spokesman for the aristocrats attempted to restore to members of the senate the right to sit as *judices* ("jurors") in the law courts, which had been transferred to the *equites* ("knights", actually the propertied group in Rome) by the legislation of Gaius Sempronius Gracchus. In order to accomplish this purpose, Drusus proposed to admit 300 of the knights to the senate, doubling the membership of that body; to grant the franchise to non-Roman Italian allies; and to decrease the price of grain distributed to the people. These and other proposals were passed, but were subsequently declared invalid because they had been enacted as a single measure. Shortly after the rejection of his proposals, Drusus was assassinated and a rebellion of the Italian allies broke out (see SOCIAL WAR).

Nero Claudius Drusus Germanicus, known also as DRUSUS SENIOR (38 B.C.–9 B.C.), younger son of an adopted member of the family, Livia Drusilla, by her first husband, Tiberius Claudius

Nero (d. 38 B.C.?). Drusus Senior was the brother of the Emperor Tiberius and stepson of the Emperor Augustus (qq.v.). He served as a general under Tiberius against the Rhaeti and Vindelici in 15 B.C., and from 13 until 10 B.C. he was governor of the three Gallic provinces. In 9 B.C. he held an army against the German peoples of the Elbe region, penetrating farther than previous Roman armies. He died after a fall from his horse. Germanicus Caesar and Claudius (qq.v.), Emperor of Rome, were his sons.

DRUZES or DRUSES, members of a Middle Eastern religious sect who live mainly in mountainous regions of Lebanon and Southern Syria. An industrious people, the Druzes have terraced the mountainsides with soil brought from river valleys. They can be differentiated from their neighbors only because of their religion, which completely dominates their habits and customs.

The basis of the Druze religion is that at various times God has been divinely incarnated in a living person, and that His last, and final, such incarnation was in the person of al-Hakim (abu-'Ali Manṣūr al-Ḥākim, 985–1021), the sixth Fatimid caliph, who announced himself at Cairo about 1016 A.D. as the earthly incarnation of God. In 1017 the new religion found an apostle in Hamzah ibn 'Ali ibn Ahmad, who became vizier to Hakim. Hamzah gave the religion form and content and coordinated its various dogmas into a single creed. The religion probably derives its name from al-Darazi (Muhammad ibn-Ismā'īl al-Darazi, d. 1019), a missionary follower of Hakim.

The Druzes believe that in Hakim God made a final appeal to man to redeem himself; and that God, incarnated as Hakim, would again return to establish the primacy of His religion. The religion itself is an outgrowth of Islam (q.v.), but is admixed with elements of Judaism and Christianity. The Druzes believe in one God whose qualities cannot be understood or defined, and who renders impartial justice. They do not believe in proselytizing. The seven cardinal principles to which they adhere are: (1) veracity in dealing with each other; (2) mutual protection and assistance; (3) renunciation of other religions; (4) belief in the divine incarnation of Hakim; (5) contentment with the works of God; (6) submission to His will; and (7) separation from those in error and from demons. They believe in the transmigration of souls, with constant advancement and final purification. The teachings demand abstinence from wine and tobacco and from profanity and obscenity. The Druzes do not pray, fast, or feast, and, with exception of the 'uggal, a privileged class, do not hold religious services. In order to protect their religion and not divulge its secret teachings, they worship as Muslims when among Muslims, and as Christians when among Christians. Jesus Christ is acknowledged by the Druzes as one of the divine incarnations.

The Druzes were under the nominal rule of Turkey from the 16th century until 1918, during World War I, but they maintained virtual autonomy by their fierce opposition to any forces sent by the sultans to subjugate them. In 1860 a conflict broke out between the Maronites, a Syrian Christian sect, and the Druzes, in the course of which several thousand Maronites were killed and large numbers driven from their homes. European powers intervened to protect the Christians, with a French force occupying Lebanon for nearly a year. A Christian governor general was appointed administrator in 1864, and a large measure of autonomy was conferred on Lebanon. These events marked the end of the political importance of the Lebanese Druzes, who until 1918 remained an aloof, conservative community. The Syrian Druzes were engaged periodically in struggles against the Turkish government until 1910, mainly on the questions of taxes and military service. During World War I most of the Druzes remained neutral. On Sept. 1, 1918, however, an armed force of Syrian and Lebanese Druzes gave assistance to the Arab leader Faisal (see FAISAL I), who in turn helped British forces capture the city of Damascus a month later. Late in 1920 the Druzes entered into negotiations with the French government, which controlled Syria through a mandate from the League of Nations. On March 4, 1921, an agreement was concluded that granted autonomy to the Syrian plateau region of Jebel ed Druze. In April, 1925, the Druzes petitioned the French authorities for a hearing to discuss French breaches of the agreement. On July 11, 1925, Gen. Maurice Sarrail (1856–1929), the high commissioner for the French mandate, ordered his delegate at Damascus to summon the Druze representatives. On arrival the petitioners were seized and exiled by the French to the distant oasis of Palmyra, precipitating a Druze revolt that gave impetus to the independence struggles of Syria and Lebanon.

According to the latest available statistics, the Druzes number about 190,000 in Syria and about 90,000 in Lebanon. Because of the Druze practice of outwardly conforming to the faith of the people among whom they live, their number in other countries of the Middle East cannot be estimated. Israel, which has recognized the Druzes since its formation in 1948, reported in a recent census (1971) a Druze population of 36,000.

DRYAD, in Greek mythology, a nymph of the trees and forests. In early legend, each dryad was born with a certain tree over which she watched. She lived either in the tree (in which case she was called a hamadryad) or near it. Because the dryad died when her tree fell, the gods often punished men for the destruction of a tree. The word dryad has also been used in a general sense for nymphs (q.v.) living in the forest.

DRYBURGH ABBEY, ruined abbey, in Berwick Scotland, 5 miles S.E. of Melrose, on the Tweed R. It contains the tomb of the Scottish writer Sir Walter Scott (q.v.) and his son-in-law, the Scottish writer John Gibson Lockhart (1794–1854). The abbey was founded in 1150 by David I (q.v.), King of Scotland.

DRY CELL. See CELL, ELECTRIC: *Primary Cells.*

DRYDEN, John (1631–1700), English poet, dramatist, and critic, born of a Puritan family in Aldwinkle, Northamptonshire, and educated at Westminster School and at Trinity College, University of Cambridge. About 1657 he went to London as clerk to a relative, Sir Gilbert Pickering (1613–68), who was chamberlain to the lord protector Oliver Cromwell (*see under* CROMWELL). Dryden's first important poem was *Heroic*

John Dryden

Stanzas (1659), written in memory of Cromwell; after the Restoration, however, he became a Royalist and celebrated the return of Charles II (q.v.), King of England, in two poems, *Astraea Redux* (1660) and *Panegyric on the Coronation* (1661). In 1663 he married Lady Elizabeth Howard (d. 1714), sister of his patron, the courtier and playwright Sir Robert Howard (1626–98).

In 1662 Dryden began to write plays as a source of income. His first attempts, including the comedy *The Wild Gallant,* failed, but *The Rival Ladies,* a tragicomedy written in 1664, was a success. During the next twenty years, he became the most prominent dramatist in England. His comedies, including *An Evening's Love; or, the Mock Astrologer* (1668), *Ladies à la Mode* (1668), and *Marriage à la Mode* (1672), are broad and bawdy; one of them, *The Kind Keeper; or, Mr. Limberham* (1678), was banned as being indecent, an unusual penalty during the Restoration. His early heroic plays, written in rhymed couplets, are extravagant in style and full of pageantry; among them are *The Indian Queen* (with Sir Robert Howard, 1664); *The Indian Emperour; or, the Conquest of Mexico by the Spaniards* (1665); and *Almanzor and Almahide; or, the Conquest of Granada* (1670). One of his later tragedies in blank verse, *All for Love; or, The World Well Lost* (1678), a version of the story of Antony and Cleopatra, is considered his greatest play and one of the masterpieces of Restoration tragedy.

In his poem *Annus Mirabilis* (1667), Dryden wrote of the events in the "Wonderful Year" 1666, chiefly of the English naval victory over the Dutch in July and of the Great Fire of London in September. In 1668 he wrote his most important prose work, *Essay of Dramatic Poesie,* the basis for his preeminent position as a critic.

Dryden was appointed poet laureate and historiographer royal in 1670. In 1681 he wrote his first and greatest political satire, *Absalom and Achitophel,* a masterful parable in heroic couplets ridiculing the Whig attempt to make the Duke of Monmouth (q.v.), rather than the Duke of York (the future King James), successor to King Charles II. His other great verse satires, all written in 1682, are *The Medall;* the second part of *Absalom and Achitophel,* written in collaboration with the poet and playwright Nahum Tate (1652–1715); and MacFlecknoe.

Although Dryden had defended his adherence to Protestantism in the poem *Religio Laici* (1682), he became a Catholic in 1685, presumably because James II (q.v.), an avowed Catholic, came to the throne in that year. The poet then wrote *The Hind and the Panther* (1687), a metrical allegory in defense of his new faith. The revolution of 1688 and the resulting succession of the Protestant king William III (q.v.), however, did not change his religious views, though he lost his laureateship and his pension because of them.

Dryden returned to writing for the stage, but without much success. He then began a new career as a translator, the most important of his translations being *The Works of Virgil* (1697). During the same period he wrote one of his greatest odes, *Alexander's Feast* (1697), which, like an earlier ode, *A Song for Saint Cecilia's Day* (1687), was written for a London musical society and set to music. In 1699 he wrote the last of his published works, metrical paraphrases of Homer, Ovid, Boccaccio, and Chaucer, under the title *Fables Ancient and Modern*; its preface is one of his most important critical essays. Dryden is buried in Westminster Abbey.

DRY DOCK. See DOCK.

DRY FARMING, or DRYLAND FARMING, method of agricultural cultivation in dry regions usually receiving less than 20 in. of rainfall a year; see AGRICULTURE; RAIN. Dry farming normally produces crops without any irrigation (q.v.), and depends mainly upon tillage methods that conserve soil moisture. It is used for crops that do not absorb excessive moisture. *See also* SOILS AND SOIL MANAGEMENT.

Conservation of moisture is achieved by various means, such as fallowing, that allows cultivation every alternate year; by the destruction of moisture-absorbing weeds; or by reduced seeding. Loss of water is minimized by farming practices such as wider spacing of furrows, or by having the furrows following the contours of the land instead of running vertically up and down hillsides.

Crops produced by the dryland-farming method are grown extensively, not intensively, and include wheat, barley, rye, corn, and potatoes. Dry farming is common in many parts of Africa, Asia, Australia, and in the dry, semiarid areas of the southwestern United States.

DRY ICE. See CARBON DIOXIDE.

DRYOPE, in Greek legend, daughter of Dryops, King of the Dryopes, a tribe of the region of Thessalia (q.v.), which settled in Euboea (q.v.). Dryope won the love of the god Apollo (q.v.), who visited her in the form of a tortoise one day while she was playing with her dryad (q.v.) friends. Later, after bearing Apollo a son, she was carried away by the dryads and transformed into a poplar.

DRYPOINT, in art, the process of engraving (q.v.) on copper or other metals by means of a needle, usually of the type used in etching (q.v.), but more obliquely ground and sometimes pointed with a diamond. Drypoint differs from line engraving in that the needle is used; line engravings are made with a burin, a type of chisel. Drypoint differs from etching in that no acid is used in the engraving process. In drypoint, the scratches of the needle cause a certain amount of turning up and accumulation of the metal beside the cut; this roughness is known as the burr. Because in printing the burr holds more ink than does a scratch made by other engraving tools, drypoint prints have a characteristic line that is richer and softer than that produced in etching and line engraving. Drypoint is often used to finish a previously etched plate, because this process makes unnecessary a recoating of the plate with varnish and an additional application of acid. The term "drypoint" is applied also to the needle used in the process, to the engraving made by the needle, and to the print made from the engraving.

The Dutch painter Rembrandt (q.v.) employed the drypoint method in finishing the plates of his engravings and later produced work in pure drypoint. More recent masters of the medium include Sir Francis Seymour Hayden (1818–1910) and Sir Muirhead Bone (q.v.) in Great Britain and painters Alphonse Legros and Jean Forain and the sculptor Auguste Rodin (q.v.) in France.

DRY ROT, decay of seasoned wood caused by the attacks of any of a number of species of saprophytic fungi, particularly *Merulius lacrymans*, *Coniophora cerebella*, and *Poria incrassata*. These fungi penetrate to the interior of timbers and consume the cellulose in the wood fibers, leaving the timbers porous, although the wood may appear sound on the surface. The decay, dry rot, is so called because of the powdery appearance of the decayed wood, but the term is misleading, because the fungi need water to live, and dry rot appears only in wood which has been exposed to moisture. The best method of preventing dry rot in any type of wood construction is to avoid dampness. In cases where dampness is unavoidable, as in outdoor construction, creosote (q.v.) or other compounds may be used to protect timbers; see FUNGICIDE. *See also* WOOD: *Durability.*

The term "dry rot" is also sometimes applied to the decay of living trees caused by bracket fungi.

DRY TORTUGAS, or TORTUGAS, group of ten coral keys or islets belonging to Florida, and forming part of Monroe Co. They lie in the Gulf of Mexico about 70 miles w. of Key West.

Among the principal islets, all of which are low and partially covered with mangrove bushes, are Bush Key, Loggerhead, East Key, and Garden Key. The last-named islet is the site of Fort Jefferson National Monument (q.v.). A marine biological station, maintained by the Carnegie Institute of Washington, is on Loggerhead Key. The entire group is a bird sanctuary, established by the Federal government in 1908.

DUALISM, in philosophy, the theory that the universe is explicable only as a whole composed of two distinct and mutually irreducible elements. In Platonic philosophy the ultimate dualism is between "being" and "non-being", that is, between ideas and matter. In the 17th century, dualism took the form of belief in two fundamental substances, mind and matter. The French philosopher René Descartes (q.v.), whose interpretation of the universe exemplifies this belief, was the first to emphasize the irreconcilable difference between thinking substance (mind) and extended substance (matter). The difficulty created by this view was to explain how mind and matter interact, as they apparently do in human experience. This perplexity caused some Cartesians to deny entirely any interaction between the two. They asserted that mind and matter are inherently incapable of affecting each other, and that any reciprocal action between the two is caused by God, Who, on the occasion of a change in one, produces a corresponding change in the other; see OCCASIONALISM. Other followers of Descartes abandoned dualism in favor of monism (q.v.).

In the 20th century, reaction against the monistic aspects of the philosophy of idealism has to some degree revived dualism. One of the most interesting defenses of dualism is that of the Anglo-American psychologist William McDougall (1871–1938), who divides the universe into spirit and matter and maintains that there is good evidence, both psychological and biological, of the spiritual basis of physiological processes. The French philosopher Henri Louis Bergson (q.v.) in his great philosophic work *Matter and Memory* likewise takes a dualistic position, defining matter as what man perceives with his senses and possessing in itself the qualities that man perceives in it, such as color and resistance. Mind, on the other hand, reveals itself as memory, the faculty of storing up the past and utilizing it for modifying our present actions, which otherwise would be merely mechanical. However, in his later writings Bergson abandons dualism and comes to regard matter as an arrested manifestation of the same vital impulse which composes life and mind.

Dualism also has an ethical aspect; namely, in the recognition of the independent and opposing principles of good and evil. This dualism is exemplified in Zoroastrianism (q.v.) and in the Manichaean heresy (*see* MANICHAEISM).

DUAL MONARCHY. *See* AUSTRIA-HUNGARY.

DUANE, James (1733–97), American jurist, born in New York City, and admitted to the bar in 1754. He served as New York attorney general in 1767. During the period preceding the American Revolution, he advocated cooperation with Great Britain. From 1774 to 1784 he served as a delegate to the Continental Congress (q.v.), where he supported the conciliatory plan of the American loyalist Joseph Galloway (1729?–1803), calling for a union of all the American colonies under a British chief magistrate appointed by the Crown. Later, however, Duane supported the Declaration of Independence (q.v.); he helped to draft the Articles of Confederation and the first New York State constitution. He was a member of the New York State senate (1782–85, 1789–90) and the first mayor of New York City (1784–89). Duane was also a U.S. district judge for New York from 1789 until his retirement in 1794.

DUANE, William John (1780–1865), American lawyer and public official, born in Clonmel, Ireland, the son of the Irish-American journalist and politician William Duane (1760–1835). At the age of sixteen, the younger Duane was brought to Philadelphia, Pa., where he worked under his father on the Jeffersonian newspaper *Aurora*. He later served in the Pennsylvania legislature. After his admission to the bar in 1815, Duane practiced law in Philadelphia and remained active in politics. In 1833 President Andrew Jackson (q.v.) appointed him secretary of the treasury. Duane was dismissed later in the year for opposing a Presidential directive to transfer government deposits from the Second Bank of the United States to private banks without authorization from Congress, *see* BANKS AND BANKING: *United States Banking System.*

DUARTE, city of California, in Los Angeles Co., about 38 miles N.E. of central Los Angeles. In addition to its fruit-packing and poultry industries, Duarte manufactures missile parts and electronic equipment. It is the site of the City of Hope tuberculosis and cancer medical center, and nearby is the Santa Fe Flood Control Dam. Settled about 1841, Duarte was incorporated in 1957. Pop. (1960) 13,962; (1970) 14,981.

DUBAI, town in the Union of Arab Emirates, and capital of the sheikhdom of Dubai, on Dubai Creek, on the Persian Gulf, about 250 miles N.W. of Muscat. Dubai is on the western side of the creek, the eastern part of the town being known as Dera. The town was the residence of the British political agent for the former Trucial States from 1954 until 1971. Known as the "Venice of the Gulf", Dubai is the chief port and commercial center of the Arab Emirates. Oil drilling in the area has largely displaced the traditional occupations of pearl diving, fishing, and camel breeding. Until 1833 the town was tributary to the sheikhdom of Abu Dhabi. Dubai is sometimes spelled Debai, Dubayy, and Dibai. Pop. (1972 est.) 80,000.

DU BARRY, Marie Jeanne Bécu, Comtesse (1743?–93), French mistress of Louis XV (q.v.), King of France, born in Vaucouleurs. She was the natural daughter of a seamstress and a tax collector. After a brief convent education, she became, at the age of fifteen, a milliner's assistant in Paris. In 1764 she became the mistress of the Chevalier Jean du Barry (1723–94) and presided over his Paris gambling house. He contrived to present her to Louis XV, who, after marrying her to the Comte Guillaume du Barry, Jean's brother, made her his official mistress. Madame du Barry had great influence with the king until his death in 1777, when she retired to her chateau of Louveciennes, near Versailles. Her supposed political intrigues appear to have been of little consequence. She was, however, a generous patron of artists and men of letters, and was celebrated for her beauty and wit. In 1792, after the outbreak of the French Revolu-

Madame du Barry

tion (q.v.), she made at least one trip to England. Her reason for returning to France is not known, although it may have been to recover jewelry that had been stolen. She was arrested on charges of conspiracy against the new French republic and was tried and guillotined.

DUBINSKY, David (1892–   ), American labor leader, born in Brest-Litovsk, Russia (now Brest, U.S.S.R.). While working in his father's bakery in Łódź, Poland (then under Russian control), he began the trade union activities that resulted in his deportation to Siberia in 1909; he escaped two years later. He went to the United States and became an American citizen in 1916. In New York City he learned to be a cloak cutter, joined the International Ladies' Garment Workers Union (q.v.), and quickly rose through the ranks to the presidency of the union, a post he held from 1932 to 1966. Under Dubinsky's leadership the union increased vastly in membership and influence. Dubinsky was an active supporter of the New Deal enunciated by President Franklin D. Roosevelt (qq.v.) and a founder of the American Labor Party in 1936, of the Liberal Party (qq.v.) of New York in 1944, and of the Americans for Democratic Action, an independent political organization, in 1947.

DUBLIN, city in Georgia, and county seat of Laurens Co., on the Oconee R., about 45 miles S.E. of Macon. Situated in an agricultural and timber area, the city is a processing and marketing center, with light manufacturing. Pop. (1960) 13,814; (1970) 15,143.

DUBLIN, county of the Republic of Ireland, in Leinster Province, in the w. central section of the country, adjoining the Irish Sea. The terrain is generally flat, except in the extreme s. portion, which contains the N. extremities of the Wicklow Mountains. The county coastline, about 70 mi. long, is indented by a number of creeks and bays, notably Dublin Bay, formed by the Howth Peninsula on the N. Dublin Bay receives the waters of the Liffey R., the only stream of consequence in the county. Several islands, including Lambay and Ireland's Eye, are attached to the county for administrative purposes. The county has numerous small farms, the chief products of which are cattle, oats, and potatoes. The fishing industry is important, producing valuable catches of salmon, brill, cod, haddock, sole, plaice, and oysters. Industrial production is confined largely to Dublin (q.v.), capital of the Republic of Ireland and administrative center and chief seaport of the county. Among the principal towns are Dún Laoghaire (q.v.), Balbriggan, and Skerries. Area, 356 sq.mi.; pop. (1971) 852,219.

Dublin, like many of the world's larger cities, is built on a river. This is the Liffey, which flows through the center of the Irish capital to empty into Dublin Bay.
Louis Goldman–Rapho-Photo Researchers

DUBLIN (Gaelic, *Baile Atha Cliath,* "Town of the Ford of the Hurdles"), capital, county borough, and seaport of the Republic of Ireland, and administrative center of County Dublin, in Leinster Province. It is at the mouth of the Liffey R., on Dublin Bay, an inlet of the Irish Sea. The city is serviced by steamship lines operation to Cork, Ireland, Belfast, Northern Ireland, and various ports in England, Scotland, and France; and by several railway systems, that provide connections with all important points in Ireland.

The city occupies a generally flat site, which is bisected in an E. and w. direction by the Liffey. The river is spanned by ten bridges, notably O'Connell's Bridge, that links the main thoroughfares of the city. Except in its s.w. portion, where the streets are narrow and crooked, Dublin is well laid out, with broad avenues and spacious squares. These are especially numerous in the s.E. and N.E. quarters, which also contain many stately old mansions. Circular Drive, a boulevard about 9 mi. long, extends along what was the periphery of the city at the end of the 19th century. Since that time, the city limits have been considerably extended. The port area, confined to the lower reaches of the Liffey, has a number of quays and basins open to vessels drawing up to 23 ft. of water. The Royal (96 mi. long) and the Grand (208 mi. long) canals, provide connections between the port area and the N. and s. branches of the Shannon R.

Dublin contains several notable suburbs, including Rathmines and Rathgar, where the homes of many of the wealthy businessmen of Dublin are located; and Glasnevin, where Joseph Addison, Jonathan Swift, Richard Brinsley Sheridan (qq.v.), and other well-known personalities once resided. In the cemetery of Glasnevin lie the remains of the Irish patriots Daniel O'Connell and John Philpot Curran (qq.v.).

Points of Interest. Most of Dublin's historic edifices are in the old section of the city, N. of the Liffey. Dublin Castle, the nucleus around which the modern town developed, formerly housed the offices of the British viceroy of Ireland. Although most of this structure, that occupies a ridge overlooking the river, was completed in the 16th century and later, parts of it date from early in the 13th century. In the vicinity of the castle is the Protestant cathedral of Christ Church, founded in 1038 and rebuilt from 1870 to 1877 according to the original design. Saint Patrick's Cathedral, a Gothic structure not far from Christ's Church, is the largest of the many churches in Dublin and the center of the Protestant faith in the country. Sometimes called the Westminster of Ireland, the cathedral was founded in 1190 and rebuilt between 1220 and 1260. The remains of Jonathan Swift, once dean of St. Patrick's, are interred in the cathedral. The University of Dublin (see DUBLIN, UNIVERSITY OF) and the Bank of Ireland building are in the old section of Dublin. Among other public buildings of the city are the Customs House, an 18th-century structure; the Four Courts, seat of the high courts of Ireland; and Leinster House, seat of Dáil Éireann (q.v.), the lower house of the bicameral national parliament. Dublin also has a number of notable statues commemorating such famous Irish citizens as the national leader Daniel O'Connell, the states-

man, orator, and essayist Edmund Burke, and poet, playwright, novelist, and essayist Oliver Goldsmith (qq.v.).

Educational institutions in Dublin include University College, a campus of the National University of Ireland. Among the excellent libraries of the city are the library of the University of Dublin, with more than 450,000 volumes; the Irish Academy Library; and the National Library. Other cultural centers include the Museum of Science and Art, that contains numerous Irish antiquities; the National Gallery, with valuable collections of painting and sculpture; and the Abbey Theatre (q.v.).

The principal unit of the Dublin park system is Phoenix Park, in the w. environs of the city. About 7 mi. in circumference, the site of this park encompasses part of the Liffey R. valley. Besides recreational facilities, Phoenix Park contains zoological gardens, several conservatories, an arboretum, and the residence of the president of the republic.

Commerce and Industry. Predominantly a commercial city, Dublin also is the principal port and trading center of Ireland. The chief industrial establishments of the city include brew-

A view of Trinity College, also known as the University of Dublin. Among its distinguished graduates are Jonathan Swift and Edmund Burke. Ian M. Keown

eries, distilleries, and plants producing electrical and electronic equipment, footwear, glass, pharmaceuticals, and processed foods. Some shipbuilding is carried on, and the city has a number of foundries and automobile-assembly plants. Livestock, agricultural products, and local industrial manufactures constitute the principal exports.

History. the first known settlement on the site of Dublin was called *Eblana,* a name that is found in the writings of the 2nd-century Alexandrian geographer Ptolemy (q.v.). The town later appears in history as *Dubh-linn* (Gael., "Black Pool"), the inhabitants of which won (291 A.D.) a military victory over the armed forces of the kingdom of Leinster. *Baile Atha Cliath,* the present official name, is believed to have been applied to the settlement at a subsequent date.

Dublin has often figured prominently in Irish history. Its inhabitants were converted to Christianity about 450 by Patrick (q.v.), later the patron saint of Ireland. The town was captured in the 9th century by the Danes. The rebellious Irish wrested control of Dublin from the Danes on a number of occasions during the next three centuries, notably in 1052, 1075, and 1124. In 1171 the Danes were expelled by the Anglo-Normans, led by Henry II (q.v.), King of England. He held his court in Dublin in the following year, and later made the town a dependency of the English city of Bristol. English overlordship in Dublin remained unchallenged until 1534, when the Irish patriot Thomas Fitzgerald (1513–37) laid brief siege to the city in the course of a rebellion.

In the 17th century, during the English civil wars known as the Great Rebellion (q.v.), Dublin was surrendered to English Parliamentary forces to prevent the city from falling to the Irish. Dublin remained under British control until the Irish insurrection of 1798, during which an attempt to seize the city ended in failure. A second attempt in 1803, led by Robert Emmet (q.v.), also ended disastrously. Further abortive insurrections occurred in Dublin in 1847 and in 1867. Dublin was the scene of some of the most severe fighting of the Irish rebellion of 1916, and of the revolution of 1919 to 1921, which resulted in the establishment of the Irish Free State. Pop. (1971) 567,866.

DUBLIN, UNIVERSITY OF, also known as TRINITY COLLEGE, the oldest and leading institution of higher learning in the Republic of Ireland. The first University of Dublin was established in 1320 in connection with Saint Patrick's Cathedral but lacked an endowment and func-

tioned poorly, finally closing with the dissolution, by Henry VIII (q.v.), of the cathedral foundation. The present foundation was chartered by Elizabeth I (q.v.), Queen of England, in 1591 as "the mother of an university" with the title of "the College of the Holy and Undivided Trinity, near Dublin". It was expected that other colleges would be formed about this nucleus, and that a university of the English type would eventually develop in its place. This expectation was never realized, and Dublin University retains to the present day the capacity to function as both a college and a university. In April, 1967, however, the Irish government announced that it planned ultimately to merge University College, Dublin (*see* IRELAND, NATIONAL UNIVERSITY OF) with the University of Dublin. The Corporation of Dublin donated to the university the grounds and the ruins of the confiscated All Hallows monastery, and a building fund was raised by local subscription. James I (q.v.), King of England, endowed the institution with £400 a year and the revenue of various estates in Ulster; and the English army in 1601 commemorated its victory over the Spanish at Kinsale (*see* O'NEILL, HUGH, 3RD BARON OF DUNGANNON AND 2ND EARL OF TYRONE) by subscribing £1800 to establish a library for the college. These and other local donations provided the main financial resources of the young college. The original constitution has been revised several times, although some of the early statutes are still in effect. A revision adopted in 1793 enabled Roman Catholics to take degrees. The college is headed by a provost, and the principal governing body is the board consisting of the provost, seven senior fellows, the three principal officers of the college, four representatives of the junior fellows, and two representatives of professors who are not fellows. Two elected representatives of the students may be invited to attend and take part in meetings of the board on a nonvoting basis.

Applicants for admission to the institution must pass an entrance examination or possess prescribed entrance qualifications. With few exceptions every student enrolls in the four-year B.A. course which offers a wide range of liberal arts subjects. The professional schools offer courses and degrees in divinity, law, medicine, dentistry, veterinary medicine, engineering, business management, music, education, and social studies. The degrees of master and doctor are awarded as higher degrees. Women have been eligible for degrees since 1904 and are eligible for all university appointments and offices on the same basis as men. The first woman fellow was elected in 1968.

The university buildings include fine examples of the 18th-century architecture for which Dublin is noted, particularly the library (1732), the dining hall (1761), and the public theater (1791). The library houses over 1,000,000 bound volumes as well as a notable collection of old Irish illuminated manuscripts including the Gospels transcribed in the 7th-century *Book of Durrow* and the unique 8th-century *Book of Kells*. Since 1801 the college has been entitled by law to receive a copy of every book published in Great Britain and Ireland. Among former students of the university were the Irish philosopher George Berkeley, the English satirist Jonathan Swift, the British statesman and orator Edmund Burke, and the British poet, playwright, and novelist Oliver Goldsmith (qq.v.). In 1969–70 enrollment totaled 4311 and the faculty numbered about 340.

DU BOIS, city of Pennsylvania, in Clearfield Co., about 44 miles N.W. of Altoona. Situated in a farming and coal-mining region, the city is a marketing and industrial center with varied manufacturing. The Du Bois campus of the Pennsylvania State Commonwealth, established in 1935, is affiliated with Pennsylvania State University. Pop. (1960) 10,667; (1970) 10,112.

DUBOIS, Eugène. *See* MAN, ANCIENT: *Pithecanthropines.*

DuBOIS, Guy Pène (1884–1956), born in Brooklyn, N.Y. Having studied painting at the New York School of Art and in Paris, duBois became art critic and columnist for several American newspapers and magazines, including the New York *American* (1906–13) and the New York *Evening Post* (1916–18), as well as editor of the magazine *Arts and Decoration* (1913–16; 1917–22). Examples of his work in oil, usually lively and always accurate depictions of the contemporary scene, are "Morning Paris Cafe" (1926) and the portrait "Jeanne Eagels" (1922), both in the Whitney Museum of American Art, New York City. His autobiography, *Artists Say the Silliest Things,* was published in 1940. His son, William Pène duBois (1916–   ), is an author and illustrator of children's books.

DU BOIS, W(illiam) E(dward) B(urghardt) (1868–1963), American writer and sociologist, born in Great Barrington, Mass., and educated at Fisk and Harvard universities and the University of Berlin. In 1895 he became the first Negro to be awarded a Ph.D. degree from Harvard. He taught history and economics at Atlanta University from 1897 to 1910. Attention was first focused on Du Bois as a spokesman for his race early in the 20th century when he disagreed openly with the views of the American educator Booker T. Washington (q.v.). Du Bois, as an ardent advocate of complete racial equality, discounted Washington's views of the Negro as a minority figure in a white society; *see* WASHINGTON–DU BOIS CONTROVERSY. Du Bois was a founder (1910) of the National Association for the Advancement of Colored People (q.v.) and, as the association's director of publications (1910–32), the editor of *Crisis,* the official organ of the N.A.A.C.P. In 1926 he visited the U.S.S.R. and thereafter became increasingly convinced that advancement of the American Negro could best be achieved through socialism (q.v.). In 1934, having left the N.A.A.C.P., Du Bois returned to teach at Atlanta University; he also served (1940–44) as editor of the university's quarterly, *Phylon.* In 1944 he again joined the staff of the N.A.A.C.P. as director of the department of special research; he remained with the organization until 1948. Du Bois, increasingly involved in the promotion of world peace and nuclear disarmament, became chairman of the Peace Information Center in New York City in 1950, but the next year the organization was declared subversive by the United States government. During the 1950's he traveled extensively behind the Iron Curtain (q.v.). Awarded the 1959 Lenin Peace Prize, Du Bois joined the Communist Party in 1961 and settled in Ghana later the same year. In 1963, shortly before his death at the age of ninety-five, he became a cit-

W. E. B. Du Bois UPI

izen of Ghana. He was then engaged in editing the *Encyclopedia Africana.*

Du Bois wrote some twenty books, including *The Philadelphia Negro* (1899), *Black Reconstruction* (1935), and a trilogy, *Black Flame: The Ordeal of Mansart* (1957), *Mansart Builds a School* (1959), and *Worlds of Color* (1961).

DUBOS, René Jules (1901–), American bacteriologist, born in Saint Brice, France, and educated at the Collège Chaptal and Institut National Agronomique in Paris. Upon his arrival in the United States in 1924, he became a research assistant and instructor in bacteriology at Rutgers University. In 1938 he was naturalized a U.S. citizen. Dubos received a Ph.D. from Rutgers in 1927 and in the same year joined the faculty of the Rockefeller Institute for Medical Research (now Rockefeller University). In 1929 Dubos isolated a bacterium that destroys the polysaccharide capsule which protects the pneumonia-causing microbe. Ten years later he isolated from soil a microbe that produces the antibiotics gramicidin and tyrocidine. This pioneer work led to the development of other antibiotics. In recent years he has concerned himself with the biological as well as physiochemical effects of environmental forces on human life. Among his books are *Health and Disease* and *Man Adapting*, both published in 1965, and *Man, Medicine and Environment,* published three years later. Dubos was named cowinner of the 1968 Pulitzer Prize for general nonfiction for his work *So Human an Animal.* In 1970 he became university professor and director of environmental studies at the Purchase campus of the State University of New York.

DUBRIDGE, Lee Alvin (1901–), American physicist and educator, born in Terre Haute, Ind. He received a B.A. degree from Cornell College in Iowa in 1922, then began a teaching assignment at the University of Wisconsin, from which he received an M.A. degree in 1924 and a Ph.D. degree in 1926. DuBridge continued his academic work at the California Institute of Technology in Pasadena, at Washington University in Saint Louis, and at the University of Rochester, N.Y. At Rochester he began his long career as an academic administrator, serving as dean of the faculty of arts and sciences. On leave from Rochester between 1940 and 1946, DuBridge headed the radar development project at the Radiation Laboratory of the Massachusetts Institute of Technology. He was named president of the California Institute of Technology in 1946; during his twenty-three-year tenure the institute became one of the leading technical schools in the United States. DuBridge gave

up the presidency of the institute to become chief science adviser to President Richard Milhous Nixon, a position he held in 1969 and 1970. Beginning in 1968 he also served as chairman of the Greater Los Angeles Urban Coalition.

DUBROVNIK (It. *Ragusa*), coastal town of Yugoslavia, in the Republic of Croatia, about 180 miles s.w. of Belgrade. An historic and picturesque town on the Dalmatian coast, Dubrovnik is a major tourist resort on the Adriatic Sea. The town faces the sea at the foot of rugged, limestone mountains and is notable for its medieval walls and fortifications. Historical buildings include a rector's palace, two monasteries, and one of the oldest pharmacies (1317) in Europe. Dubrovnik has harbor facilities in the suburb of Gruz. Silk and leather are manufactured; exports include foodstuffs and timber. A music and drama festival held here each summer attracts performers and visitors from all over the world.

The town was founded in the 7th century on a site called Ragusium by the Romans. It was under the protection of the Byzantine Empire between 867 and 1205, when it fell to Venice. The town later came under the protection of the Hungarians and Turks but governed itself as an independent republic. In the 16th century, Dubrovnik had one of the greatest merchant fleets of the Mediterranean. It remained the chief cultural center for the Yugoslavs until the 19th century. During the French Revolutionary wars, the town became a crownland of Austria-Hungary (q.v.). By the terms of the Treaty of Rapallo (1920) following World War I, it became a part of the newly created country of Yugoslavia. During World War II, Dubrovnik was occupied by the Italians and Germans. Pop. (1971 est.) 31,000.

DUBUFFET, Jean (1901–), French painter, born in Le Havre. After his first exhibition in Paris in 1925, Dubuffet spent several years painting only part-time, but he developed a distinctive style of simple, primitive images in a heavily encrusted canvas. When his paintings were exhibited in Paris in 1944, the phrase *L'Art Brut* (raw art) was used to describe his style because of its crude and often violent quality. The style helped Dubuffet gain a worldwide reputation and extensive showings of his paintings. His works are frequently collages, as for example "Coursegoules" (1956), which is composed chiefly of pebbles and grass. During the early 1960's, Dubuffet worked on a series of deft jigsawlike paintings, such as "Bank of Ambiguities" (1963), in which tiny, obscure, closely spaced figures and faces dominate the painting. His later work consisted of large painted polyes-

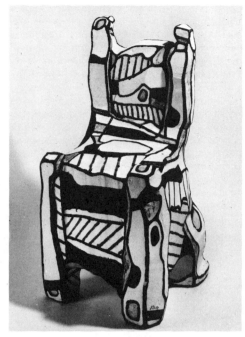

"Chaise Bleue", a cast polyester-resin sculpture by Jean Dubuffet.   Pace Gallery

ter resin sculptures. Retrospective exhibitions of his work were held in New York City at the Museum of Modern Art (1962; 1968) and the Solomon R. Guggenheim Museum (1973). At the last-named there was also a theatrical presentation, *Coucou Bazar*, produced by the artist. *See* ABSTRACT AND NONOBJECTIVE ART.

DUBUQUE, city and river port in Iowa, and county seat of Dubuque Co., on the Mississippi R., opposite the border between Wisconsin and Illinois, about 175 miles N.E. of Des Moines. Dubuque is served by six railroads and is an important market for agricultural produce. It is the center of a large wholesale and jobbing trade and of the lead and zinc mining industry of the Northwest. The city contains railway repair shops, large sash and door factories, flour and lumber mills, pork-packing houses, iron and brass foundries, breweries, and factories manufacturing hardware, leather, furniture, bricks, engines, boilers, steel ship hulls, barrels, brooms, dry batteries, plumbing supplies, clothing, oil tanks, agricultural implements, and boots and shoes. The city is the see of a Roman Catholic archbishop, and the site of Loras College (1839) for men and Clarke College (1843) for women (both Roman Catholic). The University of Dubuque (1852, Presbyterian), originally a German theological seminary which became a university in 1920, and Wartburg Seminary (Lu-

theran) are located in the city. One of the three Trappist monasteries in the United States is situated 14 miles s.w. of Dubuque.

The oldest city in the State, Dubuque was named in honor of Julien Dubuque (1762–1810), a French Canadian who settled here in 1788; a monument to him has been erected in the city. The first permanent settlement dates from 1883. Pop. (1960) 56,606; (1970) 62,309.

DU CANGE, Charles du Fresne, Sieur (1610–88), French scholar, born in Amiens, and educated at the Jesuit college there, and at Orléans, where he studied law. He later devoted himself to philology, history, and linguistics. In 1647 he became treasurer of Amiens but, because of a plague, left in 1668 for Paris, where he continued his studies until his death. Among his works are *Histoire de l'Empire de Constantinople sous les Empereurs Français* ("History of the Empire of Constantinople at the Time of the French Emperors", 1657), *Glossarium ad Scriptores Mediæ et Infimæ Latinitatis* ("Dictionary of Medieval and Late Latin", 1678), and *Glossarium ad Scriptores Mediæ et Infimæ Græcitatis* ("Dictionary of Medieval and Late Greek", 1688). The last two books, pioneering and expansive glossaries showing the historical development of medieval Latin and Greek, were accepted as standard texts for two centuries.

DUCCIO DI BUONINSEGNA (1255?–1319?), Italian painter, born in Siena. He was probably a pupil of the painter Guido da Siena (1250?–1275), and reputedly received training in art from a Byzantine master, possibly at Constantinople. Duccio was, after Giotto (q.v.), the foremost Italian artist of the late medieval period in Italy and the founder of the Sienese school (q.v.) of painting. His work brought to perfection the art of medieval Italy as influenced by Byzantine art (q.v.). Duccio's paintings are characterized by precise drawing, skillful composition, a decorative quality akin to that of the mosaic, and by deeper emotional feeling than that of the Byzantine models which he followed. His most famous work is the "Maestà" (1308–11), an altarpiece executed for the cathedral of Siena. Its front panel, 14 ft. long and 7 ft. high, represents a Madonna enthroned and surrounded by a host of angels and saints and by the Apostles; the reverse of the panel contains twenty-six scenes from the life of Christ, painted on the type of golden background characteristic of Byzantine art. Most of the panel is now in the museum of the cathedral of Siena, though several of the narrative scenes are dispersed in other collections; these include "Nativity with the Prophets Isaiah and Ezekiel" and "The Calling of the Apostles Peter and Andrew", both painted from 1308 to 1311, in the National Gallery, Washington, D.C., and "The Temptation of Christ", in the Frick Collection, New York City. Other works generally attributed to Duccio are in the Metropolitan Museum of Art in New York City, the National Gallery, and Buckingham Palace, in London.

DU CHAILLU, Paul Belloni (about 1831–1903), American explorer, born in France, probably in Paris. He spent his youth in the colony of Gabon, French Equatorial Africa, with his father, a French trader. In 1852 he migrated to the United States and later became a naturalized citizen. He led an expedition to central Africa in 1855, and returned to the U.S. four years later, bringing with him many previously unknown birds and animals, including the first gorillas ever seen in the U.S. His description of the expedition, *Explorations and Adventures in Equatorial Africa* (1861), aroused controversy, however, because it conflicted with prevailing geographical, zoological, and ethnological theories. Du Chaillu led a second expedition to Africa, confirming his first report and verifying rumors about tribes of pygmies in the forests of central Africa in *A Journey to Ashango-Land* (1867). After traveling in northern Europe from 1871 to 1874, he wrote *The Land of the Midnight Sun* (1881).

DUCHAMP, Marcel (1887–1968), French painter, born near Rouen, France. At the age of sev-

The painting, "Nude Descending a Staircase, No. 2" (1912), by Marcel Duchamp, brought down the wrath of art critics when it was first exhibited in New York City at the Armory Show of 1913.　UPI

enteen he went to Paris and early became a leading avant-garde artist. His major work of this period, "Nude Descending a Staircase" (1911), caused a scandal both at the Salon des Indépendants in Paris and at the International Exhibition of Modern Art, the so-called Armory Show, in New York City in 1913. The style of painting is derived from cubism and is closely related to the dynamic style of futurism. Like the futurists, the intention of Duchamp was to represent time on a two-dimensional surface. In 1915 he arrived in the United States, where he became a leader of the American dadaists (see DADAISM). In the United States his works were composed of "ready-mades", mass-produced objects arranged in an artistic manner. After 1923 Duchamp produced little art.

The Pekin duck is a popular commercial breed in the U.S.   UPI

DUCK, common name for the female of any of several species of water birds in the family Anatidae. The males, usually more brilliantly colored than the females, are properly called drakes, but in ordinary usage they are often also termed ducks. The duck is closely related to the swan and the goose (qq.v.), but differs from them in having a shorter neck and legs, the latter being covered with scales on the front rather than on the back. The legs are placed far back on their bodies and, although not efficient for walking, they enable the birds to swim powerfully. The plumage is dense, soft, and water-repellent. Most species have spoon- or shovel-shaped bills. The majority nest on the ground, although some species breed in hollow stumps or trees. The nests of all species are characteristically lined with down and small feathers plucked from the breasts of the parent birds. A number of species are migratory, nesting in the summer as far north as the Arctic Circle and wintering in temperate, subtropical, and tropical regions. The diet, which is varied, includes small fish and invertebrates as well as seeds, berries, and roots.

Three subfamilies of ducks are generally recognized: the Anatinae or freshwater ducks, the Fuligulinae or sea ducks, and the Merginae or

The mallard, Anas platyrhynchos, *from which most domestic breeds of duck originate.*   UPI

mergansers. A number of breeds are raised domestically and commercially for meat production. Among the most important are the Pekin duck, an all-white breed which originated in China; the mallard, found throughout the Northern Hemisphere, has a chestnut breast, a white ring around the neck, and a greenish-black head; and the Muscovy duck, a crested species native to tropical America.

For descriptions of various species of ducks, see BLUEBILL; BUFFLEHEAD; CANVASBACK; EIDER; MALLARD; MERGANSER; PINTAIL; TEAL; WIDGEON; WOOD DUCK.

DUCKBILL. See PLATYPUS.

DUCK HAWK. See HAWK.

DUCKING STOOL, in England and Colonial America, a chair, mounted at the end of a long, levered beam or pole, formerly used for the punishment of shrewish women, prostitutes, and witches. Invented in the 17th century and used into the early 19th century, the wooden device was designed to shame such offenders within a community. Ducking stools were either permanently installed along rivers or ponds, or else had wheels so that the culprit could first be paraded through the streets of the town. They worked on the seesaw principle, sometimes having hinged chairs that dipped the offender backwards into the water. The guilty party, strapped into the chair so as not to fall out, was immersed a specific number of times prescribed by the sentencing magistrate.

DUCOMMUN, Élie (1833–1906), Swiss journalist, born in Geneva. After some years as editor of the *Journal de Genève* and then of the Bern newspaper *Der Fortschritt*, he devoted his life to furthering the cause of peace. He edited and contributed to many pacifist journals, including *Progrès, Helvétie,* and *États-Unis d'Europe.* In 1891 he organized the International Bureau of Peace in Bern. In 1902 he shared the Nobel Peace Prize with the Swiss statesman Charles Albert Gobat (q.v.).

DUCTILITY. See METALS: *Physical Properties.*

DUCTLESS GLANDS. See ENDOCRINE SYSTEM; GLAND; HORMONES.

DUDEVANT, Baroness. See SAND, GEORGE.

DUDLEY, Great Britain, city and county borough of Worcestershire, England, about 10 miles N.W. of Birmingham. The city, known as Dudelei in medieval times, was of importance during the industrial revolution because of its coal and pig-iron production. The industries of Dudley include coal mines, limestone and dolerite quarries, ironworks, brass foundries, and brickworks. The lime quarries of Dudley have disclosed excellent specimens of fossils of the Silurian Period (q.v.), one of which is depicted on the municipal emblem. Pop. (1971) 185,580.

DUDLEY, name of an English family of soldiers and statesmen. Among its most important members are the following.

John Dudley, Duke of Northumberland and Earl of Warwick (1502?–53). His father, Edmund Dudley (1462?–1510), a lawyer involved in tax extortion under the English king Henry VII, was executed upon the accession of King Henry VIII (qq.v.). Dudley's mother remarried, and his stepfather gained him favor at the court of Henry VIII. He was made governor of Calais in 1538 and warden of the Scottish marches in 1542, the year he was elevated to the peerage as Viscount Lisle. He was created earl of Warwick in 1546. Upon the accession in 1547 of King Edward VI (q.v.), who was still a minor, Dudley became joint regent and lord chamberlain of England. After subduing a Scottish rebellion in 1547, he embarked on a struggle for power with the Seymour family, headed by the English nobleman Edward Seymour, Duke of Somerset (*see under* SEYMOUR). Dudley was created duke of Northumberland in 1550 and two years later disposed of his rival, Somerset, by having him tried and executed on false charges. Subsequently, he conspired to gain the succession to the English throne for his heirs by marrying his son Guildford Dudley (d. 1554) to Lady Jane Grey (q.v.). His resistance to the accession of Queen Mary I (q.v.), daughter of Henry VIII, led to his execution in 1553.

Robert Dudley, 1st Earl of Leicester (1532?–88), son of the preceding. He was sentenced to death with his father in 1553 but was pardoned by Queen Mary, who made him her master of the ordnance. He later became a favorite of Queen Elizabeth I (q.v.). The mysterious death of his wife, Amy Robsart (1532?–60), cast suspicion upon him. It was believed he had ambitions to marry the queen, who continued to show him high favor and created him earl of Leicester in 1564. Leicester later involved himself in an invalid marriage, which he kept secret, and then in a valid marriage to the widow of his rival, Walter Devereux, 1st Earl of Essex (*see under* DEVEREUX). As a result, he suffered the queen's displeasure, but in 1585 she relented and appointed him commander of an expedition to the Low Countries to assist them in their revolt against Spain. The following year he was appointed governor of the Low Countries but he was recalled in 1588 because of differences with the Dutch governing body. The queen, to whom he was reconciled, made him a lieutenant general of the forces sent to resist the Spanish Armada (q.v.). He died shortly after the Spanish defeat.

DUDLEY, Joseph (1647–1720), colonial administrator in America, born in Roxbury, Mass., and educated at Harvard College (now Harvard University). He was the son of the English colonial administrator Thomas Dudley (1576–1653). Joseph Dudley was a member of the Massachusetts General Court from 1673 to 1676 and of the upper house from 1676 to 1683. He was sent to England in 1682 to secure the continuation of the Massachusetts charter, but in an attempt to gain the favor of Charles II (q.v.), King of England, he privately advocated the establishment of royal authority in the colony. In 1686 Massachusetts was placed under a royal administration, and Dudley became president of the new provisional council for Massachusetts, New Hampshire, and part of Rhode Island under James II (q.v.), King of England. Later in the same year, he was replaced by the English colonial administrator Sir Edmund Andros (q.v.), under whom he served as judge of the superior court and censor of the press. In 1689 the Andros regime was deposed and Andros and Dudley were arrested and sent to England. Charges against both men were dismissed and Dudley returned to serve as chief justice of New York in 1691–92. He was appointed governor of Massachusetts in 1702 by Anne (q.v.), Queen of England, and remained in that post until 1715. He was a harsh and unpopular administrator, but efforts by his constituents to unseat him were unsuccessful.

DUEL (Lat. *duellum*, "combat between two", old form of *bellum*, "war"), prearranged combat with deadly weapons between two persons, generally taking place under formal arrangements and in the presence of witnesses, called seconds, for each side. The usual cause of a duel is affront or offense given by one person to the other, or mutual enmity over a question of honor. In most cases, the challenged person has the right to name the time, place, and weapons. The sword and the pistol have been the traditional dueling weapons throughout history, and duels have customarily been fought early in the morning at relatively secluded places.

The duel, in the modern, personal sense, did not occur in the ancient world, when single combats generally occurred in the context of national wars. Modern dueling arose in Teutonic countries during the early Middle Ages, when legal, judicial combat was used to decide controversies, such as guilt for crimes and ownership of disputed land. Such combat was first legalized by Gundobad, King of the Burgundi-

ans (d. 516), in 501 A.D.; *see* BATTLE, WAGER OF. The custom of judicial combat spread to France, where it became prevalent, particularly from the 10th to 12th centuries; even the Church authorized it to decide the ownership of disputed church property. The Normans brought this form of duel to England in the 11th century; *see* ENGLAND: *History.* As late as 1817, an English court authorized a judicial combat between the accuser and accused in a case of murder.

Dueling to avenge one's honor, however, has never been legalized, and its history has instead been marked by laws against it. The custom became popular in Europe after a famous rivalry between Francis I, King of France, and Charles V (qq.v.), King of Spain. When Francis declared war on Spain in 1528, abrogating a treaty between the two countries, Charles accused the French ruler of ungentlemanly conduct and was challenged by him to a duel. Although the duel did not take place because of the difficulty in making arrangements, the incident so influenced European manners that gentlemen everywhere thought themselves entitled to avenge supposed slights on their honor by similar challenges.

Dueling subsequently became particularly popular in France and occasioned so many

Robert Dudley, 1st Earl of Leicester
National Maritime Museum, Greenwich

Spectators watch a duel in 15th-century France (from a contemporary French manuscript).

deaths that Henry IV (q.v.), King of France, in 1602, declared in an edict that participation in a duel was punishable by death. Similar edicts were issued by Henry's successors, though they were rarely enforced with any strictness. The various French republican governments also outlawed dueling, making it an offense against the criminal code. Duels, however, still occur in France, though they are rarely fatal.

The duel was exceedingly popular in England, particularly during the Restoration (q.v.), as a reaction against the Puritan morality of the protectorate of the soldier and statesman Oliver Cromwell (see under CROMWELL), in the reign of George III (q.v.), King of Great Britain, during which 91 deaths resulted from 172 encounters. Numerous legislative enactments during the 17th and 18th centuries had little effect on curbing the practice. Though the English common law holds killing in a duel to be murder, juries rarely convicted in dueling cases until the custom ceased to be popular during the reign of Victoria (q.v.), Queen of Great Britain. The British articles of war were amended in 1844 to

make participants in a duel subject to general court-martial; since that date, dueling has become obsolete in the British army.

Under the imperial regime in Germany, dueling was a recognized custom in the army and navy, though each affair was subject to approval by a so-called council of honor. The German student *Mensuren* ("duels") were famous elements of German university life and were regarded as a form of sport. Every university had *Verbindungen* ("dueling clubs"), and membership in them was considered an honor. Restrictions on dueling, however, were in force even during the Empire at the end of the 19th century. The 1928 criminal code of the Weimar Republic made dueling an offense punishable by imprisonment.

In the United States, duels were common from the time of the first settlement, a duel having occurred at Plymouth in 1621. Such combats, under all sorts of conditions and with every variety of weapon, were frequent during the 18th and early 19th centuries and were usually fatal. In 1777 the American patriot Button

Gwinnett (q.v.) was killed in a duel, and one of the most famous American victims of a duel was the statesman Alexander Hamilton, who was killed by his political rival Aaron Burr (qq.v.) in 1804. The District of Columbia outlawed dueling in 1839, and, since the American Civil War, all the States have legislated against dueling, with punishments ranging from disqualification for public office to death.

By the beginning of the 20th century, dueling was almost universally prohibited by law as a criminal offense. The major factors in the suppression of dueling, however, have been social changes and social disapproval. The greatest of these social changes has been the decline of the aristocracy, since dueling was a custom reserved for the upper classes. In addition, organizations were formed to promote social disapproval of dueling, notably a British association founded in 1843 and an international league founded by European aristocrats in 1900.

See also BUSHIDO; TOURNAMENT.

DUE PROCESS OF LAW, as administered through courts of justice in accordance with established and sanctioned legal principles and procedures, and with safeguards for the protection of individual rights. It is frequently referred to in such terms as the "law of the land" and "legal judgment of his peers", expressions used for the first time in the sense of due process in the great charter of English liberty, the Magna Charta (q.v.).

In the United States the phrase "due process" first appears in the Fifth Amendment to the Constitution of the United States (q.v.), ratified Dec. 15, 1791. Because the amendment refers specifically to Federal and not State actions, another amendment was necessary to include the States. This was accomplished by the Fourteenth Amendment, ratified July 9, 1868. Thus was established at both Federal and State level that no person "shall be deprived of life, liberty, or property without due process of law".

As determined by custom and law, due process has become a guarantee of civil as well as criminal rights. Much emphasis has recently been placed by the Supreme Court of the United States (q.v.) on procedural safeguards in the administration of criminal justice in Federal and State courts. Through interpretation of the law, due process has grown to include, among other things, provision for insuring an accused person a fair and public trial before a competent tribunal, the right to be present at his trial, and the right to be heard in his own defense; the doctrine that the provisions of criminal statutes must be drawn so that reasonable persons can be presumed to know when they are breaking the law; and the principles that taxes may be imposed only for public purposes, that property may be taken by the government only for public use, and that the owners of property so taken must be fairly compensated.

See also CIVIL RIGHTS AND CIVIL LIBERTIES: *Criminal Trials and Due Process of Law.*

DUERO, river in Spain. *See* DOURO.

DUFAY, Guillaume (1400?–74), Flemish composer, born probably in Chimay, Hainault, in what is now Belgium. As a young priest and chorister he lived in Italy and France, and during most of the years 1428–37 was a singer in the papal chapel in Rome. In 1536 he was made canon of the Cathedral of Cambrai, in what is now northern France, but eighteen years at the courts of Savoy and Burgundy elapsed before he made Cambrai his permanent residence and a renowned center for music. Dufay was one of the early masters of counterpoint (q.v.), especially four-part music, and many reforms in musical notation are attributed to him. Among his compositions are magnificats, masses, motets, and songs.

DUFF, Sir Lyman Poore (1865–1955), Canadian jurist, born in Meaford, Ontario, and educated at the University of Toronto. Admitted to the bar in 1893, he served on the supreme court of the province of British Columbia from 1904 until 1906, when he became a member of the supreme court of Canada. He was chief justice of Canada from 1933 until his retirement in 1944. In 1932 he served as chairman of the Royal Commission on Transportation, popularly known as the Duff Commission, appointed to investigate Canadian railway problems during a period of economic stagnation. In 1934 he was knighted.

DUFFY, Francis Patrick (1871–1932), American Roman Catholic clergyman, born in Cobourg, Ontario, Canada, and educated at Saint Michael's College, Toronto, Catholic University, Washington, D.C., and Saint Francis Xavier College, New York City. He was ordained in 1896 and in 1898 was an unofficial chaplain to the "fighting 69th" division during the Spanish-American War (q.v.). From 1898 to 1912 he was professor of logic and metaphysics at Saint Joseph's Academy, Dunwoodie, N.Y. He became rector of the Church of Our Saviour in New York City in 1912. During World War I, he served overseas as chaplain in the United States Army, and for his bravery under fire was promoted to the rank of major and received many decorations. From 1920 to his death he was pastor of Holy Cross Church in New York City. A

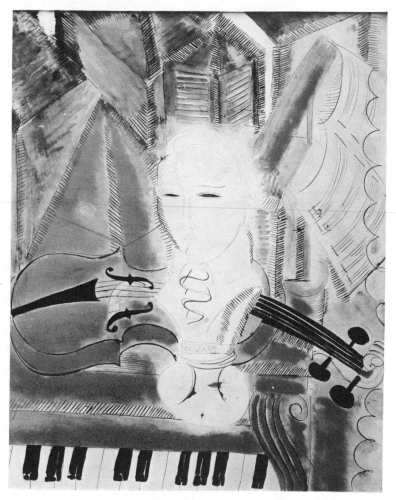

statue of Father Duffy was unveiled in Times Square, New York City, in 1937, and the area surrounding it was renamed Duffy Square two years later. His autobiography, *Father Duffy's Story,* was published in 1919.

DUFFY, Hugh (1866–1954), American baseball player, born in Cranston, R.I. He began his career in the major leagues in 1888 as an outfielder for the Chicago club of the National League. In 1893, as a member of the Boston club, he won the National League batting title with an average of .378. The following year he averaged .438, setting the all-time major-league batting record in baseball. In more than twenty-four seasons Duffy averaged .329 at bat and stole a total of 584 bases. He played for and managed clubs in Milwaukee, Wis., Philadelphia, Pa., and Providence, R.I. After his retirement as a player in 1909, he managed American League clubs in Chicago and Boston. He was elected to the

Baseball Hall of Fame in 1945; *see* BASEBALL HALL OF FAME AND MUSEUM, NATIONAL.

DUFOURSPITZE, one of the ten summits of Monte Rosa, in the Pennine Alps, and the highest peak in Switzerland. Its elevation is 15,217 ft. above sea level. *See* ALPS.

DU FRESNE, Charles. *See* DU CANGE, CHARLES DU FRESNE, SIEUR.

DUFY, Raoul (1877–1953), French painter and decorative artist, born in Le Havre, and educated there and at the École Nationale des Beaux-Arts, Paris. He was greatly influenced by the impressionists early in his career; *see* IMPRESSIONISM. In 1905 he met the French painter Henri Matisse (q.v.), then leader of the group of painters called *les Fauves* ("wild beasts"); *see* FAUVISM. Paintings by Dufy executed between 1905 and 1909 reflect the Fauvist influence. In 1909 he began to study the techniques of cubism (q.v.), but his paintings in this style were not generally well received. He had won praise meanwhile for his work in the graphic and decorative arts. The illustrations for *Le Bestiaire* (1911), a book by the French poet and novelist Guillaume Apollinaire (q.v.), are particularly noteworthy. Dufy was well known also as a designer of textiles, tapestries, and ceramics.

Gaiety, freshness, and the imaginative use of flat planes and luminous color distinguish his style, particularly after 1920. Outdoor scenes and activities at fashionable resorts are among his favorite subjects. Following a visit to the United States in 1950 he executed a series of watercolors based on impressions of New York and Boston. Dufy is represented in many leading museums of the U.S. and Europe. Among his best-known paintings are "Seascape, Le Havre" (1924–25) and "Paddock at Deauville" (1930), both at the Musée National d'Art Moderne, Paris.

DU GARD, Roger Martin. *See* MARTIN DU GARD, ROGER.

DUGONG. *See* SIRENIA.

DU GUESCLIN, Bertrand (1320?–80), Constable of France, born near Dinan, Brittany. His career began in 1341 when he entered the service of Charles de Blois, Duke of Brittany (1319–64), for whom he fought against the invading English. In 1354 he was made a knight and in 1356 he relieved the town of Rennes, which he held until the truce of Bordeaux in June, 1357; *see* HUNDRED YEARS' WAR. Later, Du Guesclin, who became known as "the Eagle of Brittany", served Charles V (q.v.), King of France who in 1364 gave him the office of lieutenant of Normandy and the title Count of Longueville. After being taken prisoner by the English at the battle of Auray in 1364, Du Guesclin was released with a large company of mercenaries, whom he then led into Spain. There he aided Henry of Trastamara, later Henry II (q.v.), King of Castile, in his war against his half brother, Pedro El Cruel (q.v.). Although Pedro, with the help of English forces, gained the first victory, Du Guesclin eventually secured the throne of Castile for Henry. From 1370, when he was made constable of France by Charles V, to his death, Du Guesclin was engaged in driving the English from the south and west of the country, thus aiding in the eventual creation of a united France.

DUHAMEL, Georges (1884–1966), French writer, born in Paris. He was educated in medicine and his first published fiction was based on his experience as a surgeon in the French army in World War I. *Vie des Martyres* (1917; Eng. trans., *The New Book of Martyres,* 1918) and *Civilisation* (1918; Eng. trans., *Civilization,* 1919),

were collections of short war stories. For the last-named, written under the pen name Denis Thévenin, Duhamel was awarded the Goncourt Prize. During his long career Duhamel wrote novels, plays, volumes of poetry and criticism, and works on philosophy, medicine, and travel. His major works were two cycles of novels, *Vie et Aventures de Salavin* (5 vol., 1920–32; Eng. trans., *Salavin,* 1936) and *La Chronique des Pasquier* (10 vol., 1933–45; Eng. trans., *The Pasquier Chronicles,* 1937–46). The first-named deals with a man determined to achieve sainthood; the last-named concerns several generations of a Parisian family. Duhamel, elected to the French Academy in 1935, wrote in a lucid, sympathetic style about the basic dignity and goodness of men.

DUIKER *or* **DUIKERBOK,** any of the small African antelopes of the subfamily Cephalophinae. They have large eyes and ears and two small, straight spikes on their convex foreheads, usually with a small tuft of stiff hairs between the spikes. Duikers rove in herds in the dense forests of South Africa and eat berries and small fruit.

The subfamily Cephalophinae is divided into three genera. In the genus *Cephalophus* the most numerous species is *C. grimmi,* which is variable in color and is about 26 in. tall. It roams throughout the southwestern forests of Africa, as do the banded duiker, *C. doriae,* and the wood antelope, *C. sylvicultor.* The second genus, *Guevei,* contains the blue duikers, pygmy antelopes of the Natal forests in southeastern Africa. They are generally about 13 in. tall and bluish gray in color. The third genus, *Sylvicapra,* contains only one species, *S. grimmia,* found throughout South Africa. *See* ANTELOPE.

DUISBURG, city and river port of Germany, in North Rhine–Westphalia State, near the border between Germany and Belgium, at the confluence of the Ruhr and Rhine rivers, about 15 miles N. of Düsseldorf.

The city, with one of the largest river harbors in the world, is the center of the Westphalian coal and iron trade and has large imports from the Americas and Sweden. Exports from the city are iron ore and coal, grain transported from other points, and many local manufactures, such as steel and brass foundry products, machinery, chemicals, textiles, plate glass, soap, starch, sugar, margarine, and malt products. Duisburg is connected with Dortmund by the Rhine-Herne Canal and in turn with North Sea ports by the Dortmund-Ems Canal.

History. Duisburg was known as *Castrum*

Deutonis to the Romans, and as *Dispargum* under the Frankish kings. In the 12th century it ranked as an imperial free city, and it joined the Hanseatic League in the 13th century. The 15th-century Church of Saint Salvator, containing the tomb of the geographer Gerhardus Mercator (q.v.), is a notable example of Gothic architecture. The modern city was formed in 1929 when the ancient Duisburg, together with several other towns, was merged with the northern suburb of Hamborn; until 1934 it was called Duisburg-Hamborn. Duisburg was one of many cities in the Westphalia-Saar Basin region that was heavily bombed by the British during World War II. After the war ended the city was included in the British zone of occupation. Pop. (1970 est.) 457,891.

DUKAS, Paul (1865–1935), French composer, born in Paris. He studied at the Paris Conservatory and in 1888 won the second prize in the competition for the Prix de Rome. In 1909 he became a teacher of composition at the conservatory. His reputation as a composer rests principally on two works: the orchestral scherzo *The Sorcerer's Apprentice* (1897), a brilliant piece of program music based on a ballad by the German poet Johann Wolfgang von Goethe (q.v.); and the opera *Ariane et Barbe-Bleue* ("Ariane and Bluebeard", 1907), one of the most important of modern French operas, performed in leading opera houses in Europe and the United States. Among other works by Dukas are the overtures *King Lear* (1883) and *Polyeucte* (1892), the Symphony in C (1896), the ballet *La Péri* ("The Genie", 1912), the Sonata in E flat minor (1901) for piano, and the *Sonnet de Ronsard* (1924) for voice and piano.

DUKE UNIVERSITY, coeducational institution of higher learning in Durham, N.C. Founded as a secondary school in 1838 in Randolph County, it was reincorporated in 1851 as Normal College. It was renamed Trinity College in 1859 and moved to Durham in 1892. In 1924, through the endowment of the American industrialist James Buchanan Duke (1856–1925), the facilities were expanded and the institution gained university status. Although it took the name Duke as a condition of the endowment, Trinity College remains the undergraduate college of arts and sciences. The university also has schools of divinity, medicine, law, engineering, forestry, and nursing, and a graduate school of arts and sciences. Degrees are awarded at all university levels. The university press publishes a number of periodicals, including *Duke Mathematical Journal, Ecology, History of Political Economy,* and *Journal of Personality.* The Law School publishes *Law and Contemporary Problems.* Duke University Medical Center is nationally known.

In 1973 the university library housed some 2,450,000 volumes and nearly 5,000,000 manuscripts. Included are special collections on British Commonwealth history, American literature and art, and the history of medicine. Student enrollment was about 9400, the faculty numbered 1125, and the endowment was about $86,800,000.

DULBECCO, Renato (1914–), Italian microbiologist and Nobel laureate.

Dulbecco was born in Catanzaro, Italy, on Feb. 22, 1914, and earned degrees in medicine and physics in Turin. He emigrated to the United States in 1947 and joined his friend Salvador Luria (q.v.) at the University of Indiana in the study of viruses that infect bacteria. After two years he became a researcher at the California Institute of Technology, where he developed techniques for studying animal-infecting viruses. He determined that viruses could cause animal cells to change their genetic material and also showed that the transformed cells induced tumors when injected into animals. This work made it possible to analyze changes in growth regulation when a cell becomes malignant, thus opening various new paths for investigating cancer.

In 1963 Dulbecco formed a research team at

John Foster Dulles   Wide World

the Salk Institute for Biological Studies in San Diego, Calif., that produced a series of discoveries on the interaction of tumor-causing viruses and host cells. In 1972 he joined the Imperial Cancer Research Fund Laboratories in London. Dulbecco was awarded the Nobel Prize for Physiology and Medicine in 1975 along with two of his former students, David Baltimore and Howard M. Temin (qq.v.).

DULCIMER, musical instrument consisting of a shallow, trapezoid-shaped resonance box with wire strings stretched across the top. The strings are attached at one end to tuning pegs. It has a compass of two or three octaves and is played by striking the strings with mallets. An ancient instrument and a remote ancestor of the pianoforte (see PIANO), the dulcimer originated in Persia (now Iran). It was introduced into Europe probably during the Crusades. The present-day instrument is used chiefly in gypsy bands in Hungary, where it is known as the *cimbalon.* The Hungarian composer Zoltán Kodály (q.v.) used the cimbalon in his orchestral suite *Háry János. See* PSALTERY; *see also* ZITHER.

DULLES, name of two American brothers who were diplomats and public officials.

John Foster Dulles (1888-1959), born in Washington, D.C., and educated at Princeton and George Washington universities and at the University of Paris. He began to practice law in New York City in 1911, and subsequently became known as an authority on international law. In 1945 he was a member of the United States delegation to the founding conference of the United Nations at San Francisco, and he later served as a U.S. delegate to the U.N. In 1945 and 1947 he served as adviser to meetings of the Council of Foreign Ministers, the formal meetings of the foreign ministers of Great Britain, the U.S.S.R., the U.S., and, in 1947, France, to discuss problems and draw up peace treaties following World War II. In 1949, he was appointed United States Senator from New York to complete the unexpired term of Senator Robert Ferdinand Wagner (q.v.) but his bid for election to a full term in the Senate in 1950 met with defeat. Dulles was named U.S. ambassador-at-large and negotiated the terms of the Japanese peace treaty signed in 1951; *see* JAPAN: *History: The 20th Century.* Dulles became secretary of state in the cabinet of President Dwight David Eisenhower (q.v.) in January, 1953, and served in that capacity until April, 1959.

Allen Welsh Dulles (1893-1969), born in Watertown, N.Y., and educated at Princeton and George Washington universities. He entered the United States diplomatic service in 1916, serving at various European and Near Eastern posts until 1926, when he resigned to practice law in New York City. He was head of the United States Office of Strategic Services in Bern, Switzerland, during World War II. From 1953 until his resignation in 1961 he was director of the Central Intelligence Agency (q.v.). In 1963-64 Dulles was a member of the Presidential commission investigating the assassination of President John F. Kennedy; *see* WARREN REPORT. He wrote several books on international affairs, including *The Secret Surrender* (1966).

DULSE, or DULCE, common name for several edible red algae which grow on rocky marine coasts. It is used as a food or condiment in several parts of the world, especially the Orient. Purple seaweeds of the genus *Porphyra,* sometimes called laver, are the most widely used for this purpose. *Porphyra laciniata* is grown in large quantities in Japan. *Rhodymenia palmata,* which is eaten in the British Isles and in other northern countries, has a purple, leathery frond. *Iridaea edulis,* eaten in s.w. England and Scotland, has a succulent, dull-purple frond. *Compare* CARRAGEEN.

DULUTH, city and port of entry in Minnesota, and county seat of Saint Louis Co., at the western extremity of Lake Superior, on the N. bank of the estuary of the Saint Louis R., opposite Superior, Wis., about 150 miles N.E. of Minneapolis. Duluth, a terminal of the Saint Lawrence Seaway (q.v.), is the third-largest city in Minnesota and, in terms of volume of cargo handled, the leading port on the Great Lakes. Duluth and Superior share an excellent natural harbor, 19 sq.mi. in area and almost completely landlocked. Entrance to the harbor is afforded by broad channels through Minnesota and Wisconsin points, enclosing the harbor. Vessels drawing up to 22 ft. of water have access to all parts of the port, including the estuary of the St. Louis R. The site of Duluth, 62.3 sq.mi. in area, occupies ground which slopes upward from the lake and river fronts to an elevation of 600 ft. A modern boulevard, Skyline Parkway, extends along the crest of this bluff for a distance of 25 mi., providing an unobstructed view of Lake Superior and the city. Among points of interest in Duluth are the Civic Center, comprising the City Hall, the Court House, and the Federal Building; the Public Library; the John Jacob Astor Trading Post, near the s.w. city limits, a replica of the stockade and blockhouses established in that vicinity early in the 19th century by the noted fur trader (see under ASTOR); the Aerial Lift Bridge, 510 ft. long, which spans the Minnesota Point entrance to the Duluth-Superior harbor; the Zoological Gar-

Duluth's new cultural center, built in 1966, is a multi-purpose complex consisting of an arena, auditorium, exhibit hall, and seven meeting rooms.

dens; and Minnesota Point, site of a United States Naval Training Station and a United States Coast Guard Station.

Duluth has various educational and cultural facilities including a modern public-school system, sixteen parochial schools, and a junior college. Schools of higher learning are the Duluth Branch of the University of Minnesota, founded in 1905, and the College of Saint Scholastica, a Roman Catholic school for women, founded in 1912. Among the cultural institutions are the Children's Museum and Art Center, which contains natural-history, ethnological, and industrial exhibits; the Bible House, with an outstanding collection of old Bibles and religious art objects; and the Duluth Symphony Orchestra. Two daily newspapers and one Sunday newspaper are published in the city.

The Duluth park system comprises more than 3200 acres, and has facilities for swimming, boating, fishing, golf, and other recreational activities. Superior National Forest, administered by the United States Forest Service, is easily accessible from the city. Duluth is the coolest large city in the U.S. during the summer season (having then a mean temperature of about 63° F.) and is popular as a summer resort.

Industry. Duluth became important as an inland port primarily because of its proximity to the Vermilion, Cuyuna, and Mesabi iron ranges, the sources for most of the iron ore produced in the U.S. Virtually all of the ore from these ranges is transported by rail to the port for transshipment. The surrounding region also produces vast amounts of grain, which ranks second only to iron ore among cargoes moving through the port. In addition, large amounts of coal are received at the port. The port is equipped with extensive cargo-handling facilities. Duluth harbor is open to navigation from about mid-April to mid-December, when it is usually closed by ice. Rail connections with important Canadian and American points are provided by seven major railway systems, including the Great Northern and the Northern Pacific. Four of the systems operate lines to the iron-ore fields.

Next to shipping, the most important industry of Duluth is manufacturing. The city produces a broad variety of products, notably steel and iron, cement, paper, leather products, food products, machinery, flour, and lumber.

History. French fur traders were active around what is now Duluth as early as 1660. In 1679, Daniel Greysolon, Sieur Duluth (1636–1710), the French explorer from whom the city takes its name, visited the region. Although John Jacob Astor established a trading station near the site of Duluth in 1817, the first permanent settlement was not founded until 1853. Four years later Duluth was chartered as a town. In 1870 it was incorporated as a city; its population was then 3131. By 1900 the population of Duluth had increased to 52,969. Pop. (1970) 100,578.

DUMA, or DOUMA, the lower house of parliament of the Russian Empire, promised on Oct. 30, 1905, by Nicholas II (q.v.), Czar of Russia, during the Revolution of 1905 and formally established by his ukase, or decree, of March 5, 1906. *See* RUSSIA: *The End of the Empire: Nicholas II.* According to this ukase, parliament consisted of the old Council of the Empire, which became the upper house, and the Duma, or lower house. No law could be passed without the consent of the assembly, but in practice this principle was rendered ineffective by political maneuvers. The members of the Duma were chosen by various electors, who in turn were elected in six curias, or subdivisions: these were large landowners, small landowners, capitalists, middle class, laboring class, and peasantry. Each group was represented according to its political influence in the empire, rather than according to its relative size. Thus, in the first Duma, the large landowning class, which numbered about 200,000, chose 2594 electors, whereas the 70,000,000 peasants chose only 1168. Demands of the Duma, such as to have the widespread persecution of the Jews brought to an end, were ignored by the government. When the Duma began to criticize governmental policy and action it was promptly dissolved, after having been in existence for 73 days. The second Duma was convened in the following year (1907). Although it contained more radicals, it also had a better organized reactionary wing. After 103 stormy days it was dissolved for opposing the arrest of several members by the czarist police. For the third Duma, which sat from 1907 to 1912, the electorate was considerably changed. Polish districts lost two thirds of their representation, and that of the peasantry and the workers of the large cities was diminished. The fourth Duma, composed almost entirely of landowners, retired military officers, and members of the clergy, convened in 1912, served through World War I, and was replaced by the Provisional Government during the Russian Revolution (q.v.) in 1917.

DUMAS, name of a French general and of his son and grandson, both of whom became famous authors.

Thomas-Alexandre Dumas, original name ALEXANDRE DAVY LA PAILLE I ERIE (1762–1806), born in the French colony of Saint Domingue (now Haiti). He was the natural son of Count Alexandre Davy de la Pailleterie and Marie Cesette Dumas (d. 1772), a Negro. He was taken to France by his father upon the death of his mother. Forbidden by his father to join the French army as a private, he enlisted under his mother's name. Dumas rose rapidly through the ranks in the revolutionary and Napoleonic armies. He served in the Italian and Egyptian campaigns of Napoleon I (q.v.) as a cavalry commander with the rank of general. Disapproving of many of the policies of Napoleon, Dumas left the army in Egypt in 1798. He was captured by the British naval forces on his way back to France and held in prison for two years.

Alexandre Dumas, known as DUMAS PÈRE (1802–70), French novelist and playwright, the son of Thomas-Alexandre, born in Villers-Cotterêts. He had little formal education. He worked as a clerk, first to a notary and then in the service of the Duc d'Orléans, later Louis Philippe (q.v.), King of France, studying French his-

Alexandre Dumas, père

tory in his spare time. The performances in Paris of an English Shakespearean company headed by Charles Kemble (*see under* KEMBLE), inspired him to write for the theater. His first works to be produced were two vaudeville reviews, both written in collaboration with other authors. The Comédie Française produced his play *Henri III et Sa Cour* ("Henry III and His Court") in 1829, and an earlier work, the romantic drama, *Christine,* in 1830. These plays established Dumas' reputation as a dramatist. They were followed by numerous works for the theater, for which he is best known in France, and by the historical novels for which he is even more famous outside of France.

Dumas was a prolific writer; about 1200 volumes were published under his name. Although many of these works were the result of collaboration or were the production of a "fiction factory" in which hired writers completed or executed his ideas, almost all of the writing bears the unmistakable imprint of his personal genius and inventiveness. His earnings were enormous but scarcely sufficient in his later years to sustain his extravagant style of living, which involved the maintenance of Monte-Cristo, as he called his estate outside of Paris, and a horde of attendant parasites, or to compensate for the losses incurred in the operation of a theater devoted chiefly to his own plays and of several newspapers. He died in comparative poverty.

The works of Dumas include the plays *Antony* (1831), *La Tour de Nesle* ("The Tower of Nesle", 1832), *Catherine Howard* (1834) and *L'Alchim-*

207

Alexandre Dumas, fils   Bettmann Archive

his plays are somewhat marred for the modern spectator by their tendency to "preach". Dumas was elected to the French Academy in 1874. Among his other well-known plays are *Le Demi-Monde* (1855), *La Question d'Argent* (1857; Eng. trans., *The Money Question,* 1915), *Le Fils Naturel* ("The Natural Son", 1858), *Un Père Prodigue* ("A Prodigal Father", 1859), and *Denise* (1885).

DUMAS, Jean Baptiste André (1800–84), French chemist, born in Alais (now Alès). He became a tutor at the École Polytechnique in Paris in 1823, and then professor of chemistry at the Sorbonne. In 1832 he founded the École Centrale des Arts et Manufactures. He was made a member of the Académie des Sciences in 1832, and became its perpetual secretary in 1868. From 1849 to 1851 he was minister of agriculture and commerce. He also served as senator and as president of the municipal council of Paris.

Dumas showed that the molecular weight of certain organic compounds is directly proportional to the vapor density of the compound, and, using this principle, he devised a valuable method for determining molecular weights, especially of gases and liquids with low boiling points. He formulated a theory on substitution, after observing that the properties of certain organic compounds were little changed when their hydrogen was replaced by an equivalent quantity of chlorine. Dumas also devised a method for the quantitative determination of nitrogen in organic substances. He wrote *Traité de Chimie Appliquée aux Arts* ("Treatise on Chemistry Applied to the Arts", 8 vol., 1828–45).

DU MAURIER, name of a British family of writers.

George Louis Palmella Busson du Maurier (1834–96), born in Paris, and educated in Paris and at University College, London. He became an analytical chemist in Bucklersbury, but in 1856 left for the Paris Latin Quarter to devote himself to painting. Later he continued his artistic training in Antwerp. While there he lost the sight of one eye, but was able to continue using his talents as a graphic artist. In 1858 he began drawing for *Punch's Almanac.* His caricatures for *Punch, Once a Week,* and the *Cornhill Magazine,* in which he satirized the middle and upper classes, are of historical value in portraying the fashionable social life of his time. He illustrated works by the British novelists William Makepeace Thackeray, George Meredith, and Elizabeth Cleghorn Stevenson Gaskell (qq.v.), and the Anglo-American novelist Henry James (q.v.). He wrote and illustrated the novels *Peter Ibbetson* (1891) and *Trilby* (1894), both of which were successfully dramatized; the former was

iste ("The Alchemist", 1839), as well as numerous dramatizations of his own fiction; his most famous novels include *Les Trois Mousquetaires* (1844; Eng. trans., *The Three Musketeers,* 1846), *Vingt Ans Après* (1845; Eng. trans., *Twenty Years After,* 1846), and *Le Comte de Monte-Cristo* (1844; Eng. trans., *The Count of Monte-Cristo,* 1846).

Alexandre Dumas, known as DUMAS FILS (1824–95), French playwright and novelist, the natural son of Alexandre, born in Paris. Dumas *fils* had an unhappy childhood because his schoolmates constantly taunted him about his illegitimacy. His first literary work was a volume of poetry, *Péchés de Jeunesse* ("Sins of Youth", 1847). The following year his first novel, *La Dame aux Camélias* (1848; Eng. trans., *Camille,* 1856), appeared, and his subsequent dramatization of this work, produced in 1852, established him as a success in the theater. The play has enjoyed lasting popularity. It has served as a vehicle for many fine actresses, including Sarah Bernhardt and, in a motion-picture version, Greta Garbo. The story was immortalized by the Italian composer Giuseppe Verdi (q.v.) in his opera *La Traviata.*

Dumas continued to write novels, but he was far more successful as a dramatist. In his view the playwright's function is highly moralistic, and nearly all of his plays are concerned with social and moral problems, such as marital infidelity and prostitution. Despite his dramatic ingenuity and his gift for dialogue and repartee,

used as a theme for an opera by the American composer Deems Taylor (q.v.).

Daphne du Maurier (1907–   ), granddaughter of George du Maurier, and daughter of the British actor-manager Sir Gerald du Maurier (1873–1934), born in London, England, and privately educated in Paris. One of her earliest works was *Gerald, a Portrait* (1935), about her father. Her work is characterized by colorful backgrounds, usually historical, and by melodramatic action. Among her other writings are *The Infernal World of Bramwell Brontë* (1961) and *Vanishing Cornwall* (1967); the novels *Jamaica Inn* (1936), *Rebecca* (1938), *Frenchman's Creek* (1941), *Hungry Hill* (1943), and *The House on the Strand* (1969); the plays *The Parasites* (1949), *My Cousin Rachel* (1952), *Mary Anne* (1954), and *The Scapegoat* (1957); and a collection of short stories, *The Breaking Point* (1959).

DUMBARTON OAKS, former private estate in Washington, D.C., now owned by Harvard University. In 1944 it was the site of the conversations, conducted by representatives of the United States, China, Great Britain, and the Soviet Union, which resulted in the Dumbarton Oaks Proposals. These constituted the basic plan from which the Charter of the United Nations (q.v.) was developed at the San Francisco Conference in 1945. The estate was deeded to Harvard in 1940 by the American diplomat Robert Woods Bliss (1875–1962). Among its notable features are a library and art collection of early Christian, Byzantine, and medieval works.

DUMBCANE, common name for plants of the genus *Dieffenbachia* of the Arum (q.v.) family (Araceae), which are frequently grown as ornamental foliage plants in conservatories, homes, and especially in public places. A full-grown dumbcane is 4 to 6 or more ft. tall with a thick, erect stem scarred by the points of detachment of dropped leaves. Usually two or more large, simple-bladed, stalked leaves arise near the single growing point at the tip of the plant. New leaves appearing at the tip of the plant periodically are tightly rolled along the long axis and point straight up. As they lengthen and unfold, they spread out more or less horizontally; old leaves hang along the stem. The leaf blade has a strong central vein with a large number of secondary veins running in pinnate arrangement from the main vein to the edge of the blade. Leaves usually have irregular areas of lighter green, yellow, or off-white that follow the veining pattern.

The leaves and stem contain dangerous quantities of microscopic, needlelike crystals of calcium oxalate. The plant takes its name from the

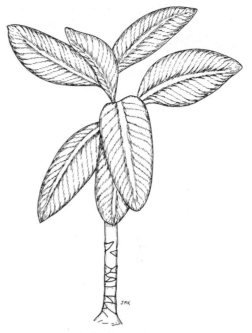

Dumbcane, Dieffenbachia seguine

fact that the intense, burning reaction which results from chewing it leaves a person speechless. In severe cases, swelling at the base of the tongue may cause the air passage of the throat to become blocked, with fatal results if not treated in time.   J.M.K.

DUMFRIES, Great Britain, border county of Scotland. Roughly oval in shape, the county contains 21 mi. of coastline on Solway Firth, toward which its surface slopes from the mountainous northern part. The county also contains extensive tablelands and rich bottomlands. Near Solway Firth are tracts of moss land, such as Lochar Moss and Nutberry Moss, which were once underwater but have been reclaimed through drainage. The county is divided into three districts (Nithsdale, Annandale, and Eskdale) by the Nith, Annan, and Esk rivers, which run N. and S. The principal lakes are Loch Skene in the N., a group around the central town of Lochmaben, and Loch Urr in the W. The raising of cattle and exporting of cattle and cattle products to England is the principal industry. At Dumfries, the county seat, and at Langholm are woolen and hosiery mills. Salmon fisheries are located along Solway Firth and the Nith and Annan rivers. Lead is mined at Wanlockhead; limestone is quarried at Keir and Carmertrees. Among the antiquities of Dumfries are the ruins of Roman stations at Birrens and the 13th-century Caerlaverock Castle, near the town of Dumfries (pop. 1969 est., 28,149). Area, 1073 sq.mi.; pop. (1971 est.) 88,065.

DUMONT, Albert Santos. See Santos-Dumont, Alberto.

DUMONT D'URVILLE, Jules Sébastien César (1790–1842), French naval officer and explorer, born in Condé-sur-Noireau. Self-educated, he went to sea at the age of seventeen. In 1820, on an expedition to the Greek archipelago, he recognized a then recently unearthed Greek statue, now known as the "Venus de Milo", as an ancient masterpiece and secured its acquisition by the French government. In 1822 he served aboard the *Coquille,* which circumnavigated the globe. Three years later he was given command of the vessel, renamed the *Astrolabe,* and was commissioned to find traces of the lost French explorer Comte de La Pérouse (q.v.). Between 1826 and 1829 d'Urville traversed the southern Australian coast, charted parts of New Zealand, and visited New Guinea, New Caledonia, and other islands in the western Pacific. At Vanikoro Island, in the Santa Cruz group, north of the New Hebrides, he found evidence that La Pérouse and his ship's company had been massacred by natives. Upon d'Urville's return, he was promoted to the rank· of captain. He embarked with the *Astrolabe* and *Zélée* in 1837, on an expedition to the South Polar regions. In 1838 he reached Palmer Land, and then Joinville island off its northern extremity. He refitted in Talcahuano, Chile, made explorations of the New Guinea and Borneo coasts, and in 1840 sailed from Hobart, Tasmania, for the Antarctic, where he discovered a coast which he called Adélie Land. This proved to be part of the continental mass and represents the French claim to the Antarctic continent. D'Urville Sea, off Adélie Land, and Cape d'Urville, West Irian, Indonesia, bear the name of the explorer, as does D'Urville island, off the coast of New Zealand. D'Urville was appointed a rear admiral on his return from the Antarctic, and wrote accounts of his voyages.

DÚNA. See Dvina.

DÜNABURG. See Daugavpils.

DUN & BRADSTREET COMPANIES, INC., a holding company comprising more than forty companies, formed in 1973. Its six main operating divisions include Dun & Bradstreet, Inc., from which the name derives; The Reuben H. Donnelley Corporation, advertising and marketing services company, including sales of Yellow Pages advertising for telephone companies; Corinthian Broadcasting Corporation, owner and operator of television stations; Moody's Investors Service, Inc., specialists in financial and investment information; Dun-Donnelley Publishing Corporation, center of Dun & Bradstreet's educational services and its book and magazine publishing division, including *Dun's Review,* the nation's oldest (since 1893) continuously published business magazine; and The Management Consulting Division, made up of William E. Hill & Co., Inc., management consultants, and the Fantus Co., Inc., plant-site location and area development specialists.

Dun & Bradstreet, Inc. The diversified business information division of the parent company is primarily known for writing reports on businesses and selling them to business clients as a basis for credit, insurance, marketing, and other business decisions. The division also publishes a reference book of credit ratings on nearly 3,000,000 companies in the U.S and Canada, primarily of manufacturing, wholesaling, and retailing firms. With headquarters in New York City, the company has more than 140 domestic offices and over 100 offices outside the U.S.

History. Dun & Bradstreet was formed in 1933 by a merger of the R. G. Dun Corporation, established in 1841 as The Mercantile Agency and operated from 1859 to 1900 under the proprietorship of the American credit specialist Robert Graham Dun (1825–1900) and The Bradstreet Company, established in 1849 by the American lawyer and businessman John M. Bradstreet (1815–63). The Mercantile Agency was the first major credit information business in the U.S. and Bradstreet the first to offer standardized credit ratings.

DUNANT, Jean Henri (1828–1910), Swiss philanthropist and founder of the Red Cross, born in Geneva. Dunant had been appalled by the condition of the wounded he saw while traveling near the battlefield of Solferino, Italy, in 1859, during the Franco-Austrian War. As a result he wrote a book, *Un Souvenir de Solferino* (1862; Eng. trans., *The Origins of the Red Cross,* 1911), suggesting that neutral organizations be established to aid wounded soldiers in time of war. His idea was supported by the Société Genevoise d'Utilité Publique, and in 1863 an international conference was held in Geneva. The Geneva Convention of 1864, planned by the meeting of 1863, established the permanent International Red Cross; see Red Cross, International: *History.* In 1901 Dunant shared the first Nobel Peace Prize with the French statesman Frédéric Passy (q.v.). Among Dunant's writings are *Fraternité et Charité Internationales en Temps de Guerre* ("International Brotherhood and Charity in Time of War", 1864).

DUNBAR, Paul Laurence (1872–1906), American poet, the son of a former slave, born in Dayton, Ohio. The best of his poems from two privately printed collections appeared in a single volume, *Lyrics of Lowly Life,* published in 1896 with an introduction by the American writer William Dean Howells (q.v.). Howells noted that Dunbar was the first Negro poet to express the lyrical qualities of Negro life and the Negro dialect. Some of Dunbar's poetry was not written in dialect; although skillful it is generally sentimental and traditional. His *Collected Poems* appeared posthumously in 1913. He also wrote four novels and several short stories. *See* NEGROES IN THE UNITED STATES: *History: New Leaders;* NEGRO LITERATURE, AMERICAN.

DUNBAR, William (1460?–1520?), Scottish poet, educated at Saint Andrews University. Virtually nothing is known of his early life. Some evidence suggests that he became a Franciscan friar and, after travels in England and France, was attached in 1500 to the court of James IV (q.v.), King of Scotland. Dunbar was the outstanding Scottish poet influenced by the work of the great English poet Geoffrey Chaucer (q.v.). The robust humor, lively imagination, and sharp satire and invective of his poetry are best shown in *The Dance of the Sevin Deidly Synnis* ("The Dance of the Seven Deadly Sins"; between 1503 and 1508). Among his other poems are *The Thrissill and the Rois* ("The Thistle and the Rose"), composed in honor of the marriage of Margaret Tudor (q.v.) and James IV in 1502, *Flyting of Dunbar and Kennedie,* and *The Twa Maryit Wemen and the Wedo* ("The Two Married Women and the Widow").

DUNBARTON, Great Britain, county in west central Scotland. In the N. and N.W. portions the peaks of the Highlands rise 2000 to 3200 ft. above sea level; this area has many scenic lakes, including Loch Lomond (*see* LOMOND, LOCH). In south Dunbarton the Kilpatrick Hills rise to 1300 ft. above sea level. Along the Clyde and Leven rivers in the S. are the Lowlands, where many farms and dairies are located. The principal crop is oats; sheep and cattle graze on the hills. Because of the purity and softness of the water of the Leven, many plants for the bleaching, dyeing, and printing of cloth and yarn have been built along the river. Other industries of Dunbarton are shipbuilding, distilling, brewing, and coal mining. Found in the county are the ruins of forts and mounds built by prehistoric peoples and the ruins of a wall built in 140–42 A.D. from the Firth of Forth to the Clyde R. by order of Antoninus Pius (q.v.), Emperor of Rome. In the Highlands are the glens where the Macgregors, the Macfarlanes, and other medieval Scottish clans made their homes, and from which they raided their neighbors in the Lowlands. The county seat is Dumbarton (pop. 1971 prelim., 25,640). Area, 246 sq.mi.; pop. (1971 prelim.) 237,549.

DUNCAN, city in Oklahoma, and county seat of Stephens Co., 90 miles S.W. of Oklahoma City. In the region surrounding Duncan are about 2300 producing oil wells. The area is also agricultural, producing wheat, oats, cotton, pecans, beef and dairy cattle, and poultry. Duncan has oil refineries, factories manufacturing asphalt and casing heads, and wholesale oil-well supply houses. The city was founded about 1890 and incorporated in 1910. Pop. (1960) 20,009; (1970) 19,718.

DUNCAN, name of two kings of Scotland.

Duncan I (d. 1040), King (1034–40), grandson of King Malcolm II Mackenneth (d. 1043), whom he succeeded. Before his accession to the Scottish throne he was ruler of the Kingdom of Strathclyde. The Scottish nobleman Macbeth (d. 1057?), who ruled the Kingdom of Moray and served Duncan as a general, killed Duncan and became king of Scotland. The tragedy *Macbeth* by William Shakespeare (q.v.) is based upon the struggle between the two kings.

Duncan II (d. 1094), King (1094), son of Malcolm III MacDuncan (d. 1093) and grandson of Duncan I. In 1093 he deposed his uncle Donald Bane (d. 1097) from the Scottish throne. Duncan ruled only for one year before he was killed by emissaries of Donald Bane, who was then restored to the throne.

DUNCAN, Isadora (1878–1927), American dancer, born Dora Angela Duncan in San Francisco, Calif. She is noted for her creation of new dance techniques based largely on the dances of the ancient Greeks. Her dancing was characterized by free, flowing movements expressive of inner emotion and inspired by waves, winds, birds, and insects. She usually appeared in a diaphanous tunic, her feet, arms, and legs bare and her long hair unbound. When she first introduced her style of dancing in America she met with strong opposition, especially from adherents of ballet (q.v.) with its traditional conventions. Eventually her ideas came into wide favor; they greatly influenced the Russian ballet and also gave rise to a new type of dancing known as "interpretive dancing" (*see* DANCE: *Modern Dance*). Among the choreographers she influenced were the Americans Agnes De Mille, Martha Graham, Ruth St. Denis, and Ted Shawn, and the Russian-American George Balanchine (qq.v.). She established schools near

Isadora Duncan   UPI

Berlin in 1904, in Paris in 1914, and in Moscow in 1921, and she toured Europe and the United States in dance recitals. Her personal life was tragic. An advocate of free love, she had two children, a daughter by the British stage designer Edward Gordon Craig (q.v.) and a son by Paris Singer (d. 1953), American heir to a sewing-machine fortune. Both children were killed in an automobile accident in 1913. She married the Russian poet Sergei Esenin (1895–1925) in 1922, but they were separated shortly thereafter. Miss Duncan lived in poverty for many years, making one final dramatic appearance in Paris before her own death in an automobile accident. Her autobiography, *My Life*, was published in 1927. A motion picture based on her life was released in 1968. She is also the subject of a biography, *The Real Isadora*, by the Russian-born U.S. writer and musician Victor Ilyich Serov (1902–), published in 1971.

DUNDALK, unincorporated suburban area of Maryland, in Baltimore Co., on the Patapsco R. and Bear Creek, adjoining the city of Baltimore and 5 miles S.E. of the downtown area. It has several residential sections and an industrial area that produces iron and steel, sheet-metal and aluminum products, engines, wire, furniture, and whiskey. The Dundalk Terminal (Harbor Field) of the Maryland Port Authority borders on the Patapsco R. and is partly within Baltimore. Pop. (1960) 82,428; (1970) 85,377.

DUNDEE, Great Britain, city and seaport of Angus County, Scotland, on the Firth of Tay,

about 40 miles N.E. of Edinburgh. The fourth largest city of Scotland, Dundee was built as a royal burgh by William the Lion (q.v.), King of Scotland, about 1200. It was granted city status by royal charter in 1889. Formerly important as a whaling and seal-fishing center, Dundee extends more than 4 mi. along the waterfront; its docks, accessible in all tides, are about 12 mi. from the North Sea. Products manufactured in the city include iron castings, machine tools, lumber, coarse linen and jute fabrics, boots and shoes, meal, flour, confectionery products, and ale. Other industries include bleaching and dyeing. An interesting landmark is Town Churches, which houses three separate churches (Saint Mary's, Saint Paul's, and Saint Clement's) under the same roof. Pop. (1971) 182,930.

DUNDEE, John Graham, 1st Viscount. *See* GRAHAM, JOHN, 1ST VISCOUNT DUNDEE.

DUNE. *See* DESERT.

DUNEDIN, city in New Zealand, on South Island, capital of Otago Province, on Otago Harbor, 15 mi. from the Pacific Ocean. The city was founded in 1848 on a site selected because of its fine harbor. Dunedin enjoyed its major growth after 1861, when the discovery of gold in the neighborhood attracted thousands of settlers from Australia. Dunedin is the seat of Otago University, containing faculties of arts, medicine, chemistry, and mineralogy; and a teachers' training college. The city is a rail center. Industry is chiefly the manufacture of woolen goods. Gold mining, sheep and cattle raising, and the processing of dairy products are the principal occupations in the surrounding region. Most of these commodities are exported; coal, timber, and manufactured goods are the leading imports. Pop. (1972 est.) 82,700.

DUNE VEGETATION, plants which grow on dunes. Although dune vegetation is commonly regarded as being composed only of xerophytes (plants especially adapted to grow under conditions of severe drought or high salt concentration), mesophytes (plants adapted to grow under conditions of medium water availability) are also commonly found upon dunes.

Both the absence of water and the instability of the sand in a dune make the initial establishment of vegetation difficult. Upon such shifting areas, the most successful species are those with underground stems which send down roots at close intervals and so extend over wide areas. Sand reeds of the genus *Ammophila*, which are common beach plants (q.v.), are the best-adapted dune plants. They are found throughout the Northern Hemisphere and are often planted to aid in preventing dunes from shifting. Among woody plants capable of growing on dunes are various species of small willow; shrubby cherries and sumacs are also abundant in many dune areas of the United States.

DUNFERMLINE, Great Britain, city of Fife County, Scotland, 3 mi. from the N. shore of the Firth of Forth and about 15 miles N.W. of Edinburgh. The city is cut from N. to S. by Pittencrieff glen, a deep ravine at the bottom of which flows the stream Lyne Burn. Dunfermline dates from about the 9th century, when the Culdees, early Celtic monks, established an abbey on the site. The present abbey was built in 1072 by Malcolm III MacDuncan, King of Scotland (d. 1093), and his queen, Margaret, who were married in Dunfermline and are buried in the abbey. Many others of Scotland's royal dead are said to be buried in Dunfermline Abbey, including Robert Bruce (q.v.), King of Scotland, who granted the city a royal charter in 1322.

The American industrialist Andrew Carnegie (q.v.), born in Dunfermline, donated to the city a public library, public baths, the 60-acre estate of Pittencrieff park and glen, and a trust fund of some $3,750,000 for the maintenance of the park, the endowment of a theater, and the promotion of the general interests of the townspeople. Dunfermline is now the headquarters of all the trusts established by Carnegie in Scotland. The chief occupation in the city is the manufacture of fine damask table linen. Other industries are bleaching and dyeing, and the manufacture of brass and iron castings, pottery, ale, soap, and cordage. Numerous coal mines are in the vicinity of Dunfermline. Pop. (1971) 51,738.

DUNG BEETLE. See SCARAB.

DUNHAM, Katherine (1910–   ), American choreographer and dancer, born in Chicago, Ill. She studied anthropology at the University of Chicago and continued her studies on the West Indies at Northwestern University. Long interested in the theater and the dance, she began her entertainment career in Chicago in 1931, performing at a Beaux Arts Ball. After a period in which she danced with the Chicago Opera Company, she studied (1936–37) native dances in Brazil and the West Indies. After her return to the United States she appeared on the stage in New York City in *Cabin in the Sky* (1940) and *Concert Varieties* (1945); she also danced in and choreographed *Carib Song* (1945) and *Bal Nègre* (1946). In 1963 she did the choreography for a Metropolitan Opera Company, New York City, production of *Aïda*. In 1945 she founded the Katherine Dunham School of Cultural Arts, of

which she became president. Her experiences with native dancing helped her to develop a distinctive choreography, which combined primitive body movements with classic ballet patterns.

DUNKERS. See CHURCH OF THE BRETHREN.

DUNKIRK, city of New York State, in Chautauqua Co., on Lake Erie, 40 miles S.W. of Buffalo. It is a port of entry, possessing a fine harbor resembling that of Dunkirk, France, after which it is named, and is served by five railroads. Dunkirk is the center of an agricultural region noted for grape cultivation. The chief industries of the city are the manufacture of stainless steel, oil-refining machinery, automobile radiators and valves, steel bridges, and leather products. Dunkirk was founded about 1809, incorporated as a village in 1837, and received a charter as a city in 1880. In 1946 the people of Dunkirk "adopted" the war-ravaged city of Dunkirk, France, donating more than $75,000 worth of recovery aid in the form of food, clothing, tools, medical supplies, and farm animals. Pop. (1960) 18,205; (1970) 16,855.

DUNKIRK (Fr. *Dunkerque*), city and seaport of France, in Nord Department, on the Strait of Dover, 28 miles N.E. of Calais. It is connected by railway and canal with the principal industrial and agricultural centers of Belgium and France. Dunkirk is a leading seaport of France and is the headquarters of large herring- and cod-fishing fleets. The harbor, which is approached by a natural roadstead, is accessible to the largest vessels. Industries in Dunkirk include the manufacture of soap, starch, beer, beet sugar, cordage, and leather. The town also contains metal foundries, distilleries, flour mills, sawmills, petroleum refineries, and shipyards. Dunkirk owes its origin to a church built in the 7th century by Saint Éloi (588?–659) in the midst of sand dunes; the name of the town means "Church on the Dunes". Historically Dunkirk shared the fortunes of Flanders, coming successively under Burgundian, Austrian, and Spanish rule. It was taken by the English in 1658, and sold to France in 1662 by Charles II (q.v.), King of England. By the Treaty of Utrecht in 1713 the French were compelled to destroy the fortifications of Dunkirk, but they were restored in 1783. In World War I the port was the object of constant attacks by the Germans, principally by air, because of its importance as an antisubmarine base. In World War II, during May–June, 1940, Dunkirk was the site of one of the great military feats of history, when more than 335,000 men of the British and other Allied forces were evacuated by small British craft that were under con-

"The Withdrawal from Dunkirk" (from an oil painting by the British artist Charles Cundall).

stant German attack; see WORLD WAR II: *The Battle of Western Europe*. Pop. (1970 est.) 28,082.

DÚN LAOGHAIRE *or* **DUNLEARY,** formerly KINGSTON, city and seaport of the Republic of Ireland, in County Dublin, on the s. side of Dublin Bay, 15 miles s.e. of the city of Dublin. The town received the name of Kingston in 1821 in honor of a visit by George IV (q.v.), King of Great Britain. Dún Laoghaire was a fishing village prior to the construction of its large harbor between 1817 and 1859. The harbor covers about 250 acres, and varies in depth from 10 to 28 ft. according to the tide. Cattle, lead ore, and granite are exported; coal, iron, timber, corn, and foodstuffs are the chief imports. Fishing is still an important occupation of the townspeople. Pop. (1971) 53,171.

DUNLAP, William (1766–1839), American playwright, painter, and art historian, born in Perth Amboy, N.J. He studied art in London under the American artist Benjamin West (q.v.) in 1784, and, after painting for a time, turned to writing plays. Dunlap was the first American professional playwright (see DRAMA: *American Drama*). His first successful play was *The Father of an Only Child* (1789). Thereafter he wrote or adapted sixty additional plays, among which are *Leicester* (1794) and *Fontainville Abbey* (1795). In 1796 he became one of the managers of the John Street Theatre, New York City, and two years later became sole director of the New Park Theatre in the same city. In 1805 bankruptcy

ended his managerial career and in 1816 he resumed his career as a painter. He became one of the foremost American painters of religious subjects. In 1826 he was one of the founders of the National Academy of Design. Among his paintings are "Calvary", "Christ Rejected", and "Bearing of the Cross". Dunlap wrote *History of the American Theatre* (1832) and *History of the Rise and Progress of the Arts of Design in the United States* (1834), both important sources for the study of early American culture.

DUNMORE, borough of Pennsylvania, in Lackawanna Co., near the Susquehanna R., about 2 miles n.e. of Scranton. The city manufactures textiles and mines anthracite coal. Dunmore was settled in 1783 and incorporated as a borough in 1862. Pop. (1960) 18,917; (1970) 17,300.

DUNMORE, 4th Earl of, John Murray (1732–1809), British colonial administrator, born in Scotland. A member of the British House of Lords from 1761 to 1770, he was appointed governor of New York in 1770 and governor of Virginia in 1771. He dissolved the Virginia assembly in 1772, 1773, and 1774 because of its revolutionary attitude. An action against the Shawnee (q.v.) Indians in 1774, which he supposedly instigated to protect his own property, became known as Lord Dunmore's War. In April, 1775, he prompted a revolutionary uprising by transferring part of the colony's gunpowder stores from Williamsburg to the British warship *Magdalen*. After a riot at the June session of the colonial legislature, Dunmore transferred the seat of government to the British man-of-war *Fowey*, anchored 12 mi. off Yorktown. The colonial burgesses declared that he had abdicated and vested a committee of safety with executive powers. Dunmore equipped a flotilla and used it to attack Hampton. After he had burned Norfolk on Jan. 1, 1776, the Americans drove him from his station on Gwynn's Island in Chesapeake Bay. Dunmore then sent his fleet to the West Indies and returned to England. He was governor of the Bahamas from 1787 to 1796. *See also* VIRGINIA: *History.*

DUNN, Oscar James (1820–71), American soldier and politician, born a slave in Louisiana. At the age of twenty-one he escaped from his owners. He served in the Union army during the American Civil War and became a captain in a regiment of Negro troops, but resigned his commission when an incompetent white man was placed over him as major. After the war he took an active part in the Reconstruction (q.v.) measures in Louisiana and became lieutenant-governor in 1868. He was the first Negro to hold an important public executive office in the United States.

DUNNE, Finley Peter (1867–1936), American newspaperman and humorist, born in Chicago, Ill. He was on the editorial staff of the Chicago *Evening Post* and Chicago *Times-Herald* from 1892 to 1897, and editor of the Chicago *Journal* from 1897 to 1900. He first attracted attention while on the *Times-Herald* with the publication of a series of sketches concerning the opinions of an Irish saloonkeeper called Mr. Dooley, who commented on American social and political life with shrewd and down-to-earth humor. The sketches were subsequently (1898) collected into a book, *Mr. Dooley in Peace and in War,* which enjoyed a wide popularity in the United States and England, and established Mr. Dooley as a household character. Mr. Dooley's adventures were continued in *Mr. Dooley in the Hearts of His Countrymen* (1898), *Mr. Dooley's Philosophy* (1900), *Mr. Dooley's Opinions* (1901), *Observations by Mr. Dooley* (1902), *Dissertations by Mr. Dooley* (1906), and *Mr. Dooley Says* (1910).

DUNNOCK, Mildred (1900?–), American stage and motion-picture actress, born in Baltimore, Md. After graduation from Goucher College, she taught school in New York City. Her first Broadway role was in *Life Begins* (1932). She played the part of Miss Ronberry in both the stage (1940) and film (1945) versions of *The Corn Is Green.* Miss Dunnock was best known for her role as the disillusioned but loyal wife and mother in *Death of a Salesman* (1946), by the American playwright Arthur Miller (q.v.).

She repeated that role in the film (1951) and television (1966) productions of the play. Other roles she performed on the stage in New York City were Big Mamma in *Cat on a Hot Tin Roof* (1957) and Hecuba in the 1963 production of *The Trojan Women.*

DUNSANY, 18th Baron Edward John Moreton Drax Plunkett (1878–1957), Irish poet, dramatist, and novelist, born in London, England, and educated at Eton College and the Royal Military College, Sandhurst. He served in the Boer War and was wounded while serving in World War I. In 1940–41 he was Byron Professor of Literature at Athens University, Greece. Lord Dunsany wrote in many different media, but was most successful as a playwright. Nearly all of his works are characterized by mysticism, fantasy, and rich, imaginative language. His stories frequently draw upon Celtic and Oriental mythology. Among his best-known plays are *The Glittering Gate* (1909), *The Gods of the Mountain* (1911), and *If* (1921). His other works include the novels *The King of Elfland's Daughter* (1924) and *The Charwoman's Shadow* (1926); the collection of short stories *The Sword of Welleran* (1908) and *Travel Tales of Mr. Joseph Jorkens* (1931); and the autobiographies *Patches of Sunlight* (1938), *While the Siren Slept* (1944), and *The Sirens Wake* (1945).

DUNSINANE, mountain in Scotland, one of the Sidlaw Hills, in Perth County, 7 miles N.E. of the city of Perth. It rises 1012 ft. above sea level, and overlooks the Carse of Gowrie and the Tay valley. The action of the play *Macbeth* by William Shakespeare took place in the surrounding area. On the summit of Dunsinane are the remains of "Macbeth's castle". Located nearby is Birnam Wood, where Macbeth, King of Scotland (d. 1057), was slain in battle by Malcolm Canmore, later Malcolm III MacDuncan, King of Scotland (d. 1093).

DUNS SCOTUS, John (1265?–1308), Scottish scholastic theologian and philosopher, born in Duns. He entered the Franciscan order and studied at the universities of Oxford and Paris. He later lectured at both universities on the *Sentences,* the basic theological textbook by the Italian theologian Peter Lombard (1100?–60?). In 1303 he was exiled from Paris for refusing to support Philip IV (q.v.), King of France, in his quarrel with Pope Boniface VIII (*see under* BONIFACE) over the taxation of church property. After a brief exile Duns Scotus returned to Paris, where he lectured until 1307. Toward the end of that year he was sent to Cologne, where he lectured until his death in 1308. His most important writings are two sets of *Commentaries on the*

215

John Duns Scotus   Bettmann Archive

Sentences and the treatises *Quodlibetic Questions, Questions on Metaphysics,* and *On the First Principle.* Because of his intricate and skillful method of analysis, especially in his defense of the doctrine of the Immaculate Conception (q.v.), he is known as *Doctor Subtilis* (Lat. "the Subtle Doctor").

In his system of philosophy Duns Scotus closely analyzed the concepts of causality and possibility in an attempt to set up a rigorous proof for the existence of God, the primary and infinite being. He held, however, that in order to know the truth in all its fullness and to fulfill his eternal destiny, man not only must make use of the insights afforded by natural knowledge, or philosophy, but also must be taught by divine revelation. Revelation both supplements and perfects natural knowledge, and, in consequence, no contradiction can exist between them. For Duns Scotus, theology and philosophy are distinct and separate disciplines; they are, however, complementary, because theology uses philosophy as a tool. In his view, the primary concern of theology is God, considered from the standpoint of His own nature, whereas philosophy properly treats of God only insofar as He is the first cause of things. With regard to the nature of theology as a science, however, Duns Scotus departs sharply from his Dominican forerunner, the Italian theologian Saint Thomas Aquinas (q.v.). Whereas Aquinas defines theology as primarily a speculative discipline, Duns Scotus sees theology as primarily a practical science, concerned with theoretical issues only insofar as they are ordered toward the goal of saving men's souls through revelation. He argues that through faith men may know with absolute certainty that the human soul is incorruptible and immortal; reason plausibly may argue the existence of such qualities of the soul, but it cannot strictly prove that they exist.

Like Aquinas, Scotus was a realist in philosophy (*see* REALISM), but he differed from Aquinas on certain basic issues. A major point of difference concerned their views of perception. Duns Scotus held that a direct, intuitive grasp of particular things is obtained both through the intellect and the senses. Aquinas maintained that intellect did not directly know the singularity of material things but only the universal natures abstracted from sense perceptions.

Duns Scotus held that universals as such do not exist apart from the human mind, but that each separate or "singular" thing possesses a formally distinct nature that it shares in common with other things of the same kind. This fact, he taught, provides the objective basis of our knowledge of essential truths. Following the Franciscan tradition established by the Italian theologian Saint Bonaventura (q.v.), Duns Scotus stressed the freedom of man and the primacy of his will and acts of love over his intellect. He avoided an arbitrary or voluntarist view of God's acts, although he pointed out that the actual existence of things depends on a free decision made by God and argued that moral obligations depend on God's will. That will, he taught, is absolutely free and not shaped or determined by particular motives. God commands an action not, as Aquinas asserts, because He sees it to be good; He makes it good by commanding it.

Duns Scotus was one of the most profound and subtle of the medieval theologians and philosophers known as Schoolmen (*see* SCHOLASTICISM). For many centuries after his death his followers, called Scotists, engaged in controversy with the adherents of Aquinas, who were called Thomists. In the middle of the 20th century the influence of Scotist philosophy was still strong within the church. Duns Scotus was a staunch supporter of the doctrine of the Immaculate Conception, which Pope Pius IX (*see under* PIUS) defined as a dogma of the Roman Catholic faith in 1854.   J.D.C. & W.N.C.

DUNSTAN, Saint (about 909–88), English prelate and statesman, born near Glastonbury, and educated by Irish clerics. He later joined the court of Athelstan (q.v.), King of England. Ordained a priest by Alphege, or Aelfheah Bishop of Winchester (954–1012), Dunstan lived as a hermit until 940 when Edmund I (q.v.), Athelstan's successor, appointed him abbot of Glastonbury. Dunstan expanded the abbey, which became a famous school under his administration. After Edred (r. 946–55) succeeded to the throne, Dunstan became virtual ruler of the kingdom and instituted policies of political unification, the establishment of royal authority, and religious reforms. When Edwy (r. 955–57) became king, Dunstan fell into disfavor for reproving his conduct, was outlawed, and fled the country. He was recalled by Edwy's successor, Edgar (q.v.), in 957, and became successively bishop of Worcester (958), bishop of London (959), and archbishop of Canterbury (960). He was again the most influential figure in the kingdom and introduced monastic reforms based on a strict observance of the Benedictine rule, with which he had become acquainted during his exile. He rebuilt churches and promoted education. When Edgar died, Dunstan succeeded in placing the king's son, later Edward the Martyr (see under EDWARD), on the throne. When Edward was murdered in 975, however, Dunstan's public career ended and he retired to Canterbury.

Dunstan was a patron saint of metalworkers. In art he was often represented holding an evil spirit's nose in a pair of tongs. His traditional feast day is May 19.

DUNTON, Walter Theodore Watts-. See WATTS-DUNTON, WALTER THEODORE.

DUODECIMAL SYSTEM. See NOTATION.

DUODENUM. See INTESTINE.

DUPLEIX, Marquis Joseph François (1697–1763), French colonial administrator, born in Landrecies. His father, a shareholder in the French East India Company, appointed him to a seat in the superior council at Pondicherry, India, in 1720. Ten years later Dupleix became superintendent of French affairs at Chandernagore in Bengal. In 1742 he was appointed governor-general of all French possessions in India. He enlarged the army and tightened its discipline and made improvements in the defenses of Pondicherry. After war broke out in Europe between France and Great Britain in 1742, Dupleix attacked the British at Fort Saint David, but was repulsed. He, in turn, repulsed the British in 1748, when they attempted to drive him from Pondicherry. For five weeks a British force under Admiral Edward Boscawen (1711–61) attacked his defenses remorselessly, but without success. Dupleix failed in his project to found a French empire in India largely because of the

energy and military genius of the British general Robert Clive (q.v.). The struggle continued until 1754, when Dupleix was recalled and repudiated by Louis XV (q.v.), King of France, who desired peace with Great Britain. Dupleix died in obscurity, having spent his personal fortune in carrying out his policies.

DUPLICATING MACHINE. See OFFICE MACHINES: *Duplicating of Drawings and Documents: Duplication of Typed Matter.*

DU PONT, family of American industrialists of French ancestry, famous as the founders and major stockholders of E. I. du Pont de Nemours & Company, Inc., the largest manufacturer of chemical products and explosives in the world. The more famous members of the family include the following.

Pierre Samuel du Pont de Nemours (1739–1817), French economist, born in Paris. His name was originally Dupont; he changed the form and later added "de Nemours" to avoid confusion with innumerable other Duponts in France. Only he and his sons used the full name. Du Pont was educated by his mother, and in his early twenties became a friend and disciple of the French economist François Quesnay (q.v.), leader of a group of economic theorists. The supporters of Quesnay's theories took the name of physiocrats (see ECONOMICS) from the book explaining Quesnay's doctrines, *Physiocratie, ou Constitution Naturelle du Gouvernement le Plus Avantageux du Genre Humain* ("Physiocraticism, or the Natural Constitution of Government Most Advantageous to Man", 1768) written by du Pont. From 1768 to 1772 he was editor of the journal of the physiocrats, *Les Ephémérides du Citoyen* ("The Citizen's Historical Calendar"). His articles favoring reforms, such as the abolition of slavery and of governmental restrictions on the economic life of the nation, aroused the anger of the government, however, and he was forced to leave France. After traveling in Germany, Sweden, and Poland, he was recalled to France in 1774 by Anne Robert Jacques Turgot (q.v.), who in that year became comptroller general of Louis XVI (q.v.), King of France. Two years later, Turgot was forced to resign, and du Pont left the government service. He returned at the request of Jacques Necker (q.v.), who became finance minister in 1776. In 1782 du Pont was entrusted by Charles Gravier, Comte de Vergennes (1717–87), then foreign minister, with the negotiations with Great Britain which led to the British recognition of American independence in the following year. He also negotiated a commercial treaty between France and England in 1786. The district

217

of Nemours elected him to the States General in 1789 and later to the Constituent Assembly, of which he was twice president. After the Assembly was dissolved (*see* FRANCE: *History*), he opened a printing and publishing business in Paris. His reactionary and Royalist views, particularly his defense of Louis XVI, led to his imprisonment, and he narrowly escaped being guillotined. In 1799 he and his sons emigrated to the United States, where he hoped to establish a colony in Virginia. The colony never materialized, but du Pont was well received in the U.S. President Thomas Jefferson (q.v.), asked him to prepare a plan for national education; the plan was not adopted in the U.S., but parts of it were later incorporated into the French education code. When Napoléon Bonaparte, later Napoleon I (q.v.), Emperor of France, began to welcome the return of the refugees from the French Revolution, du Pont returned to France in 1802. He played an important role in the negotiations for the Louisiana Purchase (q.v.), and, later, was appointed president of the Paris Chamber of Commerce. After the defeat of Napoleon I, du Pont became secretary of the provisional government preparing for the return of Louis XVIII (q.v.) to the French throne, but Napoleon's escape from Elba in 1815 forced du Pont to take refuge with his son in the U.S., where he remained. Among his works were *Mémoires sur la Vie et les Ouvrages de Turgot* ("Recollections of the Life and Works of Turgot", 1782) and *Philosophie de l'Univers* ("Philosophy of the Universe", 1796).

Victor Marie du Pont de Nemours (1767–1827), French diplomat, later American industrialist, the elder son of Pierre Samuel, born in Paris. He entered the French diplomatic service in 1787 as attaché to the French legation in the U.S., became first secretary of the legation in 1795, and in the same year, was appointed French consul in Charleston, S.C. After resigning from government service, he returned to France and in 1799 he emigrated with his father to the U.S., where he was later naturalized. For a time he was a member of the Delaware legislature and a director of the Second Bank of the United States.

Eleuthère Irénée du Pont de Nemours (1771–1834), Franco-American industrialist, the younger son of Pierre Samuel, born in Paris. He became a pupil of the French chemist Antoine Laurent Lavoisier (q.v.) in 1787, and entered the royal powder mills at Essone, where he was trained in the manufacture of gunpowder. When the French Revolution began, du Pont left the mills, and in 1791 took charge of his fa-

Eleuthère Irénée du Pont de Nemours
Du Pont Photo Library

ther's printing business in Paris. He was a Royalist and, eight years later, emigrated with his father to the U.S. Noting the poor quality of gunpowder then manufactured in the U.S., he decided to manufacture explosives. He returned to France to get plans and models of French gunpowder machinery and to obtain financial support. In 1802 he established E. I. du Pont de Nemours and Company near Wilmington, Del., and began to manufacture gunpowder. So successful were his operations that, at the time of his death, the du Pont factory was the largest of its kind in the U.S.

Samuel Francis du Pont (1803–65), American naval officer, the son of Victor Marie, born in Bergen Point, N.J. At the age of twelve, he was appointed a midshipman in the United States Navy by President James Madison (q.v.). By 1842, du Pont had reached the rank of commander, and in 1845 he was designated to assist in the organization and administration of the newly established United States Naval Academy at Annapolis. During the war between the U.S. and Mexico (1846–48) he commanded a ship. After the start of the Civil War he was promoted to rear admiral in the Union navy. In 1863 du Pont was ordered to attack Charleston, S.C. The Union ships attacked and were repulsed with great losses; when he was ordered to attack again, du Pont refused on the ground that his forces were insufficient. He was relieved of his command and retired from active duty. In 1882 by Congressional order one of the most important traffic circles in Washington, D.C., was named Du Pont Circle, and a statue of him was erected there.

Pierre Samuel du Pont (1870–1954), American industrialist, the great-grandson of Eleuthère Irénée, born in Wilmington, Del., and educated at the Massachusetts Institute of Technology. He was the acting president of E. I. du Pont de Nemours and Company, Inc., from 1909 to 1915, when he was elected president of the company. In 1920 he became president of the General Motors Corporation, returning to his family company in 1923 as chairman of the board. Under his direction the company developed to tremendous proportions.

The corporation expanded into the chemical products field, acquiring, in the period from 1915 to 1931, sixteen large chemical-products companies in the U.S., the Remington Arms Co., and a large block of the stock of the General Motors Corporation. From the time of its beginning in 1802, the company supplied nearly all the military explosives used by the U.S. in its wars; during World War I, it supplied 40 percent of the smokeless gunpowder used by all the Allies. Explosives became a minor interest of the du Pont enterprises after 1918; its products included acids, dyes, lacquers, industrial alcohol, cellulose, synthetic fibers such as rayon and nylon, and photographic film. After further expansion in World War II, the company owned eighty-three factories in twenty-three States. In a recent year, the total sales of E. I. du Pont de Nemours and Company, Inc. amounted to more than $3,000,000,000.

DUPRÉ, Jules (1811–89), French landscape painter, born in Nantes. The son of a porcelain manufacturer, his earliest art training was in decorating porcelain objects. Subsequently he studied art under various masters in Paris, where he was particularly influenced by the paintings in the Louvre of the Dutch landscape painters Meindert Hobbema (q.v.) and Salomon van Ruisdael (1600?–70). Dupré also admired the work of the contemporary French landscape artist Théodore Rousseau (1812–67), and became a member of the Barbizon school (q.v.) of painting, with which Rousseau was identified. A trip to Great Britain in 1834 enabled Dupré to study the landscapes of the British painter John Constable (q.v.), an experience which also influenced his style.

Dupré became one of the leaders of the Barbizon group, and is considered one of the founders of the modern French school of landscape painting. His work in general expresses the gloomy, the dramatic, and the tragic in nature; it is characterized by vivid and sharply contrasting colors, often applied in thick coatings, a technique known as impasto. Among his paintings are "Morning" and "Evening" (both in the Louvre, Paris), "River Scene" (Tate Gallery, London), "Hay Wagon" and "The Old Oak" (Metropolitan Museum of Art, New York City), and "Barks Fleeing Before a Storm" (Art Institute of Chicago).

DUQUESNE, city of Pennsylvania, in Allegheny Co., on the Monongahela R., 10 miles S.E. of Pittsburgh. Industries in the city include the manufacture of steel, cement, chemicals, and drugs. Duquesne was settled in 1789, incorporated as a borough in 1891, and chartered as a city in 1917. Pop. (1960) 15,019; (1970) 11,410.

DUQUESNE, FORT. *See* PITTSBURGH: *History.*

DURAN, Carolus (1837–1917), French painter, born Charles Auguste Émile Durand, in Lille. He was also known as Auguste Émile Carolus-Duran. He studied at the Lille Academy of Art

"Portrait of the Artist's Daughter" by Carolus Duran.
California Palace of the Legion of Honor — Mildred Anna Williams Collection

and at the École Suisse, Paris; his extensive copying of paintings of the old masters in the Louvre, particularly those of Leonardo da Vinci and Velázquez (qq.v.), also helped form his style, which is characterized by lifelike quality and vivid coloring. Duran was chiefly a portrait painter. He was also a notable teacher; among his pupils were the American painters John Singer Sargent (q.v.) and Will Hicok Low (1853–1932). In 1905 Duran was elected a member of the French Institute and appointed director of the French Academy in Rome. Among his works are many portraits of women and children; portraits of contemporary personages; and the paintings "The Assassination" (1868) and "Lady with a Dog" (both in the Lille Museum), and "Gloria Mariae Medici" (decoration for a ceiling in the Louvre, Paris).

DURAND, Asher Brown (1796–1886), American engraver and painter, born in South Orange, N.J. He received instruction from the American engraver Peter Maverick (1780–1831) but was largely self-taught. He established his reputation as an engraver in 1823 with "The Signing of the Declaration of Independence" after a painting by the noted American artist John Trumbull (q.v.). Subsequently Durand executed more than fifty engraved portraits of contemporary personages, including General Andrew Jackson, Henry Clay (qq.v.), and a number of American Presidents. After 1835 he devoted himself chiefly to painting, at first executing principally figure pieces and portraits, but later specializing in landscape painting, chiefly of scenes along the valley of the Hudson R. and in New England. With the American painter Thomas Cole (q.v.) he was the originator of the Hudson River school of painting (q.v.). He was one of the founders of the National Academy of Design in 1825, and was its president from 1845 to 1861. Among Durand's works are the engraving "Ariadne" after the painting by the American artist John Vanderlyn (1775–1852); and the paintings "The Wrath of Peter Stuyvesant" (New York Historical Society), "Franconia Notch" (New York Public Library), "Mountain Forest" (Corcoran Gallery, Washington, D.C.), and "In the Woods" (1855, Metropolitan Museum of Art, New York).

DURANGO, city in Colorado, and county seat of La Plata Co., about 25 miles E. of Mesa Verde National Park (q.v.). The city is in a livestock-raising, mining, and farming area. Durango has light manufacturing and is a shipping center. It is the site of Fort Lewis College, founded in 1910. Durango was founded in 1880 and incorporated in 1881. Pop. (1960) 10,530; (1970) 10,333.

DURANGO, or VICTORIA DE DURANGO, city in Mexico, and capital and largest city of Durango State, in the foothills of the Sierra Madre Mts., about 475 miles N.W. of Mexico City. The city, on a major highway, also has rail and air facilities. The region surrounding Durango is rich in minerals, particularly silver, iron, copper, gold, tin, coal, cinnabar, sulfur, and antimony. The Cerro del Mercado, a hill near the city, is estimated to have contained more than 500,000 tons of unusually pure iron ore. In addition to being a mining center, Durango is an important industrial city and commercial center for the surrounding agricultural and timber areas. Industrial establishments include iron foundries, cotton and woolen mills, sugar refineries, glassworks, flour mills, tanneries, and tobacco-processing factories. Because it has a pleasant climate and a nearby thermal iron-water spring, Durango is an important resort city. Founded in 1563, it became the political and ecclesiastical capital of the Spanish colonial province of Nueva Viscaya, which was comprised of the present-day Mexican States of Chihuahua and Durango. Pop. (1970) 150,541.

DURANT, city in Oklahoma, and county seat of Bryan Co., about 120 miles S.E. of Oklahoma City. Situated in a farming area, the city is a processing and marketing center. Manufactures include wood products and fabricated metals. It is the site of Southeastern State College, established in 1909. Durant was settled in 1870. Pop. (1960) 10,467; (1970) 11,118.

DURANT, Will(iam James) (1885–   ), American historian, born in North Adams, Mass., and educated at Saint Peter's College and Columbia University. From 1907 to 1911 he taught at Seton Hall College, and in 1917 he taught philosophy at Columbia University. He was director of adult education at the progressive Labor Temple School in New York City from 1914 until 1927, and taught at the University of California at Los Angeles in 1935. His doctoral dissertation, *Philosophy and the Social Problem*, was published in 1917. In his writing Durant tried to present complex subject matter so that it would be easily understood by the average reader. That he succeeded is proved by the success of his *The Story of Philosophy* (1926); more than 2,500,000 copies in twelve languages have been sold. Durant's historical works emphasized the story of people rather than dry, impersonal dates and events. In 1935 appeared *Our Oriental Heritage,* the first volume of his monumental and extraordinarily popular *The Story of Cvilization.* Successive volumes were *The Life of Greece* (1939), *Caesar and Christ* (1944), *The Age of Faith*

The author-philosopher Will Durant, with his wife and collaborator, Ariel.   Bettmann Archive

(1950), *The Renaissance* (1953), *The Reformation* (1957), *The Age of Reason Begins* (1961), *The Age of Louis XIV* (1963), *The Age of Voltaire* (1965), *Rousseau and Revolution* (1967), and *The Age of Napoleon* (1975). In the last five works Durant's wife, Ariel Durant (1898–), who has collaborated with her husband since their marriage in 1913, was listed as co-author. They also collaborated in writing *Interpretations of Life: A Survey of Contemporary Literature* (1970). Durant's historical works have been praised for the lively style of their narratives; they have, however, been criticized by some historians for an alleged lack of perspective.

DURANTE, Jimmy, in full JAMES FRANCIS DURANTE (1893–), American motion-picture and stage actor, born in New York City. He started his career playing the piano at local saloons. In 1923 he opened his own nightclub and that year also began his longtime association with performers Lou Clayton (1887?–1950) and Eddie Jackson. As Clayton, Jackson, and Durante, they performed in nightclubs and vaudeville for many years. In 1932 Durante appeared in his first film, *Get-Rich-Quick Wallingford.* Later he appeared on Broadway in *Jumbo* (1935) and in the films *Music for Millions* (1944), *The Great Rupert* (1950), *Yellow Cab Man* (1950), *The Milkman* (1950), and *It's a Mad, Mad, Mad, Mad World* (1963). In later years his prominent nose (which earned him the nickname "Schnozz"), raspy singing voice, and quick wit made him a prominent television personality.

DURAZZO. *See* DURRËS.

DURBAN, city and seaport of the Republic of South Africa, in Natal Province, on the Indian Ocean about 40 miles S.E. of Pietermaritzburg. The third largest city of the republic, Durban is

An aerial view of the south beach of Durban, with the city in the background.   South African Tourist Corp.

served by railroads and has international airlines. Port Natal, the name sometimes given to the harbor of the city, was accessible only to small craft until late in the 19th century, when a protective seawall and pier were constructed to form a channel entrance with an average depth of 35 to 40 ft. This entrance is kept free of silt and sandbanks by the tide and by dredging operations. The harbor is equipped with ample docking and loading facilities. Near the city is a grain elevator with a storage capacity of about 40,000 tons. Among the industrial establishments are oil refineries, machine works, railroad repair shops, a whaling station, and soap, paint, and fertilizer factories. The principal exports are coal, manganese, chrome ore, grain, wool, and sugar. The University of Durban (founded in 1909) and, for Indian students, University College Durban (1960) and the M. L. Sultan Technical College (1946) are located in the city. Durban was founded as a township in 1835, by British settlers. It grew rapidly following the discovery of gold in the Witwatersrand (q.v.) in 1884–86. Pop. (greater city; 1971 est.) 663,000.

DÜRER, Albrecht (1471–1528), German painter and engraver, born in Nuremberg. As a boy he worked with his father, a goldsmith, and from 1486 to 1489 he studied in Nuremberg with the German painter Michel Wohlgemuth (1434–1519). From 1490 to 1494 Dürer traveled, studied, and worked in various parts of Europe. After his return to his native city in 1494, he worked in Wohlgemuth's studio until 1497, when he established his own.

Dürer's career may be divided into three periods. In the first, comprising the years 1494 to about 1505, he was under the influence of the German painter and engraver Martin Schongauer (q.v.) and the Italian artists Andrea Mantegna (q.v.) and Jacopo de' Barbari (1440?–1516?). Notable among Dürer's works of this period are a portrait of his father (1497), two of himself (1498 and 1506), and the portrait "Hans Dürer" (1500); the painting "The Adoration of the Magi" (1504); and a number of engravings on copper, including "Adam and Eve" and "The Prodigal Son". The period was also marked by his execution of three masterly sets of woodcuts, the "Apocalypse" series (16 blocks, published 1498); the "Great Passion" series (12 blocks, executed in 1500); and the "Life of the Virgin" series (16 blocks, executed in 1504–05). Dürer's second period included the years between 1505 and 1520. From 1505 to 1507 he had a studio in Venice. In that city, through his study of Greek and Roman art and of the work of the Venetian masters of painting, particularly Gio-

"Self-portrait" by Albrecht Dürer.
Bavarian State Picture Collections

vanni Bellini (*see under* BELLINI), Dürer's work lost the angularity and stiffness characteristic of the German school of art. The most important works produced by Dürer during his Venetian stay are the altarpiece "Feast of Rose Garlands", commissioned by German merchants living in Venice for their chapel in the Church of San Bartolommeo; and "Christ Crucified" (1506, now in the Dresden Gallery). In 1507 Dürer returned to Nuremberg. Among the notable works he executed from 1507 to 1520 were the altarpieces "Adoration of the Trinity" (Vienna Museum) and "Adam and Eve" (Prado, Madrid); a number of portraits, including "Charles the Great" and "Emperor Sigismund" (1510, both in the Germanic Museum, Nuremberg); his copper-engraving masterpieces "Saint Jerome in His Study", "The Knight, Death, and the Devil", and "Melancolia" (1514); a number of single woodcuts, and the woodcut series "Small Passion" (37 blocks, 1509–10). From 1512 to 1519 Dürer was court painter to Maximilian I (q.v.), Holy Roman Emperor, for whom he made twenty-four of the blocks for a series of ninety known as "Triumphal Arch". Dürer also executed the woodcut series "Triumphal Procession" and made marginal pen-and-ink drawings for the emperor's prayer book. After the death of Maximilian, Dürer became court painter to Charles V (q.v.), Holy Roman Emperor.

During a stay in the Netherlands in 1520, Dürer studied the paintings of early Flemish

"The Four Horsemen of the Apocalypse", one of a series of woodcuts by Albrecht Dürer, published in 1498 to illustrate the Apocalypse. Metropolitan Museum of Art

masters, particularly Hubert and Jan van Eyck (q.v.). The rich and subtle colors in the paintings of Dürer's third period, from 1521 to 1528, are largely due to the influence of the work of the van Eycks. Dürer created in this period the portraits "An Unknown Man" (Boston Museum of Fine Arts), "Hans Imholf" (Madrid Museum), and "Hieronymus Holzschuher" (National Gallery, Berlin); the paintings "Virgin and Child" and "Madonna and Child with St. Anne" (1516 and 1519, respectively; both in the Metropolitan Museum of Art, New York City); and the work which is generally recognized as his masterpiece in painting, "The Four Apostles" (1526, Munich Gallery). He also executed (1526), in the medium of copper engraving, his portraits of the German scholars Erasmus and Melanchthon (qq.v.), who were among his many distinguished friends. In addition to his many paintings and engravings, all through his career he made numerous drawings in pencil, pen, charcoal, chalk, and other mediums. A collection of

over 100 of his drawings is in the Albertina, Vienna; other notable collections are in the British Museum and in Berlin.

Dürer is the most important and the most representative of all German artists. He was the most prominent engraver of his time and by most critics is considered one of the greatest in history. He was the foremost master of the woodcut and one of the earliest masters of the process of etching (q.v.).

DURESS, in law, illegal compulsion applied to a person to force him to commit an act he would not otherwise do. It may consist of physical restraint or violence, or of threats. Violence or threats directed against the spouse or children of a person in order to compel him to perform a particular act may also constitute duress. The courts formerly held that, to constitute duress, threats had to be of sufficient strength to overcome the resistance of a person of average firmness. They now tend to take into consideration such factors as the age, sex, and physical state of the person alleged to be under duress.

Any person who has entered into a contract (q.v.) under duress has the power to declare the contract void. The intention to repudiate the contract must be made within a reasonable time after the victim has regained the power to act free from duress. Since the contract is not automatically void, both the victim and the party guilty of applying duress will be bound by its terms if the victim does not repudiate it.

DURHAM, city in North Carolina, and county seat of Durham Co., 22 miles N.W. of Raleigh and 75 miles S.E. of Winston-Salem. The city is one of the most important centers of the tobacco industry in the United States, producing about 20 percent of all cigarettes manufactured. Other leading industries include the manufacture of hosiery and cotton goods. Durham is the site of Duke University (q.v.) and North Carolina College (chartered 1909). Bennett Place Memorial is 6 miles N.W. of the city; it marks the scene where, on April 26, 1865, General Joseph E. Johnston (q.v.) surrendered all Confederate armies remaining in the field to General William T. Sherman (*see under* SHERMAN). Durham was settled about 1855 and incorporated in 1869. Pop. (1960) 78,302; (1970) 95,438.

DURHAM, Great Britain, maritime county of N.E. England, between the Tees and the Derwent rivers. It is drained principally by the Derwent, Wear, and Tees rivers. In addition to the county town, Durham, the leading cities are the municipal boroughs of Stockton-on-Tees, Hartlepool, and Jarrow, and the county boroughs of Gateshead, Sunderland, South Shields, Darlington (qq.v.), and West Hartlepool. The E. section of the county contains rich coal fields, and is fertile, particularly in the river valleys. Oats, wheat, barley, potatoes, turnips, and rutabagas are grown, and sheep are raised, the Teesdale and Weardale breeds being particularly well known. In the w. part of the county are large wasteland areas. Durham is one of the leading coal-mining counties in England. Shipbuilding is another important industry. Of the shipyards of Great Britain, those on the Derwent R. rank second to those on the Clyde R. In addition, marble, slate, and fire clay are quarried, and machinery, locomotives, tools, chemicals, glass, earthenware, and fertilizers are manufactured.

Durham was once an outpost of the Romans. Later, it became a part of the Saxon Kingdom of Northumbria. After the Norman conquest (*see* ENGLAND: *History*) it obtained the privileges of a county palatine, and for many years its affairs were administered by the bishops of the see at the town of Durham. In 1536 Henry VIII (q.v.), King of England, stripped the bishops of much of their judicial power, and in 1646 the palatinate was abolished. It was revived after the Restoration (q.v.) and continued until 1836, when an act of Parliament removed all temporal jurisdiction and privileges from the bishopric. Area, 1015 sq.mi.; pop. (1971) 1,408,103.

DURHAM, John George Lambton, 1st Earl of. *See* LAMBTON, JOHN GEORGE, 1ST EARL OF DURHAM.

DURIAN or **DURION,** fruit tree, *Durio zibethinus,* of the Chocolate family, found in the islands of southeast Asia. It is a tall tree, with leaves resembling those of the cherry and with large bunches of pale-yellow flowers. The fruit, also called durian or durion, is about the size of a coconut and has a hard, thick rind covered with soft spines. The cream-colored meat is flavorsome, but has an unpleasant odor. The fruit contains ten or twelve seeds each as large as a walnut. When roasted, the seeds taste like chestnuts. The durian commands a higher price than any other native fruit. One tree yields about 200 fruits each year.

DURKHEIM, Émile. *See* SOCIOLOGY: *History.*

DUROCHER, Leo (Ernest) (1906–), American professional baseball player and manager, born in West Springfield, Mass., and educated there in the public schools. He joined the New York (N.Y.) Yankees, an American League club, in 1928 as an infielder. His brash self-confidence and argumentative spirit soon earned him the nickname "Leo the Lip". Transferring to the National League in 1930, he played for three seasons with the Cincinnati (Ohio) Reds. In 1933 he was traded to the Saint Louis (Mo.) Cardinals, and as a member of that team he won recognition as a star shortstop. In 1937 he joined the Brooklyn (N.Y.) Dodgers. He became manager of the Brooklyn club the next year. Under his management the Dodgers won (1941) their first National League championship in twenty-one years. Durocher remained with the Dodgers until 1948, when he became manager of the New York (N.Y.) Giants, a post he kept until 1955. His team won the National League pennant in 1951 and in 1954. In the World Series of 1954 the Giants defeated the Cleveland (Ohio) Indians in four games. From 1961 to 1964 Durocher was a coach of the Los Angeles (Calif.) Dodgers. From 1966 to the middle of the 1972 season he managed the Chicago (Ill.) Cubs. He then became manager of the Houston (Texas) Astros, retiring from baseball after the 1973 season.

DURRA or **DOURRA** or **DOORA** or **GRAIN SORGHUM,** variety of *Sorghum vulgare* (*see* SORGHUM), grown extensively in southern Asia and northern Africa. It was introduced into the southwestern United States in 1874. It is a medium-sized plant, having narrow leaves and a dry, pithy stalk, and bearing hard, round grains. Durra is a relatively nonsweet sorghum and is grown for its grain and as animal forage. The meal does not make good bread, but it is excellent as a substitute for rice in pudding.

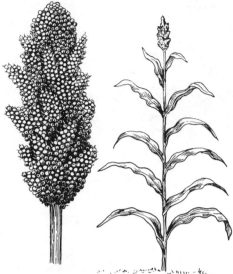

Durra, a variety of Sorghum vulgare.

DURRELL, Lawrence (1912–), British novelist and poet, born in Julundur, India, educated in India and at Saint Edmund's School, Canterbury, England. Durrell began writing poetry and novels in the 1930's. His first major success was the autobiographical novel *The Black Book* (1938). His best imaginative work was derived largely from his experiences and observations gathered during long periods of residence abroad, especially in Greece, Cyprus, and Egypt. His greatest success came with the *Alexandria Quartet,* a series of four novels originally published as *Justine* (1957), *Balthazar* (1958), *Mountolive* (1958), and *Clea* (1960). The quartet, a study of love and political intrigue in Alexandria, Egypt, tells the same story from the point of view of several of its characters, and has a complex structure and an elaborate style. His published volumes of poetry include *Collected Poems* (1960) and *The Ikons* (1966). The novel *Tunc* was published in 1968; its sequel, *Nunquam,* in 1970. *Spirit of Place: Letters and Essays on Travel* was published in 1969.

DÜRRENMATT, Friedrich (1921–), Swiss author and playwright, born in Konolfingen, and educated at the universities of Bern and Zürich.

His first play, *Es Steht Geschrieben* ("It Is Written"), was produced in Switzerland in 1947. His first major work of fiction, *Der Richter und sein Henker* (1952; Eng. trans., *The Judge and His Hangman,* 1955), is the first of several detective stories. *Die Ehe des Herrn Mississippi* (1952; Eng. trans., *The Marriage of Mr. Mississippi*) was staged in New York City in 1958 as *Fools Are Passing Through.* Dürrenmatt's best-known play, *Der Besuch der Alten Dame* ("The Old Lady's Visit"), had its premiere in Zürich in 1956. Staged in New York City as *The Visit* in 1958, it was filmed in 1964. A German operatic version by Gottfried von Einem (1918–) was first performed in 1971. *Die Physiker* (1961; Eng. trans., *The Physicists*) was produced in New York City in 1964.

DURRËS (It. *Durazzo*), city and seaport in Albania, and administrative center of Durrës District, on the Adriatic Sea, about 20 miles w. of Tiranë. The city is in a fertile region in which corn, grains, sugar beets, and tobacco are grown, and livestock is raised. An important commercial and communications center serving central Albania, the city has a power plant, a dockyard, and factories producing bricks, cigarettes, leather products, and soap. Exports include grains, hides, minerals, and tobacco. The city is linked by rail with Tiranë and Elbasan. Durrës is the seat of a Greek Orthodox Metropolitan and, since the 5th century, of a Roman Catholic archbishop. Remains of Byzantine and Venetian fortifications are outside the city.

Durrës is the ancient Epidamnus, founded about 625 B.C. by the Corcyreans, who were the ancient inhabitants of the island of Kérkira (q.v.), and by Corinthians from the Greek city Corinth (q.v.). The Romans seized the city in the 3rd century B.C., and changed the name to Dyrrachium. Durrës was under Byzantine rule in the 8th century A.D. Venice took the city in the 14th century. In 1501 the Ottoman Turks captured Durrës and held it for 414 years. In 1915, during World War I, Durrës was occupied by the Italians. The city was taken by the Austrians in 1916, subjected to Allied naval and air attacks in 1918, and reoccupied by the Italians. In 1939, Italian troops used Durrës as a point of disembarkation in the invasion of Albania. During an Italian invasion of Greece in World War II, the city suffered heavy damage. Pop. (1970 est.) 53,800.

DURYEA, name of two American brothers who were automotive engineers: **Charles Edgar Duryea** (1862–1938) and **James Frank Duryea** (1869–1967).

Charles Duryea was born near Canton, Ill., and J. Frank Duryea was born near Washburn,

The original Duryea car, first operated in 1893, is now in the National Museum, Washington, D.C.

Ill. Together they constructed and tested in 1893 a vehicle considered by many to be the first successful automobile produced in the United States; *see* AUTOMOBILE. In later years the brothers disagreed as to which of them had designed and which constructed the gasoline-powered vehicle. Charles Duryea invented the spray carburetor in 1892 and in 1893 was the first to use pneumatic tires on his cars. A four-cycle engine built by the brothers powered a car that won the first American automobile race in 1895. The two brothers founded the Duryea Motor Wagon Company in 1895, but dissolved it three years later and afterward worked separately. Charles Duryea organized the Duryea Power Company in 1900 to produce a three-cylinder car, retiring from manufacturing in 1914 to become a consulting engineer and writer on automotive problems. Frank Duryea headed the Stevens-Duryea Company, producers of the Stevens-Duryea car, and remained a leader in the auto industry.

DUSE, Eleonora (1859–1924), Italian actress, born in Vigevano. Her father was a strolling player and she made appearances with his company as a young child. In 1873 she attracted favorable attention when she appeared in Verona as Juliet in William Shakespeare's *Romeo and Juliet,* but did not achieve widespread recognition as an actress until 1878 when she appeared in Naples in *Les Fourchambault* ("The House of Fourchambault", 1878) by the French dramatist

Émile Augier (q.v.). The following year the noted Italian actor Cesare Rossi engaged her as his leading lady, and her work with his company in subsequent years gave her an international reputation. In Rossi's company and, after 1886, in her own, she made tours of Europe, Egypt, and the United States; she appeared in New York City for the first time in 1893, at the Fifth Avenue Theatre, in *La Dame aux Camélias* (1848; Eng. trans., *Camille*) by the French novelist and playwright Alexandre Dumas, fils (*see under* DUMAS).

From 1878 to 1897 Miss Duse's principal roles were those of Marguerite Gautier in *La Dame aux Camélias;* Magda in *Die Heimat,* known in the U.S. and England as *Magda,* by the German playwright and novelist Hermann Sudermann (q.v.); Santuzza, a role she created, in *Cavalleria Rusticana* (1880; Eng. trans., *Rustic Chivalry,* 1928) by the Italian writer Giovanni Verga (q.v.); and Hedda in *Hedda Gabler* and Ellida in *The Lady from the Sea,* both by the Norwegian poet and dramatist Henrik Ibsen (q.v.). In 1897 she began a close friendship with the Italian poet and playwright Gabriele D'Annunzio (q.v.). Thereafter she devoted herself principally to acting and promoting interest in D'Annunzio's plays, particularly *La Gioconda* (1898; Eng. trans., *Gioconda,* 1902) and *Francesca* (1902; Eng. trans., *Francesca da Rimini,* 1902) until her retirement from the stage in 1909, because of ill

Eleonora Duse   Bettmann Archive

machine tools, chemicals and dyes, paper and paper products, textiles, technical, scientific, and musical instruments, furniture, glass, porcelain, enamel, fire clay, cement, and beer. In addition, Düsseldorf has a large printing and publishing industry. It is the site of the University of Düsseldorf, which was founded in 1907 as the Medical Academy of Düsseldorf.

The city received the official status of a town in 1288 from Count Adolf of Berg. One of the local castles was for a long period the residence of the counts, and later the dukes of Berg. The city became the capital of the Napoleonic grand duchy of Berg in 1805; in 1815, along with the duchy, it became a part of Prussia. Düsseldorf attained importance as an industrial center in the Ruhr valley after 1870.

The city has been damaged several times during wars. After World War I it was occupied by Allied forces from 1921 to 1925. During World War II it suffered its greatest damage as a result of aerial bombardment. At the end of World War II Düsseldorf was included in the British zone of occupation. The modern city is considered one of the most beautiful in the Ruhr valley. Pop. (1972 est.) 650,377.

DUST, fine particles of organic and inorganic substances suspended in the atmosphere. Among the substances found in dust are animal and vegetable fibers, pollen, silica, bacteria, and molds. In some cities much coal and oil are burned; in those places the atmospheric dust also contains a large number of smoke particles and tarry soot particles. After a nuclear explosion, particles of radioactive dust are usually detected in the atmosphere.

No part of the lower atmosphere is entirely free from dust, although the concentration varies widely according to the locality. In an industrial city the air may contain more than 50,000,000 particles per cu.in. but in the middle of the ocean or in high mountains the count may fall to a few thousand per cu.in. The size of dust particles varies from about half a micron (.00002 in.) to several times this size. Because of their extremely small size, dust particles remain suspended in the air for long periods of time and may be carried great distances. A dust particle of the same density as water and one micron (.000039 in.) in diameter will take more than a day to fall 10 ft. In this time it can be carried hundreds of miles, even by a moderate wind. The most remarkable demonstration of the distances which dust particles may travel was given by the dust cloud thrown up by the eruption of the volcano on Krakatau (q.v.) in 1883. Clouds of volcanic dust from this eruption were carried

health. Financial losses caused her to return to the stage in 1921, and for three years, in spite of failing health, she toured Italy and played in England and the U.S. She died in April in Pittsburgh, Pa., and was buried at her summer home in Asolo, Italy.

Duse was considered one of the leading actresses of her time, in the opinion of some critics, was superior even to the renowned French actress Sarah Bernhardt (q.v.). Duse's reputation was due to her sympathetic portrayal of the sufferings of human beings, her power to convey powerful emotion, and her sense of realism, touched, however, by a poetic spirit.

DUSHANBE, formerly STALINABAD, city in the Soviet Union, and capital of the Tadzhik S.S.R. about 200 miles s. of Tashkent. It is an industrial and transportation center. Cotton and silk milling, meat packing, printing, tanning, and machine manufacturing are among the chief industries. Tadzhik V.I. Lenin State University and several other educational institutions are located in the city. Dushanbe was developed after 1929 on the site of the village of Dyushambe (or Diushambe). Pop. (1970) 373,885.

DÜSSELDORF, city in West Germany, and capital of North Rhine-Westphalia State, on the Rhine R., in the Ruhr R. valley, about 20 miles N. of Cologne, and 55 miles E. of the German borders with Belgium and the Netherlands. Manufactures include metal products, machinery and

227

several times around the world and gave rise to brilliantly colored sunsets in many countries from 1883 to 1886.

Atmospheric dust has two important physical properties: its ability to scatter light of short wave lengths (see COLOR), and its ability to serve as nuclei for the condensation of water vapor. Mist, fog, and clouds would never occur if it were not for the presence in the air of particles around which water droplets can condense.

The heavy concentration of dust in the air over large cities is a serious problem, because as much as 2000 tons of dust per sq.mi. may fall annually in such areas. Dust is also a problem in flour and sugar mills, and in coal mines; in such places a concentration of inflammable particles constitutes an explosion hazard. Silica particles in dust are destructive to machinery and to polished surfaces such as the facets of semiprecious stones, because of their hardness; they can also be injurious when inhaled (see SILICOSIS). To obtain dust-free air in manufacturing plants and other places in which dust may cause contamination or damage, air filters have been devised, using either cloth or water as the filtering medium. Dust and smoke may be removed from exhaust stacks of industrial plants by such devices as the Cottrell precipitator (q.v.). See AIR POLLUTION; SMOG.

DUST BOWL, common name applied to a large area in the southern part of the Great Plains region of the United States, much of which suffered extensively from wind erosion during the 1930's. The area included parts of Kansas, Oklahoma, Texas, New Mexico, and Colorado, and comprised a total of approximately 96,000,000 acres.

Several factors responsible for the devastation of the Dust Bowl were the character of the soil, the climate, and the types of agriculture practiced. Much of the soil is loess, a rich, finely grained soil originally deposited by the wind (see DEPOSIT); an additional large quantity of soil is outwash carried down from the Rocky Mountains by rainwater. In its primitive state, however, the area was covered with hardy grasses which held the soil in place in spite of the long recurrent droughts and occasional torrential rains characteristic of the region.

In the thirty years before World War I, a large number of homesteaders settled in the area, many of whom planted wheat and row crops. The acreage devoted to wheat in one part of the Dust Bowl region tripled between 1914 and 1919 and increased by more than 50 percent in the next decade. This expansion in wheat-growing came about partly because of the high prices current during the war and partly because of the availability of tractors, harvester-threshers, and other machinery for large-scale farming.

In 1935 about half of the Dust Bowl area was devoted to crops and one half to intensive cattle raising. Both of these land uses left the soil exposed to the danger of erosion by the winds that constantly sweep over the gently rolling land. The grass covering the cropland was plowed under, and the grass of the grazing land was cut short and trampled into the ground by large herds of cattle. A series of crop failures from 1930 to 1935 intensified the dangers of erosion. Beginning in the early 1930's, the region suffered a period of severe droughts, and the soil began to blow away. The organic matter, clay, and silt in the soil was carried for hundreds of miles by the winds, in some cases darkening the sky as far as the Atlantic coast, and sand and heavier materials drifted against houses, fences, and barns. In many places 3 to 4 in. of topsoil were blown away, and sand and silt dunes 4 to 10 ft. in height were formed. In one area in the

A roadway in the Dust Bowl is cleared of soil drifts and tumbleweed following a severe dust storm. **Wide World**

heart of the Dust Bowl it was estimated that 80 percent of the land suffered from wind erosion during the drought years, with 40 percent being severely eroded. The combined effect of crop failure and loss of the productive soil ruined a large number of farmers. Many thousands of families emigrated westward; about a third of the remaining families had to accept government relief.

Beginning in 1935 intensive efforts were made by both Federal and State governments to develop adequate programs for soil conservation and for rehabilitation of the Dust Bowl. The measures taken have included seeding large areas in grass; a three-year rotation of wheat and sorghum and of lying fallow; the introduction of contour plowing, terracing, and strip planting; and, in areas of greater rainfall, the planting of long "shelter belts" of trees to break the force of the wind. By 1940 the area subject to dangerous wind erosion amounted to less than 25,000,000 acres, and in subsequent years it has been reduced still further. See CONSERVATION; EROSION; SOILS AND SOIL MANAGEMENT.

DUTCH EAST INDIA COMPANY. See EAST INDIA COMPANY: *Dutch East India Company.*

DUTCH ELM DISEASE, disease of elm trees, caused by the fungus *Ceratostomella ulmi*. The disease is characterized by gradual yellowing of the leaves and defoliation. Eventually the infected tree dies. The fungus is transmitted from diseased trees to healthy elms by various bark-beetle carriers, notably the species *Hylurgopinus rufipes,* native to the United States, and the small European bark beetle, *Scolytus multistriatus.* See BARK BEETLE. Elm-bark beetles are highly susceptible to the chemical DDT (q.v.). The disease, widespread in the northeastern U.S., may be controlled by thoroughly spraying the trees with this insecticide. Badly diseased trees are cut down and burned, and, in addition, all dead elm wood which might serve as breeding material or might carry the fungus are removed.

DUTCH GUIANA. See SURINAM.

DUTCH HARBOR, village of Alaska, on Unalaska Island, one of the Aleutian Islands, on a small strait separating Unalaska and Akutan islands. Dutch Harbor was a major United States Navy air and submarine base in the Aleutians, built in 1941 and used during World War II. See ALEUTIAN ISLANDS.

DUTCH LANGUAGE, member of the western group of the Germanic branch of Indo-European languages (q.v.). It is the language of the inhabitants of the Netherlands, the northern half of Belgium, the northern part of Nord Department, France, and the Netherlands overseas territories. Cape Dutch, or Afrikaans, spoken in South Africa, is, although an independent tongue, to a large extent identical with "High" Dutch. The name Dutch is derived from the word *Dietsch,* meaning the vernacular, as distinguished from Latin. The modern standard language developed in stages under the successive influence of the dialects of Flanders, Brabant, and Holland, during the times of their respective political and economic hegemony. These three dialects mainly represent the West-Lower-Frankish branch of the Germanic languages, although through the Holland and West-Flemish dialects, elements of the so-called Coastal Germanic (Ingvaeonian) survived. The Dutch language may be divided into three main periods, as follows.

(1) Old Dutch, extending to about 1100. The only important, extant monument of this period is a translation of the Psalter.

(2) Middle Dutch, extending from 1100 to 1550. The language during this period underwent changes in sounds and inflections; no standard written form was at first recognized, and each writer used his own dialect. In the 13th century a determined effort was made to establish a literary Dutch, the leader in the movement being the poet Jacob van Maerlant (1235?–1300). The use of dialects, however, continued to prevail.

(3) Modern Dutch, extending from 1550 to the present day. The most important single event in the history of the language during this period was the publication from 1619 to 1637 of the *Statenbijbel,* the authorized version of the Scriptures, which did much to spread this form of Dutch in the Low Countries. The effect of this translation was similar to that of the High-German version of the Bible by the German religious reformer Martin Luther (q.v.), in establishing a standard of language and orthography that was generally recognized as authoritative. This standard language spread first in the Dutch Republic of the 17th century. In the Netherlands-speaking part of Belgium, which was under Spanish and Austrian domination during the 17th and 18th centuries, the language lost its position as a vehicle of culture until its restoration by the Flemish national movement in the 19th century. Modern Dutch and Flemish are nearly identical. After World War II, government-sponsored measures were taken to reform Dutch orthography and to effect uniformity of usage in the Netherlands and Belgium. See FLEMISH LANGUAGE AND LITERATURE.

DUTCH LITERATURE, literature written in the Dutch language (q.v.). The earliest extant examples of Dutch literature are the works of Heynrik van Veldeke (fl. about 1200), who wrote a *Life of Saint Servatius* based on a Latin source, an *Eneïde* (Aeneid) after a French original, and various love songs. During the 13th century a number of epics were produced, including *William of Orange* (1211–17) by Klaas van Haarlem (fl. early 13th century) and *Floris and Blanchefleur* (about 1250) of Diederic van Assenede (d. about 1292). A significant literature began to appear after 1250 with the work of Jacob van Maerlant (about 1225–about 1291). Called the father of Dutch literature, he wrote didactic poetry, romances of chivalry, treatises on history and government, and a *Rhyme Bible*. The new literature declined under the Burgundian domination of the Netherlands (1363–1477), when French words and forms became assimilated into Dutch; *see* NETHERLANDS, THE: *History.* During the first half of the 16th century, however, the work of the Dutch scholar and humanist Desiderius Erasmus (q.v.) led to an intensification of literary activity in the Netherlands and throughout Europe; *see* HUMANISM. The writers Dirk Volkertszoon Coornhert (1522–90) and Philip van Marnix (1538–98) directly influenced the Golden Age of Dutch literature. Coornhert wrote poetry, drama, and prose. His collected works were published in 1633. Marnix is the author of one of the most acrimonious satires ever written against the Catholic Church, *Biencorf der Heiligher Roomscher Kercke* (1569; Eng. trans., *The Beehive of the Romish Church,* 1578?).

The Influence of Humanism. The Golden Age of Dutch literature, which occupied most of the 17th century, is characterized by intellectual independence, an emphasis on Humanist values, and the suppression of foreign terms and idioms in the language. Jacob Cats (1577–1660), known as "Father" Cats, enjoyed wide popularity as a poet. His writings, expressing simple moral precepts and workaday philosophy, include *Houwelijck* ("Marriage", 1625), *Spieghel van den Ouden ende Nieuwen Tijdt* ("The Mirror of Old and New Times", 1632), *Trou-Ringh* ("The Wedding Ring", 1637), and an autobiographical volume of reminiscences (1656). Pieter Hooft (1581–1647), in contrast, reflects the spirit of the Renaissance (q.v.); his works are culturally and intellectually sophisticated, and include the tragic dramas *Geeraerd van Velsen* (1613) and *Baeto* (1626), which were modeled after the dramas of the Roman philosopher and dramatist Lucius Annaeus Seneca (q.v.); a comedy, *Warenar* (1617), adapted from the *Aulularia* of the Roman comic dramatist Titus Maccius Plautus

(q.v.); and various historical studies (1626–47). Gerbrand Bredero (q.v.), one of the founders of the Amsterdam Theater, first wrote romantic plays but achieved his greatest success in low-comedy farces. His most popular play was *De Spaansche Brabander* ("A Spaniard from Brabant", 1618).

Joost van den Vondel (q.v.) was the greatest, and one of the most prolific, poets of the Golden Age. His chief contribution to literature was twenty-four poetic dramas in the classical form. His masterpiece *Lucifer* (1654), dealing with the revolt of the angels against God, was for many years the subject of literary controversy in which one school of critics held that *Lucifer* had served as the model and source for the epic poem *Paradise Lost,* by the English poet John Milton (q.v.). Constantijn Huygens, father of the famous mathematician Christian Huygens (*see under* HUYGENS) possessed a brilliant facility with language and a mastery of form. His collected poems, *Korenbloemen* ("Cornflowers", 1658–72) were published in twenty-seven volumes.

In the latter part of the 17th century occurred a gradual slackening of this renaissance. Pieter Langendijk (1683–1756), one of the important writers of the first half of the 18th century, is the author of comedies that are still performed in the Netherlands. His best-known work, *The Mirror of Dutch Merchants* (1760), was finished posthumously by two unknown writers. Other noteworthy writers of this period were Justus van Effen (1684–1735), who imitated the English reviews with his *Hollandsche Spectator* (1731–35), and Lucas Rotgans (d. 1710), a dramatist and the author of the epic *Willem III.*

The *Verlichting.* The last quarter of the 18th century is marked by a movement known as the *Verlichting* or "enlightenment", which was characterized by an opposition to the rules and forms of classicism. Two women were among the distinguished contributors to this movement, Betje Wolff-Bekker (1738–1804) and her friend Aagje Deken (1741–1804), whose joint work produced a number of novels in letter form, among them *Sara Burgerhart* (1782) and *Willem Leevend* (1784–85). Rhijnvis Feith (1753–1824), in contrast, wrote the sentimental romances *Julia* (1783) and *Ferdinand en Constantia* (1785); didactic poems; and a number of songs still used as church hymns. Willem Bilderdijk (1756–1831) became the hero of a political and religious movement called the *Réveil.* His works include the epic poem *De Ondergang der Eerste Wereld* ("The Downfall of the Primordial World", 1810), religious poetry, such as

Left: Jacob Cats. Right: Joost van den Vondel.

Gebed (1796), and the famous *Ode van Napoleon* (1806). Johannes Kinker (1764–1845) was a philosopher, critic, and philologist best known for his attacks on the sentimental school of writing. *Maurits Lijnslager,* by Adriaan Loosjes (1761–1818), is considered a forerunner of the historical novel.

Romanticism. The 19th century opened inauspiciously with writing marked by conventionality, lack of originality, and an emphasis on form. The prose of this period includes the literary criticism of Jacob Geel (1789–1862) and the historical novels of Jacob van Lennep (1802–68) and Jan Frederik Oltmans (1806–54), both of whom were influenced by the Scottish novelist and poet Sir Walter Scott (q.v.). Everardus Johannes Potgieter (1808–75), apart from his own creative writing, was the founder, in 1837, of the review *De Gids* ("The Guide"), which served as an organ for the romantic movement in literature. His masterpiece is *Florence* (1868), a study of medieval Italy. Nikolaas Beets (q.v.), one of the most famous writers of this period, owes his reputation to a single work, *Camera Obscura* (1839), a gently humorous reflection of the life and manners of middle-class society. Pieter Hasebroeck (1812–96), writing under the pen name Jonathan, and Johannes Kneppelhout (1814–85), whose pen name was Klikspaan, both produced works that resemble Beets' *Camera Obscura.* Anna Louise Geertruida Bosboom-Toussaint (1812–86), whose name is also directly associated with the romantic movement and *De Gids,* is the author of novels influenced by the English romantics. Her works include a cycle dealing with the adventures of the British soldier Robert Dudley (q.v.) in the Netherlands (1845–55) and the fictionalized diary *Majoor Frans* (1874). Petrus Augustus de Genestet (1829–61) was a Protestant minister who enjoyed popularity as a poet of both religious and secular subjects, and Josephus Albertus Alberdingk Thym (1820–89) was a Catholic romantic. Conrad Busken Huët (1826–86), a theologian and pastor who resigned

Eduard Douwes Dekker

from his church to devote himself to literary criticism, served with Potgieter on the staff of *De Gids* and in 1872 founded his own newspaper in Batavia (now Djakarta, Indonesia). His essays and reviews were collected in twenty-five volumes (1881–88).

Eduard Douwes Dekker (q.v.), who wrote under the pen name Multatuli, anticipated the revolutionary movement in Dutch letters by some twenty years. In the novel *Max Havelaar* (1860), his style was simple and free from the formalism that had become a literary standard of the language. The success of his work did much to emancipate the next generation of writers from meaningless restrictions.

The "Eightiers". During the 1880's Dutch writers attempted to produce a major national literature comparable to the best contemporary European literary achievements. Their efforts, coinciding with a period of great economic, social, and artistic expansion in the Netherlands, are generally dated from the first issue (October, 1885) of a review called *De Nieuwe Gids* ("The New Guide"). The leaders of the "Eightiers", as the new movement was called, were the poets Willem Kloos (1859–1938), Frederik van Eeden (1860–1932), Lodewijk van Deyssel (pseudonym of Karel Alberdingk Thym, 1864–1952), and Albert Verwey (1865–1937). The poetry of Kloos, first published in *De Nieuwe Gids,* revolutionized literary diction. Van Eeden, one of the most versatile of the "Eightiers", wrote poems, criticism, novels, and dramas with equal facility. His works include the long poem *Het Lied van Schijn en Wezen* ("The Song of Seeming and Being", 1895–1922) and the novel trilogy *The Quest* (1885–1906; Eng. trans., 1907). Van Deyssel was the prophet of the movement, coining its slogans and credos and proving their validity in his writings, which include a quantity of critical writing for *De Nieuwe Gids*. During the 20th century, *De Nieuwe Gids,* in which these writers combined elements drawn from European literature and other arts, declined in influence and was replaced by Verwey's new periodical *De Beweging* ("The Movement" 1905–1920).

The reaction against the "Eightiers" was led by C. S. Adama Scheltema (1877–1924), a socialist who opposed their narrow preoccupation with "art for art's sake" and believed in art for the many rather than the few. His own poetry resembles folk art. Herman Gorter (1864–1927) wrote *Mei* ("May", 1889), one of the great poems of modern Dutch literature. The poetry of Henriëtte Roland Holst Van der Schalk (1869–1952) is identified with communism and

social rebellion; her works include *De Nieuwe Geboort* ("The New Birth", 1902), *De Vrouw in het Woud* ("The Woman in the Wood", 1912). Pieter Cornelis Boutens (1870–1943) was one of the most distinguished poets of his generation. His works include a number of translations from Greek. Of the novelists of this period, Louis Couperus (1863–1923), the author of *De Boeken der Kleine Zielen* (4 vol., 1901–03; Eng. trans., *The Book of the Small Souls,* 1932), won an international reputation. Marcellus Emants (1848–1923) was a novelist, poet, and playwright. His prose works were chiefly studies of neurotic characters. Herman Heijermans (1864–1924) was one of the most successful playwrights of the Dutch theater; his numerous social dramas include *Ghetto* (1898) and *Op Hoop van Zegen* (1900; Eng. trans., *The Good Hope,* 1928). Arthur van Schendel (1874–1946) was a novelist who used as his theme the condition of mankind bound by fate; representative of his works is *De grauwe vogels* ("Grey Birds", 1937).

Vitalism and Contemporary Literature. After World War I, a reaction to the overintellectualized literature of the early 1900's was led by Hendrik Marsman (1899–1940), who championed the cause of "vitalism", based on the concept that the poet is merely a member of, and spokesman for, the masses. Other leaders of the group include Hendrik de Vries (1896–   ), Jan Slauerhoff (1898–1936), and Anthonie Donker (1902–   ). These writers, in turn, aroused the reaction of another group who gathered around the periodical *Forum*, 1932–35, founded by the writers C(harles) Edgar du Perron (1899–1940)

Lucebert   Netherlands Information Service

Jan Wolkers
Netherlands Information
Service

and Menno ter Braak (1902–40). Contending that the "vitalists" were becoming too stylized and obscure, the *Forum* group advocated the use of simple language, realism, and an intellectual rather than emotional approach to literature. The works of Simon Vestdijk (1898–   ), perhaps the outstanding Dutch writer of the mid-20th century, clearly reflect the influence of the Austrian physician and psychoanalyst Sigmund Freud (q.v.) in this period between World Wars I and II.

The German occupation of Holland forced Dutch writers to go underground, and their literature, mostly poetry, was characterized by works expressing resistance to the invaders, hatred for the cruelties of war, and patriotism. By the end of the war, the younger generation of writers had rejected many of the theories of their predecessors, and postwar Dutch literature reflected the disillusionment brought on by the atomic age, the new welfare state, and the Cold War. To this end the writer Bert Schierbeek (1908–   ) created a new experimental prose and the poet and painter Lucebert (1924–   ) sought to express the fullness of life with intelligible simplicity. The problem of human solitude and isolation was poignantly dealt with in the fiction of Anna Blaman (1906–60). Questions concerned with personal responsibility, political commitment, often approached with skepticism and cynicism, are treated in the works of Willem Frederik Hermans (1921–   ) and Harry Mulisch (1927–   ). The younger writers of the mid-20th century show a marked interest in psychology, sociology, sexuality, and existential philosophy

(*see* EXISTENTIALISM). An outstanding modern writer is the novelist Jan Wolkers (1929–   ), who deals symbolically with love and death.

DUTCH PAINTING, body of painting executed in the Netherlands after that country proclaimed (1581) its independence from Spain. In the period preceding and immediately following independence Dutch painting was virtually indistinguishable from Flemish; it shared the Flemish characteristics of earthliness and of comparatively objective representation, as opposed to the idealization prevalent in Italian painting of the same period. The beginnings of a distinctly Dutch school coincided with the emergence during the ensuing century of the Netherlands as a mercantile power.

Dutch art was called upon in that period to play a new role and to satisfy new tastes. The Calvinist (*see* CALVIN, JOHN) spirit of the newly independent nation precluded religious art; Dutch merchants and bankers wanted secular art to grace their homes. Hence portraits, genre scenes, and landscapes were in great demand, and it was chiefly in such paintings that the genius of the 17th-century Dutch masters found expression. In their art they sought to communicate and illumine day-to-day Dutch life, in the country and in the town, in the home and in the church. They strove to effect a compelling illusion of reality and developed the means of producing that illusion through remarkable advances in artistic techniques, especially in the use of light and shadow.

The Dutch Masters. A powerful external influence was that of the Italian painter Michelan-

233

DUTCH PAINTING

Left: "Young Girl at an Open Half-Door" (1645) by Rembrandt. Below: "Banquet of Officers of the Civic Guard of Saint George at Haarlem" (1616) by Frans Hals.

"Head of a Girl" (1660) by Jan Vermeer.
Mauritshuis, The Hague

gelo da Caravaggio (q.v.), whose dramatic chiaroscuro effects were introduced into the Netherlands through the work of Gerard van Honthorst (1590–1656). Developed by nearly every important Dutch painter, the tradition reached its culmination in the work of Rembrandt (q.v.), the greatest Dutch master and one of the great painters of all time. Especially marvelous was his skill in making light seem to emanate from smoky depths. He excelled in a wide range of subjects, including historical scenes, landscapes, and portraits. Especially renowned among the portraits is a series of self-portraits done at various stages of his life. He was also one of the few Dutch painters who treated religious subjects. The profound humanity, the exaltation of suffering, and the uncanny light suggestive of an unseen presence which pervade these works remain unrivaled.

After Rembrandt, Frans Hals, Jan Vermeer, and Jan Steen (qq.v.) are regarded as the most eminent Dutch painters. Hals is best known as a portrait painter. His official group portraits of town magistrates exude a vibrant robustness and vitality, and his individual portraits exhibit this quality even more markedly. Hals also handled light and relative tone values with remarkable skill. His later paintings display less variety of color, concentrating rather on subtle gradations of only a few hues.

Of the four greatest Dutch painters, Vermeer is most representative of the Dutch school as a whole. His works reflect a serenity and inner quietude typical of many of his contemporaries. He is most famous for scenes of domestic interiors with one or two figures engaged in such occupations as reading and writing. He raises such subjects to sublime beauty through his masterly composition and the effect of bright daylight flooding through windows and virtually inundating the scene. Other outstanding painters of similar scenes include Pieter de Hooch, Gerard Terborch, and Gabriel Metsu (qq.v.).

Jan Steen excels in the depiction of humorous genre scenes. His canvases, which often portray a multitude of figures given over to unreserved merriment and hilarity, are somewhat reminiscent of the work of the Flemish painter Pieter Brueghel the Elder (*see under* BRUEGHEL.).

The development of landscape painting owes its maturity to the Dutch school, the painters of which were the first to reproduce the inherent beauty in nature for its own sake. Jacob van Ruisdael (q.v.) is regarded as the finest Dutch landscape painter. He portrayed the more brooding and tempestuous aspects of nature. His wind-racked trees, troubled skies, and cascading waters communicate in vivid form the ever-potential violence of nature. Quieter landscapes were done by other outstanding painters such as Philip de Koninck (1619–88), Meindert Hobbema, Albert Cuyp, and Jan van Goyen (qq.v.).

Among other outstanding 17th-century Dutch painters are Pieter Saenredam (1597–1665) and Emanuel de Witte (1617?–92), noted for their treatment of church interiors; and Willem Kalf (1619–93), whose still lifes were among the most impressive of the period.

Dutch Painting after the Golden Age. The Golden Age of art ended in the 18th century; the mercantile power of the Netherlands was eclipsed by that of Great Britain, and Dutch painting declined with the Dutch economy. A new group of artists, whose work largely paralleled the contemporary movements in French painting, appeared in the 19th century. Among these painters were Jacob Maris (1837–99) and Johan Barthold Jongkind (q.v.), both closely allied with the Barbizon School (q.v.) in France. Jongkind, the more distinguished of the two, produced works with a translucent quality of light foreshadowing impressionism. Another artist, Josef Israels (1824–1911), gained distinction as a painter of historical and genre scenes. The most famous and original Dutch artist of the 19th century was Vincent van Gogh (q.v.). He accomplished his greatest work in France, where he was a prominent member of the postimpressionist school; *see* POSTIMPRESSIONISM.

Pieter Cornelis Mondriaan (q.v.) is the most

235

significant Dutch painter of the 20th century. His work is totally nonobjective, consisting in his later years exclusively of rectangular shapes against a light background. He generally colored one or two of the enclosed rectangles, using only red, yellow, blue, black, and white. Mondriaan was the leader of a Dutch group known as the de Stijl, literally, the Style, which included Theo van Doesburg (1883–1931) and several other lesser-known artists who adhered to Mondriaan's esthetic theories. Ultimately, Mondriaan exerted as strong an influence on 20th-century architecture, furniture design, advertising art, fashion design, and typography as on painting.

DUTCH REFORMED CHURCH. See REFORMED CHURCHES.

DUTCH WEST INDIA COMPANY, trading company incorporated by the States-general of the Netherlands in 1621 to share world trade with the Dutch East India Company (see EAST INDIA COMPANY). In return for subsidies to the state, the West India Company was granted a monopoly of trade in the Americas and Africa, with the right of colonizing and of maintaining armed forces. The colonizing activities of the company were notable for the settlement of New Netherlands (later New York), Surinam, and Curaçao. In Brazil, the company took Bahia in 1623, but later lost it to the Spanish and Portuguese; the company established itself at Pernambuco and elsewhere until 1661, when it resigned all rights in the country. Armed forces of the Netherlands were used to enforce the sovereign rights of the company wherever possible, and to plunder Spanish and Portuguese settlements.

The trading career of the Dutch West India Company was not so successful as that of its sister company, the Dutch East India Company. In 1674 it dissolved because of financial difficulties. A new company lasted until 1794, when it collapsed in the course of the French invasion of the Netherlands. Another West India Company, formed in 1828, was completely unsuccessful.

DUTCH WEST INDIES. See NETHERLANDS ANTILLES.

DUTY. See CUSTOMS DUTIES; EXCISE.

DUVALIER, François known as PAPA DOC, (1907–71), Haitian political leader and physician, born in Port-au-Prince, and educated at the faculty of medicine of the University of Haiti. From 1934 to 1946 Duvalier served in hospitals and clinics, specializing in the treatment of the tropical disease yaws (q.v.). From 1946 to 1950 he was director-general of the National Public Health Service and secretary of labor. After 1950 Duvalier led the resistance to the presidential administration of Paul Eugène Magloire (1907–), and in 1957 he was elected president for a six-year term. In 1964 Duvalier had himself declared president for life. His dictatorial regime saw military and governmental purges, mass executions, and the institution of curfews, all enforced by the Tonton Macoute, the secret police of Haiti.

In January, 1971, the legislature amended the constitution to permit Duvalier to name his son, Jean-Claude Duvalier (1951?–) as his successor. Subsequently the people of Haiti voted their approval of the young Duvalier, who assumed the presidency of Haiti (q.v.) upon his father's death. See HAITI: History.

DUVENECK, Frank (1848–1919), American painter, etcher, sculptor, and art teacher, born in Covington, Ky. He studied with the German painter Feodor Dietz (1813–70) in Munich. In 1878 Duveneck established an art school in Munich and later taught at Florence. Among his pupils were the American painters John White Alexander (1856–1915), William Merritt Chase (1849–1916), and John Henry Twachtman (q.v.). After 1888 Duveneck was a permanent resident of Cincinnati, Ohio, where he occupied himself mainly with teaching. Among his works are a series of etchings of Venetian scenes (1880–85); a bronze monument to his wife (1888), the original of which is in the English cemetery in Florence and marble replicas of which are in the Metropolitan Museum of Art, New York City, and in other American museums; and the paintings "Portrait of an Old Woman", in the Metropolitan Museum of Art, New York City, and "Whistling Boy" (about 1872), "Young Man with a Ruff" (1873), and "Turkish Page" (1876), all in the Pennsylvania Academy of the Fine Arts, Philadelphia.

DU VIGNEAUD, Vincent (1901–), American biochemist, born in Chicago, Ill., and educated at the universities of Illinois and Rochester. In 1932 he became professor and head of the department of biochemistry in the school of medicine at George Washington University. From 1938 to 1967 he held a similar position at Cornell University Medical College. At Cornell du Vigneaud did important research on insulin, hormones, vitamins, amino acids, and on the synthesis of penicillin. His formula for the structure of the vitamin biotin (q.v.), advanced in 1942, was confirmed by synthesis in the following year. He was head of the research team which in 1953 achieved the synthesis of oxytocin, the first pituitary hormone to be produced artificially; *see* PITUITARY GLAND: *The Posterior Lobe.* For this achievement he received the 1955 Nobel Prize in chemistry. In 1956 du Vigneaud and his assistants synthesized vasopressin, another pituitary hormone.

DVINA (Ger. *Düna*), name of two rivers in the Soviet Union.

Northern Dvina. The Northern Dvina is formed by the union of the Sukhona and Yug rivers, in N. Russian S.F.S.R. After a northwesterly course of about 465 mi., it flows through Dvina Bay into the White Sea (q.v.). The main tributaries are the Vychegda, Vaga, and Pinega rivers. After its juncture with the Pinega, just below the city of Archangel (q.v.), the Northern Dvina forms an extensive delta. Frozen from December until April, the river is navigable during the warmer months from its confluence with the Vychegda R. to the White Sea. The river is used to ship timber.

Western Dvina. The Western Dvina rises in the Valday Hills (q.v.) in N.W. Russian S.F.S.R., and flows S.W. to Vitebsk (q.v.), a city in the White Russian S.S.R. It then flows N.W. through the Latvian S.S.R., emptying into the Gulf of Riga (*see* RIGA, GULF OF), 8 mi. below the city of Riga (q.v.). During normal weather conditions, the Western Dvina, which is about 635 mi. long, has a maximum depth of about 40 ft.; spring floods, however, cause the river to become as much as 55 ft. deep. Because of rapids and shallows, it is used mainly for floating timber. Hydroelectric-power stations E. of Riga produce about 50,000 kw annually. The Western Dvina is frozen from December through April.

DVINSK. *See* DAUGAVPILS.

DVOŘÁK, Antonín (1841–1904), Czech composer, born in Nelahozeves, Bohemia (now Mühlhausen, East Germany). As a child he learned to play the violin and often entertained the guests at his father's inn. At the age of fourteen Dvořák began the study of music, and in 1857 became a student at the Organ School, Prague. After completing his studies there in 1859, he became a member of the concert band of Komzák and later of the orchestra of the National Theater, Prague, with which the band was merged. He had begun to compose while still at school, but not until 1873, when his cantata *Hymnus* was performed with great success, did Dvořák receive marked public recognition. From 1873 to 1884 he composed a number of notable works, including his first series of *Slavonic Dances* (1878), and his reputation rapidly grew. In 1884 he made the first of nine trips to Great Britain. There he made many successful appearances as a conductor and composed

Antonín Dvořák, in a photograph taken in Prague in 1895.   Bettmann Archive

much music. From 1892 to 1895 he was director of the National Conservatory of Music of America, in New York City. During his stay in the United States he acquired a great liking for Negro spirituals and American Indian music. Two of his most famous works, the Symphony in E Minor ("From the New World") and the Quartet in F, known as the American quartet, were composed in the U.S. in 1893; though these works do not contain actual themes from Negro or American Indian music, they have melodies that are strongly akin in structure and spirit to these types of music. After Dvořák's return to Bohemia in 1895, he composed extensively, mainly symphonic poems and operas, and in 1901 became director of the Prague Conservatory. The day of his funeral was a day of national mourning throughout Bohemia.

Dvořák's early works were influenced by the music of the Austrian composer Franz Schubert and the German composer Ludwig van Beethoven, and throughout his career he was influenced to some extent by the work of the German composer Richard Wagner (qq.v.). Dvořák drew on Czech and Slavonic folk music in his most mature and characteristic compositions, and these works reflect both his national and racial consciousness. He is regarded as one of the most important European composers of the 19th century and as the leading Czech composer of his time. Among his pupils were the noted Czech composers Josef Suk (1874–1935) and Vítězslav Novák (1870–1949). In addition to the works mentioned above, Dvořák's compositions include nine symphonies (1865–93); the oratorios *Stabat Mater* (1876–77) and *The Specter's*

Bride (1884); the overtures *Amid Nature* (1891) and *Carnival* (1891); chamber music, including the *Dumka Trio* (1890–91) and the String Quintet, Op. 97 (1893); music for the piano, including the well-known "Humoresque" (1894); the symphonic poems *The Wood Dove* (1896) and *Heroic Song* (1897); and the operas *Vanda* (1875), *The Jacobin* (1887–88), *Rusalka* (1901), and *Armida* (1902–03).

DVORSKY, Michel. *See* HOFMANN, JOSEF CASIMIR.

DWARF, in zoology and anthropology, an undersized and often deformed animal, particularly an undersized human being under 50 in. in height. Some dwarfs have been less than 2 ft. tall when fully grown. The term midget is usually applied to physically well-proportioned dwarfs. The term pygmy (*see* PYGMIES) is applied to people whose shortness of stature is a racial trait and not the result of pathological conditions.

Cretinism (q.v.), a result of a disease of the thyroid gland, is the cause of most dwarfism in Europe and the United States. Other causes of dwarfism are mongolism (q.v.), a congenital condition with symptoms similar to those of cretinism; achondroplasia, a disease characterized by short extremities resulting from absorption of cartilaginous tissue during the fetal stage; spinal tuberculosis; and deficiency of the secretion of the pituitary gland or of the ovary. Most human dwarfs display traces of rickets (q.v.), a nutritional disorder of bone formation, although in some instances dwarfs show no signs of the disease and are physically well proportioned.

Formerly dwarfs were attractions in the entourages of kings. The growth of any part of the human body may be restricted by suitable mechanical devices, and the Romans practiced artificial dwarfing of children by such means in order to obtain court jesters. Perhaps the best known of all dwarfs was General Tom Thumb (*see* STRATTON, CHARLES SHERWOOD). The hunchbacked dwarfs at the court of Philip IV (q.v.), King of Spain, were immortalized by the great Spanish painter Diego Velázquez (q.v.). Dwarfs have often been exhibited to the public for profit.

Stories of dwarfs are familiar in folklore nearly everywhere on earth, though the greatest development of these myths seems to be among the peoples of northern Europe. The dwarf Alberich in the opera *Siegfried* by the German composer Richard Wagner (q.v.) is a well-known example.

DWIGHT, Timothy (1752–1817), American clergyman and educator, grandson of the Amer-

ican theologian Jonathan Edwards (q.v.), born in Northampton, Mass., and educated at Yale College (now Yale University). He remained at Yale for six years as a tutor and later served as a chaplain in the army during the American Revolution. Dwight was pastor at Greenfield, Conn., from 1783 to 1795 when he was chosen president of Yale College; he filled the position until his death. He was author of *Theology, Explained and Defended* (5 vol., 1818–19), and *Travels in New England and New York* (4 vol., 1821–22).

DYAKS. *See* DAYAKS.

DYCK, Sir Anthony Van. *See* VAN DYCK, SIR ANTHONY.

DYEING, process of coloring textile fibers and other substances so that the coloring matter becomes an integral part of the fiber or substance rather than a surface coating. Dyes or dyestuffs (q.v.) are chemical compounds, chiefly organic, which have a chemical or physical affinity for fibers and which are "fast", that is, tend to retain their color in the fiber under exposure to sunlight, water, detergents, and wear. Pigments are insoluble coloring compounds. *See* COLOR; PIGMENT.

History. Dyeing is an ancient art, and was practiced in Egypt, Persia, China, and India thousands of years before the birth of Christ. Little is known about the dyes used in those times, but it is probable that they included madder as a red dye and indigo as a blue dye. In the early days of the Roman Empire, garments dyed with Tyrian purple were worn by the imperial family and the nobility. This dye, which was prepared from the secretions of certain mollusks, was extremely valuable, and as late as the 4th century A.D., cloth colored with Tyrian purple was literally worth its weight in gold. Because of the value of the dyestuff, the mollusks that provided it were virtually exterminated in Roman times. The art of dyeing was greatly stimulated by the discovery in the 13th century of a purple dye, archil, made from a species of lichen. Northern Italy, where the discovery was made, became the center of dyeing in Europe. In the 16th century, explorers brought back a number of dyestuffs such as cochineal and logwood from the Americas, and these new materials were incorporated in the dyers' art. Among the other important natural dyes were quercitron, weld, fustic, brazilwood, safflower, and indigo.

The 19th century saw the development of the first synthetic dye, mauve, an organic compound derived from coal tar, which was discovered by the British chemist William Henry Perkin (q.v.) in 1856. From that time to the present a great number of synthetic and artificial dyes have been developed, and the use of natural dyes has virtually ceased.

Dye Classifications. Many thousands of dyes and a number of dyeing processes have been developed. The dye and the process used in a given operation depends on three factors: color, cost, and colorfastness.

Dyes are classified in a number of ways. They are broadly classified as direct dyes if they have the property of producing fast colors in fibers placed directly in the dye solution, and as indirect dyes if preliminary or subsequent treatment of the fiber is needed to produce a fast color. Dyes are also classified chemically according to their structures and into what are commonly called acid and basic dyes. Acid dyes contain acidic groups, such as the sulfonic and carboxyl groups, and form salts with bases. The basic dyes are those which will form salts with acids.

The chemical characteristics of textile fibers determine the dyes and dyeing methods which can be used for coloring them. Wool and silk will form salts with either acid or basic dyes and hence can be dyed directly by either type. Wool dyes more easily than silk. Cotton, on the other hand, will react only with acid dyes and cannot be dyed directly by the basic dyes.

The dyeing of synthetic fibers depends upon their composition. Viscose rayon and cuprammonium rayon, being essentially cellulose, can be directly dyed with the same compounds used for cotton. Acetate rayon (*see* CELANESE) requires the use of special dyes and indirect processes. Some types of nylon (q.v.) can be dyed directly with modified silk dyes, but in general the compounds and techniques employed are similar to those employed for cellulose acetate fibers. New synthetic fabrics usually require new types of dyes. Fabrics made of glass fiber cannot be dyed, because of the inert nature of the material, and are colored with metallic salts while the glass is molten, before the fibers are spun. *See* CHEMICAL COMPOUNDS, SYNTHETIC: *Plastics and Elastomers.*

Indirect Dyeing. Among several processes for indirect dyeing, the simplest involves the pretreatment of the textile material with a fixing solution called a mordant, followed by immersion in the dye bath. The action of the mordant permits the dye to act on the fiber. Formerly tannin was much used as a mordant, because it allowed the use of basic dyes with cotton fabrics. The classic mordant-dyeing process involves three steps: the treatment of the fabric with a solution containing the salt of a metal; a second

An Italian Renaissance painting shows wool being dyed. Alinari

bath containing ammonia; and a dye bath. The ammonia acting on the salt produces insoluble metal hydroxides, which remain in the fibers and which react with the dye solution to produce colored compounds known as lakes, which are also stable and insoluble. In a more generally used technique, the chrome-dyeing of wool, the fabric is first directly colored with a soluble dye, and then treated with sodium dichromate, which combines with the dye to form a chrome lake in the fibers.

A number of dyes are insoluble compounds, and must be chemically altered before they can be used for the coloring of fabrics. In sulfur dyes and vat dyes the insoluble dye is first chemically reduced to a soluble compound known as leuco compound. The fabric is immersed in a solution of the leuco compound, and then exposed to air to reoxidize the compound, forming the insoluble dye in the fiber. Sulfur dyes are reduced in a solution of sodium sulfide, and vat dyes in a sodium thiosulfate solution.

Another technique of indirect dyeing involves the actual formation of the dye chemical within the fibers themselves. Such developed dyes are passed through two or more baths of compounds which react with each other to create the appropriate dyestuff. A similar system is used in the production of dyes in photographic emulsions in color photography (q.v.).

239

In Burma textiles are dyed in striking colors and patterns; the cloth is then measured and packed for shipping.
United Nations

Dyeing Processes. Textiles may be dyed at any stage during their manufacture. Yarn or thread is dyed for the weaving of patterned fabrics and high-quality solid-color cloths. For less expensive solid-color fabrics, the cloth is dyed "in the piece", that is, after weaving. Colored designs can also be formed on woven cloth by several processes of selective dyeing. Dyeing machinery is in general simple in operation. For acid dyes, vats of Monel Metal and other acid-resisting alloys are commonly employed, and stainless steel vats are used for basic or neutral dye baths. When thread or yarn is dyed, it is usually wound on perforated spindles, through which the dye solution is forced under pressure to insure that the dye penetrates to all parts of the spools. Cloth dyed in the piece is usually run backwards and forwards over a set of rollers in the dye bath a number of times to insure even dyeing.

Three methods are employed for pattern dyeing. In direct printing, the cloth is run over a copper roller which has a design etched to correspond to the pattern. The dye, thickened by the addition of some substance such as starch or gelatin, is transferred to the cloth, as in the intaglio processes for printing on paper. The reverse printing method is similar except that a dye-repelling substance is applied to the cloth from the roller, and the cloth is then placed in the dye bath. This method is used, for example, for the production of white polka dots on a col-

ored ground. For discharge printing, the cloth is first dyed and then printed with a chemical that will oxodize or reduce the dye, leaving the colored cloth patterned.

See Printing Techniques; Textiles.

DYERSBURG, city in Tennessee, and county seat of Dyer Co., near the Mississippi R., about 43 miles N.W. of Jackson. The city is a processing and marketing center for the surrounding agricultural and cotton region. Dyersburg has light manufacturing and has an annual cotton festival. Pop. (1960) 12,499; (1970) 14,523.

DYESTUFFS, any of a large group of chemicals, almost exclusively organic in nature, used for the coloring of textiles, inks, food products, and other substances. *See* Color; Dyeing.

The color properties of organic compounds depend upon their structure. In general, the colored compounds used as dyes are unsaturated organic chemicals. The quality of possessing color is particularly noticeable in compounds containing certain well-defined chemically unsaturated groupings. These groups are known as chromophores (color bearers). The chromophores are not all equally effective in producing color. Dyestuffs, however, in addition to being colored, must be capable of entering and coloring cloth fibers or other substances. It has been found that certain other chemical radicals have the property of anchoring the desired dye effectively. These radicals, known as auxochromes, are acidic or basic in nature and give rise to the acid and basic dyes. In the case of some compounds the addition of an auxochrome group changes a colorless compound into a colored one in addition to acting as an anchor.

The basic raw materials of synthetic dyes are compounds such as benzene, anthracene, phenol, and naphthalene, which are derived from the destructive distillation of coal; *see* Aniline; Coal Tar. For this reason synthetic dyestuffs are often popularly known as coal-tar dyes. In many instances they are similar in structure to natural substances which were used in the dyeing art before the introduction of synthetics. From the basic materials, intermediates are manufactured by a number of chemical processes. In general these processes involve the substitution of specific elements or chemical radicals for one or more of the hydrogen atoms in the basic substance. Many dye intermediaries are known, from which a far larger number of dyes can be produced by further chemical treatment.

Dyestuffs can be classified according to their use or by their chemical structure. The chemical classification is generally made according to the nucleus of the compound. Among the more important dye groups are the azo dyes, which inclue butter yellow and Congo red; the triphenylmethane dyes, which include magenta and methyl violet; the phthalein dyes; the azine dyes, which include mauve; and the anthraquinone dyes, which include alizarin. Indigo is a vat dye, occurring in nature in the crystalline glucoside indican. An important new group of dyes are the phthalocyanine dyes, which are blue or green in color and resemble chlorophyll in chemical structure. Of all the groups of dyes the azo dyes are the most generally useful and widely employed.

See DIAZO COMPOUNDS. S.Z.L.

DYING DECLARATION, statement as to the cause of his death, made by a person who has been physically injured at the hands of another, and who has given up all hope of recovery and who subsequently dies of such injury. In English and American law, such statements are permitted to be given in evidence (q.v.). This allowance is an exception to the rule excluding hearsay evidence from the consideration of the jury.

The exception is based on the assumption that statements made by a dying person in the apprehension of death are as trustworthy as those made in open court under oath. To be admissible, however, a dying declaration must have been made by the victim of the homicide and must relate to the circumstances of the crime; it can be used only on the trial of the person charged with the death of the declarant and is equally admissible whether favorable or unfavorable to the accused.

Dying declarations made by others than the victim of a homicide are inadmissible, either in civil or in criminal cases. Thus, a confession of guilt made by a person in articulo mortis ("at the point of death") will not be received in favor of a person accused of the crime. This narrow scope of the rule has been much criticized but is almost universally maintained.

DYNAMICS, study of the effects of forces on the motions of bodies. The study of motion itself is the subject matter of kinetics; see KINETIC THEORY. Dynamics is usually divided into three branches, depending on the nature of the bodies.

Translational motion, or the dynamics of particles, concerns bodies in which the motion described is that of the center of mass of the body. Examples include the orbits of planets, rockets, and spacecraft, the trajectories of projectiles, and the analysis of vibrations. Rotational dynamics, or the dynamics of rigid bodies, concerns bodies that rotate as well as move from one place to another. The gyroscope, the rotor

of a jet engine, and the perturbations in the motions of planets are examples. The third branch is the dynamics of continuous media, concerned with the motion of fluids and similar media having little or no rigidity; see FLUID MECHANICS: Fluid Dynamics. In the study of fluid dynamics, the concepts of force and mass are replaced by those of pressure and density.

The basic elements of dynamics include displacement, velocity, and acceleration. They bear on the relationships between space and time in events involving a mass and a force. The description of a body in motion allows for the definition of mass as inertial mass; the concept can be widened to define force as well. (In rotational dynamics, the moment of inertia is equivalent to mass, and torque is equivalent to force.) The definition of mass and force permits the logical development of mechanics (q.v.) by the introduction of derived quantities such as power and energy.

History. The history of mechanics, of which dynamics is a branch, is generally traced back to the Greek philosopher Aristotle (q.v.). His theories, though they seemed reasonable, could not be demonstrated in practice. Examples are his contentions that heavy bodies fall faster than light ones and that the earth is the center of the solar system. This latter principle was challenged in the 16th century by the Polish astronomer Nicolaus Copernicus (q.v.), who proposed instead a sun-centered solar system. The German astronomer Johannes Kepler (q.v.), in his three laws of planetary motion, modified the Copernican system by accurately describing the motion of the planets as ellipses rather than circles. The Italian scientist Galileo Galilei (q.v.) is generally regarded as the founder of mechanics, however, because he first used experimental techniques. In so doing, he dispelled many of Aristotle's ideas.

It remained for the English mathematician and physicist Sir Isaac Newton (q.v.), in his famous three laws of motion, to formulate the laws of mechanics mathematically. In order to do so he also had to develop calculus (q.v.). Following Newton, a variety of techniques arose, notably in France, that together formed the basis for the highly mathematical study of analytical dynamics. In time, the study of dynamics became linked with the study of differential equations (see CALCULUS: Differential Equations), and solutions were obtained to highly complicated problems. The basis for dynamics remained, however, Newton's laws of motion (q.v.).

Newton's dynamics were accepted as valid

A graphic example of the relationship between force and mass. The kinetic energy of the golf club (accelerating force) is transferred to the golf ball (mass). The mass of the ball and the force with which it was struck determine the acceleration and final velocity.

Harold E. Edgerton

for all motions until the German physicist Max Planck (q.v.) introduced the concept of quanta of action in 1900, and the American theoretical physicist Albert Einstein (q.v.) formulated his special theory of relativity (q.v.) in 1905. Planck's theory became known as the quantum theory (q.v.), which, in turn, was superseded in the second quarter of the 20th century by quantum mechanics (q.v.), which treats of bodies that are exceptionally small, such as atoms; relativistic mechanics treats of bodies moving with speeds approaching that of light; Newton's mechanics treats of everyday experience. In the case of fluids, Newton's laws are still applicable, but they have been reformulated to treat the constituent atoms collectively, because it is impossible to treat each atom separately and then add all the separate results together. This reformulation is the basis for modern fluid mechanics.

J.D.N.

DYNAMITE, explosive, usually consisting of a mixture of nitroglycerin (q.v.) or nitrostarch, sodium nitrate, and an absorbent, such as wood flour, sawdust, or charcoal, to cushion the nitroglycerine from shock. Dynamite was invented in 1866 by the Swedish inventor Alfred Bernhard Nobel (q.v.), who used diatomaceous earth (q.v.) for the absorbent. Because of the comparative safety with which dynamite can be handled and manufactured (being much more stable that nitroglycerine or most other explosives which explode with a force comparable to its own), and because of its high shattering power, it has become the most widely used nonmilitary explosive in the United States and most other parts of the world. The nitroglycerine is often mixed with ingredients which depress its freezing point, so that the dynamite may be used under conditions of low temperature. Oxidizing agents are included in most dynamites used in the U.S. in order to reduce the amount of carbon monoxide and other poisonous fumes produced when the mixture explodes.

The strength of a quantity of dynamite depends upon its nitroglycerine content, which usually ranges from 10 to 75 percent of the mixture. Various types are manufactured according to the uses for which they are intended. The most powerful of the dynamites is blasting gelatine. When this material is mixed with wood flour and potassium nitrate, a product known as gelatine dynamite results. This water-resistant material is the most common explosive for underwater uses. A nonfreezing dynamite, useful at low temperatures, is a mixture of nitrostarch, oxidizing agents, and absorbent. For quick-acting, powerful explosions, an explosive called straight nitroglycerine dynamite, a mixture of nitroglycerine and a combustible absorbent, is used. Ammonia dynamites, which consist of the same materials as nitroglycerine dynamites with part of the nitroglycerine replaced by ammonium nitrate, are relatively safe to handle.

Dynamite is generally manufactured in sticks or cartridges about 8 in. long and from 1 to 3 in. in diameter. These cartridges are fired by detonating caps, which are inserted under the paper covering of the dynamite stick. See EXPLOSIVES.

DYNAMOELECTRIC MACHINERY, group of devices used to convert mechanical energy into electrical energy, or electrical energy into mechanical energy, by electromagnetic means; see ENERGY. A machine which converts mechanical energy into electrical energy is called a generator, alternator, or dynamo, and a machine which converts electrical energy into mechanical energy is called a motor.

Two related physical principles underlie the operation of generators and motors. The first is the principle of electromagnetic induction discovered by the British scientist Michael Faraday (q.v.) in 1831. If a conductor is moved through a magnetic field, or if a magnetic field through a stationary conducting loop is made to vary, a current is set up or induced in the conductor; see INDUCTANCE. The converse of this principle is the principle of electromagnetic reaction, first observed by the French physicist André Marie Ampère (q.v.) in 1820. If a current is passed through a conductor located in a magnetic field, the field exerts a mechanical force on it; see MAGNETISM

The simplest of all dynamoelectric machines is the disk dynamo developed by Faraday. It consists of a copper disk which is mounted so that part of the disk, from the center to the edge, is between the poles of a horseshoe magnet. When the disk is rotated a current is induced between the center of the disk and its edge by the action of the field of the magnet. The disk can be made to operate as a motor by applying a voltage between the edge of the disk and its center, causing the disk to rotate because of the force produced by magnetic reaction.

The magnetic field of a permanent magnet is strong enough to operate only a small practical dynamo or motor. As a result, for large machines, electromagnets are employed. Both motors and generators consist of two basic units, the field, which is the electromagnet with its coils, and the armature, the structure which supports the conductors that cut the magnetic field and carry the induced current in a generator or the exciting current in a motor. The armature is usually a laminated soft-iron core around which conducting wires are wound in coils.

Direct-Current (D-C) Generators. If an armature revolves between two stationary field poles, the current in the armature moves in one direction during half of each revolution and in the other direction during the other half. To produce a steady flow of unidirectional or direct current from such a device it is necessary to provide a means of reversing the current flow outside the generator once during each revolution. This reversal is accomplished by means of a commutator, a split metal ring mounted on the shaft of the armature. The two halves of the ring are insulated from each other and serve as the terminals of the armature coil. Fixed brushes of metal or carbon are held against the commutator as it revolves, connecting the coil electrically to external wires. As the armature turns, each brush is in contact alternately with the halves of the commutator, changing position at the moment when the current in the armature coil reverses its direction. Thus there is a flow of unidirectional current in the outside circuit to which the generator is connected. Direct-current generators are usually operated at fairly low voltages to avoid the sparking between brushes and commutator that occurs at high voltage. The highest potential commonly developed by such generators is 1500 volts.

A number of refinements have been made in the structure of modern d-c generators. The armatures now in use usually consist of a large number of windings set in longitudinal slits in the armature core and connected to appropriate segments of a multiple commutator. This type of armature is called a drum armature. In an armature having only one loop of wire the current produced will rise and fall depending on the part of the magnetic field through which the loop is moving. A commutator of many segments used with a drum armature always connects the external circuit to one loop of wire

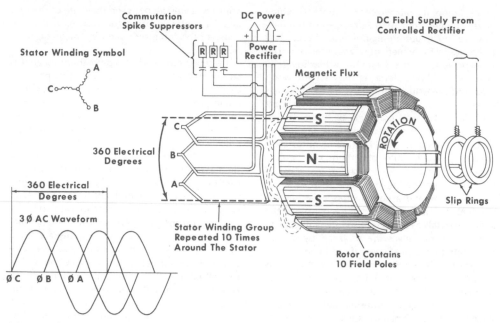

Schematic diagram of a locomotive alternator.
General Motors Corp.

moving through the high-intensity area of the field, and as a result the current delivered by the armature windings is virtually constant. Fields of modern generators are usually equipped with four or more electromagnetic poles to increase the size and strength of the magnetic field. Sometimes smaller interpoles are added to compensate for distortions in the magnetic flux of the field caused by the magnetic effect of the armature.

Direct-current generators are commonly classified according to the method used to provide field current for energizing the field magnets. A series-wound generator has its field in series with the armature, and a shunt-wound generator has the field connected in parallel with the armature. Compound-wound generators have part of their fields in series and part in parallel. Both shunt-wound· and compound-wound generators have the advantage of delivering comparatively constant voltage under varying electrical loads. The series-wound generator is used principally to supply a constant current at variable voltage. A magneto is a small d-c generator with a permanent-magnet field.

Direct-Current (D-C) Motors. In general, d-c motors are similar to d-c generators in construction. They may, in fact, be described as generators "run backwards". When current is passed through the armature of a d-c motor, a torque is generated by magnetic reaction, and the armature revolves. The action of the commutator and the connections of the field coils of motors are precisely the same as those used for generators. The revolution of the armature induces a voltage in the armature windings. This induced voltage is opposite in direction to the outside voltage applied to the armature, and hence is called back voltage or counter electromotive force (e.m.f.). As the motor rotates more rapidly, the back voltage rises until it is almost equal to the applied voltage. The current is then small and the speed of the motor will remain constant as long as the motor is not under load and is performing no mechanical work except that required to turn the armature. Under load the armature turns more slowly, reducing the back voltage and permitting a larger current to flow in the armature. The motor is thus able to receive more electric power from the source supplying it and to do more mechanical work.

Because the speed of rotation controls the flow of current in the armature, special devices must be used for starting d-c motors. When the armature is at rest it has virtually no resistance, and if the normal working voltage is applied a large current will flow, which may damage the commutator or the armature windings. The usual means of preventing such damage is the use of a starting resistance in series with the armature to lower the current until the motor begins to develop an adequate back voltage. As the motor picks up speed the resistance is gradually reduced, either manually or automatically.

The speed at which a d-c motor operates depends upon the strength of the magnetic field acting on the armature, as well as on the armature current. The stronger the field, the slower is the rate of rotation needed to generate a back voltage large enough to counteract the applied voltage. For this reason the speed of d-c motors can be controlled by varying the field current.

Alternating-Current (A-C) Generators (Alternators). As stated above, a simple generator without a commutator will produce an electric current that alternates in direction as the armature revolves. Such alternating current is advantageous for electric power transmission (*see* ELECTRIC POWER SYSTEMS) and hence most large electric generators are of the a-c type. In its simplest form, an a-c generator differs from a d-c generator in only two particulars: the ends of its armature winding are brought out to solid unsegmented slip rings on the generator shaft instead of to commutators, and the field coils are energized by an external d-c source rather than by the generator itself. Low-speed a-c generators are built with as many as 100 poles, both to improve their efficiency and to attain more easily the frequency desired. Alternators driven by high-speed turbines, however, are often two-pole machines. The frequency of the current delivered by an a-c generator is equal to half the product of the number of poles and the number of revolutions per second of the armature.

It is often desirable to generate as high a voltage as possible, and rotating armatures are not practical in such applications because of the possibility of sparking between brushes and slip rings and the danger of mechanical failures which might cause short circuits. Alternators are therefore constructed with a stationary armature within which revolves a rotor composed of a number of field magnets. The principle of operation is exactly the same as that of the a-c generator described, except that the magnetic field (rather than the conductors of the armature) is in motion.

The current generated by the alternators described above rises to a peak, sinks to zero, drops to a negative peak, and rises again to zero a number of times each second, depending on the frequency for which the machine is designed. Such current is known as single-phase a.c. If, however, the armature is composed of two windings, mounted at right angles to each other, and provided with separate external connections, two current waves will be produced, each of which will be at its maximum when the other is at zero. Such current is called two-phase a.c. If three armature windings are set at 120° to each other, current will be produced in the form of a triple wave, known as three-phase a.c. A larger number of phases may be obtained by increasing the number of windings in the armature, but in modern electrical-engineering practice three-phase a.c. is most commonly used and the three-phase alternator is the dynamoelectric machine typically employed for the generation of electric power. Voltages as high as 13,200 are common in alternators.

Alternating-Current (A-C) Motors. Two basic types of motors are designed to operate on polyphase alternating current, synchronous motors and induction motors. The synchronous motor is essentially a three-phase alternator operated in reverse. The field magnets are mounted on the rotor and are excited by direct current, and the armature winding is divided into three parts and fed with three-phase a.c. The variation of the three waves of current in the armature causes a varying magnetic reaction with the poles of the field magnets, and makes the field rotate at a constant speed which is determined by the frequency of the current in the a-c power line. The constant speed of a synchronous motor is advantageous in certain devices; however, in applications where the mechanical load on the motor becomes very great, synchronous motors cannot be used, because if the motor slows down under load it will "fall out of step" with the frequency of the current and come to a stop. Synchronous motors can be made to operate from a single-phase power source by the inclusion of suitable circuit elements which cause a rotating magnetic field.

The simplest of all electric motors is the squirrel-cage type of induction motor used with a three-phase supply. The armature of the squirrel-cage motor consists of three fixed coils similar to the armature of the synchronous motor. The rotating member consists of a core in which are imbedded a series of heavy conductors arranged in a circle around the shaft and parallel to it. With the core removed, the rotor conductors resemble in form the cylindrical cages once used to exercise pet squirrels. The three-phase current flowing in the stationary armature windings generates a rotating magnetic field, and this field induces a current in the conductors of the cage. The magnetic reaction between the rotating field and the current-carrying conductors of the rotor makes the rotor turn. If the rotor is revolving at exactly the same speed as the magnetic field, no currents will be induced in it, and hence the rotor should not turn at a

Top: Copper is used to make the rotor assembly of this alternating-current generator. Center: A disassembled 400-ampere alternator shows the workings of the stator assembly. Bottom: The conversion of a-c to d-c is performed by 60 high-current, high-voltage diodes, which have the capacity to conduct current in only one direction.   General Motors Corp.

synchronous speed. In operation the speeds of rotation of the rotor and the field differ by about 2 to 5 percent. This speed difference is known as slip. Motors with squirrel-cage rotors can be used on single-phase a.c. by means of various arrangements of inductance and capacitance which alter the characteristics of the single-phase voltage and make it resemble a two-phase voltage. Such motors are called split-phase motors or condenser motors (or capacitor motors) depending on the arrangement used. Single-phase squirrel-cage motors do not have a large starting torque, and for applications where such torque is required repulsion-induction motors are used. A repulsion-induction motor may be of the split-phase or condenser type, but has a manual or automatic switch which allows current to flow between brushes on the commutator when the motor is starting, and short-circuits all commutator segments after the motor reaches a critical speed. Repulsion-induction motors are so named because their starting torque depends on the repulsion between the rotor and the stator, and their torque while running depends on induction. Series-wound motors with commutators, which will operate on direct or alternating current, are called universal motors. They are usually made only in small sizes and are commonly used in household appliances.

Miscellaneous Machines. For special applications several combined types of dynamoelectric machines are employed. It is frequently desirable to change from direct to alternating current or vice versa, or to change the voltage of a d-c supply, or the frequency or phase of an a-c supply. The most direct method of accomplishing such changes is to use a motor operating from the available type of electric supply to drive a generator delivering the current and voltage wanted. Motor generators, consisting of an appropriate motor mechanically coupled to an appropriate generator, can accomplish most of the indicated conversions. A rotary converter is a machine for converting alternating to direct current, using separate windings on a common rotating armature. The a-c supply voltage is applied to the armature through slip rings, and the d-c voltage is led out of the machine through a separate commutator. A dynamotor, which is usually used to convert low-voltage direct current to high-voltage direct current, is a similar machine which has separate armature windings.

Pairs of machines known as synchros, Selsyns, or Autosyns are used to transmit torque or mechanical movement from one place to another by electrical means. They consist of pairs of motors with stationary fields and armatures wound with three sets of coils similar to those of a three-phase alternator. In use, the armatures of Selsyns are connected electrically in parallel to each other but not to any external source. The field coils are connected in parallel to an external a-c source. When the armatures of both Selsyns are in the same position relative to the magnetic fields of their respective machines, the currents induced in the armature coils will be equal and will cancel each other out. But when one of the armatures is moved, an unbalance is created which will cause a current to be induced in the other armature. The magnetic reaction to this current will move the second armature until it is in the same relative position as the first. Selsyns are widely used for remote-control and remote-indicating instruments where it is inconvenient or impossible to make a mechanical connection.

Direct-current machines, known as amplidynes or rototrols, which have several field windings, may be used as power amplifiers. A small change in the power supplied to one field winding produced a much larger corresponding change in the power output of the machine. These electrodynamic amplifiers are frequently employed in servomechanism (q.v.) and other control systems; see AUTOMATION. See also DYNAMOMETER; ELECTRICITY. E.C.E.

DYNAMOMETER, apparatus used to measure the mechanical power developed by an engine or other prime mover. Such apparatus is either of the absorption or transmission type. Absorption dynamometers absorb all of the mechanical power output of the engine they are measuring. This mechanical power is converted by frictional drag into heat; the dynamometer then measures, by some form of spring balance and a tachometer (q.v.), the frictional power, or measures the total heat produced with the help of a calorimeter; see CALORIMETRY. The results obtained are converted into units of power such as watts or horsepower (q.v.). The friction for absorption dynamometers may be furnished by cords, belts, or wooden blocks tightened around the engine output shaft or pulley, by liquid or air in a closed container around the shaft, or by a magnetic drag.

In transmission dynamometers, the power furnished to the device passes on to an external load. In one device of this type, called the torsion dynamometer or torquemeter, a shaft is inserted between the engine and its load. This intermediate shaft is constrained, and twists through an angle dependent upon the force that the engine develops. The dynamometer is usually calibrated in such a manner that, when its reading is multiplied by a tachometer reading, the power of the engine in horsepower is obtained directly.

DYNAMOTOR. See DYNAMOELECTRIC MACHINERY: *Miscellaneous Machines.*

DYSENTERY, acute or chronic disease of the large intestine of man, characterized by frequent passage of small watery stools, often containing blood and mucus, accompanied by severe abdominal cramps. There may be ulceration of the walls of the intestine. It may be sporadic or epidemic. Although many severe acute cases of diarrhea (q.v.) have been called dysentery, the word properly refers to a disease caused by either a specific amoeba or a bacillus that infects the colon (*see* AMOEBA; BACTERIA).

Amoebic dysentery, also called amoebic colitis, intestinal amoebiasis, and entamoebiasis, is caused by a parasite, *Entamoeba histolytica,* found in stools of infected persons. It is usually chronic and relatively painless but severe cases result in diarrhea with blood and mucus in the feces because of ulceration of the colon.

Amoebic Dysentery. Amoebic dysentery is endemic in many tropical countries, but is attributable more to unsanitary conditions than to heat. It is the most common type of dysentery in the Philippine Islands, the Malay Archipelago, and the West Indies, but also occurs in almost all temperate countries. A violent outbreak in the United States occurred in Chicago, Ill., during the late summer and fall of 1933 when a carrier visiting the World's Fair infected a large number of people through faulty plumbing connections that caused a contamination of drinking water. In 1953 an epidemic at South Bend, Ind. caused four deaths.

The disease is caused by the ingestion of freely motile or more often encysted forms of *E. histolytica.* Amoebic dysentery is most commonly spread by water or contaminated, uncooked food or from carriers. Uncooked vegetables are a common source of infection in countries where untreated human feces are used as plant fertilizers. Flies may carry the cysts to spread the amoeba from the feces of infected persons to food.

Amoebic dysentery may result in perforation of the walls of the intestine and in abcesses on the liver and lungs. Various drugs, including emetine (q.v.), arsenicals such as carbarsone, and iodine-containing preparations have been useful in treating severe cases of the disease.

Bacillary Dysentery. Bacillary dysentery is caused by certain nonmotile bacteria of the genus *Shigella*. This form of dysentery is also most prevalent in unhygienic areas of the tropics, but, because it is easily spread, sporadic outbreaks are common in all parts of the world. Characterized by intestinal pain, diarrhea with mucus and blood in the stools, and some degree of toxemia, this dysentery is usually self-limiting, and rarely manifests the more severe organ involvements characteristic of amoebic dysentery. Simultaneous infections by viruses and bacteria may occur. Bacillary dysentery is spread by contaminated water, milk, and food. Feces from active cases and those from healthy carriers as well contain immense numbers of the disease-producing bacteria. Flies, that may carry the bacteria on their feet or in their saliva and feces and desposit them on food, are also an important means of the dissemination of bacteria; ants are also believed to spread the disease.

In addition to dehydration produced by loss of water in the feces, bacillary dysentery may occasionally cause arthritis and perforation of the bowel. General debility may also result from vitamin deficiencies caused by improper digestion and absorption of food. In the treatment of bacillary dysentery, proper replacement of fluid is important. Sulfonamides, tetracycline, and streptomycin were effective in curing acute cases until drug-resistant strains emerged. Chloramphenicol is sometimes used to treat these strains.

DYSMENORRHEA. *See* MENSTRUATION.

DYSPEPSIA, condition of impaired or painful digestion resulting from failure of some phase of the normal digestive process. The cause may be physical or emotional upset. Among the physical causes are gastritis, ulcers, or gallbladder inflammation. Symptoms may include a heavy feeling in the pit of the stomach, gas, constipation, diarrhea, nausea, or heartburn. Headache or dizziness may accompany the discomfort. Treatment is prescribed according to the specific cause; such treatment may include administering drugs and placing the patient on a special diet.

See also INDIGESTION.

DYSPROSIUM, metallic element, one of the rare earths (q.v.) with at.no. 66, at.wt. 162.50, b.p. estimated 2600° C. (4712° F.), m.p. estimated 1500° C. (2732° F.), sp.gr. 8.55, and symbol Dy. Dysprosium usually occurs as the white oxide, Dy_2O_3, dysprosia, with erbium and holmium, two other rare-earth elements. It is forty-fifth in abundance among the elements in the crust of the earth. Its compounds are found in gadolinite, xenotime, euxenite, and fergusonite in Norway, the United States, Brazil, India, and Australia. Its salts are yellow or yellow green,

the most common being a chloride, $DyCl_3$, a nitrate, $Dy(NO_3)_3 \cdot 5H_2O$, and a sulfate, $Dy_2(SO_4)_3 \cdot 8H_2O$. The salts of dysprosium have an extremely high magnetic susceptibility, higher than that of any other substance except metals such as iron. The element was discovered in 1886 by Paul Émile Lecoq de Boisbaudran (1838–1912), who separated one of its compounds from an oxide of holmium. Compounds of dysprosium have no commercial uses.

DYTISCUS. *See* WATER BEETLE.

DZERZHINSK, industrial city and former resort of the Soviet Union, in the Russian S.F.S.R., on the Oka R., 20 miles s.w. of Gor'kiy. The city, a major chemical center, produces synthetic chemicals, explosives, phosphate fertilizers, alabaster, rope, flour, and lumber. Deposits of phosphates, gypsum, limestone, shale, and peat are in the vicinity. Founded in 1930 when Rastyapino was joined with two suburbs, the city grew from a population of under 9000 in 1926 to more than 100,000 by 1939. Pop. (1970 est.) 221,000.

DZHAMBUL, city of the Soviet Union, in the Kazakh S.S.R., capital of the Dzhambul Oblast, on the Talas R., 290 miles w. of Alma-Ata. Dzhambul is on the Turksib Railway in an irrigated area of orchards, truck farms, and sugar-beet and cotton fields. Industries in the city include food processing, fruit canning, metalworking, sugar refining, wool processing, distilling, and the manufacture of phosphate fertilizers. The 5th-century city of Taraz was on the site of Dzhambul; it was succeeded by Yany (or Yangi), city and capital of the Karakhanid state ruled by the Arabs following the defeat of the Chinese in 751. Yany was devastated by Genghis Khan (q.v.) in the 13th century. The modern Kazakh city called Aulie-Ata, or Auliye-Ata was founded in the late 18th century. In 1864 it was taken by the Russians. The name was changed to Mirzoyan in 1933 and to Dzhambul in 1938. Pop. (1970 est.) 188,000.

DZUNGARIA, region of China, in Sinkiang-Uigur Autonomous Region, between the Tien Shan range on the s. and the Altay Mts. on the N. On the west it is bounded by the Soviet Union and on the east by the Mongolian People's Republic.

A semidesert area, roughly triangular in shape, Dzungaria is the source of the Black Irtysh and Ili rivers. The region derives its name from the Dzungar, one of the tribes under Mongolian rule during the 17th century. In 1759 the Chinese, after long campaigns, conquered and annexed the area, settling it largely with colonists from China.

E, fifth and most frequently used letter of the English alphabet. Its form was derived without alteration from the fifth letter of the classical Latin alphabet, which had adapted it from the Greek letter *epsilon* (E, e). The letter evolved from the Semitic *he,* ∃ , which in turn had developed from the Egyptian hieratic ⚒ and the earlier hieroglyph ⊐ , the ultimate origin of the letter.

In the Semitic alphabet the letter *he* indicated a sound similar to that of the aspirate *h* in English. The Greeks adopted it with the value of long or short *e*. In eastern Greek, another long e was evolved from the Semitic *cheth* (*see* H). Thus, Greek had two types of the letter e, the long *eta,* derived from *cheth,* and the short *epsilon,* derived from *he*.

The evolution of the values of e in English is long and complicated. Starting generally with the short, open sound of *e* in the word bell and the long, closed sound of *e* in the German word *zehn,* the letter has come to represent a variety of sounds, as in the words eve, here, there, end, and maker, as well as the silent value that lengthens preceding vowels, as in mate and rule.

Among the many uses of the letter E are the following. As a Roman numeral, capital E stands for 250 or, in the form Ē, for 250,000. As an abbreviation, capital E may stand for such terms as east, eastern, Earth, Easter, and English. Capital E symbolizes, in logic, the universal negative proposition; in mathematics, the eccentricity of a curve; in chemistry, the element einsteinium; and in physics, Young's modulus of elasticity and a line in the spectrum produced by iron (*see* Fraunhofer Lines). Italicized *E* stands for energy, electromotive force (voltage), and the lowermost layer of the ionosphere (q.v.). In music, E is the name of the third note in the C major scale and the fifth note in the relative minor scale (A minor). Lowercase e may be used as an abbreviation for the stage direction "entrance"

Italicized *e* symbolizes the numerical value of the electrical charge of an electron or proton in physics and, in mathematics, represents the number that is the base of natural logarithms; see separate article on *e* in mathematics.   M.P.

e, in mathematics, number of great importance, comparable only to π (the ratio of the circumference of a circle to its diameter) in the wide variety of its applications. *e* is most commonly defined as the limit of the expression $\left(1 + \frac{1}{n}\right)^n$ as *n* becomes large without bound. Some values of this expression for increasing values of *n* are included in the following table.

CALCULATIONS OF $\left(1 + \frac{1}{n}\right)^n$ FOR INCREASING VALUES OF n

n	$\left(1 + \frac{1}{n}\right)^n$	Numerical Value
1	$(1 + \frac{1}{1})^1$	2.000
2	$(1 + \frac{1}{2})^2$	2.250
3	$(1 + \frac{1}{3})^3$	2.369
5	$(1 + \frac{1}{5})^5$	2.489
10	$(1 + \frac{1}{10})^{10}$	2.594
20	$(1 + \frac{1}{20})^{20}$	2.653
40	$(1 + \frac{1}{40})^{40}$	2.684
50	$(1 + \frac{1}{50})^{50}$	2.691
100	$(1 + \frac{1}{100})^{100}$	2.705
1,000	$(1 + 0.001)^{1.000}$	2.717
10,000	$(1 + 0.0001)^{10.000}$	2.718
∞	. . . .	2.71828...

Examination of the right-hand column of the table shows that the value of the expression becomes closer and closer to a limiting value. This limiting value is approximately 2.7182818285.

The value of *e* may also be determined by computing the limit of certain infinite series. One example of such a series is:

$$\sum_{n=1}^{\infty} \frac{1}{n!} = 1 + \frac{1}{1 \times 2} + \frac{1}{1 \times 2 \times 3} + \frac{1}{1 \times 2 \times 3 \times 4} + \cdots + \frac{1}{1 \times 2 \times 3 \cdots x(n-1)(n)} + \cdots$$

Unlike π, *e* has no simple geometrical interpretation. Like π, it is a transcendental number, that is, it is not the root of any polynomial equation $a_0 x^n + a_1 x^{n-1} + \ldots + a_n = 0$ with integral coefficients.

This number forms the base of natural, or Napierian, logarithms (q.v.). It appears in the so-called exponential function, e^x, the only function having a rate of growth equal to its size (in the language of calculus, the only function having a derivative equal to itself), and therefore the fundamental function for equations describing growth and many other processes of change. In geometry, e is a necessary component of the formulas for many curves, such as the catenary, the shape assumed by a cord suspended from its extremities. In the study of imaginary numbers (q.v.), e appears in the extraordinary equation $e^{\pi i} = -1$, in which i is the imaginary number $\sqrt{-1}$. e appears constantly in the theory of probability (q.v.). For example, if many letters are written and the corresponding envelopes addressed, and the letters are then fitted at random into the envelopes, the probability that every letter will go into a wrong envelope is very close to e^{-1}. e also appears in formulas for calculating compound interest. Even in pure theory of numbers, e crops up. Thus, the number of prime numbers in the first N numbers (if N is very large) is given by the expression $\frac{N}{\log N}$ in which log N is the natural logarithm of N, and therefore a function of e. Compare PI. J.Si. & J.McP.

EADMUND, variant form of the name ED-MUND; see articles under the latter spelling.

EADS, James Buchanan (1820–87), American inventor and engineer, born in Lawrenceburg, Ind., and self-educated. He invented a diving bell (*see* DIVING: *Diving Bells*), using it successfully to salvage sunken steamboats from rivers. In 1861 he obtained a government contract to construct a fleet of fourteen steam-powered, armor-plated gunboats to guard the western rivers during the American Civil War, and completed the task in one hundred days. Between 1867–74, he constructed his best known achievement, the steel and masonry Eads Bridge across the Mississippi R. at St. Louis, Mo., incorporating some of the most advanced engineering features at the time. In 1874 he deepened the mouth of the Mississippi R. by means of huge jetties which so directed the water that the river dredged its own channel.

The last years of his life were spent in extensive engineering operations both in America and Europe, for example, in improving harbor facilities at Toronto, Ont. and Liverpool, England, and designing a ship railway across the isthmus of Tehuantepec in Mexico.

EADWINE, variant form of the name EDWIN; see article under the latter spelling.

EAGLE, common name for a number of the largest members of the Hawk (q.v.) family in the order Falconiformes. The term is loosely used; some buzzards of the same family and some hawks are larger than the smaller eagles. Like other members of the Hawk family, the eagle is characterized by a hooked beak, and by well-developed legs and feet with the toes equipped with long, curved talons. Its keenness of vision and the strength which it displays in flight are remarkable. To a limited extent, the eagle has been used in falconry (q.v.).

From ancient times the eagle has been regarded as a symbol of courage and power because of the altitudes to which it flies, because of the great size of the larger species, and because of the inaccessibility of the mountain heights in which some species nest. In Roman myths the eagle is associated with the principal Roman deity Jupiter. It was the emblem of certain Roman legions, and of France under the Bonapartes (*see* NAPOLEON I), of Germany, of the Russian and Austro-Hungarian empires, and of the United States.

The golden eagle, *Aquila chrysaëtos,* is distributed through most of the Northern Hemisphere. In North America it is seen as far south as Mexico, although it is most common in the Rocky Mountain area and in the mountains of the Pacific Coast; east of the Mississippi R. it is relatively rare. The male grows to an average length of about 33 in. from the tip of the beak to the tip of the tail, and has a wingspread of 6½ to 7 ft. The female is larger by several inches. A characteristic of the genus is that the legs down to the toes are feathered. The plumage is dark brown shading to a sooty color on some parts, with irregular bands or mottling of a grayish color on the tail. The head and the back of the neck are covered with slightly longer feathers of a tawny hue. The name golden eagle probably is derived from the bright yellow of the beak and feet. Compared with that of other species, the beak is relatively short, but has the typical curve beginning below the fleshy base.

By preference the golden eagle builds its nest on a high ledge or rock. The nest is large and coarse, built of sticks or twigs. The female lays two, and occasionally three, eggs. Usually the nest is built at a considerable distance from other eagle nests, for one pair of birds and their young consume extraordinarily large quantities of food, and need an extensive area for their

The bald eagle, the national bird of the U.S., is an endangered species of American wildlife.   UPI

hunting ground. The diet of this species consists mainly of small birds and mammals. Legends crediting eagles with carrying off children greatly exaggerate the bird's strength; experiments have proved that no eagle can rise into the air with a load greater than 8 to 10 lb. Occasionally, however, the golden eagle carries off a newborn lamb.

Another member of the genus *Aquila* is *A. heliaca,* the imperial eagle of Asia and southeast Europe; it is smaller and darker than the golden eagle. The much smaller, spotted eagles, *A. maculata* and *A. clanga,* are found in central and southern Europe, and the dwarf eagle, *A. pennata,* is found in southern Europe and in India and Africa. *A. vindhiana* and *A. rapax* are the tawny eagles of India and Africa, respectively.

Sea Eagles.   The sea eagles or ernes inhabit coastal regions and the shores of lakes and streams, and live mainly on fish. One of these is the bald eagle, *Haliaeetus leucocephalus,* also known as the American eagle; by an act of the second Continental Congress in 1782 it became the official emblem of the U.S. The bald eagle has a range extending from Alaska as far as Florida in the east and Lower California in the west. The bird is about the size of the golden eagle, the female, slightly larger than the male, attaining a wingspread of 7½ ft. Birds in the northern range tend to be slightly larger than those in the south. The bald eagle migrates only from the coldest sections of its range. The bird is not bald, but when three years old develops white feathers on the head and neck, and also a white tail, contrasting with the rest of its plumage, which is blackish brown. The young are entirely dark. Unlike the golden eagle, the bald eagle has no feathers on the lower legs. Compared to other eagles, the bald eagle is clumsy and inexpert in hunting and fishing. For food it depends heavily on injured or dead fish cast up by whirlpools or tides. It also steals from the osprey (q.v.) when the smaller bird has caught a live fish; the eagle attacks the osprey in the air, tormenting it until the osprey drops the fish, which the eagle catches in the air. The bald eagle's nest frequently is built in the top of a tall, dead tree. A pair of bald eagles may use the same nest year after year.

A larger species is the white-tailed eagle or gray sea eagle, *H. albicilla,* of Iceland, Greenland, northern Europe, and northern Asia; its plumage is a dark, grayish color with white on the tail. *H. pelagicus,* a brown species with white shoulders, rump, and tail, inhabits northeastern Asia. Steller's sea eagle, *Thalasso-*

251

aëtus pelagicus, also called the Kamchatkan sea eagle, grows to a length of 44 in. or more. It inhabits northeastern Asia and the north Pacific islands, including islands off the coast of Alaska. It is marked with white on the forehead, breast, and wing coverts, and on the flanks, rump, and tail. *Polioateus ichthyaetus,* the fishing eagle of India, belongs in this group. Africa has several sea eagles.

Crested and Other Eagles.   One of the largest and most powerful eagles, although relatively slow in flight, is the harpy or harpy eagle, *Thrasaëtus harpyia,* of Mexico, Central America, and northern South America. It is gray, with white on the head and lower parts. The upper parts are marked with black bands, and a dark band crosses the chest. The head has a double crest. Another large, crested bird is the monkey-eating eagle, *Pithecophaga jefferyi,* of the Philippines; it, too, is sometimes called the harpy eagle.

The spotted crested eagles of the genus *Spilornis,* of India and southeast Asia, feed on reptiles and are called serpent eagles. This latter name is given also to the harrier eagles of the genus *Bastatur* and to the secretary bird. Several species of *Bastatur* and of *Circaëtus,* another genus of reptile-eaters, are found in Africa and southern Asia; *C. gallicus* appears in areas bordering the Mediterranean and in Central Europe.   W.Be. & K.AC.

EAGLE PASS,   city in Texas, and county seat of Maverick Co., on the Rio Grande, near the Mexican border, about 105 miles N.W. of Laredo. The city, a port of entry and processing and shipping center for the surrounding farm and livestock area, has varied manufacturing. Pop. (1960) 12,094; (1970) 15,364.

EAKINS, Thomas (1844–1916), American painter, born in Philadelphia, Pa. Eakins attended the Pennsylvania Academy of the Fine Arts. From 1866 to 1869 he was in Paris, studying painting and sculpture with the French artists Jean Léon Gérôme (q.v.) and Augustin Alexandre Dumont (1801–84), respectively. Eakins spent several months (1869–70) in Spain. His observation of the works of the Spanish painters Diego Rodríguez de Silva y Velásquez and Francisco José de Goya y Lucientes (qq.v.) profoundly influenced his style of painting. In 1870 he enrolled at Jefferson Medical College, Philadelphia, to study anatomy. He taught anatomy and painting at the Pennsylvania Academy of the Fine Arts (1873–86) and later at the Art Students League of Philadelphia. An inspired but unorthodox teacher, Eakins was constantly under critical pressure, particularly for his reliance on nude models. Although Eakins pro-

"The Thinker: Louis N. Kenton" by Thomas Eakins.
Metropolitan Museum of Art — Kennedy Fund, 1917

duced many paintings and some sculpture, the latter usually in collaboration, his importance was not recognized until after his death. His severe realism, in contrast to the prevailing Romantic style of the late 19th century, influenced an entire generation of American painters of the 20th century. Eakins was a meticulous craftsman, deeply interested in anatomical accuracy, but he was also aware of the possibilities of light and shadow, of subtle color gradations, and of dramatic composition. Among his most important paintings are two large-scale works depicting surgical operations, "The Gross Clinic" (1875; Jefferson Medical College) and "The Agnew Clinic" (1889; University of Pennsylvania); a group of studies of athletes, including "Between Rounds" (1899; Philadelphia Museum of Art) and "Max Schmitt in a Single Scull" (1871; Metropolitan Museum of Art, New York City); and incisive portraits such as "The Thinker: Louis N. Kenton" (1900; Metropolitan Museum of Art).

EAMES, Charles (1907–   ), American designer whose form-fitting plywood and fiberglass chairs demonstrated the feasibility of mass-producing quality contemporary furniture.

Born in Saint Louis, Mo., on June 17, 1907, Eames went to work at the age of ten after his father's death. One of his first jobs was in a steel mill, where he became a draftsman and acquired an interest in architecture. Awarded a scholarship to Washington University, he remained in school only briefly.

After several years of travel and a few unsuccessful business ventures, in the late 1930's Eames was offered a fellowship to Cranbrook Academy of Art, Bloomfield Hills, Mich. There, despite his lack of formal education, he became head of the Experimental Design Department. During this time he collaborated with Eero Saarinen, son of the Finnish-American architect Eliel Saarinen (then director of the academy), in designing a molded plywood chair, which was entered in the 1940–41 Organic Design Competition of the Museum of Modern Art. Awarded first prize, the design won considerable acclaim, but inadequate manufacturing techniques precluded its production.

During World War II Eames did set designing for Metro-Goldwyn-Mayer and research and development work for the United States Navy; but in his spare time he concentrated on furniture design, also striving to develop the necessary manufacturing processes to mass-produce the molded chair. By 1946, when the Museum of Modern Art held a one-man show of his simple, functional designs, the original chair was finally being produced and marketed.

From the 1950's onward, with the creative partnership of his wife Ray, Eames extended his work into many diversified areas of design, including graphics, films, exhibits, and architecture. (The Eames's own house, at Pacific Palisades, Calif., was a revolutionary design for its time, incorporating standardized industrial building components.) Asked to make a film conveying the nature of American life for the American Exhibition in Moscow in 1959, the Eames produced a highly sophisticated multiscreen presentation. Their camera eye also created films for World's Fairs (Brussels, Seattle, and New York City), television, and industry. Charles Eames's fascination with mathematics has resulted in the multimedia exhibit "Mathematica: A World of Numbers and Beyond", a permanent installation at the California Museum of Science and Industry, in Los Angeles, and at the Museum of Science and Industry, in Chicago.

EAR, organ of hearing and equilibrium. It is composed of three divisions—external, middle, and internal—the greater part of which is enclosed within the temporal bone.

Structure. The external ear is that portion of the auditory apparatus lateral to the tympanic membrane or eardrum. It comprises the auricle, or pinna (the external flap of the ear), and the external auditory canal, 1¼ in. in length.

The middle ear embodies the mechanism for the conduction of sound waves to the internal ear. This space or cleft extends vertically for about 15 mm and for about the same distance horizontally, but is very narrow from side to side. The middle ear is in direct communication with the back of the nose and throat by way of the eustachian tube and is traversed by a chain of three small, movable bones known as the ossicles: the malleus or hammer handle, the incus or anvil, and the stapes or stirrup. The ossicles connect the eardrum acoustically to the internal ear. The tension of the eardrum is maintained by two muscles, one attached to the stapes.

The eustachian tube, into which the tympanic cavity opens anteriorly, is about 1½ in. in length, and passes downward, forward, and inward to its opening in the nasopharynx. It is partly osseous, but chiefly cartilaginous, and allows for the passage of air into and out of the middle ear.

The internal ear, or labyrinth, is the part of the temporal bone containing the organs of hearing and equilibrium to which the ultimate filaments of the auditory nerve (*see* NERVOUS SYSTEM) are distributed. It is separated from the middle ear by the *fenestra ovalis* (oval window). The internal ear consists of membranous canals housed in a dense portion of the temporal bone and is divided into the cochlea (Gr., "snail shell"), the vestibule, and three semicircular canals. All of these canals communicate with one another.

Hearing. The structure of the ear is simpler in animals lower than mammals. The pinna is usually absent, and there is a simplified system of ossicles. Classes below the Amphibia possess only the internal ear. Sound waves are carried through the external auditory canal to the eardrum, causing it to vibrate. These vibrations are communicated to the ossicular chain in the middle ear, through which sensations are conveyed by fluid in the oval window to the organ of Corti in the cochlea and then to the tiny nerve endings leading to the auditory center located in the brain (*see* AUDITION).

The range of hearing, like that of vision, varies in different persons. The maximum range of human hearing includes sound frequencies from about 16 to 28,000 cycles per second. The least noticeable change in tone that can be picked up by the ear varies with pitch and loudness. A change of vibration frequency (pitch) corresponding to about 0.03 percent of the original frequency (or about $\frac{1}{30}$ of a note) can be detected by the most sensitive human ears in the range between 500 and 8000 vibrations per second. The ear is less sensitive to frequency changes for sounds of low frequency or low intensity. See SOUND: *Sensations of Tone.*

The sensitivity of the ear to sound intensity (loudness) also varies with vibration frequency. Sensitivity to change in loudness is greatest in the range from 1000 to 3000 cycles, where a change of one decibel can be detected, and becomes less when sound-intensity levels are lowered.

The variation in the sensitivity of the ear to loud sounds causes several important phenomena. Very loud tones produce in the ear entirely different notes (such as sum and difference tones and harmonics) that are not present in the original tone. These subjective tones are probably caused by imperfections in the natural function of the middle ear. The harshness in tonality caused by greatly increasing sound intensities, as when a radio volume control is adjusted to produce excessively loud sounds, results from subjective tones produced in the ear. The loudness of a pure tone also affects its pitch. High tones may increase as much as a whole musical-scale note; low tones tend to become lower as sound intensity increases. This effect is noticeable only for pure tones. Because most musical tones are complex, hearing is usually not affected to an appreciable degree by this phenomenon. Another phenomenon is known as masking. The production in the ear of harmonics of lower-pitched sounds may deafen the ear to the perception of higher-pitched sounds. Masking is the phenomenon that makes necessary the raising of one's voice in order to be heard in a noisy place. See also DEAFNESS; HEARING AIDS.

Equilibrium. Whereas the cochlea of the internal ear contains the essential mechanism of hearing, the semicircular canals are concerned with the sense of equilibrium; the vestibule is situated in the center of the inner ear and is separated from the middle ear by the footplate of the stapes. All three parts of the bony labyrinth contain, within a membranous lining, a gelatinous fluid called endolymph. Any motion of the endolymph agitates hair cells extending from sensory structures in the membrane; hairs in the Corti organs of the cochlea respond to vibrations of sound, and hairs in the vestibule and the semicircular canals respond to changes in the position of the head.

The three semicircular canals extend from the vestibule approximately at right angles to each other, providing sensory organs to record movements of the head in each of the three planes of space: up and down; forward and backward; and to the left or right. Lying over the hair cells in the vestibule are crystals of calcium carbonate, known technically as otoliths and popularly as ear sand. When the head is tilted, the otoliths shift, and the hairs beneath respond to the change in pressure.

When the nerves connecting with these sensory structures transmit to the brain impulses that record changes in the position of the head, contraction of various muscles is initiated. The body then endeavors by reflex movements to maintain its equilibrium in all positions. The eyes and certain sensory cells in the skin and in internal tissues also help to maintain equilibrium, but when the labyrinth of the ear is removed in animals or is diseased in man, disturbances of equilibrium invariably follow. With eyes closed, a person with disease of the internal ear may be unable to stand or even to sit up without swaying or falling.

Ear Diseases. Diseases of the external, middle, or internal ear may cause partial or total deafness, and most diseases of the internal ear are associated with disturbances of the sense of equilibrium. Diseases of the external ear include congenital and acquired malformations; inflammation caused by such factors as burns, frostbite, or skin diseases; and presence of foreign bodies in the external auditory canal. Diseases of the middle ear include perforation of the eardrum and otitis media. Diseases of the internal ear include disturbances caused by systemic and constitutional maladies, drugs and other toxic substances, injuries, circulatory disturbances, and emotional disorders.

In congenital malformations of the outer ear, the pinna and even the opening into the external auditory canal may be lacking. If the structures of the middle ear are abnormal, reconstructive and substitution surgery of the ossicular chain is possible, and hearing can be partially restored. Acquired malformations of the external ear include such conditions as cuts and wounds. Othematoma, known popularly as the cauliflower ear of boxers, is a common result of injury to the ear cartilage followed by internal bleeding and excessive production of reparative tissue.

Inflammation of the external ear may result from any condition that causes inflammation of the skin, such as dermatitis resulting from injury, burns, and frostbite. Diseases of the skin, such as erysipelas and seborrheic dermatitis, commonly affect the ear. Skin tuberculosis and

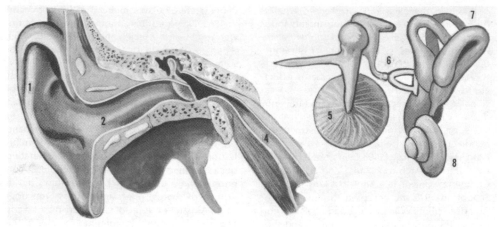

Human ear. (1) Auricle; (2) Auditory canal; (3) Middle ear; (4) Eustachian tube; (5) Membrane of the tympanum; (6) Middle-ear bones; (7) Semicircular canals; (8) Cochlea.

syphilis (q.v.) are among more uncommon diseases that also affect the external ear; see SKIN: Skin Diseases. Foreign bodies such as insects, cotton, and cerumen, the waxlike secretion of the ear, in the external auditory canal cause ear disturbances and must be removed skillfully.

Perforation of the eardrum may be caused through accidental injury by some sharp object, by forceful blowing of the nose, by a cuff on the ear, or by sudden changes in the atmospheric pressure.

Otitis media is divided into suppurative and nonsuppurative forms, either of which may be acute or chronic. Acute suppurative otitis media includes all acute infections of the middle ear caused by pus-forming bacteria, which usually reach the middle ear by way of the Eustachian tube. The most common causative agents are staphylococci, streptococci, and pneumococci; see BACTERIA: Scientific Classification. Involvement of the mastoid process (q.v.) may result as a complication of the disease, and impairment of hearing often follows because of the formation of adhesions and granulation tissue that affect the mobility of the eardrum and the ossicles. Suppurative otitis media may follow acute infectious diseases that involve the upper respiratory tract. Infections of tonsils and adenoids frequently result in suppurative infection of the middle ear; see TONSIL. Penicillin (q.v.) and other antibiotics (see ANTIBIOTIC) usually bring about subsidence of the infection, although surgery may also be required when painful distention of the eardrum necessitates its incision to permit drainage of the middle ear or destruction of mastoid cells. Chronic suppurative otitis media may result from inadequate drainage of pus in the acute form. The chronic type of the disease does not respond readily to

antibacterial agents because of irreversible pathological changes. Granulations and polyps may be removed by snare or punch forceps. Treatment of this disease includes the application of caustics, antibacterial powders, or alcoholic solutions used as ear drops. Surgery on the mastoid and middle ear may be required to prevent further hearing loss or intracranial complications.

Acute and chronic catarrhal, or nonsuppurative, otitis media is caused by occlusion of the Eustachian tube as a result of such conditions as a head cold, diseased tonsils and adenoids, sinusitis, improper blowing of the nose, or riding in nonpressurized airplanes. These conditions occur especially in persons with allergic nasal blockage, causing a condition known as aeroototis or barotitis. A serous discharge resulting from tubal blockage fills the middle ear cavity and exerts pressure on the eardrum, causing pain and impairment of hearing. Restoration of the occluded Eustachian tube to its normal patency is essential. The serous fluid may be removed by the use of an aspirating needle, by incision of the eardrum with subsequent inflation of the tube, or by inserting a tiny polyethylene tube.

Diseases of the inner ear usually affect the sense of balance and induce symptoms similar to those of seasickness (q.v.). Anemia (q.v.), hyperemia, tumors of the acoustic nerve, exposure to abnormal heat, circulatory disturbances, skull injuries, toxic states, and emotional disorders may also cause these symptoms. Ménière's disease results from lesions of the semicircular canals and produces nausea, hearing loss, tinnitus or noise in the ears, and a disturbed equilibrium. Surgical destruction of the membranous labyrinth is sometimes indicated to combat intractable dizziness by cryosurgery or ultrasonic destruction; see CRYOGENICS.

Otalgia, or earache, is not necessarily associated with external or middle-ear disease; occasionally it is caused by impacted teeth, sinus disease, diseased tonsils, nasopharyngeal lesions, or inflamed neck nodes. Treatment depends on finding the basic cause.   F.L.L.

EARHART, Amelia (1898–1937), American aviatrix, born in Atchison, Kans., and educated at Columbia University and Harvard Summer School. In 1928 she accepted the invitation of American pilots Wilmer Stutz and Louis Gordon to join them on a transatlantic flight, and thus became the first woman to make the crossing by air. In 1932 she became the first woman to fly the Atlantic alone, and at the same time established a new record for the crossing: 13 hr., 30 min. For this feat she was awarded honors by the American and French governments. In 1935 she became the first woman to fly the Pacific Ocean, crossing from Hawaii to California. Later the same year she set a new speed record by flying nonstop from Mexico City to New York City in 14 hr., 19 min. In June, 1937, she began a flight around the world, flying eastward from Miami, Fla., accompanied by Frederick J. Noonan, a navigator. Their plane disappeared on July 3, while en route from Lae, New Guinea, to Howland I. An extensive search by planes and ships of the United States Navy failed to discover any trace of the lost flyers, and their fate remains an unsolved mystery. Amelia Earhart described her first transatlantic flight in the book *20 Hrs. 40 Min.* (1928), and also wrote *The Fun of It* (1931).

Shortly after Amelia Earhart's disappearance, her husband, the book publisher George Palmer Putnam (1887–1950), edited and published *Last Flight* (1937), a book consisting largely of her diary of the last ill-fated journey, transmitted from the various stopping-places on the way.

EARLY, Jubal Anderson (1816–94), Confederate army general, born in Franklin County, Va., and educated at the United States Military Academy, West Point. He resigned from the army in 1838 to practice law, but interrupted his practice to serve during the Mexican War. At the outbreak of the American Civil War Early entered the Confederate army as a colonel in 1861 and rose to the rank of lieutenant general in 1864. Because of his defeats by the Union generals Philip Henry Sheridan in 1864 and George Armstrong Custer (qq.v.) in 1865 in

Pennsylvania, he was relieved of his command in 1865. Early fled the country at the end of the war and lived in Mexico and Canada until 1869, when he returned to Lynchburg, Va., and resumed his law practice.

EARLY ENGLISH, in architecture, term first used in the 19th century to designate a style of Gothic architecture that succeeded the Norman in Britain near the end of the 12th century. At this time the pointed arch, the pinnacle, and the buttress were introduced into British architecture. This style is often called lancet-arched because lancets, or high narrow openings, culminating in a pointed arch, were often used in groups of threes, fives, and sevens. The dogtooth ornament is also characteristic of Early English architecture. Prominent examples of the style are the Salisbury catheral (begun 1220) and parts of the transepts in the York cathedral (1230–60). As tracery and floral decoration became more profuse at the end of the 13th century, Early English merged into the Decorated Style (q.v.). *See also* GOTHIC ARCHITECTURE.

EARP, Wyatt Berry Stapp (1848–1929), American frontiersman and law enforcement officer, born in Monmouth, Ill. In 1876 Earp, who had been a stagecoach driver, railroad construction worker, surveyor, buffalo hunter, and policeman, became chief deputy marshal of Dodge City, Kans., a lawless frontier town. Within a year, having brought relative peace to Dodge City, he moved on to Deadwood in the Dakota Territory. He returned to Dodge City in 1878, and in 1879 he settled in Tombstone, Arizona Territory. There he furthered his reputation as a gunfighter, first as deputy sheriff of Pima Co. and later as deputy United States marshal for the entire Arizona Territory. Earp and three of his brothers, together with the American frontiersman John Henry ("Doc") Holliday (1852–87), participated in the famous O. K. Corral gunfight in 1881, during which they killed several suspected cattle rustlers. Earp left Tombstone in 1882, to live the rest of his life in various cities of the American West, looking after his extensive real estate and mining interests. Since his death he has become a legendary figure, hero of numerous Western novels, television programs, and motion pictures.

EARRING, type of jewelry, an ornament for the ear, attached to the lobe, and usually worn one in each ear. Originally it was a ring, with or without pendants, which was passed through a hole pierced in the ear. Sometimes the pendants were suspended from a hook instead of a ring. The wearing of earrings dates from remote times and is mentioned in the Bible, in Genesis.

Earrings made of various materials, particularly gold and other precious metals, and often decorated with gems, were worn by almost all ancient peoples. The Egyptians excelled at fine filigree work on their golden earrings; the jeweled earrings of the Greeks were of magnificent workmanship. Roman earrings were simple in form and decorated with precious stones. Among many of the Oriental peoples earrings have been worn by both men and women, but in the Western world, as among the Greeks and Romans, their use has generally been confined to women. The wearing of earrings has been periodically fashionable in Europe and America during the 20th century. The development of clip and screw fasteners has increased the popularity of earrings. In the 1960's many women had their ears surgically pierced and the wearing of pierced earrings has also increased.

EARTH, one of the planets in the solar system, the third in distance from the sun (q.v.) and the fifth largest of the planets in diameter. The mean distance of the earth from the sun is 92,897,000 mi. It is the only planet known to be capable of supporting higher forms of life, although some of the other planets also have atmospheres and water molecules.

Shape and Size. The earth is not a perfect sphere but is very slightly pear-shaped. Calculations based on perturbations in the orbits of artificial satellites reveal that the earth is an imperfect sphere because the equator bulges, or is distended, 13 mi.; the North Pole bulges 33 ft.; and the South Pole is depressed about 100 ft. The circumference of the earth at the equator is 24,902.4 mi., whereas the circumference around the poles is 42.2. mi. less. The diameter of the earth at the equator is 7926.42 mi., and at the poles, 7899.83 mi. The difference in diameters is 26.59 mi. The total area of the earth's surface is 196,950,000 sq.mi. and its volume 259,880,000,-000 cu.mi. Because the average density of the planet is 5.52, the total mass of the earth is ap-

Byzantine silver and enamel earrings dating from the 11th or 12th century. Metropolitan Museum of Art

proximately 6,595,000,000,000,000,000,000 (6595 × 10^{18}) tons.

Motion. In common with the entire solar system, the earth is moving through space at the rate of approximately 12.5 mi. per sec. or 45,000 m.p.h. toward the constellation of Hercules. The earth and its satellite, the moon, also move together in an elliptical orbit about the sun. The eccentricity of the orbit is very slight, so that the orbit is virtually a circle. The approximate length of the earth's orbit is 583,400,000 mi., and the earth travels along it at a velocity of about 66,000 m.p.h. The earth rotates on its axis once every 23 hr., 56 min., 4.1 sec. (based on the solar year). A point on the equator therefore rotates at a rate of a little over 1000 m.p.h., and a point on the earth at the latitude of Portland, Ore. (45° N.) rotates at about 667 m.p.h.

In addition to these primary motions, three other components of the total motion of the

A segmented view of the structure of the earth. American Museum of Natural History

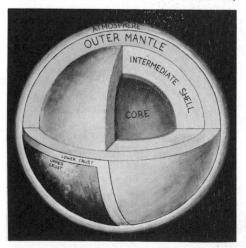

earth exist: the precession of the equinoxes (see ECLIPTIC), nutation (periodic variation in the inclination of the earth's axis caused by the gravitational pulls of the sun and the moon), and variation of latitude (see LATITUDE AND LONGITUDE).

Composition. From the scientific point of view, the entire earth is considered to consist of four parts: the atmosphere, the lithosphere, the hydrosphere, and the barysphere. The atmosphere (q.v.) is the gaseous envelope which surrounds the solid body of the planet. Although it has a thickness of more than 700 mi., about one half of its mass is concentrated in the lower 3.5 mi. The lithosphere is the solid, rocky crust of the earth, extending to a depth of perhaps 25 mi. The hydrosphere is the layer of water which, in the form of the oceans, covers approximately 70.8 percent of the surface of the earth. The barysphere, sometimes called the centrosphere, is below the lithosphere. It is the heavy interior of the earth, comprising more than 99.6 percent of the earth's mass.

The rocks of the lithosphere have an average density of 2.7, and are almost entirely made up of eleven elements, which together account for about 99.5 percent of its mass. The most abundant is oxygen (about 46.60 percent of the total), followed by silicon (about 27.72 percent), aluminum (8.13 percent), iron (about 5 percent), calcium (3.63 percent), sodium (2.83 percent), potassium (2.59 percent), magnesium (2.09 percent), and titanium, hydrogen, and phosphorus (totaling less than 1 percent). In addition, eleven other elements are present in trace amounts of from $\frac{1}{10}$ of 1 percent to $\frac{1}{50}$ of 1 percent. These elements, in order of abundance, are carbon, manganese, sulfur, barium, chlorine, chromium, fluorine, zirconium, nickel, strontium, and vanadium. The elements are present in the lithosphere almost entirely in the form of compounds rather than in their free state. The most common compounds of the earth's crust are silicates and aluminosilicates of various metals.

The lithosphere is divided into two shells, each of which has a density that increases with depth. The innermost shell contains such rock types as basalt and gabbro and has an average density of about 3.0. The upper shell is made up of rocks of the granite type with a density of about 2.7. This lighter, granitic mass may be compared to a continent floating on a basaltic sea. The surface of the earth is largely covered with sedimentary rocks and soil.

The hydrosphere consists chiefly of the oceans, but technically includes all water surfaces in the world, including inland seas, lakes, rivers, and underground waters. The average depth of the oceans is 12,447 ft., more than five times the average height of the continents. The mass of the oceans is about 1,490,000,000,-000,000,000 (1.49 × 10^{18}) short tons, or 1/4400 of the total mass of the earth.

The barysphere is divided into an outer zone, called the mantle, and an inner zone, called the core. The mantle extends from the base of the lithosphere down to approximately 1800 mi. It is solid and has a density that increases with depth, varying from 3 to 6. According to current theory, the outer part of the mantle is composed of iron and magnesium silicates. The lower part probably consists of a mixture of magnesium, silicon, and iron oxides. Seismological research has shown that the core, which has a radius of some 2175 mi., lacks rigidity and probably is liquid, that is, it consists of molecules having free movement among themselves, but tending not to become widely separated. Some geophysicists believe it to be highly compressed molten iron.

Age of the Earth. A number of methods have been suggested for estimating the age of the earth. One such method involves comparing the thickness of sedimentary deposits with the rate of the deposition of sediment at the mouths of modern rivers. Another method is to assume that the seas were originally composed of fresh water and have become salty as a result of the salts carried to them by the rivers of the continents. It is possible, therefore, to calculate the age of the planet from the total salt in the seas in relation to the amount of salt that modern rivers carry annually. Both these methods are, however, subject to large errors because of the assumption that sediment deposition and salt content of the rivers have been constant throughout geologic history. Modern knowledge of radioactivity makes possible the absolute dating of certain rocks with considerable accuracy, as the distintegration of a radioactive element occurs at a rate which is independent of the chemical or physical environment. For example, uranium–238 decays to lead 206 at a rate which results in the reduction of one half of the uranium to lead in 7,600,000,000 years. Thus, by careful comparison of the amounts of these isotopes of uranium and lead present in a rock, one can determine the age of the rock. The oldest rocks so far studied are more than 3,500,000,000 years old. The maximum time required for the formation of all the elements in the crust of the earth has been determined to be about 5,500,000,000 years. The age of the earth, therefore, is probably between 3,500,000,000 and 5,500,000,000 years. *See* COSMOGONY; DEEP-SEA DRILLING; EARTHQUAKE; GEOLOGY, HISTORICAL; GEOPHYSICS; PLANET; SEISMOLOGY.   C.C.

EARTHENWARE. *See* POTTERY.

EARTH-MOVING MACHINES, equipment used in heavy construction, especially civil-engineering projects, which often require the moving of millions of cubic feet of earth. Earth-moving machines can be divided into two groups according to function. One group moves earth from one location to another; the other excavates earth. The removal of earth or material from the bottoms of bodies of water is performed by dredges; *see* DREDGING.

The primary earth-moving machine is the heavy-duty tractor (q.v.), which, when fitted with endless tracks to grip the ground and with a large, movable blade attached in front, is called a bulldozer (q.v.). Bulldozers are used to clear brush or debris, remove boulders, and level ground. A scraper is a machine that may be pulled by a tractor or may be self-powered. It consists of a blade and a box or container. Dirt is scraped by the blade into the container; the dirt may then be released so as to form an even layer of a predetermined thickness, or be carried off for disposal elsewhere. Scrapers are used to level and contour land, as in road con-

struction. Somewhat similar are graders, self-propelled, wheeled machines with a long, inclined, vertically adjustable steel blade. Graders are primarily finishing equipment; they level earth already moved into position by bulldozers and scrapers. Lightweight tractors fitted with wheels in place of tracks are used for comparatively light construction jobs. Equipped with a backhoe, which is an open scoop attached rigidly to a hinged boom, such a vehicle can dig shallow trenches; equipped with a front-end loader, a scoop-shovel affixed to the front of the tractor, it can lift and carry gravel, stone, sand, and other construction materials.

Draglines and power shovels are the primary excavation equipment. A dragline is fitted with an open scoop supported from the end of a long boom by a wire cable. The scoop is dragged along the ground by the cable until it is filled with earth, which is then dumped elsewhere. Draglines are used primarily to excavate deep holes. Power shovels are fitted with buckets called clamshells, which dig directly into the earth and shovel it up. The bottom of the clamshell opens to dump the dirt into a truck.

An electric stripping shovel, one of the largest earth-moving machines in the world, has a 180-cubic yard bucket or clamshell with a capacity of 270 tons.

National Coal Assn.

EARTHNUT, name applied to certain tubers (*see* TUBER) roots, or underground pods which are used as human or animal food. The peanut, *Arachis hypogaea,* is sometimes called an earthnut, as is the tuber of *Conopodium denudatum* of the Carrot family. The small edible tubers or earthnuts of the European sedge *Cyperus esculentus,* also known as chufa, or earth almonds, are edible and eagerly sought by hogs. The root of the heath pea (*Lathyrus tuberosus*), a European legume, bears small edible tubers or earthnuts which are used in Scotland to flavor whiskey.

EARTHQUAKE, vibration of the crustal layer of the earth (q.v.) that is tectonic or volcanic in origin; *see* GEOPHYSICS; VOLCANISM; VOLCANO. It was formerly believed that earthquakes were generally the result of volcanic activity, but modern research in geology (q.v.) suggests that such action is a relatively unimportant cause of major earthquakes. The lack of uniformity in the composition and structure of the crust of the earth, plus the action of gravity (*see* GRAVITATION) and other factors such as centrifugal force, set up tremendous stresses both on and below the surface of the earth. When such stresses become large enough, the crust breaks. The line of such a break is called a fault. The force released by such a break sets up a series of vibrations, or waves, in the body of the earth that travel outward from the fault. These waves may be so small that they are no more dangerous than the tremors caused by passing traffic or by a waterfall, or they may be so large, particularly in the immediate vicinity of the fault, that they have sufficient force to overthrow buildings.

The waves formed by an earthquake are of two kinds: primary waves, a series of rapid compressions and expansions that travel directly outward from the source of the quake; and secondary waves, slower vibrations, perpendicular to the direction of travel. The secondary waves rather than the primary cause earthquake damage. Although the waves are usually only a few inches in magnitude, their force is extremely great, and they can be observed and recorded many thousands of miles from their source.

The location of the first movement on the fault which causes an earthquake is known as the focus or the hypocenter of the quake. The focus is commonly below the surface of the earth. The point on the surface directly above the focus, the point from which the waves apparently radiate, is called the epicenter. In most cases earthquake waves radiate out from the epicenter elliptically rather than in perfect circles.

More than 1,000,000 earthquakes occur an-

nually in all parts of the world, but most of the more serious quakes are confined to two broad belts. One of these runs along the coastline of the Pacific Ocean from Chile in South America, northward along the western coast of the United States and Alaska, westward along the Aleutian Islands, and south through Japan and the Philippine Islands to Indonesia. The other belt runs eastward from Spain through the Mediterranean basin, Turkey, the Caucasus Mts., and the Himalaya to the Malayan Peninsula and Indonesia, at which it intersects the first belt. These regions are also the area of greatest volcanic activity. The earthquake belts, which are characterized by ranges of recently formed mountains (q.v.), are believed to be regions in which the crust of the earth is comparatively weak.

Many of the earthquakes that are recorded each year occur beneath the surface of the sea. A large undersea quake produces a series of huge water waves that travel across the surface of the ocean much as the secondary earthquake waves travel through the earth. These waves are usually called tidal waves, although they have no relation to the tides. They are more correctly known as seismic sea waves or by the Japanese name *tsunami.*

Seismology (q.v.), the study of earthquakes, is a comparatively new science. It has yielded much information about the interior structure of the earth. The chief instrument of seismological research is the seismograph (q.v.), a device for recording earthquake tremors. By timing the arrival of the primary and secondary waves at a seismograph station, it is possible to determine the distance of the epicenter of an earthquake from the station; and if the distances from three widely separated stations are known, the position of the epicenter then can be accurately located.

Earthquake Prediction. Since 1960 the Seismology Data Center of the U.S. Department of Commerce at Asheville, N.C., has been maintaining and analyzing, with the help of a computer, seismology recordings of earthquakes occurring throughout the world. About 300,000 seismograms are processed annually in the hope that patterns will emerge from the data that will enable seismologists to predict earthquakes.

At the present time seismologists believe that major earthquakes may be preceded by minute changes in the earth within the earthquake zone. It is probable that large earthquakes are preceded by much smaller earthquakes detectable only by sensitive instruments. Among other

Earthquake. Plate 1. *Above: A house in a residential area of Alaska sinks to one side during one of the most violent earthquakes of the 20th century, on Good Friday, March 27, 1964. Below: A business street of Anchorage is a scene of rubble and ruin after the quake that caused 131 deaths and property losses estimated at $500,000,000.*

Earthquake. Plate 2. *Scenes of destruction near Los Angeles, Calif., after a major earthquake, on Feb. 9, 1971, struck an area of some 30,000 sq.mi. Because the disaster occurred at 6 A.M., before the work day had begun, the death toll was low.*

predictable precursors of earthquakes suggested by U.S., Soviet, Chinese, and Japanese seismologists in the mid-1970's are (1) dilatancy, or swelling due to the expansion of small cracks in rocks where a rupture might occur, producing tilts, increased seismic velocities, electrical resistivity, small local tremors, and radon (q.v.) gas emission into groundwater; (2) the shattering of deep bedrock in fault zones and the flow of groundwater into the pore space, building up pressure, lubricating the fault, and triggering an earthquake; (3) the piezoelectric effect (see CRYSTAL: *Crystallography*) from clear-weather lightning producing stresses in underlying sandstones; (4) the jet stream in the upper atmosphere creating long, slow waves in the ground surface, triggering an incipient earthquake; (5) the so-called Jupiter effect, or the alignment of the planets, activating a chain of events in which increased sunspot activity might cause changes in the earth's atmospheric circulation and thus in the rotation of the earth, inducing stresses in the earth's crust; (6) the injection of volcanic dust into the atmosphere, reducing solar insolation at the surface; this phenomenon, together with minute climatic changes associated with zonal wind-circulation patterns, could affect the earth's rotation rate much as described in (5), creating similar stresses in the earth's crust and mantle; (7) a slight drop in the level of the sea before a coastal earthquake; and (8) a minute change in the magnetic field of the earth just before a large earthquake.

Devastating Earthquakes. Historical records of earthquakes prior to the middle of the 18th century are either lacking or unreliable. Such disasters were known in ancient times, but in most instances the reports available on them in the writings of such authors as the Greek philosopher Aristotle and the Roman rhetorician Seneca (qq.v.) are accompanied by irrational and unscientific explanations of the phenomena. Among the earthquakes of antiquity of which reasonably trustworthy records exist are that which occurred off the coast of Greece in 425 B.C., making Euboea an island; that which destroyed the city of Ephesus, Asia Minor, in the year 17 A.D.; that which leveled much of Pompeii in 63; and those which partially destroyed Rome in 476 and Constantinople in 557 and again in 936. In the Middle Ages severe quakes occurred in England (1318), Naples (1456), and Lisbon (1531).

The earthquake of 1556 in the Shensi Province of China, which is estimated to have cost 800,000 lives, is on record as one of the greatest natural disasters in history. One of the more no-

table earthquakes of the 17th century is that which took an estimated 60,000 lives on the island of Sicily in 1693. Early in the 18th century the Japanese city of Edo, on the site of the present Tokyo, was destroyed with the loss of some 200,000 lives. In 1755 the city of Lisbon, Portugal, was devastated: about 60,000 persons died; the shocks were felt in southern France and North Africa; and inland waters of Great Britain and Scandinavia were agitated. Quito, now the capital city of Ecuador, was shaken by an earthquake in 1797, and more than 40,000 people lost their lives. As a result of an earthquake that ravaged the present-day State of Kutch, India, in 1819, an area of 2000 sq.mi. sank below the level of the surrounding terrain and became the bed of an inland sea. The violent eruption of Krakatau (q.v.) in Sunda Strait in 1883 was accompanied by earthquakes and tidal waves that wreaked havoc in Java and other nearby islands, and killed 36,000 people. In 1886 the first major earthquake disaster to occur in the U.S. seriously damaged the city of Charleston, S.C., with some loss of life. An earthquake in Japan took 26,000 lives in 1896.

The U.S. suffered its second severe earthquake in 1906, when the city of San Francisco, and neighboring towns and villages, were severely damaged; this disaster caused a great conflagration and, by breaking water mains, prevented its control. As a result, about 700 persons perished and property valued at $350,000,000 was destroyed. Two years later a large area of southern Italy was ravaged, with the number of deaths amounting to about 100,000. Italy was again stricken in 1915, when almost 30,000 persons living in its central regions were killed. In the earthquake that struck Kansu, China, in 1920, the number of residents who lost their lives cannot be determined precisely, but it has been estimated at between 100,000 and 200,000. One of the most severe earthquakes ever recorded struck Tokyo, Japan, and its surrounding area in 1923, killing more than 200,000 persons. Continuing shocks, tidal waves, and fires destroyed property valued at $4,500,000,000. Kansu, China, suffered again in 1932, the death toll amounting to 70,000. In 1933 a large area of southern California was affected; 115 persons died and $50,000,000 worth of property was destroyed. Early in 1939 six provinces of central Chile were ravaged, 30,000 Chileans perished, 700,000 were left homeless, and property worth $30,000,000 was demolished. Near the end of the same year an area of approximately 15,000 sq.mi. in Anatolia, Turkey, was stricken by several consecutive earthquakes that, com-

263

bined with ensuing floods and heavy snow-storms, caused 45,000 deaths.

About 2000 persons were killed in Turkey by an earthquake in 1943. On Dec. 21, 1946, a severe shock hit the Japanese islands of Honshu, Shikoku, and Kyushu, causing disastrous tidal waves. More than 1000 persons were killed. An earthquake devastated the city of Fukui, Japan, late in June, 1948. Casualties totaled more than 10,500, including about 5000 dead. About 6000 persons were killed by an earthquake in central Ecuador in August, 1949. Property damage, estimated at $86,000,000, included four towns destroyed and more than 40 others severely damaged.

One of the severest earthquakes on record occurred in Assam, India, on Aug. 15, 1950. Casualties included about 2000 killed; property damage, extending over an area of 30,000 sq.mi., was virtually incalculable. On March 18, 1953, more than 1200 persons were killed by an earthquake in northwestern Turkey. A protracted series of earthquakes devastated the Ionian islands of Cephalonia, Zante, and Ithaca in August, 1953. Among the casualties were an estimated 1000 dead. Almost the entire population (118,000) of the islands was left homeless. Between Sept. 9 and 12, 1954, earthquakes killed more than 1650 persons and left an estimated 10,000 homeless in northern Algeria. About 2000 fatalities were recorded in earthquakes in Afghanistan between June 10 and 17, 1956. In July, 1957, 2500 persons died and 100,000 were injured or made homeless in an earthquake in northern Iran.

On Feb. 29 and March 1, 1960, two earthquakes, a tidal wave, and fire entirely destroyed the city of Agadir, Morocco; the death toll was estimated at about 12,000. In the following May and June earthquakes caused tidal waves and volcanic eruptions in southern Chile, desolating ten provinces and killing 5700. Property losses totaling hundreds of millions of dollars were reported and millions of people were made homeless. The worst earth tremors in Iran's history occurred on Sept. 1, 1962, killing an estimated 12,000 persons and destroying over 200 towns and villages in a 23,000 sq.mi. area. Four fifths of the city of Skopje (pop. in 1961, 165,529), Yugoslavia, was destroyed on July 26, 1963, in an earthquake that killed over 1000 residents and injured 3350.

One of the most violent earthquakes of the 20th century struck the State of Alaska on March 27, 1964, triggering tidal waves that wreaked havoc along 2000 mi. of the Pacific coast. Property losses totaling about $500,000,000 were re-ported in Alaska alone, but the 131 deaths were fewer than is usual for such quakes.

In May, 1970, an earthquake in Peru triggered a landslide that totally buried the mountain town of Yungay; also heavily damaged was the port city of Chimbote. An estimated 50,000 people were killed. In December, 1972, two thirds of Managua, the capital city of Nicaragua, was leveled by a quake that killed about 10,000 people. An earthquake in northern Pakistan in December, 1974, caused about 5000 deaths.

The worst earthquake of modern times struck northeast China in July, 1976. The quake, centered near the city of Tangshan, caused almost 2,000,000 casualties, of which over 600,000 were killed, and incalculable economic damage. A series of aftershocks drove millions more from their homes.   C.C.

EARTHWORM, name given to certain worms in the class Oligochaeta. They have cylindrically shaped, segmented bodies that project minute bristles called setae and that taper off at both ends. Although there is a difference in shading between the upper and under surfaces, and between different parts of the body, earthworms are in general uniform in color, usually flesh red, but varying from dull pink to dirty brown. Many species grow to a length of only a few inches, but some tropical species attain a length of up to 11 ft. Large specimens of the common American species are 8 to 12 in. long. In such specimens as many as 175 segments may be present, but 130 is the usual number.

Earthworms are mostly subterranean and, in order to survive, must live in moist soil containing organic matter. They are never encountered in deserts or in pure sands. They usually live in the upper layers of the soil, but during the winter they penetrate more deeply into the soil to escape frost. During unusually hot weather they also penetrate downward, in order to avoid dehydration. They shun daylight but frequently come to the surface of the soil during the night to feed and to throw off their castings. During the daytime they appear upon the surface of the soil only under unusual conditions, such as the flooding of their burrows by excessive rainfall. Earthworms are capable of burrowing with considerable speed, especially in loose soil, by thrusting their bluntly pointed heads between particles of earth and forcing them apart or by actually swallowing much of the opposing material and excreting it after passage through their bodies. In all their movements, the short but stiff bristles along the sides of the body are of great assistance.

In burrowing, earthworms swallow large

quantities of earth that often contains considerable amounts of vegetable remains. They are able to digest the nutritive matter of the soil, depositing or casting out the remains on the surface of the earth or in their burrows.

Structure. The muscular system of the earthworm consists of an outer series of circular or transverse muscle fibers that girdle the body, and an inner series of longitudinal muscle fibers forming five principal bands and several smaller ones. The latter are employed in moving the setae. The circulatory system is likewise well developed and consists of a prominent dorsal blood vessel and at least four ventral blood vessels, running longitudinally in the body and connected with each other by a regularly arranged series of transverse vessels. These transverse vessels form a network of capillaries in the wall of the intestine and in the muscles. The dorsal vessel is provided with valves and is the true heart. Most of the pumping of blood, however, is performed by general muscular movements. The central nervous system consists of a pair of suprapharyngeal ganglia, which is often called the brain, and a ventral cord that lies beneath the alimentary canal, bearing ganglia in every segment. Although earthworms can detect the presence of light, it is believed that they have no sense organs other than those of touch. The digestive system consists of a muscu-

An earthworm, Lumbricus terrestris, *emerges from its burrow. The clitellum, a thickened portion of the body wall, can be seen as a light-colored band.*
John H. Gerard – National Audubon Society

lar pharynx, a slender esophagus, a thin-walled crop or food receptacle, a muscular gizzard used for grinding ingested earth, and a long, straight intestine, terminating at the anus.

Earthworms are hermaphrodites, with each worm having both male and female reproductive organs (*see* REPRODUCTIVE SYSTEM). Mutual cross-fertilization probably always takes place. After the eggs, containing considerable yolk, have been laid, they are buried in the earth in capsules that serve to protect the young until they are well developed. These capsules are probably formed from the secretion of the clitellum, a thickened portion of the body wall between the 29th and 35th segments. In the common American earthworm *Lumbricus terrestris* only one egg develops into a worm with the other fertilized eggs acting as nurse eggs. When the young emerge, they are small, fully developed earthworms.

Classification. Earthworms are divided into five families: Lumbricidae, in North America, Europe, and northern Asia; Moniligastridae, inhabiting India, Ceylon, Malaya, and the eastern part of Africa; Megascolecidae, inhabiting India, Australasia, Africa, and South America; Eudrilidae, inhabiting central parts of Africa; and Glossoscolecidae, inhabiting South and Central America, Africa, and southern Europe. More than 1000 species of earthworms are known. Especially well known are *L. terrestris* and *Allobophora foetida,* widely distributed in temperate and tropical lands; *Megascolides australis,* inhabiting Australia and attaining the enormous length 11 ft.; and *Glossoscolex giganteus,* inhabiting South America.

The English naturalist Gilbert White (1720–93), in his *Natural History of Selborne* (1788), was the first to recognize the important role played by earthworms in the subsoil. By being continually loosened, stirred up, and aerated by the action of earthworms, soil is made more fertile. Earthworms also form a source of food for many animals, constituting the principal food of moles and shrews. They are the most frequently used bait for fishing in the United States, where they are commonly known as angleworms.

See ANNELIDA.

EARWIG, common name for the various nocturnal insects comprising the order Dermaptera. They are of world-wide distribution, and in the United States are frequently found in the southern States. They live under the decayed bark of trees, under stones, and in old straw, and feed chiefly upon flowers and ripe fruit. They are similar to the rove beetles in appearance, but are distinguished from them by pincerlike proc-

265

esses at the posterior ends of their abdomens. The earwig was so named because of the erroneous belief that it sometimes creeps into human ears. It is completely harmless to humans, but is known to be able to transmit virus diseases that affect plants. The name earwig is also applied in the U.S. to several small centipedes in the genus *Geophilus*.

EASEMENT, in law, a privilege of advantage without profit that the owner of a parcel of land may have in the lands of another. Among the various forms of easement are the right of access (*see* ACCESS, RIGHT OF), the right to maintain a line of telephone poles, rights of light and air, and drainage (q.v.). Perhaps the best illustration of an easement is that known as a "way of necessity", which exists when one buys premises that are shut off on all sides by intervening land from access to the highway.

EAST ANGLIA, kingdom founded by the Angles about the middle of the 6th century, in the E. part of central England, comprising the modern counties of Norfolk and Suffolk. Until formed into a Danish kingdom under Guthrum (also called Guthorm or Guttorm) in 878, East Anglia was independent under its own king.

EASTBOURNE, Great Britain, county borough and seaside resort of East Sussex, England, on the English Channel, about 50 miles S.S.E. of London. It is noted for its esplanade, and is the site of Eastbourne College, founded in 1867. Eastbourne was incorporated as a town in 1883, as a county borough in 1911, and became a parliamentary division in 1918. The town suffered heavily from German air raids in World War II. Pop. (1971) 70,495.

EAST CAPE *or* **CAPE DEZHNEV,** eastern extremity of Asia, in the Chukchi National Okrug of the Soviet Union. It is a rocky promontory opposite the Seward Peninsula. The only settlement, the village of Uelen, on the N. side of the cape, has a population of about 260.

EAST CHICAGO, city and lake port of Indiana, in Lake Co., on Lake Michigan, in the industrially important Calumet region, 17 miles S.E. of the center of Chicago, Ill., and 2 mi. E. of the Illinois-Indiana line. The city comprises three sections: East Chicago (the original town), Calumet, and Indiana Harbor. The last-named, which serves as the port, is connected with the Grand Calumet R. by the 3 mi.-long Indiana Harbor Canal. East Chicago is an important manufacturing center served by several major railroads. Large quantities of coal, iron ore, oil, limestone, and other materials are unloaded from lake steamers at the docks. Steel mills and foundries, metal and oil refineries, and chemical plants are located in the city. East Chicago also has meat-packing plants, railroad-equipment shops, and factories producing valves and other machinery, cement, gypsum, and wooden boxes. The park system includes a zoological garden. East Chicago was settled and incorporated as a village in 1885 and was chartered as a city in 1890. The city grew rapidly, its population increasing from 3411 in 1900 to 35,967 in 1920. Pop. (1960) 57,669; (1970) 46,982.

EAST CLEVELAND, city of Ohio, in Cuyahoga Co., 7 mi. by rail E. of Cleveland, of which it is a residential suburb. The city contains electrical-research laboratories and plants producing electrical appliances. East Cleveland is the site of the former summer estate of the American capitalist and philanthropist John D. Rockefeller, Sr. (*see under* ROCKEFELLER), which is now a part of the municipal park system of East Cleveland and is called Forest Hills Park. The city was settled in 1799, incorporated as a village in 1895, and chartered as a city in 1911. Pop. (1960) 37,991; (1970) 39,600.

EAST DETROIT, city and residential suburb of Michigan, in Macomb Co., adjoining Detroit and 9 miles N.E. of the downtown area. The center of a truck-farming and poultry-raising area, East Detroit manufactures auto and aircraft parts and other aluminum and steel products. Founded in 1827, it was incorporated in 1924 as the village of Halfway; four years later it adopted its present name. Pop. (1960) 45,756; (1970) 45,920.

EASTER, annual festival commemorating the resurrection of Jesus Christ, and the principal feast of the Christian year. It is celebrated on a Sunday on varying dates between March 22 and April 25, and is therefore called a movable feast. The dates of several other ecclesiastical festivals, extending over a period between Septuagesima Sunday (the ninth Sunday before Easter) and the first Sunday of Advent (q.v.), are fixed in relation to the date of Easter.

Connected with the observance of Easter are the forty-day penitential season of Lent (q.v.), beginning on Ash Wednesday (q.v.) and concluding at midnight on Holy Saturday, the day before Easter Sunday; Holy Week (q.v.), commencing on Palm Sunday (q.v.), including Good Friday (q.v.), the day of the crucifixion, and terminating with Holy Saturday; and the Octave of Easter, extending from Easter Sunday through the following Sunday. During the Octave of Easter in early Christian times, the newly baptized wore white garments, white being the liturgical color of Easter and signifying light, purity, and joy.

Pre-Christian Tradition. Easter, a Christian festival, embodies many pre-Christian traditions. The origin of its name is unknown. Scholars, however, accepting the derivation proposed by the 8th-century English scholar Saint Bede (q.v.), believe it probably comes from ĒASTRE, the Anglo-Saxon name of a Teutonic goddess of spring and fertility, to whom was dedicated a month corresponding to April. Her festival was celebrated on the day of the vernal equinox; traditions associated with the festival survive in the Easter rabbit, a symbol of fertility, and in colored Easter eggs, originally painted with gay hues to represent the sunlight of spring, and used in Easter-egg rolling contests or given as gifts.

Such festivals, and the myths and legends that explain their origin, were common in ancient

Easter is ushered in with a religious service held at dawn in the Hollywood Bowl in Los Angeles, Calif.
Shostal Associates

religions. A Greek myth tells of the return of Persephone, daughter of Demeter (qq.v.), goddess of the earth, from the underworld to the light of day; her return symbolized to the ancient Greeks the resurrection of life in the spring after the desolation of winter. Many ancient peoples shared similar legends. The Phrygians (*see* PHRYGIA) believed that their omnipotent deity went to sleep at the time of the winter solstice, and they performed ceremonies with music and dancing at the spring equinox to awaken him. The Christian festival of Easter probably embodies a number of converging traditions; most scholars emphasize the original relation of Easter to the Jewish festival of Passo-

Christian pilgrims march along the Via Dolorosa ("Road of Sorrow") in Jerusalem in a procession that celebrates Good Friday, the Friday before Easter. According to tradition, it was along this route, also known as the Way of the Cross, that Jesus was led from the place of his trial to his crucifixion on Golgotha. The original Via Dolorosa is now some 30 ft. below the surface.
Boyce M. Bennett, Jr.

At the Church of the Holy Sepulcher in Jerusalem, Archbishop Emaneos of Lydda performs the ritual of the washing of the feet on Holy Thursday, part of the Greek Orthodox ceremonies celebrating Holy Week. The feet of twelve persons are washed, in commemoration of Jesus' washing of the feet of his twelve disciples after he had shared the Last Supper with them in the "upper room" (Luke 13:4–16).

Louis Goldman–Rapho Guillmette

ver, or Pesach (q.v.), from which is derived Pasch, another name for Easter. The early Christians, many of whom were of Jewish origin, were brought up in the Hebrew tradition and regarded Easter as a new feature of the Passover festival, a commemoration of the advent of the Messiah (q.v.) as foretold by the prophets.

The Dating of Easter. On the eve of Passover Christ was crucified, and shortly afterward rose from the dead. In consequence, the Easter festival commemorated Christ's resurrection. In time, a serious difference over the date of the Easter festival arose among Christians. Those of Jewish origin celebrated the resurrection immediately following the Passover festival, which, according to their ancient lunar calendar borrowed from the Babylonians, fell on the evening of the full moon (the fourteenth day in the month of Nisan, the first month of the year); by their reckoning, Easter, from year to year, fell on different days of the week.

Christians of Gentile origin, however, wished to commemorate the resurrection on the first day of the week, Sunday; by their method, Easter occurred on the same day of the week, but from year to year it fell on different dates.

An important historic result of the difference in reckoning the date of Easter was that the Christian churches in the East, which were closer to the birthplace of the new religion and in which old traditions were strong, observed Easter according to the date of the Passover festival. The churches of the West, descendants of the Greco-Roman civilization, celebrated Easter on a Sunday.

Rulings of the Council of Nicaea on the Date of Easter. Constantine I (q.v.), Emperor of Rome, convoked in 325 A.D., the Council of Nicaea (see NICAEA, COUNCILS OF). The council unanimously ruled that the Easter festival should be celebrated throughout the Christian world on the first Sunday after the full moon following the vernal equinox; and that if the full moon should occur on a Sunday and thereby coincide with the Passover festival, Easter should be commemorated on the Sunday fol-

Easter. Plate 1. "Resurrection", by Dierik Bouts, a Dutch painter of the 15th century. In the background the meeting of the risen Jesus and Mary Magdalene is portrayed, as is the Ascension.

lowing. Coincidence of the feasts of Easter and Passover was thus avoided.

The Council of Nicaea also decided that the calendar date of Easter was to be calculated at the city of Alexandria, then the principal astronomical center of the world. The accurate determination of the date, however, proved to be an impossible task in view of the limited knowledge of the 4th-century world. The principal astronomical problem involved was the discrepancy, called the epact, between the solar year and the lunar year. The chief calendric problem was a gradually increasing discrepancy between the true astronomical year and the Julian calendar, then in use.

Later Dating Methods. Ways of fixing the date of the feast tried by the Church proved unsatisfactory, and Easter was celebrated on different dates in different parts of the world. In 387, for example, the dates of Easter in France and Egypt were thirty-five days apart. About 465, the Church adopted a system of calculation proposed by the astronomer Victorinus (fl. 5th cent.), who had been commissioned by Pope Hilarius (r. 461–68) to reform the calendar and fix the date of Easter. Elements of his method are still in use. Refusal of the British and Celtic Christian churches to adopt the proposed changes led to a bitter dispute between them and Rome in the 7th century.

Reform of the Julian calendar in 1582 by Pope Gregory XIII (see under GREGORY), through adoption of the Gregorian calendar, eliminated much of the difficulty in fixing the date of Easter and in arranging the ecclesiastical year; since 1752, when the Gregorian calendar was also adopted in Great Britain and Ireland, Easter has been celebrated on the same day in the western part of the Christian world. The Eastern churches, however, which did not adopt the Gregorian calendar, commemorate Easter on a Sunday either preceding or following the date observed in the West. Occasionally the dates coincide; the most recent times were in 1865 and 1963.

Because the Easter holiday affects a varied number of secular affairs in many countries, it has long been urged as a matter of convenience that the movable dates of the festival be either narrowed in range or replaced by a fixed date in the manner of Christmas. In 1923 the problem was referred to the Holy See, which has found no canonical objection to the proposed reform. In 1928 the British Parliament enacted a measure allowing the Church of England to commemorate Easter on the first Sunday after the second Saturday in April. Despite these steps toward re-

form, Easter continues to be a movable feast. See CALENDAR.

EASTER ISLAND (Sp. *Isla de Pascua*; nat. *Rapa Nui*), triangular-shaped island belonging to Chile, in the South Pacific Ocean, about 2350 miles w. of the Chilean coast. Several craters are reminders of the volcanic origin of the island. Swept by strong trade winds, the area is warm throughout the year, and potatoes, sugar cane, taro roots, tobacco, and tropical fruits are grown in the fertile soil. The prime source of fresh water is the rain that gathers in the crater lakes. In 1772 several thousand Polynesians (q.v.) inhabited the island, but disease and raids by slave traders have reduced the number to less than 200. Since the 19th century some intermarriage has taken place between the Polynesians and the Chileans.

Spanish geographers credit the Spanish explorer and mariner Álvaro de Mendaña de Neyra (1541–95) with the discovery of Easter Island in 1566. The island was named by a Dutch explorer who landed there on Easter Sunday in 1772. The Chilean government annexed the island in 1888. An area on the w. coast is reserved by the government for the native population; the remainder is used as grazing land for sheep and cattle. A school and two hospitals are maintained by the Chilean government.

Easter Island is of considerable archeological importance both as the richest site of the megaliths (see MEGALITHIC MONUMENTS) of the Pacific island groups, and as the only source of evidence of a form of writing in Polynesia.

Very little is known about the people who made the megaliths and carved the wooden tablets. One belief is that settlement of Easter Island took place about eighteen centuries ago, although some scholars contend that the settlement occurred more recently. Archeological and botanical evidence suggests that the original inhabitants were of South American origin. The ancestors of the present Polynesian population are thought to have traveled in canoes from the Marquesas Islands, massacred the inhabitants, and made the island their home. Many archeologists believe that at the time of the invasion the megaliths, including about 600 statues, were standing throughout the island, and that many were destroyed by the Polynesians during a period of violence on Easter Island.

Largest of the extant stone monuments are the great burial platforms, called ahus, which were used to support rows of statues. The ahus were situated on bluffs and in other positions commanding a view of the sea. Each ahu was constructed of neatly fitted stone blocks set

Easter Island is famed for its tall stone statues in human form, which stand on stone platforms called akus.
Björn Bölstad–Peter Arnold

without mortar, a form of masonry (q.v.) designated by the term cyclopean (*see* CYCLOPS). The burial platform usually supported four to six statues, although one ahu, known as Tongariki, carried fifteen statues. Within many of the ahus, vaults house individual or group burials.

About 100 statues still stand on the island; they vary in height from 10 to 40 ft. Carved from tuff, a soft volcanic rock, they consist of huge heads with elongated ears and noses. Material for the statues was quarried from the crater called Rano Raraku, where modern explorers found an immense unfinished statue, almost 70 ft. long. Many of the statues on the burial platforms bore cylindrical, brimmed crowns of red tuff; the largest crown weighs approximately 30 tons.

Recent excavations have disclosed hidden caves containing decayed remains of tablets and wooden images, and numerous small wooden sculptures. The tablets are covered with finely carved and stylized figures, which seem to be a form of picture writing. Scholars believe that a tablet was inverted after the reading of each line, because the symbols in any line appear to be upside down in relation to the next line. To date, no one has been able to translate any of the tablets, and no satisfactory method of interpreting the symbols has been found. Area of the island, about 45 sq.mi.

EASTERN CHURCH, general term for the various ancient Christian communions of the Middle East and Eastern Europe. *See also* BYZANTINE EMPIRE. **1.** The earliest decisive split in Christendom took place in 451 as a result of the Council of Chalcedon (*see* CHALCEDON), which was called to consider the claims of the Monophysites (q.v.). The churches that rejected the statement of faith adopted by the council are the Armenian Church (q.v.), the Coptic Church of Alexandria (*see* COPTS), the Ethiopian Church, the Syrian Church, and the Syrian Church in India. Sometimes known as the Oriental Orthodox, these churches include today more than 22,000,000 members. **2.** The Orthodox Church (q.v.) is that in communion with the ecumenical patriarchate of Constantinople (İstanbul, Turkey). **3.** A third group of churches are those known collectively as the Churches of the Eastern Rite (*see* EASTERN RITE, CHURCHES OF THE). They recognize the authority of the Roman Catholic Church (q.v.). J.M.

EASTERN EMPIRE. *See* BYZANTINE EMPIRE.

EASTERN QUESTION. *See* EUROPE: *History: Post-Renaissance Imperialism: Bismarck.*

EASTERN RITE, CHURCHES OF THE, term designating several bodies of Eastern Christians,

271

or Uniates, now considered part of the Roman Catholic Church (q.v.). These bodies, including Greeks, Ukrainians, Russians, Copts, Armenians, Maronites, and Syrians, originally belonged to the Orthodox Church (q.v.), or espoused but have now renounced the heretical teachings of the Greek prelate Eutyches (378–455?) and of the Nestorians (q.v.). Although they accept the authority of the pope at Rome and agree with the Roman Catholic Church on matters of faith, they differ on various points of discipline, such as the procedure during the communion service, the marriage of priests, and the choice of liturgical language; see LITURGY. Leavened bread is permitted in the consecration; both bread and wine instead of merely bread may be distributed by the Uniates in communion. Before becoming deacons, priests are allowed to marry (except in the Eastern-rite dioceses of America, where priestly celibacy is required). Rather than Latin, the liturgical languages of the churches of the Eastern Rite are either those spoken by the original missionary founders or the present-day vernacular.   J.M.

EASTERN STAR, ORDER OF THE, international fraternal and benevolent society, composed of affiliated Masons and their close female relatives. The organization promotes charitable activities and distributes large sums of money for cancer research and other worthy projects. Although the actual origin of the society is not known, it is said to have been introduced into the United States in 1850 by Dr. Robert (Rob) Morris (1818–88), who wrote the first ritual in 1850. The General Grand Chapter, organized in November, 1876, has jurisdiction over all the grand chapters in the U.S., Canada, and Puerto Rico, except for the States of New York and New Jersey, which have independent grand chapters. Coldwater Chapter No. 1, Coldwater, Mich., is the first and oldest chapter. The order has about 14,000 chapters throughout the world; total membership in 1969 was about 3,000,000. The national headquarters are located in Washington, D.C. See also FREEMASONS.

EASTER REBELLION, armed uprising of Irish patriots against the rule of Great Britain in Ireland, launched on Easter Monday, April 24, 1916, and centered mainly in Dublin. The chief objectives were the attainment of political freedom and the establishment of an Irish republic. Centuries of discontent, marked by numerous rebellions, preceded the uprising. The new crisis began to develop when, in September, 1914, following the outbreak of World War I, the British government suspended the recently enacted Home Rule Bill, which guaranteed a measure of political autonomy to Ireland. Suspension of the bill stimulated the growth of the Citizen Army, an illegal force of Dublin citizens organized by the labor leader Jim Larkin (d. 1916) and the Socialist James Connolly (1870–1916); the Irish Volunteers, a national defense body; and the extremist Sinn Fein (q.v.). The uprising was planned by the leaders of these organizations, among whom were the British consular agent Sir Roger David Casement (q.v.), the educator Padhraic Pearse (1879–1916), and the poet Thomas MacDonagh (1878–1916).

Hostilities began about noon on April 24, when about 2000 men led by Pearse seized control of the Dublin post office and other strategic points within the city. Shortly after winning these initial successes, the leaders of the rebellion proclaimed the independence of Ireland and announced the establishment of a provisional government of the Irish Republic. Additional positions were occupied by the rebels during the night and, by the morning of April 25, they controlled a considerable part of Dublin. The counteroffensive by British forces began on Tuesday with the arrival of reinforcements. Martial law was proclaimed throughout Ireland. Bitter street fighting developed in Dublin, with the strengthened British forces steadily driving the Irish from their positions. By the morning of April 29, the post-office building, site of rebel headquarters, was under violent attack. Recognizing the futility of further resistance, Pearse surrendered unconditionally in the afternoon of April 29.

The British immediately brought the leaders of the uprising to trial before a field court-martial. Fifteen of the group, including Pearse, Connolly, and MacDonagh, were sentenced to death and executed by shooting. Four others, including the American-born Eamon de Valera (q.v.) received death sentences which were later commuted to life imprisonment, although de Valera and some others were granted amnesty the next year. Casement was convicted of treason and hanged. Many others prominently connected with the rebellion were sentenced to long prison terms. The uprising was the first of a series of events that culminated in the establishment in 1937 of the independent state of Eire. Casualties were about 440 British troops and an undetermined number of Irishmen. Property damaged included the destruction of about 200 buildings in Dublin. See IRELAND, REPUBLIC OF: History.

EAST GERMANY. See GERMANY.
EAST HARTFORD. See HARTFORD.
EAST HAVEN. See NEW HAVEN.

EAST INDIA COMPANY, any of a number of commercial enterprises formed in western Europe during the 17th and 18th centuries to further trade with the East Indies. The companies, which had varying degrees of governmental support, grew out of the associations of merchant adventurers who voyaged to the East Indies following the discovery in 1498 of the Cape of Good Hope route by the Portuguese navigator Vasco da Gama (q.v.). The most important of the companies were given charters by their respective governments, authorizing them to acquire territory wherever they were able and to exercise in the acquired territory various functions of government, including legislation, the issuance of currency, the negotiation of treaties, the waging of war, and the administration of justice. Historically, the most notable companies were the following.

Danish East India Company. Chartered in 1729 by Frederick IV, King of Denmark (*see under* FREDERICK), after unsuccessful attempts by Denmark to gain a share of the East India trade in 1616 and 1634, it enjoyed great prosperity in India until the advance of British power there in the late 18th century. As a consequence of the destruction of Danish naval power in the war between Great Britain and Denmark in 1801, the power of the Danish company was broken. Its principal Indian possessions, Tranquebar in Madras (now Tamil Nadu) and Serampore in Bengal, were purchased by Great Britain in 1845.

Dutch East India Company. Incorporated from a number of smaller companies by the States-General of the Netherlands in 1602, its monopoly extended from the Cape of Good Hope eastward to the Strait of Magellan, with sovereign rights in whatever territory it might acquire. In 1619 Jan Pieterszoon Coen (1587–1629), regarded as the founder of the Dutch colonial empire in the East Indies, established the city of Batavia, the present Djakarta, in Java, as the headquarters of the company. From Batavia, Dutch influence and activity spread throughout the Malay Archipelago and to China, Japan, India, Persia, and the Cape of Good Hope. During the course of the sixty-year war between Spain and the Netherlands (1605–65), the Dutch company despoiled Portugal, which was united with Spain from 1580 to 1640, of all its East Indian possessions. It supplanted the Portuguese in most of present-day Indonesia, and in the Malay peninsula, Malacca, Ceylon, the Malabar Coast of India, and Japan. During this period it was also successful in driving English rivals from the Malay Archipelago and the Moluccas. In 1632 the Dutch killed the English factors, or

agents, in Amboina, capital of the Dutch Moluccas; for this act the English government later exacted compensation. In 1652 the company established on the Cape of Good Hope the first European settlement in South Africa. At the peak of its power, in 1669, the Dutch company had 40 warships, 150 merchant ships, and 10,000 soldiers. Between 1602 and 1696 the annual dividends that the company paid were never less than 12 percent and were sometimes as high as 63 percent. The charter of the company was renewed every twenty years, in return for financial concessions to the Dutch government. In the 18th century, internal disorders, the growth of British and French power, and the consequences of a harsh policy toward the native inhabitants caused the decline of the Dutch company. It was unable to pay a dividend after 1724, and survived only by exacting levies from native populations. It was powerless to resist a British attack on its possessions in 1780, and in 1795 it was doomed by the ouster of the States-General at home by the French-puppet Batavian Republic. In 1798 the republic took over the possessions and debts of the company.

English East India Company. The most important of the various East India companies, this company was a major factor in the history of India for more than 200 years. The original charter was granted by Elizabeth I (q.v.), Queen of England, on Dec. 31, 1600, under the title of "The Governor and Company of Merchants of London Trading into the East Indies". The company was granted a monopoly of trade in Asia, Africa, and America, with the formal restriction that it might not contest the prior trading rights of "any Christian prince". The company was managed by a governor and twenty-four directors chosen from its stockholders. In early voyages it penetrated as far as Japan, and in 1610 and 1611 its first factories, or trading posts, were established in India in the provinces of Madras and Bombay. Under a perpetual charter granted in 1609 by James I (q.v.), King of England, the company began to compete with the Dutch trading monopoly in the East Indian Archipelago, but after the massacre of Amboina (see *Dutch East India Company,* above) the company conceded to the Dutch the area that became known as the Netherlands East Indies. Its armed merchantmen, however, continued sea warfare with Dutch, French, and Portuguese competitors. In 1650 and 1655 the company absorbed rival companies which had been incorporated under the Commonwealth and Protectorate by the Lord Protector Oliver Cromwell (*see under* CROMWELL). In 1657 Cromwell ordered it reorganized as the sole joint-stock company with rights to the Indian trade. During the reign of Charles II (q.v.), King of England, the company acquired sovereign rights in addition to its trading privileges. In 1689, with the establishment of administrative districts called presidencies in the Indian provinces of Bengal, Madras, and Bombay, the company began its long rule in India. It was continually harassed by traders who were not members of the company and were not licensed by the crown to trade. In 1698, under a Parliamentary ruling in favor of free trade, these private newcomers were able to set up a new company, called the New Company or English Company. The East India Company, however, bought control of this new company, and in 1702 an act of Parliament amalgamated the two as "The United Company of Merchants of England Trading to the East Indies". The charter was renewed several times in the 18th century, each time with financial concessions to the crown. The victories of Robert Clive (q.v.), a company official, over the French at Arcot in 1751 and at Plassey in 1757 made the company the dominant power in India. All formidable European rivalry vanished with the defeat of the French at Pondicherry in 1761. In 1773 the British government established a governor-generalship in India, thereby greatly decreasing administrative control by the company; however, its governor of Bengal, Warren Hastings (q.v.), became the first governor-general of India. In 1784 the India Act created a department of the British government to exercise political, military, and financial control over the Indian affairs of the company. In 1813 its monopoly of the Indian trade was abolished and in 1833 it lost its China-trade monopoly. Its annual dividends of 10.5 percent were made a fixed charge on Indian revenues. The company continued its administrative functions until the Indian Mutiny (q.v.) of 1857–58. In 1858, by the Act for the Better Government of India, the crown assumed all governmental responsibilities held by the company, and its 24,000-man military force was incorporated into the British Army. The company was dissolved on Jan. 1, 1874, when the East India Stock Dividend Redemption Act came into effect.

French East India Company (*La Compagnie des Indes Orientales*). Established in 1664 by Jean Baptiste Colbert (q.v.), finance minister of Louis XIV (q.v.), King of France. The company founded its first trading post at Surat in Bombay, India, in 1675. In 1676 it set up its principal Indian base at Pondicherry, on the Coromandel Coast. The company prospered and extended its operations to China and Persia. In 1719 the company was reorganized with the American and African French colonial companies as the Compagnie des Indes. This company, headed by the Scottish financier John Law (q.v.), suffered severely with the collapse of the Mississippi Scheme. In 1730 it lost its slave trade with Africa, in 1731 its general trade with Louisiana, and in 1736 its coffee trade with the Americas. However, the company prospered in India under the governors Benoît Dumas, from 1735 to 1741, and the Marquis Joseph François Dupleix (q.v.) from 1742 to 1754, with Dupleix directing the unsuccessful French struggles against the British control of India. The capture of Arcot in 1751 by the British soldier Robert Clive limited French control to southern India, where it remained supreme until 1761, when the British captured the French base of Pondicherry. The operations of the company were finally suspended by royal decree in 1769, and in the following year it turned over its capital of more than 500,000,000 livres to the crown. In 1785 a new company received commercial privileges, but it was abolished in 1794 during the French Revolution.

EAST INDIES, name formerly applied to the southeastern part of Asia, embracing the entire area of geographic India, the Indochinese peninsula, and the Malay Archipelago. The name "East Indies" is now applied to the Malay Archipelago alone. *See* INDONESIA, REPUBLIC OF.

EASTLAKE, residential city of Ohio (incorporated in 1947), in Lake Co., on Lake Erie, about 19 miles N.E. of central Cleveland. Pop. (1960) 12,467; (1970) 19,690.

EASTLAKE, Sir Charles Lock (1793–1865), British painter and authority on art, born in Plymouth, England. He studied with the British historical painter Benjamin Robert Haydon (1786–1846), and later at the Royal Academy in London. Eastlake first attracted wide attention by his two full-length portraits (1816) of Napoleon I (q.v.), Emperor of France. He executed these from sketches that he drew in a small boat while the British ship *Bellerophon,* on which Napoleon was a prisoner, was in Plymouth harbor. Eastlake became a member of the Royal Academy in 1830, following a fourteen-year stay in Rome. He became an arbiter of Victorian taste; he was in charge of the National Gallery in London from 1843 to 1847 and served as its first director from 1855 until his death. In 1850 he was elected president of the Royal Academy and also was knighted. He is noted for his pictures of Italian banditti and for historical and religious pantings, including "Pilgrims in Sight of Rome" (1828), "Christ Blessing Little

Children" (1829), and "Christ Weeping over Jerusalem" (1841). Among his writings on art are *Materials for a History of Oil Painting* (1847) and *Contributions to the Literature of the Fine Arts* (1848 and 1870).

EAST LANSING, city of Michigan, in Ingham Co., 87 miles N.W. of Detroit and 3 miles E. of Lansing, of which it is a residential suburb. Michigan State University, founded in 1855 as the first land-grant college in the United States, is located in the city; see LAND-GRANT COLLEGES. East Lansing was settled in 1849 and was incorporated as a city in 1907. Pop. (1960) 30,198; (1970) 47,540.

EAST LIVERPOOL, city of Ohio, in Columbiana Co., on the Ohio R., about 80 miles S.E. of Cleveland, and 44 miles N.W. of Pittsburgh, Pa. Bridges connect the city with Chester and Newell, in the panhandle of West Virginia. Factories in East Liverpool, one of the leading pottery centers in the United States, produce semivitreous porcelain ware, electrical porcelain, pottery supplies, floor tile, and clay novelties. Other industries are the manufacture of sewer pipe, drawn steel, building brick, firebrick, barrels, and paper products. The pottery industry is an outgrowth of a kiln established in 1839 by the British potter James Bennett. At that time, only yellowware was produced. Whiteware production commenced in 1872, and semivitreous china was first manufactured around 1890. With the exception of the yellow clay, which is dug in the vicinity, the raw materials are imported from England, and from Florida, North Carolina, and Kentucky. Settled in 1798 as Fawcettstown, East Liverpool was incorporated under its present name in 1834. Pop. (1960) 22,306; (1970) 20,020.

EAST LONDON, city and seaport of the Republic of South Africa, in Cape of Good Hope Province, on the E. coast of the Indian Ocean, at the mouth of the Buffalo R., about 475 miles S. of Johannesburg. A railway terminus, East London is the marketing and distributing center for the E. part of the province and is a major wool-shipping port. Important industries include food processing, automobile assembly, and the manufacture of furniture, footwear, pharmaceuticals, and textiles. East London is a popular resort city, with a pleasant temperature, fine beaches, and an esplanade extending along the waterfront. The city is the site of an art gallery, a zoo, and an aquarium. The first known specimen of a coelacanth (q.v.), a fish thought to have been extinct for several million years, was caught near East London in 1938 and is housed in the city museum. In 1847 the town was used as a British garrison and base during a war between the British and area natives; in 1848 the city was annexed to the Cape colony. Pop. (1970 prelim.) 118,298.

EAST LOS ANGELES, unincorporated suburban area of California, in Los Angeles Co., adjoining the city of Los Angeles and 4 miles E. of the downtown area. It is the site of East Los Angeles College (1945), a unit of the Los Angeles Junior College District. Pop. (1970) 105,033.

EAST LOTHIAN *or* **HADDINGTON,** Great Britain, maritime county of S.E. Scotland, bounded on the N. by the Firth of Forth and on the N.E. by the North Sea. In the southern part of East Lothian are the Lammermuir Hills (q.v.). The chief river of the county is the Tyne. Agriculture is important economically, with oats, barley, wheat, potatoes, and turnips the chief crops. Sheep are raised in the vicinity of the Lammermuirs, and fish and lobsters are caught off the North Sea coast. Coal and iron ore are mined and fireclay is quarried in the region. The principal industries are brewing and distilling and the manufacture of agricultural implements, textiles, pottery, bricks, and salt. Celts were early inhabitants of the region, and many ancient Celtic relics have been discovered. Roman relics also have been unearthed in East Lothian, notable among which are 700 oz. of Roman silverware dating from the 4th century A.D. East Lothian was part of the Saxon Kingdom of Northumbria (q.v.) until 1018, when Malcolm II Mackenneth, King of Scotland (d. 1034), incorporated it into Scotland. John Knox (q.v.), the religious reformer, was born in Haddington, the county town. Other towns, all of comparable population, are Tranent, a coal-mining center; Dunbar, a summer resort and the site in 1650 of a military victory by the English soldier and statesman Oliver Cromwell (*see under* CROMWELL); and North Berwick, noted for its beaches and golf links. Area, 267 sq.mi.; pop. (1971 est.) 56,153.

EASTMAN, George (1854–1932), American inventor and philanthropist, born in Waterville, N.Y. Eastman, who was self-educated, played a leading role in transforming photography from an expensive hobby of a few devotees into a relatively inexpensive and immensely widespread popular pastime. In 1884 he patented a roll film, the first film in roll form to prove practicable; in 1888 he perfected the "Kodak" camera, the first ever designed specifically for roll film. In 1892 he established the Eastman Kodak Company, at Rochester, N.Y., one of the first firms to manufacture standardized photography equipment on a mass-production basis. This company also manufactured the flexible transparent film, devised by Eastman in 1889, which proved vital to the subsequent development of the motion-picture industry. Eastman was associated with this company in an administrative and executive capacity until his death, and contributed much to the development of its notable research facilities. He was also one of the outstanding philanthropists of his time, donating more than $75,000,000 to various projects. Notable among his contributions were a gift of $19,500,000 to the Massachusetts Institute of Technology, and endowments of $4,500,000 and $4,000,000 for the establishment, respectively, of the Eastman School of Music in 1918 and a school of medicine and dentistry in 1921 at the University of Rochester.

See PHOTOGRAPHY: *Historical Development: 19th Century.*

EASTMAN, Max (Forrester) (1883–1969), American writer and editor, born in Canandaigua, N.Y., and educated at Williams College and Columbia University. In 1913, in association with a group of writers and artists, he founded the revolutionary periodical *The Masses,* which he edited until 1918, when it was suppressed by the government for opposing the entry of the United States into World War I. Eastman later founded and edited a similar publication, *The Liberator* (1918–22). On a visit to the Soviet Union (1922–24), he came to know many of the Soviet leaders, but he also became an opponent of the oppressive Soviet regime. His critical

works include *Enjoyment of Poetry* (1913), *The Literary Mind* (1932), and *Enjoyment of Laughter* (1936). Among his books on political science is *Since Lenin Died* (1925), which made public the previously suppressed testament of the Bolshevik leader Vladimir Ilich Lenin (q.v.) urging that Joseph Stalin (q.v.), then general secretary of the Communist Party, not be permitted to succeed Lenin as chairman of the party. Other works by Eastman include *Stalin's Russia and the Crisis in Socialism* (1939), *Marxism: Is It Science?* (1940), and *Reflections on the Failure of Socialism* (1955). He was the translator of *History of the Russian Revolution* (3 vol., 1932) and *The Revolution Betrayed* (1937), written by the Russian revolutionist Leon Trotsky (q.v.). Eastman wrote two autobiographical works, *Enjoyment of Living* (1948) and *Love and Revolution: My Journey Through an Epoch* (1965).

EASTON, city in Pennsylvania, and county seat of Northampton Co., at the junction of the Delaware and Lehigh rivers, about 55 miles N. of Philadelphia, and opposite Phillipsburg, N.J., with which it is connected by two automobile and two railway bridges. The city is served by five railroads and lies in a rich agricultural, mining, and quarrying region. Easton is an important printing center as well as a center for the manufacture of textiles, chemicals, paper products, cement and slate, electrical equipment, and iron and steel products.

Lafayette College (q.v.) is located in Easton. Notable buildings in the city include a church which was the site, in 1777, of a treaty between the Americans and the Iroquois Indians, whereby the latter agreed to remain neutral during the American Revolution. A stone house, dating from 1757, was the home of George Taylor (1716–81), one of the signers of the Declaration of Independence. A monument marks the site of the first courthouse in Northampton County, constructed in 1765 on a tract presented by the family of William Penn (q.v.) for an annual rental of one red rose.

The site of Easton was first settled in 1739, but the town was not founded until 1752, when the land was acquired from the Indians by Thomas Penn (1702–75) and John Penn (1729–95), son and grandson respectively of William Penn. The town was incorporated as a borough in 1789, and as a city in 1887. Pop. (1960) 31,955; (1970) 30,256.

EAST ORANGE. See ORANGES, THE.

EAST PATERSON, former name of ELMWOOD PARK, industrial borough of N.E. New Jersey, in Bergen Co., on the Passaic R. near Paterson. Manufactures include cement pipes, leather

Max Eastman   Editta Sherman

goods, cosmetics, and plastic, metal, and paper products. Pop. (1960) 19,344; (1970) 20,511.

EAST POINT, city of Georgia, in Fulton Co., 6 miles s.w. of Atlanta, of which it is a residential suburb. East Point has lumber, paper, textile, and cottonseed-oil mills, and food-processing and chemical plants. The city was incorporated in 1887. Pop. (1960) 35,633; (1970) 39,315.

EASTPORT, city and port of entry of Maine, in Washington Co., on Moose Island in Passamaquoddy Bay, 90 miles E. of Bangor, connected with the mainland by a bridge. It is the most easterly city in the United States. The city, which is noted for having the coolest summer climate on the east coast of the U.S., is a vacation resort and the gateway to a hunting and fishing area. The leading industries of Eastport are fishing, sardine and blueberry canning, and the manufacture of shoes, boxes, and artificial pearls. Eastport was settled in 1782 and became a port of entry in 1790. Following the Embargo Act (q.v.) of 1807, it was a notorious smuggling center. In 1814, during the War of 1812 (q.v.), Eastport was captured by the British, who held the town until 1818, when it was returned to the U.S. in accordance with the terms of the Treaty of Ghent; *see* GHENT, TREATY OF. Eastport was chartered as a city in 1893. Pop. (1960) 2537; (1970) 1989.

EAST PROVIDENCE. *See* PROVIDENCE.

EAST PRUSSIA, easternmost province of the former kingdom and State of Prussia (q.v.), divided after World War II between Poland and the Soviet Union. The capital was Königsberg (now Kaliningrad, U.S.S.R.).

EAST RIDGE, city of Tennessee, in Hamilton Co., about 5 miles S.E. of Chattanooga, of which it is a suburb. East Ridge, situated near the Georgia State line, was incorporated in 1921. Pop. (1960) 19,570; (1970) 21,799.

EAST RIDING. *See* YORKSHIRE.

EAST RIVER, strait connecting Long Island Sound and upper New York Bay, and separating Manhattan Island from Long Island. It is connected by the Harlem R. and Spuyten Duyvil Creek with the Hudson R. On its w. bank are the boroughs of Manhattan and the Bronx, and on its E. bank are those of Brooklyn and Queens. The East R. is 15 mi. long and ranges from ½ mi. to 3½ mi. in width. Its principal islands are Roosevelt, Ward's, Randall's, Riker's, and North Brother, all containing New York City institutions. The rapids of Hell Gate, between Ward's Island and Long Island, have been made navigable by blasting out the rock shoals. The Brooklyn, Manhattan, Williamsburg, Queensboro, Triborough, Hell Gate, Bronx-Whitestone, and Throgs Neck bridges span the river. Crossing under it are the Queens-Midtown and Brooklyn-Battery automobile tunnels, several rapid-transit and private-utility tunnels, and a railroad tunnel.

EAST ROCKAWAY, village of New York, in Nassau Co., on Long Island, about 5 miles s. of Hempstead, and about 18 miles S.E. of New York City. Primarily a residential community, the village is a resort and has light manufacturing. Pop. (1960) 10,721; (1970) 10,373.

EAST SAINT LOUIS, city of Illinois, in Saint Clair Co., on the E. bank of the Mississippi R., opposite Saint Louis, Mo., with which it is connected by three bridges, including the Eads Bridge, a famous early steel-arch structure built (1867–74) by the American engineer James Buchanan Eads (q.v.). The city is an important railway, manufacturing, and meat-packing center. A number of railroads serve the city, and the East St. Louis stockyards are among the most important in the United States. The city also contains iron and steel foundries, smelters, machine shops, oil refineries, rubber-reclaiming and chemical plants, railroad-equipment shops, and factories manufacturing zinc and aluminum products, electronic equipment, bottles, paint pigments, pipeline valves, roofing, brick, and building tile. East St. Louis is the site of Parks College of Aeronautical Technology of St. Louis University. In the vicinity of the city is Cahokia Mounds State Park, which contains many Indian mounds, one of which, the Cahokia, or Monk's Mound, is the largest aboriginal earthen structure in the U.S., measuring 1000 ft. in length, 720 ft. in width, and 100 ft. in height. East St. Louis was settled as Illinoisville about 1808, and was chartered as East St. Louis in 1865. Pop. (1960) 81,712; (1970) 69,996.

EATON, Margaret, known as PEGGY O'NEILL (1796–1879), wife of John Henry Eaton (1790–1856), secretary of war in the cabinet of President Andrew Jackson (q.v.). She was born Margaret O'Neale or Margaret O'Neill, the daughter of a Washington tavernkeeper, and was noted for her beauty and wit. About 1823 she married a United States Navy purser named John B. Timberlake, who died in 1828, while on duty in the Mediterranean. In 1829 she married Eaton, who in the same year became secretary of war. Because of rumors regarding her relations with Eaton while she was still Mrs. Timberlake, Mrs. Eaton was ostracized by the wives of other cabinet members and by Washington society in general. President Jackson, an old friend of the Eatons, endeavored to break down the opposition to her, and it was partly for this reason that he replaced certain men in his cabinet. Among Mrs. Eaton's supporters was Martin Van Buren (q.v.), who thereafter became more closely associated with Jackson; Van Buren was assured of the nomination for the Presidency in 1836 in preference to the former Vice-President John C. Calhoun (q.v.), whose wife had opposed Mrs. Eaton. In later years, while her husband was minister to Spain, Mrs. Eaton was popular in the society of Madrid. Some time after the death of Eaton she married an Italian dancing master, then about twenty years old, from whom she was subsequently divorced.

EATON, Theophilus. *See* CONNECTICUT: *History;* DAVENPORT, JOHN; NEW HAVEN.

EATONTOWN, borough of New Jersey, in Monmouth Co., about 4 miles w. of Long Branch. Manufactures in the borough include precision instruments. Nearby are Monmouth Park, a racetrack, and Fort Monmouth, an army base. Pop. (1960) 10,334; (1970) 14,619.

EAU CLAIRE (Fr., "Clear Water"), city in Wisconsin, and county seat of Eau Claire Co., at the confluence of the Chippewa and Eau Claire rivers, about 160 miles N.W. of Madison, and 85 miles E. of Saint Paul, Minn. The surrounding area is noted for dairying and lumbering. Eau Claire is the commercial center of N.W. Wisconsin. Served by railroad, it is at the head of navigation on the Chippewa R. The city contains creameries, machine shops, packing houses, pickling works, paper mills, and factories manufacturing refrigerators, railroad equipment, aluminum ware, and tires and inner

tubes. Eau Claire is the site of a State teachers college and of two county hospitals. The city was settled about 1848 and grew rapidly between 1870 and 1880 with the development of the lumber industry. It was chartered as a city in 1872. Pop. (1960) 37,987; (1970) 44,619.

EBAN, Abba Solomon (1915–), Israeli statesman, born in Cape Town, Union of South Africa, and educated at the University of Cambridge, England, from which he received an M.A. degree in 1938. Eban served in the British army from 1939 until 1944, when he became an instructor at the Middle East Center for Arabic Studies of the British Foreign Office. Eban's association with the United Nations began in 1946 when he acted as U.N. liaison officer for the Jewish Agency for Palestine. He served as U.N. ambassador from the provisional as well as the permanent government of Israel, from 1948 to 1959. In 1950 he received an additional appointment, Israeli ambassador to the United States. In 1959 Eban was elected to the Knesset (parliament). Minister of education and culture in 1960–63 and deputy prime minister in 1963–66, Eban served as foreign minister in 1966–74. He wrote *My People: The Story of the Jews* (1968) and *My Country* (1972).

EBBINGHAUS, Hermann (1850–1909), German psychologist, born in Barmen (now part of Wuppertal), and educated at the universities of Bonn, Halle, and Berlin. He taught at the universities of Berlin, Breslau (now Wrocław, Poland), and Halle. A pioneer in the field of experimental psychology, Ebbinghaus performed important experiments on the value of repetition in memory, using nonsense syllables which he invented. He also devised the Ebbinghaus completion method tests for measuring the intelligence of children. He is the author of *Über das Gedächtnis* (1885; Eng. trans., *Memory: A Contribution to Experimental Psychology*, 1913).

EBENEZER (Heb., "the stone of help"), in the Old Testament, the name of a place marked by a monumental stone set up by the prophet Samuel (q.v.) in recognition of the divine assistance received by the Israelites in a battle with the Philistines (1 Sam. 7:10-12).

Earlier, the Israelites and the Philistines had fought two battles at another site, also called Ebenezer (1 Sam. 4:1-11). The Israelites were defeated, and in the second battle the Ark of the Covenant (q.v.) was captured. This site may have been N.E. of modern Jaffa (q.v.). *See also* PHILISTINES.

EBERS, Georg Moritz (1837–98), German Egyptologist and novelist, born in Berlin, and educated at the universities of Göttingen, Ber-

Abba Eban addressing the United Nations General Assembly. **United Nations**

lin, and Jena. In 1865 he became a lecturer on Egyptology at the University of Jena, and in 1870 moved to Leipzig, where he was professor at the university from 1870 to 1889. Between 1869 and 1873 he traveled twice to Egypt, and on the second journey found the famous hieratic medical papyrus which bears his name and which he edited in 1874. It is now in the library of the University of Leipzig. His first important scientific work was *Egypt and the Books of Moses* (1867–68). In addition to scientific works on Egyptology, Ebers wrote historical novels with an Egyptian setting, in an attempt to popularize Egyptian studies. His most successful novel was *An Egyptian Princess* (3 vol., 1864).

EBERT, Friedrich (1871–1925), German socialist political leader, born in Heidelberg. He was the first president of the post-World War I German Republic ("Weimar Republic"). Ebert learned the saddler's trade. He joined the Social Democratic Party, becoming a member of its central committee in 1905. He was elected to the Reichstag in 1912 and a year later became the recognized leader of his party. During World War I he led the majority wing of the Social Democratic Party in the Reichstag in supporting a policy of national defense. He favored a negotiated peace and opposed the creation of a republic in Germany, supporting instead a liberalized monarchy. In October, 1918, he induced his party to support and participate in the new government that had the German statesman Prince Max of Baden (1867–1929) as its chancellor. However, the desire of the people for an end to the war and the abolition of the monarchy manifested itself by mutiny in the navy and by strikes led by the radical Spartacists, headed by Karl Liebknecht and Rosa Luxemburg (qq.v.). Ebert and his party then pressed for the immediate abdication of William II (q.v.), Emperor of Germany. On Nov. 9, 1918, Prince Max turned the government over to Ebert, and on the following day William II went to Holland. As chancellor, Ebert was successful in putting down the Spartacist revolts. He was elected president of the new republic by the parliament assembled at Weimar in February, 1919. In 1920 Ebert faced an insurrection headed by the German monarchist Wolfgang Kapp (1858–1922). The Kapp Putsch was suppressed with the aid of the workers, called out on a general strike; but a new crisis arose when many of the workers refused to return to their jobs, demanding various governmental reforms and more severe punishment of the Kappists than had been meted out by Ebert's government. The attempt to maintain the general strike was put down by force, in the

course of which a number of workers were killed. In 1922 the Reichstag extended Ebert's term as president to 1925. In 1923 he suppressed an attempt by Adolf Hitler and General Erich Ludendorff (qq.v.) to establish a dictatorship in Bavaria.

See also GERMANY: *History: The Weimar Republic.*

EBIONITES (Heb. *ebyōn*, "poor"), name applied in the 2nd and 3rd centuries to a group of Jewish Christians who retained much of Judaism in their beliefs. The sect is supposed to have originated when the old church of Jerusalem was dispersed by an edict of the Roman Emperor Hadrian (q.v.) in 135 A.D.; some of the Jewish Christians migrated westward across the Jordan R. into Peraea (now in Jordan), cutting themselves off from the main body of the Christian Church. They adopted a conservative Pharisaic creed (*see* PHARISEES) at first, but after the 2nd century, some of these Judaistic Christians espoused a mixture of Essenism (*see* ESSENES), Gnosticism, and Christianity (qq.v.). According to the 2nd-century Christian prelate and writer Irenaeus (q.v.), they differed from orthodox Christians in denying the divinity of Christ and in considering Paul (q.v.) an apostate for having declared the supremacy of Christian teaching over the Mosaic law (*see* PENTATEUCH; TORAH). The 3rd-century Christian writer and theologian Origen (q.v.) classified the Ebionites in two groups, those who believed in the Virgin Birth and those who rejected it. Both the Sabbath (q.v.) and the Christian Lord's Day were holy to them, and they expected the establishment of a Messianic kingdom in Jerusalem. Until the 5th century, remnants of the sect were known to have existed in Palestine and Syria.

EBONY, hard, heavy, and dark-colored heartwood of various species of trees belonging to the genus *Diospyros*. The wood is highly prized for cabinetmaking and other types of woodwork. The best quality is black, takes a high polish, and is obtained from *D. ebenum,* a large tree of India, Ceylon, and other tropical countries. Logs of this species of ebony are often found in which the heartwood is 2 ft. in diameter and 10 to 15 ft. in length. Cadoobergia wood, which has a striped appearance, also comes from *D. ebenum.* Ebony of good quality is obtained in the East Indies from *D. melanoxylon.* The heartwood of *D. tomentosa,* which grows in northern Bengal, also yields good-quality ebony. Calamander wood comes from *D. hirsuta.* The American species, *D. virginiana* and *D. texana,* supply a fairly good quality of ebony which is chiefly used as a veneer.

Many imitations of ebony are current. Green ebony, also called Jamaica or American ebony, comes from a leguminous tree *Byra ebenus*. Its hard, dark-brown heartwood takes a high polish. Several other leguminous trees also share the name ebony, notably *Ebenus cretica*, which yields the red or brown ebony of Crete. German ebony is simply stained yew wood. Bastard ebony is produced by the tropical tree *Jacaranda ovalifolia*, of the family Bignoniaceae, and is exported from Brazil.

EBRO (anc. *Iberus* or *Hiberus*), river of N.E. Spain, rising in the Cantabrian Mts. in Santander Province, and emptying into the Mediterranean Sea (q.v.) after a southeasterly course of about 465 mi. The Ebro is the only major river of Spain which flows into the Mediterranean. Its principal tributaries are the Ega, Aragón, Arba, Gallego, and Segre, from the N., and the Jalón, Huerva, Aguas, Martín, Guadalope, and Mataraña, from the S. The Ebro is important to irrigation, and drains an area of almost 32,000 sq.mi. Ocean-going vessels are able to ascend the river only to the city of Tortosa, a distance of about 20 mi.

During the Spanish Civil War (1936–39), the Ebro was of tactical importance to the Republican government. Late in July, 1938, Spanish Loyalists started an offensive alongside the river which halted the progress of the army of General Francisco Franco (q.v.) for the rest of the year. *See* SPAIN: *History.*

EÇA DE QUEIROZ, José Maria (1845–1900), Portuguese novelist, born in Póvoa de Varzim, and educated at the University of Coimbra. He entered the consular service in 1872, and after serving successively in Havana, Cuba, and in Newcastle-on-Tyne and Bristol, England, he was appointed in 1888 to a post in Paris, where he remained until his death. His early work showed the influence of French naturalism, but he later developed an individual style that was a mixture of fantasy and reality. He instituted a revolutionary development in Portuguese prose and was the founder of the realist school of Portuguese writers. His works include *The Mystery of the Cintra Road* (with Ramalho Ortigão, 1870), *The Crime of Father Amaro* (1875), *Cousin Basil* (1878), *The Maisas* (1880), *The City and the Mountains* (1901), and *Contos* (1902). *See* PORTUGUESE LITERATURE.

ÉCARTÉ, card game, originating in France in the 19th century, played by two players with a deck from which all cards from the deuce to the six have been removed. The cards rank, in descending order, K, Q, J, A, 10, 9, 8, 7. Five cards are dealt to each player in two rounds, one of three and one of two cards, and the eleventh card is turned up to indicate trumps. If it is a king, the dealer scores one; if the king of trumps is in either hand, the holder scores one, providing he announces it before playing his first card. If the nondealer is not satisfied with his hand, he may propose to discard. The dealer may either accept or refuse. If he accepts, each player discards as many cards as he pleases, an equivalent number of cards being dealt from the stock. After taking the new cards, the nondealer may propose again, and the dealer may again accept or refuse. On refusal of the dealer, or on completion of the discard and redeal, the hand is played. The nondealer leads the first card. The highest card of the suit led wins the trick, except that trumps win over other suits. The second player must follow suit and is required to take the trick if he can, and with a trump card, if he is out of the suit led. The trick-winner leads after each succeeding trick. In scoring, three tricks count one point; five tricks count two. If the nondealer plays without proposing, and fails to make three tricks, or if the dealer refuses the first proposal and fails to make three tricks, the opponent scores two points. The game is five points.

See CARDS, PLAYING: *Card Games.*

ECCLES, Sir John Carew (1903–), Australian physiologist, born in Melbourne, and educated at the universities of Melbourne and Oxford. Eccles was director of the Kanematsu Memorial Institute of Pathology in Sydney, Australia, from 1937 to 1944. He taught physiology at the University of Otago, Dunedin, New Zealand, from 1944 to 1951 and at the Australian National University, Canberra, from 1951 to 1966. From 1966 to 1968 he was a member of the American Medical Association Institute for Biomedical Research, Chicago, and in 1968 he joined the faculty of the College at Buffalo of the State University of New York. Eccles shared the 1963 Nobel Prize in medicine and physiology with the British biophysicists Alan Lloyd Hodgkin (q.v.) and Andrew Fielding Huxley (*see under* HUXLEY) for their work in neurophysiology. Eccles was cited for his explanation of the transmission of signals from one nerve cell to the next along a nerve fiber. He was knighted in 1958.

ECCLESIASTES, book of the Old Testament (*see* BIBLE), in the King James Version, ECCLESIASTES, OR THE PREACHER. The English name is derived from a Greek term, roughly defined as "one who participates in or addresses an assembly", which appears in the title verse of the book in the earliest important Greek version of the Old

Testament, the Septuagint (see BIBLE: *Manuscripts, Versions, Editions, and Translations*). The Greek term is a rendering of a Hebrew proper noun, *Qoheleth,* the precise meaning of which is not clear. Because *Qoheleth* identifies himself as "the son of David, king in Jerusalem" (1:1), by implication the book has been traditionally ascribed to the Israelite King Solomon (q.v.).

Ecclesiastes consists of twelve chapters containing a series of generally pessimistic reflections on the purpose and nature of life. The conclusion, stated at the very beginning of the work, is that "all is vanity" (1:2). Pursue wisdom and wealth, cultivate pleasure, labor faithfully, deplore injustice and wickedness; the end is always the same, "vanity and vexation of spirit" (4:4). The coupling of this recurrent theme with assumptions that natural phenomena are cyclic (1:4–7, 3:1–8), and even preordained (3:15), leads the author to hedonistic, cynical doctrines (8:15–9:10, 12:1–8) so antithetical to the spirit of the earlier Old Testament books that the rabbis originally sought to suppress the book. Its popularity and its ascription to Solomon, however, eventually secured Ecclesiastes a place in the third section, the Writings, of the Hebrew canon (see BIBLE, CANON OF THE).

Modern scholarship now attributes the book to the 3rd century B.C., at a time when the Jews were being subjected to the influence of various Greek philosophic systems, such as Epicureanism and Stoicism (qq.v.). Ecclesiastes is part of the Wisdom literature of the Old Testament (see BIBLE: *The Old Testament*), which includes the books of Job and Proverbs (qq.v.).

ECCLESIASTICAL COURTS, tribunals exercising jurisdiction in religious matters. In its broadest sense, the term ecclesiastical court is applied to any former or existing tribunal established by religious authority. In a more restricted sense, it is applied only to the tribunals of the Christian Church, which are also sometimes called Courts Christian and are now found in the Roman Catholic Church (q.v.) and in many Protestant churches, as well as in the Church of England (q.v.) and other Anglican churches. Included are the bodies established by some United States Protestant denominations to legislate with respect to church policy and administration, and to exercise church discipline.

The Courts Christian originated among the Christian brethren, under the Romans, prior to the adoption of Christianity by Constantine I (q.v.), Emperor of Rome, in the 4th century A.D. The Christians, as a persecuted sect, had no access to the Roman courts; Roman courts, moreover, were pagan and were proscribed by Christian leaders on religious and moral grounds. The Christians therefore needed their own courts, which were simple tribunals whose chief function was the arbitration of disputes among the brethren, with bishops acting as the arbitrators.

After Christianity became the state religion of Rome, the ecclesiastical courts were incorporated into the Roman judicial system. The Christian Church developed on a pontifical and hierarchical basis and its power grew; the simple courts of primitive Christianity underwent a corresponding development. In time they comprised a complex system exercising jurisdiction delegated by the pope in his capacity as the supreme judicial power in the Christian Church. Then, as the secular power of Rome declined and its institutions decayed, the ecclesiastical courts began to assume jurisdiction in secular affairs.

In the Middle Ages (q.v.), the Church reached the zenith of its power: it became a world state, the popes became temporal potentates, and canon law (q.v.) and the jurisdiction of the ecclesiastical courts were extended to embrace virtually the entire range of human relationships. Extension of the jurisdiction of the ecclesiastical courts was facilitated by the dual character of the princes of the Church, as functioning ecclesiastics, that is, bishops, archbishops, cardinals, and popes; and as powerful landowners and temporal rulers. When courts established by secular authority resisted the incursions of the ecclesiastical courts into their jurisdictions, the ecclesiastical courts fought persistently for supremacy. The protracted struggle that ensued shaped much of the legal history of the latter Middle Ages. Beginning in the 13th century, the great judicial power of the Church was manifested especially through the tribunal commonly called the Holy Office, created to ferret out and punish heresy; see INQUISITION, THE.

The Reformation (q.v.) was a basic cause of the decline of the ecclesiastical courts. Other causes included the rise of representative government, the separation of judicial from executive and legislative powers of government, and the separation of church and state. All these factors combined to reduce gradually the power and jurisdiction of ecclesiastical courts to their present limited extent.

A remnant of the former extensive jurisdiction of the ecclesiastical courts survives in the three papal tribunals, the Sacred Penitentiaria, Sacred Roman Rota, and Apostolic Signatura, which comprise the judicial branch of the

Roman Curia. In Great Britain, which has an established church, the ecclesiastical courts derive their authority nominally from the crown; the principal tribunals are called Archdeacon's Court, Bishop's or Consistory Court, Chancery Court of York, Court of Arches, and Final Appeal Court, the latter comprising the Judicial Committee of the Privy Council. In the Protestant sections of Germany, and in the Netherlands, Switzerland, and other countries where Protestantism is nonepiscopal, ecclesiastical courts have virtually ceased to exist. See also HIGH COMMISSION, COURT OF.

ECCLESIASTICAL HISTORY. See CHRISTIAN CHURCH, HISTORY OF THE.

ECCLESIASTICAL LAW. See CANON LAW.

ECCLESIASTICAL YEAR. See CHRONOLOGY; EASTER; SAINT.

ECCLESIASTICUS (Lat., "ecclesiastical", meaning "of the church"), book of the Old Testament Apocrypha (see BIBLE: The Apocrypha), in the King James Version, THE WISDOM OF JESUS THE SON OF SIRACH, OR ECCLESIASTICUS. The book was written some time between 195 and 171 B.C. by Jesus the son of Sirach (Heb. Joshua ben Sira). The author is thought to have been a scholar who taught wisdom in an academy in Jerusalem. He is the only author of an apocryphal book to have attached his own name to his work (50:27). About 130 B.C., a Greek translation was made from the Hebrew original by a person who claimed in an added preface (ever since part of the book) to be a grandson of the author. Because of the great popularity earned by the book, it was translated subsequently into numerous other languages; the Greek text, however, is the only one to have survived in its entirety.

Ecclesiasticus mainly consists of a series of loosely related maxims and other sayings of a proverbial nature, much in the manner of the book of Proverbs (q.v.). Throughout, the author offers instruction on how to conduct oneself wisely in all areas of life. He identifies wisdom with the divine law (24:23), but his counsels are more concerned with ethics (q.v.) than they are with divine revelation. In addition to its numerous, diverse instructions, Ecclesiasticus contains several long poems that celebrate wisdom (1:1–20, 24:1–22), praise God and His wonderful works (42:15–43:33), and praise the venerable patriarchs and prophets of Israel (chapters 44–49). Ecclesiasticus is similar in spirit to the Wisdom literature of the Old Testament (see BIBLE: The Old Testament), such as the books of Ecclesiastes, Job (qq.v.), and Proverbs. Some scholars regard it as the final outstanding specimen of that form of literature and the first example of

the kind of Jewish thought developed subsequently by the Pharisaic and Sadducean schools (see JUDAISM; PHARISEES, SADDUCEES).

Although highly regarded by early Jewish commentators, who often cited it, Ecclesiasticus was excluded from the Hebrew canon (see BIBLE, CANON OF THE). The rabbis who closed the canon felt that the period of divine inspiration had ended soon after the time of the Hebrew priest and reformer Ezra (q.v.); thus, Ecclesiasticus, which clearly was written long after Ezra's time, could not have been divinely inspired. Early Christians, however, accepted it along with several other books regarded as spurious by the Jews. Since then, both the Orthodox Church (q.v.) and the Roman Catholic Church have decreed it to be canonical (see DEUTEROCANONICAL BOOKS), and Protestants, following the German religious reformer Martin Luther (q.v.), have rejected it as Apocryphal.

ECHEGARAY Y EIZAGUIRRE, José (1832–1916), Spanish playwright and statesman, born in Madrid. He was a professor of mathematics and physics at the Madrid engineering school from 1854 to 1868. From 1868 to 1874 he served in several Spanish cabinets as minister of commerce, education, and finance, serving as finance minister again in 1905. He first began writing plays in 1874 and wrote more than sixty dramas in prose and verse. In 1904 Echegaray shared the Nobel Prize in literature with the Provençal poet Frédéric Mistral (q.v.). Plays by Echegaray include O Locura o Santidad (1876; Eng. trans., Madman or Saint, 1912), El Gran Galeoto (1881; produced in the United States as The World and His Wife, 1908), and Mariana (1892).

ECHIDNA, also called PORCUPINE ANTEATER, name applied to two of the three existing genera of the order Monotremata, or egg-laying mammals. The species Tachyglossus aculeatus, found in Australia, is about 12 to 18 in. long, exclusive of a short tail, and has a broad body mounted upon short, strong legs. The legs have powerful claws, adapting the animal for rapid digging into hard ground. The back is covered with stiff spines, mixed with long, coarse hairs. The head is small, and the nose is prolonged into a slender snout. The toothless mouth has an extensile, glutinous tongue suitable for catching ants and other small insects. Mating occurs once a year. The female lays one egg, or rarely two eggs, after a gestation period of 27 to 28 days. The female then places the egg in a pouchlike area of abdominal skin, where it hatches after about two weeks. The offspring is carried in the pouch until it becomes able to walk. The echidna of Tasmania, *T. setosus,* is similar to *T. aculeatus* but is somewhat larger. The echidna of New Guinea, commonly known as the *spiny anteater,* is of a related but distinct genus, *Zaglossus.* It has a long, curved beak and grows as long as 30 in. In locations where ants and termites are abundant, the smaller echidnas make excellent pets, being long-lived and, despite their bristly coat, gentle in disposition.

See MONOTREMES.

ECHINODERMATA, phylum of marine animals, typified by starfishes, having a symmetrical and more or less hard external skeleton. Most adult echinoderms have an apparent radial symmetry, being divided into five equal rays or arms. Even within a single family, some species have soft, leathery body walls and others have firm, almost immovable so-called shells. This diversity is due mainly to variation in the amount of mineral matter deposited in the body wall. The body walls are often covered with knobs, tubercles, or spines. Echinoderms have well-developed alimentary canals, suspended in and distinct from the general body cavity and provided with both mouth and anus. A combined respiratory and locomotory system of complicated structure, called the water-vascular system, occurs only in the members of this phylum. It consists of a ring vessel about the mouth, from which a number of tubes radiate to what are known as *ambulacral areas,* one in each ray. The tubes are connected to the tube feet, which are extensible, saclike tentacles or suckers that project from the surface of the body through pores in the plates. In some cases the tube feet assist in conveying food to the mouth. The nervous systems, blood-vascular systems, and reproductive systems of echinoderms are well developed. The sexes are separate. The eggs, when hatched, produce bilaterally symmetrical, freeswimming larvae, which differ somewhat in form in the different classes. Three types of larvae have been distinguished among the various species, and have been given the names auricularia, bipinnaria, and pluteus.

About 3000 living species of echinoderms are known. They are found in all the seas on the globe and at all depths, but are most abundant in the warm seas of the tropics. Echinodermata include the classes Asteroidea starfish; Crinoidea, sea lily; Echinoidea, sea urchin; Holothurioidea, sea cucumber; Ophiuroidea, brittle star; and the extinct Blastoidea and Cystoidea. *See* BRITTLE STAR: CRINOIDEA; ECHINOIDEA; HOLOTHURIOIDEA; STARFISH.

ECHINOIDEA, class of marine animals in the phylum Echinodermata (q.v.), consisting of the sea urchins and other somewhat similar species. They have unattached, disk-shaped shells and movable spines. Scattered over the surfaces of sea urchins are microscopic, buttonlike bodies called *sphaeridia,* which are thought to be organs of balance. Sea urchins also have a complicated chewing apparatus called Aristotle's lantern, consisting of five converging jaws and accessory ossicles, or small bonelike parts. Echinoids feed on various types of organic matter, including plants, small animals, and waste material. Some species are occasionally used as food. The class Echinoidea comprises the orders Cidaroida, Centrechinoida, and Exocycloida. The Cidaroida are primitive sea urchins without gills about the mouth; Centrechinoida are sea urchins having gills around the mouth; and Exocycloida are sand dollars (q.v.), many of which are flattened and show both radial and bilateral symmetry.

ECHO. *See* ACOUSTICS; SOUND: *Refraction, Reflection, and Interference.*

ECHO, in Greek mythology, a nymph who loved the handsome youth Narcissus (q.v.).

ECK, Johann, (1486–1543), German theologian and outstanding opponent of the Reformation (q.v.), born Johann Mayer in Eck (now Egg), and educated at the universities of Heidelberg; Tübingen, Cologne, and Freiburg im Breisgau. In 1510 he became professor of theology at Ingolstadt, where he remained for thirty years. He had already acquired recognition as the defender of the established order when, in 1517, Martin Luther (q.v.), the German inaugurator of the Reformation, sent him copies of his 95 theses. In the following year Eck circulated his

Echidna, Tachyglossus aculeatus

Obelesci ("Obelisks"), attacking Luther. These were answered by the German religious reformer Karlstadt (q.v.), who challenged Eck to a public disputation that took place at Leipzig, Germany, in June and July, 1519. Eck first disputed with Karlstadt about grace and free will (qq.v.), defending the Roman Catholic viewpoint with great ability. He then contended with Luther about the primacy of the pope, penance, purgatory (qq.v.), and indulgences and pressed the charge of Hussite heresy against the reformer; *see* HERESY; HUSSITES; INDULGENCE. Although the arbitrators tendered no verdict, public opinion gave the victory to Eck. In 1520 he went to Rome, then returned as papal legate (q.v.) to enforce the papal bull of June 15, (*see* BULL, PAPAL), which condemned Luther as a heretic. The bull was unpopular, and Eck continued the struggle against the Reformation and defended Catholicism at the Augsburg Diet in 1530 (*see* AUGSBURG CONFESSION) and the religious conferences at Worms (q.v.) in 1540 and Ratisbon (now Regensburg) in 1541. His most important work was *De Primatu Petri* ("On the Primacy of Peter", 1519). His polemics against Luther are collected in *Operum Johannis Eckii contra Lutherum* (5 vol., 1530–35).

ECKENER, Hugo (1868–1954), German airship designer and navigator, born in Flensburg. After studying economics at the universities of Munich, Berlin, and Leipzig, he took up the study of the construction and navigation of zeppelins in 1908. He became an instructor in naval aviation during World War I, and in 1920 became a director of the Zeppelin Company, of which he later became part owner and president. He made flights by dirigible to the United States from Germany as commander of the *ZR3* in 1924, and again in 1928 as commander of the *Graf Zeppelin,* which he had built. He repeated his trips to the U.S. several times and in 1929 arranged for a round-the-world cruise which was successfully completed. His work for the development of air transportation by dirigible was nullified when the *Hindenburg,* of which Eckener was in command, crashed and burned at Lakehurst, N.J., on May 6, 1937. See AIRSHIP.

ECKERMANN, Johann Peter (1792–1854), German writer, born in Winsen, and educated at the University of Göttingen. Eckermann met the German poet and dramatist Johann Wolfgang von Goethe (q.v.) in 1823 and became his close friend. He aided Goethe in preparing the final edition of his works; he also edited writings of Goethe that were published posthumously. In collaboration with the German literary scholar Friedrich Wilhelm Riemer (1774–

1845), Eckermann brought out a complete edition of Goethe in forty volumes (1839–40). Eckermann is best known for his *Gespräche mit Goethe* (3 vol., 1836–48; Eng. trans., *Conversations with Goethe,* 1839).

ECLECTICISM (Gr. *eklegein,* "to pick out"), in philosophy, the formulation of a system of thought by choosing from the doctrines of other, already developed systems. The eclectic philosopher combines what he regards as the most plausible doctrines, although often these doctrines do not make an integral unity.

Eclecticism manifested itself to a great extent among the Greeks, beginning about the 2nd century B.C. This period was marked by a loss of the vigor of the spirit of intellectual inquiry which had motivated the great Greek philosophers, such as Plato and Aristotle (qq.v.), to develop unified cosmologies in their search for truth. The later Greek philosophers, such as Antiochus of Ascalon (1st century B.C.), who combined Stoicism and Skepticism (qq.v.), and Panaetius (2nd century B.C.), who based his thought on Stoicism and Platonism, adopted the doctrines that pleased them most. Roman thinkers, who never developed an independent philosophic system, were notably eclectic; Marcus Tullius Cicero (q.v.), for example, combined elements of Stoicism, the Peripatetic philosophy (q.v.), and Skepticism in his philosophical works, without regard for their essential disunity.

Among the early Christian philosophers, Clement of Alexandria (150?–220? A.D.) and Origen (q.v.) developed their works by selecting elements of Greek metaphysics and combining them with Hebrew thought expressed in the Old and New Testaments. Later, Johannes Eckhart (1260?–1327?), a German theologian and mystic, formulated a system of Christian philosophy based on the Greek philosopher Aristotle and his medieval Arabic commentators, on Neoplatonism (q.v.), and Hebrew doctrine.

The modern school of eclectic philosophy arose in France during the 19th century; its most distinguished figure was Victor Cousin (q.v.), who tried to unite the idealism of the German philosopher Immanuel Kant (q.v.) with the philosophy of Common Sense and the inductive doctrines of the French philosopher and mathematician René Descartes (q.v.).

ECLIPSE, in astronomy, the obscuring of one celestial body by another, particularly that of the sun or a planetary satellite. Two kinds of eclipses involve the earth: those of the moon, or lunar eclipses; and those of the sun, or solar eclipses; *see* MOON; SUN. A lunar eclipse occurs

 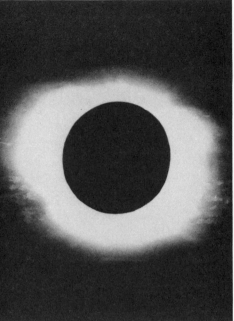

Scientists studied the total eclipse of the sun in June, 1973, from a ship off the coast of Mauritania, West Africa. In the photograph (left) the moon is observed only seconds before it totally eclipsed the sun (right) for 5 min. 32 sec., one of the longest eclipses in history.
Wide World

when the earth is between the sun and the moon, and its shadow darkens the moon. A solar eclipse occurs when the moon is between the sun and the earth, and its shadow moves across the face of the earth. Transits and occultations are similar astronomical phenomena, but are not as spectacular as eclipses because of the small size of these bodies as seen from earth; see TRANSIT.

Lunar Eclipses. The earth, lit by the sun, casts a long, conical shadow in space. At any point within that cone the light of the sun is wholly obscured. Surrounding the shadow cone, also called the umbra, is an area of partial shadow called the penumbra. The approximate mean length of the umbra is 857,000 mi.; at a distance of 239,000 mi., the mean distance of the moon from the earth, it has a diameter of about 5700 mi.

A total lunar eclipse occurs when the moon passes completely into the umbra. If it moves directly through the center, it is obscured for about two hours. If it does not pass through the center, the period of totality is less and may last for only an instant if the moon travels through the very edge of the umbra.

A partial lunar eclipse occurs when only a part of the moon enters the umbra and is obscured. The extent of a partial eclipse can range from near totality, when most of the moon is obscured, to a slight or minor eclipse, when only a

small portion of the earth's shadow is seen on the passing moon. Historically, the view of the earth's circular shadow advancing across the face of the moon was the first indication of the shape of the earth.

Before the moon enters the umbra in either total or partial eclipse, it is within the penumbra and the surface becomes visibly darker. The portion that enters the umbra seems almost black, but during a total eclipse, the lunar disk is not completely dark; it is faintly illuminated with a red light refracted by the earth's atmosphere, which filters out the blue rays. Occasionally a lunar eclipse occurs when the earth is covered with a heavy layer of clouds which prevent light refraction; the surface of the moon is invisible during totality.

Solar Eclipses. The length of the moon's umbra varies from 228,000 to 236,000 mi., and the distance between the earth and the moon varies from 222,000 to 253,000 mi. Total solar eclipses occur when the moon's umbra reaches the earth. The diameter of the umbra is never greater than 167 mi. where it touches the surface of the earth, so that the area in which a total solar eclipse is visible is never wider than

285

The corona during a total solar eclipse. UPI

167 mi. and is usually considerably narrower. The width of the penumbra shadow, or the area of partial eclipse on the surface of the earth, is about 3000 mi. At certain times when the moon passes between the earth and the sun, its shadow does not reach the earth. At such times an annular eclipse occurs in which an annulus or bright ring of the solar disk appears around the black disk of the moon.

The shadow of the moon moves across the surface of the earth in an easterly direction. Because the earth is also rotating eastward, the speed of the moon shadow across the earth is equal to the speed of the moon traveling along its orbit, minus the speed of the earth's rotation. The speed of the shadow at the equator is about 1060 m.p.h.; near the poles, where the speed of rotation is virtually zero, it is about 2100 m.p.h. The totality path of a solar eclipse and the time of totality can be calculated from the size of the moon's shadow and from its speed. The maximum duration of a total solar eclipse is about 7.5 min., but these are rare, occurring only once in several thousand years. A total eclipse is usually visible for about 3 min. from a point in the center of the path of totality.

In areas outside the band swept by the moon's umbra but within the penumbra, the sun is only partly obscured and a partial eclipse occurs.

At the beginning of a total eclipse, the moon begins to move across the solar disk about an hour before totality. The illumination from the sun gradually decreases and during totality (and near totality) declines to the intensity of bright moonlight. This residual light is caused largely by the sun's corona, or the outermost part of the sun's atmosphere. As the surface of the sun narrows to a thin crescent, the corona becomes visible. At the moment before the eclipse becomes total, brilliant points of light, called Baily's beads (q.v.) flash out in a crescent shape. These points are caused by the sun shining through valleys and irregularities on the lunar surface. Baily's beads are also visible at the instant when totality is ending, called emersion. Just before, just after, and sometimes during totality, narrow bands of moving shadows can be seen. These shadow bands are not fully understood but are thought to be caused by irregular refraction of light in the atmosphere of the earth. Before and after totality, an observer located on a hill or in an airplane can see the moon's shadow traveling eastward across the earth's surface like a swiftly moving cloud shadow. During the total solar eclipse in March, 1970, striking pictures of the 100-mile wide dark umbral spot were made from the air as it moved up the East coast of the United States at about 1500 m.p.h.

Frequency of Eclipses. If the earth's orbit, or the ecliptic (q.v.), were in the same plane as the moon's orbit, two total eclipses would occur during each lunar month, a lunar eclipse at the time of each full moon, and a solar eclipse at the time of each new moon. The two orbits, however, are inclined, and, as a result, eclipses occur only when the moon or the sun is within a few degrees of the two points, called the nodes, where the orbits intersect.

Periodically both the sun and the moon return to the same position relative to one of the nodes, with the result that eclipses recur at regular intervals. The time of the interval, called the saros, is a little over 6585.3 days or about eighteen years, nine to eleven days, depending on the number of intervening leap years, and eight hours. The saros corresponds almost exactly to nineteen returns of the sun to the same node, 242 returns of the moon to the same node, and 223 lunar months. The disparity between the number of returns of the moon and the number of lunar months is the result of the nodes moving westward at the rate of 19.5° per year. An eclipse that recurs after the saros will be a duplicate of the earlier eclipse, but will be visible 120° farther west on the earth's surface, because of the rotation of the earth during the third of a day included in the interval. Lunar eclipses recur forty-eight or forty-nine times and solar eclipses sixty-eight to seventy-five times before slight differences in the motions of the sun and moon eliminate the eclipse. The saros has been known since the time of ancient Babylonia (q.v.).

During one saros approximately seventy

eclipses take place, usually twenty-nine lunar and forty-one solar of which ten are total, forty-one are partial. The minimum number of eclipses that can occur in a given saros year is two, and the maximum seven. On the average, four eclipses take place each year.

During the 20th century 375 eclipses have taken or will take place: 228 solar and 147 lunar. The last total eclipse of the sun visible in the United States in this century was calculated by astronomers to occur over the State of Washington on Feb. 26, 1979.

Observation of Eclipses. Many problems of astronomy can be studied only during a total eclipse of the sun. Among these problems are the size and composition of the solar corona and the bending of light rays passing close to the sun because of the sun's gravitational field; *see* RELATIVITY. The great brilliance of the solar disk and the sun-induced brightening of the earth's atmosphere make observations of the corona and nearby stars impossible except during a solar eclipse. The coronagraph, a photographic telescope, permits direct observation of the edge of the solar disk at all times. Today, scientific solar eclipse observations are extremely valuable, particularly when the path of the eclipse traverses large land areas. An elaborate network of special observatories may provide enough data for months of analysis by scientists. Such data may provide information on how minute variations in the sun affect weather on earth, and how scientists can improve predictions of solar flares that could endanger astronauts.

See also ASTRONOMY. F.H.

ECLIPTIC, in astronomy, the apparent great-circle annual path of the sun in the celestial sphere, as seen from the earth. It is so named because eclipses occur only when the moon is on or near this path. The plane of this path, called the plane of the ecliptic, intersects the celestial equator (the projection of the earth's equator on the celestial sphere) at an angle of about 23° 27'. This angle is known as the obliquity of the ecliptic, and is approximately constant over a period of millions of years, although at present it is decreasing at the rate of 48 seconds of arc in each century, and will decrease for several millenniums until it reaches a minimum of 22° 54', after which it will again increase.

The two points at which the ecliptic intersects the celestial equator are called nodes or equinoxes. The sun is at the vernal equinox about March 21st, and at the autumnal equinox about September 23rd. Halfway on the ecliptic between the equinoxes are the summer and winter solstices. The sun arrives at these points about June 21 and December 22, respectively. The names of the four points correspond to the seasons beginning in the northern hemisphere on these dates. The equinoxes do not occur at the same points of the ecliptic every year, for the plane of the ecliptic and the plane of the equator revolve in opposite directions. The two planes make a complete revolution with respect to each other once every 25,868 years. The movement of the equinoxes along the ecliptic is called the precession of the equinoxes. A correction for precession must be applied to celestial charts in order to find the true position of the stars at any particular time.

The ecliptic is also used in astronomy (q.v.) as the fundamental circle for a system of coordinates called the ecliptic system. Celestial latitude is measured north and south of the ecliptic; celestial longitude is measured east and west of the vernal equinox.

In astrology (q.v.), the ecliptic is divided into twelve arcs of thirty degrees each, called the signs of the Zodiac. These signs or "houses of heaven" have been named after the constellations through which the ecliptic passes; *see* ZODIAC.

ECLOGUES. *See* PASTORAL POETRY; THEOCRITUS; VERGIL.

ÉCOLE DES BEAUX-ARTS, official name ÉCOLE NATIONALE ET SPÉCIALE DES BEAUX-ARTS DE PARIS, French government school of the fine arts, considered one of the most important art schools in the world. The École took its present official name in 1793 with the union of the Academy of Painting and Sculpture, founded by the French cardinal and statesman Jules Mazarin (q.v.) in 1648, and the Academy of Architecture, founded by the French statesman Jean Baptiste Colbert (q.v.) in 1671. For a long time the school was administered by the Académie des Beaux-Arts of the Institute of France (q.v.), but since 1863 the school has been supervised by an official of the national government assisted by a board chosen from among the most prominent artists of France.

Among the courses given at the École are architecture, painting, engraving, and sculpture; among the supplementary courses offered are drawing, history of art, history and theory of architecture, aesthetics, and geometry. The school provides free tuition to men and women between the ages of sixteen and thirty. The courses cover from eight to ten years. Candidates for admission must pass severe entrance examinations, and students take part in competitive examinations every six months. In addition to their work in the regular courses, students work outside of the school in the studios of various professors, who charge a fee. The École has an extensive library dating from its origin and comprising photographs and engravings as well as books; it also has a collection of paintings, engravings, and copies of statues. The number of students enrolled ranges between 2000 and 2500, and the school has about 55 instructors. The École administers the competitions for the Grand Prix de Rome (q.v.).

ECOLOGY, branch of biology dealing with the interrelations of plants and animals with their environment. Ecology is specifically concerned with the adaptation of species to physical conditions such as temperature, pressure, and the presence of free oxygen in air or its absence in water, and with physical and behavioral modifications that enable a species to prosper in the same habitat with other organisms. Animals with protective coloring and plants equipped to attract insects that assist in pollination (q.v.), for example, illustrate adaptation (q.v.) to biological factors in the habitat. Ecology is also concerned with both physical and biological influences on the number and distribution of members of a species, as well as with influences on the organization of the biological community as a whole. Inevitably ecology overlaps with many other sciences, including geography, geology, meteorology, oceanography, and demography (qq.v.). It is a relatively new science, but its importance is increasing as the exploding human population makes urgent demands on resources, and as technological advances more and more affect and threaten natural and human environment.

The German biologist Ernst Heinrich Haeckel (q.v.) introduced the term "oecology", the study of an animal's or plant's home or place in nature, in 1869. Originally, most ecological investigations were quests for evidence to support the theory of natural selection (q.v.) advanced by the British naturalist Charles Robert Darwin (*see under* DARWIN). Plant and animal ecology developed as separate fields within botany and zoology (qq.v.), respectively. Recently, ecology has been divided less by differences in the subjects under study than by the scope of such studies. The traditional subfields of plant and animal

With advanced technological methods man can alter his environment to meet his needs. An elaborate irrigation system has made this area of Arizona suitable for farming; a portion of the raw desert, which originally covered the entire area, can be seen in the foreground.
E. E. Hertzog — U.S. Bureau of Reclamation

ecology have been replaced by the ecology of populations, the ecology of communities, and the ecology of man. Within each of these three subfields, research may be directed toward theory, general knowledge, practical applications, or any combination of these goals. For example, various theories posit that plants with many small layered leaves are essentially adaptable to sunny environments, but that plants having a single layer with a few large leaves are adapted to shade. In fact, most plants in open fields have small leaves in many layers, and the ground cover in a deep, shaded forest usually has only a few large leaves in a single layer. Strains of field crops with unusually high productivity, moreover, have been developed by selecting and breeding individual plants that show a genetic tendency to have many layers of small, vertically oriented leaves. *See* PHOTOPE-RIODISM.

Ecology of Populations. A population consists of the locally interbreeding members of a species of plant or animal. Populations may be segregated in different habitats because of differences in physical or chemical factors. The earth is divided into temperature zones from the equator to the poles; temperature zones may be determined by altitude as well as latitude; *see*

Zebra and wildebeest graze together in Nairobi National Park, Kenya. Detailed studies made in East Africa have shown that a delicately balanced ecology exists between plants and animals, which is in danger of destruction by man. Pan American World Airways

LATITUDE AND LONGITUDE. Bodies of water may differ in their salt content, and may also be zoned vertically by variation in light penetration, aeration, and pressure. Populations are suitably adapted to each type of habitat. White birch trees that are planted beyond the southern limit of their proper range are often killed by late frosts, because they send out their leaves when the length of a spring day reaches the length appropriate to leafing time in their northern home. Among animals, the freshwater crayfish (q.v.) illustrates selection by a chemical factor. Because this crustacean needs water with much calcium carbonate in order to make its outer skeleton, it flourishes in regions where limestone is abundant, but is not found where granite predominates.

For many animals the direct effect of physical and chemical factors in the environment may be less important than the direct effect on them through plants. Plants provide the food supply of the herbivores, which in turn support the carnivores; *see* CARNIVORA. For some species, grass, shrubs, or trees are necessary as protective

289

The clownfish, Amphiprion percula (left), lives in symbiotic relationship with the sea anemone. It darts unharmed into the poisonous tentacles, and in turn probably provides the anemone with scraps when it feeds.

Arthur W. Ambler —
National Audubon Society

The brush-tailed phalanger (above, left), a marsupial of Australia, is perfectly adapted to spending its waking hours at night. The egret (above, right), an inhabitant of the Florida Everglades, is well adapted to its swampy habitat. Long legs enable it to wade through deep pools while stalking fish, which it spears with a sharp beak.   UPI

cover. Plants may also affect animals by modifying the local climate, by increasing humidity, or by decreasing light. Animals living at ground level in a dense tropical forest, for example, must be adapted to perpetual twilight.

Because plants and animals profoundly affect each other, any habitat has a characteristic community of species bound together by a web of interrelations, such as competition, dependency, and predation. Animals of the same species may be in competition for limited space in which to breed and forage. Red-winged blackbirds, for example, divide a marsh into exclusive territories. Similarly, members of different species may be in competition. Red-winged and yellow-headed blackbirds defend their respective territories against individuals of the opposite species, as well as against their own species. On the other hand, the members of a single species may cooperate. The complicated division of labor among both ants and bees is well known. Among members of different species, relationships of varying dependency occur. Legumes, including beans and their relatives, are able to survive in exhausted or poor soil when assisted by nitrogen-fixing bacteria that live in nodules on the roots of the plants; see NITROGEN FIXATION. Forest trees make their locality habitable for plants adapted to shade. Several species of bees and wasps subsist by pollinating only a few species of orchids, which in turn depend entirely on these visitors for their pollination. See also COMMENSALISM; SYMBIOSIS.

Each species in a community has an optimum population density for its habitat. If its numbers are too few, the species risks local extinction in the event of severe weather or an increase of enemies. On the other hand, excessive numbers of the species may exhaust the food supply. Theoretically any species could increase without limit, but populations are usually held in check by starvation, disease, or predation. Predators, although they may destroy many members of a species, are not necessarily dangerous to the survival of that species. In Norway a decrease in the number of hawks was followed by an increase in willow grouse, victims of the hawks. Subsequently, epidemics began to occur among the grouse nearly every year instead of about once in four years. Whereas formerly the hawks had weeded out many of the weaker individuals, diseased birds now survived long enough to spread infection through a grouse population, and eventually the grouse were again reduced in numbers. Such variations in a population are the rule rather than the exception; natural populations are in a dynamic balance rather than a static one. Variations may be extreme, as in the sudden growths or plagues of small herbivorous animals. Unusually favorable conditions, especially a superabundant food supply, may allow a sudden increase in a particular species. Predators cannot check such spurts of population growth, since the predator always has a lower rate of reproduction (q.v.) than its prey. Parasites, however, can accomplish what predators cannot. Viruses, bacteria, and protozoans multiply faster than their hosts, and conditions are ripe for an epidemic when the host species reaches a certain density. It is noteworthy that excess numbers of herbivores are checked more often by disease than by failure of the food supply. The almost worldwide spread of the viral disease myxomatosis, which decimated the vast rabbit populations in countries as far apart as Australia and Great Britain in the 1950's, is a good example of this process. See BACTERIA; DISEASES OF ANIMALS; PARASITE; VIRUS.

Plants may use biochemical weapons against their predators and competitors. For example, tobacco plants synthesize nicotine (q.v.), which is a natural insecticide (q.v.), and the roots of walnut trees exude a natural herbicide. Many such chemicals had previously been assumed to be useless by-products of the normal chemistry of a plant. See DISEASES OF PLANTS.

Ecology of Communities. A community consists of the interdependent plants and animals that live in one place. Terrestrial communities vary geographically from tropics through temperate and boreal, or northern, zones to tundra; see ZONE. The dominant vegetation changes correspondingly from broad-leaved evergreens through deciduous trees and evergreen conifers (see TREE) to shrubs, mosses, and lichens (qq.v.).

Within particular temperature zones, the amount of available moisture generally determines the main type of vegetation. Because plants take water from the soil and lose it to the air by evaporation, the seasonal distribution of rainfall and its ratio to evaporation are more important than total annual precipitation. Although in desert areas the annual precipitation may be as high as 15 in., it occurs within a short season, and most of the water is quickly evaporated from the ground. The lack of adequate year-round moisture in the soil is the factor that accounts for the absence of trees in the prairies of the United States. Locally, climatic formations are modified by edaphic influences, that is, by the physical and chemical character of the soil. The structure and texture of soil determine its capacity for holding water, as well as the amount of atmosphere contained in the pores between soil particles. Sandy soil holds less water than does soil containing a large proportion of clay or organic matter. On the other hand, in fine-textured, hard-packed soil, plant roots can get little oxygen. *See* HUMIDITY; PHOTOSYNTHESIS; RAIN; SOILS AND SOIL MANAGEMENT.

Aside from losses through consumption by herbivores, plant life is affected by animals, including man, in various ways. Earthworms play an important role in aerating soil, just as insects do in pollination of plants. The seeds borne within burs are spread as the bur clings to animal fur, and various berry seeds are distributed in animal droppings. Grazing herbivores discourage seed-bearing plants in favor of those that spread by means of rhizomes. Chronic pollution of air or water has drastic effects on the plant community. Conversely, the plant community affects the animal community. For example, the variety of birds that nest in a community is determined by the distribution of foliage among layers from ground cover to forest canopy, but is not greatly affected by the particular species of plants present. Agriculture, animal husbandry (qq.v.), and urbanization (*see* CITY) have greatly altered the type of vegetation found over wide regions of the earth, as have climatic changes such as those that accompanied the passing of the great glaciers (*see* GLACIER). Any plant community is subject to change continually, however, for its environment is always being modified by the plants themselves, which shade each other and contribute humus to the soil. Pioneering plants, or those capable of starting a new ecological cycle, on sand dunes or on a rocky surface are eventually succeeded by prairie or forest vegetation that is adapted to the changed conditions which the pioneering plants helped to bring about. Successive plant associations, beginning with microscopic seaweeds, will in time convert a salt marsh to grassland.

A prevailing pattern of interrelationship in an ecological community is that of predation, the linking chain of the eaters and the eaten. As the links usually progress from larger to smaller species, their relative numbers increase, that is, a waterside community includes far more fish than fish-eating birds, far more miniscule crustaceans than fish, and a still vaster population of microscopic algae. Of great importance in ecology is the study of pathways by which nutrients, pesticides, and household and industrial wastes pass through communities; *see* SEWAGE DISPOSAL. For example, sewage can be treated to reduce it to sterile inorganic nutrients. If these nutrients are discharged copiously enough into natural waters, the increase in nitrates and phosphates may cause algae to grow so abundantly that light cannot penetrate much below the surface of the water, and algae far below the surface die and decay. Furthermore, oxygen in the water is depleted by the bacteria that cause decay, and without oxygen animals in the water die. The resulting mass of partial decomposition or natural sewage can be almost as much of a nuisance and a menace to public health as the original, untreated human sewage.

Ecology of Man. The ecology of man is concerned with such factors as climate, geographical distribution of natural resources, and man's own effect on his environment. It is regarded as a branch of sociology (q.v.), because it deals with the social and technological environment created by man himself, as well as with his physical and biological environment.

Research in human geography has been concerned with man's efforts to adapt his food, clothing, habitations, and habits to conditions as diverse as those prevailing, for example, in arctic regions or in the tropics. Closely related are studies in medical geography. The control of malaria (q.v.), for example, requires the study not only of man but also of the malarial parasite, its alternative hosts, and its vectors, or carriers, the anopheline mosquitoes, and, further, the study of mosquito-eating birds and fish, and of local factors of climate, vegetation, and topography (*see* MAP), which may help or hinder extermination of the mosquitoes or their enemies.

Inevitably, the ecology of man interlocks with the study of natural populations and communities. For example, man benefits greatly from studies of the relationship between plants and their environment. Such studies can lead to the development of special strains of plants that are highly productive, naturally resistant to pests and diseases, or tolerant of different environmental conditions, including those in the urban environment.

M.I.T. Study. A computer study made in 1972 by a group of scientists at the Massachusetts Institute of Technology (M.I.T.) for the Club of Rome, an international group of scholars, predicted disaster for the earth ecosystem by the year 2100 unless growth in population, industry and economy was drastically limited. The M.I.T. scientists fed such data as birthrates, death rates, resource depletions, city growth, land use, food production, power needs, waste production, and many other facts into a computer. From the data, the computer calculated various long-range trends. The scientists programmed several variables that might change the trends. Then they calculated the earth ecosystem's ability to cope with these trends. The study indicated that within one hundred years the earth would be severely crowded with humans and dangerously polluted. Available living space, food, and minerals would be in short supply, and many existing animals would then be extinct. This amounted to a prediction of veritable disaster.

Criticism of the Report. Many scientists, educators, political leaders, and businessmen disagreed with this gloomy forecast of ecological disaster. These critics stated that no study could reliably predict social and political variables that might completely alter world environment trends. Furthermore, they said, the study did not take into account beneficial technological developments and an increasing environmental concern of a large part of the earth's population. Substitutes would be found for scarce resources, and better means of recycling and reusing waste products would probably be developed. Nonpolluting power sources, such as solar energy, would probably come into use. As agricultural technology developed, more and more food would be produced on the available land. Finally, nation after nation might be expected to reach or closely approach zero population growth.

See also AIR POLLUTION; ANIMALS, GEOGRAPHICAL DISTRIBUTION OF; CITY PLANNING; CLIMATE; CONSERVATION; EVOLUTION; GEOGRAPHY; HEREDITY; PLANNED PARENTHOOD; PLANTS, GEORGRAPHICAL DISTRIBUTION OF; SEWAGE DISPOSAL; WATER POLLUTION.   H.S.H.

ECONOMETRICS, branch of economics (q.v.) that uses mathematical methods and models; calculus, probability, statistics, linear programming (qq.v.), and game theory (see GAMES, THEORY OF), as well as other areas of mathematics, are used to analyze, interpret, and predict various economic factors and systems, such as price and market action, production cost, business trends, and economic policy.

ECONOMIC ADVISERS, COUNCIL OF. *See* PRESIDENT OF THE UNITED STATES, THE.

ECONOMIC AND SOCIAL COUNCIL, one of the six principal organs of the United Nations (q.v.), composed of representatives of twenty-seven nations. Nine members are elected each year for a three-year term by the General Assembly (q.v.) of the U.N. In 1971 the General Assembly adopted an amendment to the U.N. Charter enlarging the Council to fifty-four members. Until the amendment is ratified, the Council continues to meet as a twenty-seven member body. The responsibilities of the Economic and Social Council (ECOSOC) are first, economic and financial, and second, social, humanitarian, and cultural. The council operates mainly through a number of standing committees; six functional commissions, on population, statistics, human rights, social development, narcotic drugs, and status of women; and four regional commissions. ECOSOC holds a plenary session semiannually, with innumerable meetings of committees and commissions in the interim. At plenary sessions, the Council's work is divided among three sessional committees, the Economic Committee, the Social Committee, and the Coordination Committee. These committees meet as fifty-four-member bodies; pending the ratification of the Charter amendment, however, only the twenty-seven Council members have the right to vote. The decisions reached at council meetings, in which each member has one vote and a simple majority rules, are forwarded as recommendations to the General Assembly (q.v.) for review and approval or disapproval.

The four regional commissions of ECOSOC are modeled after the parent body, but reflect the geographical diversity of resources and needs. Each commission is headed by an executive secretary with the rank of Undersecretary-General of the U.N. Their staffs are part of the U.N. Secretariat. The Economic Commission for Europe, with thirty-three members and headquarters at Geneva, Switzerland, and the Economic Commission for Asia and the Far East (thirty-one members) at Bangkok, Thailand, were established in 1947. The Economic Commission for Latin America (twenty-nine members) was set up in 1948 at Santiago, Chile; and the Economic Commission for Africa (forty-two members) was established in 1958 at Addis Ababa, Ethiopia. The African commission is the only one that does not admit nonregional members; the U.S. and several European countries are nonregional members of the other regional groups.

Programs and projects of the commissions are formulated in annual sessions of the member nations with representatives of the specialized agencies and other U.N. units. A regional commission may make recommendations to any member government but may not take action without the consent of that government. This regional cooperation has stimulated progress in agriculture, industry, education, housing, electrical power, transportation, trade, and the environment.

The Economic and Social Council is also linked, less directly, with a number of autonomous units, each of which has its own head-quarters, budget, legislative and executive bodies, and its own secretariat. Of these units, twelve are intergovernmental; that is, they are organized apart from the U.N. by the nations that provide their basic budget. These twelve are the International Labor Organization, International Telecommunication Union, Universal Postal Union, World Meteorological Organization, Food and Agriculture Organization, World Health Oganization, International Monetary Fund, International Bank for Reconstruction and Development, with its two subsidiaries, the International Finance Corporation and the International Development Association; International Civil Aviation Organization; United Nations Educational, Scientific, and Cultural Organization; Inter-Governmental Maritime Consultative Organization; and International Atomic Energy Agency and the General Agreement on Tariffs and Trade. See separate articles on these agencies.

Except for the International Atomic Energy Agency, which was established under the aegis of the U.N., and the General Agreement on Tariffs and Trade, which cooperates with the U.N. on the secretariat and intergovernmental levels, all of these units are known as specialized agencies, with formal agreements stipulating their relationship to the U.N. The first four antedate the U.N. itself by a number of years. Through these agencies flow almost all of the resources that the U.N. has poured into low-income countries to improve social and economic conditions.

Other autonomous units within the orbit of ECOSOC are the United Nations Development Program, United Nations Industrial Development Organization, United Nations Conference on Trade and Development, United Nations Children's Fund, United Nations Institute for Training and Research, United Nations Office of the High Commissioner for Refugees, World Food Program, and the recently established United Nations Environment Program.

See also separate articles on most of the units named.   J.A.J. & K.M.

ECONOMIC DEVELOPMENT ADMINISTRATION, agency of the United States Department of Commerce, established in 1965. The agency, often referred to as the E.D.A., provides financial and technical assistance to aid the economic development of areas of the United States with high unemployment or low family-income levels. It cooperates with county and State officials in organizing and operating multi-county development districts and multi-State

economic development regions. Communities must make long-range plans for economic growth in order to be eligible for E.D.A. financial assistance, in the form of grants and loans for public works and industrial and commercial projects that help generate employment opportunities.

The agency conducts a nationwide research and technical-assistance program to help find causes of and solutions to problems that block economic growth. The program includes feasibility studies, market studies, and management counseling for new industrial firms and small businesses operating in redevelopment areas.

ECONOMIC OPPORTUNITY, OFFICE OF. See POVERTY.

ECONOMICS, social science concerned with the production, distribution, exchange, and consumption of goods and services. The older term for the science is political economy.

The development of economics as a social science has been responsive to social conditions of which it is itself a part. Thus the agricultural economy of the 18th and preceding centuries resulted in the formulation of one group of economic theories and practices, whereas the period of the Industrial Revolution (q.v.) and after resulted in the formulation of another set of theories and practices. The first modern exposition of economics as a social science was the *Inquiry into the Nature and Causes of the Wealth of Nations* (1776) by the Scottish philosopher and economist Adam Smith. The development of economic thought since the time of Adam Smith has paralleled the growth in economic institutions and the increasing complexity of the problems of contemporary life. The advance in theory has comprised more and more extensive investigation of the laws of production, distribution, exchange, and consumption of wealth (q.v.), whereas the advance in practice has concerned itself with the application of those laws to the understanding and solution of social problems.

HISTORY

Long before economics achieved the status of a science, economic problems occupied men's minds. The principal Greek writers, the philosophers Plato and Aristotle and the historian, soldier, and essayist Xenophon, subordinated economic to ethical and moral considerations. They viewed the primary object of life to be self-knowledge, not the acquisition of riches, and they did not regard wealth as of fundamental importance to the individual or the state. Plato in his *Republic* wrote of an ideal society in which the ills of society would be corrected by

Adam Smith, author of Wealth of Nations.

a communistic state. Aristotle in his *Politics* defended the institution of private property and formulated ideas concerning the functions of money (q.v.), but condemned the taking of interest (q.v.) on the ground that money was "barren". Both Plato and Aristotle were prejudiced against trade and commerce, feeling that to live by trade was undesirable.

The economic ideas of the Romans were borrowed from the Greeks and showed the same contempt for trade and commerce and the same condemnation of interest. The orator, statesman, and man of letters Marcus Tullius Cicero, the statesman and author Marcus Porcius Cato the Elder, and the scholar Marcus Terentius Varro wrote on agricultural problems, a field that they deemed worthy of philosophic consideration.

During the Middle Ages the economic ideas of the Church found expression in the *corpus juris canonici* or the canon law (q.v.). The canonists condemned usury, which signified any loan interest, and regarded trade and commerce as inferior to agriculture. With the development of commerce the canonists formulated the just–price doctrine *justum pretium,* teaching that every commodity had a just price or value, which it was sinful for the seller to try to exceed.

Mercantilism. The development of modern nationalism during the 16th century shifted attention to the problem of increasing the wealth and power of the various national states. The economic policy of the statesmen of that time, known as mercantilism, sought to encourage national self-sufficiency; *see* MERCANTILE SYSTEM. Exports were encouraged and imports discouraged in order to secure to the state the maximum amount of bullion or specie on the basis of a favorable balance of trade.

The English merchant and economic writer Thomas Mun, the English physician, statistician, and political economist Sir William Petty (1623–87), the Scottish philosopher and historian David Hume, and the Scottish statesman James Archibald Stuart-Wortley-Mackenzie, 1st Baron Wharncliffe (1776–1845), were the principal British writers who explained or extolled mercantilism.

Physiocrats. In the 18th century a reaction developed in England and France against the narrow and restrictive policies of mercantilism. In France the reaction found its expression in the writings of the physiocrats, principally the French economists François Quesnay, Jean Claude Marie Vincent de Gournay (1712–59), the economist and statesman Anne Robert Jacques Turgot, Baron de l'Aune, and the Irish economist Richard Cantillon (1680?–1734). The physiocrats taught the doctrine of natural laws, proclaimed the maxim of laissez-faire, claimed that agriculture alone yielded a net surplus beyond the expenses of production, maintained that the revenue of the state should be raised by a single direct tax levied upon land, and extolled free trade (*see* SINGLE TAX, THE).

In England the reaction against mercantilism developed toward the end of the 18th century, and a movement in favor of agriculture and against government restrictions on business was the result.

Adam Smith. The publication in 1776 of Adam Smith's *Wealth of Nations* marked the first serious attempt made to study economics apart from the sister sciences of politics, ethics, and jurisprudence. Smith gave great weight to the causal nature of economic phenomena. Through his emphasis on consumption, rather than on production, the scope of economics was considerably broadened. He was the first economist to present a well-rounded treatment of value and distributive shares. He called attention to the importance of permitting each individual to follow his own self-interest as a means of promoting national prosperity. His discussion of the division of labor and his support of free trade policies were significant contributions to the development of economic thought. *See also* SMITH, ADAM.

David Ricardo, adherent of the classical school of economics.

Classical Theory. The writings of the classical or orthodox school of economists, during the first half of the 19th century, began the formulation of a body of economic principles based on the study of the economic process as a whole. This school comprised economic doctrines that were developed between 1776 and the 1850's primarily by Adam Smith, the English economists David Ricardo and Thomas Robert Malthus, and the British utilitarian philosopher and economist John Stuart Mill. Ricardo was the first to emphasize the problem of the distribution of wealth. He adopted as the basis of his theory of distribution the law of population developed by Malthus in his book, *An Essay on the Pinciple of Population* (1798). Malthus believed, as a result of his historical and statistical investigation, that population continually outstrips the means of subsistence and that this condition would always tend to keep wages low. Ricardo believed that as population increased, society would be forced to resort to poorer and poorer soils in order to obtain food, with the result that an increasing share of the product of industry would go to the landlord in the shape of economic rent. Ricardo's theory of distribution held that with an increasing share of the product of industry going to rent, (q.v.) wages (q.v.) would receive a constant or slowly increasing amount, and profits would dwindle both absolutely and

relatively. Ricardo also made contributions to the knowledge of monetary phenomena and international trade. He was outstanding in his use of the deductive method of economic analysis. Other British classical economists were the Scottish philosopher and historian James Mill and John Ramsay McCulloch (1789–1864).

Probably the leading exponent of classical economics was John Stuart Mill, who started as a follower of Ricardo, adopting his theories of value, rent, wages, and profits. In his *Principles of Political Economy* (1848), however, he observed that although the production of wealth resulted from the operation of natural laws, the distribution of wealth was subject to the conventional laws regulating society. The materialistic and pessimistic doctrines of the classical economists earned for economics the epithet of "the dismal science".

Opposition to the classical theory of distribution came from the socialist writers and others. The classical doctrine had supported laissez-faire and the system of private capitalist enterprise; socialism protested against both of these concepts. The early academic and utopian socialism of the social philosopher Comte de Saint-Simon and the historian Louis Blanc in France, and the Irish landowner and political economist William Thompson (1785?–1833) and the British social reformer Robert Owen in

John Stuart Mill, champion of utilitarianism.

Great Britain was subordinated in importance to the scientific socialism of the German revolutionist Karl Marx. Marx built his theories on a materialistic interpretation of history, directing his conclusions against those fundamental institutions of the social order that the classical economists took for granted.

Other writers who attacked the classical doctrines were the sociologists, the most famous of whom was the French philosopher Auguste Comte. He maintained that it was impossible to develop a helpful science of economics distinct from history, ethics, and politics. The historical school of writers, which developed in Germany in the middle of the 19th century, denied that economic science could discover laws that held true for all times and all places. They emphasized the importance of inductive methods (*see* INDUCTION) and the study of legal institutions, custom, and ethics in their relation to economic life. The German economist and historian Gustav von Schmoller (1838–1917) was the outstanding exponent of the historical school.

The Austrian school of economists, among whom the leader was the statesman Eugen Böhm-Bawerk (1851–1914), directed their criticism against the classical economists' theory of value, and developed the concept of the marginal utility theory of value; *see* VALUE.

The early American economists also reacted against the classical theories. Daniel Raymond (1786–1849?) and Henry Charles Carey (1793–1879) were the most influential of the early American economists. They were outstanding exponents of the doctrine of protection by government regulation as opposed to the classical laissez-faire doctrine.

20th-Century Theory. The economic writings of the early 20th century both in England and America employed both the deductive and the historical methods of economic analysis. Economists maintained, with respect to the theory of value, that supply and demand, cost of production, and marginal utility exert an influence in the determination of values. The leading economists in this period in England and America were the Englishman Alfred Marshall and the Americans Frank William Taussig (qq.v.), John Bates Clark (1847–1938), and Edwin Robert Anderson Seligman (1861–1939).

During and after World War I the industrial countries of Europe experienced an inflation, followed by a sharp fall of prices in 1920–21. In the United States the prosperity of the 1920's was followed by one of the country's worst depressions; *see* BUSINESS CYCLE. These economic crises focused the attention of classical-minded

economists on the problem of economic instability. The British economist, John Maynard Keynes, challenged the generally accepted idea that a lowering in interest rates and wages during a recession would automatically stimulate business investment and bring about greater employment. He proposed that government spending should compensate for business investment when it was too low to maintain high employment rates. After World War II, Keynes' theories profoundly influenced the economic policies of such capitalist countries as the U.S., Great Britain, and Canada. The application of these theories was facilitated by a group of American economists, including Simon Smith Kuznets, recipient of the Alfred Nobel Memorial Prize in economics, who in the 1930's developed the concept of national income (q.v.), the aggregate of all earnings arising from goods and services produced in a country during a specified period of time. Kuznets also developed the concept of the gross national product (q.v.), the total market value of goods and services produced in a country during a specified period of time. These concepts provided an approach to measuring aggregate investment, saving, and other economic magnitudes involved in testing and applying Keynes' theories in the U.S. economy. Keynes' theories were later expanded and enlarged upon in the U.S. by a group of econo-

John Maynard Keynes, authority on modern economic problems, with Mrs. Keynes. UPI

mists who called their concept New Economics. Paul A. Samuelson, another recipient of the Nobel Memorial Prize became one of the leading theorists of this school.

Some classical economists, however, have disagreed with Keynes' diagnosis of the causes of the Great Depression, which was the case study for his theory of employment, interest, and money. The most notable American opponent of Keynes has been the economist Milton Friedman, who collected evidence to show that the factor of quantity and availability of money was more crucial than levels of private investment and government spending in causing the depression. Friedman holds that economic stability would result from steady annual increases in the money supply. In the 1960's and 1970's, as economies became more complex and the Keynesian theories were not readily solving economic problems, Friedman's theory of money gained more importance. Many economists recognized the role that the money supply—the quantity of money available and the degree of stability in the economy's demand for money—played in stabilizing a given economy.

The survival of capitalism has concerned many 20th-century economists. The Austrian-American economist Joseph Alois Schumpeter (1883–1950) maintained that changes in the leadership of business enterprise, as the adventurous owner-entrepreneur is replaced by the professional salaried manager, will cause capitalism to evolve toward socialism. Economists also have been concerned that the growth of big corporations would undermine capitalism by repressing price competition. The American economist John Kenneth Galbraith proposed that competition is being replaced by a situation of countervailing power in which the power of corporate sellers is neutralized somewhat because they must deal with other corporate enterprises, powerful unions, and other institutions as potent as themselves.

Many American economists have come to accept the concept of a "mixed economy", combining private initiative with a certain amount of government control. Increasing governmental activity in the economy has added to fears that the trend will ultimately lead to socialism.

At the same time, some centrally planned economies are moving away from the rigidity of their economic systems. The Union of Soviet Socialist Republics (q.v.) has introduced incentives into its system, as proposed by Soviet economist Yevsei Grigorievich Liberman (1897–), by abolishing excessive regulation and allowing profitability to help improve efficiency in production. Yugoslavia has moved even further away from a controlled economy, with workers' councils participating in management and sharing in profits.

The study of all economic systems begins with the analysis of the principles of production, distribution, and resource allocation in case of scarcity in the means of production (land, labor, capital, or management) in relation to a limited amount of goods available for consumption.

Specific economic concepts and problems are treated under the topics Capital; Capitalism; Collectivism; Consumption; Currency; Debt, National; Division of Labor; Finance; Foreign Trade; Free Trade and Protection; Monopoly and Competition. See also separate articles on many of the economists and men of letters whose life dates are not given in the article.

ECTODERM. *See* Embryology: *Normal Development.*

ECUADOR, republic on N.W. coast of South America, bounded by Colombia on the N., Peru on the E. and S., and the Pacific Ocean on the W. and including the Galápagos Islands in the Pacific, 600 mi. w. of the mainland. It straddles the equator and extends from about long. 75°30′ W. to about long. 81°10′ W. Ecuador is the second smallest country of South America, exceeding only Uruguay in size. The area, including the Galápagos Islands, is 115,000 sq.mi.

THE LAND

Ecuador is divided into four geographic regions. The Costa, or coastal plain, covers a little over a quarter of the area of the country; the Sierra, or central highlands, extends as a double row of high and massive mountains enclosing a narrow, inhabited central plateau; the Oriente, or eastern jungle, covering about half of the country, consists of gentle slopes E. of the Andes; and the Archipiélego de Colón (Galápagos Islands) includes 6 larger and 9 smaller islands containing many volcanic peaks, mostly extinct.

The Sierra region lies between two chains of the Andes, the Western and Eastern Cordilleras, which have more than a dozen peaks over 16,000 ft. high. Cotopaxi (19,347 ft.), the highest active volcano in the world, is located in the Cordilleras. *See* Volcano.

Climate. Although Ecuador lies on the equator (as the name implies), the country has a wide range of climates because of the varying altitudes. The Costa is generally hot and humid, with a mean annual temperature of 83° F. On the Sierra the temperatures range between 45° and 70° F., depending on the altitude. The city of Quito, which is 9350 ft. above sea level, has a

Plaza Independencia in the center of Quito, the capital of Ecuador. In the background (right) is the inactive volcano Pichincha. Panagra

mean annual temperature of 55° F. The Oriente is warmer and more humid than the Costa; temperatures throughout the year approach 100° F. and year-round rains total about 80 in.

Natural Resources. Forests, an important resource of Ecuador, cover some 70,000 sq.mi. Gold, silver, lead, and salt are of some value; and deposits of copper, iron, coal, and sulfur have been found.

Plants and Animals. Along the N. part of the coast, and within the inner portion of the S. coast, tropical jungles abound. In some places the jungles extend up the slopes of the Andes as wet, mossy forests. Mountain slopes of 10,000 ft. and higher are covered with paramo grass. Both flanks of the Cordilleras, as well as the Oriente, are densely forested up to 10,000 ft. The highland valleys have few native trees, but do support Temperate Zone plants such as potatoes and corn.

The animal life of Ecuador is extremely varied. Larger mammals include the bear, jaguar, and wildcat; and among the smaller mammals the weasel, otter, and skunk are found. A variety of reptiles, including the lizard, snake, and crocodile, thrives on the slopes of the Andes and along the coastal lowlands. Birds are the most varied group; and many North American birds migrate to Ecuador during the northern winter.

The Galápagos Islands, with many unusual native animals, serve as a wildlife sanctuary.

THE PEOPLE

Approximately 80 percent of the population of Ecuador is composed of Indians and mestizos (persons of mixed blood); the remainder is equally divided between Europeans (chiefly of Spanish descent) and Negroes. The population is primarily rural; the majority lives in villages of one hundred persons or less.

Population. The population of Ecuador (census 1974) was 6,500,845; the United Nations estimated (1974) 6,950,000. The overall population density is about 63 per sq.mi. (U.N. est. 1974). Compared to other South American countries, Ecuador is densely inhabited. About 60 percent of the people live on the Sierra and about 30 percent live on the Costa; the remainder of the population is scattered within the Oriente and Galápagos Islands.

Political Divisions and Principal Cities. Ecuador is divided into twenty provinces, which are subdivided into cantons and urban and rural parishes.

Quito, the capital, is situated in the N. Andes and has a population (1970) of 528,094. Guaya-

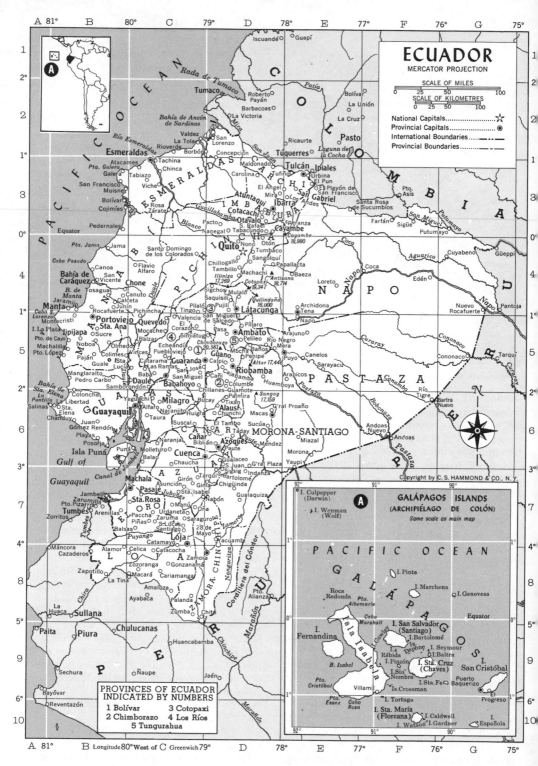

ECUADOR
MERCATOR PROJECTION

SCALE OF MILES
SCALE OF KILOMETRES

National Capitals......................☆
Provincial Capitals....................◉
International Boundaries.............
Provincial Boundaries...............

GALÁPAGOS ISLANDS
(ARCHIPIÉLAGO DE COLÓN)
Same scale as main map

Copyright by C. S. HAMMOND & CO., N. Y.

PROVINCES OF ECUADOR
INDICATED BY NUMBERS
1 Bolívar   3 Cotopaxi
2 Chimborazo   4 Los Ríos
       5 Tungurahua

Longitude 80° West of Greenwich 79°

INDEX TO MAP OF ECUADOR

View of the 16th-century town of Otavalo, an Andean market place in Ecuador where Indians meet to buy and sell their wares and exchange news.   United Nations

quil, in the s.w., has a population of about 701,227, and is the principal port and commercial center.

Language and Religion. The chief and official language is Spanish. The great majority of the population of Indian stock residing in rural areas speaks Quechua, the original language of the Inca.

Most Ecuadorian Indians became converts to the Roman Catholic faith during the years following the conquest of Peru and Ecuador by the Spanish. Roman Catholicism became the state religion in 1863, but by 1889 a liberal movement resulted in a partial severance of church from state. A decree of 1904 placed the church under state control, properties of religious orders were confiscated, and absolute freedom of religion

was introduced. Today Roman Catholicism is the faith of about 95 percent of the population. The Indians of the Oriente maintain ancient animistic religions; and various Protestant sects comprise less than 1 percent.

Education. A campaign to reduce the high illiteracy rate was started in 1944; it lowered the rate from 43 percent to 30 percent within about twenty years. Education is free and compulsory for all children between the ages of six and fourteen.

ELEMENTARY AND SECONDARY SCHOOLS. In the late 1960's, about 975,500 pupils were enrolled in about 7500 primary schools; and some 195,000 students in about 720 secondary schools.

UNIVERSITIES AND COLLEGES. The country has seven universities and two polytechnic institutions. Three of the institutions of higher learning are located in Guayaquil, and the rest in Quito, Cuenca, Loja, and Manabí. Total annual enrollment amounted to some 31,330 students in the late 1960's.

Culture. Since the inhabited regions vary greatly in their ethnic makeup, Ecuador is a country of contrasting cultural patterns. The highland Indians, the descendants of tribes conquered by the Inca, still play traditional Indian songs on ancient-style flutes and panpipes (*see* Latin-American Music). The Oriente is populated almost entirely by Indians whose tribes escaped both Inca and Spanish rule and whose customs resemble those of the Amazon basin Indians. Along the coast descendants of Spanish settlers and Negro slaves have intermingled to produce a culture that combines Spanish and African characteristics.

Libraries and Museums. The National Library, built in Quito in 1792, is one of the oldest in the country, and contains about 55,000 volumes. The university libraries in Quito and Cuenca also have extensive collections. Other libraries are maintained in the larger cities and the universities. *See* Spanish-American Literature.

Many museums in Ecuador preserve artifacts and records of historic interest. There are several historical and archeological museums in Quito; and, near Cuenca, a private museum has on display an excellent collection of Inca and pre-Inca objects.

Archeology. In the s. highlands of Ecuador ceramic and gold objects have been found in abundance; the former suggest the possibility of seaborne cultural influences from the Maya (q.v.) of Central America. Along the n. coast, the Esmeraldas culture produced gold ornaments and large copper disks decorated with high-relief human and animal figures. Various clay figurines have also been found.

The Manabí culture, to the s. of the Esmeraldas, is known for its platform mounds, enclosures, and tombs which were cut directly into the natural rock. Some archeologists see a similarity between the Manabí style of stone carving, with its low-relief figures and geometrical designs, and that of the Tiahuanaco culture found in Bolivia. East of the Ecuadorean Andes, pottery finds in the region of the Napo R. show startling similarities to ceramics of the Marajó culture of the Amazon estuary in Brazil (q.v.). *See* Peruvian Archeology.

THE ECONOMY

Agriculture is the basis of the economy. In 1967, however, an industrial development law was passed, which brought about the establishment of factories manufacturing textiles, electric appliances, pharmaceuticals, and other products. In the early 1970's about 1,000,000 kw hours of

An Andean Indian craftsman in typical native dress poses near his straw mats at a provincial fair.
United Nations

electricity were produced. In a recent year budget figures showed revenue of $169,000,000 and expenditures of about $229,000,000.

Agriculture. The cultivated area (less than 7 percent of the country) lies primarily on the Sierra and the Costa. Bananas are the chief crop;

and sugar, cocoa, and coffee are of some importance. In the late 1960's the annual banana production was about 118,000,000 stems. Sugar production amounted to about 209,000 tons annually in the same period.

Forest and Fishing Industries. Ecuador is the chief source of balsa wood, with an annual export yield of about $3,000,000. Other forest products include kapak, mangrove bark, tagua nuts (vegetable ivory), and rubber.

The waters surrounding the Galápagos Islands comprise one of the richest tuna fisheries in the world. Shrimp are also found in abundance. The value of fish and fish products in the early 1970's amounted to about $9,600,000 annually.

Mining. Gold, silver, lead, and salt are mined

in Ecuador, the last-named under government monopoly. Petroleum resources, which were first uncovered in the early 1920's and are still being discovered today, form a major industry. The deposits are the property of the country, but large, taxable concessions have been made to foreign concerns. Petroleum production in 1970 totaled about 191,000 metric tons.

Manufacturing. Traditionally, Ecuadorian industry was confined to the manufacture of goods for local consumption. Under the Industrial Development Law of 1965, plants have been established for the manufacture of textiles, refrigerators, pharmaceuticals, and batteries. In 1970 Ecuador produced 458,000 tons of cement.

Currency, Banking, and Trade. The unit of currency is the sucre, consisting of 100 centavos (1 sucre equals U.S.$0.0425; 1973). The Banco Central del Ecuador is the bank of issue.

At Puerto Bolívar, bananas, one of the chief exports, are loaded for shipment to the U.S., the major consumer of goods from Ecuador. United Fruit Company

Bananas are the principal export, and were valued at some $123,000,000 in 1970. Exports of coffee totaled $50,500,000; and of cocoa, $22,300,000. Other exports are sugar, castor-oil seed, pharmaceuticals, straw hats, balsa wood, rice, and fish products. The total value of exports in 1970 was about $233,000,000. In 1972 the first shipment of oil was made from U.S.-operated fields in Oriente. The project was reported to make Ecuador the second-largest oil exporter in Latin America, after Venezuela.

The chief imports are machinery, construction materials, and transportation and communication equipment. Imports in 1970 totaled about $296,000,000.

Transportation. The highway system comprises about 10,000 mi. of roads, of which 2700 mi. are all-weather roads. The Pan-American Highway (712 mi. in Ecuador) runs through the country from N. to S. The nationalized railroads transport freight and passengers over about 600 mi. of rail.

Ecuador has seven seaports. Guayaquil, which is connected by air and rail to all of the major cities, is the main port of entry. Many rivers, including the Guayas, Daule, and Vinces, have been dredged and are now navigable.

Communications. The major cities and towns are connected by radiotelephone; telegraph and cable services link Ecuador with all parts of the world. Radio stations number about 300, and receivers about 1,700,000. Television sets in use number about 890,000.

Labor. The total labor force numbers about 1,500,000, of which more than 50 percent is employed in agriculture, and 15 percent in manufacturing and construction. The remainder is engaged in services or the professions. Skilled workers make up only about 10 percent of the labor force, and manual workers about 85 percent.

Labor unions have a total membership of about 110,000 (exclusive of the maritime and railway-workers unions, for which figures are not available).

The largest union federation is the Confederación de Trabajadores Equatorianos (C.T.E.), with 200 affiliates.

GOVERNMENT

In a military coup in February, 1972, the government of Ecuador was overthrown. The constitution of 1967 was abrogated, and that of 1945 was reinstated.

Central Government. The constitution vests executive power in a president elected by direct popular vote for a four-year term; he cannot serve two consecutive terms. The president appoints his cabinet without congressional approval, but cabinet members may be removed from office by formal congressional censure. The president is commander in chief of the armed forces. He is responsible for convoking congress and holds extraordinary powers in time of national emergency.

A council of state, comprising the cabinet and some members of the congress and the Supreme Court and whose principal function is to defend the constitutional system, has special powers when congress is not in session.

HEALTH AND WELFARE. Effective programs designed to check communicable diseases have been instituted. The country has succeeded in eliminating yellow fever and has greatly reduced the incidence of malaria and tuberculosis. Malnutrition and infant mortality, however, still pose serious problems.

A government-sponsored social-security program in existence since 1942 provides farmers, domestic workers, artisans, and professional men with such benefits as health, accident, maternity, and unemployment insurance, as well as old-age pensions.

Legislature. Legislative power is vested in a two-chamber congress: a Senate and a Chamber of Deputies. Most of the senators are popularly elected for four years; "functional" senators are selected to represent cultural, business, and racial groups. Deputies are popularly elected for two years by a system of proportional representation.

Political Parties. The strongest parties in the country are the Conservative and the Radical Liberal parties. The former, supported primarily by large landowners, is the political spokesman for the Roman Catholic Church; the latter, supported by businessmen, advocates separation of church and state. A number of smaller parties comprise the opposition to one or both of these parties.

Local Government. Each province is administered by a governor, who is appointed by the president, and a popularly elected provincial council. Urban cantons popularly elect a municipal council, which, in turn, elects the council officers. Each rural canton and each parish is administered by an official who is appointed by the president.

Judiciary. The judicature comprises a Supreme Court of five judges; fifteen superior courts, of which four have six judges and eleven have three judges; and numerous lower courts. Criminal cases are heard before a "special jury", consisting of one judge and three members of the bar. Capital punishment is prohibited.

Defense. A two-year term of conscription is compulsory for all male citizens. The armed forces comprise an army, navy, and air force, totaling about 32,000 in strength.

HISTORY

Architectural remains of ancient civilizations dating back thousands of years, and probably related to the Maya civilization of Central America, have been discovered in Ecuador. Neither these civilizations nor the later Inca left written records of their cultures. Inca civilization was centered in and around Cuzco and the Lake Titicaca area in Peru. The Inca dominated the Indian tribes of Ecuador and provided the major military obstacles to the early Spanish invaders.

The Spanish first landed on the coast of what is now Ecuador in 1526, led by Bartolomé Ruiz. Spanish conquistadores under the leadership of Francisco Pizarro (q.v.) invaded the country in 1532 and two years later were in control of the area. Pizarro, acting in the name of the Spanish crown, appointed his brother Gonzalo (1506?–1548) governor of Quito on Dec. 1, 1540. A short time later Francisco Pizarro was assassinated, and Gonzalo Pizarro led a rebellion against Spain. His independent rule lasted until April 9, 1548, when crown forces defeated his army at Jaquijaguana, and Gonzalo Pizarro was executed.

Colonial Ecuador was at first a territory directly under the rule of the viceroyalty of Peru, one of the two major administrative divisions of 16th-century Spanish America. In 1563 Quito, as Ecuador was then called, became a presidency, or a judicial district of the viceroyalty. From 1717 to 1723 the Quito presidency was under the authority of the viceroyalty of Nueva Granada in Bogotá, but it was then returned to the authority of the viceroy of Peru.

The first revolt of the colonists against Spain took place in 1809, but the republican forces, led by General Antonio José de Sucre (q.v.), chief lieutenant of Simón Bolívar (q.v.), did not win final victory until 1822. Ecuador became the Department of the South, part of the confederacy known as the Republic of Colombia, or Great Colombia, which included Venezuela and Colombia.

Independence. In 1830 Ecuador gained independence under its present name. The first president, Gen. Juan José Flores (q.v.), was a hero of the wars for independence, and represented the arch-conservatives in the city of Quito. In 1833 a civil war broke out between the conservatives of Quito and the liberal elements of Guayaquil. It was the first of a long series of revolutions between the two factions, which resulted in the subsequent rise of three outstanding dictators in Ecuadorian history: Flores, Gabriel García Moreno (1821–75), former leader of the Conservative Party, and revolutionist and political leader Eloy Alfaro (1842–1912). During the second period of rule by President Alfaro (1907–11), a new, more liberal constitution was introduced and remained in effect for twenty-two years.

Ecuador followed the United States into World War II against the Axis Powers. For Ecuador, the end of World War II coincided with a waning of liberal influence. In 1944 liberal President Carlos Alberto Arroyo del Río (1893–   ), formerly president of the Chamber of Deputies, was forced from office and replaced by former president José María Velasco Ibarra (1893–   ), who had held office in 1934–35, and who was supported by the conservative faction. A new constitution, promulgated on Dec. 31, 1941, remained in force into the 1960's.

In 1947 Velasco Ibarra was deposed by a military group which was almost immediately ousted by counterrevolutionaries; the latter installed Carlos Julio Arosemena Tola (1895–1952) as provisional president. Galo Plaza Lasso (1906–   ), a former ambassador to the U.S., was elected president in June, 1948.

In early 1948 Ecuador attended the 9th Inter-American Conference in Bogotá, Colombia, and became a signatory of the charter of the Organization of American States (q.v.). Long-standing

A ceramic head of an old man, found in Esmeraldas Province, is representative of Indian craft of more than 500 years ago. Museum of the American Indian

border disputes with Peru were revived in 1941 and again in 1950. Both times the issue was submitted to arbitration. In 1944 most of the disputed area was awarded to Peru; no boundaries were changed following the 1950 incident. In 1960, reviving the dispute, Ecuador unilaterally nullified the territorial settlement of 1944.

Political Instability. In 1952 Velasco Ibarra, this time the candidate of a coalition of left- and right-wing groups, was chosen president for the third time, holding office until 1956. In the presidential elections that year, the conservative candidate Camilo Ponce Enríquez (1913–76) won a close victory over a liberal candidate. Velasco Ibarra ran as an independent candidate in the elections of 1960. Sharply critical of the conservative economic policies of the Ponce government, he promised widespread reforms and was elected by a wide margin in June. Velasco Ibarra, forced to resign in November, 1960, was succeeded by Vice-President Carlos Arosemena Monroy (1920–   ). On Aug. 17, 1961, Ecuador signed the charter of the Alliance for Progress, a document providing for extensive U.S. aid to signatories over a ten-year period. In July, 1963, Arosemena was ousted by a military junta, which implemented economic and social reforms in a series of decrees, including one for agrarian reform, but soon faced mounting demands for a return to constitutional government. The following month a ten-year national development plan proposed by Ecuador was approved by an Alliance for Progress commission, thus opening the way for negotiation of loans to finance development projects. The junta confirmed plans for elections in June, 1966, and installed a cabinet more acceptable to the opposition. In early 1966 demonstrations by merchants and students provoked government retaliation and triggered a countrywide upheaval.

Three consecutive governments held power in 1966: the junta, the provisional administration of Clemente Yerovi Indaburu (1905–   ), and the interim government of President Otto Arosemena Gómez (1921–   ). The junta was deposed in March. A constituent assembly was elected in October, and in the following month that body elected Arosemena Gómez as interim president. Arosemena encountered widespread opposition but survived a difficult initial period. A new constitution was promulgated in May, 1967. In June, 1968, Velasco again was elected president, and in 1970 he assumed dictatorial powers. In February, 1972, Velasco was overthrown by a military coup headed by General Guillermo Rodríguez Lara (1924–   ), chief of the army, who assumed the presidency.

Among the first acts of the new regime was establishment of a five-year economic plan, stressing agriculture, housing, and industry. In August, 1972, the first exports of petroleum were made from new fields, developed and operated by U.S. companies, which made Ecuador the second-largest exporter of petroleum in Latin America, after Venezuela. In 1973 the government took back the oil concessions granted to the U.S. firms, refused compensation, and agreed with Venezuela on technological cooperation in their petroleum industries.

ECUMENICAL COUNCILS. *See* COUNCIL; ECUMENICAL MOVEMENT.

ECUMENICAL MOVEMENT, movement for worldwide cooperation and unity among Christian churches. The term "ecumenical" is derived from the Greek *oikoumenē*, "inhabited"; thus, ecumenical councils (*see* COUNCIL) of the church, the first of which was held at Nicaea in 325, were so designated from the first because representatives attended from churches throughout the known inhabited world. In the 19th century, "ecumenical" came to denote to the Roman Catholic Church (q.v.) a concern for Christian unity and for a renewal of the church that might in part result from it. To Protestants who have pioneered in and advanced the modern ecumenical movement since early in the present century, the term has applied not only to Christian unity but, more broadly, to the worldwide mission of Christianity.

Until the present century, only sporadic efforts were made to reunite a Christendom shattered, through the centuries, by schisms, the Reformation (q.v.), and other divisions and disputes; *see* CHRISTIAN CHURCH, HISTORY OF THE. The pressure toward unity was influenced in the 19th century by the development of such organizations as the missionary and Bible societies and the Young Men's Christian Association and Young Women's Christian Association (qq.v.), in all of which Protestants of varying denominations joined in support of common causes. At the start of the 20th century, the unity movement was almost exclusively Protestant.

Purposes of Ecumenism. The World Missionary Conference of 1910, held in Edinburgh, saw the beginning of modern ecumenism. From it flowed three streams of ecumenical endeavor: evangelistic, service, and doctrinal. Today, these three aspects are furthered through the World Council of Churches (q.v.), constituted in 1948; in the mid-1970's it included 271 churches with about 400,000,000 members.

Of the three concerns of modern ecumenism, the evangelical one brought about the formation, in 1921, of the International Missionary Council, comprising seventeen national mission organizations. The council coordinated mission strategy and aided new churches.

The service efforts made by Christians across denominational and national boundaries came to fruition in 1925, in Stockholm, when the Universal Christian Conference on Life and Work was convened to study the application of the Gospel to industrial, social, political, and international affairs. The Life and Work movement went forward under the slogan "service unites but doctrine divides". The third movement germinated by the Edinburgh Conference was, as noted, doctrinal. After years of preparation by clerics who had long shared a vision of a united church, in 1927 the First World Conference on Faith and Order was convened. The conference concluded that "God wills unity . . . (and) . . . however, we may justify the beginnings of disunion, we lament its continuance".

A second Conference on Faith and Order met in Edinburgh in 1937, the year in which another Life and Work Conference met at Oxford University. Delegates to the two conferences agreed that their work should be coordinated, and in 1938 a provisional committee was named to establish a "body representative of the churches". Formation of the World Council of Churches, which was to have come about in 1941, was delayed for seven years by World War II. Ultimately, in 1961, the missionary stream of Protestant ecumenical endeavor joined with the service and doctrinal currents as the International Missionary Council merged with the World Council of Churches.

The impulse to unity was acted upon almost solely by Protestants until 1920, in which year the Ecumenical Patriarchate of Constantinople (İstanbul, Turkey) issued an encyclical summoning all Christians to search for reunion. Eastern Orthodox churches have been members of the World Council since it was constituted. See ORTHODOX CHURCH.

Ecumenism continued to flourish among Protestants and Eastern Orthodox; for example, in 1950 the National Council of Churches was formed by twenty-nine denominations in the United States; see NATIONAL COUNCIL OF THE CHURCHES OF CHRIST IN THE UNITED STATES OF AMERICA. But the Roman Catholic Church remained, as it had been throughout this period of modern ecumenism, uncompromising in its rejection of the movement. From the Roman Catholic viewpoint, church unity could mean nothing less than the return of schismatic "sects" to the "one true Church". An encyclical issued in 1928 by Pope Pius XI (see under PIUS) had reemphasized this position, and as recently as 1954, Catholics were forbidden to attend the second assembly of the World Council of Churches.

The Second Vatican Council. Change came in 1959, when Pope John XXIII (see under JOHN) proposed the calling of a second Vatican Council (see VATICAN COUNCILS), to complete the work of the Vatican Council of 1870. Renewal and reunion were high on the agenda, and the world followed the proceedings closely. The pontiff created a Secretariat for Promoting Christian Unity. Breaking precedent, in 1961 he permitted Catholic observers officially to attend the third assembly of the World Council of Churches.

Also through his influence, when Vatican II opened in Saint Peter's Basilica (q.v.) in 1962, Protestant and Orthodox observers were accorded places of honor and included in all working sessions. The 2500 Catholic bishops who attended the four council sessions (1962–65) dealt with Christian unity. Their decree on ecumenism, promulgated in 1964, spoke not of "schismatics", but of "separated brethren", and it deplored sins against unity committed over the years by Catholics and non-Catholics alike.

On the death of Pope John, in 1963, his successor, Pope Paul VI (see under PAUL), made known his intention to continue John's ecumenical advances, describing unity as "the object of permanent interest, systematic study, and constant charity". The policy was emphasized by a number of major gestures. In 1964, the pope and the Orthodox ecumenical patriarch had a warm, historic meeting in Jerusalem, the first meeting of the heads of their two churches in more than 500 years. Two years later, the archbishop of Canterbury, head of the Anglican Communion (q.v.), visited Pope Paul. And in 1967, the pontiff visited the Orthodox patriarch in Turkey.

At the close of Vatican II, a Joint Working Group was established between the Vatican and the World Council of Churches. Numerous official dialogues were started in many countries between Catholics and Protestants. Significantly, the Joint Working Group declared in 1967 that there are not two ecumenical movements, but only one. Furthermore, at the fourth assembly of the World Council, in 1968, a Jesuit theologian speaking of Catholics as partners with other Christians in the quest for the unity "that is Christ's will for His Church", broached the possibility of Roman Catholic membership in the World Council.

An Era of Change. Ecumenism is changing. Consolidation of Protestant churches has progressed rapidly. A study completed in 1969 showed that since 1925, 130 denominations in 21 countries had combined into 38 united churches. In 1969, too, 121 denominations were engaged in 46 unification conferences in 29 countries; among the most comprehensive of these conferences was the Consultation on Church Union in the U.S., held by representatives of 9 denominations.

In areas other than that of unity, such as peace, international development studies, and relief for India and the secessionist Nigerian province of Biafra, the Roman Catholic Church and World Council churches pooled their resources. Furthermore, in the U.S., the urban crisis caused Christian churches to join with Jewish groups to achieve racial justice.

Ecumenical leaders make clear that they are not seeking a Christian unity that would gloss over basic theological differences. There remain many obstacles, such as papal authority, Mariology, contraception, and even a general fear of "bigness". But ecumenists believe that much progress can result from a continuing stress on the many points on which the churches agree.

See also MISSIONARY MOVEMENTS; PAPACY; THEOLOGY.   E.C.B.

ECZEMA, also called TETTER or SALT RHEUM, an inflammatory, chronic, vascular, noncontagious disease of the skin caused by allergy and hypersensitivity. The term is loosely used to include many skin conditions more properly included under dermatitis (q.v.). Eczema is characterized by a number of cutaneous lesions, such as macules, papules, pustules, vesicles, scales, and crusts. Macules are nonelevated skin spots, but papules are hard, circular, and elevated. Pustules are papularlike lesions which contain pus, and vesicles are small skin blisters which contain fluid. Eczematous lesions are usually accompanied by an exudation of serous fluid and by intense itching. One third to one half of all cutaneous affections are eczematous diseases.

EDAM, town of the Netherlands, in North Holland Province, on the IJsselmeer (formerly the Zuider Zee), about 10 miles N.E. of Amsterdam. In 1357, William V of Bavaria, Count of Holland (d. 1389), granted the town civic rights. In the 17th century, Edam was a shipping and shipbuilding center. Large silt deposits formed in the harbor, however, and commercial traffic moved to other ports, with a consequent decline in shipbuilding. Edam's Great Church, or Church of Saint Nicholas, completed in the 14th century, is noted for its stained glass windows and carved woodwork.

Cheesemaking is the principal industry in Edam, and the town gives its name to all of the sweet-milk cheese processed throughout North Holland; see CHEESE. Leather, cordage, and sails are also manufactured. Pop. (1971 est.) 18,495.

EDDA, name given to two famous collections of Old Icelandic literature. The origin of the word is doubtful; scholars have variously traced its derivation from the Old Norse word *edda*, "great-grandmother", because the stories told are reminiscent of folktales recounted by old women; from Oddi, the native locality of Saemund (1056–1133), an Icelandic historian once thought to have written one of the *Eddas*; and from the Old Norse word *ōthr*, "poetry". The term is properly given only to the *Prose Edda*, or *Younger Edda*, a work written by the Icelandic historian Snorri Sturluson (*see* SNORRI STURLUSON) in the 13th century. The first historical use of the term *Edda* in describing Snorri's writings occurred in the *Uppsala Codex*, transcribed about 1300 and considered the most important manuscript of the work. The *Poetic Edda* or *Elder Edda* was discovered in 1643 by an Icelandic bishop, Brynjolf Sveinsson (1605–75), who erroneously ascribed it to Saemund and named it the *Edda of Saemund the Wise.*

Content of the *Eddas*. The *Prose Edda* is primarily a guide to the poetry of the scalds, the ancient Scandinavian poets. It has five sections: *Formáli* (Prologue), *Gylfaginning* (The Deception of Gylfi), *Bragaroethur* (The Sayings of Bragi), *Skaldskaparmál* (The Art of Poetry), and *Háttatal* (List of Meters). The prologue is an account of the Biblical story of the Creation and the Flood. The next two sections relate ancient Scandinavian myths, and they are the most important source for modern knowledge of that subject. The fourth section consists of instructions and rules for writing scaldic verse, and the fifth is a technical commentary on poetry written by Snorri in honor of Haakon IV (*see under* HAAKON), King of Norway.

The *Poetic Edda* is a collection of more than thirty poems, composed between the 9th and 12th centuries, concerning ancient Scandinavian myths and heroes. None of the poets is known by name, and the poems may have been written in the British Isles, Norway, Denmark, or Iceland. Many of the poems are incomplete; they were apparently written down in the 12th century after having been handed down by word of mouth. The work is approximately divisible into two sections, one concerning the gods and the other concerning human heroes. The most remarkable of the lays of the Gods is the *Völuspá* (The Prophecy of the Völva, or

Sibyl), which narrates the Creation and prophesies the end of the world. The second section is, for the most part, the story of Sigurd, the German Siegfried. *See* ICELANDIC LITERATURE: *The Saga*; NIBELUNGENLIED.

EDDINGTON, Sir Arthur Stanley (1882–1944), British astronomer and physicist, born at Kendal, England, and educated at Owens College (now Manchester University), and Trinity College, University of Cambridge. He was chief assistant at the Royal Observatory at Greenwich from 1906 to 1913, when he became professor of astronomy at Cambridge. From 1921 to 1923 he was president of the Royal Astronomical Society. He was knighted in 1930. Eddington helped clarify the theory of relativity (q.v.), but his most important scientific work was on the evolution, constitution, and motion of stars. His book *The Internal Constitution of the Stars* (1926) was a classic on this subject. The following year he wrote *Stars and Atoms,* a popular condensation of the same material. Thereafter he was best known as a popularizer of science, and his work *The Nature of the Physical World* (1928) was one of the most widely read books on abstract science ever published. His later works, however, were regarded by some scientists as being too metaphysical to be of great value.

EDDOES. *See* TARO.

EDDY, Mary Baker (1821–1910), founder of the Church of Christ, Scientist, born in Bow, N.H. Because of physical frailty she received most of her early education at home from her brother. She was widowed a few months after her marriage in 1843. She married twice again, in 1853 to an itinerant homeopathist whom she divorced twenty years later, and in 1877 to Asa Gilbert Eddy (d. 1882), a recruit to her new religion. Mrs. Eddy's only child, a son by her first husband, was born in 1844. From that year until 1862, she was continually plagued by ill health from which she constantly sought relief. In 1862 she went to Portland, Maine, to consult Dr. Phineas Parkhurst Quimby (1802–66), a mental healer. Quimby restored her health temporarily after a brief treatment, and for several years she followed Quimby's method of healing. She suffered further serious injury to her health as a result of a fall and attributed her recovery from this injury to a spiritual revelation she received upon reading the Bible, especially the passage on Christian healing in Matt. 9:2. She dated her discovery of Christian Science (q.v.) from that revelation in 1866. Mrs. Eddy spent the remainder of her life formulating and teaching her doctrines. *The Science of Man* (1870) was the first of her works on Christian Science; from its date of publication to 1880 she taught her system in Lynn, Mass. In 1875 her most important book, *Science and Health with Key to the Scriptures,* was published. She founded the Christian Science Association in 1875–76 and three years later obtained a charter for the Church of Christ, Scientist. She organized the Massachusetts Metaphysical College in Boston (1881) for the purpose of training practitioners, or mental healers. She closed the college when conflicts occurred among the students in 1889. In 1892 she reorganized the Church in Boston, centralizing control of the new Mother Church, The First Church of Christ, Scientist, in her own hands. She later retired, leaving the management to a board of directors, but retained control of church affairs as pastor emeritus until shortly before her death at her home in Chestnut Hill, near Boston. She founded The Christian Science Publishing Society, established in 1883, and organized and edited various publications connected with the Church. Among her other works are *Christian Healing* (1886), *Retrospection and Introspection* (an autobiography, 1891), *Church Manual* (1895–1908), and *The First Church of Christ, Scientist, and Miscellany* (1913).

EDDY CURRENTS, electric currents induced in masses of metal which either rotate in relation to a magnetic field, or which are stationary under a varying magnetic field. They are called eddy currents because they travel in a circular path in the metal, or behave as eddies. They are also known as Foucault currents after their discoverer, the French physicist Jean Bernard Léon Foucault (q.v.). An appreciable amount of

Mary Baker Eddy

energy is lost in electromagnetic machinery through eddy currents, because the energy of such currents goes into heat which is wasted. To reduce this loss, motor and generator armatures, as well as transformer cores and parts of other electric devices in which eddy currents are found, are constructed of thin, insulated metal plates. This method of construction prevents eddy currents from traveling through the length of the armature, and effectively eliminates them. The plates are often made of silicon steel, which has a high specific resistance, another factor in reducing eddy currents. The use of eddy currents is of great importance for screening effects in high-frequency electronic devices. If a conductor needs to be insulated from the effects of a high-frequency oscillation in its neighborhood, the conductor may be surrounded with a sheet of conducting material, called a screen or shield. The oscillation will induce eddy currents in the screen, and these currents will in turn set up a field opposite to that of the oscillation, protecting the conductor within it. An example of such screening is found in shielded cable. The common automobile speedometer is based on the principle of eddy currents; see SPEEDOMETER.

See also DYNAMOELECTRIC MACHINERY; ELECTRICITY; TRANSFORMER.

EDDYSTONE ROCKS, group of gneiss (q.v.), or granitelike rocks in the w. end of the English Channel, 9 mi. off the coast of Cornwall and Devon counties, and 14 miles s.w. of the Plymouth breakwaters. They have been the cause of many shipwrecks. Four lighthouses have been constructed on or near the rocks, only to be destroyed by storms or fire. Constructed in 1698, 1709, 1759, and 1882, the lighthouses have been excellent examples of how engineering design concepts advanced over the years. The first lighthouse was destroyed in a storm in 1699. The second, known as Rudyerd's Tower, was built of bolted oak timbers; it was destroyed by a fire in 1755. The third, known as Smeaton's Tower, named after its designer, the British engineer John Smeaton (1724–92), incorporated interlocking stonework, using a mortar composed of quicklime, clay, sand, and crushed-iron slag to bind the stones. This structure is possibly the first in which concrete was used since Roman times. The rocks upon which the structure rested began to crumble during the 19th century, and in 1877, the construction of the fourth lighthouse, named the J. N. Douglass Tower, after its designer, was begun. It employed bronze bolts to reinforce the interlocking stone, a technique that was later used in the construc-

tion of many other lighthouses, and was completed in 1882.　　　　　　　　　　　　K.B.H.

EDE, town of Nigeria, Western State, on the Oshun R., 45 miles N.E. of Ibadan. The town is on a railroad. Cotton is grown in the area, and local industries include cotton weaving, cottonseed milling, and cacao and palm processing. The town is the home of Timi of Ede, a local Yoruba chief. Pop. (1971 est.) 162,617.

EDELMAN, Gerald Maurice (1929–), American biochemist, born in New York City and educated at Ursinus College and the University of Pennsylvania. In 1960, after receiving a PH.D. degree at Rockefeller University, he joined the faculty. He shared the 1972 Nobel Prize in medicine and physiology with the British biochemist Rodney Robert Porter. Edelman was cited for his independent research, begun in 1959, on the chemical structure of antibodies, blood proteins that help the body defend itself against infection (*see* IMMUNITY).

EDELWEISS, common name for a densely wooly perennial herb, *Leontopodium alpinum,* in the Compositae (q.v.) family, found at high altitudes in Asia and Europe. The inconspicuous blossoms are borne in heads surrounded by wooly, petal-shaped leaves. The edelweiss is readily cultivated in gardens in the United States and Europe and grows best on coarse, sandy loam. The flower is the floral emblem of Switzerland.

EDEMA, general term for the accumulation of excess fluid in any body tissue, cavity, or organ, except bone. Accumulation in tissue is called hydrops; in the pleural cavity, hydrothorax; in the cranium, hydrocephalus; and in the abdominal cavity, ascites. Generalized edema is referred to as dropsy. Major causes are heart or kidney failure, low blood serum protein (*see* BLOOD: *Blood Plasma*) after starvation or liver failure, shock (q.v.), and impaired return of blood from extremities. Subcutaneous edema always appears first in feet and ankles, to which fluid gravitates. Treatment involves stimulating the kidney (q.v.) to excrete excess fluid, digitalis (q.v.) for heart failure, proper diet in starvation or liver failure, and other specific therapy. Allergy (q.v.) and injury can cause localized subcutaneous edema.　　　　　　　　　　　D.S.T.

EDEN (Heb., "delight"), also called Garden of Eden or Garden of Paradise, in the first three chapters of the book of Genesis (q.v.), the first residence of man; *see* ADAM AND EVE. Because contemporary scholars tend to regard the Biblical descriptions as imaginary, endless controversy has revolved around the question of the geographic location of Eden. The name Eden is probably connected with Edinn (the Sumerian name for the plain of Babylon), and the author of Genesis may have had in mind the verdant landscape of Mesopotamia. Eden is mentioned in other Old Testament books as a place of extreme fertility (Isa. 51:3, Ezek. 28:13, 31:9, Joel 2:3), and the name continues to connote an ideal setting.

EDEN, (Robert) Anthony, 1st Earl of Avon (1897–1977), British statesman, born in Bishop Auckland, Durham, England, and educated at Eton College and Christ Church College, University of Oxford. He served as a captain, brigade major, and a general-staff officer during World War I, and was awarded the Military Cross. His political career began in 1923, when as a Conservative Party candidate he was elected to the House of Commons; from 1926 to 1929 he was parliamentary secretary to Sir (Joseph) Austen Chamberlain (q.v.), then secretary of state for foreign affairs. Eden became parliamentary undersecretary of the British foreign office in 1931; three years later, he was appointed lord privy seal and privy councilor. In 1935 he was appointed minister without portfolio for League of Nations (q.v.) affairs and, in the same year, became secretary of state for foreign affairs. Eden resigned his office in 1938 because of his disagreement with the appeasement policy adopted by Prime Minister (Arthur) Neville Chamberlain (see under CHAMBERLAIN), with the signing of the Munich Pact (q.v.). Eden was appointed secretary of state for war in 1940, and again served as minister of foreign affairs from

Anthony Eden UPI

1940 to 1945 under Prime Minister Winston Leonard Spencer Churchill (q.v.). From 1942 to 1945 he was also leader of the House of Commons. After the election victory of the Labour Party (q.v.) in 1945, Eden was a leading member of the opposition in the House; following victory by the Conservatives in 1951 he again became foreign secretary in the new Churchill cabinet. Upon Churchill's retirement in April, 1955, Eden was appointed prime minister. His policy of armed intervention during the Suez Canal crisis in late 1956 caused widespread controversy, and he resigned in January, 1957; see ISRAEL; SUEZ CANAL.

Eden was knighted in 1954 and created earl in 1961. He wrote *Days for Decision* (1949), a collection of his speeches; a trilogy of World War II memoirs, *Full Circle* (1960), *Facing the Dictators* (1962), and *The Reckoning* (1965); and *Towards Peace in Indo-China* (1966). *See also* GREAT BRITAIN: *History: Between the Wars: The Postwar Period.*

EDERLE, Gertrude Caroline (1906–   ), American swimmer, born in New York City. In 1924 she held eighteen world swimming records and was on the United States Olympic swimming team. On Aug. 6, 1926, she became the first woman to swim across the English Channel and set a new time record. She swam from Cape Gris-Nez, France, to Dover, England, a distance of 35 mi., in 14 hr., 31 min., using the American crawl stroke. The previous record had been 16 hr., 23 min. She later became a professional swimmer and a swimming instructor.

EDESSA (Aramaic, *Urhai*; modern Turk. *Urfa*), the Greek name of an ancient Mesopotamian city. The Arabs believed it to be the Ur of the Chaldees associated with the Hebrew patriarch Abraham (q.v.). The known history of Edessa dates from the conquest of Persia by the Macedonian warrior Alexander III (q.v.), known as the Great. The Christian religion was established there in the 3rd century, and numerous monasteries were built in the city. After the 5th century Edessa came under control of the Muslims and remained so until 1097, when the Crusaders made it the capital of a Latin principality which survived until 1144; see CRUSADES. The city was sacked by the Ottoman Turks in 1147, and for the next several centuries constantly changed hands. In 1637 the Turks regained it permanently. It was renamed Urfa by the Turks in the 15th century.

EDGAR, or EADGER, known as EDGAR THE PEACEFUL (944–75), Saxon King of the English (959–75), younger son of King Edmund I (q.v.). In 957, during the rule of his brother, King Edwy

(d. 959), Edgar was chosen by the Mercians and Northumbrians to be their sovereign. Two years later he succeeded to the entire English kingdom. One of his first acts was to recall Saint Dunstan (q.v.), whom Edwy had exiled. Edgar made Dunstan bishop of Worcester and of London and archbishop of Canterbury. His reign was notable for the establishment of national consolidation, the reformation of the clergy, the improvement of the judiciary system, and the formation of a fleet to defend the coast against the Northmen (q.v.).

EDGE HILL, BATTLE OF, first battle of the Great Rebellion (q.v.) in England. It was fought on Sunday, Oct. 23, 1642, on Edge Hill, an elevated ridge in Warwickshire, near the Warwickshire-Oxfordshire border. The forces involved were the Royalists led by Charles I (q.v.), King of England and the Parliamentarians led by Robert Devereux, 2nd Earl of Essex (*see under* DEVEREUX), each with approximately 14,000 infantry and cavalry troops. The outcome of the battle was indecisive militarily, exhausting equally the strength of both armies. Essex finally retired from Edge Hill on Oct. 24, forfeiting the victory to Charles. The English soldier and statesman Oliver Cromwell (*see under* CROMWELL) fought in the battle as a captain in the Parliamentarian forces.

EDGEWORTH, Maria (1767–1849), British novelist, daughter of the English author and inventor Richard Lovell Edgeworth (1744–1817), born in Oxfordshire, England. She spent the greater part of her life in Edgeworthstown, Ireland, and, while acting as her father's assistant in managing his estate, she acquired a knowledge of the Irish peasantry that was of importance in her writing. She was greatly influenced by her father's ideas on education, especially evident in her books for children and her works of nonfiction. Her first work, *Letters to Literary Ladies* (1795) dealt with the importance of education for women; *The Parent's Assistant* (1796) is a collection of children's stories, each with a clearly drawn moral. *Practical Education* (1798) was written in collaboration with her father.

Maria Edgeworth is most noted, however, for her novels of Irish life, which were the first works of fiction to present a careful study of Irish provincial and peasant life and manners. Her first novel, *Castle Rackrent,* published anonymously in 1800, was an immediate success. *The Absentee* (1812), one of her best works, depicts the evils of the system of absentee landlords. Her novels of English life, like her other works, are distinguished by humor, sprightly dialogue, and a clear style. The heroine

of her *Belinda* (1801) was one of the first women in the English novel to abandon the simper and smelling salts that characterized women in Gothic novels (*see* GOTHIC ROMANCE), and this book is considered by some to have had an influence on the 19th-century British novelist Jane Austen (q.v.). After her father's death in 1817, Maria completed his *Memoirs* and traveled abroad. Her last novel, *Helen,* appeared in 1834.

EDICT OF NANTES, decree giving partial religious freedom to the Huguenots (q.v.), proclaimed by Henry IV (q.v.), King of France, in 1598 and revoked by Louis XIV (q.v.), King of France, in 1685.

The Edict of Nantes ended the series of religious wars between Catholics and Protestants that ravaged France from 1562 to 1598; *see* FRANCE: *History.* During these wars, several ineffective treaties were concluded, embodying privileges for the Huguenots. The Edict of Nantes included the religious provisions of these treaties and added a number of others.

By the terms of the edict, the Huguenots were granted liberty of conscience throughout France. They were allowed to build churches and hold religious services in specified villages and the suburbs of any city except episcopal and archiepiscopal cities, royal residences, and within a five-mile radius of Paris; Huguenot nobles were permitted to hold services in their homes. Followers of the faith were granted civil rights and the right to hold official positions. Four universities or schools (at Montauban, Montpellier, Sedan, and Saumur) were permitted to be Huguenot. A special court, composed of one Huguenot and fifteen Catholics and called the *Chambre de l'Édit* ("the Chamber of the Edict") was established for Huguenot protection in the *parlement* of Paris (*see* PARLIAMENT); subsidiary chambers were established in the provincial *parlements.* Huguenot pastors were paid by the government, as were Catholic priests. As a guarantee of protection, 100 fortified cities were given to the Huguenots for eight years.

The provisions of the Edict of Nantes were never fully carried out, even during the reign of Henry IV. Catholic persecution of the Huguenots persisted, and in 1681 erupted in undisguised brutality. The edict was revoked by Louis XIV in 1685; as his reason for revocation of the decree, he said that there were no more Huguenots in France.

EDINA, suburban residential village of Minnesota, in Hennepin Co., on Minnehaha and Nine Mile creeks, adjoining the southwestern corner

A view of Edinburgh. Castle Rock (left, rear), dating from the 6th century, overlooks the Gothic spires of the monument to Sir Walter Scott (right) in East Princes Gardens. Famous Princes Street is at the far right.

British Travel Assn.

of Minneapolis. Pop. (1960) 28,501; (1970) 44,046.

EDINBURG, city in Texas, and county seat of Hidalgo Co., in the Lower Rio Grande valley, about 10 miles N. of McAllen. The city is in an ir-rigated agricultural area that produces cotton, truck crops, and citrus fruits. The city manufac-tures metal products and oil-field equipment. Edinburg is the site of Pan American College, es-tablished in 1927. Pop. (1970) 17,163.

EDINBURGH, former name of the Scottish county of Midlothian (q.v.).

EDINBURGH, Great Britain, city, royal burgh, and capital of Scotland, and county seat of Midlothian (formerly Edinburgh) County, 2 miles S. of the Firth of Forth and about 40 miles E. of Glasgow. Edinburgh is the second-largest city in Scotland, after Glasgow.

Among notable public buildings in Edinburgh are Holyrood Palace, a 16th-century royal resi-dence, the site of the murder of David Rizzio, a favorite of Mary, Queen of Scots (qq.v.); Parlia-ment House, built in 1640, which became the seat of the supreme courts when the Scottish parliament was dissolved by the Act of Union (q.v.) in 1707; the General Register House (1774), archive for national records; and Edin-burgh Castle, which contains the 11th-century Saint Margaret's Chapel, the 15th-century Pal-ace, or King's Lodging, and the Scottish National

War Memorial, built by public subscription after World War I. The ecclesiastical buildings in-clude the parish Church of Saint Giles (1100), Saint Giles Cathedral, the two Greyfriars churches (occupying separate halves of the same building), Tron Church, Saint Cuthbert's Church, Saint Andrew's Church, and Saint George's Church.

Among the many monuments in Edinburgh are those commemorating the Scottish literary figures Robert Burns, Robert Louis Stevenson, and Sir Walter Scott; the British naval hero Ho-ratio Nelson; and the soldier and statesman Ar-thur Wellesley, 1st Duke of Wellington (qq.v.). A life-sized statue of Abraham Lincoln (q.v.), sixteenth President of the United States, and a freed slave honors Scotsmen who died in the American Civil War. A memorial marks the spot where the Solemn League and Covenant of 1643 was signed; see COVENANTERS. Other points of in-terest include the Princes Street Gardens; the house of the Protestant reformer John Knox (q.v.); the Robert Louis Stevenson Memorial House, and King Arthur's seat, an 822-ft. hill from which Arthur (q.v.) is said to have watched his forces defeat the Picts (q.v.). Facing Salisbury Crags are scenic spots described by Sir Walter Scott in his novel The Heart of Midlothian.

Because of its educational institutions and scientific and literary associations, Edinburgh is often called "the modern Athens". Among the scientific institutions are the Royal College of Surgeons, founded in 1505, the Royal College of Physicians (1681), and three astronomical ob-

One of the highlights of the Edinburgh International Festival is the Scottish Command Military Tattoo, which is held in front of Edinburgh Castle. The mounted band of the French Guards, pictured here, rehearses for the tattoo.

British Information Services

servatories. Edinburgh University, founded in 1583, the youngest of Scottish universities, was one of the first in Great Britain to admit women. Other important schools are the Royal High School, Edinburgh Academy, Heriot-Watt University, Fettes College, and Merchiston Academy, the last two modeled on Eton and Harrow in England. Various institutions for theological training are maintained by the United Free Church, the Church of Scotland, and the Roman Catholic Church. Notable libraries, both in Parliament House, are the Signet Library of 110,000 volumes, and the Advocates' Library of about 550,000 volumes; the latter is the largest library in Great Britain and one of the five entitled to receive a copy of every book published in Great Britain. Other cultural institutions include the Royal Scottish Academy and the National Gallery of Scotland.

For three weeks, in late August and early September, the city is the site of the annual Edinburgh International Festival, established in 1947, featuring programs of music, drama, dance, motion pictures, and the fine arts.

Commerce and Industry. Edinburgh has been known for its printing industry since the early 16th century. The principal modern industrial establishments in the city are paper mills, tanneries, iron and brass foundries, breweries and distilleries, and factories manufacturing rubber products, electric fittings, cordage, hosiery, soap, machine tools, food products, and chemicals. Edinburgh is also a market center for agricultural produce and has a number of cattle and grain markets and slaughterhouses.

History. The site of Edinburgh was occupied by the Romans for more than 300 years; thereafter control of the area reverted to the British tribes. The Britons were later conquered by Picts from the south, who made Edinburgh Castle their seat until they were overthrown in the early 7th century by the Saxons under Edwin (q.v.), King of Northumbria. The city was named for Edwin. For a long period, possession of the territory was in question, and tenure was short-lived. In the 11th century the region, known as Lothian, was conquered by Malcolm II Mackenneth, first King of Scotland (d. 1034). It was subsequently resettled by Anglo-Saxons and Normans under Malcolm MacDuncan, King of Scotland (d. 1093). King Robert Bruce (q.v.) granted Edinburgh a charter in 1329, and the city became the national capital in 1437, following the assassination of James I (q.v.), King of Scotland, at Perth, the former capital. In 1482 James III (q.v.) issued the Golden Charter, which gave the city the right to impose and collect taxes. A general charter was granted Edinburgh in 1603 by James VI, King of Scotland. In that year, however, Edinburgh lost much of its national stature when James VI became James I (q.v.), King of England and departed for London.

Although the early Scottish kings did much to expand the city, basic improvements were not made until the 19th century. In that period the former bed of the Nor'Loch, the main obstacle to the integration of the city and an unsanitary area, was drained completely and a road was built across it, connecting the old and new sections of the city. Old Town, or West Edinburgh, lies amid a group of hills and valleys dominated by Edinburgh Castle. To the east is New Town, which began to take shape near the end of the 18th century and was merged with the ancient burgh in 1856. Portobello and parts of several parishes were incorporated into Edinburgh in 1896; parts of South Leith, Duddingston, and other areas were included in 1900; and Leith, four parishes, and many villages to the south and west became part of the city in 1920.

Population. The population of Edinburgh (1971 prelim.) was 448,895.

EDINBURGH, UNIVERSITY OF, coeducational institution of higher learning, located in Edinburgh, Scotland. The university was established in 1583 by the town council of Edinburgh under a royal charter granted the year before by James VI, King of Scotland, later James I (q.v.), King of England. The institution began operating as a college of arts; a chair of theology was added in 1642, and one in medicine in 1685. After a reorganization in the 18th century, the school was given the status of a university and, in addition to the three courses of study already provided, offered courses in law, science, and music.

By acts of Parliament in 1858 and 1889, the university was made independent of the authority of the Edinburgh town council and became a self-governing corporation composed of the registered graduates, the student body, the professors, the principal, the rector (elected triennially by the matriculated students), the vice-chancellor, and the chancellor. The Universities Act of 1858 also instituted the university court, a governing body consisting of the rector (who presides), the principal, the lord provost of the city of Edinburgh, and eleven assessors representing both university and city. The university court administers the university's property and finances, and it appoints examiners, lecturers, and certain professors. The curricula and discipline of the university are supervised by the senatus academicus, which includes the principal, the professors, and certain lecturers; the decisions of the senatus are subject to approval by the university court. The general council, composed of all the persons listed above, is an advisory body except for one function, the election of the chancellor.

The older buildings of the present university, which date from 1789, were erected on the site of the Church of Saint Mary in the Field, the "Kirk o' Field" where the second husband of Mary, Queen of Scots, Henry Stewart, Lord Darnley (qq.v.), was murdered in 1567. M'Ewan Hall, a famous structure in the early Italian Renaissance style, built between 1888 and 1897, is used for all public and academic functions. Other buildings include the school of music, 1858; the medical school, built between 1878 and 1888; the John Usher Institute of Public Health, for training in bacteriology and chemistry, 1902; and the King's Buildings, for scientific studies and engineering, opened in 1924.

The collection of the university library was begun in 1580 with 300 books given to the town council of Edinburgh by Clement Little, an advocate; in 1649, a notable addition was made to the collection with the books of the Scottish poet William Drummond (1585–1649) of Hawthornden, who had studied at the university. The library contains more than 1,000,000 bound volumes and approximately 35,000 manuscripts, some of great value. The Royal Scottish Museum is part of the university structure, and the Royal Infirmary is associated with the medical school.

The income of the university is derived from legacies and endowments, parliamentary grants, and student fees. In 1901, the American manufacturer and philanthropist Andrew Carnegie (q.v.) established a £2,000,000 fund for the four Scottish universities; half the income from the fund was allocated as tuition fees for Scottish students.

After three years of work or a four-year honors course of study the university awards either the master of arts or the bachelor of science degree. Both degrees are the approximate equivalent of an American baccalaureate degree. The degrees of master (distinct from the master of arts) and doctor are conferred as higher degrees in specific fields. Edinburgh was one of the first universities in Great Britain to admit women (1889) to its undergraduate colleges, and three dormitories for women were built in 1916. In 1972–73 the student enrollment was about 11,000 and the teaching staff numbered 1500.

EDIRNE, formerly ADRIANOPLE (anc. *Hadrianopolis* or *Adrianopolis*), city of Turkey in Europe, and capital of Edirne Province, about 125 miles N.W. of İstanbul. The city is on both banks of the Tunja R., at its confluence with the Meric. Edirne lies in the center of the fertile Thracian coastal plain, and is a marketplace for fruit, wine grapes, and other agricultural produce. The principal items manufactured in the city are silk, cotton, linen, woolen goods, leather articles, and tapestries. Raw silk, rose water, attar of roses, opium, wax, and "Turkey-red" dye are among the products exported from the city and province.

Originally known as Uskadama or Uskodama when it was part of E. Thrace, the city was rebuilt and renamed by the Roman emperor Hadrian (q.v.) about 125 A.D. It was the focal point of the battle of Adrianople (378 A.D.), in which the Romans under Emperor Valens (q.v.) were defeated by the Goths (q.v.). Edirne was then conquered by the Avars, followed by the Bulgarians, and finally by the Crusaders. In 1361 the Turks gained control of the city, and it was the residence of the Turkish sultans until 1453. Edirne constantly changed hands during the Russo-Turkish wars of 1828–29 and 1877–78, and the Balkan Wars (q.v.) of 1912–13. Pop. (1970) 54,885.

EDISON, urban township of New Jersey, in Middlesex Co., on the Raritan R., adjoining New Brunswick. Several residential and industrial communities are included in the township. The industrial section produces aluminum, creosote, lumber, cosmetics, paint, heating and air-conditioning equipment, pharmaceuticals, electrical and electronic equipment, chemicals, and glass, plastic, and metal products. Menlo Park is the site of part of the Edison Laboratory National Monument, commemorating the laboratory used by the American inventor Thomas A. Edison (q.v.) from 1876 to 1887 while he worked on the incandescent light bulb and other inventions. The communities of Stelton and Bonhamtown were settled in the 17th century; the Raritan Industrial Park, formerly the Raritan Arsenal, adjoins the latter. In Piscataway is Saint James Episcopal Church, which has historical items from the 17th and 18th centuries. Incorporated in 1693, Edison was formerly called Raritan Township. Pop. (1960) 44,799; (1970) 67,120.

EDISON, Thomas Alva (1847–1931), American inventor, born in Milan, Ohio. He attended school for only three months, in Port Huron, Mich. When he was twelve years old he began work as a newsboy on the Grand Trunk Railway, devoting his spare time mainly to experimentation with printing presses and with electrical and mechanical apparatus. In 1862 he published a weekly, known as the *Grand Trunk Herald,*

Thomas Alva Edison

printing it in a freight car that also served as his laboratory. For saving the life of a stationmaster's child, he was rewarded by being taught telegraphy. Although he became an excellent telegraphic operator, he was too erratic and fond of experimentation to remain at one job for any length of time. While working as a telegraph operator, he made his first important invention, a telegraphic repeating instrument that enabled messages to be transmitted automatically over a second line without the presence of an operator.

Edison next secured employment in Boston, Mass., and devoted all his spare time there to research. He invented a vote recorder, which, although possessing many merits, was not sufficiently practical to warrant its adoption. He also devised and partly completed a stock-quotation printer. Later, while employed by the Gold and Stock Telegraph Company of New York, N.Y., he greatly improved their apparatus and service. By the sale of telegraphic appliances, Edison earned $40,000, and with this money he established his own laboratory in 1876. Afterward, he devised an automatic telegraph system that made possible a greater speed and range of transmission. Edison's crowning achievement in telegraphy was his invention of machines for quadruplex and sextuplex telegraphic transmission, which followed a duplex system he had previously devised. These inventions made possible simultaneous transmission of several mes-

sages on one line, and thus greatly increased the usefulness of existing telegraph lines. Important in the development of the telephone, which had recently been invented by the American physicist and inventor Alexander Graham Bell (*see under* BELL), was Edison's invention of the carbon telephone transmitter.

In 1877 Edison announced his invention of a phonograph by which sound could be recorded mechanically on a tinfoil cylinder. Two years later he exhibited publicly his incandescent electric light bulb, his most important invention, and the one requiring the most careful research and experimentation to perfect (*see* ELECTRIC LIGHTING). This new light was a remarkable success; Edison promptly occupied himself with the improvement of the bulbs, and also of the dynamos for generating the necessary electric current.

In 1887 Edison moved his laboratory from Menlo Park, N.J., to West Orange, N.J., where he constructed a large laboratory for experimentation and research. In the following year he invented the kinetoscope, the first machine to produce motion pictures by a rapid succession of individual views. Among his later noteworthy inventions was the Edison storage battery (an alkaline, nickel-iron storage battery), the result of many thousands of experiments. The Edison storage battery was extremely rugged and had a high electrical capacity per unit of weight. He also developed a phonograph in which the sound was impressed on a disk instead of a cylinder. This phonograph had a diamond needle and other improved features. By synchronizing his phonograph and kinetoscope, he produced, in 1913, the first talking moving pictures. Other discoveries by Edison include the electric pen, the mimeograph, the microtasimeter (used for the detection of minute changes in temperature), and a wireless telegraphic method for communicating with moving trains. At the outbreak of World War I, Edison designed, built, and operated plants for the manufacture of benzene, carbolic acid, and aniline derivatives. In 1915 he was appointed president of the United States Navy Consulting Board, and in that capacity made many valuable discoveries. His later work consisted mainly of improving and perfecting previous inventions. Altogether, Edison patented more than 1000 inventions. Few, if any, great scientific discoveries can be credited to him, but by his skill and ingenuity, he was able to surpass in practical achievements many scientists with broad academic backgrounds.

In 1878 Edison was appointed Chevalier of the Legion of Honor of France, and in 1889 was made Commander of the Legion of Honor. In 1892 he was awarded the Albert medal of the Society of Arts of Great Britain, and in 1928 received the Congressional gold medal "for development and application of inventions that have revolutionized civilization in the last century". In 1929 he was universally honored on the fiftieth anniversary of the invention of the incandescent lamp. In 1955 his West Orange, N.J., home and laboratory were established as the Edison National Historic Site.

EDISON NATIONAL HISTORIC SITE. See EDISON, THOMAS ALVA.

EDMONTON, city and provincial capital, central Alberta, Canada, on the North Saskatchewan R. Edmonton is the hub of central and N. Alberta, and the principal transshipment point for goods moving to and from the Canadian Arctic and Alaska. Of major importance to the economy of the city is the oil and gas industry. Within 300 miles of Edmonton lie the Leduc and Pembina oil fields and the tar sand deposits near Fort MacMurray, potentially one of the largest reserves in the world. Major oil and gas pipelines, some with connections to the United States, pass through the city. Indeed, Edmonton uses natural gas from the nearby fields as its main source of fuel. Also mined in the region are coal, precious metals, and uranium ore. Edmonton is the second largest meat-processing center in Canada; its other industries include furniture and bedding, foodstuffs, clothing, brick, and soap.

In 1795 both the North West Company and Hudson's Bay Company (q.v.) built fur-trading forts on the river near the present site of the city. Fort Edmonton, the Hudson's Bay Company post, was a supply center for the fur trade of the Northwest. The Canadian Pacific Railroad arrived in the area in 1891. In 1892 Edmonton was incorporated as a town and in 1904 as a city. Rapid growth of the city began when the rail connection with Calgary was completed in 1905. Pop. (1976) 461,361; Census Metropolitan Area 554,228.

EDMUND, Saint or **EADMUND, Saint,** also known as SAINT EDMUND THE MARTYR (841?–70), King of the East Anglians (855–70). He was, according to tradition, born in Nuremberg, the son of the Saxon king Alkmund. Nothing is recorded of Edmund's reign until the invasion made in the years 866 to 870 by the Danes, against whom he led the East Anglians in the battle of Hoxne (870). His forces were defeated by the Danes and he was slain. It is said that Edmund was martyred for his refusal to deny Christianity and to rule his kingdom in vassalage to the Danish overlords. The remains of the king, who was canonized, lie in Bury Saint Edmunds, England.

EDMUND I, or EADMUND I, known as EDMUND THE DEED-DOER or EDMUND THE MAGNIFICENT (922?–46), Saxon king of England (940–46), the son of King Edward the Elder (*see under* EDWARD). He participated in the Battle of Brunanburh in 937, and succeeded his half brother Athelstan (q.v.) as king in 940. In that year Olaf Sitricson (*see under* OLAF), a Dane who ruled part of Ireland, became king of Northumbria, a territory bordering on that of the English kingdom. In 944, on the breaking of a treaty by Olaf, Edmund drove the Northman king from Northumbria. In 945 Edmund occupied the kingdom of Strathclyde, west of Northumbria, and turned it over to his ally Malcolm I MacDonald, King of Scotland (d. 954). The following year Edmund was stabbed to death by a robber. He was succeeded by his brother Edred (d. 955).

EDMUND II, or EADMUND II, known as IRONSIDE (980?–1016), Saxon king of the English (1016), son of King Ethelred (q.v.). When Ethelred died (1016), Edmund was chosen king by the people of London, but Canute II (q.v.), King of Denmark, who was leading an invasion of England, secured the support of the council (*witan*) at Southampton and of Edric (d. 1017), Ethelred's son-in-law. Edmund met the Danes in battle, winning several engagements and relieving Canute's siege of London. He was defeated at Assandun (now Ashington), however, through the treachery of Edric, who had pretended to desert Canute. A truce was arranged between Canute and Edmund; Edmund was permitted to rule the south of England until his death, when it reverted to Canute.

EDMUND RICH, Saint (1175–1240), English prelate, born in Abingdon, Berkshire. He was educated at the University of Oxford, where he later taught logic (1219–26). About 1227, having acquired fame as a preacher in Paris as well as in England, he was commissioned by the pope to preach the Sixth Crusade (*see* CRUSADES: *Sixth Crusade*) throughout England. Six years later, at the instance of Pope Gregory IX (1147–1241), he was appointed archbishop of Canterbury. As archbishop, he instituted reforms in courts and monasteries and among the clergy. When Rich disputed with Henry III (q.v.), King of England, over the latter's attempt to appropriate Church revenues, the king worked through the papal legate (*see* PAPAL LEGATE) to nullify the power of the archbishop. Rich is the author of a treatise on asceticism (q.v.) that has had considerable influence on later English religious writing. He was canonized about 1249; his feast day is on Nov. 16.

EDMUNDS, George Franklin (1828–1919), American lawyer and legislator, born in Richmond, Vt. He was a member of the Vermont legislature from 1854 to 1859 and of the State senate from 1861 to 1862. He was elected to the United States Senate in 1866 and served continuously until his resignation in 1891. Edmunds was instrumental in securing passage of the act that provided for a Federal Electoral Commission (see ELECTORAL COMMISSION OF 1877), on which he served. An act bearing his name passed in 1882 provided for the suppression of polygamy in the territories, and was aimed specifically at Utah, where Mormons were in control (see REORGANIZED CHURCH OF JESUS CHRIST OF LATTER-DAY SAINTS). Edmunds was the author of the greater part of the Sherman Antitrust Act (q.v.), passed in 1890, and was president *pro tempore* of the Senate during the term of President Chester Alan Arthur (q.v.). After his retirement from the Senate, Edmunds became noted as an expert on constitutional law.

EDO. *See* TOKYO.

EDOM (Heb., "red"), in the Old Testament, surname of Esau (q.v.), a son of Isaac and twin brother of Jacob (qq.v.). The figure of Esau in the story of Jacob and Esau (Gen. 25–28) is generally taken to represent the nation of Edom, as indicated in Gen. 36:8 ("Esau is Edom"). According to the story, Esau, upon leaving his father's house, went to the Mount Seir region, which he called "Edom". Thus Edom is sometimes called "Seir" or "Mount Seir" in the Old Testament. The area referred to, called Idumaea by the Greeks, is the narrow, fertile plateau that extends some 50 miles s. of the Dead Sea toward the Gulf of Aqaba, in what is now mostly Jordanian territory.

According to Deut. 2:12 this region was originally inhabited by the Horites; they are now identified as the Hurrians, a non-Semitic race whose forebears may have been the aborigines of the land and cave dwellers. The Edomites achieved statehood before Israel did. Although there was a blood relationship between the two nations, as shown by the Biblical story, they were mutually hostile. The story may derive from Edomite sources.

EDUCATION, process by which a person learns facts and skills and develops abilities and attitudes. More specifically, education denotes the methods by which a society hands down from one generation to the next its knowledge, culture, and values. The individual being educated develops physically, mentally, emotion-

ally, morally, and socially. The work of education may be accomplished by an individual teacher, the family, a church, or any other group in society. Education is usually carried out by the school, the agency that employs men and women who are professionally trained for this task; see TEACHING AND TRAINING OF TEACHERS. The history of education is concerned with theories, methods, administration, and problems of schools and other agencies of information, both formal and informal, throughout the world from ancient times to the present. *See also* ACADEMY; UNIVERSITIES AND COLLEGES. See separate entries on eras, educators, scholars, philosophers, and educational theorists whose life dates are not given in this article.

Early Systems of Education. The oldest systems of education in history had two characteristics in common: they taught religion and they promoted the traditions of the people. In ancient Egypt the temple schools taught not only religion but also the principles of writing, the sciences, mathematics, and architecture. Similarly in India, much of the education was carried on by priests. India was the fountainhead of the Buddhist doctrines that were taught in its institutions to Chinese scholars; they, in turn, spread the teachings of the Indian philosopher Gautama Buddha to the various countries of the Far East. Education in ancient China stressed philosophy, poetry, and religion, in accord with the teachings of the Chinese philosophers Confucius, Lao-Tzu, and other great thinkers. The Chinese system of civil-service examination, which originated more than 4000 years ago and was used in China until the present century, made it possible to select the best scholars for important posts in the government.

The methods of physical training that prevailed in Persia and were highly praised by several Greek writers apparently served as the model for the educational system of Sparta (q.v.).

The Bible and the Talmud (qq.v.) were the basic sources of information about the aims and methods of education among the ancient Jews (q.v.). Jewish parents were urged by the Talmud to teach their children such subjects as vocational knowledge, swimming, and a foreign language. Today, religion serves as the base for education in the home, the synagogue, and the school. The Torah (q.v.) has remained the foundation of Jewish education; see JUDAISM.

Basic Traditions of the Western World. The educational systems in the countries of the Western world were based upon the religious tradition of the Jews, both in the original form

A music lesson in a Greek schoolroom (5th century B.C.). Bettmann Archive

and in the version modified by Christianity. A second tradition was derived from education in ancient Greece, where Socrates, Plato, Aristotle, and Isocrates were the influential thinkers on education. The Greek aim was to prepare intellectually well-rounded young people to take leading roles in the activities of the state and of society. In later centuries, Greek concepts served as bases for the liberal arts, the teaching of the various branches of philosophy, the cultivation of the aesthetic ideal, and the promotion of gymnastic training.

Following the Hellenistic period, Greek influences on education were transmitted primarily through such thinkers as the writer Plutarch, who urged the education of parents as the first essential step in the education of children.

Roman education, after an initial period of intense loyalty to the old religious and cultural traditions, approved the appointment of Greeks as teachers of Roman youth both at Rome and at Athens. For the Romans the teaching of rhetoric and oratory were important. According to the Spanish-born Roman educator, Quintilian who lived in the 1st century A.D., the proper training of the orator was to be organized around the study of language, literature, philosophy, and the sciences, with particular attention to the development of character. Roman education transmitted to the Western world the Latin language and those languages directly derived from it, the Romance languages, as well as classical literature, engineering, law, and the administration and organization of government.

Christianity as a Guiding Force. As the Roman Empire was deteriorating, Christianity (q.v.) was becoming a potent force in the countries of the Mediterranean region and in several other areas in Europe. The earliest types of Christian education were the catechumenal, or neophyte, schools for converts; the more advanced catechetical, or question-and-answer, schools for Christians; and the episcopal, or cathedral, schools, that trained priests. The early Fathers of the Church, especially Saint Augustine, wrote on educational questions in the light of the newly understood Christian concepts. The Greek Fathers were generally well disposed toward pagan writings; the Latin Fathers opposed them on moral grounds.

Many monasteries or monastic schools as well as municipal and cathedral schools were founded during the centuries of early Christian influence. Among these was that of Saint Benedict (q.v.) at Monte Cassino, Italy, in 539. Collections, or compendia, of knowledge, centered on the seven liberal arts: the *trivium*, composed of grammar, rhetoric, and logic, and the *quadrivium* of arithmetic, geometry, astronomy, and music. During the 5th to the 7th centuries these compendia were prepared in the form of textbooks by such scholars as the Latin writer Martianus Capella (fl. 5th cent.) from northern Africa, the Roman historian Cassiodorus, and the Spanish ecclesiastic Isidore of Seville. Generally, however, such works tended to disseminate the

321

EDUCATION

existing knowledge, rather than to introduce new knowledge or encourage its discovery.

The Middle Ages. In Western Europe, two revivals of learning took place in the 9th century, one on the Continent, under the Frankish emperor Charlemagne, and one in England, under King Alfred the Great. Charlemagne, realizing the value of education, brought the cleric and educator Alcuin of York from England to set up a palace school at Aachen (q.v.). King Alfred became a scholar himself and established educational institutions in England; he also encouraged monasteries to expand their educational work. Ireland had centers of learning from which many monks were sent out to teach in Continental countries. Between the 8th and the 11th centuries the highly cultivated Moorish conquerors of Spain revived the Roman university in the capital city of Córdoba. This became a center for the study of philosophy, ancient culture, science, and mathematics.

Elsewhere, Babylonia had had Jewish academies for many centuries; Persia and Arabia from the 6th to the 9th centuries had institutions for research and the study of science and language; and centers of Muslim learning were established in 859 at Al Qarawiyin University at Fez, in Morocco. In 970 at Cairo, Egypt, Al-Azhar University was founded.

During the Middle Ages the doctrines of Scholasticism (q.v.) were widely taught in Western Europe. Scholasticism was the principle of using logic to prove that Christian theology was reconcilable with the pre-Christian philosophical concepts of Aristotle. A leading teacher of Scholasticism was the churchman Anselm of Canterbury, who, like Plato, promoted the concept that ideas alone are real. Another cleric, Roscelinus de Compiègne (1050–1120?), following the principles of Aristotle, taught nominalism (q.v.), or the rejection of universal ideas as mere labels, and insisted on the reality of concrete things.

Other great Scholastic teachers were the French theologian Peter Abelard, the pupil of Roscelinus, and the Italian philosopher and theologian Saint Thomas Aquinas. The renown of such teachers attracted many students and was chiefly responsible for the establishment of universities in the north of Europe beginning in the 12th century. All during the Middle Ages the chief repositories of learning were the monasteries. These organizations maintained archives that preserved the manuscripts of the preceding classical culture.

At about this time several universities were opened in Italy, Spain, and other countries, with students traveling freely from one institution to another. The northern universities, such as those in Paris, Oxford, and Cambridge, were ad-

Students in a medieval monastery receiving instruction from a monk. **Bettmann Archive**

ministered by the professors; the southern, such as Bologna, Italy, by students. Medieval education also took the form of apprenticeship training, preparation for service as in the case of urban schools and feudal knights (see Feudalism). As a rule, however, education was the privilege of the upper classes, whereas the lower segments of society were forced to remain steeped in perpetual ignorance.

Of significance to the development of higher learning during the Middle Ages were the Muslims and the Jews, both of whom were outside the Christian society that dominated Europe. Not only did these groups promote education within their own societies, but they also served as translators and as intermediaries who brought ancient Greek thought and science to the attention of the European scholars.

Humanism and the Renaissance. The Renaissance that started in the late 14th century and continued for about two centuries was the period in which interest in the culture of ancient Greece and Rome saw a revival. The sophisticated ideas of the ancient classical world were acquired through the discovery of the old manuscripts preserved in the monasteries. Many excellent teachers of the Greek language and literature had also migrated from Constantinople, in Turkey, to Italy, beginning with the Greek scholar Manuel Chrysoloras in 1397. Among the discoverers of classical manuscripts were the Italian humanists Francesco Petrarch and Poggio Bracciolini.

The spirit of education during the Renaissance was best exemplified by the schools established by the Italian educators Vittorino da Feltre (1378–1446) in Mantua (1425) and by Guarino da Verona (1374–1460). These educators introduced into their schools such subjects as the sciences, history, geography, music, and physical training. These immensely successful schools influenced the work of other educators and indeed served as examples for educators more than 400 years later. Among the other Renaissance contributors to education theory were the Dutch humanist Desiderius Erasmus, the German educator Johannes Sturm, the French essayist Michel de Montaigne, and the Spanish humanist and philosopher Juan Luis Vives (1492–1540). The major emphasis of this period was on the classical Greek and Latin subjects taught in the so-called Latin grammar school, which, originating in the Middle Ages, became the chief secondary school of Europe until the early part of the 20th century.

The Influence of Protestantism. Protestantism was a form of Christianity deriving from the Reformation (q.v.) instituted by the German religious reformer Martin Luther in the early 16th century. Schools were established within this tradition to teach reading, writing, arithmetic, and catechism on the elementary level; and the classical subjects, such as Hebrew, mathematics, and science on the secondary level; see EDUCATION, ELEMENTARY; EDUCATION, SECONDARY. In Switzerland, another branch of Protestantism was founded by the French theologian and reformer John Calvin, whose academy at Geneva, established in 1559, was an important educational center. The modern practice of the control of education by government can be traced to the policies of Luther, Calvin, and other religious and educational leaders of the Reformation.

Roman Catholic Influences. The Roman Catholics also made use of Renaissance educational ideas in the schools that they already conducted, or had quickly established, in an effort to offset the growing influence of Protestantism through their Counter-Reformation; see REFORMATION: *Counter-Reformation.* This synthesis was accomplished in the schools of the Society of Jesus, organized by the Spanish ecclesiastic Saint Ignatius Loyola in 1540, with the approval of Pope Paul III (see under PAUL). The Jesuits (q.v.), as the members of the society were called, set up a system of schools that has succeeded in transplanting Catholic education to many countries since the 16th century.

Growth of the Sciences in the 17th Century. The 17th century, a period of rapid growth of the various sciences, was marked by the founding in 1660 of the Royal Society of London for Improving Natural Knowledge. This institution and other learned organizations simplified the exchange of scientific and cultural information and ideas among the scholars in the different countries of Europe. The new scientific subjects were introduced into the courses of study in the universities and the secondary schools. Christ's Hospital in London, England, was probably the first secondary school to teach science with any degree of competence. It served as the model for the establishment of the first scientific secondary school in Russia, the Moscow School of Navigation and Mathematics, in the early 18th century. The importance of science was set forth in the writings of the 16th-century English statesman and philosopher Francis Bacon, who stressed the principle of learning by the inductive process. This means that the student is encouraged to observe and examine many things with his senses and his mind before coming to a conclusion about them.

EDUCATION

During the 17th century, many outstanding educators in other countries exerted their influence. The German educator Wolfgang Ratke (1571–1635) pioneered in new methods of more rapid teaching of the vernacular, the classical languages, and Hebrew. René Descartes, the 16th-century French philosopher, emphasized the role of logic as the fundamental principle of rational thinking, and logic to this day has remained the basis of education in France. In the 17th century the English poet John Milton presented an encyclopedic program of secondary education, with classical learning as a means of achieving morality and completing the person of well-rounded intellect. The English philosopher John Locke recommended a curriculum and method of education, including physical training, that was based upon empirical examination of demonstrable facts before reaching conclusions. In *Some Thoughts Concerning Education* (1693), Locke advocated a number of reforms, including the emphasis on things in place of books, learning through travel, and variety of subject matter. Locke would advise the student to study a tree rather than a book about trees; to go to France rather than read a book about France. The doctrine of formal mental discipline, namely the ability to strengthen the faculties or powers of the mind by exercising them in the use of logic and the refutation of fallacies, often attributed to Locke, was a major influence on the educational thinkers of the 18th and 19th centuries. The French educator Jean Baptiste de la Salle, founder of the Institute of the Brothers of the Christian Schools in 1684 in France, established a seminary for teachers in 1685 and thereby became a pioneer in the systematic education of teachers.

Perhaps the greatest educator of the 17th century was Jan Amos Komensky, the Protestant bishop of Moravia, better known by his Latin name Comenius. His work in education brought him invitations to teach throughout Europe. He wrote a widely read, profusely illustrated textbook for the learning of Latin, called *Orbis Sensualium Pictus* (1658; Eng. trans. *The Visible World,* 1659). In his *Didatica Magna* (1628–32; Eng. trans., *Great Didactic,* 1931) he laid emphasis on furthering the educational process through the stimulation of pupil interest and by teaching with reference to concrete things rather than to verbal description of them. His educational objective can be summed up in the phrase on the title page of the *Great Didactic,* "teaching thoroughly all things to all men". His efforts in behalf of universal education earned him the title of "Teacher of Nations".

Another influential educator, August Hermann Francke (1663–1727) of Germany, made his influence felt in the late 17th and subsequent centuries. Francke, a Lutheran minister, served as professor of theology at the University of Leipzig, and later as professor of Hebrew at the University of Halle, near which he also held a pastorate. His major achievements were in the areas of secondary, teacher, and adult education; international missions training; the modernization of the curriculum; and the network of schools, the *Franckesche Stiftungen,* that are still in existence after nearly three centuries.

The Spread of European Ideas to Other Continents. From the 16th century onward, European education began to penetrate into Africa, Asia, the Western Hemisphere, and other parts of the world. The educational institutions set up in Central and South America and portions of North America were the work of educators from Spain and Portugal. England and France were mainly responsible for establishing schools in what are now the United States and Canada. Although colleges and universities were set up in the New World, students there would often go to Europe for higher education in the older institutions; *see* EDUCATION, HIGHER.

The 18th Century: Rousseau and Others. The 18th century saw the rise of a school system in Prussia, the beginnings of formal education in Russia under Czar Peter the Great and his successors, the development of schools and colleges in colonial America, and the educational reforms that resulted from the French Revolution (q.v.). Late in the century the Sunday school movement was inaugurated in England by the philanthropist and newspaper publisher Robert Raikes (1735–1811) for the benefit of poor and working children (*see* SUNDAY SCHOOLS); the same period also saw the start of the monitorial method of teaching, whereby hundreds of children could be taught by one teacher with the aid of pupil monitors or assistants. Both plans pointed the way to the possibility of mass education.

The foremost educational theorist of the 18th century was Jean Jacques Rousseau, who was born in Geneva, Switzerland, but whose influence reached throughout Europe and beyond. In his *Émile* (1762), he insisted that children should be treated as children rather than as miniature adults and that the personality of the individual must be cultivated. Among his concrete suggestions were the teaching of reading at a later age and the study of nature and society by direct observation. His radical proposals, however, were to be applied to boys only; girls

were to receive a conventional education. *See also* CHILD PSYCHOLOGY; COEDUCATION.

The educational contributions of Rousseau were largely in the realm of theory. It remained for his followers, however, to put his ideas into successful practice. The German educator Johann Bernhard Basedow and others opened schools in Germany and elsewhere on the basis of the idea of "everything according to nature".

The 19th Century and the Rise of National School Systems. The most influential of all the followers of Rousseau was the Swiss educator Johann Heinrich Pestalozzi, whose ideas and practices influenced schools in every corner of every continent. The principal aim of Pestalozzi was to adapt the method of teaching to the natural development of the child. To attain this objective, he worked toward the harmonious de-

325

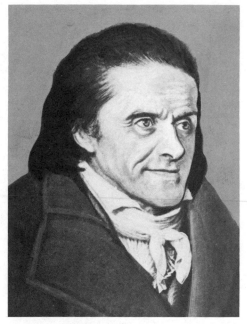

Johann Heinrich Pestalozzi, late 18th-century Swiss educational reformer.

velopment of all the faculties (head, heart, and hand) of the learner. Among the other influential educators of the 19th century were Friedrich Froebel of Germany, the father of the kindergarten (q.v.), which was introduced in America in 1856; Johann Friedrich Herbart, also of Germany, who introduced the principles of psychology and philosophy into the science of education, and whose ideas spread to America toward the end of the century; Horace Mann and Henry Barnard, the foremost American educators, who brought to the United States the doctrines of Pestalozzi and other European educators; the British philosopher Herbert Spencer, who advocated scientific knowledge as the most important subject matter to be taught in school; and Bishop Nikolai Frederik Severin Grundtvig (1783–1872) of Denmark, whose educational ideas became the basis for the internationally famous folk-high-school movement.

The 19th century was the period when national school systems were organized in England, France, Germany, Italy, and other European countries. The newly liberated nations of Latin America, especially Argentina and Uruguay, looked to Europe and the U.S. for models for their schools. Japan, which had just emerged from its traditional status and was trying to westernize its institutions, drew upon the experience of several European countries and the U.S. in the establishment of a modern school and university system.

Also significant in the 19th century was the widespread organizing of missionary education in the undeveloped areas of the world, particularly in Africa and Oceania. Education in colonial areas such as India was given attention by the administrative powers. In general, however, the vast majority of the people in the colonial and underdeveloped regions received little, if any, formal education.

The 20th Century: Child-Centered Education. At the beginning of the century, education apparently took its cue from a book written by the Swedish feminist and educator Ellen Key (1849–1926). Her book *The Century of the Child* (1900), translated into many languages, inspired so-called progressive educators in various countries. Progressive education was a system of teaching based upon the needs and potentials of the child, rather than on the needs of society or the precepts of religion. It had existed in idea and in fact under other names all through history, from ancient Greece through 19th-century Europe and America, and had appeared in varying forms in different parts of the world. Among the influential progressive educators were Hermann Lietz (1868–1919) and Georg Kerschensteiner (1854–1932) of Germany, Bertrand Russell of England, and Maria Montessori of Italy. Especially influential in America, and even on a worldwide scale, was the American philosopher and educator John Dewey. The activity program, which was developed from the theories of Dewey, stressed the educational development of the child in terms of his needs and interests. This program became the major method of instruction for many years in the elementary schools in the U.S. and other countries.

Since the Russian Revolution (q.v.) of 1917, the Soviet Union has been an object of educational interest. Particularly since 1957, when the Soviet Sputnik (*see* ASTRONAUTICS: *Space Age Programs*), the first artificial earth satellite, was launched into space, indicating the advanced state of Soviet technological learning, Soviet schools have attracted large numbers of foreign visitors, especially from underdeveloped countries. Contributing to the international interest in Soviet education were the educational theories and practices arising out of Marxist-Leninist ideology, as well as the work of Anton S. Makarenko (1888–1939), the exponent of the rehabilitation of juvenile delinquents and of collective education. *See* LENIN, VLADIMIR ILICH; MARX, KARL; UNION OF SOVIET SOCIALIST REPUBLICS: *Education.*

The current century has been marked by the expansion of the educational systems of the industrial nations, as well as the emergence of school systems among the newer, developing nations in Asia and Africa. Compulsory elementary education has become nearly universal, but evidence indicates that very large numbers of children, perhaps 50 percent of those of school age, are not attending school. In order to improve education on the elementary and adult levels, the United Nations Educational, Scientific, and Cultural Organization (q.v.) inaugurated literacy campaigns and other educational projects. The aim of this organization is to put every child everywhere into school and to eliminate illiteracy. Some progress has been noted, but it has become obvious that considerable time and effort are needed to produce universal literacy.

For information on national systems of education, see the section on *Education* in the articles on individual countries.　　　　　W.W.B.

EDUCATION, ADULT. Formal adult education dates from the Middle Ages, but it became more regular in Great Britain in the late 18th century. In the 19th century the Danish folk high-school movement (*see* EDUCATION) influenced adult education throughout Europe and the United States. The beginnings of informal adult education in the U.S. can be traced to the New England town meeting (*see* TOWN), which was a center for open debate and discussion of public issues, and served as a clearinghouse for information. Although some societies for the dissemination of knowledge, such as Benjamin Franklin's "Junto" group (1727), were founded before the American Revolution, it was not until the U.S. was well established that a great number of philanthropic and humanitarian organizations had begun to reach all classes of American society with organized discussions, lectures, and debates. Libraries for working people and agricultural and mechanical institutes became popular with the spread of the concept of bettering oneself through education. The first tax-supported public library was founded in Peterborough, N.H., in 1833, and after that date the growth of public libraries was extremely rapid.

Employers and philanthropists began to endow such institutions for adult education as the Cooper Union for the Advancement of Science and Art (q.v.) in New York City (1857) and Peabody Institute (1859) in Baltimore, Md. The lyceum (a movement organized in 1826 to provide lectures, concerts, and other cultural and educational activities) became important in

rural as well as urban areas, and by the late 1830's more than 3000 communities had lyceums. Even larger audiences were attracted to the Chautauqua movement, founded near Chautauqua Lake, New York, in 1874 by the American Methodist Episcopal minister John Heyl Vincent (q.v.), and the American inventor and philanthropist Lewis Miller (1829–99). Originally a center for religious instruction in the form of a summer camp meeting, Chautauqua became the prototype of institutions established to further popular education in the United States. The concept of summer school originated at the institution, as did the development of home study courses or correspondence education (q.v.). Evening schools and college extension courses for adults were established elsewhere and spread rapidly throughout the nation after 1880. Chautauqua, which evolved from an assembly to a cultural university, today is an institute offering a variety of courses in such subjects as religion, education, and the humanities.

In the 20th century organized adult education flourished in Germany, Great Britain, the Soviet Union, Switzerland, and the U.S. In Britain the Workers' Educational Association, which was founded in 1903, established branches throughout the country, where literature, lectures, and later, motion pictures on public issues and educational matters were provided. The Education Act of 1944 prescribed facilities for education for adults as well as for children. Trade unions, political parties, and religious groups organized programs for adult education. In the U.S.S.R., the Communist government, faced with the tremendous task of education in a country where more than 60 percent of the population was illiterate, established a variety of institutes and extension classes for adults, and was therefore successfully able to wipe out illiteracy.

Adult education became an early concern of the U.S. government. In 1862 President Abraham Lincoln (q.v.) signed the Morrill Act, which led to the establishment of land-grant colleges offering training in agriculture and the mechanical arts. The Hatch Act (1887) made possible the extension of scientific agricultural knowledge to farmers. With the rapid rise of immigration into the U.S. after 1890, enlarged programs of day and evening classes were offered in such subjects as citizenship and the English language. Since 1914, when the Federal Extension Service (q.v.) was established, the U.S. has participated in programs of education in agriculture and homemaking in rural communities. In 1926 the

The summer encampment at Chautauqua Lake, near Chautauqua, in southwestern New York State. Adherents of the Chautauqua movement cheer a speaker (from an 1880 newspaper engraving).
Granger Collection

American Association for Adult Education was founded to serve as a clearinghouse for hundreds of member organizations engaged in adult education.

During the period from 1930 to 1941 enrollment in adult educational activities almost doubled what it had been in the previous decade. This increase in enrollment was due to such factors as the desire for self-improvement in order to increase employment opportunities and additional leisure time because of unemployment. A further reason was the establishment of adult-education projects by the Federal government as part of its relief program. The Work Projects Administration (q.v.) was notably engaged in adult education. The W.P.A. program concerned itself especially with the 10 percent of the population which was illiterate in 1930. In 1960 the national illiteracy rate was 2.4 percent, but in 1970 it had declined to about 1 percent.

Such institutions as the New School for Social Research and the People's Institute of Cooper Union in New York devoted themselves almost entirely to adult education. Public libraries instituted readers' advisory services, compiling special reading lists as guides to education which could be acquired entirely through reading; the so-called *Reading with a Purpose* series became a major concern of the American Library Association. Adult classes were organized by municipal museums. The most prominent type of adult education became the public evening classes established fifty years earlier. These classes offered both vocational and nonvocational courses, and during the 1930's, more than 2,000,000 persons were enrolled in them.

New Aspects. Adult education received its greatest impetus with the passage of the G.I. Bill of Rights (see VETERANS ADMINISTRATION). The law enabled many veterans of World War II, and of the Korean and Vietnam wars, to take not only secondary and higher education courses, but virtually any course offered in the whole spectrum of adult education. In the 1960's Congress passed legislation to provide funds for adults

Above: The modern courtyard and library of the New School for Social Research, in New York City, founded in 1919 for university-level adult education. Below: A lay volunteer teaches Alaskan Eskimos to read and write; a large proportion of adult education is accomplished by itinerant teachers.

who had not completed grammar school. The Federal government also supported programs for the training and rehabilitation of handicapped persons. Increased attention was also given to the various educational needs of the aged.

Television has assumed an increasing role in adult education. By 1972, some 190 educational television stations were operating in the U.S. Noncommercial television comprises two categories: instructional (I.T.V.), an extension of the classroom in which the teaching is formal, and educational or public television, which includes both informational and broadly cultural programs. In addition to the educational television stations, the 690 commercial stations and three national networks also perform an important role in adult education. News programs, documentaries, discussion programs, and music and drama series have disseminated information and cultural material to millions of television viewers. Some courses of a more formal educational value are offered by commercial stations in early-morning time periods. In such courses, college credit is received by those students who pass the required tests given during the television course. See RADIO AND TELEVISION BROADCASTING: *Current Trends in Programming: Educational Broadcasting.*

So strong has the adult-education movement become in the United States that in the mid-1970's more than 16,000,000 adults were engaged in formal or informal educational activities conducted by the diverse schools, colleges, agencies, and organizations. Another increasingly popular form of adult education is home study, or correspondence education; in a recent year some 8,000,000 adults were taking correspondence courses. W.W.B.

EDUCATION, AMERICAN COUNCIL ON. See AMERICAN COUNCIL ON EDUCATION.

EDUCATION, ELEMENTARY, earliest program of education for children, beginning generally at the age of five or six and lasting from six to eight years. In most countries elementary education is compulsory for all children. In the larger communities of the United States a year of kindergarten often precedes the first grade of the eight-year elementary course. In such communities special provisions, either in the form of special classes or schools, are provided for children who are physically or mentally handicapped. The purpose of the elementary school is to introduce children to the skills, information, and attitudes necessary for proper adjustment to their community and to society. Basically, the subjects taught are reading, writing,

spelling, mathematics, social studies, science, art, music, physical education, and handicrafts. These are often supplemented with the teaching of other subjects, such as the study of a foreign language. Over the years new subject matter has made the elementary school curriculum more advanced than heretofore.

Upon completion of their elementary schooling, pupils continue their education in a junior high school or a senior secondary or high school.

See also GRAMMAR SCHOOL. W.W.B.

EDUCATION, GRADUATE. See EDUCATION IN THE PROFESSIONS; UNIVERSITIES AND COLLEGES.

EDUCATION, HIGHER, period of advanced study following the completion of secondary education (*see* EDUCATION, SECONDARY). The duration of the study may be from four to seven years or more, depending upon the nature and complexity of the programs pursued. The institution providing higher education may be either a college or university or a type of professional school. A junior college, such as those maintained in many municipal school systems, offers a two-year program of general education that serves either as terminal schooling or as preparation for more specialized study in a four-year college or university. When the basic course of study is successfully completed, usually at the end of four years, the graduate receives a bachelor's degree; *see* DEGREE, ACADEMIC. He may continue for a master's degree, generally requiring an additional year or two, and then for a doctor's degree, which normally requires the candidate to submit a dissertation and to complete a minimum of two or three years of further studies. Higher education, which usually includes some general education, is a time for specialized study to qualify the individual for professional activity or for employment in higher positions in business, industry, and government. In recent years, especially in the United States, the trend has been toward requiring a greater number of courses common to all students in order to counteract a growing tendency toward overspecialization.

See also EDUCATION IN THE PROFESSIONS; UNIVERSITIES AND COLLEGES. W.W.B.

EDUCATION IN THE PROFESSIONS, preparation of students for work in a field that requires higher specialized training and is governed by a specific code of ethics. Such training is given in a university or in a special institute or school on a postgraduate level. Except for engineering, one usually cannot undertake professional education in the United States before successfully completing his studies for a bachelor's degree.

Graduation from a professional school is a prerequisite, not only for entrance into the learned and technical professions, such as theology, medicine, law, and engineering, but also for such professions as library service, optometry, pharmacy, social work, and architecture. In journalism or business administration, on the other hand, it is still possible to achieve professional success without training in a professional school, possibly because such achievement is so clearly the result of demonstrable skill rather than formal training.

The idea of formal professional training in law and engineering originated in ancient times, chiefly in Egypt, Greece, and Rome. The medieval universities offered instruction in law, medicine, and theology. Great impetus was given to professional technical and medical education as a result of the scientific discoveries and inventions beginning in the 16th century. Modern technical education stems from the 18th-century German mining institutes and the École Polytechnique of France, founded in 1794.

In colonial America, most colleges functioned primarily as theological schools. Medicine was first taught at the University of Pennsylvania in 1765 and at Columbia (King's) College in New York City in 1767. Legal education began in 1779 with George Wythe (q.v.) as professor of law and police at the College of William and Mary in Williamsburg, Va. The first law school in America was established by Judge Tapping Reeve (1744–1823) in Litchfield, Conn., about 1784. This Litchfield Law School, a private institution that existed until 1833, numbered among its students Aaron Burr, John C. Calhoun, and Horace Mann (qq.v.). A permanent law faculty was instituted at the University of Maryland in 1816, followed by the establishment of the Harvard Law School, in Cambridge, Mass., in 1817. Other early examples of professional colleges were the Philadelphia College of Pharmacy, founded in 1821, and the Baltimore College of Dental Surgery, founded in 1840.

The first engineering school in the United States was the U.S. Military Academy (q.v.), founded in 1802, which developed in 1817 into an engineering school like the École Polytechnique of Paris. The first civilian engineering school was the Rensselaer School (now Rensselaer Polytechnic Institute), opened in 1824 in Troy, N.Y. Although Harvard, Yale, Dartmouth, Brown, and Michigan taught engineering before the American Civil War, not until the Morrill Act of 1862 did engineering schools achieve rapid growth; see LAND-GRANT COLLEGES. Although a college or university is accredited by the appropriate regional accrediting association, the professional organizations and associations visit, evaluate, and accredit its various professional schools. The persistence of these associations in defining acceptable standards of training and in evaluating the programs of the schools has been largely instrumental in keeping professional education at a high level.

See EDUCATION, HIGHER; EDUCATION, MEDICAL; ENGINEERING; UNIVERSITIES AND COLLEGES.   W.W.B.

EDUCATION IN THE UNITED STATES, programs of instruction offered to children, youths, and adults in the United States through schools and colleges operated by State and local governments, as well as private and religious groups. According to law, the public schools are open to "all the children of all the people" and are financed by tax revenue. Public elementary and secondary schools are free, without regard to race, religion, or social and economic status; see EDUCATION, ELEMENTARY; EDUCATION, SECONDARY; GRAMMAR SCHOOL. Compulsory-attendance laws in all States require that children, generally between the ages of seven and sixteen, be enrolled in school. In contrast to most foreign countries, the U.S. has no centralized system of education; it consists of fifty State-controlled school systems and that of the District of Columbia, which is under Federal control, and those of outlying systems, such as Puerto Rico and Guam. The Constitution of the United States (q.v.) does not deal specifically with education. Under the Tenth Amendment, public school education is left to the control of the States, but the Preamble and the elastic clause of the Constitution are often interpreted as allowing certain types of Federal support of education. Private and religious schools do not receive direct public funds.

The Colonial Era. During the colonial period, education was recognized as a function of government. The legislatures of the various colonies passed laws requiring that apprentices receive basic instruction in reading, religion, and vocational training. In 1642 the legislature of the Massachusetts Bay Colony ordered the local governments to insure, under penalty of a fine, that children be taught "to read and understand the principles of religion and the capitall lawes of this country". A stricter law, passed by the colony in 1647, directed that all towns having a population above a certain number of people were to provide elementary- and secondary-school facilities. Most of the other New England colonies soon followed the example of Massachusetts. To many historians and educators, the American public-school system is based upon

A 19th-century American schoolroom in New England.

the law of 1647, often called the "Old Deluder Satan Act". This law foreshadowed the contemporary practice of community maintenance and administration of schools. The idea of local support through taxation may be traced to the colonial era when the towns raised taxes, paid the teachers, and supervised the schools. A town school was often directed by an education com-

Daguerreotype of Horace Mann, famous Massachusetts educator, made before 1855.

mittee that later became the local school board or board of education; and the churches and towns of colonial America frequently cooperated in controlling publicly supported schools.

Education of Women. In colonial times a few towns allowed girls to learn to read the Bible and to write, but they were generally segregated in separate classes and seldom advanced beyond the most basic education. Significant reform for female education took place after the American Revolution by which time most elementary schools were coeducational; after the Civil War most American public high schools became coeducational. In 1837 Mount Holyoke Seminary, now Mount Holyoke College, was established through the efforts of the American educator Mary Lyon (q.v.); four years earlier, Oberlin College in Ohio had begun to allow women to attend classes. Many State universities, following the lead of the private colleges, admitted women and granted them degrees. During the second half of the 19th century professional schools began to admit women. Most universities today accept women, and many famous women's colleges are changing to coeducational institutions. *See also* COEDUCATION.

Land Grants as an Aid to Education. Public educational facilities for children were much more limited in the Middle- and Southern Colonies than in New England. The concept of higher public education, however, as well as the first State universities, originated in the South near the end of the 18th century; *see* EDUCATION, HIGHER. Land grants for schools were made by colonial legislatures, as in Massachusetts and Connecticut, and such grants were also provided by the newly established State governments of Georgia, Massachusetts, and New York. The Federal government, nevertheless, had the greatest interest in land grants for education. The Northwest Land Ordinance of May 20, 1785, passed by the Congress of the Confederation (see ARTICLES OF CONFEDERATION) four years before the adoption of the U.S. Constitution, reserved areas in six States in the Midwest for educational purposes. The ordinance provided that "there shall be reserved the lot No. 16 of every township, for the maintenance of public schools, within the said township". Accordingly, the township was divided into thirty-six lots, or sections, each of which consisted of an area of one square mile.

The continuing interest of the Federal government in educational programs was evidenced in the Northwest Land Ordinance of July 13, 1787. In this document, affecting the territory northwest of the Ohio R., Congress declared that "Religion, morality, and knowledge being necessary to good government and the happiness of mankind, schools and the means of education shall forever be encouraged". Although the ordinance specified no land for schools, on July 23, 1787, the Congress ordained that Section 16 be reserved for public schools, and that Section 29 "be given perpetually for the purpose of religion". At the Constitutional Convention and during the first decade of the new nation, many plans were formulated for a national educational system. Eventually, however, the Constitution left general education to the States. In 1799 President George Washington (q.v.) bequeathed in his will a fund to found a national university, but the plan was never carried through. Nor did similar proposals advanced earlier by the American physician Benjamin Rush and the statesman James Madison (qq.v.) ever materialize.

Although the Constitution makes no reference to education, the Federal government has undertaken certain educational activities, as well as giving financial aid to State governments in order to improve their educational systems. First, the U.S. government organized public-school systems in territories that were later admitted as States. A Congressional act in 1802 granted the newly established State of Ohio Federal land for institutions on every educational level; and this became standard practice for other States when they joined the Union. Between 1800 and 1850, the U.S. government also gave the States, for school purposes, funds derived from land sales; see LAND-GRANT COLLEGES. The United States Surplus Revenue Loan of 1837 made a Federal surplus fund of $28,000,000 available to the State governments, and most States applied this money, or a part of it, toward support of their schools. The educational contributions of the Federal government during the first half of the 19th century included the establishment of a public-school system in the District of Columbia in 1804, as well as the founding of the Library of Congress in 1800, the United States Military Academy at West Point in 1802, and the United States Naval Academy (qq.v.) at Annapolis in 1845. The Federal government also made land grants to two private religious institutions in the District of Columbia: $25,000 to Columbian University, a Protestant institution, in 1832; and $25,000 to Georgetown College, a Catholic institution, in 1833.

The Rise of State School Systems. Possibly fearing Federal control, the States began to establish their own systems of elementary schools, high schools, and normal schools for teachers. In 1784 New York State organized a school system and in 1812 appointed a State superintendent of schools. Before State school systems began to function effectively, private citizens formed associations in the major cities in order to devise educational means. Thus, the Free School Society of New York City operated schools from 1805 to 1852 and then turned them over to the New York City board of education, which had been created in 1842. Another educational organization was the Society for the Promotion of Public Schools of Philadelphia, organized in 1827.

Perhaps the most important event in the development of State school systems was the appointment of Horace Mann (q.v.) as secretary of the board of education of Massachusetts. Although confined to the position of State superintendent of schools, the educator raised public-school standards throughout the nation, as well as facilities for the training of teachers. Outstanding educators in other States were Henry Barnard (q.v.) in Connecticut, John Davis Pierce (1797–1882) in Michigan, and Calvin Henderson Wiley (1819–87) in North Carolina. At first, the public schools were financed in various ways: by lottery; by grants from State legislatures; by permanent school funds derived from license fees, local taxes, fines, and the sale of public lands; and by the unpopular rate bill, which determined tuition fees according to the number of children in a family. After State governments passed laws for financing free school systems, the rate bill was abandoned.

John Dewey, bronze bust by the 20th-century British sculptor Sir Jacob Epstein.

Columbia University — Collection Teachers College Library

Federal Leadership, 1850–1900. The Federal government increased its aid to education in the second half of the 19th century. The Morrill Act, passed by Congress in 1862, granted 20,000 acres of public lands to the States for each representative in Congress. The proceeds from these land sales were used for establishing agricultural- and mechanical arts colleges, in which scientific and classical subjects would be taught, as well as military science. These were the first land-grant colleges. The second Morrill Act (1890) helped State colleges and universities in the Middle Western and Far Western States, and the Hatch Act (1887) aided them in organizing agricultural experimental farms for the people of the respective States; see AGRICULTURAL EXPERIMENT STATION. Support was also given by the Federal government for education of the deaf and the blind; see DEAF-MUTE. From 1865 to 1871, various institutions founded under the aegis of the Freedmen's Bureau, were devoted to the education of black citizens; see NEGROES IN THE UNITED STATES. A law passed by Congress on March 2, 1867, established a Department of Education, which is now called the Office of Education and is a division of the Department of Health, Education, and Welfare; see EDUCATION, OFFICE OF. From 1870 to 1890, various bills were introduced in Congress for the financing of public education by the U.S. government through the sale of public lands or direct money grants. Because of opposition by political and

religious groups, however, none was passed.

Compulsory school attendance was required by the Massachusetts laws of 1642 and 1647, but it was not until 1852 that the first specific law for compulsory school attendance was passed, once more by Massachusetts. Children between the ages of eight and fourteen were required to attend school for at least twelve weeks, six of them consecutive, each year. Despite opposition, on the ground that a compulsory school was undemocratic, thirty-two States had passed attendance laws by 1900. The last State to do so was Mississippi, in 1918.

Public education in the 19th century was expanded through the establishment of high schools, municipal colleges, State colleges and universities, and normal schools which were later called teachers colleges. The first public-school kindergarten (q.v.) was opened in Saint Louis in 1873. In 1874 a decision by the Michigan Supreme Court in the famous Kalamazoo Case recognized the legal right of a town to support high schools by public taxes. Private schools and colleges, and religious institutions, multiplied during this period.

Federal Legislation in the 20th Century. In the early 20th century, Congress passed more laws to improve education: the Smith-Lever Act (1914) for extension work in agriculture and home economics at the land-grant colleges; the Smith-Hughes Act (1917), which provided funds to public high schools for vocational training; the Smith-Sears Act (1917) for vocational training of disabled veterans; and the Vocational Rehabilitation Act of 1920 for the vocational training of disabled civilians; see REHABILITATION, VOCATIONAL: *Background of Rehabilitation.* These were supplemented by similar laws in the 1930's. Moreover, the U.S. government aided education during the depression of the 1930's through the Federal Emergency Relief Administration (1933–34) and the National Youth Administration (1935–42); the Public Works Administration (1933–43); the Work Projects Administration (1935–43); and the Civilian Conservation Corps (1937–42). The government began to support school-lunch programs in 1935, and made such aid permanent through the National School Lunch Act of 1946. During World War II Congress passed the G.I. Bill of Rights (1944) to provide educational benefits for war veterans. In 1952 it extended educational benefits to veterans of the Korean War. Important post-World War II legislation included the Fulbright Act (1946) and the Smith-Mundt Act (1948), which provided for exchange of professors, students, and research experts with foreign

Roy Stevens – Ford Foundation

Above: A teacher at a Ford Foundation-sponsored class at New York Medical College asks children to decide which is a plastic banana and which is real; preschool education is designed to develop in children conceptual knowledge. Below: During an elementary-school tour through a scientific research laboratory, young students are fascinated by billions of electrons passing through a Crookes' tube; such tours are enjoyable and serve to acquaint children with science.

Westinghouse

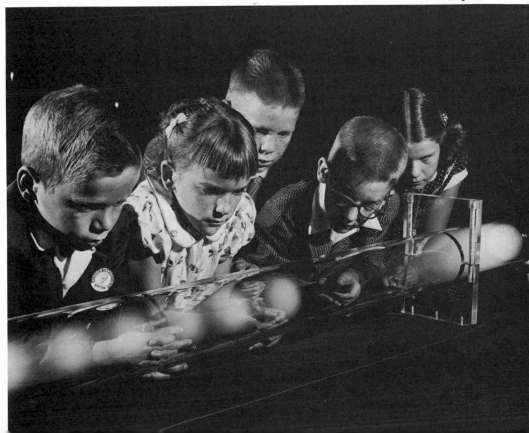

nations; and the National Defense Education Act (1958), which aided the teaching of science, mathematics, and foreign languages during the period of international tension following the Soviet launching (1957) of Sputnik the first artificial earth satellite; *see* ASTRONAUTICS. The Peace Corps (q.v.), established in 1961, trained young men and women as teachers and technical specialists, in which capacities they served in developing countries.

In the late 1960's the U.S. government showed its commitment to education for the disadvantaged by establishing such programs as the Head Start Program, which provides education to such preschool children, and the Job Corps, which provides instruction to school dropouts. *See* POVERTY; PRESCHOOL EDUCATION.

The Role of the Supreme Court. Decisions of the Supreme Court of the United States (q.v.) were crucial to the recent development of education in the nation. In the Oregon School Case (1925), the Court forbade the States to force parents to send their children to public schools. A

decision in the Everson Case (1947) permitted States to furnish public bus transportation for pupils attending parochial schools. A series of decisions, from the Gaines Case (1938) to related cases such as *Brown vs. Board of Education* of Topeka, Kans., in 1954 ordered the admission of Negroes to all public schools and colleges, and thus terminating the so-called separate but equal doctrine in effect in many Southern States for decades. The transportation of public-school pupils as a means to achieving racial integration, often referred to as "busing", has been a controversial issue in recent years. In 1971 the Court unanimously upheld the constitutionality of busing, but in 1974 it limited busing to within school-district lines.

Trends in the 20th Century. The 20th century was marked also by the emergence of the public junior-high school, the first of which was established in Richmond, Ind., in 1896, and the community college. The first public junior college was established in Joliet, Ill., in 1902. Private education, too, developed during the 20th century; and private philanthropic foundations contributed large amounts of money to help finance private and public education (*see* FOUNDATION).

A teacher leads her students in a discussion at Aspira, an organization in New York City that helps Puerto Rican high school students to prepare themselves for college. UPI

America drew often and extensively on European educational ideas, particularly those of the Swiss educator Johann Heinrich Pestalozzi and the German educators Friedrich Wilhelm August Froebel and Johann Friedrich Herbart (qq.v.); *see* EDUCATION: *The 19th Century and the Rise of National School Systems.* Herbart's opinions became popular because of the work of William Torrey Harris (1835–1909), a philosopher who served with distinction as superintendent of schools in St. Louis, Mo., and as United States Commissioner of Education (1889–1906). The so-called progressive movement in education was initiated by the American educator Francis Wayland Parker (1837–1902), who introduced a curriculum and teaching methods based upon the principles of child growth, development, and interest. The American philosopher, psychologist, and educator John Dewey (q.v.) directed (1896–1904) an experimental elementary school in Chicago, Ill., upon similar ideas; it was to have a great deal of influence upon elementary education. Coinciding with the development of progressive education was that of the intelligence- and achievement-testing movement, the origins of which were traceable to the work of the French psychologists Alfred Binet (q.v.) and Théodore Simon (1873–1961); *see* PSYCHOLOGICAL TESTING. Other influential educators of the 20th century included the Americans Granville Stanley Hall, a pioneer in the study of the psychology of adolescence; Edward Lee Thorndike (qq.v.), whose field was educational psychology and measurements; William Heard Kilpatrick (1871–1965), proponent of group activities and class projects and foremost disciple of Dewey; Abraham Flexner (*see under* FLEXNER), whose influence improved the quality of medical education; Robert Maynard Hutchins, a commentator on the imperfections of higher education; James Bryant Conant, whose observations on secondary education led to considerable change and improvement; and Jacques Martin Barzun (qq.v.), university administrator, author, and historian.

Types of American Education. Current theories of education in force in the U.S. include essentialism, progressivism, perennialism, and reconstructionism.

Essentialism is concerned with the transmission of cultures and traditions to each generation. It is concerned with subject matter, the impact of the teacher, the importance of character building, and the like. Progressivism, according to the disciples of Dewey and Kilpatrick, is concerned with the development of the thinking ability of a child, his problem-solving techniques, and his creative contribution to society. Perennialism, which overlaps with essentialism, emphasizes the training of the mind according to traditional principles. Reconstructionism, an outgrowth of progressivism, stresses the role of the school as an agent for the general improvement of society.

Youthful Peace Corps volunteers draw on their college specialties to help people around the world. Here, Bill Dewey, of Fillmore, Calif., works with a Guatemalan farmer to build a hog pen.   Ann Anderson – Peace Corps

Education Plans in the United States. The Gary Plan, a part of the progressive movement in American education, developed between 1908 and 1915 in Gary, Ind. Its purpose was to reorganize school building for the most efficient use of space, into teaching, laboratory, gymnasium, and auditorium areas. The Dalton Plan, developed in Dalton, Mass., in 1919, divided students' work into so-called contract units to be completed within announced deadlines. The Winnetka Plan, developed in 1919 in Winnetka, Ill., also separated curriculum into contract units, and encouraged the students to work together creatively on group projects.

School Enrollment. According to the U.S. National Center for Educational Statistics, the enrollment in U.S. schools and colleges in the mid-1970's was as follows: kindergarten through grade eight, 35,021,000; grades nine through

337

twelve, 15,633,000; higher education, 9,023,000; total enrollment, 59,677,000. The decade of the 1970's saw a leveling off of the rapid growth of school enrollment that had occurred since World War II. Even so, it was estimated that 89 percent of those aged 16 and 17 years was in school, as well as 46 percent of 18- and 19-year-olds and 23 percent of those aged 20 to 24. About 36 percent of all those aged 25 and over had completed high school, and 15 percent had completed four or more years of college. In 1950 the median figure for school years completed was 9.3 percent for persons 25 years or older. In 1976 it was 12.4 percent.

For further information regarding State education systems, see separate articles on individual States.

See also EDUCATION, ADULT. W.W.B.

EDUCATION, MEDICAL, branch of education devoted to training doctors in the practice of medicine. In 18th-century colonial America, prospective physicians either apprenticed themselves to established practitioners or went abroad to study in the traditional schools of London, Paris, and Edinburgh. Medicine was first taught formally by specialists at the University of Pennsylvania, beginning in 1765, and in 1767 at King's College, now Columbia University, which was the first institution in the colonies to confer the degree of Doctor of Medicine. Following the American Revolution, the Columbia medical faculty (formerly of King's College) was merged with the College of Physicians and Surgeons, chartered in 1809, which survives as a division of Columbia University.

In 1893 the Johns Hopkins Medical School required all applicants to have a college degree and was the first to afford its students the opportunity to further their training in an affiliated teaching hospital. The growth of medical schools affiliated with established institutions of learning was paralleled by the development of proprietary schools of medicine run for personal profit, most of which had low standards and inadequate facilities. Abraham Flexner (see under FLEXNER), between 1910 and 1912, wrote two books exposing the inadequacies of most proprietary schools. Subsequently, the American Medical Association and the Association of American Medical Colleges laid down standards for course content, qualifications of teachers, laboratory facilities, affiliation with teaching hospitals, and licensing of practitioners that survive to this day.

In 1970 the United States had 85 four-year medical colleges accredited by the Council on Medical Education, formed by the two associa-

tions. Graduates, after a year of internship, receive licenses to practice if they pass an examination administered either by a State board or by the National Board of Medical Examiners.

See also EDUCATION IN THE PROFESSIONS.

EDUCATION, MILITARY, training of the officers and enlisted men, including draftees, of a nation's military forces. The primary distinction between military and other forms of education is that military education is directed toward the goal of preparing the soldier to react quickly and automatically under the stress of combat. He must not only learn specific skills, but also be disciplined sufficiently to use those skills instinctively in combat. In addition, qualified soldiers may receive a more formal education to enable them to advance intellectually and professionally.

In the United States Army (q.v.), training and education may be divided into five categories:

1. Individual and unit training is designed to prepare a soldier for warfare. Individually he receives simulated combat training, is taught the use of weapons, and is physically conditioned. As a member of a military unit, he takes part in field exercises and maneuvers that train him to act as a member of a group.

2. Precommission schooling trains selected individuals for duty as commissioned officers. Officer candidate schools (O.C.S.) prepare them for appointments as second lieutenants in the Army Reserve or Regular Army. Reserve Officers Training Corps (R.O.T.C.) programs in high schools and colleges prepare students for commissions as second lieutenants in the Army Reserve. The United States Military Academy (q.v.) at West Point, N.Y., prepares individuals for commissions as second lieutenants in the Regular Army. Graduates also receive a B.S. degree.

3. The United States Continental Army Command operates an Army service school system that offers 600 courses in 350 military specialties. In addition, branches of the Army operate their own training centers.

4. A general education development (G.E.D.) program offers academic courses from the grammar-school through the graduate-school level. This program uses both classroom instruction and correspondence courses.

5. Selected personnel, primarily officers, are sent to civilian colleges and universities at government expense to obtain higher degrees or to take courses in advanced technical fields.

Officers in specific branches of the service receive a basic education in that branch when they join and between their fourth and eighth year of commissioned service are given ad-

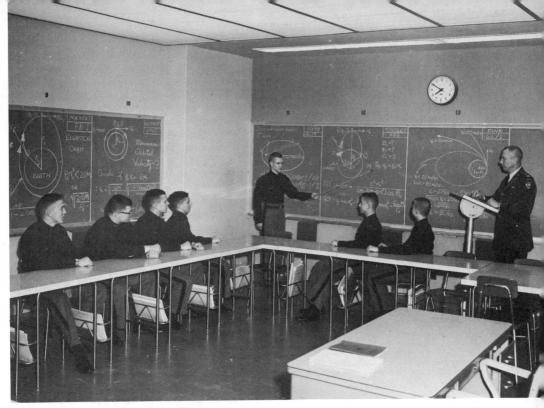

Education at the U.S. Military Academy in West Point, N.Y., traditionally stresses small class sections of not more than 12 to 15 cadets, as in this freshman class studying mathematics. U.S. Army

vanced training. After ten to fifteen years of service, officers are selected for advanced training at the U.S. Army's senior tactical school, the Command and General Staff College, at Fort Leavenworth, Kansas. The college prepares officers for duty as commanders and general staff officers at the division, corps, and field army level.

The Army War College at Carlisle Barracks, Pa., prepares selected officers for duty as commanders and general officers at the highest levels of military service.

The other branches of service have institutions similar to the Command and General Staff College and the Army War College. In addition, the Department of Defense maintains joint service schools, the National War College (q.v.), and the Industrial College of the Armed Forces, both in Washington, D.C., and the Armed Forces Staff College, in Norfolk, Va., for the training of officers selected for promotion to the highest levels of authority in the Department of Defense. The other major powers have similar institutions.

History. Until the French Revolution, officers acquired their knowledge of tactics and strategy informally, chiefly from the practical experience gained in battle and the study of the writings of the great military leaders of the past. For enlisted men, only rigid, unthinking obedience to the commands of their superiors was required. With the growth of large national armies during and after the French Revolution, the problems of command became more complex. The increasing variety and power of the armaments, the elaborate defensive fortifications, and the planning necessary to equip, supply, and maintain armies in the field required professionally trained officers. This need led first to the establishment of the first academies for training officers in the arts of war. Louis XV (q.v.), King of France, established l'École Militaire in 1751 to train noblemen as military officers. Frederick II (q.v.), King of Prussia, established the Ritterakademie in 1765, and the Royal Military Academy was established at Wollwich, England, in 1741 as an artillery school.

But the need for professional officers specifically trained in the technologies developed by the industrial revolution (q.v.) and the application of these technologies in war resulted in the establishment of institutions specifically designed to provide a professional military education. The U.S. Military Academy (q.v.) was established in 1802. The École Special Militaire was founded the same year at Fontainebleau,

339

Cadets at the U.S. Military Academy receive military instruction and training primarily during the summer months. During a cadet's second year at the Academy he spends two months at nearby Camp Buckner in rigorous field and tactical training. Here a cadet crosses a stream during a field exercise.   U.S. Army

France, and transferred to Saint-Cyr in 1808. The Royal Military Academy, Sandhurst, England, was established in 1799. The Kriegsakademie, Berlin, Prussia, was established in 1810. Following the Russian Revolution in 1917, the Soviet Union established the Suvorov Military and Nakhimov Naval Schools to prepare selected individuals for commissions as army and navy officers in the Soviet armed forces.

In most European armies until the beginning of World War I, students for the academies were recruited from the aristocracy and the well-to-do upper middle class. Officers were usually well educated, had private means, and felt socially superior to the men they commanded. As a result of World Wars I and II, the general trend has been toward an increased democratization of the military forces. Officer candidates are now almost universally selected on the basis of merit. Enlisted men have been given much wider latitude to act independently in battle, and are expected to do so. The complexity of modern armaments has accelerated this trend, and officers and enlisted men are increasingly required to act in cooperation with each other rather than as leaders and followers.

See also ARMY; UNITED STATES AIR FORCE ACADEMY; UNITED STATES COAST GUARD ACADEMY; UNITED STATES NAVAL ACADEMY.   E.A.W.

EDUCATION, NATIONAL SYSTEMS OF. *See* EDUCATION IN THE UNITED STATES and separate articles on individual countries.

EDUCATION, OFFICE OF, agency of the United States government within the Department of Health, Education, and Welfare (q.v.). The office was established by Congress in 1867 to promote the progress of education in the U.S. In 1869 it became part of the U.S. Department of the Interior (q.v.). It was transferred to the Federal Security Agency in 1939 and to the Department of Health, Education, and Welfare in 1953.

The initial function of the Office of Education was to collect and distribute information on education in the U.S. Since the passage of the National Defense Education Act in 1958, its major function has been to administer Federal funds allocated by Congress to improve the quality of American education. Subsequent education legislation has increased these funds to several billion dollars annually. Financial aid is directed to programs developed by State educational agencies, local school districts, colleges, and other educational agencies and institutions. The agency administers, for example, a multi-billion-dollar program of Federal aid to elementary, junior, and senior high schools, authorized under the Elementary and Secondary Education Act of 1965; the largest part of these funds is marked for special programs to help raise the quality of education for children from low-income families. Other programs range from kindergarten to post-graduate study. Nearly all of the 19,000 public-school districts and 2500 institutions of higher education in the U.S. participate. In the field of higher education the agency administers programs to strengthen colleges and universities and provide loans and grants to needy students.

Among the publications of the Office of Education are *American Education,* published 10 times a year; *Research in Education,* published monthly; and the annual *Education Directory.*

EDUCATION, PHYSICAL. *See* PHYSICAL EDUCATION.

EDUCATION, SECONDARY, program of public education immediately following elementary schooling (*see* EDUCATION, ELEMENTARY). It begins generally at the age of twelve to fourteen and continues from four to six years. Some types of secondary education, such as vocational schooling, are terminal and prepare the student for employment upon graduation. Others lead to advanced training in colleges, universities, or technical schools. In the United States, secondary education comprises the junior and senior high schools. In many foreign countries, this

Young men interested in careers in telecommunications study the electrical circuit of a radio receiver at a National Telecommunications Administration training institute in Paraguay. *United Nations*

level of education often embraces the junior or community college as well as the first two years of university training. The purpose of secondary education is to expand the basic knowledge of subjects already studied, including the systematic study of literature, foreign languages, sciences, mathematics, social studies, and other subjects essential for physical and intellectual development and to prepare students as future citizens. In some countries, such as the U.S.S.R., military training is also required of students.

W.W.B.

EDUCATION, TECHNICAL, instruction in a skill or procedure usually of a mechanical type and at a level between that of the professional scientist or engineer and that of a skilled craftsman. Technicians support scientists and engineers by designing, developing, producing, and maintaining machines and materials. The work of a technician is more limited in scope than that of scientists and engineers and is usually considered to be practical rather than theoretical in its orientation.

In industry, jobs for technicians range from those that are narrow in scope and require relatively limited technical understanding, such as the routine inspection of parts, to those that require a considerable level of mathematical, scientific, and applied technological ability, such as engineering aide, instrumentation technician, draftsman, and tool designer.

Educational Programs. A technical education is acquired in a number of ways. Many learn on the job and supplement their practical experi-

ence with correspondence courses and evening school. The armed forces train a large number of technicians, particularly in electronics. Increasing numbers of technicians receive their education in trade schools, technical high schools, vocational-technical schools, community or junior colleges, or in technical institutes. The trend is toward education beyond the high school, with more skilled technicians and technologists completing either two or four years of college. In the late 1960's the median number of school years completed by technicians was about fourteen years, compared to twelve years for all workers.

A great diversity of courses and programs are available. Some schools offer technical training in only a single field; others in a variety of fields. Some schools combine agricultural and industrial training within the same school; other schools train skilled craftsmen as well as technicians. Junior or community colleges offering courses primarily for craftsmen and technicians include courses in the liberal arts, or the technical courses may be offered in a separate division of a liberal-arts-oriented junior college. Some senior colleges are now providing a four-year baccalaureate program in engineering technology.

Development in America. The first technical institute in the United States was the Lyceum, founded in Gardiner, Maine, in 1822 to provide

Science education for teachers. High-school teachers in Afghanistan carry out an experiment in the chemistry laboratory of Kabul University. *United Nations*

a suitable education for farmers and mechanics in a two-year course. A number of mechanics institutes were founded in the 1820's to provide lectures, libraries, and classes for their members, but the spread of free public schools tended to eliminate the need for this type of school. The only such institute that developed into the present-day technical institute was the Ohio Mechanics Institute, founded in Cincinnati in 1828.

The Rensselaer Polytechnic Institute, founded in Troy, N.Y., in 1823, to provide an education in the sciences for interested workmen and others gradually evolved into a school of engineering and graduated its first class of civil engineers in 1835. Other early technical institutes that later became engineering colleges include the Polytechnic Institute of Brooklyn and the Cooper Union for the Advancement of Science and Art, both in New York City; Drexel Institute of Technology (now Drexel University) in Philadelphia; the Carnegie Institute of Technology in Pittsburgh, Pa. (now Carnegie-Mellon University); and the California Institute of Technology at Pasadena, Calif.

Pratt Institute, which opened in 1877 in New York City, was one of the best-known early technical institutes. Its first courses were intended for experienced industrial craftsmen with a high-school background and two years of practical experience. In 1895 Pratt Institute introduced an adaptation of the curriculum followed by the German *Technikum,* which emphasized the practical applications of engineering. Pratt Institute gradually changed, however, into a school offering regular four-year engineering programs.

Recognition of the excellence of Russian technical schools, as shown by Russian exhibits at the Philadelphia Centennial Exposition (1876), further improved technical instruction in the U.S. by placing increased emphasis on acquiring basic skills prior to workshop practice.

Government and Professional Support. In 1917 Congress passed the Smith-Hughes Act to promote vocational education. Congress broadened the scope of this program several times and in 1958 authorized the training of technicians under the National Defense Education Act. In 1963 Congress expanded this program of vocational and technical education still further. In the mid-1970's the total number of secondary, postsecondary, and adult students in Federally aided vocational and technical education classes was estimated to exceed 13,000,000. The greatest enrollments were in home economics, trade and industry, office skills, and agriculture.

The standards in technical education have gradually risen since World War II. In 1944 the Engineers Council for Professional Development assumed responsibility for accrediting technical institutes offering programs in engineering technology. The approved engineering technology curriculum leads usually to an associate or bachelor's degree in engineering technology. In the late 1960's about 150 approved curricula were being followed in 45 institutions.

See also EDUCATION, VOCATIONAL.

L.C.A. & WILLIAM W. BRICKMAN

EDUCATION, VOCATIONAL, instruction in skills necessary for persons who are preparing to enter the labor force or who are at work (or unemployed) and need training or retraining in the technology of their occupation.

The impact of technology upon occupations,

the tendency of employers to set higher educational requirements, and the need for employees with specialized training have made vocational preparation imperative. Part-time programs are essential in order to provide occupational mobility among workers and to overcome the effects of job obsolescence. *See also* AUTOMATION.

In the United States, vocational-education programs are conducted in the public schools, both secondary and postsecondary, and are financed in part by Federal funds. Other programs are conducted by business and industry, by labor organizations, by the armed forces, and by a number of private schools. Programs in both public and private institutions are usually general in scope, providing training for several jobs in an occupational cluster; programs conducted by business, industry, and the armed forces usually focus on particular institutional interests. Under the Vocational Education Amendments (1968), vocational programs are administered by the U.S. Office of Education.

Range of Programs. Vocational-education programs range from short-unit (ten weeks or less) to long-term programs up to two years in length. The programs include numerous occupational areas, such as office, agricultural, distributive, trades, health, and technical. The scope of vocational education is broad, ranging from occupations requiring little skill to those requiring a high degree of skill and scientific knowledge. Jobs requiring minimum training are not generally included in formal programs because the necessary skills can be readily learned on the job. In 1973, 29 percent of vocational enrollment was in home economics, 22 percent in trade and industry, 20 percent in office work, and 8 percent in agriculture.

Many of the public and private schools offering vocational instruction operate on a so-called open-door policy; that is, anyone may attend who can profit from the instruction. The goal of the public-school program is to provide access for all persons to high-quality instruction that will meet occupational opportunities.

Almost 8,800,000 students were enrolled in public-school vocational-education programs annually in the early 1970's. The number enrolled in private vocational schools and in business and industrial programs is unknown. Every State department of education in the U.S. employs staff specialists in vocational education.

Vocational Guidance. Vocational guidance and vocational education have their origin in the 20th century. Although the vocational-guidance and vocational-education movements developed separately during the early 1900's, they later became closely associated.

The basic principle of vocational guidance is that a person is better equipped to make his occupational plans after (1) recognizing his own characteristics; (2) examining the requirements of various occupations; and (3) matching the two sets of facts under the guidance of a skilled counselor.

Various standardized tests have been developed to measure skills, aptitudes, interests, and other abilities and traits. School records and consultation with guidance specialists assist students further with occupational selection. In recent years the U.S. Office of Education has increased emphasis on the concept of career education, which seeks to integrate academic learning with specific job skills.

Work Experience. An imperative aspect of vocational guidance is knowledge of the world of work. It has been established that ignorance of the variety of ways in which people earn a living has been a greater deterrent to freedom of occupational selection than any barrier of ethnic

A young student is taught industrial skills in a modern, government-operated vocational school in Sicily.
Standard Oil Co. (N.J.)

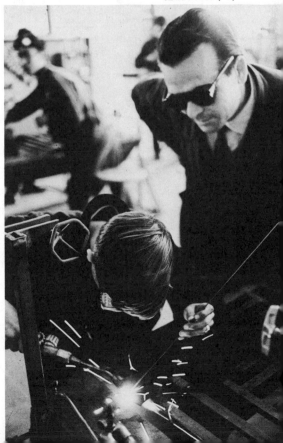

or cultural origin. To help solve this problem schools provide opportunity for students to study the occupational world and enable them to gain actual work experience as part of their educational preparation. The value of work experience in education, from the standpoints of vocational education and vocational guidance, has long been recognized and is emphasized in the contemporary guidance of youth.

Vocational education and vocational guidance have had the active support and participation of the trade unions because both contribute to the labor goal of an educated labor force.

The two national professional associations concerned with vocational education and vocational guidance are the American Vocational Association and the National Vocational Guidance Association. Accreditation is accomplished by the National Association of Trade and Technical Schools. *See also* CORRESPONDENCE EDUCATION; EDUCATION IN THE PROFESSIONS; EDUCATION, TECHNICAL; Four-H (4-H) CLUBS.   M.L.B. & W.W.B.

EDWARD, *or* EADWARD, the name of three Saxon kings of the English.

Edward, called EDWARD THE ELDER (870?–925), King (899–925), son of King Alfred (q.v.).

He succeeded as king of the Angles and Saxons in 899, despite a rebellion led by his cousin Ethelwald with the support of the Danes of Northumbria and East Anglia. After a protracted struggle he defeated the Danes, and in 912, upon the death of his brother-in-law Ethelred, Alderman of Mercia, he annexed the cities of London and Oxford and their environs. The Danes submitted formally in 918, and soon thereafter the sovereignty of Edward was acknowledged by the North Welsh, the Scots, the Northumbrians, and the Welsh of Strathclyde. He was succeeded by Athelstan (q.v.).

Edward, called EDWARD THE MARTYR (963?–978), King (975–78), son of King Edgar the Peaceful (q.v.), whom he succeeded in 975. His reign was marked by agitation against the monasteries, which had been defended by Edgar and his adviser Saint Dunstan (q.v.). After a reign of three years Edward was murdered, probably by his stepmother Elfrida, whose son acceded to the throne as Ethelred II (q.v.).

Edward, called EDWARD THE CONFESSOR (1002?–66), King (1042–66), son of King Ethelred II. During most of the rule of the Danish kings of England who followed Canute II (q.v.), Ed-

Edward the Confessor, King of England, established Westminster Abbey as an expression of his devotion to religious works. The abbey church was consecrated about 1066.   Ewing Galloway

ward lived at the court of the dukes of Normandy. In 1041 Hardecanute (q.v.) invited Edward to England, and the following year Edward succeeded to the English throne, largely because of the support of Godwin, Earl of Wessex (d. 1053). Edward married Godwin's daughter Edith, but soon gave his favor to the enemies of Godwin, who was harassed and for a brief time exiled. Perhaps because of Godwin's popularity in England, a reconciliation was effected about 1052. Godwin's son Harold, later Harold II (q.v.), King of England, became one of Edward's advisers, and another son, Tostig (d. 1066), became his favorite. In 1055 Edward made Tostig Earl of Northumbria, but the earl's rule was so oppressive that a rebellion broke out in 1065, and Edward was forced to exile Tostig. Thereafter Edward's health failed, and he was unable to attend the consecration of Westminster Abbey (q.v.), which he had founded. He was succeeded by Harold II, the last Saxon king of England. Less than a century after his death Edward was canonized.

EDWARD, known as THE BLACK PRINCE (1330–76), Prince of Wales, son of Edward III (q.v.), King of England. During his lifetime, he was called Edward of Woodstock, from his place of birth; the name "Black Prince" was given him because of the black armor he wore. In 1346 Edward accompanied his father on the English campaign in Normandy (see HUNDRED YEARS' WAR), and during the battle of Crécy (see CRÉCY, BATTLE OF), the prince distinguished himself by his command of the right wing of the English army.

In 1355 Edward was appointed his father's lieutenant in Gascony. He led the English army in a series of raids across southern France, and in 1356 defeated a French army at Poitiers, took prisoner John II, King of France (see under JOHN), and returned in triumph to England with his captive. In 1361, during the short peace following King John's ransom, Edward married his cousin Joan, Countess of Kent (1328–85), known as "the fair maid of Kent". A year later, having been created prince of Aquitaine and Gascony by his father, he crossed to the English possessions in southern France. As ruler of those lands, Edward became, under feudal law, a vassal of the French king.

The prince was a successful ruler, but he estranged the Gascon nobles, who believed that he was curtailing their feudal rights. After almost six years of peace, Edward, in 1367, led an expedition to Spain in order to restore Pedro el Cruel (q.v.), the deposed king of Castile, to his throne. During the successful Spanish campaign, Edward contracted an illness from which he never recovered; Pedro furthermore refused to repay to Edward the vast sums that had been expended on his behalf. On his return to Aquitaine, the prince levied taxes to pay for the expedition, but the disgruntled nobles protested to their feudal lord, Charles V (q.v.), King of France. The prince refused to answer to the charges against him, and Charles renewed the war against England. A revolt against Edward spread through Aquitaine and Gascony and, despite his illness, the prince led his troops against the city of Limoges, capturing it in 1370 and massacring its defenders. A year later he returned to England and resigned his principality.

During the last years of his life, Edward was a leader of the political faction that rebelled against the misrule of Edward's younger brother, John of Gaunt (q.v.), Duke of Lancaster. However, he finally succumbed to his illness and was buried in Canterbury Cathedral, in which parts of his armor still hang.

EDWARD I, called LONGSHANKS (1239–1307), King of England (1272–1307), of the house of Plantagenet, born in Westminster, the eldest son of Henry III (q.v.), King of England. He married Eleanor of Castile (q.v.) in 1254. In the struggles of the barons against the crown for constitutional and ecclesiastical reforms, Edward took a vacillating course. When warfare broke out between the crown and the nobility (see BARONS' WAR), Edward fought on the side of the king, winning the decisive battle of Evesham in 1265. Five years later he left England to join the Seventh Crusade (see CRUSADES). Following his father's death in 1272, and while he was still abroad, Edward was recognized as king by the English barons; in 1273, on his return to England, he was crowned.

The first years of Edward's reign were a period of the consolidation of his power. He suppressed corruption in the administration of justice, restricted the jurisdiction of the ecclesiastical courts to church affairs, and eliminated the papacy's overlordship over England.

Upon the refusal of Llewelyn ab Gruffydd (d. 1282), ruler of Wales, to submit to the English crown, Edward began the military conflict that resulted, in 1284, in the annexation of Llewelyn's principality to the English crown. In 1290 Edward expelled all Jews from England. War between England and France broke out in 1293 as a result of the efforts of France to curb Edward's power in Gascony. Edward lost Gascony in 1293 and did not again come into possession of the duchy until 1303. About the same year in which he lost Gascony, the Welsh rose in rebellion.

345

Greater than either of these problems was the disaffection of the people of Scotland. In agreeing to arbitrate among the claimants to the Scottish throne, Edward, in 1291, had exacted as a prior condition the recognition by all concerned of his overlordship of Scotland. The Scots later repudiated him and made an alliance with France against England. To meet the critical situations in Wales and Scotland, Edward summoned a parliament, called the Model Parliament by historians because it was a representative body and in that respect was the forerunner of all future parliaments. Assured by Parliament of support at home, Edward took the field and suppressed the Welsh insurrection. In 1296, after invading and conquering Scotland, he declared himself king of that realm. In 1298 he again invaded Scotland to suppress the revolt led by Sir William Wallace (q.v.). In winning the battle of Falkirk in 1298, Edward achieved the greatest military triumph of his career, but he failed to crush Scottish opposition. The conquest of Scotland became the ruling passion of his life. He was, however, compelled by the nobles, clergy, and commons to desist in his attempts to raise by arbitrary taxes the funds he needed for campaigns. In 1299 Edward made peace with France and married Margaret, sister of Philip III, King of France (*see under* PHILIP). Free of war with France, he again undertook the conquest of Scotland in 1303. Wallace was captured and executed in 1305. But no sooner had Edward established his government in Scotland than a new revolt broke out and culminated in the coronation of Robert Bruce (q.v.) as king of Scotland. In 1307 Edward set out for the third time to subdue the Scots, but he died en route.

EDWARD II (1284–1327), King of England (1307–27), of the house of Plantagenet, born in Caernarvon, Wales, the fourth son of Edward I (q.v.), King of England, and his first wife, Eleanor of Castile (q.v.). The deaths of his elder brothers made the infant prince heir to the throne; in 1301 he was proclaimed prince of Wales, the first heir apparent in English history to bear the title. The prince was idle and frivolous, with no liking for military campaigning or affairs of state. Believing that the prince was being badly influenced by his close friend Piers Gaveston (d. 1312), a Gascon knight, Edward I banished Gaveston. On his father's death, however, Edward II recalled his favorite. Gaveston incurred the opposition of the powerful English barony. The nobles were particularly angered when in 1308 Edward made Gaveston regent for the period of the king's absence in France, where he went to marry Isabella of France (1292–1358), daughter

Edward II

of Philip IV (q.v.), King of France. In 1311 the barons, led by Thomas, Earl of Lancaster (1277?–1322), forced the king to appoint from among them a committee of twenty-one noblemen and prelates called the lords ordainers. They proclaimed a series of ordinances that transferred the ruling power to themselves and excluded the commons and lower clergy from Parliament. After they had twice forced the king to banish Gaveston, and the king had each time recalled him, the barons finally had the king's favorite kidnapped and executed (1312).

In the meantime Robert Bruce (q.v.) had almost completed his reconquest of Scotland, which he had begun shortly after 1305. In 1314 Edward II and his barons raised an army of about 100,000 with which to crush Bruce, but in the attempt to raise the siege of Stirling were decisively defeated (*see* BANNOCKBURN, BATTLE OF). For the following eight years the Earl of Lancaster virtually ruled the kingdom. In 1322, with the aid of barons opposed to Lancaster, and with the advice and help of two new royal favorites, the baron Hugh le Despenser the elder, and his son Hugh le Despenser the younger (*see under* DESPENSER, LE), Edward defeated Lancaster in battle and had him executed. The Despensers thereupon became virtual rulers of England. They summoned a Parliament in which the commons had a voice and which repealed the ordinances of 1311 on the ground they had been passed by the barons only. The repeal was a great step forward in English constitutional development, for it meant that thenceforth no law passed by Parliament was valid unless the House of Commons approved it.

Edward again futilely invaded Scotland in 1322, and in 1323 signed a thirteen-year truce with Robert Bruce. In 1325 Queen Isabella accompanied the prince of Wales to France, where, in accordance with feudal custom, he did homage to Charles IV, King of France (*see under* CHARLES) for the fief of Aquitaine. Isabella, who desired to depose the Despensers, allied herself to a number of barons who had been exiled by Edward II. In 1326, with their leader Roger de Mortimer (1287–1330), Isabella raised an army and invaded England. Edward and his favorites fled, but his wife's army pursued and executed the Despensers, and imprisoned Edward. In January, 1327, Parliament forced Edward to resign and proclaimed the prince of Wales king as Edward III. The same year Edward II was murdered in Berkeley Castle, Gloucestershire, in which he had been held for several months.

EDWARD III (1312–77), King of England (1327–77), of the house of Plantagenet, born in Windsor, the eldest son of Edward II (q.v.). In 1327 he was proclaimed king by Parliament. During Edward's minority, England was nominally ruled by a council of regency, but the actual power was in the hands of the king's mother, Isabella of France (1292–1358), and her paramour, Roger de Mortimer (1287–1330). In 1330 the young king took the power into his own hands, had Mortimer hanged, and confined his mother to her home.

Edward began a series of wars almost directly after he had control of England. Taking advantage of civil war in Scotland in 1333, he invaded the country, defeated the Scots at Halidon Hill, England, and restored Edward de Baliol (*see under* BALIOL), to the throne of Scotland. De Baliol was deposed, and later attempts by Edward to establish him permanently as king of Scotland were unsuccessful. In 1337 France came to the aid of Scotland. This action was the culminating point of a series of disagreements between France and England, and Edward declared war on Philip VI (q.v.), King of France

(*see* HUNDRED YEARS' WAR). In 1340 the English fleet destroyed a larger French fleet off Sluis, the Netherlands, an action resulting in a truce that, although occasionally disturbed, lasted for six years.

War broke out again in 1346. Edward, accompanied by his eldest son, Edward (q.v.), the Black Prince, invaded Normandy and won a great victory over France in the battle of Crécy (*see* CRÉCY, BATTLE OF). He captured Calais in 1347, and a truce was reestablished. Edward returned to England, where he maintained one of the most magnificent courts in Europe. About 1348 he instituted the Order of the Garter (*see* GARTER, ORDER OF THE). The war with France was renewed in 1355, and again the English armies were successful. The Peace of Calais, in 1360, gave England all of Aquitaine, and Edward renounced his claim, first made in 1328, to the French throne.

The English king continued to assert his will both domestically and abroad. In 1363 he concluded an agreement with David II (q.v.), King of Scotland, uniting the two kingdoms in the event of David's death without male issue. Three years later Edward repudiated the papacy's feudal supremacy over England, held in fief since 1213. He renewed his war with France, disavowing the Peace of Calais. The English armies were unsuccessful this time; after the truce of 1375, Edward retained only a few of the former vast English possessions in France.

The king had, by this time, become senile. He was completely in the power of an avaricious mistress, Alice Perrers (d. 1376), who, with the help of Edward's fourth son, John of Gaunt (q.v.), dominated England. Alice Perrers was banished by Parliament in 1376, but John of Gaunt continued his struggle for the control of England with Edward's successor and grandson, Richard II (q.v.). *See* ENGLAND: *History: The Plantagenets: Baronial Revolt: Dynasties of Lancaster and York.*

EDWARD IV (1442–83), King of England (1461–70; 1471–83), of the house of York, son of Richard Plantagenet, 3rd Duke of York (*see* YORK, HOUSE OF), born in Rouen, France. He inherited the title earl of March. During the Wars of the Roses (*see* ROSES, WARS OF THE), and following the defeat of the house of York in the battle of Ludlow in 1459, Edward was driven from England by Henry VI (q.v.), King of England, and head of the house of Lancaster. Following his return to England and the death of his father in the Battle of Wakefield in 1460, Edward became head of the house of York. He defeated the Lancastrians in the Battle of Mortimer's Cross in 1461 and was acclaimed king by Parliament, which also declared Henry VI a usurper and traitor. Edward was crowned in June, 1461. In giving thanks in person to the House of Commons, he set a historic precedent. Despite the civil war that continued intermittently until 1471, when all Lancastrian resistance was crushed and Henry VI was taken prisoner, Edward fostered the commerce of his realm. During his reign, printing and silk manufacturing were introduced in England.

Edward's marriage to Elizabeth Woodville, a commoner, and his efforts to create a new nobility more amenable to his interests, angered the older nobles and alienated Richard Neville, Earl of Warwick (*see under* NEVILLE), who had been his loyal supporter. Warwick later made an alliance with the Lancastrians and, in 1470, drove Edward from the throne and into exile in Holland. Henry VI again became king of England. Supplied with funds by his brother-in-law, Charles (q.v.) the Bold, Duke of Burgundy, Edward returned to England in 1471, raised a large army, and won decisive victories over his enemies at Barnet and Tewkesbury. Thereafter the crown was securely in his possession. The later years of his reign were, for the most part, uneventful. The most notable incident of this period was a short war with France in 1475, which was terminated by an arrangement whereby Louis XI (q.v.), King of France, agreed to pay Edward an annual subsidy. The autocratic rule of Edward IV paved the way for the despotism of the Tudors (*see* TUDOR). Edward was succeeded by his son Edward V (q.v.).

EDWARD V (1470–83), uncrowned King of England (1483), of the house of York (q.v.). Born in Westminster, the eldest son of King Edward IV (q.v.), he was created prince of Wales in 1471. As a result of the power struggle between his paternal uncle Richard, Duke of Gloucester (later King Richard III), and his maternal uncle Anthony Woodville, 2nd Earl Rivers (1442?–83), both Edward and his brother Richard, Duke of York (1472–83), were confined in the Tower of London (q.v.) after their father's death in April, 1483. They were not seen again outside the tower. Because the duke of Gloucester, crowned as Richard III on June 25, 1483, had a strong motive for killing them, it is reasonable to suppose that he had them assassinated before his own death in August, 1485. No circumstantial evidence exists, however. It is possible, for instance, that they survived him and were later slain by Richard's successor, Henry VII (q.v.) of the house of Tudor (q.v.), to whose title they would have been a threat. The belief that

Richard instigated their murder was advanced by Tudor historians. *See* RICHARD III.

EDWARD VI (1537–53), King of England and Ireland (1547–53), of the house of Tudor, born in Hampton Court, the only son of Henry VIII (q.v.) and Jane Seymour (*see under* SEYMOUR), his third wife. Edward succeeded to the crown upon the death of his father early in 1547. Upon his accession, his maternal uncle, Edward Seymour, 1st Earl of Hertford, was named lord protector and duke of Somerset. In 1547 the protector used as a pretext for war with Scotland an alleged violation by the Scots of an agreement to give Mary, Queen of Scots (q.v.), in marriage to Edward; in the same year, the forces he dispatched to invade that country defeated the Scots at Pinkie.

Both Edward and the protector strongly favored the principle of the Reformation (q.v.), and did much to establish Protestantism in England. The body of edicts known as the Six Articles, enacted in the reign of Henry VIII, was repealed, and a new service book, the first *Book of Common Prayer* (q.v.), was prepared and came into general use in the Anglican Church.

In 1552 John Dudley (*see under* DUDLEY), Duke of Northumberland, whose enmity the protector had incurred, accused the latter of dangerous ambitions. The young king was persuaded to consent to the execution of the protector, and subsequently was completely controlled by Dudley. In 1553 the king, who had always been of frail constitution, became seriously ill of tuberculosis. Shortly before Edward's death Dudley induced him to sign a will depriving his half sisters, later Mary I and Elizabeth I (qq.v.), of their claim to the royal succession. The right of succession fell to Lady Jane Grey (q.v.), who had married Dudley's son. However, Lady Jane Grey was deposed by Mary, who became queen in 1553.

EDWARD VII (1841–1910), King of Great Britain and Ireland, and Emperor of India (1901–10), born in Buckingham Palace, London, the eldest son of Queen Victoria and Prince Albert (qq.v.). From 1841 to 1901 the future king was known as Albert Edward, Prince of Wales. He studied at the universities of Edinburgh, Oxford, and Cambridge. In 1860 he visited Canada, inaugurating the custom of good-will visits by members of the British royal family, particularly the prince of Wales, to British dominions and foreign countries.

In 1863 he married Alexandra (q.v.), eldest daughter of Christian IX (*see under* CHRISTIAN), King of Denmark. The prince and princess then assumed much of the burden of court ceremonials and public functions, which Queen Victoria had laid aside on going into virtual retirement after the death of the prince consort in 1861. Albert Edward traveled extensively. In Russia and France, particularly, he made valuable personal contacts in political and social circles. At home, his popularity was increased both as prince of Wales and as king by his interest in sports, notably yachting and horse racing; his horses won the Derby in 1896, 1900, and 1909, and the Grand National at Liverpool in 1900.

Albert Edward succeeded to the throne in 1901. From the beginning of his reign he adopted a policy of promoting international amity in Europe, where political tension had been mounting. His visits to various European capitals from 1901 to 1904 and return visits to him by European rulers were of importance in causing the signing of arbitration treaties in 1903–04 between Great Britain and France, Spain, Italy, Germany, and Portugal, respectively. He was also instrumental in promoting two agreements that strengthened the position of Great Britain on the Continent, the Entente Cordiale (q.v.) of 1904 between France and Great Britain, and a pact between Russia and Great Britain in 1907. In 1909 the king and queen paid a diplomatic visit to William II (q.v.), Emperor of Germany, in Berlin that temporarily dispelled German suspicion that the increasingly friendly relations between Great Britain and France and Russia were aimed at weakening Germany.

Because of his efforts to increase international amity the king became known as Edward "the Peacemaker". In 1910, because of declining physical health, Edward went to Biarritz, France, for rest. He died there of a heart attack following a bronchial attack. Three daughters and two sons were born of the marriage between Edward and Alexandra. The sons were Prince Albert Victor, Duke of Clarence (1864–92), and George, Duke of York, who succeeded Edward as George V (q.v.). In 1896 Edward's youngest daughter, Princess Maude Charlotte Mary Victoria (1869–1938), married Prince Charles of Denmark, who later became Haakon VII, King of Norway (*see under* HAAKON).

EDWARD VIII, in full EDWARD ALBERT CHRISTIAN GEORGE ANDREW PATRICK DAVID (1894–1972), King of Great Britain and Northern Ireland, and Emperor of India (Jan. 20–Dec. 11, 1936), born in White Lodge, Richmond Park, England. In 1907 Edward entered the naval preparatory college at Osborne. He studied at the Royal Naval College, Dartmouth, from 1909 to 1911. When he attained the rank of midshipman in 1911, he was assigned to the H.M.S.

Edward VII, known as the Peacemaker.

Hindustan, on which he served for three months. In 1912 he entered Magdalen College, University of Oxford. At the outbreak of World War I in 1914, Edward left Oxford to join the Grenadier Guards. During the war he served in France, Italy, Flanders, and Egypt. Part of the year 1919 he spent investigating industrial and social conditions in his own duchy of Cornwall and in various British industrial cities. Later that year he undertook the first of a long series of official tours, during which he traveled through Canada and payed a brief visit to the United States. He proved himself a successful ambassador of good will and promoter of trade on his subsequent trips to countries in the British Commonwealth. During the late 1920's and early 1930's he was an active supporter of slum-clearance projects, aid to the unemployed, and improvement of the working conditions of British miners. He was also interested in the expansion of British industry.

Reign. Upon the death of his father, King George V (q.v.), in January, 1936, Edward was proclaimed King Edward VIII. Before long, rumors began to circulate concerning his alleged romance with an American, Mrs. Wallis Warfield Simpson (1896–   ), then married to a London shipping broker, her second husband.

On Oct. 20, 1936, Prime Minister Stanley Baldwin (q.v.) counseled Edward, as king and head of the Church of England, to remove all cause for the rumors. A week after the meeting between the prime minister and the king, Mrs. Simpson was granted her second divorce, which was to become final in six months. In November, the king declared in a secret interview with Baldwin that he intended to marry Mrs. Simpson even if that meant his abdication. A morganatic marriage was proposed, but the cabinet was unwilling to accept this compromise; the government wanted the king to choose between the throne and marriage. Public opinion was divided on the issue; many people were in favor of the king marrying whomever he chose, while others upheld the government position. At length the king determined to abdicate in favor of his brother, the Duke of York who became GEORGE VI (q.v.), King of Great Britain. Edward said in his abdication (q.v.) broadcast on Dec. 11, 1936: "I have found it impossible . . . to discharge my duties as King as I would wish to do without the help and support of the woman I love." He received the title Duke of Windsor from his brother, and left England, settling at Enzesfeld, Austria, where he lived until his marriage to Mrs. Simpson in June, 1937.

Duke of Windsor. Because his wife was not accorded the privileges of a royal duchess in England, the Duke of Windsor did not return to his native country for eight years. In 1937 he visited Germany, where he observed social and housing conditions and paid visits to the German dictator Adolf Hitler (q.v.). After the outbreak of World War II in 1939, he was commissioned a major general in the British Expeditionary Force and engaged in liaison work in France. He was governor of the Bahama Islands from 1940 to 1945. In 1945, not accompanied by his wife, he visited England and was reunited with his mother, Dowager Queen Mary (q.v.). After the end of World War II the duke lived as a private British citizen, chiefly in the U.S. and France. At the funeral of George VI in February, 1952, the duke took part in a British royal ceremony for the first time since his abdication. The duke and duchess were not present at the coronation of his niece, Elizabeth II (q.v.), Queen of Great Britain. The queen met the duchess for the first time during her reign in March, 1965, at the bedside of the duke, who was recovering from an eye operation. The duke wrote *A King's Story* (1951) and *Windsor Revisited* (1960). *A King's Story*, a film biography of the duke's life, was released with narration by Orson Welles (q.v.) in 1967.

EDWARD, LAKE, or EDWARD NYANZA, lake of E. central Africa, in the Democratic Republic of the Congo and Uganda, 3240 ft. above sea level. It has an area of about 830 sq.mi. and is connected on the N.E. with Lake George (or Lake Dweru), in Uganda, by means of the Kazinga Channel, which is about 25 mi. long. Lake Edward is fed by the Rutshuru R., a headstream of the White Nile. The lake has only one outlet, the Semliki R. at the N.W. end. High escarpments run along the w. shore of the lake, and mountains rise on the N.W. shore. The water is brackish with mineral salts. Many fish and crocodiles live in the lake, and waterfowl abound on its shores. The American explorer Sir Henry Morton Stanley (q.v.) discovered the lake in 1889. The lake was formerly called Albert Edward Nyanza.

EDWARDS, Jonathan (1703–58), American Congregational clergyman and theologian, born in East Windsor, Connecticut Colony. A child prodigy, at ten he wrote an essay on the nature of the soul. At the age of thirteen he entered the Collegiate School of Connecticut, now Yale University; he graduated in 1720 as valedictorian of his class. After two additional years of study in theology at Yale, he preached for eight months in a New York church and then returned to Yale as a college tutor, studying, at the same time, for his master's degree. He was ordained in 1727 and received a call to assist his grandfather, Solomon Stoddard (1643–1729), pastor of the church at Northampton, Massachusetts Bay Colony, which had one of the largest and wealthiest congregations in the colony.

When Edwards was twenty-six his grandfather died and the young man became pastor at Northampton. He was a firm believer in Calvinism and the doctrine of predestination (qq.v.); there existed in the New England colonies, however, a tendency to belief in Arminianism (q.v.; see also METHODISM). In 1731, in Boston, Edwards preached his first public attack on Arminianism and, in a sermon entitled "God Glorified in Man's Dependence", called for a return to rigorous Calvinism. Three years later he delivered a series of powerful sermons on the same subject in his own church; the series included the famous "Reality of Spiritual Light", in which the preacher combined Calvinism with mysticism (q.v.), religious experience directly given and experienced.

He was a notable pulpit orator. The result of his 1734–35 sermons was a religious revival (see REVIVALS, RELIGIOUS), in which a great number of conversions were made; Edwards received 300 new members into his church. Some of the converted were so obsessed by his fiery descrip-

Jonathan Edwards

tions of eternal damnation as to have contemplated suicide. In 1740 the British evangelist George Whitefield (q.v.) visited Edwards. Together, the two men started a revival movement that, becoming known as the Great Awakening, developed into a religious frenzy engulfing all New England. The conversions were characterized by convulsions and hysteria on the part of the converts; and the harshness and appeal to religious fear in one of Edwards' sermons, "Sinners in the Hands of an Angry God", caused his congregation to rise weeping and moaning from their seats. By 1742 the revival movement had grown out of control, and for the next sixty to seventy years it had the effect on American religion of preventing any attempt at a liberal interpretation of doctrine.

In Northampton, Edwards' sermons created a demand for sterner religious discipline. Eventually, however, his congregation turned against him because of his high-handedness and bigotry. He instituted disciplinary proceedings in church against young people who had been reading what he considered improper books; later, he objected strongly to the Halfway Covenant, a New England church custom that permitted baptized persons to have all the privileges of church membership except commun-

ion although they had not openly professed conversion. A council representing ten congregations in the region dismissed Edwards in 1750. The following year he received a call to Stockbridge, in Massachusetts, then on the frontier, where he became pastor of the village church and missionary to the Housatonic Indians. During his next seven years in Stockbridge, he wrote his most important theological works. Among them was *A Careful and Strict Enquiry into . . . Notions of . . . Freedom of Will . . .* (1754), in which he denied that man has self-determined will that can initiate acts not known or decreed beforehand by God; it remains one of the most famous theological works ever written in America.

In 1757, Edwards accepted the presidency of the College of New Jersey (later Princeton University). He was inaugurated in 1758, but five weeks later died as the result of an inoculation against smallpox, which was then epidemic. Among his other works are *A Treatise Concerning Religious Affections* (1746), *Dissertation Concerning the End for Which God Created the World* (1754), and *The Great Christian Doctrine of Original Sin Defended* (1758).

EDWIN, or EADWINE (Lat. *Aeduinus*) (585?– 633), King of Northumbria (616–33), a kingdom made up of Deira (comprising the eastern part of the modern county of York) and Bernicia (modern Northumberland and southeastern Scotland). Edwin was the son of Ella, King of Deira (d. 588). Upon the death of Ella, Deira was invaded by Ethelfrith, King of Bernicia (d. 616), and the infant Edwin was taken into North Wales where he was brought up. Later he lived as an exile under the protection of Redwald, King of East Anglia (d. 627), now Norfolk and Suffolk counties. Repeated attempts by Ethelfrith to have Edwin put to death led to a battle in 616 in which Ethelfrith was killed; Edwin became king of Northumbria. He extended his power over a large part of England, his authority stretching as far west as the islands of Anglesey and Man, and as far north as the town of Edinburgh, which bears his name. In 625 Edwin married Ethelburh, the sister of Eadbald, King of Kent (d. 640). Ethelburh was a Christian, and in 627 Edwin was converted to Christianity. The champion of the old pagan religion, Penda (577?–655), ruler of the centrally located kingdom of Mercia, then formed an alliance with Caedwalla, King of North Wales (d. 634), against Edwin. Their forces met at Hatfield in 633 and Edwin's army was overwhelmingly defeated; Edwin was killed in the battle. After his death, the kingdom of Northumbria fell apart and

Christianity was for a time extinguished in northern England.

EEL, any elongated, snake-shaped fish of the order Anguilliformes, comprising more than 400 species classified into twenty-six families. After hatching from eggs, all eels have a larval stage in which they are transparent, very thin, pelagic (oceanic) forms called leptocephali. Although most leptocephali are only a few inches long, larger specimens (up to 6 ft.) have been reported, suggesting the possibility of a yet unknown adult 40 ft. or more in length, and furnishing an explanation for accounts of "sea serpents". After spending their larval lives in the ocean, freshwater eels metamorphose into round-bodied young eels, called elvers, who seek streams in which they develop into adult, yellow eels. The adults, upon reaching the next, or silver, stage, have become rich in nutrients and fat. At this stage, they are prized in Europe and Japan for food; they swim downstream to the ocean or possibly to the Sargasso Sea, for spawning. The European eel, *Anguilla rostrata,* a freshwater species, spends three years as a leptocephalus, drifting to Europe in the Gulf Stream in this form, but later spawning in an area southeast of Bermuda. Another species, the American eel, *A. vulgaris,* spends a year as a leptocephalus. Among all species of eels reaching adulthood, the size range is from less than 1 ft. to 10 ft. long.

Most species of eels are entirely marine (ocean living), their lives being spent among reefs or on sand or mud bottoms. A few species are bathypelagic (living several hundred feet deep in the ocean). One is the snipe eel, which has long, thin jaws containing very small teeth. A few species live at even greater depths. Freshwater eels are catadromous; that is, they live most of their lives in lakes and streams and return to the ocean to spawn.

All eels are carnivorous but most are slimy, have teeth, and are generally harmless to man. The moray (q.v.), however, is considered vicious and has attacked swimmers and divers. Although freshwater eels are eaten, the flesh of a few tropical marine species has been found to be extremely toxic. Some eel-shaped fishes, and others bearing "eel" as part of their names, such as the lamprey, hagfish, electric eel, cusk eel, and eelpout, are of unrelated orders and are not true eels.

See CONGER EEL; ELECTRIC FISH; LAMPREY.

EFFIGY MOUNDS NATIONAL MONUMENT, area in N.E. Iowa, containing 191 known prehistoric Indian burial mounds dating from about 500 B.C. to about 1200–1300 A.D. Twenty-nine of the mounds are bird- or bear-shaped. Artifacts of several prehistoric Indian cultures have been found in the mounds. The monument is administered by the National Park Service (q.v.). *See* MOUND BUILDERS.

EFT. *See* NEWT.

EGADI ISLANDS, or AEGADIAN ISLES (anc. *Aegates*), group of islands in the Mediterranean Sea, belonging to Italy, 6 to 23 mi. off the w. coast of Sicily. The major islands are Favignana, Marettimo, and Levanzo. In 241 B.C. a Roman fleet defeated the Carthaginians near these islands, bringing to a close the First Punic War (*see* PUNIC WARS). The islands are now a part of the province of Trapani, in Sicily. The chief industry of the islands is fishing, particularly for tuna and anchovy. Area, 15 sq.mi.; pop. (1971 prelim.) 4461.

EGBERT, or ECGBERHT or ECHBRYHT (775?–839), King of Wessex (802–39), and first Saxon king recognized as sovereign of all England (828–39). He was the son of a Kentish noble but claimed descent from Cerdic (d. 534), founder of the kingdom of Wessex, the kingdom of the West Saxons in southern England. During the rule of Offa, King of Mercia (d. 796), over most of England, Egbert lived in exile at the court of Charlemagne (q.v.), Holy Roman Emperor. Egbert regained his kingdom in 802. His reign was marked by the conquest of the neighboring kingdoms of Kent, Cornwall, and Mercia. By 830 Egbert was also acknowledged as sovereign of East Anglia, Sussex, Surrey, and Northumbria, and was given the title Bretwalda (AS. "ruler of the British"). During succeeding years he led expeditions against the Welsh and the Northmen. The year before his death he defeated a combined force of Danes and Welsh at Hingston Down in Cornwall. He was succeeded by his son Ethelwulf (d. 858), the father of Alfred (q.v.).

EGG, ovum or female reproductive body of multicellular animals, particularly the complex structure produced by birds, reptiles, and certain mammals that matures outside the body of the parent (*see* EMBRYOLOGY; FERTILIZATION). From the anatomical point of view, eggs consist of a minute speck of protoplasm, the germ, tread, or cicatricle, from which the animal develops, and a much larger amount of food material, the yolk. In addition all eggs have some form of protective coating, either a shell or a covering membrane.

The structure and development of eggs of different species vary with the conditions under which the egg is produced and matures. Animals which deposit their eggs to hatch outside their bodies are described as oviparous; those which produce eggs with soft coverings that mature within the body (and which therefore give birth to living young) are called viviparous; and those which produce hard or tough shelled eggs that mature within the parents' bodies are said to be ovoviviparous. Morphologically, the latter group, though they give birth to living young, are oviparous. An egg that contains little yolk is either retained and nourished by the mother, or, if deposited outside the body, develops quickly into a self-sustaining form such as a larva (q.v.). The number of eggs produced varies with the likelihood of their survival. When conditions militate against the survival of eggs, as in the case of fish eggs, which are often eaten by other animals, a large quantity of eggs is produced—as many as 14,000,000 in the case of the turbot. The number of individuals that can develop from a single egg varies from one to several hundred, the latter number being produced by certain chalcid flies.

Mammals of only one order, the Monotremata (see MONOTREMES), deposit eggs outside their bodies. These are the duckbill and the echidnas, whose eggs have thin, parchmentlike shells and a large yolk.

Eggs of Birds. Besides the germ and yolk, the eggs of birds contain an albuminous mass, the white, which is an additional source of nourishment for the developing chick. The egg is enclosed in a tough double membrane, the *membrana putaminis,* which in turn is covered by a hard, three-layered shell chiefly composed of calcium carbonate. The shell serves to protect the egg from the weight of the parents' bodies during incubation. All birds, with the exception of the mound birds, incubate their eggs by body heat. See BIRD: *Structure: Reproductive System.*

Eggs of Reptiles. The majority of reptiles lay eggs, although some species of snakes bear their young alive. Reptile eggs in general have leathery coverings that range in thickness from thin, parchmentlike layers to thick shells resembling those of birds' eggs. The eggs of many lizards have soft shells. In the eggs of all reptiles there is a large amount of yolk. The number of eggs laid by different species varies from a dozen to as many as a hundred in the case of pythons. Pythons, alone among reptiles, incubate their eggs (see REPTILES); most reptilian species either bury their eggs in shallow ground, where they are warmed by the sun, or lay them in underground burrows. A few species, such as the crocodile, incubate their eggs in beds of fermenting vegetable matter. Some lizards lay almost mature eggs, and the young lizards break out of the shells as soon as the eggs are deposited. In some species of lizards the eggs are completely incubated and hatch in the oviduct or egg passage of the parent.

Eggs of Amphibia. Among the amphibia, only certain species of newts and salamanders bear live young. The eggs of frogs and toads are spherical, are usually covered with a gelatinous substance, and eggs are laid in long strings or in masses. The eggs vary in size from a few hundredths of an inch in diameter, as in the case of the eggs of the common toad, to a half inch in

Loggerhead shrikes hatching from eggs.
Robert H. Wright —
National Audubon Society

diameter, as in the case of the eggs of a large Malayan frog. Most species deposit their eggs in water, sometimes attaching them to water plants, but others lay the eggs in damp moss or attach them to the limbs or leaves of trees overhanging the water. In several species of toads the eggs are carried on the back or legs of the father or mother until they are hatched. Water-dwelling newts and salamanders commonly lay their eggs in water, but the land-living species usually deposit them in holes in moist ground.

Eggs of Fishes. Only certain species of fish bear their young alive. Among the elasmobranches, some, such as the spotted dogfish, lay eggs that resemble those of birds, containing a white as well as a yolk and covered with a horny shell. The eggs of the dogfish are flattened and have tendrils at the end by which the mother fish attaches them to objects underwater. The eggs of the bony fishes are usually spherical in shape, surrounded by a tough capsule. In some cases they are deposited on the bottom and then covered with sand or gravel, as in the case of salmon eggs; in others the eggs are laid in gelatinous masses that float on the surface. The egg mass of the angler fish covers an area of 60 to 90 square feet. Some species, such as the catfish, carry their eggs in their mouths until they hatch. The primitive hagfishes lay cylindrical eggs with hook-shaped processes at either end by which the eggs are linked together.

Eggs of Invertebrates. The eggs of lower animals, the invertebrates, exhibit the widest variety in form. This variation is especially evident in the eggs of the mollusks, crustaceans, and insects. Mollusk eggs vary from those of the squid, which are laid in a number of cylindrical cases attached to one another like the strands of a mop, to the eggs of certain snails of the genus *Bulimus,* which have hard shells and resemble pigeons' eggs in size and shape. Females of most higher crustaceans carry their eggs attached to appendages on the underside of the body. The water flea lays two kinds of eggs, small "summer eggs", carried in a pouch on the female's back, and larger "winter eggs" carried in a fold of the animal's carapace until fertilized. Normal reproduction takes place by the hatching of the summer eggs, but, in conditions of severe cold or the drying up of the pools in which the animals live, the winter eggs are fertilized by the male and deposited. They may then lie in a dormant state for years until conditions are favorable for hatching. The eggs of insects are characterized by great variety of form as well as by the intricate markings that appear on the shells of many species.

Eggs as Food. Because of their content of food material intended for the nourishment of the developing embryo, eggs of many different animals are used as food by men in all parts of the world. The eggs most commonly eaten are those of the domestic hen, but duck eggs and the eggs of other birds are also commonly used as food. The eggs, or roe, of various fishes, especially sturgeon and salmon, are processed as a relish called caviar and considered a delicacy. In some countries turtle eggs are used for food purposes, as are the eggs of ants and other insects. Primitive races sometimes eat the eggs of other reptiles, such as lizards.

The typical hen's egg, which weighs about 2 oz., contains about 13 percent protein and 10 percent fat. Its energy value is approximately 80 calories. Egg yolks are also a source of several vitamins, including A, B, D, and E. The chief components of egg yolk are lecithin, lutein, cholesterol, vitellin, and livetin. Egg white is approximately 85 percent water. The remaining 15 percent is chiefly albumen, with smaller amounts of egg globulin, ovomucoid, glucose, and certain inorganic salts.

The production of eggs for food in the United States takes place chiefly on small diversified farms, although in recent years an increasing number of farmers have confined themselves exclusively to poultry and egg production, particularly in the eastern States. Eggs are usually sold in the shell, but an increasing proportion of the nation's egg production is marketed in the form of frozen whole eggs or dehydrated yolks, whites, or whole eggs. The production of powdered eggs (dehydrated whole eggs) increased almost 800-fold between 1940 and 1944 as a result of the demand during World War II for eggs in this form for shipment overseas.

Eggs to be marketed are graded according to weight and appearance and are candled to detect staleness or blood clots within the egg. The process of candling involves inspecting the egg by transmitted light (originally a candle flame). A good egg appears clear and translucent when viewed in this manner; stale eggs are noticeably darker.

Several methods are used for the storing and preservation of eggs. In the home, eggs are preserved by placing them in some liquid, such as lime water or water glass, which seals the pores of the shells and prevents air from entering the interior. Commercially, eggs are preserved in cold storage at a temperature slightly below freezing. If an egg is cooled below 21° F. (−6° C.), the white thickens permanently. Where appearance is not important, as in the case of eggs used in baking or candy making, eggs are usually removed from their shells and stored frozen at a temperature of about −4° F. (−20° C.).

The per-capita consumption of eggs used for food purposes in the U.S. averages slightly more than one egg each day. Eggs are used industrially in the manufacture of animal foods, fertilizers, drugs, paints, and adhesives. *See* AGRICULTURE: *Agriculture in the United States.*

EGGERTSVILLE, unincorporated suburban area of New York, in Erie Co., part of Amherst town, adjoining Buffalo on the N.E. and 6 mi. from the downtown area. Pop. (1970 est.) 55,000.

EGGPLANT, or AUBERGINE or GUINEA SQUASH, common name for a fruit-bearing East Indian herb, *Solanum melongena,* of the Nightshade family (Solanaceae). The common eggplant is the variety *esculentum* of *S. melongena.*

Common eggplant, the variety esculentum *of* Solanum melongena   United Fresh Fruit and Vegetable Assn.

Other varieties include *depressum,* the dwarf eggplant, and *serpentium,* the snake eggplant, which has long, slender, curved fruits. The common variety bears from two to five purple, white, or yellowish skinned fruits that vary in diameter from 2 to 8 in. and somewhat resemble an egg in shape. Eggplants are cultivated for their edible, watery, grayish pulp. About 26,400 tons of eggplant are grown annually in the United States.

Although the eggplant is a perennial, it is widely grown in temperate climates as an annual. The plants grow slowly, and they are damaged by temperatures below 50° F. When grown in gardens in the northern part of the U.S., the plants must be germinated and grown under glass for approximately five weeks before being transplanted outdoors.

EGLANTINE or **SWEETBRIER,** common name for *Rosa eglanteria* (formerly called *R. rubigi-*

nosa) of the Rose family (Rosaceae). It is a dense shrub, often 6 ft. tall, and its stems bear hooked prickles. The upper side of the leaf is dark green, the underside being much lighter in color. The leaves have a pleasant aromatic odor. The flowers, which occur as inflorescences of one to three blossoms, are bright pink and sweet-scented, and have short stems. The fruit is orange-red or scarlet. Native to Europe, the plant has been widely cultivated in the United States.

The name eglantine has been used for two other roses, the Austrian brier, *R. foetida,* and the dog rose, and is also sometimes applied to the honeysuckle. *See* ROSE: *Wild Roses.*

EGMONT, Lamoral, Comte d', Prince of Gavre (1522–68), Flemish general and statesman, born in Hainault (now in Belgium). His victories at Saint Quentin (1557) and Gravelines (1558), in the war between Spain and France over the Low Countries, made him a popular hero, and he was appointed governor of Flanders and Artois by Philip II (q.v.), King of Spain. He joined William I (q.v.), Prince of Orange, in protesting against the infringement of Flemish liberties and the introduction of the Inquisition (q.v.) into the Netherlands. In 1565 Egmont made a trip to Spain to inform Philip of the great resentment felt toward his policies. After his return, when insurrections arose, Egmont took action against heretics in Flanders, indicating his submission to Philip's policies. When Fernando Alvarez de Toledo, Duke of Alva (q.v.), was sent in 1567 to restore order in the country, Egmont and the Flemish soldier Philip de Montmorency, Count of Horn (1518–68), remained there in spite of warnings from the prince to leave the country, and Alva had them imprisoned. They were condemned to death by the Blood Council and beheaded in Brussels; this event was used to date the beginning of the revolt of the Netherlands from Spanish rule. The German dramatist Johann Wolfgang von Goethe (q.v.) used incidents in Egmont's life as the basis for his poetic drama *Egmont* (1788), for which the German composer Ludwig van Beethoven (q.v.) wrote (1810) incidental music and the *Egmont Overture.*

EGO, in psychoanalysis, term denoting the central part of the personality structure that deals with reality and is influenced by social forces. According to the psychoanalytical theories developed by the Austrian physician Sigmund Freud (q.v.), the ego constitutes one of the three basic provinces of the mind, the other two being the id and the superego (qq.v.). The id is the only innate, totally unconscious component of the psyche and harbors the biological instinctual drives. The superego, which is largely conscious, develops early in life as a result of unconscious identification with parental images, and functions as the "conscience". Although rooted in the unconscious, the ego is in direct touch with reality. Formation of the ego begins at birth in the first encounters with the external world of people and things. The ego learns to modify behavior by controlling those impulses which are socially unacceptable. Its role is that of mediator between unconscious impulses and acquired social and personal standards. *See* PSYCHOANALYSIS.

In psychology ego means the conscious self or "I". It was viewed by some philosophers, notably the 17th-century Frenchman René Descartes and the 18th-century German Johann Gottlieb Fichte (qq.v.), as the sole basis of reality; the universe was said by them to exist only in the individual's knowledge and experience of it. Other philosophers, such as the 18th-century German Immanuel Kant (q.v.), proposed two forms of ego, one perceiving and the other thinking.

EGRET, name given to various species of heron (q.v.), especially those having white plumage and bearing long, soft plumes on the lower parts of their backs during the breeding season. Among the best-known European species are the greater egret, *Casmerodius albus,* and the lesser egret, *Egretta garzetta.* In the southern part of the United States three species of heron

are known as egrets: the American egret, *Casmerodius albus egretta,* 41 in. in length; the snowy egret, *Leucophoyx thula,* 24 in.; and the reddish egret, *Dichromanassa rufescens,* 29 in. The reddish egret occurs in two color phases, one white and the other slate blue with a red head and neck. All three American egrets were nearly exterminated because hunters indiscriminately slaughtered the adult birds during the nesting season for their valuable plumes, known in the millinery trade as aigrettes. Protective legislation subsequently insured the perpetuation of these species.

The cattle egret, *Bubulcus ibis,* native to Africa, recently became established in the U.S. It was not seen in the Western Hemisphere before 1937, when it appeared in British Guiana. Authorities believe the bird may have been carried across the Atlantic Ocean by the trade winds. Initially observed in the U.S. in 1942, the birds were estimated in the late 1950's to number more than 2000, mostly in Florida. The cattle egret is 20 in. in length and white with a buff-colored back. It stays close to grazing cattle and feeds mainly on insects.

EGYPT, ARAB REPUBLIC OF, historically EGYPT, and from 1958 to 1971 named UNITED ARAB REPUBLIC, an independent nation in the Middle East, occupying the N.E. corner of Africa and the Sinai Peninsula (q.v.) of S.W. Asia. Bounded on the N. by the Mediterranean Sea, on the E. by Israel and the Red Sea, on the S. by the Sudan, and on the W. by Libya, Egypt is located approximately between lat. 31°40′ N. and lat. 22° S. and long. 25° E. and long. 35°30′ E. The country has a maximum length from N. to S. of about 675 mi. and a maximum width, near the S. border, of about 780 mi. The total area is approximately 387,000 sq.mi.

THE LAND

Less than 14,000 sq.mi. of the land area of Egypt is settled or under cultivation. This territory consists of the valley and delta of the Nile River (q.v.) and a number of desert oases. The remaining 96 percent of the country consists of the Libyan Desert in the w., a part of the Sahara (q.v.), and the Arabian Desert, which borders the Red Sea and the Gulf of Suez (qq.v.), in the E. The Libyan Desert includes a vast expanse called the Great Sand Sea; the 7000-sq.mi. Qattara Depression, which reaches depths of 440 ft. below sea level; and the oases of Siwa, Khârga, Baharîya, Farâfra, and Dakhla. Much of the Ara-

Since ancient times, floodwaters from the Nile River has irrigated Egyptian land, turning the parched soil into fertile cropland. Modern dams help control the annual overflow and divert water to still barren parts of the country. **Paris Match**

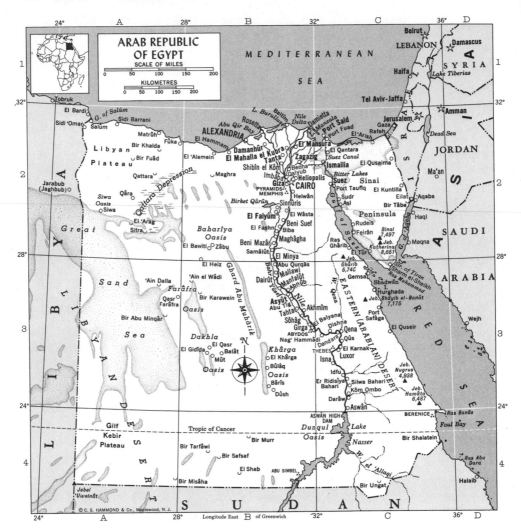

ARAB REPUBLIC
OF EGYPT
SCALE OF MILES
0   50   100   150   200
KILOMETRES
0   50   100   150   200

bian Desert rests on a plateau, rising gradually eastward from the Nile valley to elevations of 2000 ft. in the E. and broken along the Red Sea coast by jagged peaks as high as about 7000 ft. above sea level. In the extreme S., along the border with the Sudan, is the Nubian Desert, an extensive region of dunes and sandy plains. The Sinai Peninsula consists of sandy desert in the N. and rugged mountains in the S., with summits looming more than 7000 ft. above the Red Sea. Jebel Katherina (8651 ft.) on the peninsula is the highest elevation in Egypt.

The Nile enters Egypt from the Sudan and flows N. for about 960 mi. to the Mediterranean Sea. Just N. of the Sudan border lies Lake Nasser, a huge reservoir formed by the Aswân High Dam (q.v.). The lake is more than 300 mi. long and 10 mi. across at its widest point. South of a

point near the town of Idfu, the Nile valley is rarely more than 2 mi. wide. From Idfu to Cairo, for a length of nearly 525 mi., the valley is about 13 to 14 mi. in width, with most of the arable portion, about 10 mi. wide, on the w. side. In the vicinity of Cairo the valley merges with the delta, a fan-shaped plain, the perimeter of which occupies about 155 mi. of the Mediterranean coastline. Silt deposited by the Rosetta (Rashid), Damietta (Dumyât), and other distributaries has made the delta the most fertile region in the country. A chair of four shallow lakes extends along the seaward extremity of the delta. Another lake, Birket Qârûn, about 30 mi. long and 5 mi. wide, is situated in the desert N. of the town of El Faiyûm. Geographically and traditionally the Nile valley is divided into two regions, Lower Egypt and Upper Egypt, the

INDEX TO MAP OF ARAB REPUBLIC OF EGYPT

former consisting of the delta area and the latter comprising the valley s. of Cairo.

Although Egypt has about 1800 miles of coastline, two thirds of which are on the Red Sea, indentations suitable as harbors are confined to the delta. The Isthmus of Suez, which connects the Sinai Peninsula with the African mainland, is traversed from the Mediterranean to the Gulf of Suez by the Suez Canal (q.v.).

Climate. The climate of Egypt is characterized by a hot season from May to September, and a cool season from November to March. Extreme temperatures during both seasons are moderated by the prevailing N. winds. In the coastal region temperatures range between a mean maximum of 99° F. and a mean minimum of 57° F. The annual rainfall, from 8 to 12 in., is confined almost entirely to the area contiguous to the Mediterranean; less than 3 in. falls in the s. part of the country. Wide variations of temperature occur in the deserts, ranging between a mean annual maximum of 114° F. during daylight hours and a mean annual minimum of 42° F. after sunset. During the winter season desert temperatures often drop to 32° F.

Natural Resources. Egypt has a wide variety of mineral deposits, some of which, such as gold and red granite, have been exploited since an-cient times. The chief mineral resource of contemporary value is petroleum, found mainly in the Red Sea coastal region and at El 'Alamein on the Mediterranean. Other minerals include coal, phosphates, manganese, lead, iron, titanium, sulfur, clay, nitrates, barite, and salt.

Plants and Animals. The vegetation of Egypt is confined largely to the Nile delta, the valley, and the oases. The most widespread of the few indigenous trees is the date palm. Others include the sycamore, tamarisk, acacia, and carob. Trees that have been introduced from other lands include the cypress, elm, eucalyptus, mimosa, myrtle, and various types of fruit trees. The alluvial soils of Egypt, especially in the delta, sustain a broad variety of plant life, including the grape, many kinds of vegetables, and such flowers as the lotus, jasmine, and rose. In the arid regions alfa grass and several species of thorn are common. Papyrus (q.v.), once prevalent along the banks of the Nile, is now limited to the extreme s. of the country.

Because of its arid climate Egypt has few indigenous wild animals. Gazelles are found in the deserts, and the fox, hyena, jackal, wild ass, boar, jerboa, and ichneumon inhabit various areas, mainly the delta and the mountains contiguous to the Red Sea. Among the reptiles of

Egypt are lizards and several kinds of poisonous snakes, including the asp and the horned viper. The crocodile and hippopotamus, common in the lower Nile and Nile delta in antiquity, are now restricted to the upper Nile. Bird life is abundant, especially in the Nile delta and valley. The country has about 300 species of birds, including the sunbird, golden oriole, pigeon, plover, pelican, flamingo, heron, stork, duck, quail, and snipe. Birds of prey include eagles, falcons, vultures, owls, kites, and hawks. Many species of insects are found in Egypt, beetles, mosquitoes, flies, and fleas being especially numerous. About 100 species of fish are found in the Nile and the deltaic lakes.

Waterpower. Prior to 1960 most of the electrical power produced in Egypt was generated by thermal plants. Generators installed on the Aswân High Dam on the Nile in 1960 are now producing about 1,900,000,000 kw hours annually. The twelve turbines on the Aswân High Dam, completed in 1970, increased the production of electric power to some 10,000,000,000 kw hours annually, compared with the previous total annual output of about 6,000,000,000 kw hours.

THE PEOPLE

Most Egyptians are descended from the successive Arab settlements after the Muslim invasion, mixed with the indigenous pre-Islamic popula-

In accordance with religious custom, Egypt's Muslim women traditionally wear the yashmak, a veil which covers the lower half of the face from public view. Usually made of cloth, the more ornate type shown here is reserved for festive occasions.   UPI

Another traditional Egyptian scene: a desert tribesman, mounted on a camel, passes slowly by an ancient pyramid.
Camera Press

tion. This mixture has given the inhabitants of the Nile valley physical characteristics that set them apart from the other Mediterranean peoples of the region. They are somewhat more stocky in build and have darker skins. Egyptian society is predominantly rural. Approximately 75,000 nomadic herdsmen, mostly Bedouins (q.v.), roam the deserts.

Population. The population of Egypt (census 1966) was 30,075,858; the United Nations estimated (1971) 34,130,000. Almost 99 percent of the population lives within the Nile valley, which comprises only 4 percent of the total area. The population density is 88 per sq.mi. (U.N. est. 1971).

Political Divisions and Principal Cities. Egypt is divided for administrative purposes into twenty-five governorates. The capital and largest city is Cairo (q.v.), which has a population of 5,126,000 (1971 est.). Other important cities with 1970 estimated populations are Alexandria, the principal port, 2,032,000; Port Said, which is at the Mediterranean entrance to the Suez Canal and is a major coaling station, 313,000; and Suez, the s. terminus of the canal and a port, 315,000.

Religion. More than 90 percent of the Egyptians are Sunnite Muslims; see ISLAM: *Islamic Law*. The Coptic Church, a Christian denomination, has more than 1,000,000 adherents and constitutes the largest religious minority; see

COPTS; MONOPHYSITES. Approximately 250,000 people belong to the Greek Orthodox, Roman Catholic, Armenian, and various Protestant churches. The country has a small Jewish community.

Language. Arabic is the national language of Egypt. Greek and Armenian are still heard in Cairo and Alexandria, and Berber is spoken in a few villages in the w. oases. French and English are common second languages among the educated.

Education. An elementary education is free and compulsory for all children between the ages of six and twelve. Graduates of the primary schools may attend either a general intermediate school, which prepares for a secondary education, or a technical intermediate school specializing in industrial and agricultural subjects. The secondary-school system is similarly divided into general schools, with curricula designed to prepare students for a university education, and technical schools.

ELEMENTARY, INTERMEDIATE, AND SECONDARY SCHOOLS. In the late 1960's about 3,500,000 children attended almost 8000 elementary schools. In the same period the country had approximately 1250 general intermediate schools and 15 tech-

Alexandria's location at the westernmost mouth of the Nile makes it a popular recreation area as well as the chief port. Egyptian State Tourist Administration

Students at the Cairo School for Handicrafts (above) work with inlaid ivory, fashioning book covers and jewelry boxes; the school trains youngsters in the ancient arts and crafts of the land. In specially designed laboratories (below), students use microscopes in their scientific research. Egypt's educational system, designed to preserve the old as well as teach the new, is one of the most advanced in the Arab world.

nical intermediate schools with enrollments of about 736,000 and 8000, respectively. General secondary schools numbering about 300 and secondary technical schools numbering about 200 had about 260,000 students and 153,000 students, respectively.

UNIVERSITIES AND COLLEGES. Al-Azhar University at Cairo, founded in 972 as a school of Islamic studies, is the oldest continually existing institution of higher learning in the world. Faculties of engineering, medicine, business administration, and agriculture were added in 1961, and women were admitted for the first time in 1962. In the late 1960's about 8000 students were enrolled at the university and 25,000 at affiliated institutes. The largest institution of higher education in Egypt is the University of Cairo, with more than 65,000 students. Other universities, with their approximate enrollments, are Ain Shams, 38,000; Alexandria, 33,000; Asyût, 10,000; and the American University in Cairo, 1300. Two new universities are being developed at Tanta and El Man-sûra around existing faculties of medicine established there in 1962. In addition, Egypt has a number of colleges and institutes of art and music.

Culture. Cultural activities are directed by the ministry of culture. Egypt has various cultural facilities including the Pocket Theater, the National Puppet Theater, the Opera House, and the National Symphony. Since the early 1960's there has been a growing interest in folk dancing, which is performed by two national dance groups. Egypt is the principal film-making country in the Arab world. *See also* EGYPTIAN ARCHEOLOGY; EGYPTIAN ARCHITECTURE AND ART; EGYPTIAN LANGUAGE AND LITERATURE; EGYPTIAN RELIGION for information on the cultural heritage of the nation.

THE ECONOMY

With the promulgation of a series of laws beginning in 1961 the economy of Egypt was rapidly socialized. Foreign trade, wholesale trade, banking, insurance, and most manufacturing enterprises were taken over by the government. Although agriculture, urban real estate, and some manufacturing concerns remained in private hands, stringent regulations were imposed. An economic-development plan introduced in 1960 brought about a considerable expansion of industry and increase in production during the succeeding five years. The plan was replaced in 1965 by a seven-year plan which, however, was less successful, partly because of insufficient foreign investment, and a comparatively modest three-year plan was introduced in 1967. Losses suffered during the Arab-Israeli War of June,

1967 (see *History*, below), and the general economic dislocation which persisted afterward seriously retarded social and economic development. Egypt's economic ills were a major reason for the peace efforts of the late 1970's: the country could not afford another war. The expected public and private investment under the development plan for 1973–83 was in the neighborhood of $20 billion. Recent annual budget figures show revenues of about $2.85 billion and expenditures of about $2.84 billion.

Agriculture. Egypt is predominantly an agricultural country, about 60 percent of the labor force being engaged in farming or herding. The pattern of land ownership was greatly altered by the Agricultural Reform Decree of 1952, which limited individual holdings to about 200 acres, a figure revised in 1961 to about 100 acres. Lands requisitioned by the government were distributed to the peasants (fellahin), but in the mid-1960's, 5.4 percent of the peasants still owned almost 50 percent of the land, in holdings averaging more than 18 acres each; the remaining 94.6 percent averaged about 2 acres each. An economic gap thus remains between the middle-class farmers and the vast majority of the fellahin. Government programs are now expanding arable area through reclamation, irrigation, and the use of advanced technology.

The yields of Egyptian farmlands are now among the highest in the world. Yields of more than 500 lb. per acre make Egypt the world's most important producer of long-staple cotton. Annual production in the mid-1970's was about 382,000 metric tons. Yields of corn, averaging about 35 bu. per acre, are also the highest in the world, with annual production reaching some 2,781,000 tons. Other leading crops, in metric tonnage for the same period, include rice (2,423,000) and wheat (2,033,000). Also produced are sugarcane, millet, barley, vegetables, citrus fruits, mangoes, dates, figs, and grapes.

The principal pastoral industry of Egypt is the breeding of beasts of burden. The livestock population in the mid-1970's included 2,102,000 cattle, almost 2,000,000 sheep, 1,533,000 asses, and 32,000 horses and mules.

Fishing. Egypt has a flourishing fishing industry. According to the latest available figures, the annual catch was more than 106,000 tons, about 75 percent of which was taken from inland waters. The most productive areas are the sardine fisheries of the Mediterranean coast and the Rosetta and Damietta mouths of the Nile, the shallow deltaic lakes, and Birket Qârûn. The Nile fisheries s. of the delta yield about 10 percent of the annual catch.

Egyptian workers take a rest period during the construction of the Aswân High Dam which was planned in the 1950's and completed in 1968. UPI

Mining. Annual production of crude petroleum, the most important mineral product of Egypt, was about 2,600,000 tons in the early 1950's, approximately 3,820,000 tons in the early 1960's, and by the late 1960's had reached about 7,800,000 tons. As a result of the discovery in the 1950's and 1960's of large new fields in the El 'Alamein and Gulf of Suez areas, the figure had reached 16,404,000 tons by 1970. Production fell again during the early 1970's to a low of 7,472,000 tons in 1974. In 1975, however, production rose to 8,428,000 tons, and in 1976 Western companies were enlisted in a major exploration effort. It was hoped that production would triple by 1980. In addition, during the mid-1970's an Italian consortium built a pipeline to carry 80,000,000 tons of petroleum a year from the Gulf of Suez to the Mediterranean.

Other important products of the mining industry, with mid-1970's output in metric tons, include phosphate rock (404,000), iron ore

(560,000), salt (500,000), and manganese (2100).

Manufacturing. Initial moves toward industrialization in Egypt in the 19th century were frustrated by the European powers, chiefly Great Britain, which preferred to have the country remain a market for their manufactured goods. During and after World War I new efforts resulted in the development of a small industrial base capable of meeting some of the domestic demand, and during World War II this base was greatly expanded, especially in the area of textiles. After the overthrow of the monarchy in the early 1950's, the government assigned top priority to industrial expansion. By the mid-1960's, after the completion of the first Five-Year Plan (1960–65), the total value of industrial production, including electric power and mining output, had reached some $2.71 billion annually, and by 1971–72 the gross value of manufacturing was more than $3.2 billion.

The most important products of Egyptian industry in the mid-1970's, with output in metric tons, include cotton yarn (179,000), cotton textiles (120,000), jute yarn and fabrics (31,600),

Large bore tubes bring crude oil from offshore wells in the Gulf of Suez. Crude petroleum is Egypt's most important mineral product. UPI

wool yarn (10,900), wool fabrics (7100), refined sugar (534,000), sulfuric acid (198,000), hydrochloric acid (2300), nitrogenous fertilizers (100,200), tobacco products (4718), paper products (113,000), cement (3,263,000), and motor-vehicle tires (364,000 units). These and other industries employed a total of about 651,400 persons in 1971–72.

Smaller-scale industrial enterprises of significance to the economy include tanning, brewing, and the manufacture of pottery, perfumes, handicrafts, cottonseed oil, flour and other processed foodstuffs, and asphalt.

Currency and Banking. The basic unit of currency is the Egyptian pound (valued at U.S.$2.58; 1977), consisting of 100 piastres. The Central Bank of Egypt, set up by government decree in August, 1960, controls government banking, commercial banks, and the issue of notes by the National Bank.

Commerce and Trade. The principal imports of Egypt are agricultural products and foodstuffs, chemicals, mining and quarrying machinery, metal products, and transport equipment. The principal suppliers are the United States, West Germany, Great Britain, the Soviet Union, Italy, and Czechoslovakia. Because of rapid population growth the country has become more and more dependent upon imports and food grants, especially for wheat, flour, and meat. The three major exports of Egypt are raw cotton, rice, and oil. The chief customers for these and other exports are the Soviet Union,

Czechoslovakia, India, West Germany, and the U.S.

Despite large-scale investments and tight government controls, Egypt has a very serious balance of payments problem. This problem existed even before the Arab-Israeli War of June, 1967. Four major sources of foreign currency earnings before the 1967 war were cotton, oil, Suez Canal revenues, and tourism. In 1966 Suez Canal tolls totaled $227,000,000 and the tourism industry brought in another $100,000,000.

As a result of the war, however, the Suez Canal, revenues from which covered almost half of the deficit in the trade balance, was closed, and rising anti-Western sentiment in Egypt resulted in the decline of tourism. Loss of the oil fields of the Sinai Peninsula, which was occupied by Israeli troops, cuts into Egypt's earnings by an estimated $56,000,000 a year. Damages inflicted upon the vital Suez refineries in the Israeli air attack of October, 1967, amount to an estimated $162,000,000, excluding the annual cost of having Egyptian oil refined abroad.

The country's balance of payments problem grew worse during the mid-1970's as imports rose rapidly. In 1975, $3.71 billion in imports were recorded, but exports covered only $1.40 billion of this amount. The picture began to brighten in the late 1970's as oil production increased and the Suez Canal was reopened. There was a rapid increase in tourism as Egypt appeared to move toward peace with Israel.

Transportation. Egypt has approximately 2800 mi. of railroads. The principal line links Aswân and points northward in the Nile valley. The inland waterways of Egypt, including the Nile R., navigable throughout its course in the country, and more than 11,000 mi. of irrigation canals in the Nile delta, are extensively utilized for transportation. Camel caravans are employed to a limited extent in the desert regions.

Two highways connect Cairo with Alexandria. Other highways connect Cairo to Port Said, Suez, and El Faiyûm. The total length of roads is 16,140 mi., of which less than half are paved. International airlines provide regular services between Cairo and major world centers. Egyptair, the government-owned airline, also provides domestic and foreign services. The major ports are Alexandria and Port Said, both served by numerous shipping companies. The Suez Canal, 107 mi. long, which was closed from 1967 until mid-1975, produced toll fees of about $590,000,000 in 1976.

Communications. The Egyptian press is the most developed in the Arab world. All newspapers and periodicals are under the control and ownership of the Arab Socialist Union, as are all publishing houses. The most important newspaper is the authoritative *al-Ahram* (circulation 400,000), which often reflects the views of the government. The organ of the Arab Socialist Union is *al-Gomhouria*. In the mid-1970's there were 14 daily newspapers with total circulation of 773,000 and 24 nondailies with 920,000 circulation.

Egypt has three news agencies that also serve other countries in the Arab world. A national broadcasting corporation presents programs in Arabic, English, French, Greek, Italian, and German. In 1974 more than 5,100,000 radio sets were in use. Television services are carried over three channels with a total of 28 hours daily. Television receivers numbered about 610,000 in 1974.

GOVERNMENT

Egypt is governed by a constitution promulgated on Sept. 11, 1971. The constitution provides for an Arab socialist state with Islam as the official religion. It also stresses social solidarity, equal opportunity, and popular control of the means of production.

Central Government. The head of state is the president of the republic, who is nominated by the People's Assembly and elected by the people. The president is elected for a six-year term and has the power to formulate general state policy and supervise its execution. He can dissolve the People's Assembly, appoint and dismiss cabinet ministers, attend cabinet meetings, and issue decrees during emergencies. Also, the president declares war after approval by the People's Assembly, ratifies treaties, commutes penalties, orders plebiscites, and acts as commander in chief of the armed forces.

HEALTH AND WELFARE. Despite progress in the 20th century, particularly in the health of urban populations, there was much still to be done, especially in rural areas. By the mid-1970's, according to the latest available statistics, the country had about 7500 doctors and 76,600 hospital beds (one for every 464 persons). From the 1960's, concentrated efforts have been made by the ministry of health to establish "rural combined" centers, each serving about 15,000 to 20,000 people. The aim of the centers is to coordinate medical, educational, social, and agricultural services through village councils. Great progress has been made in stamping out diseases such as cholera, smallpox, and malaria.

Legislature. Legislative authority is vested in the People's Assembly, which exercises control over the executive. Its members are elected for a five-year term and half of them are always from the worker and farmer groups. The People's Assembly is empowered to approve the budget, make investigations, levy taxes, and approve government programs or withdraw confidence from the cabinet or any of its members.

Political Parties. From 1961 to 1977 the Arab Socialist Union (A.S.U.) was the only legal political party in Egypt. When a multiparty system was introduced in 1977, the A.S.U. was replaced by three new parties—the Arab Socialist Party, a moderate group closely tied to President Anwar el-Sadat; the Liberal Socialist Party, a conservative organization; and the National Progressive Unionist Party, a leftist group.

Local Government. Egypt is divided into twenty-five governorates, each headed by a governor appointed by the president. The governors are aided by councils, of which most of the members are elected.

Judiciary. Judicial authority is vested in an independent judicial system. The courts are di-

vided into four categories. The supreme court is the highest judicial body. It renders final judgments in civil and criminal matters and is composed of a chief justice, 4 deputy chief justices, and 36 justices. Below it are five courts of appeal situated in the important governorates. In each governorate there is a primary tribunal which hears both civil and criminal cases. At the lowest level are summary tribunals which are branches of the primary tribunals situated in various districts headed by a single judge.

Defense. Military service is compulsory for all males over eighteen. The total strength of the Egyptian defense forces is about 342,500. A national guard of about 500,000 has received increased attention since the June, 1967, war with Israel. The army consists of 3 mechanized infan-

An Egyptian destroyer (foreground) carrying President Anwar el-Sadat heads down the Suez Canal on June 5, 1975, breaking a chain stretched across the waterway and formally reopening the canal, which had been closed since the June, 1967, war. UPI

Egyptian military manpower continues to spiral. Military service is compulsory for all males over eighteen years of age. Paris Match

try divisions, 3 armored divisions, 5 infantry divisions, and various separate brigades. Naval personnel number 17,500 officers and men. Air force personnel are estimated at 30,000.

HISTORY

The origins of ancient Egyptian civilization, which is regarded by many scholars as one of the fountainheads of Occidental culture, cannot be established with certainty. Evidence accumulated through recent archeological research indicates that the first known inhabitants of the Nile delta and valley may have borrowed substantially from the culture of Mesopotamia, in particular from that of Sumer (q.v.). It is known, for example, that before the end of the fifth millennium B.C., when Egypt had yet to emerge from the Neolithic phase of the Stone Age, Sumerian civilization had already reached the city-building stage. Similarly, long before the Egyptians succeeded in welding a national cul-

ture, Sumerian civilization had achieved extraordinary advances in the arts and sciences. In the view of some authorities, these accomplishments profoundly influenced subsequent developments in Egypt. For further information relating to the following account, *see* EGYPTIAN ARCHEOLOGY; EGYPTIAN ARCHITECTURE AND ART; EGYPTIAN LANGUAGE AND LITERATURE; EGYPTIAN RELIGION.

The history of the development and growth of Egyptian civilization is, like attempts to identify its intellectual foundations, largely a process of conjecture based on the discoveries of archeology. A science known as Egyptology, this process has been facilitated by the remarkable abundance in the country of enduring ruins, tombs, and monuments, many of which contained invaluable specimens of the culture of the ancients. In addition, the ancients frequently adorned their temples and monuments with inscriptions, executed in hieroglyphics (q.v.). These inscriptions, undecipherable until after the discovery in 1799 of an inscribed slab of basalt now known as the Rosetta Stone (q.v.), and the hieratic writings found on the papyri of Egyptian antiquity, provide priceless data regarding ancient Egypt.

In establishing the framework of ancient Egyptian history, scholars have relied, to a considerable extent, on extant fragments of a record written in Greek by Manetho, an Egyptian priest of the 3rd century B.C. Although Manetho's division of the history of Egypt into thirty periods, each dominated by a ruling dynasty, is generally accepted in Egyptology, other fragments of his chronology which have been preserved are considered questionable. Most of the ancients, in particular those who lived prior to 2000 B.C., failed to establish in their inscriptions and papyri a chronological relationship among the successive dynasties. Many dates after 2000 B.C. have been determined by scientific verification of ancient astronomical records, but scholars differ widely on the general chronology of the dynasties. The chronology employed in this article is that propounded by the American Egyptologist William C. Hayes (1903–63), head curator of the Egyptian Art department of the Metropolitan Museum of Art in New York City. A tabulation, according to Hayes' chronology, of the dynasties, together with their names, follows.

THE DYNASTIES OF ANCIENT EGYPT*

OLD KINGDOM

Number	Name	Reign
I	Thinite	3100–2980
II	Thinite	2980–2780
III	Memphite	2780–2680
IV	Memphite	2680–2560
V	Memphite	2560–2420
VI	Memphite	2420–2280
VII and VIII	Memphite	2280–2242

MIDDLE KINGDOM

IX and X	Heracleopolitan	2242–2052
XI	Theban	2134–1991
XII	Theban	1991–1778
XIII	Theban	1778–1625
XIV	Xoite	1778–1594
XV and XVI	Hyksos	1694–1600
XVII	Theban	1600–1567

NEW KINGDOM

XVIII	Diospolite	1567–1320
XIX	Diospolite	1320–1200
XX	Diospolite	1200–1085
XXI	Tanite	1085–950
XXII	Bubastite	950–730
XXIII	Tanite	817–730
XXIV	Saite	730–715
XXV	Ethiopian	713–656
XXVI	Saite	665–525
XXVII to XXX	Persian	525–332

* All dates are B.C.; chronology suggested by William C. Hayes in *The Scepter of Egypt* (N.Y., Harper & Bros., 1953) and followed in *The Cambridge Ancient History*, 2nd edition.

General agreement exists on the division of Egyptian historical periods before the first millennium B.C. into the Old, Middle, and New Kingdoms, but there is still considerable disagreement on the dates. Some historians assign the first two dynasties to an archaic period pre-

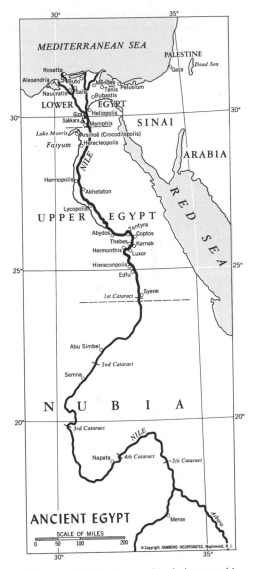

ANCIENT EGYPT

SCALE OF MILES

0   50   100   200

© Copyright HAMMOND INCORPORATED, Maplewood, N. J.

ceding the Old Kingdom and include several intermediate periods. One chronology gives the following dates: Old Kingdom, 2680–2280; first intermediate period, 2280–2065; Middle Kingdom, 2065–1785; second intermediate period, 1785–1580; New Kingdom, 1580–1085. Another chronology dates the periods of ancient Egyptian history as follows: Old Kingdom, 2815–2294; first intermediate period, 2294–2132; Middle Kingdom, 2132–1777; second intermediate period, 1777–1573; New Kingdom, 1573–1090. Still another chronology lists Old Kingdom, about 2780–about 2270; Middle Kingdom, about 2143–1790; and New Kingdom, 1555–1090.

The immediate predynastic period of Egyp-

369

tian history is marked by a flourishing Aeneol-
ithic culture, of which many specimens, including pottery, copper products, and art objects,
have been excavated, usually from graves. This
circumstance, as well as the prevalence of amu-
lets representing various forms of animal life, indicates the beginnings of the belief in personal
survival after death and of the animistic panthe-
ism (q.v.) that characterize the theological systems of ancient Egypt. Philological and anthro-
pological evidence indicates that the people
then inhabiting the Nile delta and valley were
descendants of the Hamitic branch of the Caucasian race. The tiny communities in which they
lived evolved in the course of time into towns.
These became in turn the nuclei of the prin-
cipalities or political divisions, later known as
nomes to the Greeks, which are a traditional
characteristic of Egyptian political geography.
Before the expiration of the predynastic period,
regional groupings of the nomes were combined into two strong kingdoms. These kingdoms initiated another traditional feature of
Egyptian political geography, encompassing in
their dominions the territories belonging to
what are now Lower and Upper Egypt.

The Old Kingdom (3100–2242 B.C.). According
to Manetho and the American historian James
Henry Breasted (1865–1935), classical Egyptian
history begins with the unification, in about
3100 B.C., of the Lower and Upper kingdoms by
Menes, the ruler of Upper Egypt (fl. early 4th
cent. B.C.). The capital of his realm, which is usually referred to as the Old Kingdom, was the city
of This, known also as Thinis. From its name is
derived the name of the I and II Dynasties, the
Thinite. Menes' reign, which lasted 62 years according to Manetho, was distinguished by two
enduring accomplishments, the foundation of
the city subsequently called Memphis (q.v.) and
the introduction of the basin system of irrigation in the Nile valley. Little is known regarding
the other kings of the Thinite dynasties. It is
probable that toward the end of II Dynasty the
first mastaba, an elaborate above-ground tomb,
was constructed. Some of the art of this period
was influenced by that of Mesopotamia, a region with which the Egyptians had extensive
commercial relations. The golden age of ancient
Egypt began during the rule of Zoser (fl. in the
first half of the 27th century B.C.), founder of III
Dynasty. This dynasty is also known as the first
Memphite dynasty, because Memphis was the
seat of the royal government. Besides extending
his dominions into the Sinai Peninsula, Zoser
encouraged the development of the arts and
sciences. His counselor, the physician Imhotep,

who epitomized the burgeoning culture of the
period, probably designed the Step Pyramid, the
first great structure of stone known in history.
This mausoleum, situated at Saqqara, initiated a
series of engineering projects that culminated,
during the next dynasty, in the famous pyramids
(q.v.) of Giza. Zoser's successor Snefru, or Sne-
feru, the first important warrior king of Egypt,
brought his realm to new heights of prosperity,
promoting commerce and the mining of copper, and conducting successful expeditions
against the Nubians and Syrians.

Egyptian civilization reached a peak in its development during IV Dynasty (the second Memphite), and this high level was generally maintained throughout the following Memphite
dynasties. The Egyptian government had already
evolved into a theocracy, in which the pharaohs, as the kings were called, were both absolute ruler and god. This centralization of authority was a prerequisite for the launching and
execution of colossal undertakings. The mono-
lithic Egyptian social structure, resting on slaves
and on the forced labor of the peasants during
the off season for farming, insured the necessary
leisure for the men of learning who planned the
undertakings. The three great pyramids of Giza,
which were built by the first, third, and last of
the rulers of IV Dynasty, Khufu (q.v.), Khafre (fl.
2565 B.C.), and Menkure (fl. 2525? B.C.), respectively, remain as indestructible symbols of the
high cultural level of this dynastic period, a span
of about 150 years. The splendor of these accomplishments in the field of engineering, however, was approximated in every field of endeavor known to the ancients, including
architecture, sculpture, painting, navigation, the
industrial arts and sciences, and astronomy. The
major achievement of the Memphite astronomers was the establishment of a solar calendar,
based on a year of 365 days and consisting of
twelve thirty-day months, plus an additional period of five days following the expiration of the
twelfth month: see CALENDAR: *Ancient Calen-
dars.* The failure of the astronomers to provide
for the remaining six hours of the solar year is
responsible for much of the confusion in modern times regarding ancient Egyptian chronology (see CHRONOLOGY). Among other outstanding achievements of the Memphite period were
the invention of the sundial, the water clock,
and several mathematical formulas, notably that
for computing the area of a circle. In the science
of medicine, the Egyptians of the Old Kingdom
displayed a remarkable knowledge of physiology, surgery, the circulatory system of the
blood, and asepsis.

The descendants of the Memphite generations preserved the civilization of the Old Kingdom for many centuries. In certain respects, chiefly in the field of art, they added to it. They did not exceed it, however. Much of the culture of the Old Kingdom was eventually lost to posterity, but enough survived to exercise a considerable influence on the course of subsequent antiquity, particularly the ancient civilizations of the Hebrews and Greeks.

The IV Dynasty was followed by four other Memphite dynasties, all grouped, by the usual system, in the Old Kingdom. During the reign of the final king of V Dynasty, the Egyptians inaugurated the practice of inscribing religious texts on the walls of the inner chambers of the pyramids, preserving for posterity a record of their earliest writings. Ptahhotep, the most distinguished sage of Egyptian antiquity, lived during V Dynasty. The following dynasty was notable for the reign of Pepi I (r. about 2590–70 B.C.), who was a vigorous administrator and warrior. During the reign of his son, Pepi II (r. about 2566–2476 B.C.), the authority of the throne was successfully challenged by the Egyptian nobility, leading to the decline and eventual disintegration of the Old Kingdom. As a consequence of this internal strife, Dynasties VII and VIII (2280–2242 B.C.) represent an extremely obscure period of Egyptian history.

The Middle Kingdom (2242–1567 B.C.). Although Dynasties IX and X, known as the Heracleopolitan dynasties because their capital was the city of Heracleopolis, succeeded in establishing a measure of stability in Egypt, nothing approaching the former glory of the kingdom was accomplished until the seizure of the throne by the nomarch, or count, of Thebes (q.v.). About 2160, he founded the XI Dynasty, the first of three successive Theban dynasties that ruled for nearly 400 years. A vigorous cultural renaissance developed under the Theban pharaohs, the most important of whom were Amenemhet I (*see under* AMENEMHET) and Sesostris I (r. about 1980–35). During their reigns, considerable territory, mainly Nubian, was annexed to the kingdom, a canal (now partly the Ismailia Canal) was dug between the Nile and the Red Sea, and a vast engineering project in what is now El Faiyûm Province was completed, reclaiming a large flooded area. The Theban architecture, art, and jewelry reveal an extraordinary delicacy of design. The period was considered the golden age of Egyptian literature. According to some accounts, the Jewish patriarch Abraham made his visit to Egypt in 1935 B.C., the final year of the reign of the first Sesostris.

The Egyptian nomarchs during the XIII and XIV Dynasties once again plunged Egypt into a state of political anarchy. Aided by the resultant turmoil and disunity, foreign invaders easily

conquered the country in the 18th century B.C., sacking and destroying many of its cities. The conquerors, called Hyksos (q.v.), were apparently of mixed stock, the predominant element of which was Semitic. The pharaohs of the Hyksos dynasties, the XV and XVI, kept only Lower Egypt under their direct administration, leaving Upper Egypt to tributary native princes. About the middle of the 16th century B.C., the viceroy of Thebes rebelled against his foreign sovereign and established the XVII Dynasty. The struggle to expel the Hyksos from Lower Egypt culminated in victory, about 1567 B.C. under the leadership of the Theban Ahmose I (*see under* AHMOSE).

The New Kingdom (1567–10th cent. B.C.). Ahmose I established the XVIII Dynasty, known as the first Diospolite dynasty for Diospolis ("City of God"), a name later applied to Thebes by the

One of two colossal statues of Amenhotep III (left), who reigned during the XVIII Dynasty. The statues, 70 ft. high, are near Thebes. They are sometimes referred to as the Colossi of Memnon because the Greeks associated them with their mythological hero Memnon. The temple at Deir el-Bahri (below), built by Queen Hatshepsut, is one of the greatest monuments of the same dynasty. The queen ruled Egypt for some two decades, while her husband Thutmose II and his son by another wife, Thutmose III, were thrust into the background. After her death in about 1482 B.C. she was buried in a tomb in the mountains behind the temple. Hatshepsut called herself a king and her statues depict her as a male. Luis Villota

Greeks. Under the Diospolite pharaohs of the XVIII Dynasty, notably those named Ikhnaton and Thutmose (qq.v.), Egypt became an imperial power, the limits of which extended from deep within the ancient north African Kingdom of Nubia (q.v.) to the Euphrates R. The architectural accomplishments of the dynasty rivaled in splendor many of the monuments and edifices erected during the Old Kingdom. One of the most magnificent is the temple at Deir el-Bahri (near the site of Thebes), built for Hatshepsut (q.v.), a queen of the dynasty and the first woman of consequence known in history. Other achievements of the XVIII Dynasty include the construction of Luxor and of Hermonthis, now El Karnak (q.v.), which rank among the great Egyptian cities of antiquity. Amenhotep IV, or Ikhnaton, the last important ruler of the dynasty, forcefully suppressed the pantheistic religion of the kingdom, introducing a solar monotheism. The new creed, highly unpopular among his people, was abandoned after the brief reign of his son-in-law and successor Tutankhamen (q.v.), the pharaoh whose tomb in the Valley of the Kings, near Luxor, was discovered in 1922.

Several capable pharaohs, including Harmhab, Seti I and Seti II (see under SETI), and Ramses II (see under RAMSES), ruled Egypt during the XIX Dynasty, but none was able to regain the imperial possessions lost by revolt during the reign of Ikhnaton. The Jewish exodus from Egypt probably occurred in 1290 B.C., in the reign of Ramses II. From 1200 to 1085 B.C., the period of the XX Dynasty, the pharaohs, mainly named Ramses, maintained peaceful relations with their neighbors. They were generally weak and incompetent rulers, however, and under them the kingdom was weakened by internal divisions, with the priesthood gradually achieving dominance in Egyptian political life. Subsequent internal strife led to the overthrow of the XXI Dynasty by Sheshonck (r. about 945–924), a general and the head of a Libyan family of Heracleopolis. He established his capital at Bubastis (q.v.), from which Bubastite, the name of the XXII Dynasty, is derived. Sheshonck won some signal victories over the Jews (Kings I), who knew him as Shishak, and otherwise strengthened the kingdom. His successors in the dynasty, which endured for 200 years, were unable to maintain unity in Egypt, which once again fell under the sway of the nomarchs. The XXIII and XXIV Dynasties were ineffectual, short-lived regimes, and the XXV, consisting of Ethiopian pharaohs, became involved in war with Assyria. The Assyrians conquered Egypt in 670 B.C., forcing Taharka, last pharaoh of the XXV Dynasty, to take refuge in the extreme south of the kingdom. The XXVI Dynasty was established by Psamtik I (see under PSAMTIK), a native prince whom the Assyrians had installed in 663 B.C. as regent. In 660 B.C. he rebelled against the Assyrian overlords, then engaged in war with the Babylonians, and proclaimed Egyptian independence. A brief resurgence of cultural achievement, reminiscent of former epochs, occurred during the XXVI Dynasty. In addition, one of its pharaohs, Necho II (r. about 609–593 B.C.), won a notable victory in Palestine (about 608 B.C.) over Josiah's army. Necho was severely defeated in battle by Nebuchadnezzar II, King of Babylonia (see under NEBUCHADNEZZAR) about three years later. Apries (r. about 588–69? B.C.), a later pharaoh of the dynasty, was deposed about 569 B.C. by Ahmose II, who withstood attacks by both the Babylonians and Persians. In 525 B.C., however, his son and successor Psamtik III was conquered by Cambyses II, King of Persia (see under CAMBYSES).

Egypt now became a province of Persia and was ruled for nearly two centuries by Persian kings. These comprised the XXVII to XXX Dynasties. Their control, challenged on several occasions by native rebellions, ended in 332 B.C., when Alexander III (q.v.), King of Macedonia, followed up his series of victories over the Persians by occupying Egypt. He founded the city of Alexandria (q.v.) in the next year. On Alexander's death, in 323 B.C., Ptolemy I (see under PTOLEMY), one of his generals, received the governorship of Egypt and Libya. Hostilities subsequently developed between Ptolemy and other of Alexander's generals, over whom he won a succession of victories. In 305 B.C. he established Egypt as an independent monarchy, taking the title of king. The country prospered under his rule, and Alexandria soon became the foremost commercial and cultural center of the world. The kingdom flourished for nearly 200 years under the Ptolemies. On the accession in 203 B.C. of Ptolemy V, great-great-grandson of the first Ptolemy, their domain became a virtual protectorate of Rome. This state of affairs continued until the deaths in 30 B.C. of the last of the line, Cleopatra VII (see under CLEOPATRA) and her son Ptolemy XIV. From that time until 640 A.D., Egypt was successively a province of the Roman and Byzantine empires.

Egypt under the Caliphate (640–1914). Between 640 and 646, control of Egypt was wrested from the Byzantine Empire by the Arab general Amr ibn-al-As (594?–664). In the course of the next few centuries the country became one of

The Mosque of Mohammed Ali, one of the more than 400 mosques in the older section of Cairo, and a dominant landmark. It was built (1830–48) by Mohammed Ali Pasha (Mehemet Ali), Ottoman viceroy of Egypt, who is often called the founder of modern Egypt. Of the many buildings he erected, the mosque is considered his masterpiece. Surmounted by a major dome, semidomes, smaller domes, and minarets, it is built in the style of the Ottoman mosques of Istanbul.   Luis Villota

the main strongholds of the Caliphate (see CA-LIPH), with virtually all of the Egyptians except the Copts embracing Islam. The Fatimid, claimants of the Caliphate, overran Egypt between 969 and 973, and established a new capital at Cairo (q.v.). Their rule, severely shaken by the first and second Crusades, was ended in 1171 by Saladin (q.v.), founder of the Ayyubid Muslim dynasty; see CRUSADES. Under the Ayyubids Egypt became the political and cultural center of the Islamic world. The Mamelukes (q.v.), slave troops in the service of the Ayyubids, revolted against their masters in 1250, establishing a new Muslim dynasty in Egypt. This lasted until 1517, when the country was conquered by the Ottoman Turks.

Despite the general incompetence of the Turkish viceroys (known as khedives after 1867) and their oppressive rule, Ottoman control of the country continued without interruption until Napoléon Bonaparte, later Napoleon I (q.v.), Emperor of France, invaded Egypt in 1798. With the help of the British, the Turks expelled the French in 1802. Thereafter, the Turks re-

tained nominal control of Egypt for more than a century, but both the British and French governments frequently intervened in Egyptian affairs during this period. Nationalist discontent culminated in 1881 in a general uprising, led by Ahmed Arabi Pasha (1839–1911), an Egyptian officer and revolutionary. The revolution was crushed by the armed forces of Great Britain in the following year. In fact though not in law, Egypt then became a virtual possession of Great Britain.

Protectorate and Kingdom   (1914–1953). In World War I (q.v.), in December, 1914, the British government proclaimed a protectorate over Egypt, traditionally regarded by British military strategists as a key position in the imperial defense system. The Turkish khedive was deposed, and Hussein Kamil (1850–1917) was proclaimed Sultan of Egypt. His brother Fuad succeeded him in 1917. Chiefly as the result of another nationalist rebellion, the British protectorate was terminated in March, 1922, and Egypt became an independent monarchy, with Fuad I (q.v.) as king. Great Britain, however, retained its rights in the Anglo-Egyptian Sudan (see SUDAN, REPUBLIC OF THE: *History*), held its positions along the Suez Canal (q.v.), and continued its occupation of Cairo, Alexandria, and other Egyptian cities.

Because of British influence in Egyptian affairs, political tension increased sharply in the country during the 1920's. In 1929 the Egyptian parliament, controlled by the Wafd (Nationalist) Party, was dissolved by King Fuad. Mustafa el-Nahas Pasha (1876–1965), the Wafd leader, resigned as premier, and a new government was formed. The constitution of 1923 was replaced in 1930 by a new constitution, which increased the powers of the king. New parliamentary elections, characterized as fraudulent by the Wafdists, were won in 1931 by a Conservative coalition. The dictatorial government established by the Conservatives lasted until December, 1934, when a more liberal cabinet assumed office. One of its first official acts was to abolish the constitution of 1930 and reintroduce the constitution of 1923.

Fuad's son Faruk I (q.v.) succeeded to the throne in 1936. In the same year, Great Britain and Egypt negotiated a treaty of alliance, to be effective for twenty years. Under the terms of this agreement, Great Britain conditionally agreed to the withdrawal from Egyptian soil of all British troops except those guarding the Suez Canal and assumed responsibility for the defense of Egyptian frontiers in the event of war. Great Britain also undertook, under the treaty, to train and equip an Egyptian army.

Following the outbreak of World War II, Alexandria became an important military base of the Allies. The armed forces of Italy invaded Egypt from Libya in 1940, and Italian airplanes bombed Alexandria, Cairo, and other Egyptian cities. Despite these and later acts of aggression by the Axis powers (q.v.), the Egyptian government maintained a cautious neutrality throughout the war. In 1942 a German advance that threatened to engulf Alexandria and the Suez Canal was stopped by the British at El 'Alamein, a short distance west of Alexandria. Egypt became a charter member of the United Nations in 1945.

In 1946 Great Britain ended its military occupation of Alexandria and other Egyptian cities. Negotiations between the British and Egyptian governments relative to revisions of the treaty of alliance of 1936 broke down in 1947, mainly because of disagreements regarding the Anglo-Egyptian Sudan.

After the establishment in May, 1948, of Israel (q.v.) in Palestine, Egypt and other nations of the Arab League (q.v.) began hostilities against the new state. The Egyptians won several minor victories during the early stages of the conflict, but were severely defeated later in 1948. On Feb. 24, 1949, the Egyptian government concluded an armistice with Israel. Subsequent attempts by the United Nations to arrange a peace treaty ended in failure, and Egypt continued wartime prohibitions against passage of Israel-bound ships through the Suez Canal.

The Wafd Party won a decisive victory in the national elections of January, 1950, and the Wafdist leader Mustafa el-Nahas Pasha became premier again. His program included proposals for industrialization, land reform, reorganization of the army, and British evacuation of the Sudan and the Suez Canal zone.

On Nov. 16, 1950, el-Nahas demanded the immediate withdrawal of British forces from these areas. The British government replied on Nov. 21 that amendment of the treaty of 1936 by mutual consent was a prerequisite to any change in the status quo. Subsequent negotiations between the two governments were inconclusive. On Oct. 15, 1951, the Egyptian parliament abrogated the treaty of 1936.

Following bloody battles between Egyptian police and British troops, and rioting in Cairo, Premier el-Nahas decreed martial law for all Egypt on Jan. 26, 1952. The next day King Faruk, citing the failure of the government to maintain "security and order", removed it from office. During the next six months the premiership changed hands four times. The marked political instability was largely due to intragovernmental strife over the Anglo-Egyptian crisis.

Early in the morning of July 23 a group of middle-ranking army officers, organized by Lieutenant Colonel Gamal Abdel Nasser (q.v.), ousted the existing government, installed former premier Aly Maher Pasha (1883–1960) as "emergency premier", and proclaimed the Palestine war hero Major General Mohammed Naguib (q.v.) as commander-in-chief. In a radio broadcast to the populace later that day, Naguib ascribed Egyptian military weakness, political chaos, and economic troubles to bribery and corruption in high office. King Faruk was forced to abdicate on July 26; his six-month-old infant son succeeded to the throne as Ahmed Fuad II.

With the enthusiastic support of large sections of the people, the revolutionary regime abolished all noble titles, impounded the royal properties, raised army pay, increased income taxes, and launched investigations of fraud and graft in former administrations. Apparently because Aly Maher opposed land redistribution, he was replaced on Sept. 7 as premier by Naguib. An Agricultural Reform Decree, promulgated on Sept. 9, limited individual holdings of farm land to 200 acres and provided that holdings in excess of that amount be distributed to peasants with less than 5 acres.

The constitution of 1923 was nullified in December. In January, 1953, Naguib dissolved all political parties and proclaimed a three-year suspension of constitutional government. The dictatorship was formalized on Feb. 10, when Naguib ruled that all power would be vested in himself and a thirteen-member "Army Council of the Revolution".

Meanwhile Anglo-Egyptian relations had gradually improved. A pact on Feb. 19 between the two countries stipulated that, after a three-year transitional period, Sudan would be free to choose its future status: independence, union with Egypt, or membership in the Commonwealth of Nations.

The Republic. On June 18 the Army Council of the Revolution deposed Ahmed Fuad II, proclaimed Egypt a republic, and named Naguib its first president and premier. Nasser was appointed deputy premier. The initial land redistribution, provided for by the Agricultural Reform Decree, was made on July 23.

In January, 1954, the Egyptian government outlawed the Muslim Brotherhood, an organization of extreme nationalists, and arrested seventy-eight of its leaders on charges of illegal political activity. Events in February disclosed a hitherto unpublicized struggle for supremacy between Naguib and Nasser. The dispute centered on the opposition of Nasser and the majority of the Council to reinstatement of constitutional rule, a policy favored by Naguib. Between Feb. 22 and April 18 Nasser twice replaced Naguib as premier. Naguib was permitted to retain the presidency until Nov. 14, however, when he was placed under house arrest on charges of complicity in a plot to assassinate Nasser. The council assumed the functions of the president and Nasser, retaining the premiership, emerged as the real ruler of Egypt.

Egypt and Great Britain meanwhile had signed on Oct. 19 a seven-year treaty designed to settle the long-standing Suez dispute. By the terms of the treaty, which superseded that of 1936, British troops were to evacuate the Suez Canal zone by June 18, 1956, and certain installations in the area, such as ammunition and petroleum storage depots, were to remain under the control of British personnel. The treaty stipulated further that Egypt was to be responsible for the security of the zone, that Great Britain had the right to reoccupy the area in case of

armed attack upon Egypt, any other member of the Arab League, or Turkey, and that Egypt was to gain complete control of the zone after seven years. Following ratification of the treaty, withdrawal of British forces proceeded on schedule.

Sudan proclaimed itself an independent republic on Jan. 1, 1956. Neither Egypt nor Great Britain objected to the Sudanese move.

On Jan. 16 the Nasser regime promulgated a new constitution, which was approved by 99.8 percent of the electorate in a plebiscite held on June 22. The voters also elected Nasser president under the new constitution.

The Egyptian economy had made considerable progress since 1952. The Egyptian government started new industries, brought desert areas under cultivation, and improved the health conditions of the people. Despite improved economic conditions, the peasant masses were hardly better off than before 1952 because of the extraordinarily rapid growth of population. As part of its program to accelerate economic growth, the Nasser government developed plans to construct a vast dam at Aswân on the Nile R.; see Aswân High Dam.

Relations between Egypt and Israel deteriorated steadily during 1955. Recurring border incidents threatened constantly to erupt into full-scale warfare. In September, 1955, Egypt arranged to buy military equipment from the Soviet Union and Czechoslovakia. The arms deal, besides marking the first major Soviet penetration of the Middle East, introduced a period of mounting Egyptian-Israeli tensions. Concurrently the Nasser regime displayed increasing hostility toward the Western democracies and open friendliness toward the Communist bloc of states.

Early in 1956 the Egyptian government began negotiations with the United States and other countries for a $1.2 billion loan to finance the Aswân dam project. The U.S. government subsequently offered to participate in the loan, but the offer was withdrawn on July 19. Within the next few days Great Britain and the International Bank for Reconstruction and Development (q.v.), or World Bank, also refused to help finance the dam. It was maintained that the project was financially unsound because Nasser had heavily mortgaged the national income to pay for matériel purchased from the Communist nations.

On July 26 Nasser nationalized the Suez Canal. In his statement proclaiming seizure of the waterway he asserted that revenues from the canal would be used to finance the Aswân project. Nasser's action was greeted with enthu-

The two 65-ft.-high statues of Ramses II (right) before his temple at Abu Simbel are in the impersonal style of sculpture used for temple ornament. The temple was moved from its original site in the mid-1960's to protect it from the waters rising behind the Aswân High Dam.

Trans World Airlines

Left: The Great Sphinx of Giza and the pyramid of Khafre. The pyramid was built as the tomb of Khafre, a king of the IVth Dynasty of Egypt, and the head of the Sphinx is a portrait of him.   Trans World Airlines

Egypt. Plate 1.

Below: Egyptian sailing vessels ply quiet waters in a countryside setting.   John G. Ross — Trans World Airlines

An Egyptian craftsman works on a tapestry. Villagers learn the traditional art of weaving such handsome hangings without formal training.

Egyptian Government Tourist Office

Egypt, Plate 2.

Below: The mosques of Egypt are ornamented with glowing mosaics (left), such as the detail shown here. A tapestry (right) created by a village artist. Museums buy artistic woven goods from the most expert of these craftsmen.

Egyptian Government Tourist Office

The modern section of Cairo, with the tall arabesque Cairo Tower, symbol of today's Egypt. In the background the large structure with the drum-shaped base is the Television Building, housing the city's television and radio studios and the offices of the Ministry of Information. Cairo is not only the capital of the Arab Republic of Egypt; it is also its economic, financial, and cultural center. With several universities, the largest of which is the University of Cairo, it is the country's center of higher education as well, attracting students from all over the Middle East.

Luis Villota

siasm in Egypt and other Arab nations, but with consternation in Great Britain, France, and the U.S. The Western countries charged Egypt with flagrant violation of treaties guaranteeing international control of the canal. Great Britain and France threatened to use force, if necessary, to insure freedom of navigation on the waterway.

During the next few months the powers concerned made repeated efforts to negotiate a new agreement with Egypt. However, a twenty-two nation conference on Aug. 16–23 in London, a five-nation mission on Sept. 3–9 to Cairo, United Nations discussions Oct. 5–12 in New York, and various informal talks held afterward produced no positive results. The Egyptian position was backed by the Soviet Union.

On Oct. 29 Israeli troops invaded the Sinai Peninsula of Egypt with the declared objective of wiping out bases from which raids had been

launched against Israel. The next day the British and French governments demanded that Israel and Egypt withdraw their forces from the Suez Canal area. Israel accepted the demand, but Egypt rejected it, whereupon British and French aircraft attacked Egyptian airfields and military installations. By Nov. 2 the Israelis had advanced to within 10 mi. of the canal, gained control of almost all of the peninsula, and captured many thousands of Egyptian soldiers. The U.N. General Assembly called for a cease-fire on Nov. 2, but Anglo-French air raids continued. Having destroyed the bulk of the Egyptian air force, British and French forces invaded the Suez Canal area on Nov. 5. The next day Great Britain, France, and Israel, yielding to American pressure and Soviet threats to "crush the aggressors . . . through the use of force", accepted the U.N. cease-fire demand. The invaders undertook to withdraw from Egypt on condition that a specially constituted U.N. police force take their place. In the days following, the governments of the Soviet Union and of Red China indicated that "volunteers" might be "permitted" to help Egypt expel the "aggressors". Talk of "volunteers" stopped after the U.S. government warned on Nov. 14 that it would oppose, through the U.N., the entry of any new forces in the Middle East. The first U.N. police contingents reached Egypt on Nov. 15. During December all of the British and French forces in the Suez Canal area were withdrawn. On Dec. 26, 1956, a U.N. salvage team started work on removing the ships which Egypt had sunk in the canal in order to close it to navigation; the canal was fully cleared by April, 1957.

Nasser stated early in 1957 that Egypt recognized the right of ships of every country, except Israel, to use the canal and would agree to arbitration to settle the claims of former canal owners to compensation. He insisted, however, that all tolls be paid to the autonomous Egyptian body established to operate the waterway. This requirement was resisted only by Great Britain and France, but during the spring of 1957 those countries authorized their shipowners to make payments to the Egyptian authority. After the Egyptian terms were accepted generally a substantial volume of traffic again began to move through the waterway.

During 1957 Egypt placed increasing reliance on the U.S.S.R. for economic and military assistance. The U.S.S.R. bought twice as much Egyptian cotton during 1957 as it had in the previous year and also replaced the military equipment and warplanes which Egypt had lost in the Sinai campaign. In October, Egypt, supporting the Soviet and Syrian stand that Syria was in danger of invasion by Turkey, dispatched troops by sea to the Syrian port of Latakia. However, the charges that Turkey harbored aggressive intentions against Syria were abandoned soon afterward.

On Feb. 1, 1958, the governments of Egypt and Syria proclaimed the union of their two countries as the United Arab Republic, with Nasser as the first president. The new state was described as the first step in uniting all Arab nations. Several of the Arab countries, however, showed an inclination to mistrust the alliance. On Feb. 14, in an apparent countermove to the Egyptian-Syrian union, Jordan and Iraq announced that they would form a union; the latter subsequently was constituted as the Arab Federation (see JORDAN: History). Support for the U.A.R. was expressed on the other hand by Yemen (now the Yemen Arab Republic), which

on March 8, allied itself with the republic in an entity designating the United Arab States. Under this grouping, Yemen, while remaining an independent monarchy, unified its armed forces with those of the U.A.R. and pursued a foreign policy in common with it.

Tensions within the Arab World. In 1961 the union of Syria and Egypt that created the U.A.R. was dissolved. As early as 1958 there had been Syrian complaints that control of the state was concentrated in Egyptian hands and that Syria, economically the stronger region, was being neglected in favor of Egypt. Nationalization of financial institutions in the summer of 1961 was particularly resented by some élements in Syria, and on Sept. 28 an army revolt broke out there. An independent Syrian government was soon organized. President Nasser decided not to oppose the Syrian revolt, and in December he also dissolved the loose federation between the U.A.R. and Yemen on the ground that Yemen's feudal regime was incompatible with the aims of his country.

In February, 1962, elections were held for a National Congress of Popular Forces to draft a U.A.R. constitution. When the congress convened in May, Nasser presented a charter setting forth principles for an "Arab Socialist Union". The charter was approved by June 30. In September Nasser reorganized the government, creating an executive council and a presidential council to share his burden of administrative responsibility. When the royal government of Yemen was overthrown during the same month, the U.A.R. offered support to the revolutionary regime and thus augmented the tensions present in its relationship with monarchist Saudi Arabia, which supported the deposed ruler. See YEMEN ARAB REPUBLIC.

During early 1963 coups in Iraq and Syria brought to power regimes of the Ba'athist parties, which favored Arab unity, and in March both countries began merger talks with the U.A.R. A federal agreement was signed by the three countries but was renounced later by Nasser on July 22, after quarrels developed between him and Ba'athist factions that feared his domination. In 1964 Iraq again moved toward closer association with the U.A.R., although no immediate merger was envisioned. In March a new provisional U.A.R. constitution was promulgated and elections were held for a National Assembly.

During 1964 President Nasser began to pursue a more accommodating policy toward the other Arab states in the face of the decision by Israel to use the water supply of Lake Tiberias (the Sea of Galilee). This was manifested by two Arab summit meetings in January and September, 1964, which resulted in an agreement to build a dam in Jordan and Syria to divert the river. Also a joint Arab command was set up under a U.A.R. general to counter possible Israeli moves against the proposed diversion project. More significantly, with Libyan financial aid, a beginning was made toward the establishment of the Palestine Liberation Organization.

During 1964 a variety of factors caused a resumption of the cold war between the Arab countries. The Syrians were continually pressing the U.A.R. for a more militant attitude toward Israel, and the continued Egyptian presence in Yemen further alienated Faisal (q.v.), King of Saudi Arabia. While the relations of the U.A.R. with Jordan and Morocco had improved, the sudden call by President Habib Bourguiba (q.v.) of Tunisia for Arab-Israeli negotiations on the basis of the 1947 partition of Palestine by the United Nations (q.v.) greatly angered the Arab world. Diplomatic relations with Tunisia were severed amid charges of U.A.R. attempts to interfere in the domestic affairs of other Arab states. In August, 1965, agreement was reached at Jeddah between President Nasser and King Faisal to settle the Yemeni conflict in stages. The arrangement was aborted when agreement could not be reached by the warring Yemeni factions, and U.A.R. forces remained in Yemen until their final departure late in 1967.

On the international scene during 1964–65 there was a new rapprochement with the Soviet Union, and a corresponding deterioration in Egyptian relations with the West, except France. Continued American support of Israel and British presence in Aden were important factors. The revelation of the secret arms aid to Israel by West Germany brought a severing of relations with that country and Egyptian recognition of East Germany.

On the domestic scene President Nasser was reelected in a referendum in March, 1965, and during August visited the Soviet Union. Meanwhile there were signs of discontent in mid-1965 that culminated in an abortive attempt by the Muslim Brotherhood to take power. The regime reacted by conducting widespread arrests and purging the Ministry of the Interior. A new government was formed headed by Zakaria Muhyi Al-Din (1918–) replacing Prime Minister Ali Sabri (1920–), who became secretary general of the Arab Socialist Union. A well-known pragmatist, Muhyi Al-Din instituted measures to reduce foreign spending, tightened internal security, and successfully attracted foreign aid from France, Japan, Italy, Kuwait, and the International Monetary Fund.

War with Yemen. Despite these efforts the U.A.R. foreign exchange reserves became depleted and it became necessary to sell large quantities of gold on world markets. In September, 1966, Muhyi Al-Din was replaced by an officer-technocrat, Sidky Sulayman (1919–), who had been minister of the Aswân High Dam. The changeover signified the continuation of the expensive involvement of the U.A.R. in Yemen and a generally leftist orientation in ideological terms.

The civil war in Yemen continued to promote Egyptian-Saudi conflict and in November, 1966, Egyptian aircraft bombed Saudi villages near the Yemeni border. Meanwhile King Faisal began to organize a Pan-Islamic coalition to counter the Arab Socialist States headed by the U.A.R. In July, 1966, President Nasser moved to postpone the Arab summit conference planned for September in the context of worsening relations with Saudi Arabia, Tunisia, and Jordan. In the meantime relations with Syria were strengthened and on Nov. 4, 1966, a joint defense treaty was signed, aimed against Israel. This coincided with the increase of guerrilla activity directed from Syria against Israel, culminating in fighting around Lake Tiberias. On May 12, 1967, Israeli Premier Levi Eshkol (1895–1969) threatened to invade Syria. The U.A.R. reacted by moving large numbers of troops into the Sinai in accordance with the mutual defense pact with Syria, and asked the U.N. to withdraw its Emergency Force, whose presence on the Egyptian side of the border had been originally requested by the U.A.R.

Six-Day War and Its Consequences. On May 23, 1967, President Nasser declared the closing of the Straits of Tiran to Israeli shipping. With the support of the U.S. and Britain, Israel declared that the Gulf of 'Aqaba was an international waterway and considered the blockade an act of war. Meanwhile all Arab leaders declared their support for the U.A.R. Early on June 5 Israel launched an air and ground attack against the U.A.R. and fighting spread to the Syrian and Jordanian frontiers. Within hours the bulk of the Arab air forces were destroyed, and Israeli troops controlled the Sinai, the west bank of the Jordan R., and the Golan Heights of Syria by June 10.

President Nasser resigned soon after the conclusion of hostilities, but within twenty-four hours he rescinded his resignation amid tumultuous demonstrations of support. As he moved to begin the task of reconstruction, the military high command was purged, and armaments were acquired from the Soviet Union to rebuild the armed forces. The economic losses, especially the loss of revenues from the canal and the Sinai oil fields, were compensated by grants from Saudi Arabia, Kuwait, and Libya. At the Arab summit conference of Aug. 29, 1967, in Khartoum, a rapprochement was achieved between the U.A.R. and Saudi Arabia on Yemen, and the oil embargo against the West was ended. By December, 1967, the U.A.R. armed forces had been withdrawn from Yemen.

On the political front, the Arab Socialist Union began to assume an increasingly leftist orientation, and Soviet influence registered a significant increase through the injection of a large number of specialists into the Egyptian armed forces and a persistent Soviet naval presence in Alexandria and Port Said.

Death of Nasser. On the international scene in the postwar period the U.A.R. emerged as a relative moderate in the Arab world as compared with Syria and Algeria, which advocated total guerrilla warfare against Israel. On July 23, 1970, Nasser announced acceptance of a U.S. proposal for a cease-fire along the Suez Canal as

a preliminary step toward peace negotiations. Jordan and Israel announced their acceptance a few days later. Although the guns were stilled, attempts at negotiation failed, as the Israeli government accused the U.A.R. of violating the cease-fire by moving Soviet-built antiaircraft missiles into the canal area. On Sept. 28, 1970, President Nasser died of a heart attack. In a national plebiscite on Oct. 15, Vice-President Anwar el-Sadat (q.v.) was elected to succeed him.

The Sadat Regime. On May 14, 1971, President Sadat announced the defeat of an alleged plot to oust him, and he ordered the arrest of six of his ministers and many other officials. The grounds of the conspiracy, he reported, was opposition to his agreement (April 17) to join Egypt with Libya and Syria in a confederation. A new cabinet was formed and both the military and police pledged support to Sadat.

In other developments the Aswân High Dam was officially dedicated on Jan. 15, 1971, with the Soviet President Nikolai Viktorovich Podgorny (1903–   ) in attendance, and an important new oil field was discovered 160 miles w. of Cairo on April 1. In September a short-lived union of Egypt with Syria and Libya was effected; the loose linking was named the Federation of Arab Republics. At the same time Egypt changed its

President Gamal Abdel Nasser steps from armored vehicle as he arrives at site of Egyptian military maneuvers in 1970.   UPI

name from United Arab Republic, in use since 1958, to Arab Republic of Egypt.

In 1972 President Sadat made several moves affecting Egyptian foreign policy. After visits to Moscow in February and April, it seemed clear that the Soviet Union was refusing to meet fully the Egyptian demands for arms. On July 18 Sadat ordered the ouster of some 5000 Soviet military advisers and technicians and announced that Soviet-supplied military equipment and installations belonged to Egypt. A planned merger between Egypt and Libya, announced in August, 1972, was called off after disagreements over foreign and domestic policy in 1973.

In March, 1973, Sadat dismissed the cabinet and then assumed the premiership. A few days later he declared himself military governor, giving him the power to declare martial law.

The October War. On Oct. 6, 1973, Egypt and Syria entered the fourth Arab-Israeli war. Israel was unprepared, and Egyptian forces moved across the Suez Canal and within a few days had advanced 10 mi. into the Sinai Peninsula. By mid-October, however, Israel had seized the initiative against Syria and, concentrating on the Sinai front, was able to push back the Egyptian forces. Attempts to establish a cease-fire in late October were unsuccessful, and a more permanent cessation of hostilities was arranged in mid-November, largely through the efforts of U.S. Secretary of State Henry A. Kissinger. Egyptian and Israeli officials conferred directly for the first time since 1956, and the two countries exchanged prisoners of war. Although Egypt did not win the October war, it effectively challenged the 1967 boundaries and regained complete control of the Suez Canal.

In December, 1973, a conference aimed at stabilizing the Middle Eastern situation began at Geneva; Egypt and Israel also held bilateral talks there. Beginning on Jan. 11, 1974, Kissinger conducted intensive—but not face-to-face—talks between the two countries by shuttling between Cairo and Jerusalem, and on Jan. 18 an agreement providing for disengagement on the Sinai front was signed separately by Egypt and Israel. The accord, put into effect by early March, provided for a 6-mi.-wide Egyptian forward position along the entire east bank of the Suez Canal, separated from Israeli forces by a buffer zone, which was policed by a U.N. Emergency Force.

Egypt resumed full diplomatic relations with the U.S. in February. Kissinger was unable to secure a second disengagement agreement in 1974, but on Sept. 1, 1975, through his mediation efforts, Israel and Egypt initialed a new accord.

President Anwar el-Sadat of Egypt addresses the Knesset (parliament) on Nov. 20, 1977, during his dramatic visit to Israel, the first by an Arab leader since the nation's establishment. William Karel–Sygma

Israel agreed to pull back another 12 to 26 mi. and to surrender the Sinai oil fields captured from Egypt during the 1967 war; in exchange, Egypt agreed to allow nonmilitary cargoes bound to and from Israel to pass through the Suez Canal, which had been reopened on July 6.

In domestic affairs Sadat loosened his control of the country in 1974. In September he relinquished the premiership to Abdul Aziz Hegazy (1923–), who, early in 1975, was succeeded as premier by Mamdouh Salem (1918–). Egypt's economy fared poorly in 1975, and by early 1976 the country's debt to the Soviet Union was estimated at $4 billion. In September, 1976, Sadat

A small model in wood from a tomb of the Middle Kingdom (2242–1567 B.C.). The figure at right is playing a stringed instrument, and the three at left are clapping in time and singing while their master and mistress listen.
Federico Borromeo-Scala

was elected to a second six-year term as president of Egypt, and candidates supporting him won a large majority in the People's Assembly in general elections held the following month.

In a dramatic gesture designed to foster a Middle Eastern settlement, Sadat visited Jerusalem, the capital of Israel, for three days in November, 1977. He met there with Israeli leaders and addressed Israel's parliament. The visit quickly led to peace talks between Egyptian and Israeli officials, but the negotiations soon became deadlocked, mainly because Israel refused to meet Sadat's demand that it eventually relinquish virtually all of the territory it had captured in 1967. Leaders of most other Arab states severely criticized Sadat for his diplomatic initiative. The peacemaking process was renewed in September, 1978, when Sadat and Israeli Premier Menachem Begin (q.v.) agreed, during a conference held under U.S. auspices near Washington, D.C., on a framework for negotiating a peace treaty between their countries by mid-December, 1978.

EGYPTIAN ARCHEOLOGY, scientific investigation of the material remains of ancient Egypt for the purpose of studying its history and culture. Intensive research and excavation in the Nile R. valley have resulted in the development of archeological methods that have done much to advance the science of archeology (q.v.) in general. Scholars have been attracted to Egyptology, the study of Egyptian antiquities, since the 16th century; scientific expeditions have been sent to Egypt since 1798. This early and sustained interest in the Nile R. valley derives, to a great extent, from the multiplicity of Egyptian relics. These relics are in a remarkable state of preservation, having resisted decomposition for thousands of years because of the extraordinarily dry climate of Upper, or southern, Egypt. The soil, which consists of silt and sand, is comparatively dry and easily removable, thus providing ease in the excavation of monuments and relics. Recent excavations in Lower, or northern, Egypt have led to the hope that significant information can be won from this part of the Arab Republic of Egypt also, even if not in such quantity as in Upper Egypt.

Another major factor in the progress of Egyptology was the Egyptian religion (q.v.). Because of their veneration of the dead, the Egyptians furnished their elaborately constructed tombs with all manner of objects used in life, thus depositing a continuous and detailed record of their daily existence. Even when the tombs were new, however, they were despoiled by thieves; not until 1922 was a royal tomb discovered relatively intact. The sumptuous furnishings of this tomb, which was the burial place of Tutankhamen (q.v.), an insignificant XVIII Dynasty king, indicate that the tombs of important pharaohs originally must have been magnificent beyond imagination.

History. The first archeological expedition to Egypt comprised a group of scientists who accompanied Napoléon Bonaparte, later Napoleon I (q.v.), Emperor of France, on his Egyptian campaign in 1798. One of the most important archeological discoveries of the journey was the Rosetta Stone (q.v.), which bore inscriptions in hieroglyphics (q.v.), demotic, or popular, Egyptian, and Greek; *see* EGYPTIAN LANGUAGE AND LITER-ATURE. In 1822 the French scholar Jean François Champollion (q.v.) deciphered the hieroglyphics, which provided the key to understanding the language of the ancient Egyptians (*see* EGYPTIAN LANGUAGE AND LITERATURE). The findings of Napoleon's commission are presented in the *Description de l'Egypte* (21 vol., 1809–28), which focused much popular interest on ancient Egypt. European museums began to collect Egyptian antiquities indiscriminately. In 1828, Champollion, accompanied by the Italian Egyptologist Ippolito Rosellini (1800–43), explored Egypt from Alexandria to Wadi Halfa. Led by Karl Richard Lepsius (q.v.), a commission sent by Frederick William IV (q.v.), King of Prussia, recorded the texts of all the ancient inscriptions then visible in *Denkmäler aus Ägypten und Äthiopien* ("Monuments of Egypt and Ethiopia", 12 vol., 1849–59); this work has remained one of the valuable sources for the study of Egypt, because the inscriptions are the most important feature of many monuments. Dozens of explorers and collectors dug in Egypt until, in 1858, the Egyptian government appointed the French Egyptologist Auguste Edouard Mariette (1821–81) conservator of monuments. For more than

twenty years Mariette was the only archeologist permitted to excavate in Egypt. Under his direction the Museum of Antiquities was established, and all portable discoveries were placed there, his purpose being to control the plunder and sale of antiquities. After the death of Mariette, his successor, Sir Gaston Maspero (1846–1916), helped put into effect a more liberal policy.

The British occupation of Egypt in 1882 was followed, in the same year, by the establishment of the Egypt Exploration Fund for scientific excavation and study. A new era of directed excavation was begun in the Nile valley. Under the direction of the Swiss Egyptologist Edouard Naville (1884–1926), the sites of such ancient towns as Pithom in the land of Goshen (q.v.) were uncovered. Sir Flinders Petrie (q.v.), one of the most famous archeologists to work with the fund, systematized scientific excavation by instituting strict records and catalogs of all objects found, no matter how unimportant they seemed. Such Egyptologists as Francis Griffith

The Egyptians were superb artificers in metal and glass, as these objects from the time of Thutmose III (about 1501–1447 B.C.) give evidence. (Left to right) Silver canister, turquoise-blue glass goblet, silver cup, gold dish, gold beaker. Metropolitan Museum of Art

(1862–1934), Ernest Arthur Gardner (1862–1939), and Percy Edward Newberry (1869–1949) discovered new and important data, notably in the ancient cities of Tanis, Bubastis (qq.v.), and Naucratis.

Since the beginning of the 20th century, an ever-increasing volume of archeological data has resulted from scientific excavation in Egypt. So detailed is this information that most Egyptian relics can now be dated merely from internal evidence, without the help of inscriptions. Tombs and graves have been some of the richest sources of archeological study. The most sensational of such discoveries occurred in 1922 when the tomb of King Tutankhamen (q.v.) was unearthed in excavations of the British archeologists Howard Carter (q.v.) and George Edward Herbert, 5th Earl of Carnarvon (*see under* HERBERT). The tomb was almost intact and contained, in addition to the mummy, numerous priceless relics of the XVIII Dynasty. Another great discovery, deemed by archeologists to be even more significant than the Tutankhamen find, was the 125-ft.-long funeral ship of Khufu (q.v.), the first king of the IV Dynasty. The funeral ship was intended to carry the soul of Cheops to reunion with the sun. In June, 1954, it was found in a sealed chamber, unearthed accidentally in the course of road construction on the south side of the Great Pyramid at Giza. Sumptuously furnished for the solar journey, the ship was in an excellent state of preservation.

Findings. The oldest evidences of Egyptian civilization are flint and chert tools found in the shallow graves of Stone Age inhabitants of the Nile valley. The paleolithic Egyptians, who were hunters living on the desert edge of the river valley, developed during the Neolithic Age into shepherds; as they learned to control the waters of the annual Nile flood they became farmers. Before the prehistoric period ended, the Egyptians had contact with people from the Middle East who invaded Egypt from the north. More advanced culturally than the Egyptians, the Middle Easterners may have introduced into Egypt the use of metal and the concept of writing, which greatly stimulated the growth of civilization. The influence of Middle East culture is evidenced by the conception of Egyptian gods, which united deities in human form, brought from the north, with the animal deities of Africa.

A series of ruined tombs discovered at Abydos (q.v.) in 1897 was one of the first evidences of the earliest dynastic culture. Only scattered inscriptions and tombs, however, fill in the cultural outline of the years 3400–2700 B.C. In the III Dynasty, an extraordinary development of construction in stone began, due probably to the influence of Imhotep (fl. about 2780 B.C.), the chief minister of Zoser (fl. 28th century B.C.); in less than 200 years construction reached a climax in the Great Pyramid at Giza, near Cairo; *see* EGYPTIAN ARCHITECTURE AND ART; PYRAMIDS. This development in building was accompanied by great achievements in every cultural field, notably in science. One of the greatest Egyptian contributions to world knowledge was a calendar that was introduced probably in 2780 B.C. (*see* CHRONOLOGY). By observing the stars the Egyptians knew that the approximate length of the year was 365 days. They dated their first day from the heliacal rising of the star Sirius in mid-July, which corresponded with the beginning of the annual Nile flood. Mathematics was a formal study as early as the III Dynasty. Because landmarks were periodically obliterated by the floods, geometry was a necessity for measuring land, and the accurate construction of the pyramids required a mastery of measurement in two and three dimensions. Egyptian mathematicians knew how to find the area of a triangle if the sides were known, and the area of a circle with a given radius. Their method for determining the area of the circle involved dividing it up into small, approximately triangular strips. The Egyptians possessed an excellent knowledge of medicine and bone surgery; *see* TREPANNING. Physicians constituted a special caste, and there were at least two medical schools, administered independently of the temples.

During the V Dynasty, the classical age of ancient Egypt, the enduring characteristics of Egyptian civilization were finally set. After the V Dynasty, alterations occurred only in those details, such as dress, which had nothing to do with religion. Such details, however, were comparatively rare, because few countries have been so dominated by religion as ancient Egypt (*see* EGYPTIAN RELIGION). Even in costume, the classical tradition was important. Great nobles of the XXVI Dynasty had themselves depicted in the V-Dynasty dress of more than 2000 years earlier; even as late as the time of the Roman pharaohs the ceremonial dress of rulers was that of the classical dynasty.

The conquest of Egypt by the Hyksos (q.v.) brought a cultural lull, and then a revival embellished with foreign influences. After the Egyptian conquest of the Near East by pharaohs of the New Kingdom, Asian influences, notably from Babylonia, appeared, especially in the great monuments which were built with the spoils of conquest. During the XXVI Dynasty, a revolt against Asian influences occurred, but the neoclassicism of the period, though sometimes beautiful in artistic expression, was only an inaccurate imitation of the classic V Dynasty. A second attempt to return to classic forms occurred after the Persian conquest of Egypt, but it was even less successful. The spirit of the great Egyptian culture was fading, and, by the time of the Roman conquest, Egyptian civilization was no longer an independent creative force.   R.H.

EGYPTIAN ARCHITECTURE AND ART, specifically architecture and art of ancient Egypt. Because of extensive archeological activity, much is known, and with great certainty, about ancient Egyptian culture; *see* EGYPTIAN ARCHEOLOGY. With the possible exception of Sumer (q.v.), Egypt was the first country in history to develop a great artistic culture. The arts and crafts of the Nile valley dominated the basin of the eastern Mediterranean for more than 2000 years, from about 2900 B.C., when the first important artistic surge took place, to about 600 B.C., when cultural dominance passed to the Greeks. Egyptian arts, governed by an immutable religion, were controlled by tradition as few other national cultures have been; *see* EGYPTIAN RELIGION. Once established, these artistic conventions were absolute. In only one instance, during the reign of Ikhnaton (q.v.), was a major, although unsuccessful, revolt staged against the conventions. The revolt was an outgrowth of Ikhnaton's naturalistic religion. The develop-

ment of Egyptian art is generally divided into four main periods: the Old Kingdom (3100–2242 B.C.); the Middle Kingdom (2242–1567 B.C.); the New Kingdom (1567–332 B.C.); and the Greco-Roman period (332 B.C.–about 300 A.D.).

Architecture The oldest stone structures are those built by the Egyptians. Wood was scarce, granite and limestone were abundant, and a peasant population provided a bountiful labor supply for some of the most despotic monarchies in history. Given these conditions, elaborate construction in stone was a logical development and was a major endeavor as early as the III Dynasty. Such construction began and remained as a corollary to religion, being limited throughout Egyptian history almost entirely to permanent abiding places for the dead, in tombs, and for the gods, in temples. Even royal palaces were usually made of mud brick, and stone was used only for details, such as thresholds.

Egyptian religious architecture had several definite characteristics. It was marked by a post-and-lintel style of construction. This style was simple but on an enormous scale, and the buildings were made of huge blocks piled one on another. Secondly, it was distinguished by use of

The statue of Ramses II overshadows that of his wife in the Temple of Amon at El Karnak, in central Egypt. One of the most notable builders of the New Kingdom, Ramses erected statues of himself in many parts of Egypt. **Luis Villota**

the column, which appeared in two major forms. One represented a palm tree with a crown of foliage as the capital. The other was a bundle of papyrus stalks with a capital in the form of a papyrus bud, a papyrus flower resembling an inverted bell, or a cluster of closed lotus buds. A third characteristic of Egyptian religious architecture was the use of the colonnade and the clerestory, which originated in Egypt. By raising the hypostyle roof (roof resting on columns) above the surrounding parts of the building and placing a stone lattice under it, Egyptian architects lighted a building without using windows. A fourth characteristic was the inward slope of the outer walls, a carry-over from the slope of mud-brick walls.

Old Kingdom builders concerned themselves chiefly with tombs, of which the pyramids (q.v.), or royal tombs, were the greatest achievement. The Egyptian sepulcher developed progressively from the predynastic heap of sand above a shallow grave to a rectangular stone structure, or mastaba, above a stone burial chamber. Eventually a still more splendid tomb for royalty was the step pyramid, achieved by piling mastaba on mastaba. In later tombs the steps were filled in, thus attaining the pure pyramidal form. The tomb pyramid was the center of an architectural group that included also a chapel adjoining the tomb, a covered causeway leading to it, and a valley temple. Numerous pyramids, in six groups, are clustered around Memphis (q.v.), the capital of the Old Kingdom. Three pyramids at Giza (q.v.) are the largest, and of these the greatest is that of Khufu (q.v.). The base of the Great Pyramid covers 13 acres and the structure was originally 480 ft. high.

Because isolated tombs in the desert attracted thieves, Middle Kingdom pharaohs and nomarchs (provincial rulers) began to have their tombs cut into rock or cliffs. Among the most famous of these rock-cut tombs are those of the nomarchs at Beni Hasan. Equally famous are the tombs found in the cliffs of the Valley of the Kings, near Thebes (q.v.); for example, the tomb of King Tutankhamen (q.v.). The entrances were concealed, and the pyramid chapel became a mortuary temple, constructed at some distance from the tomb itself. The temples became more and more elaborate. Architects began to embellish the buildings with intricate facades, porticoes, colonnaded interiors, and relief sculpture. A striking example of these monuments was the mortuary temple of Queen Hatshepsut (q.v.) at Deir el-Bahri. It rises in colonnaded terraces of white limestone from the plain to the cliff in which the tomb of the queen was hidden.

Under the dynasties of the New Kingdom, after the expulsion of the Hyksos (q.v.), structures of extraordinary size and splendor were built. The XVIII and XIX dynasties perfected the style of temple architecture which remained constant from that time until the decline of Egyptian culture. In this style, a road bordered by sphinxes (see SPHINX) led to a high-walled enclosure concealing the temple proper. The gateway to the enclosure was flanked by two massive pylons, in front of which often were placed obelisks or colossal statues. The gateway led to an open court lined with columns, which extended to the hypostyle hall, the foremost part of the sanctuary. Behind the hall was the inner sanctuary, an isolated shrine in a dark, colonnaded hall surrounded by small chapels. The unity of this simple plan was destroyed by later rulers, who made additions to such great temples as those at Luxor, El Karnak (qq.v.), and Philae. The Temple of Amon (q.v.) at El Karnak, the most monumental in Egypt, was built over a period of 2000 years, beginning in the Middle Kingdom and continuing to the 1st century B.C. The hypostyle hall of the temple, built during the XIX Dynasty, measures 170 ft. by 329 ft.; in the central nave stand 12 of the highest (70 ft.) columns in Egypt; the aisles are formed by 122 columns in 9 rows.

During the New Kingdom, surface decoration of monuments was full and varied. The columns and walls were covered with designs. The favorite form of decoration was extremely low relief or incised sculpture, brilliantly colored, and arranged in systematic series of panoramic pictures, according to an elaborate mythological or religious system (see *Sculpture,* below).

The greatest Egyptian builders were the pharaohs of the New Kingdom, notably Thutmose I, II, and III (*see under* THUTMOSE), Amenhotep II and III (*see under* AMENHOTEP), and Ramses II and III (*see under* RAMSES). After the Persian conquest no important buildings were erected until the Greco-Roman period, when a revival of the classic architectural forms produced such temples as that of the Egyptian divinity Horus (q.v.) at Idfu, the best-preserved example of temple architecture in Egypt.

Sculpture. Portraits and carvings in relief were two forms of Egyptian sculpture. Portraiture developed early and as an adjunct of religion. According to Egyptian religion, if the human body, although mummified, should perish, a statue as nearly identical as possible could serve for it in the afterlife. Old Kingdom sculptors were skilled in carving. They were able to work in extremely hard materials such as basalt and dio-

Egyptian Architecture and Art. Plate 1. *Above: Hieroglyphics from the tomb of Harmhab, an Egyptian ruler of the XIXth Dynasty. Below: A wall painting of a man plowing with oxen, found in Thebes.*

Above: Statue of Tutankhamen, Egyptian ruler of the XVIIIth Dynasty, whose tomb was discovered in 1922 in the Valley of the Kings, near Luxor. Below: Polychrome head of a funerary statuette dating from 2500 B.C., in the period of the Egyptian Old Kingdom.

Egyptian Architecture and Art. Plate 2

Wooden statuette of a walking man, dating from about 2300 B.C., in the period of the Egyptian Old Kingdom.

rite, used for a famous seated statue of Khafre, a IV Dynasty ruler. The head of the Great Sphinx of Giza is also a portrait of Khafre.

The sculptors of the Old Kingdom began the convention of designing all statues to be viewed from the front and so that a central axis divided them into two equal symmetrical parts. Some statues were given crystal eyes and were painted in flat, brilliant colors. Color was also occasionally used to add details, such as jewelry, not carved in the stone. When royalty was portrayed, the sculptor stylized his portrait to give an impression of majestic serenity rather than any sensitive characterization of his subject. Part of the stylization was due to the difficulty of working in extremely hard stone. Statues of people in the lower classes, however, tended to be more individualized, because softer materials were frequently used and because stylization for religious purposes was less necessary. Two of the most famous examples of this latter type are a IV Dynasty wooden figure now known as "Sheik el-Beled" (because it resembled the chief of the natives who helped in the excavation) and a seated V Dynasty figure, "The Scribe", in limestone painted red.

Old Kingdom reliefs were carved so low that they resemble painting more than sculpture. The conventions of relief sculpture are evident in these carvings, which covered the walls of tomb chapels and depicted scenes from everyday living, such as hunting and farming, in order to provide the dead with necessities and pleasures of life. The human figure was portrayed with the head and legs in profile and the trunk and eyes facing the observer. The carvers were gifted with extreme sensitivity to design, and the composition of every panel was balanced with the greatest of care. This attention to design and balance was an integral part of Egyptian art in general. Perspective was unknown; distance, for example, was expressed by placing the farther object on top of the nearer. Little attention was paid to visual reality, except for some animal figures, and the dominating outline was stylized and angular rather than freely curved.

With the development of temple architecture during the Middle and New Kingdoms, a type of colossal sculpture was created, as an integral part of the temple structure, and was used chiefly as embellishment for facades and interiors. Notable examples of these massive figures are the 65-ft.-high seated statues of Ramses II in front of his temple at Abu-Simbel (q.v.). These simple, stylized figures are impersonal portraits of the pharaoh they represent. As the temples

Ceramic figure of a hippopotamus with a lotus-blossom design, dating from the Middle Kingdom.

The head of Queen Nefertiti (left), in painted limestone, with eyes made of rock crystal. Nefertiti, the wife of Ikhnaton, lived in the 14th century B.C. During her husband's reign, sculptors were encouraged to turn away from the stiff, static tradition of Egyptian art, and her bust bears witness to the skill they achieved in lifelike representation. By contrast, the sculptured relief (below), from a temple of the XXX Dynasty, 4th century B.C., is rigid and conventional.

Egyptian Museum, Berlin

Metropolitan Museum of Art – Rogers Fund

Wall painting of the XVIII Dynasty (1567–1320 B.C.) showing fishermen and (right) a scribe.
Metropolitan Museum of Art

became more elaborate, reliefs were used to cover their walls. On the inside walls, carvings usually pictured the pharaoh worshipping the god. The outside carvings recorded the wars and hunts of the pharaoh.

The religious revolution of Ikhnaton, during the XVIII Dynasty, turned the attention of artists to nature and against the artificial convention, just as the pharaoh turned from conventional religion to a conception of the sun as the one great creator of nature. This naturalistic tendency of the Amarna school (from Tell el-Amarna, Ikhnaton's capital) is notably illustrated in two portrait heads, those of Ikhnaton and his wife, Nefertiti (fl. 14th cent. B.C.). The head of the pharaoh is a thorough characterization, rather than an abstract portrayal of majesty, and is almost effeminately delicate. The portrait of the beautiful Nefertiti, in painted limestone with rock-crystal eyes, is notable for its expression of grace and charm. Examples of an even more radical departure from tradition are the portrait heads of Ikhnaton, found at El Karnak, which are extremely naturalistic representations verging on caricature. The composition of reliefs of the Amarna school is vigorous, and although the human figures are conventionally distorted, the animals are carved with extraordinary freedom and vitality. In the tomb of Tutankhamen, who married one of Ikhnaton's daughters and was influenced by his father-in-law, was found a small statue with the head turned slightly, a startling departure from tradition. In the pursuit of his solar monotheism, Ikhnaton

defaced monuments sacred to other gods, causing the failure of his religious reform and resulting in a reaction in art and a return to strict convention, dictated by the priests. The traditional forms were thenceforth monotonously repeated, although statues and reliefs continued to be superbly decorative. The neoclassicism of the XXV and XXVI dynasties produced beautiful sculpture. These creations were imbued with a delicacy never permitted under the Old Kingdom. In the Middle Kingdom sculptors carved royal portrait statues remarkable for stylistic refinements. The sculpture of the Greco-Roman period was extremely decadent and often took the form of a tasteless combination of classic Roman and Egyptian styles.

Painting and Minor Arts. Painting was used chiefly as a subsidiary of or substitute for relief sculpture. During the Old Kingdom little painting was done, except to color statues and reliefs. Gradually, however, painting developed into a major form of artistic expression. During the Middle and New Kingdoms, particularly the XII to the XIX dynasties, elaborate murals depicting the world of the dead were extensively used as tomb decorations. One reason for this development may have been the difficulty of carving the rough surfaces of rock-cut tombs. Painted murals were subject to the same conventions as reliefs, except during the Amarna period, when naturalism and realism superseded the strict

393

Wall painting showing Apuy (second from left), a sculptor during the reign of Ramses II, and his wife receiving gifts. The two figures at the right, his son and daughter, are presenting bouquets. The painting is from Apuy's tomb at Thebes. Metropolitan Museum of Art

rules. Even the naturalistic painters, however, used orderly arrangements, and borders were used to set off the parts of a panel. The colors used in painting were also governed by rule. The artists painted in distemper and achieved contrast by using varied simple colors in brilliant tones rather than by showing differences of light and shade. Thus, Egyptian men were portrayed with red complexions, and women with yellow faces. The god Amon was usually blue. Mountains were represented by yellow with red spots, and bodies of water were signified by blue or green zigzag lines.

Egyptian potters never attained the distinction of many other Egyptian artists and craftsmen. Nonetheless, they did produce notable glazed pottery, particularly a brilliant blue-glazed faïence. Beads and tiles as well as vessels were made of glazed pottery, and the material was commonly used for ushabtis, small statues placed in tombs to do menial duties in the world beyond. Jewelry, an important part of the Egyptian costume, was highly developed and became lavish and intricate. Collar necklaces, breastplates, bracelets, and clasps were usually of gold and were inlaid with semiprecious stones or enamel. The jewelry and metalwork of the XII Dynasty are considered the most beautiful ever produced in Egypt, and European goldsmiths have rarely surpassed this work. By the time of the New Kingdom the use of gold was extremely lavish. Furniture and chariots were heavily encrusted with the metal, and the innermost coffin of Tutankhamen was solid gold.

The patterns used in pottery and metalwork were also traditional. Nature themes, such as the conventionalized lotus and papyrus, and religious symbols such as the sun and royal asp, were commonly used. The veneration of the scarab, or dung beetle, resulted in almost a separate craft dedicated to this insect. The image of the scarab in pottery was used as an amulet beginning late in the Old Kingdom. From the time of the XII Dynasty images of this insect were used primarily as seals, and were made of stone, pottery, or crystal, often set in rings or mountings of gold. R.H.

EGYPTIAN LANGUAGE AND LITERATURE, specifically, language and literature of ancient Egypt. The Egyptian language is Semitic in structure, although it has African characteristics. The main features of the language were contributed by the Asian nomads who invaded Egypt during the predynastic era; *see* EGYPT: *History.* Egyptian is a language with almost 5000 years of recorded use, from I-Dynasty inscriptions to Coptic writings (*see* Copts) of the 14th century A.D. Spoken and written Egyptian differed considerably. Most of the hieroglyphic inscriptions (*see* Hieroglyphics) on tombs, temples, pillars, and statues were written in a stilted style, and approximations of the living speech exist only in such documents as business records and letters.

Language. Spoken Egyptian developed in four stages. The language of the Old Kingdom (3100–2242 B.C.) persisted as a classical language, similar to modern usage of Latin or Greek, during almost all of ancient Egyptian history. A colloquial form of Old Egyptian was used for popular speech from the VI to the XVIII dynasties. Demotic, or popular, speech developed after the XVIII Dynasty and was used to the end of the Greco-Roman period. The last stage was Coptic, a combination of Egyptian and Greek, written in Greek characters.

Three forms of written Egyptian were developed: archaic hieroglyphics; hieratic, an abbreviated form of hieroglyphics; and demotic, a conventionalized and abbreviated form of hieratic. The signs used represented ideograms, determinatives, syllables of a word, or the most important single letters. The hieroglyphics were written either horizontally or vertically, according to the direction in which signs representing birds faced. Generally lines of hieroglyphics read from right to left.

The first modern attempt to solve the meaning of Egyptian hieroglyphics was made in the 17th century by a German Jesuit, Athanasius Kircher (1601–80). He was unsuccessful, as were all the Egyptologists after him until the discovery of the Rosetta Stone (q.v.), an inscription in three languages: old hieroglyphics, demotic Egyptian, and Greek. Several scholars contributed to the solution of the hieroglyphics in this inscription, particularly the British Egyptologist Thomas Young (q.v.). It was finally solved in 1822 by the French archeologist Jean François Champollion (q.v.), who discovered that the hieroglyphics spelling proper royal names were alphabetical signs. In the course of subsequent investigations, Champollion discovered the use of determinatives, or signs attached to words to specify their meanings, and ideograms, or pictorial symbols of words. A complete Egyptian grammar was developed on the basis of Champollion's work. In 1856 the French Egyptologist Vicomte Emmanuel de Rougé (1811–72) was able to read for the first time almost the complete text of a celebrated Egyptian poem concerning the exploits of the ancient Egyptian king Ramses II (*see under* Ramses) in his war with the Hittites (q.v.).

Literature. The oldest collection of Egyptian writings comprised religious inscriptions found on V- and VI-Dynasty pyramids and called, collectively, the Pyramid Texts or *Book of the Dead* (q.v.). Many of them were handed down from predynastic times. In addition to charms for the protection of the dead in the next world, the texts included myths, religious poems, and lyrically expressed philosophy. The secular literature of the Old Kingdom, a sterner period than those that followed it, included collections of aphorisms dealing with such matters as moderation, the treatment of inferiors, and submission

Hieroglyphs carved on a stela of the XXX Dynasty (4th century B.C.). Metropolitan Museum of Art

to authority. The most notable of these collections were those of the great viziers Imhotep (fl. 28th cent. B.C.) and Ptahhotep (fl. 25th cent. B.C.). The *Proverbs of Ptahhotep* was a particularly famous compilation and was used as a school text.

The classical age of Egyptian literature was during the Middle Kingdom (2242–1567 B.C.) in the XII Dynasty. A literature of entertainment was developed during this period. Writers pre-

epics, which were long and rhetorical, were inscribed on temple walls. The most celebrated of them is called the *Poem of Pentewere,* or *Pentaur* (the name of the scribe who copied it on papyrus), and relates the events of the battle of Ramses II against the Hittites, under the walls of the Syrian city of Kadesh. The most notable literary compilation of the New Kingdom is the *Book of the Dead,* an accumulation of advice and formulas written to help the dead attain

Hieroglyphic spelling of the word "Egypt".
Bettmann Archive

sented folk tales and stories of pure imagination in a rhetorical, formal manner which was regarded as the perfect style. These writings were immensely popular and included such tales as *The Shipwrecked Sailor,* the prototype of Sinbad in the *Arabian Nights* (q.v.). Another story, *The Tale of Sinuhe,* was so famous that it was placed in tombs to entertain the dead. *The Tale of the Eloquent Peasant* is significant because it deals with the injustice of the law to the lower classes. Some of this literature was written for a literate public of nobles and rich courtiers. The *Song of the Harper,* for example, was recited during banquets to remind the guests that life was brief and the passing hour should be enjoyed. Most of the literature of the period was written in poetic form. This literature, however, also includes pure poetry, such as love songs and hymns. The first known example of a poem in rigid strophe was a hymn to the king Sesostris III (fl. 19th cent. B.C.). A form of theater developed from the dramatic presentations during funeral ceremonies of the life and death of the god Osiris (q.v.).

These literary forms were continued during the New Kingdom (1567–332 B.C.) when writers composed such famous tales as *The Doomed Prince* and *The Two Brothers.* New Kingdom poetry includes some beautiful hymns to the sun god, written during the reign of Ikhnaton (q.v.), which are comparable in form and thought to the Biblical psalms. In addition to stories and lyric poetry, epic narrative was developed during this period, influenced, probably, by the position of Egypt as an empire. These

eternal life (*see* EGYPTIAN RELIGION). Many of the charms and texts included in the *Book of the Dead* originated in predynastic times, but the first definitive form of the book was made by priests of the New Kingdom.

Literary endeavor in ancient Egypt lost all vitality near the close of the New Kingdom. After the conquest of Egypt by Macedonia and, later, Rome, Egyptian literature and language were supplanted by the Greek literary style and language. The Greek alphabet was eventually adapted to native Egyptian dialects, resulting in Coptic. The Coptic literature, however, dealt almost wholly with Christian doctrine, notably in a collection entitled *Acts of the Saints.*   R.H.

EGYPTIAN RELIGION, specifically, the religion of ancient Egypt. The religious beliefs of the ancient Egyptians were the dominating influence in the development of their culture, although a true religion, in the sense of a unified theological system, never existed among them. The Egyptian faith was an unorganized collection of ancient myths, nature worship, and innumerable deities. The most influential and famous of these myths developed a divine hierarchy and explained the creation of the earth.

Origins in Myth and Nature. To begin with only the ocean existed. Then Ra, the sun, came out of an egg (a flower, in some versions) that appeared on the surface of the water. Ra brought forth four children, the gods Shu and Geb and the goddesses Tefnut and Nut. Shu and Tefnut became the atmosphere. They stood upon Geb, who became the earth, and raised up Nut, who became the sky. Ra ruled over all. Geb and Nut later had two sons, Set and Osiris (q.v.), and two daughters, Isis (q.v.) and Nephthys. Osiris succeeded Ra as king of the earth, helped by Isis, his sister-wife. Set, however, hated his brother and killed him. Then Isis embalmed her husband's body with the help of the god Anubis, who thus became the god of embalming. The powerful charms of Isis resurrected Osiris, who became king of the nether world, the land of the dead. Horus (q.v.), who was the son of Osiris and Isis, later defeated Set in a great battle and became king of the earth.

From this myth came the conception of the ennead, a group of nine divinities, and the triad, consisting of a divine father, mother, and son. Every local temple in Egypt possessed its own ennead and triad. The greatest ennead, however, was that of Ra and his children and grandchildren. This group was worshiped at Heliopolis (q.v.), the center of sun worship. The origin of the local deities is obscure. Some of them were taken over from foreign religions and some were originally the animal gods of prehistoric Africa. Gradually, they were all fused into the complicated religious structure. Comparatively few local divinities became important throughout Egypt. In addition to those already named, the important divinities included the male Amon, Thoth (qq.v.), Ptah, Khnemu, and Hapi, and the female Hathor, Mut, Neit, and Se-

khet. Their importance increased with the political ascendancy of the localities where they were worshiped. For example, the ennead of Memphis was headed by a triad composed of the father Ptah, the mother Sekhet, and the son Imhotep. Therefore, during the Memphite dynasties of the Old Kingdom (3100–2242 B.C.), Ptah became one of the greatest gods in Egypt. Similarly, when the Theban dynasties ruled Egypt most importance was given to the ennead of Thebes, headed by the father Amon, the mother Mut, and the son Khonsu. As the religion became more involved, true deities were sometimes confused with human beings who had been glorified after death. Thus Imhotep, who was originally the chief minister of the III Dynasty ruler Zoser (fl. 28th cent. B.C.), was later regarded as a demigod. During the V Dynasty the pharaohs began to claim divine ancestry and from that time on were worshiped as sons of Ra. Minor gods, some merely demons, were also given places in local divine hierarchies.

The gods were represented with human torsos and human or animal heads. Sometimes the animal or bird expressed the characteristics of the god. Ra, for example, had the head of a

A wall painting depicting the deceased and his wife plowing the fields of the blessed. From a tomb in Thebes (about 2000 B.C.). Metropolitan Museum of Art

Anubis, jackal-headed god of the dead, prepares a mummy, while the goddesses Isis and Nephthys mourn. From a tomb painting. Brian Brake-Rapho Guillumette

hawk, and the hawk was sacred to him because of its swift flight across the sky; Hathor, the goddess of love and laughter, was given the head of a cow, which was sacred to her; Anubis was given the head of a jackal because of the jackals which ravaged the desert graves in ancient times; Mut was vulture-headed and Thoth was ibis-headed; Ptah was given a human head, but he was occasionally represented as a bull, called Apis (q.v.). These sacred animals were venerated because of the gods to which they were attached, but they were never worshiped until the decadent XXVI Dynasty. The gods were also represented by symbols, such as the sun disk and hawk wings which were worn on the headdress of the pharaoh.

The only important god who was worshiped with consistency was Ra, chief of cosmic deities from whom early Egyptian kings claimed descent. Beginning with the Middle Kingdom

(2242–1567 B.C.), Ra worship acquired the status of a state religion, and the god was gradually fused with Amon, during the Theban dynasties, becoming the supreme god Amon-Ra. During the XVIII Dynasty the pharaoh Amenhotep III (*see under* AMENHOTEP) renamed the sun god Aton, an ancient term for the physical solar force. Amenhotep's son and successor, Amenhotep IV, instituted a revolution in Egyptian religion by proclaiming Aton the true and only god. He changed his own name to Ikhnaton (q.v.), meaning "Aton is satisfied". This first great monotheist was so iconoclastic that he had the plural word "gods" deleted from monuments, and he relentlessly persecuted the priests of Amon. Ikhnaton's sun religion failed to survive, although it exerted a great influence on the art and thinking of his time, and Egypt returned to the ancient, labyrinthine religion of polytheism after Ikhnaton's death.

Burial Ritual. The burial of the dead was of religious concern. Egyptian funerary rituals and equipment eventually became the most elaborate that the world has ever known. The Egyptians believed that the vital life force was composed of several psychical elements, of which the most important was the ka. The ka, a duplicate of the body, accompanied the body throughout life and, after death, departed from the body to take its place in the kingdom of the dead. The ka, however, could not exist without the body, and every effort had to be made, therefore, to preserve the corpse. Bodies were embalmed and mummified according to a traditional method supposedly begun by the mummification of the god Osiris by his wife Isis. In addition, replicas of the body in wood or stone were put into the tomb in the event that the mummy was destroyed. The greater the number of statue-duplicates in his tomb, the more chances the dead man had of resurrection. As a final protection, exceedingly elaborate tombs were erected to protect the corpse and its equipment. *See* EGYPTIAN ARCHITECTURE AND ART.

After leaving the tomb, the souls of the dead supposedly were beset by innumerable dangers, and the tombs were therefore furnished with a copy of the *Book of the Dead* (q.v.; *see also* EGYPTIAN LANGUAGE AND LITERATURE). Part of this book, a guide to the world of the dead, consisted of charms designed to overcome these dangers. After arriving in the kingdom of the dead, the ka was judged by Osiris, the king of the dead, and forty-two demon assistants. The *Book of the Dead* contained instructions for proper conduct before these judges. If the judges decided the dead man had been a sinner, his ka was condemned to hunger and thirst or to be torn to pieces by horrible executioners. If the decision was favorable, the ka went to the heavenly realm of the fields of Yaru, where grain grew 12 ft. high and existence was a glorified version of life on earth. All the necessities for this paradisiacal existence, from furniture to reading matter, were, therefore, put into tombs. As payment for the afterlife and his benevolent protection, Osiris required the dead to perform tasks for him, such as working in the grain fields. Even this duty could, however, be obviated by placing small statuettes, called ushabtis, into the tomb to serve as substitutes for the dead man when he was summoned to do menial duties. *See* EGYPTIAN ARCHEOLOGY; SUN WORSHIP. — R.H.

EHRENBURG, Ilya Grigoryevich (1891–1967), Russian novelist and journalist, born in Kiev. He spent most of his youth in Moscow, where the Russian writer Maksim Gorki (q.v.) was a frequent guest of the Ehrenburg family. Ilya at-

Ilya Grigoryevich Ehrenburg   UPI

tended the First Moscow Gymnasium, but was expelled in 1907 for leading a student strike. In 1908, after serving an eighteen-month prison term for illegal political activities, he left Russia and settled in Western Europe. He returned to Russia in 1917, but became so disillusioned by the excesses of the Russian Revolution and its aftermath that in 1921 he again left the country and remained abroad for two decades. During this period he lived mainly in Paris and was a notable correspondent for the Soviet newspaper *Izvestia,* for which he covered the events of the Spanish Civil War and the fall of Paris in World War II.

Ehrenburg was a prolific author; in addition to poetry and newspaper and magazine articles, he wrote more than two dozen novels. His writings brought him into frequent disfavor with the Soviet government. During the rule of the Soviet political leader Joseph Stalin (q.v.), Ehrenburg was an apologist for the Soviet regime. After the death of Stalin, however, Ehrenburg wrote *The Thaw* (1954), a novel critical of Stalinism. His first novel, *Extraordinary Adventures of Julio Jurenito and His Disciples* (1921), is considered by some critics to be his best. Among his other novels are *The Self Seeker* (1925), *A Street in Moscow* (1927), *The Fall of Paris* (1941), and *The Storm* (1947). Ehrenburg received two Stalin Prizes, one for each of the last two works.

EHRLICH, Paul (1854–1915), German bacteriologist, born in Strehlen (now Strzelin, Po-

Paul Ehrlich

land), and educated at the universities of Breslau, Strassbourg, Freiburg, and Leipzig. In 1890 he became professor at the University of Berlin, and a member of the newly formed Institution for Infectious Diseases. In 1896 he became director of the Royal Institute for Serum Research. Ehrlich conducted research on immunity and on the histology of blood, and later developed methods for staining nerve cells and the tuber-

cle bacillus. In 1909 he discovered Salvarsan, a chemical used with dramatic success in the treatment of syphilis (q.v.), and the first synthetic chemotherapeutic agent. In 1908 Ehrlich shared the Nobel Prize in medicine and physiology with the Russian bacteriologist Élie Metchnikoff (q.v.). *see* CHEMOTHERAPY.

EICHENDORFF, Baron Joseph von (1788–1857), German poet, born in Lubowitz (now Lubowice Raciborski, Poland), and educated at the universities of Halle and Heidelberg. He became a member of the religious Romanticist circle of the German critic and philosopher Friedrich von Schlegel (*see under* SCHLEGEL) and his wife. From 1813 until 1844, Eichendorff served the Prussian government, acting as councilor on Roman Catholic affairs in the ministry of public worship and education. Many of his lyrical poems were set to music by such composers as Robert Schumann (*see under* SCHUMANN) and Felix Mendelssohn (*see under* MENDELSSOHN). A number of his poems were translated into English in the collection *The Happy Wanderer and Other Poems* (1925). His other works include *From the Life of a Good-for-Nothing* (1826) and *A History of German Poetry* (1857).

EICHMANN, Karl Adolf. *See* ISRAEL: *History: Domestic Affairs in the Early 1960's*; WAR-CRIMES TRIALS: *Tokyo and Other Trials.*

EIDER *or* **EIDER DUCK,** common name for several large sea ducks of the genus *Somateria,* and of allied genera, in the family Anatidae. They inhabit the shores and rocky inlets of northern America, Europe, and Asia. The female eider lines her nest with soft gray down taken from her breast. After she lays her eggs, she also covers them with the down, thus helping to

American eider, Somateria mollissima

Arthur W. Ambler – National Audubon Society

The Eiffel Tower, seen from across the Seine River. French Government Tourist Office

protect them during the period of incubation. Eiderdown, which is light and warm, is used to fill quilts and pillows.

The American eider, *S. mollissima,* inhabits Europe and the northeastern part of North America. It is slightly less than 2 ft. in length. The female is pale brown, tinged red, and has transverse marks of dark brown. The male is similar in color when young, but after the spring of its third year, its underbody is colored black, and its upper surfaces are colored creamy white.

Other species in the same genus include the king eider, *S. spectabilis,* and the northern eider, *S. mollissima borealis.*

EIFFEL, Alexandre Gustave (1832–1923), French engineer, born in Dijon, and educated at the École Centrale. He constructed the iron bridge over the Garonne R. at Bordeaux in 1858, and the viaduct of Garabit in Cantal. He de-

signed the Eiffel Tower (q.v.) for which he received the Legion of Honor (q.v.). Eiffel also designed the locks for the unsuccessful French effort to build a canal across the isthmus of Panama (*see* PANAMA CANAL: *History*). His later investigations were in connection with aerodynamics. He was particularly interested in air resistance, and built a wind tunnel in which the effects of air currents from power fans could be studied on immovable models.

EIFFEL TOWER, skeleton iron tower, 934¼ ft. high, in the Champ de Mars in Paris, designed and built by the French engineer Alexandre Gustave Eiffel (q.v.). It was planned as a feature of the World's Fair held in Paris, May 6 to Nov. 6, 1889, and was completed on March 31 of that year. The lower section of the tower consists of four arched columns resting on masonry piers. Each of the four piers provides a supporting base 330 ft. square. The columns curve toward each other until they unite in a single column, 620 ft. above the ground. Platforms are at the 189-ft., the 380-ft., and the 906-ft. levels; on the first of these is a restaurant. The platforms, each with its own observation deck, are reached by staircases and elevators. In the construction of the tower about 7000 tons of iron were used. The cost was estimated to be more than $1,000,000. The French government provided $292,000 and the remainder was provided by Eiffel, who was reimbursed by the receipts from admission fees. The Eiffel Tower has played an important part in scientific research. At an early date it was utilized as a radio-broadcasting station. Daily time signals, under international agreements, are dispatched from the tower throughout the world. Near the top of the tower, where searchlights are mounted, are a meteorological observatory and physical and biological laboratories. The Eiffel Tower has become a great tourist attraction, as it affords a superb view of the city.

EIGEN, Manfred (1927–), German chemist, born in Bochum, and educated at Georg August University of Göttingen, at which Eigen taught physical chemistry from 1951 to 1953. In 1953 he became associated with the Max Planck Institute for Physical Chemistry in Göttingen; he was named director of the institute in 1964. Eigen shared the 1967 Nobel Prize in chemistry with the British chemists Ronald George Wreyford Norrish and George Porter (qq.v.) for their studies of high-speed chemical reactions. Eigen experimented with reactions occurring at speeds up to 1/10,000,000 of a second.

EIGHTEEN BENEDICTIONS. See PRAYER, JEWISH.

EIGHT-HOUR DAY. See HOURS OF LABOR.

EIJKMAN, Christiaan (1858–1930), Dutch physician, born in Nijkerk, and educated at the University of Amsterdam. Working (1886–97) on the island of Java, he found that fowl fed a diet consisting exclusively of polished rice developed polyneuritis, a disease closely resembling beriberi (q.v.) in man, but fowl fed unpolished rice remained healthy. Eijkman was able to conclude, on the basis of his research, that disease could be caused by depriving the body of certain essential, but unknown, substances, later defined as vitamins. Beriberi was later found to be caused by a deficiency of vitamin B_1, or thiamine. For his work in the field of nutrition, Eijkman was awarded the 1929 Nobel Prize for medicine and physiology jointly with the British biochemist Sir Frederick Cowland Hopkins (q.v.). See VITAMIN: Vitamin B Complex.

EINAUDI, Luigi (1874–1961), Italian economist and statesman, born in Carru, Cuneo Province, and educated at the University of Turin. In 1896 he began to write on economic subjects for a Turin daily newspaper, and by the early 1900's his articles were appearing in a number of influential publications in Great Britain and the United States, as well as in Italy. In 1900 he was appointed professor of economics and finance at the University of Turin. In 1919, having acquired an international reputation as an economist and educator, he was named a life member of the Italian senate. Einaudi opposed the regime of the fascist dictator Benito Mussolini (q.v.) and in 1943, he was forced to flee to Switzerland. Upon his return to Italy after World War II, Einaudi was appointed director of the Bank of Italy in 1945, served as a member of the Constituent Assembly in 1946–47, and held the posts of vice-premier and minister of the budget in the government of Premier Alcide De Gasperi (q.v.) in 1947–48. In May, 1948, the parliament elected him to a seven-year term as the first president of the Republic of Italy. See ITALY: History: Republic of Italy.

EINBECK, town of West Germany, in Lower Saxony State, on the Ilm R., 40 miles S. of Hanover. Since the 15th century the town has been noted for the brewing of Einbecker beer, from which the name bock beer is derived. Other industries of Einbeck are the manufacture of linen, carpets, beet sugar, chemicals, soap, and bicycles. Einbeck grew up around a cathedral chapel reputed to contain the blood of the Saviour and visited by throngs of pilgrims. From the 14th to the 16th centuries the town was the seat of the princes of Grubenhagen and later became a member of the Hanseatic League (q.v.). Because of its fortifications, the town assumed importance during the Seven Years' and Thirty Years' wars. In 1761 the fortifications were razed by the French. Pop. (1971) 18,906.

EINDHOVEN, city of the Netherlands, in North Brabant Province, on the Dommel R., 55 miles S.E. of Rotterdam. After the founding of an electrical industry in 1891, the city developed into a large industrial and railroad center. The electrical plant manufactures many different appliances and is the largest such plant outside the United States. Other industries include the manufacture of motor vehicles and tobacco products. Eindhoven was heavily bombed by the Allies during World War II. Pop. (1972) 189,209.

EINHARD or EGINHARD (770?–840), biographer of Charlemagne (q.v.), Holy Roman Emperor, born in the Main R. valley, and educated at the monastery in Fulda (now in West Germany). By 796 he was sent to the palace school at Charlemagne's court where he became a pupil and friend of the English scholar and ecclesiastic Alcuin (q.v.). Einhard found favor with the emperor, who appointed him superintendent of public buildings. Einhard was later appointed tutor to the emperor's grandson, Lothair I (*see under* LOTHAIR), and was given large estates. Einhard is noted for his *Life of Charlemagne,* the best primary source on the subject. His collected correspondence is also an important source for the history of the time.

EINSIEDELN ("Place of the Hermits"), town of Switzerland, in Schwyz Canton, on the Alpbach R., 2910 ft. above sea level, about 20 miles S.E. of Zürich. The town was originally the Benedictine abbey of Einsiedeln, which thousands of pilgrims have visited annually since the Middle Ages to worship before the statue of the Blessed Virgin, kept in the chapel of the abbey. The statue, to which miraculous powers have been ascribed, was donated by the Abbess Saint Hildegard (q.v.); *see* MIRACLE. Einsiedeln was originally under the protection of the counts of Rapperswil. The old pilgrims' way leads over Etzel Pass (3146 ft. above sea level) from Rapperswil on Lake Zürich. The monastery was destroyed or damaged by fire four times before the 17th century. The present buildings, dating from the early 18th century, are in the Italian style and are surrounded by walls. The monastery was plundered by French troops in 1798. Einsiedeln is the birthplace of the 16th-century physician Paracelsus (q.v.). Pop. (1970) 10,020.

EINSTEIN, Albert (1879–1955), German-born American theoretical physicist, born in Ulm, and educated at the Technische Hochschule in Zürich, Switzerland, and at the University of Zürich. His childhood was spent mainly in Munich, Germany, where his father had established an electrical business. In 1894, because of financial problems, Einstein's family emigrated from Germany to live with relatives in Milan, Italy. Later in the same year Einstein joined his family in Milan and within 6 months, taught himself calculus (q.v.) and other advanced subjects. He then went to Switzerland to continue his formal education. From 1896 to 1900 he attended the Technische Hochschule while supporting himself as a tutor of mathematics and physics. In 1902, after becoming a naturalized Swiss citizen, he secured a position as patent examiner with the Swiss Patent Office in Bern. During the next few years the modest financial security that this post provided enabled him to do research in his spare time and to obtain his doctorate.

Early Publications. In 1905 Einstein published three papers that revolutionized man's image of the physical universe and helped lay the foundation for the nuclear age. One of the papers, which appeared in the scientific journal *Annalen der Physik* ("The Physics Annals"), offered an explanation of the photoelectric effect, which concerns the emission of electrons from metal surfaces exposed to light. Theoretically, this study represented a cornerstone of the quantum theory (q.v.) and, practically, it made

Albert Einstein, a bust cast in bronze by Sir Jacob Epstein (1933).   Tate Gallery

possible many great inventions, including television and automation systems; *see* PHOTOELECTRIC CELL; QUANTUM MECHANICS. In another paper he analyzed mathematically the theory of the Brownian movement (q.v.) and provided a method for determining the dimensions of molecules. The third paper, his initial presentation of the special theory of relativity, described the relativistic nature of uniform motion and the interdependence of space and time; *see* RELATIVITY. One of the far-reaching conclusions of this paper postulated the equivalence of mass and energy (qq.v.), as expressed in his famous equation $E = mc^2$ in which energy equals mass times the velocity of light squared. The validity of the equation was dramatically demonstrated many years later by the enormous power released in atomic explosions; *see* ATOM AND ATOMIC THEORY; NUCLEAR ENERGY; NUCLEAR WEAPONS.

Major Works. In 1915 Einstein published his paper *General Theory of Relativity,* developing a revolutionary concept of gravitation (q.v.). This work, which vastly extended the scope of the special theory of relativity, held that the forces of gravity and of inertia are equivalent, and led to several astronomical predictions. Verification of the predictions was obtained following World War I, and Einstein's fame spread throughout the world. He was universally acclaimed as one of the great intellectual giants of all time.

In his theory of relativity, Einstein had achieved the unification of such concepts as space and time, mass and energy, and inertia and gravitation, each of which had been considered in classical physics as independent and absolute. The later years of his life were devoted to the development of the unified field theory (q.v.), a hypothesis combining the concepts of electromagnetic and gravitational fields of force; see ELECTROMAGNETIC RADIATIONS. In this theory he attempted to interrelate all the forces of the universe in one set of laws governing the behavior of nuclear particles as well as that of the stars. Einstein's long search for such a synthesis ended a few months before his death with the completion of a simplified set of formulas published posthumously in 1956; these formulas failed, however, to provide predictions that may be compared with the results of observations. His work on a unified field theory represented the affirmation of his philosophic belief in a well-ordered universe, in which individual events may be predicted according to immutable laws of cause and effect.

By 1909, while he was still employed as a patent examiner, his work had achieved such recognition in scientific circles that he was offered posts at several universities. After teaching successively at the University of Zürich, the German University of Prague, the Technische Hochschule in Zürich, and the University of Leiden in the Netherlands, he was appointed director of the Kaiser Wilhelm Institute of Physics in Berlin in 1913, and the next year was elected a member of the Prussian Academy of Science and provided with a yearly stipend so that he might devote himself exclusively to research. He refused, however, to resume German citizenship at that time and retained his Swiss nationality until after the establishment of the Weimar Republic in 1919.

When the German dictator Adolf Hitler (q.v.) came to power in 1933, Einstein was in Belgium on a lecture tour. Because he was Jewish and because of his outspoken stand against National Socialism (q.v.), the German government instituted many reprisals against him in his absence. He was expelled from the Prussian Academy of Science, his citizenship was revoked, his property confiscated, and a price was set upon his head. Many nations offered Einstein refuge. After spending a few months in seclusion in England, he went to the United States and became a naturalized American citizen in 1940. In 1933, he was appointed a life member of the Institute for Advanced Study at Princeton, N.J. He served as professor of theoretical physics and head of the mathematics department until 1945, when he became professor emeritus.

A Leader in Science. The greatest scientist of his time, Einstein was a man with a profound sense of social responsibility. He was a humanitarian who believed passionately in social justice and who often championed unpopular causes which he deemed worthy of his support. Although a confirmed pacifist, he was responsible for initiating the U.S. atomic-bomb project. Fearing that the National Socialists would achieve world domination if they developed an atomic weapon first, he wrote a letter to President Franklin Delano Roosevelt (q.v.) in August, 1939, urging the U.S. to undertake nuclear research urgently. Following World War II, he attempted to arouse the world to the dangers of atomic warfare and devoted much energy to the promotion of world peace, which he believed attainable only through total disarmament (q.v.) and some form of world government. Einstein was an ardent supporter of the effort to establish a homeland for the Jewish people and in 1952 was invited by the Israeli government to succeed the Russian-born chemist and Zionist leader Chaim Weizmann as president of Israel (qq.v.), but he declined; see ZIONISM.

Honorary degrees were conferred upon Einstein by many universities, including Oxford and Cambridge in England; Harvard and Princeton in the United States; Geneva, Switzerland; Paris, France; and Brussels, Belgium. In 1921 he was awarded the Nobel Prize in physics for his work on the photoelectric effect and he received a number of other awards including the Copley Medal of the Royal Society (1925), the Gold Medal of the Royal Astronomical Society (1926), and the Franklin Institute Gold Medal (1935). His writings include *The Meaning of Relativity* (1923); *Investigation on the Theory of the Brownian Movement* (1926); *About Zionism* (1931); *Builders of the Universe* (1932); *Why War?* (1933), with the Austrian physician Sigmund Freud (q.v.); *The World As I See It* (1934); *Evolution of Physics* (1938), with the Polish physicist Leopold Infeld (1898–1968); and *Out of My Later Years* (1950).   G.G. & L.A.Bo.

EINSTEINIUM, radioactive, transuranic element with at.no. 99, at.wt. 254, and symbol Es. The element, named in honor of the American scientist Albert Einstein (q.v.), was discovered in 1952 in the debris produced by a thermonuclear explosion; *see* NUCLEAR ENERGY. The isotope first identified had an atomic mass of 253 and a half-life of 20 days. Subsequently, a relatively long-lived isotope, einsteinium-254, was prepared synthetically. Einsteinium is available only in trace quantities, although small amounts are now being produced by reactor irradiation. No practical applications of the element are foreseen. *See* TRANSURANIUM ELEMENTS.

EINTHOVEN, Willem (1860–1927), Dutch physiologist, born in Samarang, Java, and educated at the University of Utrecht. He became professor of physiology at the University of Leiden in 1886, serving in that capacity until his death. For his discovery of the principle of the electrocardiograph, he was awarded the Nobel Prize in medicine and physiology in 1924; *see* HEART: *Heart Diseases*. He wrote extensively for scientific journals.

EIRE. *See* IRELAND, REPUBLIC OF.

EISENACH, city of East Germany, in Erfurt District, at the junction of the Nesse and Hörsel rivers, about 32 mi. by rail w. of Erfurt. Industries include worsted spinning, woodworking and cabinetmaking, brewing, granite quarrying, lumbering, and the manufacture of pigments, pottery, alabaster ware, and shoes. The city is noted as a summer resort. A commanding position above the city is occupied by the Wartburg, the 11th-century castle of the landgraves of Thuringia. In 1207 the landgrave Hermann I (d. 1217) presided there over the *Sängerkrieg,* or "minstrels' contest", upon which the German composer Richard Wagner (q.v.) based his opera *Tannhäuser.* The German religious reformer Martin Luther (q.v.), in 1521, worked on his translation of the Bible in one of the castle rooms. In the city are the Lutherhaus, in which the reformer took refuge in 1498, and the house in which the German composer Johann Sebastian Bach (q.v.) was born. One of Eisnach's schools, the Gymnasium, was attended by Luther and Bach, and now contains a Wagner museum and the museum of Thuringia. Other notable buildings include the former ducal palace of the Duchess Hélène of Orléans, built in 1742; the late-Gothic Saint George's Church, which contains a statue of Bach; St. Nicholas' Church, dating from the 12th century; and the Klemda, a small castle dating from 1260.

Eisenach was founded in 1070 near the older town of Isenach or Isenacum. The district of Eisenach was a principality until it was partitioned in 1498, and was a Saxon duchy at various times between 1596 and 1741. After World War II, it was included in the Soviet occupation zone of Germany. Pop. (1972) 50,674.

EISENHOWER, Dwight David (1890–1969), American army officer and thirty-fourth President of the United States, born in Denison, Texas, where his father worked as a mechanic in the railroad shops. Two years after Eisenhower's birth the family moved to a small farm in Abilene, Kans., where the future general and President spent most of his boyhood and youth. He entered the United States Military Academy at West Point, N.Y., in 1911 and gained recognition as an outstanding athlete before graduation. He married Mamie Geneva Doud (1896–   ) in 1916 and they had two sons. One died in childhood; the other, John Sheldon Doud Eisenhower (1922–   ), later followed a professional Army career. He was appointed ambassador to Belgium in 1969.

During World War I and between the two world wars Eisenhower served in the United

Dapper in his lieutenant's uniform, a youthful Dwight David Eisenhower poses with his bride, the former Mamie Doud, in 1916. **Gallery of Modern Art**

Above: Toasting the Allied victory in Europe in 1945 are, left to right, Field Marshal Sir Bernard L. Montgomery, General Dwight D. Eisenhower, Soviet Marshal Georgi K. Zhukov, and British Air Chief Marshal Sir Arthur Tedder and an unindentified officer. Below: President Eisenhower's public appearances always drew large and enthusiastic crowds. He is pictured surrounded by admirers in Cleveland, Ohio. UPI

States Army in a variety of staff positions. He held the temporary rank of brigadier general at the beginning of World War II. With the rank of full general in 1943, Eisenhower became Supreme Commander of the Allied forces in Europe, and directed the invasions of Sicily, Italy, Normandy, and Germany; see WORLD WAR II: *The European War.* After serving as chief of the general staff, he resigned in 1948 to become president of Columbia University. At the request of President Harry S. Truman (q.v.) he subsequently returned to Europe to accept the command of the armed forces of the North Atlantic Treaty Organization (q.v.), known as NATO.

As a soldier and war hero, the general, popularly called "Ike", had never expressed any political interests. In 1952, however, his supporters in the Republican Party (q.v.) nominated Eisenhower for President after defeating the more conservative wing of the party that preferred Senator Robert Alphonso Taft (q.v.) of Ohio. With Richard Milhous Nixon (q.v.), then Senator of California, as his running mate, Eisenhower won 33,936,234 votes against 27,314,992 for his Democratic opponent, Adlai Ewing Stevenson, Governor of Illinois (*see under* STEVENSON). In the 1956 Presidential election Eisenhower received 35,590,472 votes, and Stevenson 26,022,752 votes.

As President, Eisenhower selected advisors from the leaders of American business and industry. Describing himself as "an economic conservative and a social progressive", he pledged to reduce governmental interference in the economic life of the country and to encourage programs designed to achieve equal opportunity for all individuals. A notable event of his first term was the 1954 decision of the Supreme Court of the United States (q.v.), declaring segregation in public schools unconstitutional; see INTEGRATION. In 1957 Eisenhower, acting on this decision, sent Federal troops to enforce a court order calling for integration of a high school in Little Rock, Ark. A bill creating a U.S. Commission on Civil Rights was signed by the President in 1957; see CIVIL RIGHTS AND CIVIL LIBERTIES. Controversy over the investigative procedures of Senator Joseph Raymond McCarthy (q.v.) of Wisconsin also marked the first term of Eisenhower's administration. When a period of financial recession occurred in 1957, Eisenhower asserted his leadership to win from Congress a series of measures calculated to stimulate business and industrial activity. These measures included a tax cut, lower credit rates, a program of space exploration (*see* ASTRONAUTICS: *Space Ex-*

President Eisenhower and his successor, President John F. Kennedy, take a pensive stroll at Camp David, Maryland (1962). 	Gallery of Modern Art

ploration), extended foreign aid, increased welfare coverage under Social Security laws, and major appropriations for highway construction.

In foreign affairs, Eisenhower redeemed his 1952 campaign pledge to "go to Korea" with a view to settling the Korean War (q.v.). A truce was arranged in 1953. Acting on the advice of his secretary of state, John Foster Dulles (*see under* DULLES), Eisenhower sent United States Marines to Lebanon (q.v.) in 1958 to prevent possible Communist aggression, and he guaranteed the security of Formosa against threats from Communist China; see FORMOSA: *History.* After the French withdrew from Indochina, Eisenhower supported the government of South

Vietnam against Communist insurgents (see VIETNAM: *History*), but he refused to commit large numbers of combat troops to Southeast Asia. Several meetings with leaders of the Soviet Union were climaxed by the visit of the Soviet premier Nikita S(ergeyevich) Khrushchev (q.v.) to the U.S. in 1959. In 1961 Eisenhower delivered his last Presidential address, urging Americans to "guard against the acquisition of unwarranted influence" by forces that he called the "military-industrial complex". He warned that this combination of interests in modern American life represented a "potential for the disastrous rise of misplaced power" that could threaten "our liberties or democratic processes". See UNITED STATES OF AMERICA: *History: Administrations of the 1950's and 1960's.*

In his retirement at Gettysburg, Pa., Eisenhower was frequently consulted by Presidents John Fitzgerald Kennedy and Lyndon Baines Johnson (qq.v.). As a leader in war and peace, he had suffered six heart attacks, two of them while serving as the nation's Chief Executive, before a fatal attack on March 28, 1969, at the age of seventy-eight. As are all Chief Executives, he was given a State funeral and was interred at the Eisenhower Center, Abilene, Kans., on April 2, 1969.

Throughout his career Eisenhower refused to exploit his personal assets for political advantage. He was often irritated by problems of patronage, and his legislative achievements usually resulted from the efforts of the moderates of both parties rather than from the work of the Republicans alone. With his unique gift for promoting compromise in difficult human relationships, "Ike" generated trust, goodwill, and a sense of security. He was among the most popular of American Presidents.

EISENHOWER, Milton Stover (1899–), American educator and public official, brother of President Dwight D. Eisenhower (q.v.), born in Abilene, Kans., and educated at Kansas State College of Agriculture and Applied Science (now Kansas State University of Agriculture and Applied Science). After serving from 1924 to 1926 as United States vice-consul at Edinburgh, Scotland, he joined the U.S. Department of Agriculture, first as special assistant to the secretary and later as director of information. Between 1941 and 1943 he held positions in several war agencies of the U.S. government. Later in 1943 he began his career as an academic administrator as president of Kansas State College. From 1950 to 1956 he was president of Pennsylvania State College (after 1953, Pennsylvania State University); and in 1956 he became president of

Johns Hopkins University, of which he was named president emeritus in 1967. Eisenhower served on diplomatic and investigative commissions under five successive Presidents of the United States, beginning with Harry S. Truman (q.v.). In 1968 and 1969 he was chairman of the National Commission on Causes and Prevention of Violence, which in its final report urged a reordering of national priorities and the diversion of Federal funds from defense to domestic spending to combat the "rising tide of individual violence".

EISENSTEIN, Sergei Mikhailovich (1898–1948), Russian stage and motion-picture director whose creative film-editing techniques and writings on film theory earned him lasting worldwide repute as a master of montage and the use of symbols.

Eisenstein, born Jan. 23, 1898, in Riga (now in the Latvian S.S.R.), studied engineering at the Petrograd Institute of Civil Engineering from 1915 to 1918, when he enlisted in the army. His army experience with an amateur theater group contributed to his decision to pursue a theatrical rather than an engineering career. About 1920 he became a scene designer at the experimental Proletkult Theatre; this experience inspired him to study at the State School for Stage Direction, and soon he began to direct Proletkult productions. His unconventional ideas on dramatic art included contrasting images to stir an emotional reaction in the audience.

Eisenstein made his first full-length motion picture, *Strike*, with the Proletkult collective in 1924. A well-known sequence in this film, depicting the struggle of striking workers, contains scenes of cattle being slaughtered intercut with scenes of workers being shot by government soldiers. His next film, *Potemkin*, completed in 1925, is considered a silent-film masterpiece. Commissioned by the Soviet government to commemorate the 1905 revolution, Eisenstein produced one of the most famous sequences in silent films. Using a long flight of steps in Odessa as his setting, the director intercut detail shots with action scenes: close-ups of guns and faces contrast with scenes of fleeing civilians and attacking soldiers. His skill in creating powerful impact by manipulating visual composition was widely heralded after *Potemkin*.

Eisenstein's other notable films are *Ten Days That Shook the World* (1927); the abandoned project *Que Viva Mexico!* (1931), which was reedited and released first as *Thunder Over Mexico* (1933) and later as *A Time in the Sun* (1939); *Alexander Nevsky* (1938); *Ivan The Terrible*, Part I (1944); and *Ivan The Terrible*, Part II,

A scene from the motion picture Potemkin, directed by Sergei M. Eisenstein.
Museum of Modern Art

completed in 1946 and released (only outside the U.S.S.R.) in 1958. He was about to begin work on the third part of *Ivan* when he died in Moscow on Feb. 11, 1948. Eisenstein's passion for and understanding of the potentialities of film made him one of the greatest innovators in the history of cinema.

His published writings, widely read by film students, are *Film Sense* (1942), *Film Form* (1949), *Notes of a Film Director* (1958), and *Film Essays* (1968).

EISTEDDFOD (Welsh, "a sitting of learned men"), national music and literary festival held annually in Wales to promote Welsh language, literature, music, and customs. The week-long ceremony is a revival of the ancient Welsh custom of assembling bards for competition among themselves, for the regulation of poetry and music, and for the licensing of duly qualified candidates to the position of recognized bards or minstrels. The Gorsedd, or assembly, now occurs on the second day (Tuesday) of the festival to confer degrees of four grades upon the modern equivalent of the Welsh bards. The history of Eisteddfod antedates the Christian era.

EL AAIÚN, or EL AIÚM, town and capital of Western Sahara (formerly the overseas Province of Spanish Sahara), and capital of El Aaiún District, located on the Saguia el Hamra R., about 30

miles E. of its mouth on the Atlantic Ocean, and about 550 miles S.W. of Casablanca. The town is an artificially constructed, irrigated oasis that grows grains and vegetables. Fish are caught off the developing port area, and phosphate deposits have been discovered to the S. El Aaiún is the site of a museum of Saharan culture. The modern town, which was built in 1938, remained under Spanish control until Dec. 11, 1975, when it was occupied by Moroccan troops; the last of the Spanish forces withdrew on Dec. 20. The town's name is also spelled El Aiún. Pop. (1971 est.) 25,500.

ELAGABALUS. See ROME, HISTORY OF: *The Empire: Decline and Fall (193–476)*.

ELAM (Elamitic *Haltamtu*; Persian *Huwaja*; Gr. *Susiana* or *Elymais*; Sum. and Heb. *Elam*), kingdom of ancient Asia, situated N. of the Persian Gulf and E. of the Tigris R., and corresponding approximately to the present-day province of Khuzistan, Iran. The capital of Elam was Susa, today the city of Shush. Other leading cities included Awan, Simash, Madaktu, and Dur-Untash, the site of present-day Tchoga-Zembil, Iran. During various periods of Elamite history the rulers entitled themselves "kings of Anshan and Shushan"; the exact location of Anshan, a district of the kingdom, is not certain.

The site of one of the earliest civilizations,

Elam dates back to the 6th millennium B.C. The inhabitants, known as the Elamites, spoke an agglutinative language unrelated to the Sumerian, Semitic, or Indo-European languages. After 3000 B.C. the Elamites, under the influence of the system of writing developed by the neighboring Sumerians, began to record their language in a native semi-pictographic script known as Proto-Elamite. About 2200 B.C. this script was replaced by the cuneiform (q.v.) of the Sumerians and Akkadians.

From early times Elam influenced greatly the politics of neighboring Mesopotamia. The Elamites destroyed the city of Ur about 1950 B.C.; *see* SUMER. Subsequently they exerted considerable influence on the rulers of Babylonia (q.v.). After the capture in 1550 B.C. of Babylonia by the Kassites (q.v.); however, the country suffered a political decline which persisted for about 350 years.

Elam experienced a political revival under King Shutruk-Nahhunte I (r. about 1200 B.C.), who conquered Babylonia, deposed the Kassite dynasty, and placed his son on the throne. King Shilhak-Inshushinak (r. 1154–1140 B.C.), a great administrator and patron of art and learning, created the first Elamite empire. Under his rule the borders were greatly extended, the literary use of the Elamite language was revived, and an architectural and sculptural renaissance took place. Shortly after his death Elam was conquered by the Babylonian king Nebuchadnezzar I. A new Elamite kingdom appeared about the middle of the 8th century, but it was subjected to constant attacks by Assyria. About 635 B.C. the

Assyrians, under the leadership of Ashurbanipal, sacked Susa and annexed the country. Subsequently Elam was overrun by Media (q.v.). Under the Persian king Cyrus the Great, it was incorporated into the Persian Empire.

The native language of Elam was used for administrative purposes until about the 4th century B.C.; thereafter it probably was used only as a spoken vernacular. According to Arabic writings the Elamite language continued to be spoken in what is now Khuzistan until about the 10th century A.D.

See separate articles on many of the persons and places mentioned.   S.N.K.

ELAND, common name for either of two African antelopes comprising the genus *Taurotragus,* the largest of all true antelopes. The species *T. oryx* has smooth, short hair when young, later developing a broad, deep-fringed dewlap extending to the knees. Its strong horns, which rise straight upward, are about 28 in. long in large bulls, and a little longer, but more slender, in cows. The other, larger species, *T. derbianus,* attains a height of about 6 ft. and a weight of about 1500 lb.

ELASTICITY, property of a material that causes it to resume its original size and shape after having been compressed or stretched by an external force. In science and in common language, terms such as stiffness, tensile strength, and resilience are often used to describe elasticity. The applied force creates stress within the material, expressed as units of force per unit area, and causes a deformation called strain.

Stress and strain are determined by the molecular structure of the material (*see* MOLECULE).

A herd of South African eland, Taurotragus oryx.
South African Tourist Corp.

The distance between molecules in a stress-free material depends on a balance between molecular forces of attraction and repulsion. When an external force is applied, the molecular distances change and the material becomes deformed. The shift in molecular spacing causes stress within the material. The stress force is usually equal and opposite to the applied force. When the force is removed, the molecules return to their balanced position, and the elastic material regains its original shape.

If an applied force separates the molecules to the extent that they are unable to return to their original positions, the material is permanently deformed or broken apart. This maximum amount of elastic deformation is the elastic limit of the material. Below the elastic limit, stress is directly proportional to strain. This relation is known as Hooke's law, after the British physicist Robert Hooke (q.v.), who first expressed it. Rubber, which is commonly considered an elastic substance, does not follow Hooke's law because it differs molecularly from ordinary solids.

The various types of stress-strain deformation are called the elastic moduli of a material. Young's modulus is a ratio of deformation in length; the shear modulus is a ratio of lateral displacement or shear; and the bulk modulus is a ratio of compressibility of volume. The bulk modulus can be applied to liquids and gases as a measure of compressibility.

ELASTOMER. See CHEMICAL COMPOUNDS, SYNTHETIC: *Plastics and Elastomers;* RUBBER, SYNTHETIC.

ELATH. See ISRAEL; NEGEV.

ELBA (anc. *Ilva* or *Aethalia*), mountainous island of Italy, in the Mediterranean Sea, forming part of Livorno Province, 7 miles S.W. of the mainland port of Piombino and about 35 miles E. of Corsica. Elba is 18 mi. long from E. to W. and from 3 to 10 mi. wide; it forms part of a sunken mountain range that extends S.W. from the Italian mainland to the island of Sardinia. The highest point is Monte Capanne, 3340 ft. above sea level. The climate is mild and the soil is fertile, but other than the growing of a small amount of fruit and wine grapes, farming is neglected because of rich mineral deposits. Since ancient times Elba has been famous for iron ore deposits. The chief city is Portoferraio, or "iron port", home of about half the island's residents. Other mineral deposits are tin, copper, lead ores, granite, sandstone, and marble. Most of the inhabitants of the island are employed in the mining industry. The extraction of sea salt, fishing, and winemaking are other industries.

Elba is chiefly known as the residence of Napoleon I (q.v.), Emperor of France, after his first abdication, from May 4, 1814, to Feb. 26, 1815, when he escaped and returned to France. He enjoyed full sovereignty over the island, with the title of emperor and an income of 2,000,000 francs a year. During his stay he had the road built connecting Portoferraio with the town of Porto Longone. The villa San Martino that he occupied still stands, 4 miles S.W. of Portoferraio, between the forts Stella and Falcone, erected by Cosimo I de' Medici (*see under* MEDICI). Elba had been given to France in 1802; after Napoleon escaped from the island, it was restored to Tuscany, which became part of Italy in 1860. Area, 86 sq.mi.; pop. (1971 prelim.) 26,830.

ELBASAN, or ELBASANI, city in Albania, and capital of Elbasan District, on the Shkumbi R., 20 miles S.E. of Tiranë. The city is the terminus of a railroad to Durrës (q.v.) and a market center for the area, which grows tobacco, olives, fruit, grapes, cotton, grains, and vegetables. Industries include production of olive oil, wine, cigarettes, leather, textiles, flour, and handicrafts. A 15th-century fortress in Elbasan contains a museum of antiquities. The present city was built by the Turks in 1466 on the site of ancient Scampa, on the Via Egnatia. Pop. (1970 est.) 41,700.

ELBE, river of Czechoslovakia and Germany, one of the chief rivers of central Europe. It is 706 mi. long and rises at about 4600 ft. in N.W. Czechoslovakia. Flowing generally N.W., the Elbe courses through the central part of East Germany and constitutes about 150 mi. of the frontier between East Germany and West Germany. The river continues N.W. through West Germany until it empties into the North Sea at Cuxhaven. Major cities along the Elbe include Ústí nad Labem, Czechoslovakia; Dresden, East Germany; and Hamburg, West Germany. Among the chief tributaries of the Elbe are the Vltava R., Czechoslovakia, and the Saale R., East Germany; it is connected by canals with the Oder R. in Czechoslovakia and with the Rhine and Weser rivers in West Germany. More than 500 mi. of the Elbe, from the North Sea to Prague, Czechoslovakia, are navigable, and the river has been an important commercial route since the 13th century. On April 27, 1945, at the close of World War II (q.v.), American and Soviet forces converged at Torgau (now in East Germany) on the Elbe R.

ELBLĄG (Ger. *Elbing*), city and port of Poland, capital of Elbląg Province, about 40 miles S.E. of Gdansk. It is on the Elbląg R., which empties into Frisches Haff, an inlet of the Baltic Sea. A canal connects Elbląg with the E. arm of the Vistula R. The city is an industrial center; manufactures include locomotives, machinery, metal goods, textiles, and cigars. Before World War II the city was a part of East Prussia, Germany. Soviet troops captured Elbląg in February, 1945; in the same year the Potsdam Agreement (*see* POTSDAM CONFERENCE) ceded part of East Prussia including Elbląg to Poland. Pop. (1971 est.) 90,800.

EL'BRUS *or* **ELBRUZ,** mountain in the Soviet Union, the highest summit of the Caucasus Mountains, and the highest peak in Europe. It is an extinct volcano with two craters and reaches a height of 18,481 ft. above sea level. El'brus is in the N.W. part of the Georgian S.S.R.

ELBURZ RANGE, mountain range in N. Iran, extending S.E. from the border between Iran and the Soviet Union and along the shores of the Caspian Sea. The range marks the limit of the Iranian Plateau. The Elburz has an average altitude of about 5000 ft. The highest peak, Demavend, is 18,376 ft. above sea level.

EL CAJON, suburban residential city of California, in San Diego Co., on El Cajon Creek in the Cajon Valley, 12 miles E. of San Diego. The surrounding region produces citrus fruits, grapes, avocados, and vegetables. Industries in the city include fruit and vegetable packing and the manufacture of automobile, aircraft, and missile parts; dairy products; business machines; and metal, lumber, and wood products. El Cajon is the site of Grossmont College. Nearby, to the s.w., is Mt. Helix, which has an amphitheater, famous for Easter sunrise services, that affords an excellent view of the San Diego area. The site of the city was originally a part of the El Cajon Rancho. The land was opened for settlement in 1869, and the city was incorporated in 1912. Pop. (1960) 37,618; (1970) 52,273.

EL CANO, Juan Sebastián de. *See* CANO, JUAN SEBASTIÁN DEL.

EL CENTRO, city in California, and county seat of Imperial Co., in the Imperial Valley (q.v.), about 150 miles S.E. of Los Angeles, and 10 miles N. of the Mexican border. The city, which is 49 ft. below sea level, is the center of a fertile agricultural region that was desert until, by irrigation from the Colorado R., it was converted into one of the most important fruit and vegetable-growing sections of the United States. Food processing and the production of gypsum are the principal industries. The city was settled in 1906 and incorporated in 1907. Pop. (1960) 16,811; (1970) 19,272.

EL CERRITO, suburban residential city of California, in Contra Costa Co., on the w. slopes of the Berkeley Hills, on Cerrito Creek, adjoining Richmond and 8 miles N. of Oakland. Industries include production of instruments and business machines, furniture, asphalt, metal and clay products, and quarrying and construction equipment. Settled in 1823 and called Cerrito de San Antonio, the city developed after the Rancho San Pablo was subdivided. It was then named County Line and was later renamed Rust; in 1917 the city was incorporated as El Cerrito. Pop. (1960) 25,437; (1970) 25,190.

ELCHE (anc. *Ilici*), town of Spain, in Alicante Province, 16 miles s.w. of the city of Alicante and about 4 miles E. of the Mediterranean Sea. Dates, olives, cereal grains, and pomegranates are cultivated; and woolens, brandy, wine, and olive oil are manufactured. The city's Iberian origin is indicated by the "Lady of Elche", a painted bust of the 5th century B.C. Elche, occupied by Carthaginians, Greeks, and Romans, was made an episcopal see by the Goths. It lost importance during the Moorish period, but retains much of its Moorish architectural character. Pop. (1970) 122,663.

ELDER, *or* ELDERBERRY, common name for trees or shrubs of the genus *Sambucus* of the Honeysuckle family (Caprifoliaceae). About twenty species occur in widely distributed areas. The common elder of Europe, *S. nigra,*

Red-berried elder, Sambucus pubens

grows to 30 ft. in height and is sometimes cultivated in North America. It has large compound leaves, dense flat clusters of cream-colored flowers, and, later, black berries. The American or sweet elder, *S. canadensis,* common along roads and in neglected meadows in the United States, resembles *S. nigra,* except that it has white flowers and purplish-black berries. Its thick, soft stems break easily and are filled with a white, cottony pith. The red-berried elder, *S. pubens,* another species found in the U.S., is noted for its vivid scarlet fruit. Other species are generally similar, with variation in size, flower color, and color of the berries. Some elder are cultivated as hedge shrubs.

The berries of many elder are used for making wines and jellies. The plants themselves, however, and especially the roots, contain active principles that produce severe purging if eaten. Children have been poisoned by using blowguns that they have fashioned from the stems. Animals usually avoid elder.

ELDER, title given to officers in certain churches. The term has had various meanings. In the Old Testament, an elder was a tribal or family head, usually somewhat older than other men of the society; *see also* PATRIARCHY. The Israelite elders were officials of civil and religious government; the lay members of the later Sanhedrin (q.v.) were also termed elders. In the early Christian Church, elders were administrative officials of local congregations, who served along with deacons and bishops; *see also* BISHOP. The title is retained in some modern denominations, notably the Church of Jesus Christ of Latter-day Saints.

See also MORMONS.

EL DORADO, city in Arkansas, and county seat of Union Co., about 110 miles S.E. of Little Rock, and 15 miles N. of the Louisiana boundary. It is served by several railroads. El Dorado is the headquarters of the State oil industry and the trade center for the surrounding agricultural area. Extensive petroleum deposits, discovered in 1921, are nearby, and the city has large oil refineries. El Dorado was settled in 1843 and was incorporated in 1870. Pop. (1960) 25,292; (1970) 25,283.

EL DORADO, city in Kansas, and county seat of Butler Co., on the Walnut R., about 30 miles N.E. of Wichita. The city, surrounded by a livestock, grain, and oil-producing region, is a refining and shipping center for oil, and manufactures oil-field equipment. It is the site of Butler County Community Junior College, founded in 1927. Pop. (1960) 12,523; (1970) 12,308.

EL DORADO (Sp. "The Gilded One"), term applied in the New World by the 16th-century Spanish to the legendary chief of an Indian tribe said to inhabit an area in the northern part of South America. In Indian folklore, the chief was enormously wealthy. At yearly festivals he would cover his entire body with gold dust. The term came to be applied also to his city or country, supposedly abounding in gold and precious stones. The fabled golden city was sometimes referred to in the legend as Manoa or Omoa. The stories inspired the Spanish to expend vast sums in sending out exploring parties, most of which returned decimated by privation and disease. The most celebrated expedition was that of the Spanish explorer Francisco de Orellana (q.v.), who went (1540–41) down the Amazon R. to its mouth in an unsuccessful attempt to find the city. The German adventurer Philip von Hutten (1511?–46) in 1541 led an exploring party from Coro, a German settlement on the Venezuelan coast, and searched as far as the Omagua region, near the Amazon R. In 1595 the English explorer Sir Walter Raleigh (q.v.) took up the search and, upon his return to England, published a manifestly romantic account of his voyage, in which he described Manoa as being on an island in Parimá Lake, in Guiana. For more than two centuries, until the existence of the lake was disproved, it was marked on maps. The name El Dorado has come to be applied to any place of fabulous wealth or of opportunities for acquiring sudden wealth. In literature, especially in poetry, frequent references have been made to the legend.

ELEANOR OF AQUITAINE (1122?–1204), Queen Consort of France (1137–52), and Queen Consort of England (1154–1204). She inherited the Duchy of Aquitaine from her father in 1137, the same year in which she was married to Louis VII (q.v.), King of France. She accompanied her husband on the Second Crusade to the Holy Land (*see* CRUSADES: *Second Crusade (1147–49)*), where it was rumored that she committed adultery. The scandal, coupled with the fact that she had not borne the king a male heir, resulted in a divorce in 1152 under the pretext of blood kinship between her and the king. Later that year Eleanor married and gave her possessions to Henry Plantagenet, Count of Anjou, who in 1154 became Henry II (q.v.), King of England. In 1170 the queen induced her husband to invest their son Richard the Lion-Hearted (*see* RICHARD I) with her personal dominions of Gascony, Aquitaine, and Poitou. When Richard and his brothers rebelled against their father in 1173, Eleanor, already alienated from the king because of his unfaithfulness, supported her sons. Consequently, she was placed in confinement until 1185. After her release she secured the succession of her son Richard, who had become heir apparent at the death in 1183 of his eldest brother. From the death of King Henry II in 1189 until Richard's return from the Third Crusade in 1194, Eleanor ruled as regent. During this time she foiled the attempt of her son John (*see under* JOHN) in 1193 to conspire with France

Eleanor of Aquitaine   Bettmann Archive

against the new king. After the return of Richard, she arranged a reconciliation between the two brothers. Eleanor continued to be prominent in public affairs until she retired to the abbey in Fontevrault, France, where she died.

ELEANOR OF CASTILE (d. 1290), Queen Consort of England (1272–90), daughter of Ferdinand III (q.v.), King of Castile and León. In 1254 she married Prince Edward, later Edward I (q.v.), King of England, the eldest son of King Henry III (q.v.). In 1270 she accompanied Edward on the Seventh Crusade (*see* CRUSADES). During their absence from England, Henry III died (1272) and Edward succeeded to the throne. Two years later, following their return from the Middle East, Edward and Eleanor were crowned king and queen of England.

ELEATIC SCHOOL, Greek school of philosophy that flourished in the 6th and 5th centuries B.C. Eleatic thought is opposed to both the materialist philosophy of the Ionian school and the theory of universal flux propounded by the Greek philosopher Heraclitus (q.v.). According to the Eleatics the universe is an essentially changeless unity which, being infinite in time and space, is beyond the cognition of the human sense. Only through philosophical reflection, they asserted, can ultimate truth be known. Sensory observations yield merely a limited and distorted view of reality. The name Eleatic is derived from the Greek city of Elea, in southern Italy, the home of Parmenides and Zeno (qq.v.), the leading exponents of the school. Scholars differ as to whether the school was founded by Xenophanes (q.v.) or Parmenides. Many of the Eleatic doctrines were based upon the teachings of Xenophanes, while Parmenides developed the Eleatic doctrines into a system of metaphysics. Eleatic philosophy served as a basis for the metaphysical system of the later Greek philosopher Plato (q.v.).

ELECAMPANE, common name for a hardy, perennial herb, *Inula helenium,* of the Thistle family (Compositae). The plant grows to a height of about 3 ft. to 5 ft., and has large, toothed leaves, and yellow flowers with three-notched rays. The thick, branching root is bitter to the taste, has a camphorlike smell, and contains inulin, a carbohydrate used in medicine. Elecampane is found from England to southern Europe, and in Asia as far east as the Himalaya. It grows wild in North America, from Nova Scotia as far south as Georgia and as far west as Ontario and Minnesota. The root of the elecampane was cultivated in ancient times and was used in medicine as a diuretic and a diaphoretic.

ELECTIONS, procedures through which the members of an organization or of a governmental jurisdiction, such as a State or nation, select a person or persons to hold offices of authority. Elections may also register choices between alternate courses of action, and they may be conducted by ballot (q.v.), by a show of hands, or by oral voting. In the public affairs of Western democracies, elections usually select executive, legislative, administrative, and some judicial officials. Those who participate by voting are known collectively as the electorate.

ELECTION PROCEDURE

Before officials are selected by election, they are usually nominated as candidates from among all the individuals who aspire to a particular office. In Great Britain, a person may be nominated for a position in the House of Commons by presenting a petition bearing the signatures of as few as ten qualified voters, although he stands little chance of election until he is adopted by a local major party organization. In the United States, aspirants have been nominated by caucus, convention (qq.v.), and primary elections (see below). Historically, the caucus has not been adequately responsive to the popular will. The same criticism has been made against the conventions that generally nominated most candidates in the U.S. until the early part of the 20th century. Candidates for President and Vice-President are still selected by national conventions, and in the States of Connecticut, Dela-

Elecampane, Inula helenium

Arthur W. Ambler—
National Audubon Society

ware, Indiana, and New York, conventions still serve in the selection of candidates for both State and national offices. In most States, however, the direct party primary, or nominating election, is the method of selecting candidates for all legislative offices, and often for many executive and administrative positions.

Primary Elections. In the U.S., nominating elections have usually been regarded as party elections. The regulations for a closed primary, which is used by most States today, may require the voter to register as a member of a political organization or in some other way indicate his choice of a political party before he can receive a ballot. In other States, the open primary allows a voter to choose his party ballot in such a way that he need not publicly reveal his affiliation; in some of these States no requirement of party affiliation is made when the voter registers. In the State of Washington, the tradition of party elections has been disrupted by the blanket primary, which presents the voter with a ballot on which are printed the names of all candidates for nomination by all parties and which permits him to participate in the nomination of more than one party, provided only that he cast a single vote in reference to each office. Widely prevalent in the U.S. is the nonpartisan primary, common for judicial and school elections. In the nonpartisan primary no party designations are made on the ballot; each voter is free to vote for one or more candidates for office. A frequent feature of the nonpartisan primary is the election of officers at the primary when they win a specified majority of the votes cast.

In most primary elections, the aspirant who wins a plurality of the votes becomes the candidate of his group or party. In an effort to prevent the nomination of a minority candidate—one whose total votes number less than the combined total of his opponents' votes—some States have instituted a preferential primary. The essential feature of a preferential primary is that voters indicate the order of their preference among the aspirants. In such elections, an aspirant's total vote will combine the votes cast for him as first preference, second preference, and so forth, and the aspirant with the highest total is named the candidate. Nine States and a number of cities have run-off elections, which are held to nominate a candidate if the primary election fails to produce a majority vote. In a run-off election, voters choose between the two aspirants who received the highest totals in the earlier primary.

Several States have so-called Presidential primaries, in which delegates to the national nomi-

Voters cast paper ballots in the Presidential election of 1860.   Bettmann Archive

nating conventions are chosen. Because these delegates are usually pledged to support a particular candidate for President, such primaries are often taken as an indication of the strength of the candidate in the electorate as a whole. Movements for the establishment of a nationwide Presidential primary election have, however, been unsuccessful so far.

General Elections. By participating in general elections, voters determine which of the nominated candidates shall hold office. Such elections are called direct elections if the electorate makes this ultimate choice; they are called indirect elections if the electorate chooses instead a group of representatives who then make the final selection. Thus in the U.S., the election of a Congressman by his constituency is direct, as is the election of members of the House of Commons in England. On the other hand, the naming of the President of the U.S. by an Electoral College (q.v.) and the selection of the British prime minister by members of Parliament (q.v.) are indirect elections. The American tradition favors direct election and is based on the assumption that officials so elected, and subject to reelection, are more responsive to the will of the electorate than are officials chosen indirectly.

Elections have not always been used to achieve democratic results. In some countries, in some States of the U.S., and in some private organizations, the electorate has often in practice been restricted to the membership of one or more groups or parties. In some general elections, the choice before voters has been a positive or a negative vote for a single candidate. The frequency of elections is also an important factor in the democratic dimension of public affairs. In the U.S., elections for national legislative positions are held at fixed intervals and on specified dates. Presidential elections and most other general elections are held on the first Tuesday after the first Monday in November. Elections for State and local offices may occur on other dates, and provisions for certain special elections may also be made. In other countries, however, notably some European parliamentary democracies, the executive branch of the government can, within specified limits, dissolve the legislative branch and call for a new election of legislative members.

Still another consideration in this regard is the variety of public matters that are open to the elective process and the number and the kinds of officials subject to election. In some countries, the electorate selects a party, rather than individual candidates, so that the legislative body may reflect a wide scope of organized political opinion; see PROPORTIONAL REPRESENTATION. In such countries, both the executive and administrative officials are usually elected indirectly. By contrast, the officials to be selected in some U.S. State and municipal elections may include executives, legislators, judges, commissioners, and dozens of other administrators. These elections are consistent with the tradition of direct elections, and they often require a so-called long ballot of some complexity; *see* BAL-

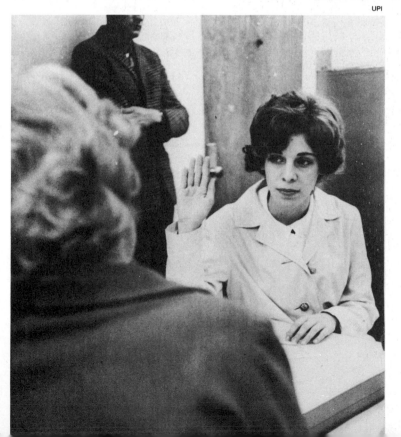

Above: Recent voters registration drives have greatly increased the number of voters from minority groups. Left: A girl registers to vote in Georgia, which opened its voting rolls to eighteen-year olds in 1943. About twenty-seven years later, in 1970, the Supreme Court of the United States upheld the constitutionality of a previously passed law that gave the right to vote to eighteen-year olds in Federal elections; many States later accepted this age limit for elections to State offices as well.

LOT. Voters at such elections may also be asked to approve or reject financial propositions such as tax levies and bond issues, and in the States that provide for direct legislation they may even be asked to vote directly for or against specific pieces of legislation that have been officially initiated by the voters themselves or referred to them; see INITIATIVE; RECALL; REFERENDUM.

HISTORY

Historically, elections have been identified with the rise of democracy (q.v.). In the city-states of ancient Greece, often cited as examples of pure democracies, members of the council of state were chosen by lot from a list of candidates selected by the *demes,* or local governments. The citizens of ancient Rome elected important public officials and voted on public matters. Little is known of medieval election practices. Suffrage (q.v.) was very limited in the Middle Ages (q.v.). Among the early Teutonic tribes, the freemen elected their kings; later heredity became the basis for kingship. From the mid-13th century until the beginning of the 19th century, the German monarchs and the emperors of the Holy Roman Empire (q.v.) were elected by the princes of the realm, who were called electors; see ELECTORS, GERMAN IMPERIAL. Medieval Venice chose its doges, or chief magistrates, by a complicated system of indirect elections involving an intermediate electoral body selected by lottery. Some countries chose their rulers by lot.

In England, the method of selecting the members of parliament was not defined by law in the early history of that institution. The statesman Simon de Montfort (q.v.) summoned a parliament in 1265, calling for representatives of counties and boroughs. Subsequently, an informal and irregular system of electing parliamentary representatives developed with procedures varying from county to county. Many elections took place at mass meetings following a reading by the sheriff of a writ of election. A number of abuses which developed later were eliminated by law in the latter half of the 19th century.

United States. In 1787 the Constitution of the United States (q.v.) provided for the election of the chief executive in Article II, Section 1, and the members of the national legislature in Article I, Section 2. A number of election abuses, however, led in the latter part of the 19th century to the adoption of the Australian, or secret, ballot and to the practice of registering voters prior to election day; see REGISTRATION. Voting machines were first used in the U.S. in 1892, in the city of Lockport, N.Y.

During the 19th century the electorate in the U.S. grew considerably. Most of the States en-

franchised all white, male adults, although the so-called poll tax (q.v.) was retained. The Fifteenth Amendment to the U.S. Constitution, Section 1, (ratified in 1870) broadened the electorate still further by enfranchising the former Negro slaves; in elections held during the period of Reconstruction (q.v.), Negroes were elected to high office for the first time in American history. Subsequent legislation, however, as well as extralegal practices in a number of States, ended frequently the participation of Negroes in elections; see DISCRIMINATION; NEGROES IN THE UNITED STATES.

During the post-Civil-War period the primary system of selecting candidates for public office became widespread. By 1900, primaries were regulated by law in most States. The Nineteenth Amendment to the Constitution, Section 1, (ratified in 1920) enfranchised women; see WOMAN SUFFRAGE. The major development in U.S. elections since 1920 has been the struggle to end the de facto disenfranchisement of Negroes in the South and to establish election districts that are approximately equal in population; see CIVIL RIGHTS AND CIVIL LIBERTIES; ELECTORAL REFORM.

ELECTORAL COLLEGE, collective name for the electors who nominally choose the President and Vice-President of the United States. This group comprises the electors from the separate States who are selected by the voters in Presidential elections. Each State is entitled to a number of electors equal to the total number of Senators and Representatives it sends to the U.S. Congress. Thus, each State has at least three electors.

History and Later Changes in the System. The electoral method was devised by the drafters of the Constitution of the United States (q.v.), who hoped thereby to entrust the responsibility to men whose choice would be unaffected by partisan politics. In Article II, Section 1, of the Constitution, the mode of selecting electors is delegated to the separate State legislatures, and the voting procedure to be followed by the electors is carefully defined. According to the electoral procedure originally specified in the Constitution, the electors were to vote for the two most qualified persons without specifying which was preferred for President and which for Vice-President. The candidate receiving the greatest number of electoral votes, provided he received the votes of a majority of the electors, would be President, and the candidate winning the second largest number of votes would be Vice-President. A serious flaw in this procedure was revealed in the election of 1800, when Thomas Jefferson (q.v.) was the Presidential candidate of the Democratic-Republican (later the Democratic) Party and Aaron Burr (q.v.) was the candidate for Vice-President. The electors, by voting strictly for candidates of their party, gave Burr and Jefferson the same number of votes. As the Constitution provided, the election was referred to the House of Representatives, in which a protracted struggle took place, requiring thirty-six ballots before Jefferson was chosen President and Burr Vice-President. As a consequence, in 1804 Congress enacted and the States ratified the Twelfth Amendment, providing for separate electoral votes for President and for Vice-President.

Another important change resulted from a serious dispute in the Presidential election of 1876 in which the Republican, Rutherford Birchard Hayes, and the Democrat, Samuel Jones Tilden (qq.v.), were the candidates. The dispute involved the validity of the electoral votes of four States, and the outcome was crucial, since Tilden needed just one of the twenty-two votes to have a majority and Hayes needed all twenty-two to win. Under existing law, it was the duty of Congress to resolve the dispute, but Congress found itself deadlocked. Finally, the issue was settled through the creation of the Electoral Commission of 1877 (q.v.), which chose Hayes on a strict party vote, eight to seven. Later, in 1887, Congress enacted a law that gave the States almost exclusive power to resolve all controversies regarding the selection of Presidential electors and that made mandatory, except in cases in which electors vote "irregularly", the acceptance by Congress of all certificates of election duly made by the States. The enactment also provided that Congress may intervene to settle a dispute over the election of the Presidential electors of a State only when the State is unable to do so.

Apart from the changes described above, the procedure worked out by the framers of the Constitution is substantially the one in use today. The Twenty-third Amendment, however, adopted in 1961, permits residents of the District of Columbia to vote for three electors in the same manner as residents of the States. Through its power of apportioning Representatives among the States, Congress determines the number of Presidential electors to which each State is entitled. At the present time the total of State and District of Columbia electors is 538; a simple majority of 270 is necessary for election. Presidential electors meet in each State at a place designated by the State legislature, usually the State capitol. By decision of Congress, they meet to vote simultaneously in all the States, on the first Monday after the second Wednesday in December of Presidential election years. On January 6, following the meeting of the electors, their votes are counted in the presence of both Houses of Congress.

Current Significance. Electoral procedure is unchanged, but the significance of the Presidential electors has changed. As political parties developed and vied for power, party interests became the dominant factors influencing the votes of the electors. Another development was of even greater importance. Before 1820, most of the State legislatures applied their constitutionally granted power of selecting Presidential electors by appointing them. But as suffrage in the U.S. was broadened after 1800 and the electorate began to exercise greater political influence, the States instituted the direct, popular election of Presidential electors. By 1828 this practice had been adopted in all of the States except South Carolina, where it was not instituted until 1868. To attend this change, political parties began to present lists of Presidential electors who were tacitly pledged to vote for the candidates of their party. Thus originated the practice of the electors of a State voting as a unit, a procedure which was subsequently made mandatory in most of the States and which has aroused serious criticism. A challenge to the "winner-take-all" system of awarding electoral votes was rejected by the U.S. Supreme Court in January, 1969; the action of the high court was a unanimous affirmation of a lower-court ruling. Mississippi and Alabama allow slates of unpledged electors to be placed on the ballot. If the unpledged electors win, the electoral vote of the State may be split among the candidates.

Occasionally an elector pledged to one candidate has voted for another. Technically an elector may vote as he wishes, and such votes have usually been validated by Congress. Critics consider this a weakness in the present system.

Critics of the electoral method contend that the true sentiments of the voters are distorted by the winner-take-all system, as well as by the fact that population and voter turnout are not accurately reflected. Critics point to the fact that a candidate receiving a plurality of the popular vote in a State whether the margin is 1 vote or 1,000,000 carries all the electoral votes of that State, and they conclude that in effect the minority is disfranchised at an intermediate stage of the electoral process. The winner-take-all system is largely responsible for the fact that a candidate could be elected President even though he polled fewer popular votes than his opponent. Should a candidate receive a minority of the popular vote nationally but carry a sufficient number of States to assure him of a majority of the electoral votes, he would be elected, and the will of the majority would be frustrated through the legal and normal operation of the Electoral College. Critics point to the dispute caused by the election of 1876 and also to the election of 1888, in which Stephen Grover Cleveland (q.v.), the defeated candidate, polled 5,540,050 popular votes to 5,444,337 for Benjamin Harrison (q.v.); however, Cleveland received only 168 electoral votes to Harrison's 233. The popular-vote totals for major Presidential candidates in recent years have been relatively close, with the exception of 1964, and such situations may be repeated. In the 1968 Presidential election a strong third-party candidate attempted to win enough electoral votes to raise the possibility that the election would be decided when the electors met, or, failing that, in the House of Representatives. Although the move failed, it has prompted renewed demands for reform or abolition of the Electoral College. Many critics point out that the only system that can guarantee election of the popular choice is direct popular election.

The table below, reflecting the 1970 census, lists the number of electors by States. The District of Columbia is represented in the Electoral College by three members. B.B.

Alabama	9	Montana	4
Alaska	3	Nebraska	5
Arizona	6	Nevada	3
Arkansas	6	New Hampshire	4
California	45	New Jersey	17
Colorado	7	New Mexico	4
Connecticut	8	New York	41
Delaware	3	North Carolina	13
Florida	17	North Dakota	3
Georgia	12	Ohio	25
Hawaii	4	Oklahoma	8
Idaho	4	Oregon	6
Illinois	26	Pennsylvania	27
Indiana	13	Rhode Island	4
Iowa	8	South Carolina	8
Kansas	7	South Dakota	4
Kentucky	9	Tennessee	10
Louisiana	10	Texas	26
Maine	4	Utah	4
Maryland	10	Vermont	3
Massachusetts	14	Virginia	12
Michigan	21	Washington	9
Minnesota	10	West Virginia	6
Mississippi	7	Wisconsin	11
Missouri	12	Wyoming	3

ELECTORAL COMMISSION OF 1877, commission created by congressional enactment to resolve the disputed United States Presidential election of 1876. Rutherford Birchard Hayes (q.v.), the Republican candidate, had polled 4,033,950 popular votes; Samuel Jones Tilden (q.v.), the Democratic nominee, had polled 4,284,885 votes, winning a popular majority of 250,000 votes. Tilden, however, had only 184 uncontested electoral votes, one short of a major-

ity in the Electoral College; Hayes had 163. The electoral votes of Florida (4), Louisiana (8), Oregon (3), and South Carolina (7), 22 in all, were contested.

The Republicans charged that in Florida, Louisiana, and South Carolina the Democrats had achieved popular majorities by intimidating Negro voters. The charge of intimidation was obviously true, but it was never proved; it is doubtful that the outcome of the election was changed because of such intimidation. Nevertheless, the Republican-dominated governments in these States set up electoral bodies, called returning boards, which cast electoral votes for Hayes. In retaliation, the Democrats in Oregon made use of a convenient technicality to oust a Hayes elector and replace him with a Tilden man, throwing the entire electoral vote of the State into dispute.

The first attempts of Congress to resolve these disputes ended in a deadlock: the majority of the Senate was Republican, and the House of Representatives was predominantly Democratic. Both sides, however, finally agreed to the creation of a bipartisan commission of fifteen men to settle the matter. Legislation enacted on Jan. 29, 1877, provided for a commission of five Senators (three Republicans and two Democrats), five Representatives (three Democrats and two Republicans), and four Supreme Court associate justices (two Republicans and two Democrats) who were to name a fifth justice. The fifth justice was nominally nonpartisan but in actuality a Republican.

The commission considered the disputed returns on a State-by-State basis in alphabetical order. Hayes was awarded the returns from Oregon and South Carolina by a unanimous vote of the commission, and the returns from Florida and Louisiana by a vote of 8 to 7. Thus Hayes, who had received a minority of the popular vote, received a one-vote majority of the electoral vote and became the nineteenth President of the United States; William Almon Wheeler (q.v.), his running mate, was designated Vice-President.

Involved in the Hayes-Tilden dispute were two issues: one was the question as to whether Congress or the States had the power to resolve disputes over the validity of electoral votes; the second and more important question was whether it is consistent with democratic principles and practices for a candidate receiving a minority of the popular vote in a Presidential election to become President through the votes of the electors.

On the first issue, the commission adopted

The electoral commission of 1877.   Bettmann Archive

the viewpoint of the Republicans, who held that the commission had no power to pass on the action of the States in certifying electoral returns, and that any attempt to do so would constitute an invasion of the sovereignty of the States. In 1887 this view was incorporated into a law which gave the States exclusive power, subject to certain restrictions, to resolve disputes over the votes of Presidential electors. The graver problem concerning the relation of the Presidential electors to the will of the voters was not considered by the commission and remains unresolved. For further details on both problems, *see* ELECTORAL COLLEGE.

ELECTORAL REFORM, elimination of undemocratic, dishonest, and corrupt practices in the conduct of public elections. Reform is usually effected by statutory enactments that contain provisions for accomplishing one or more of the following ends: a change in the qualification of voters in order to include in the electorate certain categories of citizens previously barred from voting; a revision of procedures for selecting candidates and arranging elections to assure that voters will be able to register an effective choice; the definition and outlawing of corrupt practices employed to influence the outcome of elections. See BALLOT; CAUCUS; ELECTIONS; SUFFRAGE.

Among the practices that have been the objects of electoral reform are actual or threat-

ened physical violence against voters; concealed pressures such as those exercised by some employers; bribery, consisting of gifts of money or other rewards for voting as directed; impersonation of duly qualified voters by others, called personation; voting more than once, called repeating; shifting voters from districts where the result is certain, to others where it is doubtful, called colonization; nullification of ballots by altering or defacing them; stuffing of ballot boxes; false counting of ballots; and a variety of other practices.

Electoral Reform in Great Britain. In Great Britain the purchase of votes was long a common practice. Efforts to eliminate bribery and other forms of electoral corruption were embodied in acts passed by Parliament in 1729, 1809, 1827, 1842, 1854, 1868, and 1883. The 1883 law, known as the Corrupt and Illegal Practices Prevention Act, defined as corrupt practices, undue influence, personation, treating (the offer by a candidate for office to a voter of food or drink in a public place), and seven specific forms of bribery. These practices were made statutory offenses, punishable by fines, jail sentences, and loss of political rights for seven years. Under the terms of the act, the elections of Parliamentary candidates found guilty of any of the above corrupt practices are voided.

Electoral Reform in the United States. After the establishment of the United States, the first significant State legislation against electoral frauds was enacted in 1890 by New York State. It listed the amounts that candidates for various offices might legally spend and required candidates to file itemized accounts of campaign expenditures. Violations of the law were punishable by imprisonment and loss of office. Subsequently, the law was extended to include the treasurers of political committees as well as the candidates they sponsored. Illegal registration, the use of false naturalization papers, personation, and bribery were made punishable by jail sentences up to five years. Bribe givers were also disqualified from holding office, and bribe takers were disfranchised for five years. In 1909 New York State prohibited candidates from soliciting donations and forbade all corporations, except political organizations, from making campaign contributions or spending money for political ends. A one-year prison sentence and a $1000 fine were established as punishment for the violation of this law.

About the time of the enactment of the New York legislation, Massachusetts forbade the practice of influencing voters with offers of employment and appointments to office, publication of unsigned political advertisements, subsidizing of newspapers to support candidates, contributions by certain corporations to political parties, and payment by political committees of naturalization fees for prospective voters. Other States also enacted electoral reform laws. Oregon established a maximum amount of money that candidates might legally spend in pursuit of election and arranged to pay a part of their campaign expenses. Kansas prohibited a candidate from spending more than 10 percent of the yearly salary of the office to which he seeks election. Most States now require publication by candidates of financial statements of campaign expenses both before and after election day.

A Federal law enacted in 1925 repealed all previous Federal election laws and provided that treasurers of political committees, operating in two or more States, had to file with the clerk of the House of Representatives sworn statements containing the names and addresses of all contributors of $100 or more, the names and addresses of all persons receiving $10 or more from the moneys collected by the committees, and the purposes for which the disbursements were made. Candidates for Congress were required to submit itemized accounts of contributions made to their cam-

paign expenses both before and after election. Limits were placed on the amounts candidates were allowed to expend in campaigning. Candidates for public office, Congressmen, and Federal employees were prohibited from soliciting campaign contributions among government workers. National banks and corporations organized under Congressional charter were forbidden to make contributions to the campaign funds of candidates for Congressional seats and for the Electoral College (q.v.).

In 1939 a drastic and far-reaching measure, known as the Hatch Act (q.v.), was passed by Congress. Designed to discourage the spoils system (q.v.) of political patronage in favor of a genuine merit system for selecting and training employees in the civil service (q.v.), the Hatch Act prohibits certain types of political activity on the part of Federal employees. Violation of this central provision of the Hatch Act was made punishable by loss of position, among other things.

Electoral practices aimed at preventing Negroes from exercising their legal right to vote was the particular focus of electoral reform in the 1950's and 1960's. The most sweeping reforms were embodied in the Voting Rights Act of 1965. This law provided for automatic suspension of literacy tests and other voter qualification devices if they were applied in a discriminatory way; gave Federal voting examiners the authority to register voters in areas not meeting certain voter participation requirements; authorized the U.S. attorney general to investigate the validity of State poll taxes; placed restrictions on new State voting laws; and it made interference with voting rights conferred by the law a criminal offense. Supplementing these laws was the Twenty-Fourth Amendment to the Constitution of the United States (q.v.), ratified in 1964, prohibiting poll taxes as a qualification for voting in Federal elections; see POLL TAX.

On June 22, 1970, the Voting Rights Act of 1965 was extended for an additional five years. A second division of the law lowered the voting age to eighteen. In December, 1970, the Supreme Court of the United States (q.v.) upheld the vote for eighteen-year-old citizens in Federal elections. At the same time the Court ruled that Congress acted unconstitutionally in lowering the voting age to eighteen in State and local elections. This problem was solved by the Twenty-Sixth Amendment to the Constitution, ratified in 1971, providing that citizens eighteen years of age or older could not be denied the franchise "on account of age".

A major concern of supporters of electoral reform has been the establishment of election districts that are nearly equal in population. In districts that are unequal, a disproportionate power has often been given to small numbers of voters, especially those in sparsely populated areas. In 1962 in Tennessee, for example, one third of the voters elected two thirds of the legislators, and under the circumstances one rural vote equaled twenty urban votes. Such conditions have caused reformers to support the movement for "one man, one vote", which reached a significant achievement with the decision of the Supreme Court in the case of *Baker vs. Carr* (1962). The Court then declared unconstitutional the kind of disproportionate representation found in Tennessee and said the principle of "one man, one vote" must govern State legislative apportionment if the States are to satisfy Constitutional requirements. The Court further clarified its position in 1963 by outlawing the Georgia county-unit system, under which all the votes assigned to each county went to the candidate who won a majority of its popular vote. It ruled in 1964 that the "one man, one vote" rule applied to both houses of State legislatures. After these decisions, most legislatures were reapportioned, often with significant changes in political power.

Increasing concern over the use of money in elections led to the passage of the campaign financing act of 1972. Although it placed limits on the amount of individual contributions and on the amount that could be spent on media advertising, its most significant feature was its provision for full disclosure of all contributions and disbursements on behalf of candidates. Before it went into effect on April 7, 1972, the campaign committee to reelect President Richard M. Nixon had raised at least $23,900,000. The Watergate scandals (*see* WATERGATE), inextricably involved with the misuse of campaign contributions, led to the resignation of Nixon in 1974 and to the passage of the campaign financing act of 1974. This act placed strict limits on individual and group contributions, provided for limits on campaign expenditures, and required full and periodic disclosures. A full-time bipartisan Federal Elections Commission was established on Jan. 1, 1975, to enforce this complex law. Its most novel provision was for the partial Federal financing of Presidential campaigns, both primary and general.

R.E.Bu.

ELECTORAL VOTES. *See* ELECTORAL COLLEGE.

ELECTORS, GERMAN IMPERIAL, group of ecclesiastical and secular German princes invested with the power of electing the king of Germany,
who in turn was crowned emperor of the Holy Roman Empire (q.v.) by the pope. Originally, all the princes of the empire voted in the election of the German king. In 1263, however, Pope Urban IV (*see under* URBAN) issued two bulls recognizing the authority of seven German potentates to choose the king. Nevertheless, the authority and membership of this electorate was not definitely settled until 1356 when the Golden Bull (q.v.) was issued by Charles IV, who was known as the Holy Roman Emperor (*see under* CHARLES). The bull named to the electorate the archbishops of Cologne, Mainz, and Trier, the margrave of Brandenburg, the duke of Saxony, the count palatine of the Rhine, and the king of Bohemia.

From that time the composition of the electorate remained unchanged until 1623 when the vote of the count palatine was transferred to the duke of Bavaria during the Thirty Years' War (q.v.). In 1648 an eighth electoral vote was added so that the count palatine could vote again, and in 1692 a ninth vote was created for the electorate of Hannover. The number of electors reverted to eight in 1778 after extinction of the Bavarian ducal line. With the dissolution of the Holy Roman Empire in 1806, the German Imperial Electorate was also dissolved.

ELECTRA, in Greek mythology, daughter of Agamemnon, King of Mycenae, and Queen Clytemnestra (qq.v.). After the murder of Agamemnon by Clytemnestra and the queen's lover Aegisthus (q.v.), Electra sent her brother Orestes (q.v.) to safety at the court of an uncle. She herself stayed behind in Mycenae, living in poverty under constant surveillance while Clytemnestra and Aegisthus ruled the kingdom. Electra sent frequent reminders to Orestes that he must return to avenge the death of their father. At the end of seven years Orestes and his friend Pylades came secretly to Agamemnon's tomb. There they met Electra, who had come to pour libations and offer prayers for vengeance. Orestes revealed his identity to his sister, then proceeded at once to the palace where he killed Aegisthus and Clytemnestra. Electra later married Pylades, Orestes' constant companion. *See* ATREUS, HOUSE OF.

ELECTRICAL ENGINEERING. *See* ENGINEERING: *Fields of Engineering: Electrical Engineering. See also* DYNAMOELECTRIC MACHINERY; ELECTRICITY; ELECTRIC-POWER SYSTEMS.

ELECTRICAL MACHINE. *See* ELECTROSTATIC MACHINE.

ELECTRICAL UNITS, units used to express quantitative measurements of all types of electrostatic and electromagnetic phenomena and of the electrical characteristics of components of electrical circuits; *see* ELECTRIC CIRCUIT; ELECTRICITY; ELECTRIC METERS. The basic electrical units are part of the centimeter-gram-second system (*see* C.G.S. SYSTEM), but because, in most cases, these units are either too large or too small for convenient measurement, a number of practical units have been adopted for use in engineering.

Basic Units. The elemental unit of electricity is the charge on a single electron or proton (qq.v.). The symbol for this unit is e'' or, frequently, simply e. The C.G.S. unit of electrical charge is the electrostatic unit (e.s.u.), which is defined as the quantity of electricity which, when concentrated at a point in a vacuum, will repel a like charge 1 cm away with a force of 1 dyne. The e.s.u. is equal to 2,082,400,000 elemental units, or the aggregate charge carried by this number of electrons or protons.

The basic unit of electrical current or flow is the statampere, which is defined as a current of 1 e.s.u. per sec. The statvolt, the basic unit of electromotive force, or potential difference, is the difference in potential that exists between two points when 1 erg of work is required to force 1 e.s.u. of electricity between those two points.

Electromagnetic Units. Besides the electrostatic units of charge, current, and potential difference, a parallel group of basic electromagnetic units exists. The basic magnetic unit, comparable to the elemental unit of electricity, is the unit magnetic pole, defined as a point magnetic pole that in a vacuum will act on a similar pole 1 cm away with a force of 1 dyne. The unit used to measure the strength of magnetic fields is the oersted. A field that acts on a unit magnetic pole with a force of 1 dyne has a strength of 1 oersted. The electromagnetic unit of electric current is called the abampere. If a current of 1 abampere flows in a wire 1 cm long, the wire is pushed sidewise with a force of 1 dyne by a magnetic field of 1 oersted acting at right angles to the wire. The abcoulomb is the quantity of electricity passing any point in a circuit in 1 second when a current of 1 abampere is flowing in the circuit. The abvolt, the electromagnetic unit of potential difference, is the potential difference between two points when 1 erg of work is necessary to move 1 abcoulomb of electricity from one point to the other. *See also* POTENTIAL.

The mathematical relationships between the electrostatic and electromagnetic units follow: 1 e.s.u. equals 0.000000000033356 abcoulombs; 1 statampere equals 0.000000000033356 abamperes; and one statvolt equals 29,979,600,000 ab-

volts. This last figure is exactly equal to the velocity of light through a vacuum, expressed in centimeters per second, as predicted by the electromagnetic-wave theory of the British physicist James Clerk Maxwell (q.v.). *See* ELECTROMAGNETIC RADIATIONS.

Practical Units. The unit of electrical current in common use is the ampere, which is defined as 0.1 abamperes. The practical unit of electrical quantity is the coulomb, the amount of electricity passing a given point in a circuit in 1 second when a current of 1 ampere is flowing. The volt is the practical unit of potential difference. It is equal to 100,000,000 abvolts and can be defined as the potential difference existing between two points when 1 joule (10,000,000 ergs) of work is required to move 1 coulomb of electricity from one of the points to the other. The unit of electrical work is the watt. It represents the generation or use of electrical energy at the rate of 1 joule per sec. The kilowatt is equal to 1000 watts.

Because of the difficulty of making measurements in terms of the absolute units, the practical units are also defined for purposes of practical standardization as follows: the ampere is the amount of current that will deposit 0.001118 g of silver per sec. if passed through a silver nitrate solution; the ohm is the resistance of a column of mercury 106.3 cm in length and 1 sq. mm in cross-section at a temperature of 0° C. (32° F.); the volt is the electromotive force necessary to produce a current of 1 ampere through a resistance of 1 ohm. The volt is also defined in terms of a standard voltaic cell, known as the Weston cell, which has poles of cadmium amalgam and mercurous sulfate and an electrolyte of cadmium sulfate. A volt is defined as 0.98203 of the potential of this standard cell at 20° C. (68° F.).

In all the practical electrical units the conventional prefixes of the metric system are used to indicate fractions and multiples of the basic units. Thus a micromicrofarad is a trillionth of a farad, a microampere is a millionth of an ampere, a millivolt is a thousandth of a volt, a millihenry is a thousandth of a henry, a kilowatt is 1000 watts, and a megohm is 1,000,000 ohms.

Resistance, Capacitance, Inductance. All components in electrical circuits exhibit one or more of the characteristics of resistance, capacitance, and inductance. The commonly used unit of resistance is the ohm, which is the resistance of a conductor in which a potential difference of 1 volt causes a current flow of 1 ampere. The capacitance of a condenser is measured in farads. A condenser of 1 farad capacitance will exhibit a change in potential difference of 1 volt

424

between its plates when 1 coulomb of electricity is transferred from one plate to the other. The henry is the unit of inductance. A coil has a self-inductance of 1 henry when a change in current of 1 ampere per sec. produces a countervoltage of 1 volt. In a transformer, or in any two magnetically coupled circuits, a mutual inductance of 1 henry is that inductance which will induce a voltage of 1 volt in the secondary when there is a change of 1 ampere per sec. in the primary.

See also CELL, ELECTRIC; ELECTROCHEMISTRY.

ELECTRIC ARC, type of continuous electric discharge (q.v.), giving intense light and heat, formed between two electrodes in a gas at low pressure or in open air. It was first discovered and demonstrated by the British chemist Sir Humphrey Davy (q.v.) in 1800.

To start an arc, the ends of two pencil-like electrodes, usually made of carbon, are brought into contact and a large current (about 10 amperes) is passed through them. This current causes intense heating at the point of contact, and if the electrodes are then separated, a flamelike arc is formed between them. The discharge is carried largely by electrons traveling from the negative to the positive electrode, but also in part by positive ions traveling in the opposite direction; *see* ION; IONIZATION. The impact of the ions produces great heat in the electrodes, but the positive electrode is hotter, because the electrons impinging on it have greater total energy. In an arc in air at normal pressure, the positive electrode reaches a temperature of 3500° C. (6332° F.).

The intense heat of the electric arc is often utilized in special furnaces to melt refractory materials; *see* ELECTROTHERMIC FURNACE. Temperatures of about 2800° C. (5072° F.) can easily be attained with such a furnace. Arcs are also used as a high-intensity light source. Arc lights have the advantage of being concentrated sources of light, because some 85 percent of the light intensity comes from a small area of the tip of the positive carbon electrode. Such lamps were formerly much used for street lighting, but are now chiefly employed in motion-picture projectors. Mercury-vapor lamps and sodium-vapor lamps are enclosed arc lamps in which the arc is maintained in an atmosphere of mercury or sodium vapor at reduced pressure; *see* ELECTRIC LIGHTING.

ELECTRIC BATTERIES. *See* CELL, ELECTRIC.

ELECTRIC CABLE. *See* CABLE, ELECTRIC.

ELECTRIC CELL. *See* CELL, ELECTRIC.

ELECTRIC CHAIR, specially constructed seating device, employed in United States prisons to inflict the death sentence on a convicted criminal by passing a strong electric current through his body; *see* ELECTROCUTION. *See also* CAPITAL PUNISHMENT.

ELECTRIC CIRCUIT, path of an electric current. The term is usually taken to mean a continuous path composed of conductors and conducting devices and including a source of electromotive force that drives the current around the circuit. A circuit of this type is termed a closed circuit, and a circuit in which the current path is not continuous is called an open circuit. A closed circuit in which there is a direct connection with no appreciable resistance, inductance (qq.v.), or capacitance between the terminals of the source of electromotive force is called a short circuit. *See* ELECTRICITY: *Current Electricity.*

Current flows in an electric circuit in accordance with several definite laws. The basic law of current flow is Ohm's law, named for its discoverer, the German physicist Georg Simon Ohm (q.v.). Ohm's law states that the amount of current flowing in a circuit made up of pure resistances is directly proportional to the electromotive force impressed on the circuit and inversely proportional to the total resistance of the circuit. The law is usually expressed by the formula $I = E/R$, where I is the current in amperes, E is the electromotive force in volts, and R is the resistance in ohms; *see* ELECTRICAL UNITS. Ohm's law applies to all electric circuits for both direct current (DC) and alternating current (AC), but additional principles must be invoked for the analysis of complex circuits and for a-c circuits also involving inductances and capacitances.

A series circuit is one in which the devices or elements of the circuit are so arranged that the entire current (I) passes through each element without division or branching into parallel circuits.

When two or more resistances are in series in a circuit, the total resistance may be calculated by adding the values of such resistances. If the resistances are in parallel, the total value of the resistance in the circuit is given by the formula

$$R_{total} = \cfrac{1}{\cfrac{1}{R_1} + \cfrac{1}{R_2} + \cfrac{1}{R_3} + \cdots}$$

In a parallel circuit, electrical devices, such as incandescent lamps or the cells of a battery, are arranged to allow all positive (+) poles, electrodes, and terminals to be joined to one conductor, and all negative (−) ones to another conductor so that each unit is, in effect, on a parallel branch. The value of two equal resistances in parallel is equal to half the value of the component resistances, and in every case the value of resistances in parallel is less than the value of the smallest of the individual resistances involved. In a-c circuits, or circuits with varying currents, circuit components other than resistance must be considered; see below.

If a circuit has several interconnected branches, two other laws are applied in order to find the current flowing in the various branches. These laws, discovered by the German physicist Gustav Robert Kirchhoff (q.v.), are known as Kirchhoff's laws of networks. The first of Kirchhoff's laws states that at any junction in a circuit through which a steady current is flowing, the sum of the currents flowing to the point is equal to the sum of the currents flowing away from that point. The second law states that, starting at any point in a network and following any closed path back to the starting point, the net sum of the electromotive forces encountered will be equal to the net sum of the products of the resistances encountered and the currents flowing through them. This second law is simply an extension of Ohm's law.

The application of Ohm's law to circuits in which there is an alternating current is complicated by the fact that capacity and inductance are always present. Inductance makes the peak value of an alternating current lag behind the peak value of voltage, while capacitance makes the peak value of voltage lag behind the peak value of the current. Capacitance and inductance inhibit the flow of a-c current, and must be taken into account in calculating current flow. The current in an a-c circuit can be determined graphically by means of vectors or by means of the algebraic equation

$$I = \frac{E}{\sqrt{R^2 + \left(2\pi fL - \frac{1}{2\pi fC}\right)^2}}$$

in which L is inductance, C is capacitance, and f is the frequency of the current. The quantity in the denominator of the fraction is called the impedance of the circuit to alternating current, and is sometimes represented by the letter Z; then Ohm's law for a-c circuits is expressed by the simple equation $I = E/Z$. G.D.F.

ELECTRIC DISCHARGE, equalization of an electrical potential difference by means of a flow of current, particularly applied to such flows in gases; see ELECTRICITY. If the potential gradient between two conductors in air at normal pressure reaches a value of about 30,000 volts per cm, the gas surrounding the conductors is ionized and a flow of ions is set up; see

ION; IONIZATION. This flow usually causes a faint violet glow or luminosity in the gas, creating a visible corona at the surface of the conductor. As the voltage gradient increases, the corona gradually gives place to a brush discharge, a number of fine filaments of light emanating from the negative conductor and resembling the bristles of a brush. If the potential gradient increases still further, a comparatively large current begins to flow, giving a bright light all the way between conductors, and tending to drain the conductors completely of electric charge. This discharge takes the form of a spark or an arc between the two conductors. A spark is an abrupt, severe discharge of short duration, whereas an arc, which often follows the spark, is continuous. For certain conductor spacings the spark may occur at once without prior appearance of visible corona. Lightning (q.v.) usually takes the form of a rapid series of large spark discharges.

In a gas under reduced pressure, another form of discharge known as a glow discharge is observed. When the potential gradient reaches a sufficiently high value, the gas between the conductors shines luminously. The color of this glow depends on the gas used. The phenomenon of glow discharge is employed in fluorescent and neon light tubes. See ELECTRIC ARC; ELECTRIC LIGHTING. See also CELL, ELECTRIC.

ELECTRIC EEL. See ELECTRIC FISH.

ELECTRIC EYE. See PHOTOELECTRIC CELL.

ELECTRIC FISH, common name for a group of unrelated fishes which emit electrical discharges. The organs adapted for this purpose consist of groups of highly compact nerve endings. For example, in small so-called electric eels (which are not true eels), a typical nerve-ending cell is about 1/10 mm long and has an electric voltage of 0.14 volts. The average small electric eel has about 230 of these nerve-ending cells per centimeter of length, and is capable of developing 30 to 32 volts per centimeter, or slightly more than 75 volts per inch. These cells are concentrated in the tail, which occupies about four fifths of the total length of the fish. Large electric eels have fewer nerve-ending cells per unit of length, but each cell is larger. They are capable of emitting a discharge of 450 to 600 volts. If the organs are exhausted from numerous discharges in a short interval, they will not function until they have had sufficient rest. Discharges are emitted by electric fish in order to stun their prey while hunting, or in self-defense.

The most important groups of electric fish are the electric eels, the electric catfish, and the electric rays. Of the three, the electric eels emit

Electric catfish, Malapterurus electricus
New York Zoological Society

the most powerful shocks. These fish comprise the genus *Electrophorus* of the family Electrophoridae, and are native to the Orinoco R. and the rivers of the Amazon basin in South America. The discharge organs of the electric eel include a small so-called pilot organ, which continuously emits electricity, and a large high-voltage organ which supplies most of the power to the intermittent discharges. The electric eel is capable of stunning large animals with its shock.

The electric catfish, *Malapterurus electricus,* of the Nile R., emits weaker discharges than does the eel, and has a discharging mechanism slightly different from that of the eel. Its electric shock organ consists of a membrane of nerve endings that extends over the entire back. *See* CATFISH.

The electric rays of the family Torpedinidae are found in oceans in many parts of the world. A typical genus of this family is *Torpedo,* common in many parts of Europe. Fish of this genus have two electric discharge organs between the head and pectoral fins. *See* RAY.

ELECTRIC FIELD. *See* ELECTRICITY: *Electrostatics;* FIELD. *See also* MAGNETISM: *Magnetism and Electricity.*

ELECTRIC FURNACE *or* **ELECTROTHERMAL FURNACE.** *See* ELECTROTHERMIC FURNACE; FURNACE.

ELECTRIC GENERATOR. *See* DYNAMOELECTRIC MACHINERY.

ELECTRIC HOME APPLIANCES, machines and devices that use electric power to facilitate performance of household chores.

Models of a hand-operated washing machine first appeared in the 1850's; however, the first patent on an electrically operated home appliance was granted for an electric iron in 1882. At the World's Columbian Exposition of 1893 in Chicago, Ill., many early versions of present-day kitchen appliances were exhibited in an "electric kitchen". Shortly before 1900, electric coffee makers and toasters were devised, and a clothes washer driven by a motor was invented in 1908. The electric refrigerator first appeared in 1915, and electric ranges, washers, and vacuum cleaners came into wide use in the decade between 1920 and 1930. Electric clothes dryers were introduced to the public early in the 1930's. Today, the electric home-appliance industry in the United States produces some seventy varieties of appliances. In the early 1970's the retail value of electric home appliances was more than $9,000,000,000 annually.

Electric home appliances can be divided into two general classes. One class uses electricity to power a motor that turns gears, cams, or shafts to operate the appliance. Examples include dishwashers, clothes washers, vacuum cleaners, mixers, blenders, can openers, and knife sharpeners. The motors can be controlled manually by on-off switches or automatically by contact switches connected to the motor circuit. The length of time for which the appliance operates can be controlled by an electric or mechanical timer, also connected to the motor circuit. In refrigerators and freezers, the electrically driven motor operates a compressor. The temperature within the appliance is maintained automatically by a temperature-sensitive switch connected to the motor circuit. Among other appliances that use electricity to power a motor are food-disposal units and floor polishers. The disposal unit rotates an impeller to force food down against a grinding ring. Food waste is pulverized and then forced down the drain by running water. The floor polisher has circular attachments (brushes, buffers, and similar equipment) that are spun by an electric motor.

In the second class of home appliances, electricity is used to produce heat through resistor coils. The heat, in turn, is used to operate the appliance. Examples of these appliances include electric ranges, ovens, irons, coffee makers, toasters, frying pans, hot plates, and rotisseries. The amount of heat supplied to the appliance is controlled either manually, by turning a rheostat, or automatically, by a thermostat connected to the electric circuit that switches the current on and off to maintain the desired temperature. Some appliances use both motors and heating coils. Examples include clothes washers, clothes dryers, certain automatic dishwashers, and rotisseries. The electronic range, a recent development, does not heat itself. It produces high-energy waves that penetrate food, transforming energy to heat within the food.

Many household devices that, strictly speaking, are not classified as appliances because they do not help to perform the usual household tasks also make use of electricity. These include electric shavers, electric clocks, electric blankets, electric fans, electric shoe polishers, electric power-tools, and air-conditioning units.

Of the many factors that have contributed to the increased use of electric appliances in the home, three of the more important are the saving of time and personal effort, the rising cost of certain household services, and the scarcity of labor. Today a housewife may rent or purchase a machine to shampoo her rug rather than call upon a professional rug-cleaning service. She may also find a home hair dryer or electric curlers more convenient and less expensive than have the work done at a beauty parlor.

ELECTRIC INSULATION. See DIELECTRIC; INSULATION: *Electric Insulation.*

ELECTRICITY, property of matter that, when stationary or static, produces forces on objects in regions where it is present, and that, when in motion, produces magnetic effects. Electric and magnetic effects are caused by the relative position and movement of positively and negatively charged particles of matter. So far as electrical effects are concerned, these particles are either neutral, or positive or negative; see ATOM AND ATOMIC THEORY. Electricity is concerned with the positively charged particles, such as protons, that repel one another and negatively charged particles, electrons, that also repel one another; see ELECTRON; PROTON. Negative and positive particles, however, attract each other. This behavior may be summarized as: like charges repel and unlike charges attract.

Electrostatics. A common manifestation of electricity is the repulsive or attractive force between two stationary bodies. Electrically, they exert an equal force on one another. The electric charge on each body may be measured in statcoulombs or the electrostatic unit of charge, abbreviated to e.s.u. The force between particles bearing charges q_1 and q_2 can be calculated by Coulomb's law, $F_{elec} = k \frac{q_1 q_2}{r^2}$ that is, the force is proportional to the product of charges, divided by the square of the distance that separates them. The constant of proportionality k is called the dielectric constant and depends on the medium surrounding the charges. This law is named after the French physicist, Charles Augustin de Coulomb, who developed the equation.

Every electrically charged particle is surrounded by a field of force. This field (q.v.) may be represented by lines of force showing the direction of electrical stresses within the field. To move a charged particle from one point in the field to another requires work. The amount of energy needed to perform such work on a particle bearing a unit charge is known as the "potential difference" between these two points. The difference is usually measured in volts; see ELECTRICAL UNITS. The earth, a large conductor, which may be assumed to be substantially uniform electrically, is commonly used as the zero reference level for potential (q.v.). Thus the potential of a positively charged body is said to be a certain number of volts above the potential of the earth, and the potential of a negatively charged body is said to be a certain number of volts below the potential of the earth.

ELECTRICAL PROPERTIES OF SOLIDS. The first manmade electrical phenomenon to be observed was the property displayed by certain resinous substances, such as amber, which become negatively charged when rubbed with a piece of fur or woolen cloth, and then attract small objects. Such a body has an excess of electrons. A glass rod rubbed with silk has a similar power to attract uncharged objects and attracts negatively charged objects even more strongly. The glass has a positive charge, which can be described either as a deficiency of electrons or an excess of protons.

When some atoms combine to form solids, one or more electrons are often liberated and can move with ease through the material. Electrons are easily liberated in some materials, which are known as conductors. Metals, particularly copper and silver, are good conductors; see CONDUCTOR, ELECTRICAL.

Materials in which the electrons are tightly bound to the atoms are known as insulators, nonconductors, or dielectrics; *see* DIELECTRIC; INSULATION. Glass, rubber, and dry wood are good examples.

A third kind of material is a solid in which a relatively small number of electrons can be freed from their atoms in such a manner as to leave a "hole" where each electron had been. The hole, representing the absence of a negative electron, behaves as though it were positively charged. An electric field will cause both negative electrons and positive holes to move through the material, thus producing a current of electricity. Such a solid, called a semiconductor, generally has a higher resistance to the flow of current than a conductor such as copper but a lower resistance than an insulator such as glass. If most of the current is carried by the negative electrons, the semiconductor is called "n-type". If most of the current is carried by the positive holes, the semiconductor is said to be "p-type".

If a material were a perfect conductor, a charge would pass through it without resistance (q.v.), and a perfect insulator would allow no charge to be forced through it. No substance of either type is known at room temperature. The best conductors at room temperature offer a low resistance (but not zero) to the flow of current. The best insulators offer a high resistance (but not infinite) at room temperature. However, most metals lose all their resistance at temperatures near absolute zero; this phenomenon is called *superconductivity*.

ELECTRIC CHARGES. One quantitative tool used to demonstrate the presence of electric charges is the electroscope (q.v.). This device also indicates whether the charge is negative or positive, and it determines and measures the intensity of radiation (q.v.). As first used by the British physicist and chemist, Michael Faraday, the device is shown in Fig. 1. The electroscope consists of

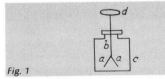
Fig. 1

two leaves of thin metal foil (a,a) suspended from a metal support (b) inside a glass or other nonconducting container (c). A knob (d) collects the electric charges; charges, either positive or negative, are applied to the metal support and travel to both leaves. The like charges repel one another, and the leaves fly apart, the distance between them depending roughly on the size of the charges.

Three methods may be used to charge an object electrically: (1) by contact with another object of dissimilar substance (such as contact between amber and fur), followed by separation; (2) by contact with another charged body; and (3) by induction.

The effect of electrical charges on conductors and nonconductors is shown in Fig. 2. A nega-

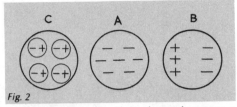
Fig. 2

tively charged body, A, is shown between a neutral conductor, B, and a neutral nonconductor, C. The free electrons in the conductor are repelled to the side of the conductor away from A, whereas, the positive charges are attracted to the nearer side. The entire body B is attracted toward A, because the attraction of the unlike charges that are close together is greater than the repulsion of the like charges that are farther apart. The forces between electrical charges vary inversely according to the square of the distance between the charges. In the nonconductor, C, the electrons are not free to move, but the atoms or molecules of the nonconductor reorient themselves so that their constituent electrons are as far as possible from A; the nonconductor is also attracted to A, but less strongly than the conductor.

The movement of electrons in the conductor B of Fig. 2 and the reorientation of the atoms of the nonconductor C gives these bodies positive charges on the sides nearest A and negative charges on the sides away from A. Charges produced in this manner are called induced charges.

Electrical Measurements. The flow of charge, current, in a wire is measured in terms of the number of coulombs per second going past a given point on a wire. One coulomb per second equals 1 ampere, a unit of electric current named for the French physicist, André Marie Ampère. See description under *Current Electricity,* below.

When 1 coulomb of charge travels across a potential difference of 1 volt, the work it does equals 1 joule. This definition facilitates transitions from mechanical to electrical quantities. One joule equals 10^7 ergs; *see* JOULE, JAMES PRESCOTT.

A widely used unit of energy in atomic physics is the electron volt (ev). This is the amount of energy gained by an electron that is acceler-

Thomas Alva Edison holds his "Edison Effect" lamp, in which he passed a weak electric current between a heated filament and a cold electrode; the famous inventor thus laid the basis of modern electronics.

Lewis Studios

ated by a potential difference of 1 volt. This is a small unit and is frequently multiplied by 1,000,000 or 1,000,000,000, the result being abbreviated 1 mev or 1 bev.

Current Electricity. If two equally and oppositely charged bodies are connected by a metallic conductor such as a wire, the charges neutralize each other. This neutralization is accomplished by means of a flow of electrons through the conductor from the negatively charged body to the positively charged one. (Note: in some branches of electrical engineering, electric current has been conventionally assumed to flow in the opposite direction, that is, from positive to negative.) In any continuous system of conductors electrons will flow from the point of lowest potential to the point of highest potential. A system of this kind is called an electric circuit. The current flowing in a circuit is described as direct current (DC) if it flows continuously in one direction, and as alternating current (AC) if it flows alternately in either direction.

Three interdependent quantities determine

the flow of direct currents. The first is the potential difference in the circuit, which is sometimes called the electromotive force (e.m.f.) or voltage. The second is the rate of current flow. This quantity is usually given in terms of the ampere, which corresponds to a flow of about 6,250,000,000,000,000,000 electrons per second past any point of the circuit. The third quantity is the resistance of the circuit. Under ordinary conditions all substances, conductors as well as nonconductors, offer some opposition to the flow of an electric current, and this resistance necessarily limits the current. The unit used for expressing the quantity of resistance is the ohm, which is defined as the amount of resistance which will limit the flow of current to 1 ampere, in a circuit with a potential difference of 1 volt. This relationship is known as Ohm's law and is named after the German physicist Georg Simon Ohm, who discovered the law in 1827. Ohm's law may be stated in the form of the algebraic equation $E = I \times R$, in which E is the electromotive force in volts, I is the current in amperes, and R is the resistance in ohms. From this equation any of the three quantities for a given circuit can be calculated if the other two quantities are known. Another formulation of Ohm's law is $I = E/R$. See ELECTRIC CIRCUIT; ELECTRIC METERS.

When an electric current flows through a wire, two important effects can be observed: the temperature of the wire is raised, and a magnet or a compass needle placed near the wire will be deflected, tending to point in a direction perpendicular to the wire. As the current flows, the electrons making up the current collide with the atoms of the conductor and give up energy, which appears in the form of heat. The amount of energy expended in an electric circuit is expressed in terms of the joule, which is equivalent to 0.738 foot pounds. Power expended is measured by the watt, which is equal to one joule per second. The power in a given circuit can be calculated from the equation $P = E \times I$ or $P = I^2 \times R$. Power may also be expended in producing mechanical work, electromagnetic radiation such as light or radio waves, and chemical decomposition.

Electromagnetism. The movement of a compass needle, near a conductor through which a current is flowing, indicates the presence of a magnetic field (see MAGNETISM) around the conductor. When currents flow through two parallel conductors, the magnetic fields of the conductors attract each other when the current flow is in the same direction in both conductors, and repel each other when the flows are in opposite directions. The magnetic field caused by the current in a single loop of wire is such that if the loop is suspended near the earth it will behave like a magnet or compass needle and swing until the wire of the loop is perpendicular to a line running from the north and south magnetic poles of the earth.

The magnetic field about a current-carrying conductor can be visualized as spreading radially outward from the conductor in the same manner as ripples created when a stone is dropped into water. The direction of the magnetic lines of force in the field is counterclockwise when observed in the direction in which the electrons are moving. The field is stationary about the conductor so long as the current is flowing steadily through the conductor.

When a conductor moves so as to cut the lines of force of a magnetic field, the field acts on the free electrons in the conductor, displacing them and causing a potential difference and a flow of current in the conductor. The same effect occurs whether the magnetic field is stationary and the wire moves, or the field moves and the wire is stationary. When a current begins to flow in a conductor, a field moves out from the conductor. This field cuts the conductor itself and induces a current in it in the direction opposite to the original flow of current. With a conductor such as a straight piece of wire this effect is very slight, but if the wire is wound into a helical coil, the effect is much increased because the fields from the individual turns of the coil cut the neighboring turns and induce a current in them as well. The result is that such a coil, when connected to a source of potential difference, will impede the flow of current when the potential difference is first applied. Similarly when the source of potential difference is removed, the magnetic field "collapses" and again the moving lines of force cut the turns of the coil. The current induced under these circumstances is in the same direction as the original current, and the coil tends to continue the flow of current. Because of these properties, a coil resists any change in the flow of current, and is said to possess electrical inertia, or inductance. This inertia has little importance in DC circuits, because it is not observed when current is flowing steadily, but it has great importance in AC circuits. See *Alternating Currents*, below.

Conduction in Liquids and Gases. When an electric current flows in a metallic conductor, the flow is in one direction only, inasmuch as the current is carried entirely by electrons. In liquids and gases, however, a two-directional flow is made possible by the process of ionization; see ELECTROCHEMISTRY. In a liquid solution, the positive ions move through the solution from points of high positive potential to points of low positive potential; the negative ions move in the opposite direction. Similarly, in gases, which may be ionized by radioactivity, by the ultraviolet rays of sunlight, by electromagnetic waves, or by an electric field of high potential gradient, a two-way drift of ions takes place to produce an electric current through the gas; see ELECTRIC DISCHARGE.

Sources of Electromotive Force. To produce a flow of current in any electrical circuit, a source of electromotive force or potential difference is necessary. The available sources are as follows: (1) electrostatic machines, which operate on the principle of inducing electric charges by mechanical means (see ELECTROSTATIC MACHINE); (2) electromagnetic machines, in which current is generated by mechanically moving conductors through a magnetic field or a number of fields (see DYNAMOELECTRIC MACHINERY); (3) voltaic cells, which produce an electro-

431

motive force through electrochemical action (*see* CELL, ELECTRIC); (4) devices that produce electromotive force through the action of heat (*see* THERMOELECTRICITY); (5) devices that produce electromotive force by the action of light (*see* PHOTOELECTRIC CELL; SOLAR POWER); and (6) devices that produce electromotive force by means of physical pressure (for example, the piezoelectric crystal, for which *see* CRYSTAL: *Crystallography*).

Alternating Currents. When a conductor is moved back and forth in a magnetic field, the flow of current in the conductor will change direction as often as the physical motion of the conductor changes direction. Several devices generating electricity operate on this principle, producing an oscillating form of current called alternating current. Alternating current has several valuable characteristics, as compared to direct current, and is generally used as a source of electric power and light, both for industrial installations and in the home.

The most important practical characteristic of alternating current is that the voltage or the current may be changed to almost any value desired by means of a simple electromagnetic device called a transformer. When an alternating current passes through a coil of wire, the magnetic field about the coil expands and collapses and then expands in a field of opposite polarity and again collapses. If another conductor or coil of wire is placed in the magnetic field of the first coil, but not in direct electric connection with it, the movement of the magnetic field induces an alternating current in the second coil. If the second coil has a larger number of turns than the first, the voltage induced in the second coil will be larger than the voltage in the first, because the field is acting on a greater number of individual conductors. Conversely, if the number of turns in the second coil is smaller, the secondary, or induced, voltage will be smaller than the primary voltage.

The action of a transformer makes possible the economical transmission of electric power over long distances. If 200,000 watts of power is supplied to a power line, it may be equally well supplied by a potential of 200,000 volts and a current of 1 ampere or by a potential of 2000 volts and a current of 100 amperes, because power is equal to the product of voltage and current. The power lost in the line through heating is equal to the square of the current times the resistance. Thus, if the resistance of the line is 10 ohms, the loss on the 200,000-volt line will be 10 watts, whereas the loss on the 2000-volt line will be 100,000 watts or half the avail-

able power; *see under* ELECTRIC POWER SYSTEMS.

The magnetic field about a coil in an a-c circuit is constantly changing, and the coil constantly impedes the flow of current in the circuit, because of the quality of the inductance mentioned above. The relationship between the voltage impressed on an ideal coil (that is, a coil having no resistance) and the current flowing in the ideal coil is such that the current is at a zero value when the voltage is at a maximum, and the current is at a maximum when the voltage is at zero. Furthermore, the changing magnetic field induces a potential difference in the coil that is equal in magnitude and opposite in direction to the impressed potential difference. In practice, coils always exhibit resistance and capacitance as well as inductance.

If a condenser, also called a capacitor, is placed in an a-c circuit, the current is proportional to the size of the condenser and to the time rate of the change of the voltage across the condenser; *see* CONDENSER, ELECTRICAL. Therefore, twice as much current will flow through a condenser that has a capacity or size of two farads as in a condenser of one farad capacity. In an ideal condenser, the voltage is exactly out of phase with the current. No current will flow when the voltage is maximum because then the rate of change of voltage equals zero. The current will be maximum when the voltage equals zero because then the rate of change of voltage will be maximum. Current flows through a condenser even if there is no direct electrical connection between its plates because the voltage on one plate induces an opposite charge on the other plate.

It follows from the above effects that if an alternating voltage is applied to an ideal inductance or capacitance no power is expended. In all practical cases, however, a-c circuits contain resistance as well as inductance and capacitance, and power is actually expended. The amount of power depends on the relative amounts of the three quantities present in the circuits.

History. The knowledge that amber acquires the power to attract light objects when rubbed is believed to date back at least to the Greek philosopher Thales of Miletus, who lived about 600 B.C. Another Greek philosopher, Theophrastus, in a treatise written about three centuries later, stated that this power is possessed by other substances. The first scientific study of electrical and magnetic phenomena, however, did not appear until 1600 A.D., when the researches of the English physician William Gilbert were published. Gilbert was the first to

Electricity. Plate 1. *Above: Over-all view of an array of power generators in a hydroelectric dam installation. Below: Aesthetic considerations influence the design and appearance of bulky power-transmission systems across the land. These colorful devices are 500-kilovolt oil circuit breakers, in which the breakers are immersed in oil to break the arc that forms across the terminals when an automatic interruption of current occurs.*

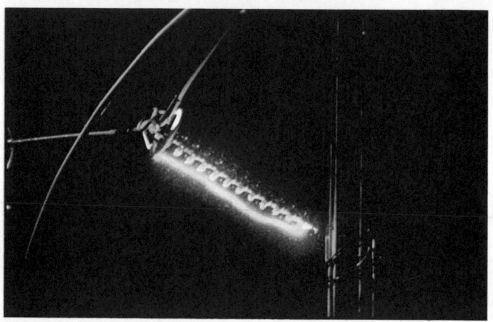

Above: A striking photograph of an electric-discharge flash over insulation devices in a power-transmission line.

Electricity. Plate

Left: A modern 69-kilovolt oil circuit breaker and high-voltage circuit-opening device. These switching devices automatically regulate powerful electric circuits, interrupting the transmission of power under abnormal conditions such as overloads and short circuits.

apply the term "electric" (Gr. *elektron*, "amber") to the force that such substances exert after rubbing. He also distinguished between magnetic and electric action.

The first machine for producing an electric charge was described in 1672 by the German physicist Otto von Guericke. It consisted of a sulfur sphere turned by a crank on which a charge was induced when the hand was held against it. The French scientist Charles François de Cisternay Du Fay (1698–1739) was the first to make clear the two different types of electric charge: positive and negative. The earliest form of condenser, the Leyden jar (q.v.), was developed in 1745. It consisted of a glass bottle with separate coatings of tinfoil on the inside and outside. If either tinfoil coating was charged from an electrostatic machine a violent shock could be obtained by touching both foil coatings at the same time.

The American scientist and diplomat Benjamin Franklin spent much time in electrical research. His famous kite experiment proved that the atmospheric electricity that causes the phenomena of lightning and thunder is identical with the electrostatic charge on a Leyden jar. Franklin developed a theory that electricity was a single "fluid" existing in all matter, and that its effects could be explained by excesses and shortages of this fluid.

The law that the force between electric charges varies inversely with the square of the distance between the charges was proved experimentally by the British chemist Joseph Priestley about 1766. Priestley also demonstrated that an electric charge distributes itself uniformly over the surface of a hollow metal sphere, and that no charge and no electric field of force exists within such a sphere. Charles Augustin de Coulomb invented a torsion balance to measure accurately the force exerted by electrical charges. With this apparatus he confirmed Priestley's observations and showed that the force between two charges was also proportional to the product of the individual charges. Faraday, who made many contributions to the study of electricity in the early 19th century, was also responsible for the theory of electric lines of force.

The Italian physicists Luigi Galvani and Alessandro Volta conducted the first important experiments in electrical currents. Galvani produced a current by putting two dissimilar wires into the muscle of the leg of a frog. Volta in 1800 announced the first man-made electrochemical source of potential difference, a form of electric battery. The fact that a magnetic field exists around an electric current flow was demonstrated by the Danish scientist Hans Christian Oersted in 1819, and in 1831 Faraday proved that a current flowing in a coil of wire could induce electromagnetically a current in a nearby coil. The British physicist, James Prescott Joule, and the German scientist, Hermann Ludwig Ferdinand von Helmholtz, about 1840 demonstrated that electric circuits obeyed the law of the conservation of energy and that electricity was a form of energy.

One of the most important contributions made to the study of electricity in the 19th century was the work of the British mathematical physicist James Clerk Maxwell, who investigated the properties of electromagnetic waves and light and developed the theory that the two are identical. His work paved the way for the German physicist Heinrich Rudolph Hertz, who produced and detected electric waves in the atmosphere in 1886, and for the Italian engineer Guglielmo Marconi, who in 1896 harnessed these waves to produce the first practical radio signaling system; see RADIO.

The electron theory, which is the basis of modern electrical theory, was first advanced by the Dutch physicist Hendrik Antoon Lorentz in 1892. The charge on the electron was first accurately measured by the American physicist Robert Andrews Millikan in 1909. The widespread use of electricity as a source of power and light is largely due to the work of such pioneering American engineers and inventors as Thomas Alva Edison, Nikola Tesla, and Charles Proteus Steinmetz. See separate articles on persons whose birth and death dates are not given.

See also ELECTRONICS.   E.C.E.

ELECTRICITY, TERRESTRIAL. *See* TERRESTRIAL ELECTRICITY.

ELECTRIC LIGHTING, illumination by means of any of a number of devices that convert electrical energy into light (q.v.). The types of electric lighting devices most commonly used are the incandescent lamp, the fluorescent lamp, and the various types of arc and electric-discharge vapor lamps; see ELECTRIC ARC.

Technology of Electric Lighting. If an electric current is passed through any conductor, other than a perfect conductor, a certain amount of energy is expended that appears in the form of heat in the conductor; see CONDUCTOR, ELECTRICAL. Inasmuch as any heated body will give off a certain amount of light at temperatures over 525° C. (977° F.), a conductor heated above that temperature by an electric current will act as a light source. The incandescent lamp consists of a filament of a material with a high melting

435

point sealed inside a glass bulb, from which the air has been evacuated, or which is filled with an inert gas. Filaments with high melting points must be used, because the proportion of light energy to heat energy radiated by the filament rises as the temperature increases, and the highest efficiency as a light source is obtained at the highest filament temperature. The first practical incandescent lamps employed carbon filaments, but modern lamps are universally made with filaments of fine tungsten wire, which has a melting point of 3380° C. (6116° F.); see TUNGSTEN. The filament must be enclosed either in a vacuum or in an inert atmosphere, since otherwise the heated filament would react chemically with the surrounding atmosphere. The use of an inert gas instead of a vacuum in the bulb of an incandescent lamp has the advantage of slowing evaporation of the filament, thus prolonging the life of the lamp. In most modern incandescent lamps, a mixture of argon with a small amount of nitrogen or krypton (qq.v.), or with halogen gases (see HALOGENS), is used to fill the bulb. Radical changes in incandescent lamp design have resulted from the substitution of compact fused-quartz glass tubes for glass bulbs.

Types of Lamps. Electric-discharge (q.v.) lamps depend on the ionization and the resulting electric discharge (qq.v.) in vapors or gases at low pressures, if an electric current is passed through them. Representative examples of these types of devices are the mercury-vapor arc lamp, which gives an intense blue-green light and is used for photographic and roadway illumination; and the neon lamp (q.v.), which is employed for decorative sign and display lighting. Newer electric-discharge lamps add other metals to mercury and phosphor on the enclosing bulbs to improve color and efficacy. Glasslike, translucent ceramic tubes have led to high-pressure sodium vapor lamps of unprecedented lighting power.

The fluorescent lamp is another type of electric discharge device used for general-purpose illumination. It is a low-pressure mercury vapor lamp contained in a glass tube, which is coated on the inside with a fluorescent material known as phosphor. The radiation (q.v.) in the arc of the vapor lamp causes the phosphor to become fluorescent. Much of the radiation from the arc is invisible ultraviolet light (see ULTRAVIOLET RADIATION), but this radiation is changed to visible light, if it excites the phosphor. Fluorescent lamps have several important advantages. By choosing the proper type of phosphor, the light from such lamps can be made to approximate

the quality of daylight. In addition, the efficacy of the fluorescent lamp is high. A fluorescent tube taking 40 watts of energy produces as much light as a 150-watt incandescent bulb. Because of this illuminating power, fluorescent lamps produce less heat than incandescent bulbs for comparable light production.

An advance in the field of electric lighting is the use of electroluminescence, known commonly as panel lighting. In panel lighting particles of phosphor are suspended in a thin layer of nonconducting material such as plastic. This layer is sandwiched between two plate conductors, one of which is a translucent substance, such as glass, coated on the inside with a thin film of tin oxide. With the two conductors acting as electrodes (see ELECTRODE), an alternating current is passed through the phosphor, causing it to luminesce. Luminescent panels may serve a variety of purposes, for example, to illuminate clock and radio dials, to outline the risers in staircases, and to provide luminous walls. Applications of panel lighting are restricted, however, because the current requirements for large installations are excessive. See FLUORESCENCE AND PHOSPHORESCENCE.

A number of different kinds of electric lamps have been developed for special purposes such as photography (q.v.) and floodlighting. These bulbs are generally shaped to act as reflectors when coated with an aluminum mirror; see OPTICS: *Curved Mirrors.* One such lamp is the photoflood bulb, an incandescent lamp which is operated at a temperature higher than normal to obtain greater light output. The life of these bulbs is limited to 2 or 3 hr., as against 750 to 1000 hr. for the ordinary incandescent bulb. Photoflash bulbs used for high-speed photography produce a single high-intensity flash of light, lasting a few hundredths of a second, by the ignition of a charge of crumpled aluminum foil or fine aluminum wire inside an oxygen-filled glass bulb. The foil is ignited by the heat of a small filament in the bulb.

History. The earliest experiments in electric lighting were conducted by the British chemist Sir Humphry Davy (q.v.), who produced electric arcs and who also made a fine platinum wire incandescent by passing a current through it in air. Beginning about 1840 a number of incandescent lamps were patented, but none were commercially successful until the American inventor Thomas Alva Edison (q.v.) produced his carbon-filament lamp in 1879. During the same period various arc lamps were introduced. The first practical arc lamp was installed in a lighthouse (q.v.) at Dungeness, England, in 1862. The Amer-

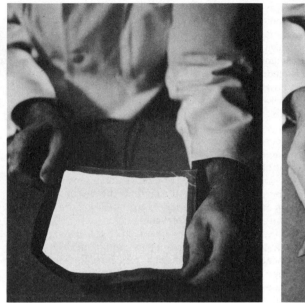

ican pioneer in electrical engineering, Charles Francis Brush (q.v.), produced the first commercially successful arc lamp in 1878. Tungsten filaments were substituted for carbon filaments in incandescent lamps in 1907, and gas-filled incandescent lamps were developed in 1913. The fluorescent lamp was introduced in 1938.

See LAMP.   ILLUMINATING ENGINEERING SOCIETY

ELECTRIC METERS, instruments for measuring and indicating magnitudes of electrical values, such as current, charge, potential, and power, and the electrical characteristics of circuits, such as resistance, capacity, and inductance. The information is usually presented in terms of defined, standard electrical units, which principally are the ohm, volt, ampere, coulomb, henry, farad, watt, and joule; see ELECTRICAL UNITS. In that all forms of matter exhibit one or more electrical characteristics, electrical measurements may be taken from an essentially unlimited number of sources.

Basic Meter Mechanisms. By their nature, electrical values cannot be measured by direct observation. Therefore some property of electricity must be used in analog application to produce a physical force that can be observed and measured. For example, in a galvanometer, which was the earliest type of meter devised, the force existing between a magnetic field and a pivoted, current-carrying coil within the field causes an observable deflection of the coil. Because the deflection is proportional to the current, a calibrated scale is employed to measure

the electric current. Electromagnetic action between currents, force action between electric charges, and the heating effect caused by conductor resistance are some other examples of indirect methods used for electric meter analog readouts.

Meter Calibration. To insure uniformity and accuracy, electric meters are calibrated according to the accepted standards of measurement for the given electrical unit (such as volt, ampere, ohm, and watt) as established in the United States, for example, by the National Bureau of Standards (q.v.).

Primary Standards and Absolute Measurements. The primary standards for the ohm and ampere are based upon internationally accepted definitions of these units in terms of mass, conductor dimension, and time. The measurement techniques which employ these basic units are accurate and reproducible. Absolute ampere measurements, for example, involve the use of a weighing-balance scheme that measures the force between a set of fixed coaxial coils and a moving coil. Absolute measurements of current and potential difference are of importance primarily in laboratory work, and for most purposes relative measurements are sufficient. The meters described in the following paragraphs are all intended for relative measurements.

Measurements of Current. Galvanometers are

437

the main instruments used to detect and measure current. They depend on the fact that force is generated by an electric current flowing in a magnetic field. The mechanism of the galvanometer is so arranged that a small permanent magnet or electromagnet sets up a magnetic field that generates a force when current flows in a wire coil adjacent to the magnet. Either the magnet or the adjacent coil may be movable. The force deflects the movable member by an amount proportional to the strength of the current. The movable member may have a pointer or some other device to enable the amount of deflection to be read on a calibrated scale.

In the D'Arsonval galvanometer, a small mirror attached to a movable coil reflects a beam of light on a scale about 3 ft. away from the instrument. This arrangement involves less inertia and friction than does a pointer, and consequently greater accuracy is achieved. The instrument was named after the French biologist and physicist, Jacques d'Arsonval (1851–1940), who devised the first reflecting galvanometer. He also conducted experiments with the mechanical equivalent of heat and in high-frequency oscillating current of low voltage and high amperage, d'Arsonval current, used in the treatment of certain diseases (diathermy treatment). The addition of a scale and proper calibration converts a galvanometer into an ammeter, the instrument used for measuring electric current in amperes, and d'Arsonval was also responsible for inventing a direct-current (DC) ammeter.

Only a limited amount of current can be passed through the fine wire of a galvanometer coil. When large currents must be measured, a shunt of low resistance is attached across the terminals of the meter. Most of the current is bypassed through this shunt resistance, but the small current flowing through the meter is still proportional to the total current. By taking advantage of this proportionality, a galvanometer can be used to measure currents of hundreds of amperes. Galvanometers are usually named according to the magnitude of the currents they will measure. A microammeter is calibrated in millionths of an ampere and a milliammeter in thousandths of an ampere.

Ordinary galvanometers cannot be used for the measurement of alternating currents (AC), because the alternation of the current would produce deflection in both directions. However, an adaptation of the galvanometer, called an electrodynamometer, can be used to measure alternating current by means of electromagnetic deflection. In this meter a fixed coil, in series with the moving coil, is employed in place

of the permanent magnet of the galvanometer. Because the current in the fixed and in the moving coil reverses at the same instant, the deflection of the moving coil is always in the same direction, and the meter gives a constant current reading. Meters of this type can also be used to measure direct currents. Another form of electromagnetic meter is the iron-vane meter or soft-iron meter. In this device two vanes of soft iron, one fixed and one pivoted, are placed between the poles of a solenoid coil through which is passed the current to be measured. The current induces magnetism in the two vanes, causing the same deflection no matter what the direction of the current. The amount of the current is ascertained by measuring the deflection of the moving vane.

Meters which depend on the heating effect of an electric current are used to measure alternating current of high frequency. In thermocouple meters, the current passes through a fine wire which heats a thermocouple junction; the electricity generated by the thermocouple is measured by an ordinary galvanometer. In hot-wire meters, the current passes through a thin wire which heats and stretches. This wire is mechanically linked to a pointer which moves over a scale calibrated in terms of current.

Measurement of Voltage. The instrument most generally used to measure potential difference or voltage is a galvanometer, with a high resistance in series with the coil. When such a meter is connected across a battery, or to two points in an electrical circuit between which a potential difference exists, a small current (limited by the series resistor) will pass through the meter. The current is proportional to the voltage, and the latter quantity can be measured if the galvanometer is calibrated appropriately. By using the proper values of series resistors, one galvanometer can be used to measure a large range of voltages. The most accurate instrument for the determination of voltage, resistance, or direct current is the potentiometer, which indicates an unknown electromotive force by comparing it with a known value.

For the measurement of a-c voltages, a-c current meters having high internal resistance, or similar meters with high series resistance, are employed.

Other methods for measuring the value of a-c voltages depend on vacuum tubes and electronic circuits (see ELECTRONICS) and are especially useful in measurements at high frequencies. One such device is the vacuum-tube voltmeter. In the simplest form of this meter an a-c voltage is rectified by a diode tube, and the rectified current is measured by an ordinary galvanometer. Other such voltmeters employ the amplifying characteristics of electronic tubes to measure extremely small voltages. The cathode-ray oscilloscope can also be used for voltage measurements, because the deflection of the electron beam is proportional to the voltage impressed on the deflection plates or coils.

Miscellaneous Measurements. The most accurate measurements of resistance are made with a galvanometer in a circuit called a Wheatstone bridge, named after the British physicist, Sir Charles Wheatstone (q.v.). This circuit consists of three known resistances and an unknown resistance connected in a diamond pattern. A d-c voltage is connected across two opposite points of the diamond, and a galvanometer is bridged across the other two points. When all four of the resistances bear a fixed relationship to each other, the currents flowing through the two arms of the circuit will be equal and no current will flow through the galvanometer. By varying the value of one of the known resistances, the bridge can be made to balance for any value of unknown resistance, which can then be calculated from the values of the other resistors. Similar bridges, substituting known inductances and known capacitances for the resistance arms of the bridge, are employed in the measurement of the inductance and capacitance of circuit components. Bridges of this type are usually known as a-c bridges, because a-c sources are used rather than d-c sources. These bridges are often balanced by means of a telephone receiver rather than a galvanometer. When the bridge is unbalanced, a tone will be heard in the receiver, corresponding to the frequency of the a-c source, but when the bridge is balanced, no tone will be heard.

The power consumed by any part of an electric circuit is most easily measured by a wattmeter, an instrument resembling the electrodynamometer. The wattmeter has its fixed coil connected so that the whole current of the circuit passes through it, and the moving coil is connected in series with a high resistance so that the current passing through it is proportional to the voltage of the source. The resulting deflection of the moving coil depends on both the current and the voltage and can be calibrated directly in power, since power is the product of voltage and current. The watt-hour meter, also known as a service meter, is a device to measure the total energy consumed in a circuit such as a home electrical circuit. It resembles the wattmeter, except that the movable coil is replaced by a motor armature. The armature, which is regulated by a magnetic governor, revolves at a speed proportional to the amount of power consumed. The armature shaft is geared to a series of dials which indicate the total energy consumed. *See also* ELECTRICITY; ELECTROSCOPE; TELEMETRY. G.D.F.

ELECTRIC MOTOR. *See* DYNAMOELECTRIC MACHINERY.

ELECTRIC-POWER SYSTEMS, systems for the transformation of other types of energy into electric energy and the transmission of this energy to the point of consumption. The production and transmission of energy in this form have important economic advantages. Such systems permit power generation by large machines that are comparatively cheap to build and operate in terms of cost per unit of power delivered. Electric-power systems also make possible the utilization of hydroelectric power at a distance from the source. Alternating current (AC) is generally used in modern power systems, because it has the important advantage of being easily converted to higher or lower voltages by means of transformers; *see* TRANSFORMER. Thus each stage of the system can be operated at an appropriate voltage. Such an electric-power system consists of six main elements: the power station, a set of transformers to raise the generated power to the high voltages used on the primary transmission lines, the primary transmission lines, the substations at which the power is stepped down to the voltage of the secondary transmission lines, the secondary transmission lines, and the transformers that lower the secondary voltage to the amount used by the consumer.

In a typical system the generators at the central station deliver a voltage of from 1000 to 26,000 volts (higher voltages being undesirable because of difficulties of insulation and the danger of electrical breakdown and damage). This voltage is stepped up by means of transformers to values ranging from 138,000 to 500,000 volts for the primary transmission line (the greater the voltage on the line, the less the current and consequently the less the power loss, the loss being proportional to the square of the current). At the substation the voltage is stepped down again by transformers to a distribution level such as 2400 or 4160 volts or 15, 27, or 33 kilovolts. Finally the current is stepped down once again at the transformer near the point of use to 240 or 120 volts (the low voltage requires more costly, heavier conductors that lessen the hazards of fire and electric shock).

The modern development of high-voltage electronic rectifying tubes and semiconductor

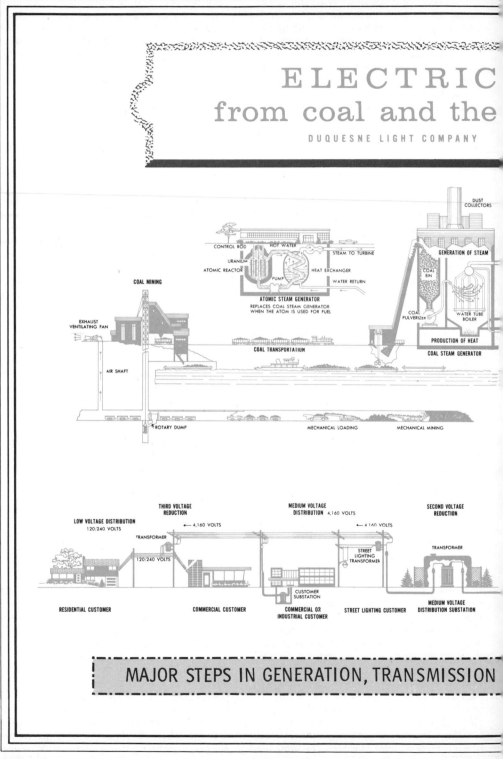

ELECTRIC
from coal and the
DUQUESNE LIGHT COMPANY

DUST COLLECTORS

CONTROL ROD   HOT WATER   STEAM TO TURBINE   GENERATION OF STEAM

URANIUM
ATOMIC REACTOR   HEAT EXCHANGER   COAL BIN
PUMP   WATER RETURN
ATOMIC STEAM GENERATOR
REPLACES COAL STEAM GENERATOR
WHEN THE ATOM IS USED FOR FUEL   COAL PULVERIZER   WATER TUBE BOILER

COAL MINING   PRODUCTION OF HEAT

EXHAUST VENTILATING FAN   COAL TRANSPORTATION   COAL STEAM GENERATOR

AIR SHAFT

ROTARY DUMP   MECHANICAL LOADING   MECHANICAL MINING

THIRD VOLTAGE REDUCTION   MEDIUM VOLTAGE DISTRIBUTION 4,160 VOLTS   SECOND VOLTAGE REDUCTION

LOW VOLTAGE DISTRIBUTION 120/240 VOLTS   ← 4,160 VOLTS   ← 4,160 VOLTS

TRANSFORMER   TRANSFORMER

120/240 VOLTS   STREET LIGHTING TRANSFORMER

CUSTOMER SUBSTATION

RESIDENTIAL CUSTOMER   COMMERCIAL CUSTOMER   COMMERCIAL OR INDUSTRIAL CUSTOMER   STREET LIGHTING CUSTOMER   MEDIUM VOLTAGE DISTRIBUTION SUBSTATION

MAJOR STEPS IN GENERATION, TRANSMISSION

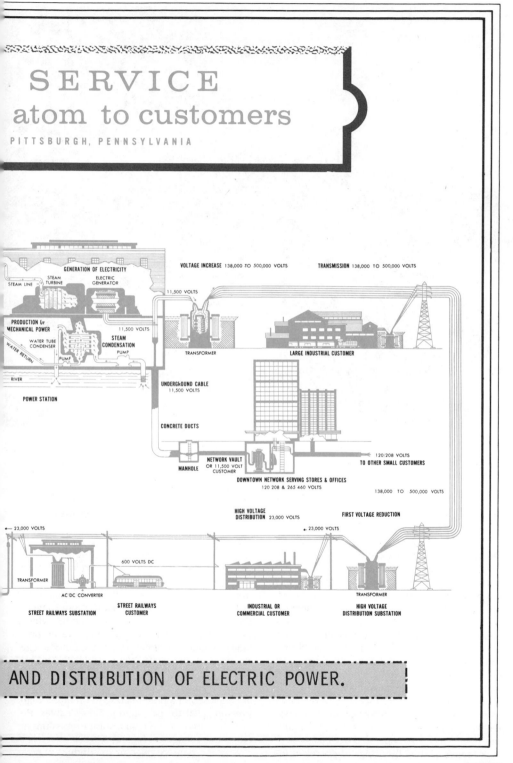

SERVICE
atom to customers
PITTSBURGH, PENNSYLVANIA

GENERATION OF ELECTRICITY

VOLTAGE INCREASE 138,000 TO 500,000 VOLTS   TRANSMISSION 138,000 TO 500,000 VOLTS

STEAM LINE   STEAM TURBINE   ELECTRIC GENERATOR

11,500 VOLTS

PRODUCTION Or MECHANICAL POWER

WATER TUBE CONDENSER   11,500 VOLTS   STEAM CONDENSATION

WATER RETURN   PUMP   PUMP

TRANSFORMER   LARGE INDUSTRIAL CUSTOMER

RIVER

POWER STATION

UNDERGROUND CABLE 11,500 VOLTS

CONCRETE DUCTS

120/208 VOLTS
TO OTHER SMALL CUSTOMERS

NETWORK VAULT OR 11,500 VOLT CUSTOMER

MANHOLE

DOWNTOWN NETWORK SERVING STORES & OFFICES
120 208 & 265 460 VOLTS

138,000 TO 500,000 VOLTS

HIGH VOLTAGE DISTRIBUTION 23,000 VOLTS   FIRST VOLTAGE REDUCTION

← 23,000 VOLTS   ← 23,000 VOLTS

600 VOLTS DC

TRANSFORMER

TRANSFORMER

AC DC CONVERTER

STREET RAILWAYS SUBSTATION   STREET RAILWAYS CUSTOMER   INDUSTRIAL OR COMMERCIAL CUSTOMER   HIGH VOLTAGE DISTRIBUTION SUBSTATION

AND DISTRIBUTION OF ELECTRIC POWER.

The huge control panel of Commonwealth Edison's Zion Station, a 2200-megawatt nuclear power plant in Zion, Ill. The installation helps to supply the Chicago area with electric power.   UPI

rectifiers makes possible the conversion of high-voltage AC to high-voltage DC for power distribution, thus avoiding capacitive and inductive losses in transmission (see below). An 800 kilovolts DC line extends from Portland, Oreg., to Los Angeles, Calif.

The central station of a power system consists of a prime mover, such as a water or steam turbine, which operates an electric generator. About 80 percent of the electric power generated in the United States is generated in steam plants driven by coal, oil, or gas. About 18 percent is generated by hydroelectric plants, and the rest by diesel and internal-combustion plants and by nuclear-power plants.

The primary lines of high-voltage transmission systems are usually composed of wires of copper, aluminum, or copper-clad or aluminum-clad steel, which are suspended from tall lattice-work towers of steel by strings of porcelain in-

sulators. By the use of clad steel wires and high towers, the distance between towers can be increased, and the cost of the transmission line thus reduced. In modern installations with essentially straight paths, high-voltage lines may be built with as few as six towers to the mile. In some areas high-voltage lines are suspended from tall wooden poles spaced more closely together. For secondary distribution lines, wooden poles are generally used rather than steel towers. In cities and other areas where open lines create a hazard, insulated underground cables are used for distribution. Some of these cables have a hollow core through which oil circulates under low pressure. The oil provides temporary protection from water damage to the enclosed wires if the cable develops a leak. This type of cable has been largely superseded by pipe-type cable in which three cables are enclosed in a pipe filled with oil under high pressure (200 lb. per sq.in.). These cables are used for transmission and subtransmission of current at voltages as high as 345,000.

Another type of electrical conductor now

being used experimentally for secondary power-transmission lines and for primary distribution up to 15,000 volts, is polyethelene-insulated sodium (q.v.). Metallic sodium has economical advantages over conventional copper and aluminum conductors in that it is light in weight. Moreover, the flexibility of the sodium cable affords greater ease of installation in both underground and overhead power cable applications. Extensive tests have indicated that such systems are tough and resilient, and can withstand considerable abuse. Electrical conductivity of sodium ranks just below copper and aluminum. A major problem with sodium cables is that the metal reacts chemically with water, and must be protected from moisture. See CABLE, ELECTRIC.

Any electric-distribution system involves a large amount of supplementary equipment for the protection of generators, transformers, and the transmission lines themselves. In addition, the system often includes devices that are designed to regulate the voltage delivered to consumers and to correct the power factor of the system.

To protect all elements of a power system from short circuits and overloads, and for normal switching operations, circuit breakers are employed. These breakers are large switches that are actuated automatically in the event of a short circuit or other condition that produces a sudden rise of current. Because an arc is formed across the terminals of the circuit breaker at the moment when the current is interrupted, some large breakers (such as those used to protect a generator or a section of primary transmission line) are immersed in oil to quench the arc. In large air-type circuit breakers, as well as in oil breakers, magnetic fields are used to break up the arc. Small air-circuit breakers are used for

protection in shops, factories, and in modern home installations but usually, in residential electric wiring, fuses are employed for the same purpose. The fuse (q.v.) consists of a piece of alloy with a low melting point, inserted in the circuit, which melts, breaking the circuit, if the current rises above a certain value.

Power Failures. Companies began to pool power in 1928, and now nearly all electric utilities in the U.S. and Canada have joined in various grid systems. The linking grids allow electricity generated in one area to be shared with others. Each pooling company gains an increased reserve capacity, use of larger, more efficient generators, and compensation, through sharing, for local power failures.

The first major grid-system breakdown occurred on Nov. 9, 1965. It started in a plant of the Hydroelectric Power Commission of Ontario in Queenston, Ontario, Canada. An automatic control device that regulates and directs current flow failed, causing a circuit breaker to remain open. A surge of excess current was transmitted through the northeastern U.S. Generator safety switches from Rochester, N.Y., to Boston, Mass., were automatically tripped, cutting generators out of the system to protect them from damage. Power generated by more southerly plants rushed to fill the vacuum and overloaded these plants, which automatically shut themselves off. The power failure enveloped an 80,000-sq.mi. area including the cities of Boston, Buffalo, N.Y., Rochester, and New York City. A similar daylight power failure began in Philadelphia, Pa., on June 6, 1967, affecting

Section cut through a hydroelectric-power plant on Raccoon Mt., one of many built by the Tennessee Valley Authority. Large quantities of water are channeled into the powerplant chamber from the reservoir, to drive the generators that produce electricity, before being discharged into Lake Nickajack, about 6 mi. west of Chattanooga, Tenn.

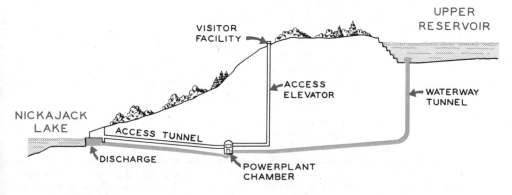

UPPER RESERVOIR

VISITOR FACILITY

ACCESS ELEVATOR

WATERWAY TUNNEL

NICKAJACK LAKE

ACCESS TUNNEL

DISCHARGE

POWERPLANT CHAMBER

parts of four States. In July, 1977, lightning knocked out a transformer in New York State; resulting load imbalances triggered an automatic shutdown of the entire grid serving New York City and Westchester Co. In spite of protective devices installed after the 1965 blackout, power was lost to all five boroughs of the city for periods of time ranging from 4½ to 25 hr., depending on the locality.

Voltage Regulation. Long transmission lines have considerable inductance and capacitance as well as resistance. When a current flows through the line, inductance and capacitance have the effect of varying the voltage on the line as the current varies. Thus the supply voltage varies with the load. Several kinds of devices are used to overcome this undesirable variation, in an operation called regulation of the voltage. They include induction regulators and three-phase synchronous motors (called synchronous condensers), both of which vary the effective amount of inductance and capacitance in the transmission circuit. Inductance and capacitance react with a tendency to nullify one another. When a load circuit has more inductive than capacitive reactance, as almost invariably occurs in large power systems, the amount of power delivered for a given voltage and current is less than when the two are equal. The ratio of these two amounts of power is called the power factor. Because transmission-line losses are proportional to current, capacitance is added to the circuit when possible, thus bringing the power factor as nearly as possible to 1. For this reason, large capacitors are frequently inserted as a part of power-transmission systems.

Power Production in the United States. The total electric power producing capacity (installed capacity) in the U.S. in the mid-1970's was about 550,400,000 kw; of this total, hydroelectric plants accounted for 57,000,000 kw, and thermal and nuclear plants the remainder. Approximately 2.12 trillion kw hours per year were being generated from all sources; this represented about 35 percent of the total world output of electricity. The demand for electricity generated by utility companies was growing at about 4.5 percent per year in the mid-1970's, as against a growth rate of nearly 8 percent at the beginning of the decade. Federally owned projects accounted for 236 billion kw hours of the U.S. total. Texas led the U.S. in installed generating capacity and was the leading State in electricity generated. The next leading States in both installed capacity and in production of electricity were California, Pennsylvania, New York, Ohio, and Illinois.

Congress authorized the use of atomic energy for the production of commercial power in the U.S. in 1954. The first nuclear-power plant to provide electricity for U.S. consumers was the 90,000-kw installation completed in Shippingport, Pa., in 1957. In the mid-1970's there were about 60 reactors in the U.S. with an installed capacity of 47,000,000 kw. According to U.S. government estimates, another 14,000,000 kw would be installed by 1981.

For explanation of technical terms *see* ELECTRICITY. *See also* INTERIOR, DEPARTMENT OF THE; TENNESSEE VALLEY AUTHORITY.   E.C.E.

ELECTRIC RAILWAYS. *See* MONORAIL; RAILROADS: *Electrification.*

ELECTRIC RAY. *See* ELECTRIC FISH; TORPEDO.

ELECTRIC SHOCK TREATMENT. *See* MENTAL DISORDERS.

ELECTROCARDIOGRAPH. *See* HEART: *Heart Diseases.*

ELECTROCHEMISTRY, that part of the science of chemistry which deals with the interrelationship of electrical currents, or voltages, and chemical reactions, and with the mutual conversion of chemical and electrical energy; *see* CHEMISTRY: *Major Divisions of Chemistry: Physical Chemistry;* ELECTRICITY; ENERGY. In the broadest sense, electrochemistry is the study of chemical reactions which produce electrical effects and of the chemical phenomena that are caused by the action of currents or voltages.

Most inorganic and some organic chemical compounds, when in a molten state or when dissolved in water or other liquids, become ionized; that is, their molecules become dissociated into positively and negatively charged components, which have the property of conducting an electric current; *see* IONIZATION. If a pair of electrodes (*see* ELECTRODE) is placed in a solution of an electrolyte, or an ionizable compound, and a source of direct current is connected between them, the positive ions in the solution move toward the negative electrode and the negative ions toward the positive. Upon reaching the electrodes, the ions may gain or lose electrons and be transformed into neutral atoms or molecules, the nature of the electrode reactions depending upon the potential difference, or voltage, applied.

The action of a current on an electrolyte can be understood from a simple example. If the salt copper sulfate is dissolved in water, it dissociates into positive copper ions and negative sulfate ions. When a potential difference is applied to the electrodes, the copper ions move to the negative electrode, are discharged, and are deposited on the electrode as metallic copper.

The sulfate ions, when discharged at the positive electrode, are unstable and combine with the water of the solution to form sulfuric acid and oxygen. Such decomposition caused by an electric current is called electrolysis.

In all cases, the quantity of material evolved at each electrode when current is passed through an electrolyte follows a law discovered by the British chemist and physicist Michael Faraday (q.v.). This law states that the quantity of material transformed at each electrode is proportional to the quantity of electricity passed through the electrolyte; and that the weight of the elements transformed is proportional to the equivalent weights of the elements, that is, to the atomic weights of the elements divided by their valences.

All chemical changes involve a regrouping or readjustment of the electrons in the reacting substances; hence all such changes may be said to be electrical in character. To produce an electrical current from a chemical reaction, it is necessary to have a reducible substance, that is, a substance that can gain electrons easily; and an oxidizable substance, one that can give up electrons easily. A reaction of this kind can be understood from the operation of a simple type of electrochemical cell. If a zinc rod is placed in a dilute solution of sulfuric acid, the zinc, which oxidizes readily, will lose electrons, and positive zinc ions will be liberated into the solution. The free electrons stay in the zinc rod. If the rod is connected through a conductor to an inert-metal electrode placed in the sulfuric acid solution, the electrons will flow around this circuit into the solution, where they will be taken up by the positive hydrogen ions of the dilute acid; inert metals used for such electrodes include gold and platinum. The combination of the electrons and the ions produces hydrogen gas, which appears as bubbles on the surface of the electrode. The reaction of the zinc rod and sulfuric acid thus produces a current in the external circuit. An electrochemical cell of this kind is known as a primary cell. Cells of this type are usually known as voltaic cells.

In the storage battery or accumulator, commonly known as a secondary cell, electrical energy is fed to the cell from an outside source and stored within it in the form of chemical energy. The chemical reaction of a secondary cell is reversible, proceeding in one direction when the cell is being charged, and in the opposite direction when it is discharging. Because the reaction is of this type, a secondary cell can be recharged and discharged again and again, whereas a primary cell is often useless as a source of current after the reaction is complete.

Industrial Applications. Electrolytic decomposition is the basis for a number of important extractive and manufacturing processes in modern industry. Caustic soda, an important chemical in the manufacture of paper, rayon, and photographic film, is produced by the electrolysis of a solution of common salt in water; see ALKALIES. The reaction produces chlorine and sodium. The sodium in turn reacts with the water in the cell to yield caustic soda. The chlorine evolved is a valuable by-product used in pulp and paper manufacture.

An important industrial use of electrolysis is in the electrolytic furnace, which is employed in the manufacture of aluminum, magnesium, and sodium. In this furnace the resistance of a charge of metallic salts is used to heat the charge until it becomes molten and ionizes. The metal is then deposited electrolytically. See ELECTROTHERMIC FURNACE.

Electrolytic methods are also employed in the refining of lead, tin, copper, gold, and silver. The advantage of extracting or refining metals by electrolytic processes is that the deposited metal is of great purity. Electroplating (q.v.), another industrial application of electrolytic deposition, is used to deposit films of precious metals on base metals and to deposit metals and alloys, as strengthening or wear-resistant coatings, on metal parts.   S.Z.L.

ELECTROCUTION, method of inflicting the death penalty upon criminals by using an electric current. In the late 1960's, electrocution was the official method of capital punishment (q.v.) in twenty States of the United States and in the District of Columbia, compared with the use by ten States of lethal gas, the next most common method. Death resulting from electrocution is assertedly painless, with loss of consciousness being virtually instantaneous.

Although only a small electric current is required to cause death in human beings, the electrical resistance of the human body is so high that a large voltage is required to force even this small current through the body. In U.S. prison practice an alternating current of about 2000 volts is used for electrocution. The criminal to be electrocuted is strapped into a specially constructed chair. One electrode is applied to the scalp, the other to the calf of one leg. The electrodes are moistened with a salt solution to ensure adequate contact. Death ensues within two minutes after the current has started to flow through the body.

ELECTRODE, component of an electric circuit (q.v.) that connects the conventional wiring of the circuit to a conducting medium such as an electrolyte or a gas. The electrically positive electrode is called the anode and the negative electrode the cathode. The ordinary dry cell employs a carbon anode and a zinc cathode in contact with an electrolytic solution. Arc-lamp electrodes are made of carbon, and the electrodes used in arc welding are made of flux-coated metal; see ELECTRIC ARC. The electrodes of vacuum tubes are fabricated from carbon and various metals and alloys, depending on the size and purpose for which the tubes are used. The electrolytic furnace (see ELECTROTHERMIC FURNACE), used in the production of aluminum, employs carbon anodes and cathodes of molten aluminum.

See also ELECTROPLATING.

ELECTRODEPOSITION. See ELECTROPLATING.

ELECTROENCEPHALOGRAPH. See SURGERY: *Recent Developments.*

ELECTROLUMINESCENCE. See LUMINESCENCE.

ELECTROLYSIS. See ELECTROCHEMISTRY.

ELECTROLYTE. See ELECTROCHEMISTRY; ELECTROTHERMIC FURNACE; IONIZATION.

ELECTROLYTIC DISSOCIATION. See ELECTROCHEMISTRY; IONIZATION.

ELECTROLYTIC FURNACE. See ELECTROTHERMIC FURNACE.

ELECTROMAGNET. See INDUCTION; MAGNETISM.

ELECTROMAGNETIC INDUCTION. See INDUCTION.

ELECTROMAGNETIC RADIATIONS, waves produced by the oscillation or acceleration of an electric charge in a magnetic field. Examples are light, heat, and radio waves. Electromagnetic waves need no material medium for transmission. Thus light and radio waves can travel through interplanetary and interstellar space from the sun and stars to the earth. Electromagnetic radiation may be arranged in a spectrum which extends from waves of extremely high frequency (10^{23} cycles per sec.) and short wavelength (3×10^{-15} m) associated with cosmic rays to waves of very low frequency (1 cycle per sec.) and great wavelength (3×10^8 m) propagated by commutated direct current. Within these extremities, the spectrum is divided into several frequency bands, among which are gamma rays, hard and soft X rays; ultraviolet, visible, and infrared light; microwaves of radar, television, and shortwave radio; long-wave radio; induction heating, and power waves. Regardless of the frequency, wavelength, or method of propagation, electromagnetic waves travel 186,272 mi. (3×10^{10} cm) per sec. in a vacuum. The properties of electromagnetic waves depend on their frequency, which is important in determining heating effect, visibility, penetration, and other characteristics of a particular kind of radiation. All the components of the electromagnetic spectrum, regardless of frequency, have in common the typical properties of wave motion (q.v.), including diffraction and interference (qq.v.).

The theory of electromagnetic waves originated with the British physicist James Clerk Maxwell (q.v.). In a series of papers published in the 1860's, he analyzed mathematically the theory of electromagnetic fields and predicted that visible light was an electromagnetic phenomenon. Subsequent experiments verified all of his basic experiments.

Physicists had known since the early 19th century that light is propagated as a transverse wave, but they originally assumed that the wave was mechanical in nature, requiring some medium for propagation of the energy. As experiments demonstrated that light could travel through the best laboratory vacuum, the medium for its propagation was postulated as an extremely diffuse substance, called ether, present even in a vacuum. According to Maxwell's theory of electromagnetic waves, the wave motion is not of a material substance, but of electric and magnetic fields, vibrating with the same frequency and in the same phase, at right angles to each other and to the direction of propagation. Although Maxwell did not discard the concept of ether, his theory made it unnecessary to assume any medium for the transmission of radiant energy. Following the promulgation of the special theory of relativity (q.v.) in 1905, it became obvious that the existence of a material ether could never be proved experimentally, and the concept was abandoned.

Also at the beginning of the 20th century, it was found that the wave theory could not account for all the properties of radiation. In 1900 the German physicist Max Planck (q.v.) demonstrated that the emission and absorption of radiation occurs in finite corpuscles of energy, known as quanta. The corpuscular concept was also postulated in 1904 by the German-born American physicist Albert Einstein (q.v.) to account for the energies of electrons emitted by a metal surface exposed to light; see QUANTUM THEORY. Other phenomena, occurring in the interaction between radiation and matter, can be explained only by the quantum theory. Thus, modern physicists were forced to recognize that electromagnetic radiation has both wave and corpuscular properties. The quantum characteristics are particularly apparent in the high-fre-

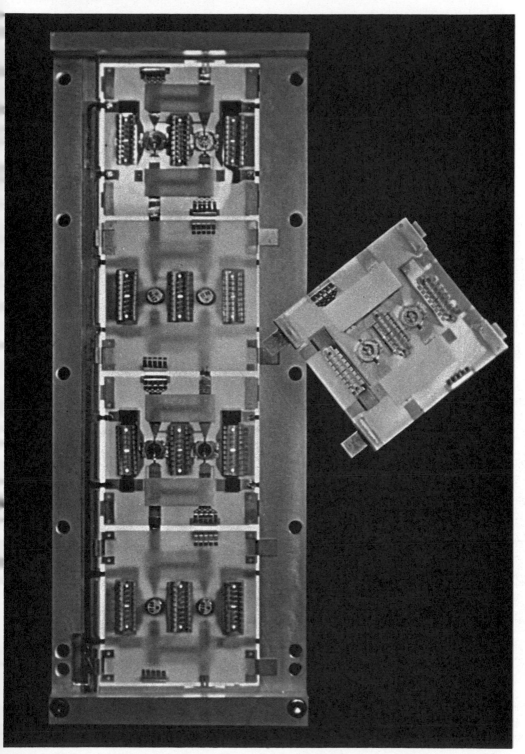

Electronics. Plate 1. *A four-stage microwave amplifier employing integrated circuits, magnified two times. Amplifiers of different powers can be assembled merely by increasing or decreasing the number of stages. Such amplification devices are used today in high-performance telephone radio-relay repeaters and radar-receiving systems.*

Electronics. Plate 2. *Right: The complex structure of modern transistorized circuits is illustrated by these integrated-circuit devices that are bonded to gold patterns laid down on a ceramic base. This process forms a complex electronic circuit in a small, rugged package. Below, left: A spinel ingot, just removed from the furnace of a crystal-manufacturing plant of the Union Carbide Corporation, is used to make a new type of silicon-on-spinel wafers for thin-film circuits. These are employed in a wide range of electronic components for household, industrial, and military equipment. Below, right: The minute size and the economy of electronic circuits today is illustrated by these sealed-junction integrated circuits, compared with the size of a coin. Hundreds of these circuits can be made at one time on a slice of silicon. The greatly magnified slice in the background reveals arrangements of individual circuits.*

Bell Telephone Laboratories

quency bands of the electromagnetic spectrum; see SPECTRUM; X RAY. The parallel concept that matter also exhibits the same duality of characteristics as radiation was developed in 1925 by the French physicist Louis Victor, Prince de Broglie (1892–   ); see QUANTUM MECHANICS.

See also ELECTRONICS: Maser; LASER.

ELECTROMOTIVE FORCE. See ELECTRICITY.

ELECTRON, elementary particle having a mass equivalent to 9.108×10^{-28} grams and an electrical charge equal to 4.802×10^{-10} electrostatic units (e.s.u.), or statcoulombs; see ELECTRICAL UNITS. Its charge, which is the elemental unit of electricity (q.v.), may be either positive or negative. In general usage the term electron designates the negative electron, known also as the negatron. The positive electron is usually called a positron (q.v.). The negative electron is a basic constituent of all atoms; see ATOM AND ATOMIC THEORY. Both kinds of charged electrons spin about their axis, and the magnetic property of matter stems mainly from this electron spin. Opposite spins result in either positive or negative charge. Electrons spinning in opposite directions form electrically neutral pairs.

The flow of an electric current in a conductor is caused by the drifting of free electrons in the metal. Heat conduction is also primarily a phenomenon of electron activity; see HEAT. In vacuum tubes a heated cathode emits a stream of electrons that may be used to amplify or rectify an electric current; see RECTIFICATION; VACUUM TUBES, THERMIONIC. If such a stream is focused into a well-defined beam, it is called a cathode-ray beam. Cathode rays (q.v.) directed against suitable targets produce X rays; directed against the fluorescent screen of a television tube, the beam of electrons produces visible images. The beta rays emitted by radioactive substances also consist of electrons; see RADIOACTIVITY; X RAY. See also BETATRON; ELECTRONICS.   R.H.

ELECTRON AND ION DETECTION. See CLOUD CHAMBER; IONIZATION CHAMBER; SCINTILLATION COUNTER.

ELECTRONIC MUSIC, music that requires knowledge or use of electronic devices to produce or manipulate sound during its composition and performance. The sound may be produced entirely through electrical means, as by an electronic sound synthesizer, a complex system of generators that can originate and control sound. Sounds may be produced also by nonelectronic means and then altered and combined by electronic devices, such as a tape recorder. The essential feature is that electronic devices are necessary in the compositional process. Electronic music is thus distinguishable

from music composed in the traditional manner but played on an electronic instrument, such as the electronic organ or electric guitar, or from music transferred to an electronic medium, such as a phonograph or radio.

Electronic music first appeared in 1948 in Paris, France, where a group of engineers and composers recorded sounds from everyday life on magnetic tape and patched them together in various ways, sometimes purposely distorting the original sounds in the process. Music composed in this manner is called *musique concrète* (Fr., "concrete music") because it uses actual, or concrete, sounds from the real world as opposed to artificial, or abstract, sounds produced by musical instruments.

In the 1950's sound synthesizers were developed, principally in the United States. Synthesizers enable composers to produce sounds electronically in almost any range, tone quality, and volume. In the 1960's computers were linked to many sound synthesizers in order to automate some steps in the sound-producing process. By 1970 the techniques and devices of electronic music had begun to be used by composers of popular music. Also in this decade, composers were increasingly incorporating both electronic and traditional sound sources in the same works. One reason for the growing popularity of electronic music has been the development of relatively inexpensive synthesizers, such as those manufactured by the American engineer Robert A. Moog (1934–   ). Leading serious composers in the electronic-music field include the German Karl Heinz Stockhausen (1928–   ), who published the first electronic score in 1956; the French-American Edgard Varèse (1885–1965); the Americans Otto Luening (1900–   ) and Milton B. Babbitt (1916–   ); and the Russian-American Vladimir Ussachevsky (1911–   ).

See also MUSIC: History: The 20th Century.

J.V.

ELECTRONICS, category of applied physics and engineering that deals with the conduction of electricity and with the design and application of devices whose operation depends on the flow of electrons; see ELECTRICITY; ELECTRON.

Electrons are emitted in radioactive substances as beta rays; see RADIOACTIVITY. The electron itself, however, is completely stable. Electrons are always in motion and the volume of an atom consists almost entirely of the cloud of electrons surrounding the nucleus (q.v.); see ATOM AND ATOMIC THEORY. The freedom of electrons to move from atom to atom depends in part on the strength of the forces binding them to their parent atoms. This force varies greatly from element to element. Electrons have an inherent negative electric charge and are repulsed from other negative electric charges and attracted toward positive electric charges.

Conductor. Electricity is the passage of electrons through a conductor (a substance through which an electric current passes easily) or an evacuated space. Electrons do not flow spontaneously but only when pressure in the form of an external electric charge is exerted against them by a battery or an electric generator. In metallic conductors, such as copper, aluminum, gold, silver, or sodium, the electric current is carried by so-called free electrons that are not bound tightly to any particular atom and can wander through the conductor. In an insulator, on the other hand, are very few free electrons and it is difficult to obtain any flow of electricity at all; see INSULATION: *Electric Insulation.*

When the temperature (q.v.) of a conductor is increased, the electrons moving through the conductor move at a higher velocity. Increasing the temperature sufficiently enables the electrons to acquire enough energy to overcome the forces holding them in the conductor, and they are emitted from the surface of the conductor. This phenomenon is similar to that in which molecules of water are emitted from the surface of the liquid when the temperature is increased to the boiling point; the molecules boil away. The number of electrons that will be emitted from a conductor depends on the temperature of the conductor.

Semiconductor. A semiconductor is a substance in which the ability to conduct electrons is weak, midway between a good conductor and a good insulator. The chief semiconducting substances in use today are the elements silicon and germanium (qq.v.). These elements are modified in character by having added to them small amounts of other substances, called impurities. Certain impurities, such as antimony, have an excess of electrons; in such cases the material is called an n-type (for negative) semiconductor. If an n-type semiconductor is connected to a battery, the electrons drift away from the negative pole of the battery as in any other electric circuit, producing a small current of electricity.

If, on the other hand, the semiconductor is modified with an impurity such as gallium, that has a shortage of electrons, the material is called a p-type (for positive) semiconductor. The locations in the impurity to which free electrons would be attracted if available are called "holes". When a p-type semiconductor is connected to a battery, the "holes" tend to drift away from the negative pole of the battery. The effect resembles that of a positive current of electricity flowing through the semiconductor in a direction opposite to the normal flow of electricity. *See also* ELECTRIC CIRCUIT; INTEGRATED CIRCUIT; PRINTED CIRCUIT; TRANSISTOR.

Electron Tubes. Electron tubes, or thermionic vacuum tubes, are devices in which the flow of electrons is manipulated in order to control the flow of electricity in an electric circuit. Without electron tubes, radio, television, and long-distance telephone communication would be impossible; see VACUUM TUBES, THERMIONIC.

Diode. The simplest electron tube is a diode. It contains two electrodes, one negative (called the cathode) and the other positive (called the anode). Air is evacuated from the tube to increase the efficiency of operation. Electrons enter the diode through the cathode. The cathode is heated, causing a "cloud" of electrons to be emitted from and form about it. The electron cloud develops a negative charge of electricity called a space charge as it increases in size. The limit of the cloud is reached when the space charge is great enough to repel one electron for every emitted electron that joins the cloud.

If the anode is now made positive with respect to the cathode, the electrons making up the space charge are attracted to the anode, and an electric current will flow through the diode. Connecting a source of alternating current between the cathode and anode will enable a current to flow through the diode, but only when the alternating current is on the positive half of its cycle; that is, when the anode is positive with respect to the cathode. The result will be a pulsating flow of direct current through the diode; see RECTIFICATION. The effect is called half-wave rectification. By connecting two diodes to a suitable transformer so that each anode is alternately positive, both halves of the alternating current cycle can be made positive and the pulsations will be smoothed out. This effect is called full-wave rectification. In addition to their use in rectifying voltages, diodes are employed to prevent an electric current from flowing in the wrong direction in a circuit. See TRANSISTOR for a discussion of the use of semiconductors as diodes.

Triode. In 1907 the American inventor Lee de Forest (q.v.), known as the "father of radio", patented a device incorporating his discovery that the flow of electrons through a diode could be regulated if between the cathode and anode a third electrode was introduced in the form of a fine wire mesh. This resulting three-electrode

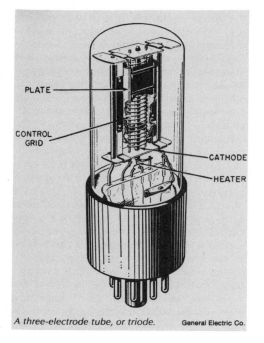

A three-electrode tube, or triode. General Electric Co.

tube is called a triode. The wire mesh is called the control grid and it usually encircles the cathode closely. Giving the control grid a slightly negative potential with respect to the cathode causes it to repel a portion of the electrons flowing toward the anode. (This negative potential on the control grid is called the bias or grid bias.) A small change in the grid bias produces a much larger change in the current flowing through the triode. Increasing the grid bias sufficiently stops the current flow altogether. Regulating the grid bias makes it possible for the triode to amplify an a-c voltage or convert a d-c voltage into an a-c voltage. *See* TRANSISTOR for a discussion of the use of semiconductors as triodes.

Amplification. A simplified schematic circuit diagram of a triode amplifier is shown in Fig. 1. The triode, represented by the large circle, contains the cathode C, the anode A, and the control grid G. The cathode is supplied with electrons and heated at the same time by the A battery. A positive voltage is supplied to the anode by the B battery. Current flows from the A battery, through the triode, to the B battery. A load resistor L in the anode circuit controls the voltage drop through the anode circuit. The control grid G is given a fixed negative potential with respect to the cathode by the C battery. An outside source of alternating current, represented by the symbol S, is connected to the grid bias circuit. As the a-c voltage varies from its minimum to maximum values, the voltage of the grid bias varies with it. This variation in turn causes the current flowing to the anode and through the load resistor L to vary. The changes in current flow across the load resistor produce much larger voltage variations in the anode circuit than exist in the a-c source S. In other words, the original a-c voltage has been amplified. The amplification factor, or ratio of anode voltage to grid bias voltage, can be 1:1500 or more. If further amplification is required, another amplifier circuit can be connected to the circuit shown in Fig. 1. It is thus possible to amplify the strength of faint signals many millions of times.

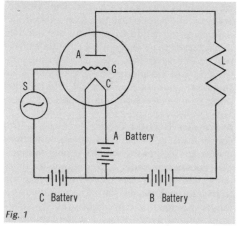

Fig. 1

Oscillators. Oscillators are used to produce high-frequency signals in radio, television, and radar (qq.v.) equipment. The ability to tune radios and television sets to stations transmitting signals at different frequencies depends on oscillator circuits in the receiving sets. A simplified schematic circuit diagram of an oscillator circuit is shown in Fig. 2. The tuned circuit consists of an inductor coil L_1 and a condenser C

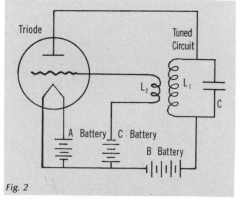

Fig. 2

451

connected in parallel; see CONDENSER, ELECTRICAL; INDUCTANCE. By choosing an inductor coil and condenser with suitable characteristics, the voltage in the anode circuit can be made to oscillate at any desired frequency. The oscillator circuit is said to *resonate* at the desired frequency; see RESONANCE. A smaller inductor coil L_2 connected to the grid bias circuit is placed adjacent to inductor coil L_1 so that the resonant frequency is induced in inductor coil L_2. This causes the voltage in the grid bias circuit to oscillate at the resonant frequency, and the oscillator circuit becomes self-sustaining.

Pentodes. Pentodes are five-electrode tubes used in television sets and other circuits in which high frequencies are used. Pentodes operate much more efficiently than triodes and have an amplification factor about one hundred times that of the average triode. Pentodes have two additional grids located between the control grid and the anode. These additional grids suppress undesirable electrical effects that occur when an electron tube is operated at very high frequencies.

Microwave Electron Tubes. Even the best of conventional pentodes have serious limitations if they are used at the extremely high frequencies common in radar and microwave equipment, because the time it takes for an electron to pass through the tube at these frequencies is longer than the duration of one cycle. The electrons only vibrate uselessly within the tube. Special types of electron tubes such as the klystron and magnetron (see Figs. 3 and 4) have been developed to overcome these difficulties. These devices operate on a resonance principle in which the energy of the electrons is transferred to hollow cavities in much the same way that air blown across the top of a hollow tube of the proper dimensions, as in organ pipes and other wind instruments, will cause the tube to resonate at a given frequency. When resonant cavities of the proper dimensions are chosen,

the energy of the electrons as they pass the opening of the cavity is converted into electromagnetic energy of the desired frequency. Coaxial cables connected to the resonant cavity then conduct the signal to other equipment.

Maser. A maser (acronym for *M*icrowave *A*mplification by *S*timulated *E*mission of *R*adiation) is an amplifying device used in radio astronomy to amplify the extremely weak microwave signals originating in outer space. The great advantage of a maser is that it amplifies very weak signals without adding any extraneous noise of its own; this virtue is not possessed by the amplifying devices so far described. The principle of operation depends on the fact that atoms have ground states and excited states; see QUANTUM THEORY: *The Bohr Atom.* Atoms can be excited if they absorb energy from an outside source, one potential source being a high-frequency radio signal. The radio signal must produce exactly that amount of energy which the atoms must absorb if they are to jump to a higher energy state. When the excited atoms return to their original ground state, they emit electromagnetic radiation of the same frequency as the absorbed radio signal; see ELECTROMAGNETIC RADIATIONS. In order to amplify incoming microwave signals, the atoms comprising the maser must first be excited by a suitable high-frequency signal. If, while in the excited state, they absorb an additional amount of electromagnetic radiation (that of a signal originating in outer space), they absorb the energy of that signal also. When they drop back to the ground state, the signal they emit will be amplified, or greater than the amount of energy absorbed originally. If the excited atoms pass through a resonance cavity before they drop back to their original ground state, the signal will be amplified further. The amplified signal is then transferred to conventional microwave equipment for further amplification. *See also* LASER.

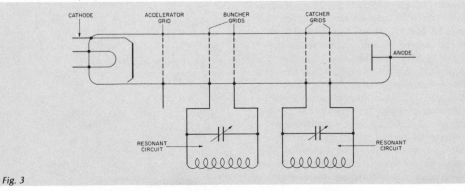

Fig. 3

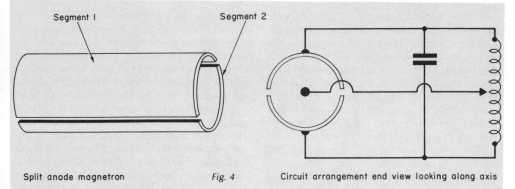

Segment I   Segment 2

Split anode magnetron   Fig. 4   Circuit arrangement end view looking along axis

Cathode-Ray Tube. A cathode-ray tube (or CRT) is an electron tube containing at one end a cathode and a device called an "electron gun" that "fires" a stream of electrons against a luminescent screen at the opposite end of the tube. A bright spot of light appears wherever the electrons strike the screen. Cathode-ray tubes are used to make many kinds of sensitive electrical measurements in instruments called oscilloscopes; a CRT may serve as a picture tube in television receivers, a visual display screen in radar-receiving equipment, or as a visual readout device in computer installations.

Electrons are emitted from a heated cathode in the electron gun. A series of grids having a positive potential with respect to the cathode accelerate the electrons as they pass. The electrons next pass through a series of doughnut-shaped anodes that focus the stream of electrons so that they strike the luminescent screen as a fine point. Between the electron gun and the screen are either two sets of electric deflecting plates or two sets of magnetic deflecting rings. Electric deflecting plates are used in small CRT's, whereas magnetic deflecting rings are used in large CRT's in which a large deflection is required, as in television tubes. Assuming the CRT contains electric deflecting plates, a horizontal pair controls the up-and-down motion of the electron beam and a vertical pair controls the left-to-right motion of the beam. In each pair of plates, one plate has a negative charge of electricity, and the other plate has a positive charge. If the charges are equal in value, the beam will strike the center of the luminescent screen. If the charges are unequal, the electron beam will be deflected. The amount of deflection depends on the voltage applied to the plates. Usually, the horizontal plates are connected to an external electric signal, the voltage of which is being measured. As the external signal varies, so will the spot of light on the face of the tube, which will move up or down in re-

sponse to the changes in voltage. The vertical deflecting plates are controlled by an internal circuit. If the voltage of the vertical plates is varied in a periodic manner, the beam of electrons can be made to sweep periodically across the face of the tube from left to right. In this way the variations of the external electric signal are spread out and can be studied more easily.

The magnetic deflecting rings work in an altogether analogous manner, except that the electron beam is deflected by variations in the strength of the magnetic fields through which the beam must pass.

Gas Tubes. Evacuated electron tubes require high voltage levels in order to produce large

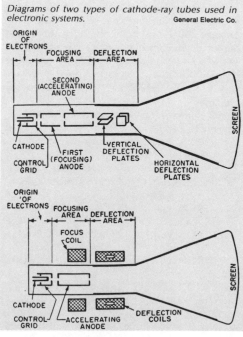

Diagrams of two types of cathode-ray tubes used in electronic systems.   General Electric Co.

current flows through the tubes. This condition makes evacuated tubes unsuitable when high voltages must be rectified. To overcome this difficulty, heated-cathode, gas-filled tubes are used. Some of the gases used include mercury vapor, neon, krypton, and argon. The passage of an electric current through a gas-filled tube depends on the fact that the gas can be ionized (that is, capable of conducting a current of electricity) at low voltages. Once the gas is ionized, large amounts of current flow through the tube. The current flow is constant in spite of any instability in the voltage. This feature makes gas-filled tubes useful when the output voltage must be controlled very closely, as in radio transmitters operating at a fixed frequency. *See* ELECTRIC DISCHARGE; IONIZATION.

A thyratron is a hot-cathode, gas-filled tube containing a control grid similar to the control grid in a triode. Current will not flow through the thyratron until the grid bias is below a certain critical level. The moment it drops below that value, a large current begins to flow through the thyratron. Current will not flow otherwise, regardless of the positive voltage at the anode. Any further change in the grid bias will not affect the continued operation of the thyratron. Current flow can be stopped only by reducing the positive voltage at the anode below a certain critical value. Thyratrons are used as relays, rectifiers in high-power circuits, and as electronic switches.

Cold-cathode, gas-filled tubes are also used in electronic circuits. In cold-cathode tubes, the voltage difference between the cathode and anode determines the moment at which the gas ionized and current begins to flow through the tube. Cold-cathode tubes are used as voltage regulators, as stroboscope lamps, and to rectify voltages.

An ignitron is a special gas-filled diode designed to handle currents of several hundred amperes. Ignitrons are used in automatic arc-welding equipment.

See also AUTOMATION; BLIND, AIDS FOR THE; BOMBSIGHT; COMPUTER; FACSIMILE; HEARING AIDS; NAVIGATION; SONAR.   G.D.F.

ELECTRON MICROSCOPE. *See* MICROSCOPE: *Electron Microscopes.*

ELECTRON VOLT. *See* ACCELERATORS, PARTICLE; NUCLEAR ENERGY

ELECTROPHONES. *See* MUSICAL INSTRUMENTS: *Electrophones.*

ELECTROPHORESIS, phenomenon of migration of suspended particles, liquid or solid, through a fluid, that is either gaseous or liquid, as a result of the imposition of an electric field

between electrodes immersed in the fluid; *see* ELECTRICITY; ELECTRODE. In an emulsion of rubber latex in an aqueous medium, for example, the rubber droplets tend to acquire an electrical charge by adsorption (q.v.) of ions; *see* ION; IONIZATION. If a voltage is applied between a pair of electrodes in the emulsion, the rubber particles migrate toward the electrode which has a charge opposite to their own. If this electrode has a particular shape, the rubber particles deposited on it will coalesce to form an article of this shape; this is the process by which surgical rubber gloves and other electroformed articles are manufactured. Similarly, many automotive parts are coated with paint by an electrophoretic deposition process. The Cottrell precipitator (q.v.) deposits smoke particles by electrophoresis on an electrode mounted in a smokestack, thus reducing their emission into the atmosphere. If the suspended particles tend to migrate toward the cathode, the negative electrode, the process is termed cataphoresis; if they migrate toward the anode, the positive electrode, it is called anaphoresis. Electroosmosis is a related phenomenon in which the solid phase is held immobile, and the liquid migrates due to the imposed electric field. *See also* ELECTROCHEMISTRY; ELECTROPLATING.   S.Z.L.

ELECTROPLATING, *or* ELECTRODEPOSITION, electrochemical process for depositing a thin layer of metal on, usually, a metallic base. Objects are electroplated to prevent corrosion, to obtain a hard surface or attractive finish, to purify metals (as in the electrorefining of copper), to separate metals for quantitative analysis, or, as in electrotyping, to reproduce a form from a mold. Cadmium, chromium, copper, gold, nickel, silver, and tin are the metals most often used in plating. Typical products of electroplating are silver-plated tableware (*see* SILVERWARE: *Silver Plate*), chromium-plated automobile accessories, and tin-plated food containers.

In the process of electroplating, the object to be coated is placed in a solution, called a bath, of a salt of the coating metal, and is connected to the negative terminal of an external source of electricity. Another conductor, often composed of the coating metal, is connected to the positive terminal of the electric source. A steady direct current of low voltage, usually from 1 to 6 volts, is required for the process. When the current is passed through the solution, atoms of the plating metal deposit out of the solution onto the cathode, the negative electrode (q.v.). These atoms are replaced in the bath by atoms from the anode (positive electrode), if it is composed of the same metal, as with copper and silver.

Otherwise they are replaced by periodic additions of the salt to the bath, as with gold and chromium. In either case an equilibrium between the metal coming out of solution and the metal entering is maintained until the object is plated. Nonconducting materials may be plated by first being covered with a conducting material such as graphite. Wax or plastic patterns for electrotype and recording disks are coated in this way.

To insure a strong and closed bond between the object to be plated and the plating material, the object must be cleaned thoroughly by dipping it into an acid or caustic solution, or by making it the anode in a cleaning bath for an instant. To eliminate irregularity in the depth of the plate, and to insure that the grain at the surface of the plate is of good quality and conducive to polishing, the current density (amperes per square foot of cathode surface) and temperature must be carefully controlled. Colloids (see COLLOIDAL DISPERSION) or special compounds are often added to the bath to improve the surface uniformity of the plate.

Some metals, notably chromium, have poor throwing powers, that is, they tend to plate heavily on projections while leaving crevices or parts distant from the anode entirely bare. See ELECTROCHEMISTRY; PRINTING TECHNIQUES: *Electrotyping.*

ELECTROSCOPE, device for measuring small electric charges or potential differences. In simplified form the electroscope consists of two lightweight conductors suspended in a container of glass or other insulating material. The two conductors are electrically connected to a third conductor which is outside the container. When the outside conductor is touched to a charged body, the two conductors inside the container become charged with similar charges and repel each other. By measuring how far the conductors are forced apart, the amount of the charge can be calculated. The inside conductors in the earliest electroscopes consisted of two oblongs of gold leaf joined at one end; see ELECTRICITY: *Static Electricity;* ELECTRIC METERS.

ELECTROSTATIC MACHINE, in electricity, device for generating an electrical charge by electrostatic means; see ELECTRICITY: *Electrostatics.*

The first electrostatic machine was developed by the German physicist Otto von Guericke (q.v.) and was described by him in 1672. It consisted of a sphere of sulfur so mounted that it could be rotated by a crank. The experimenter built up a charge on the sphere by holding his hand against it while the sphere was revolved. A number of improvements were subsequently made in Guericke's device. A glass plate was substituted for the sphere and leather pads for the human hand, and contacts were arranged for picking up the charge as it was generated. All of these machines operated by friction and were only moderately efficient. Later electrical machines employed the principle of electrostatic induction and made possible the generation of extremely high voltages; see INDUCTANCE.

The simplest type of induction machine is the electrophorus, invented by the Italian physicist Count Alessandro Volta (q.v.) in 1775. A circular plate of insulating material is rubbed with woolen cloth and becomes negatively charged. A metal plate equipped with an insulating handle is then placed on top of the insulating plate, and has a negative charge induced on its top surface and a positive charge on its underside; see INSULATION. If the negative charge is removed by touching the plate with the finger and the plate is then removed by its insulating handle, the plate carries a strong positive charge. Similar induced charges can be picked up from the insulating plate repeatedly by going through the same procedure, without renewing the original charge.

The classic type of electrostatic induction machine was that invented by the British engineer James Wimshurst (1832–1903) in 1878. The Wimshurst machine consists of two glass plates mounted close to each other on a single shaft and arranged to revolve in opposite directions. On the outside of each plate a number of segments of tinfoil are mounted near the edge. By means of collecting brushes, each pair of diagonally opposite segments on each plate is successively connected electrically and neutralized as the plates revolve. Other brushes are arranged to pick up the charges from another pair of individual segments and carry them to an outside circuit. As the plates are turned, a small accidental charge (which always exists) on any one of the segments will induce an opposite charge on the passing segments of the other plate, and these charges will in turn induce charges on the segments of the first plate. The neutralizing and pick-up connections are so arranged that half of each plate is positive and half negative and that a continuous unidirectional current flows through the outside circuit.

With the development of dynamoelectric generators (see DYNAMOELECTRIC MACHINERY), electrostatic machines fell into disuse and were employed chiefly for demonstrating electrostatic principles in the classroom. In recent years, however, several practical uses for these machines have been discovered. The most important use is the generation of extremely high voltage for nuclear research; see VAN DE GRAAFF GENERATOR. During World War II an adaptation of the Wimshurst machine was developed in Germany for supplying high voltages for lightweight cathode-ray equipment. This generator was no larger than a man's hand, but could generate potentials as high as 10,000 volts.

ELECTROSTATICS. See ELECTRICITY: *Electrostatics*; ELECTROSTATIC MACHINE.

ELECTROTHERMIC FURNACE, or ELECTRIC FURNACE or ELECTROTHERMAL FURNACE, any of several types of electrically heated devices used industrially for melting metals or firing ceramics (qq.v.).

The simplest type of electrothermic furnace is the resistance furnace in which heat is generated by passing a current through a resistance element surrounding the furnace (q.v.), or by utilizing the resistance of the material being heated. The heating element in an externally heated furnace may take the form of a coil of metal wire wound around a tube of refractory material, or it may be a tube of metal or other resistive material such as carborundum. Resistance furnaces are particularly useful in applications in which a small furnace, with precisely controlled temperatures, is needed. Small resistance furnaces find wide application in laboratories and in shops for the heat treatment of tools. Larger furnaces are used for firing ceramics and melting brass. The highest temperature at which resistance furnaces are operated, for example, in the manufacture of graphite, is in the neighborhood of 4100° C. (7366° F.).

Electric-arc furnace is the most widely used type of electrothermic furnace for the production of quality alloy steels, and range in capacity from 500 lb. to 200 tons. In these furnaces the heat is generated by an arc struck between the metal being heated and one or more electrodes suspended above the metal; see ELECTRIC ARC. A typical form of arc furnace has three electrodes, fed by a three-phase power supply, giving three heating arcs. The electrodes are made of graphite or carbon.

The most recently developed type of electrothermic furnace is the induction furnace, consisting of a crucible in which a metallic charge is heated by eddy currents induced magnetically. Around the crucible is wound a coil through which high-frequency alternating currents are passed. The magnetic field of this coil sets up eddy currents in the metal in the crucible. Induction furnaces have a number of ad-

vantages, chief among them being the speed at which metal can be melted. At comparatively low frequencies the induced eddy currents exert a stirring action on the molten metal. Because the higher frequencies are the most effective for heating, some induction furnaces have two coils, one for high-frequency current and one for low-frequency. The earlier types of induction furnaces operated at frequencies between 60 and 60,000 cycles per sec., but some modern furnaces are designed to use frequencies of 1,000,000 cycles or more per sec. See INDUCTANCE.

A special type of furnace, called an electrolytic furnace, is used in the production of aluminum, magnesium, and sodium. In the electrolytic furnace, a salt is fused by the heat generated by the passage of a large electric current, and is at the same time electrolyzed so that the pure metal is deposited at one electrode. See ALUMINUM; ELECTRICITY; ELECTROCHEMISTRY.

ELECTROTYPING. See PRINTING TECHNIQUES: *Electrotyping*.

ELECTRUM, native alloy of gold and silver found in many parts of the world, but most abundantly in the western United States and the Ural Mts. of the Soviet Union. The color of electrum ranges from pale yellow to white, depending upon the amount of silver found in the specimen. It may also contain copper and some other metals. Electrum was used for coinage as early as the 8th century B.C. in Asia Minor.

ELEGY, originally, in classical Greek and Roman literature, a poem composed of distich (q.v.) couplets. Classical elegies were often songs of lamentation, but elegies were also written on a variety of other themes, such as love or politics. Ancient poets who used the elegiac form include Callimachus, Catullus, Tibullus, Propertius, and Ovid (qq.v.).

In modern poetry (since the 16th century), elegies have been characterized not by their form but by their content, which is invariably melancholy and centers on death. The best-known elegy in English is *Elegy Written in a Country Churchyard* (1751), by the British poet Thomas Gray (q.v.), who in it treats of not just a single death but the human condition as well. Other famous elegies are *In Memoriam* (1850), by the British poet Alfred Lord Tennyson (q.v.); *Le Lac* (1820), by the French poet Alphonse de Lamartine (q.v.); and *When Lilacs Last in the Dooryard Bloom'd* (1866), by the American poet Walt Whitman (q.v.).

In music, the term "elegy" is often applied to a plaintive or mournful composition; see MUSIC.

ELEMENTS, CHEMICAL, substances that cannot be decomposed, or broken into more elementary substances by ordinary chemical means. Elements were at one time believed to be the fundamental substances, but have, in recent times, been separated into their constituent electrons, neutrons, and protons (qq.v.), the fundamental particles of all matter. *See also* ATOM AND ATOMIC THEORY; CHEMISTRY.

More than 100 chemical elements are known to exist in the universe. Although several of these, the so-called transuranium elements (q.v.), have not been found in nature, they have been produced artificially by bombarding the atomic nuclei of other elements with charged nuclei or nuclear particles. Such bombardment can take place in an accelerator such as the cyclotron (q.v.), in a nuclear reactor, or in a nuclear explosion; *see* ACCELERATORS, PARTICLE. The transuranium elements include neptunium (at.no. 93), plutonium (94), americium (95), curium (96), berkelium (97), californium (98), einsteinium (99), fermium (100), mendelevium (101), nobelium (102), and lawrencium (103). Scientists of the Soviet Union reported the discovery of element 104 (which they called kurchatovium) in 1964 and of element 105 in 1967. Scientists in the United States, however, disputed their claims and announced that they had discovered element 104 (proposed name, rutherfordium) in 1969 and element 105 (proposed name, hahnium) in 1970. In 1974 both countries claimed the discovery of element 106.

Chemical elements are classified as metals and nonmetals. The atoms of metals are electropositive, and combine readily with the electronegative atoms of the nonmetals; *see* ACIDS. A group of elements called metalloids, or transition elements, intermediate in properties between the metals and the nonmetals, are some-

Name	Symbol	Atomic Number	Atomic Weight*	Name	Symbol	Atomic Number	Atomic Weight*
Actinium	Ac	89	227	Neon	Ne	10	20.182
Aluminum	Al	13	26.98	Neptunium	Np	93	237
Americium	Am	95	243	Nickel	Ni	28	58.71
Antimony	Sb	51	121.75	Niobium			
Argon	Ar	18	39.942	(Columbium)	Nb	41	92.91
Arsenic	As	33	74.91	Nitrogen	N	7	14.007
Astatine	At	85	210	Nobelium	No	102	254
Barium	Ba	56	137.35	Osmium	Os	76	190.2
Berkelium	Bk	97	249	Oxygen	O	8	15.999
Beryllium	Be	4	9.013	Palladium	Pd	46	106.4
Bismuth	Bi	83	208.99	Phosphorus	P	15	30.973
Boron	B	5	10.82	Platinum	Pt	78	195.08
Bromine	Br	35	79.913	Plutonium	Pu	94	242
Cadmium	Cd	48	112.40	Polonium	Po	84	210
Calcium	Ca	20	40.08	Potassium	K	19	39.098
Californium	Cf	98	251	Praseodymium	Pr	59	140.91
Carbon	C	6	12.010	Promethium	Pm	61	147
Cerium	Ce	58	140.12	Protactinium	Pa	91	231
Cesium	Cs	55	132.90	Radium	Ra	88	226
Chlorine	Cl	17	35.455	Radon	Rn	86	222
Chromium	Cr	24	52.01	Rhenium	Re	75	186.21
Cobalt	Co	27	58.94	Rhodium	Rh	45	102.90
Copper	Cu	29	63.54	Rubidium	Rb	37	85.48
Curium	Cm	96	247	Ruthenium	Ru	44	101.1
Dysprosium	Dy	66	162.50	Samarium	Sm	62	150.34
Einsteinium	Es	99	254	Scandium	Sc	21	44.96
Erbium	Er	68	167.26	Selenium	Se	34	78.96
Europium	Eu	63	152.0	Silicon	Si	14	28.09
Fermium	Fm	100	253	Silver	Ag	47	107.875
Fluorine	F	9	19.00	Sodium	Na	11	22.990
Francium	Fr	87	223	Strontium	Sr	38	87.63
Gadolinium	Gd	64	157.25	Sulfur	S	16	32.064
Gallium	Ga	31	69.72	Tantalum	Ta	73	180.94
Germanium	Ge	32	72.60	Technetium	Tc	43	99
Gold	Au	79	197.0	Tellurium	Te	52	127.60
Hafnium	Hf	72	178.49	Terbium	Tb	65	158.92
Helium	He	2	4.003	Thallium	Tl	81	204.38
Holmium	Ho	67	164.93	Thorium	Th	90	232.04
Hydrogen	H	1	1.0079	Thulium	Tm	69	168.93
Indium	In	49	114.81	Tin	Sn	50	118.69
Iodine	I	53	126.90	Titanium	Ti	22	47.90
Iridium	Ir	77	192.2	Tungsten			
Iron	Fe	26	55.85	(Wolfram)	W	74	183.85
Krypton	Kr	36	83.80	Uranium	U	92	238.06
Lanthanum	La	57	138.91	Vanadium	V	23	50.95
Lawrencium	Lw	103	257	Xenon	Xe	54	131.29
Lead	Pb	82	207.20	Ytterbium	Yb	70	173.03
Lithium	Li	3	6.940	Yttrium	Y	39	88.92
Lutetium	Lu	71	174.98	Zinc	Zn	30	65.38
Magnesium	Mg	12	24.32	Zirconium	Zr	40	91.22
Manganese	Mn	25	54.94				
Mendelevium	Md	101	256				
Mercury	Hg	80	200.60				
Molybdenum	Mo	42	95.95				
Neodymium	Nd	60	144.26				

* Atomic weight of the most abundant or best known isotope, or (in the case of radioactive isotopes) the isotope with the longest half-life, relative to atomic weight of Carbon-12 = 12.

times considered a separate class. When the elements are arranged in the order of their atomic numbers (a number proportionate to the net positive charge on the nucleus of an atom of an element), elements of similar physical and chemical properties occur at specific intervals; see PERIODIC LAW. These groups of elements with similar physical and chemical properties are called families, examples of which are the alkali metals, the rare earths (q.v.), and the halogens (q.v.).

The unit for atomic weight of the elements is one twelfth of the weight of the carbon-12 atom, which is arbitrarily set at twelve; see ATOM AND ATOMIC THEORY: *Atomic Weight.* The atomic number, atomic weight, chemical symbol, and alternate name (if any) of each of the known elements are given in the preceding table.

See separate articles on each element.

When two atoms have the same atomic number, but different atomic weights, they are said to be isotopes. Many natural isotopes are known for some elements, whereas other elements occur in only one isotopic form. Hundreds of synthetic isotopes have been made by physicists. A few of the natural isotopes, and many of the synthetic ones, are unstable; see ISOTOPE; RADIOACTIVITY.   S.Z.L.

ELEPHANT, common name for an herbivorous mammal, the largest land animal now extant. It is characterized especially by an elongated prehensile snout called the trunk, which is an extension of the nose and upper lip. Two species, *Elephas maximus* of India and southeast Asia, and *Loxodonta africana* of Africa south of the Sahara, are the only living representatives of the family Elephantidae and the order Proboscidea. In Pleistocene times, however, elephants of various species were widely distributed in Europe, Africa, Asia, and North America. Dwarf elephants inhabited the islands of the Mediterranean; in Crete, fossils of elephants only 3 ft. high have been found. *See also* MAMMOTH; MASTODON.

Physical Characteristics. The average male Indian elephant is about 9 to 11 ft. tall. The male African elephant averages 1 to 2 ft. taller, and weighs from 5 to 7½ tons. Females are smaller, the African female being 8 to 8½ ft. tall. An African subspecies, the pygmy elephant, grows to a height of about 6 ft.

Members of the African and Indian species are easily distinguished, especially in profile. The Indian elephant has a domed head and an arched back, so that a depression appears between head and shoulders. The forehead is slightly concave. In the African elephant, the forehead is convex, and does not have a depression behind the head. The back is not arched, but slightly hollow; this species is tallest at the

African elephant, Loxodonta africana
Trans World Airlines

shoulder. The African elephant can be distinguished also by a series of conspicuous transverse ridges on the trunk, and by its enormous ears, usually about 2½ ft. wide and 3½ ft. long, and sometimes larger. When the ears are spread in a listening position, the distance from tip to tip may be 10 ft. By comparison the ears of the Indian elephant appear modest.

The hearing of the elephant is not remarkable, and its sight is poor. The elephant's sense of smell, however, is phenomenal; the animal can detect on the wind the scent of a human being from an amazing distance. The nostrils are at the tip of the trunk. This extraordinary nose functions also as a hose and as an arm. To drink, the animal sucks up water with the trunk and then squirts it into the mouth. In hot weather the elephant cools itself by spraying water on its back. To pull, lift, or carry, it coils its trunk around an object. On the tip of its trunk the African elephant has two fingerlike projections, an upper and a lower, which are of nearly the same size and can be used much like a finger and thumb. In the Indian species, however, only the upper "finger" is well developed.

The body and legs of both species are thick and sturdy. The head is proportionally large; the great skull, consisting largely of porous bone and enclosing large air spaces, affords space for the attachment of the powerful muscles needed to support and operate the trunk and tusks. The brain, although small in proportion to the skull and body, is larger than that of man, and highly convoluted.

Projecting from the upper jaw are the tusks, a pair of elongated incisors. Elephant tusks provide the finest ivory (q.v.), and most of the world's supply comes from Africa, where these animals have been nearly exterminated by ivory hunters. In southern Africa the tusks of the male average about 6 ft. in length, and weigh 40 to 60 lb. each; in the northern part of central Africa the average weight is 70 lb., and tusks weighing 100 lb. each are not unusual. Those of the female are smaller, as are those of the Indian species. The Indian female has poorly developed tusks, or none at all. In a subspecies native to Ceylon, the males also are usually tuskless.

Besides these exaggerated incisors, the elephant uses one molar tooth on each side of the upper and lower jaws. As a tooth wears down, it is pushed forward, falls out, and is replaced by another from the back.

A single calf, weighing about 200 lb. and covered with hair, is born after a gestation period of 21 months. It is not mature until 14 years old. The adult elephant is thick skinned and very

nearly hairless. In color, the members of both species are dark gray or grayish brown, but the African elephant is darker and has a rougher skin. The rare and highly valued "white" elephants of Asia, with pinkish or light gray skins, are albinos, or, more usually, semialbinos. In the wild state the elephant lives in forests, savannahs, and river valleys. The diet of the Indian species consists mainly of grass, leaves, bamboo shoots, fruit, especially plantains, and the young twigs and tender inside bark of certain trees. The African elephant does not eat grass, but does eat relatively coarse bark, and chews thick roots and branches to extract the sap, spitting out the pulp afterward. The daily food requirements are about ¼ ton of green fodder and 50 gal. of water. A peculiarity of the African species is that its members invariably sleep standing up. In both Asia and Africa, elephants ordinarily travel in small herds. They are slow moving and placid, and generally timid when approached by men. A wounded elephant, however, is extremely dangerous.

Use of Elephants. Because of their great strength, elephants are used extensively as work animals in India, especially for lifting and carrying heavy burdens such as timber. They do not breed well in captivity, so wild elephants must be captured and trained. When tame, they are used for hunting, herding, and training the wild ones. In Africa, elephants are not generally domesticated.

In ancient times, elephants were used in war. A Greek tablet at Adulis on the Red Sea relates that about 243 B.C. an Egyptian ruler conquered considerable territory in Asia Minor with the aid of elephants captured in Abyssinia (Ethiopia). The Carthaginians used elephants against the Romans; thirty-seven of these animals accompanied the great army that the Carthaginian general Hannibal (q.v.) led across the Alps in 218 B.C.

ELEPHANTA (Hindu, *Gharapuri*), small island of India, situated in Bombay harbor, between Bombay and the mainland. It is more than 4 mi. in circumference, and contains rice fields and stone quarries. The island is famous for four temple caves, carved out of rock and containing sculptured figures of Hindu deities. The greatest of these caves, supported by pillars cut out of the rock, is 130 ft. long, 123 ft. wide, and 18 ft. high. In the center of the cave is a striking three-headed bust representing the Hindu gods Brahma, the creator, Vishnu, the preserver, and Siva (qq.v.), the destroyer. Compartments surrounding the bust contain numerous other religious sculptures. The caves are believed to date at least from the 10th century A.D. The European

The three-headed bust at Elephanta. Left to right: Brahma, Vishnu, and Siva.   Government of India Tourist Office

name of the island is derived from a large stone elephant which once stood near the landing place.

ELEPHANTIASIS, disease of the lymphatics (q.v.), in human beings, characterized by an enormous enlargement of the infected area. The skin of this area, which becomes thick, hard, and often fissured, resembles the hide of an elephant. Elephantiasis is sometimes accompanied by passage of lymphatic fluid (chyle) and blood in the urine, and is associated with, or caused by, obstruction and rupture of the lymphatic vessels of the affected part. The parts of the body most frequently affected are the limbs, particularly the lower ones, and the genitals. In some cases the scrotum or leg becomes so enlarged that the infected person cannot move about unaided. Severe elephantiasis is endemic in many parts of the tropics, especially in India, tropical Africa, southeastern Asia, and many east Indian and South Pacific islands. It is also common around the Caribbean Sea. The disease is usually the result of filariasis, a disease caused by filariae (*see* FILARIA), or roundworms, lodged in the lymphatic system. If repeated infections occur over a number of years, elephantiasis may develop. The disease may be treated surgically but it cannot be cured.

ELEPHANT SEAL. *See* SEAL.

ELEPHANT'S EAR *or* **ELEPHANT EAR,** common name for about eight species of large herbs of the genus *Colocasia* in the Arum family (Araceae), native to tropical Asia and Polynesia. The large leaves, which give the plant its name, may reach a length of 3 ft. in some species. Several species of elephant's ear are grown as house and garden plants in the United States, including *C. antiquorum,* with shield-shaped leaves edged and veined in purple. Taro (q.v.), *C. esculenta,* which grows in the islands of the Pacific, has large edible underground tubers. Like other members of the Arum family, elephant's ear contain calcium oxalate, which produces a burning sensation and sometimes swelling in the mouth and throat if the leaves are eaten. *See also* ARUM.

ELEUSINIAN MYSTERIES, sacred rituals that were the most important of the religious festivals in ancient Greece. Like the Eleusinia, a biennial festival in honor of the Greek divinities Demeter and Persephone (qq.v.), the Eleusinian mysteries derived their name from the town of

Eleusis, in Attica, about 14 mi. west of Athens. Long before the rise of Athens, the people of Eleusis observed the mysteries, which were subsequently adopted by Athens as an official festival. The Eleusinian priesthood was retained in charge. The most important part of the festival, the initiation of the candidates, took place every year for centuries in the Telesterion at Eleusis. This initiation climaxed a series of rituals which began early in the spring with the celebration of the Lesser Mysteries at Agrae, near Athens. At that time the mystoe, the candidates for the first of four stages in the revelation of the mysteries, were told the legend of Demeter and Persephone, the latter of whom was referred to as Kore (Gr., "the maiden"). Purification rites were also part of the ceremony of the Lesser Mysteries. The autumn ceremonies, called the Greater Mysteries, began with the fetching of sacred objects from Eleusis to Athens by youths known as ephebi. The ceremonies included an address by a priest to the candidates, a cleansing in the sea, a sacrificial rite, and a great procession from Athens to Eleusis, where the initiation occurred in secret ceremonies.

It is believed that the tale of Demeter's search through the underworld for her daughter Persephone, which was probably enacted at the initiation, was related to the seeking after immortality and happiness in a future world, the presumed purpose of the ceremonies. The Eleusinian mysteries were celebrated probably until the 4th century A.D., when Alaric I (q.v.), King of the Visigoths, destroyed Eleusis. Near the village of Lefsina, on the site of Eleusis, modern archeologists have found the remains of the Telesterion and other sacred buildings. See MYSTERIES, CLASSIC.

ELEVATED RAILROADS, or ELEVATED RAILWAYS, street railroads running on tracks supported above ground level to permit the flow of traffic underneath. The tracks are usually supported by continuous girders resting on pillars. Initially introduced in 1867 in New York City (q.v.) where the roads were congested with horsedrawn carriages, wagons, and street cars, the first 4-mi.-long system did not prove popular until 1872. Thereafter, the system that operated in Manhattan grew rapidly, partially as a result of the profits made from land speculation along the right of way. Brooklyn, which was not part of New York City at the time, had its first elevated-railroad system in 1885. The motive power of the New York system was initially supplied by a continuous cable, but small steam locomotives pulling five or six wooden cars soon

replaced this; see LOCOMOTIVE. The main drawbacks of the system were the rumble and dirt of the trains and the unsightly girders of the supporting structure.

Electric traction, which had proved efficient, economical, and quieter in street railways, was first introduced on an overhead railway in 1893 in Liverpool, England; see RAILROADS: Electrification. In the same year, an electric railway was opened in Chicago, Ill., and at the turn of the century, the Brooklyn and New York City systems were also electrified. For a short while elevated electric railroads spread rapidly; by 1904 Manhattan had 117 mi. of track, and in Chicago the system was developed to form a loop of tracks around the central business district from which the lines radiated. Elevated railroads were constructed in Boston, Mass., in 1901, and in Philadelphia, Pa., elevated lines were built as an extension of the subway system; see SUBWAY. Elevated railways were also built in Paris, France, and Berlin, Germany.

With the increasing growth of automobile traffic, the girder structures led to increased congestion, and the growing subway system, which proved faster, more economical, and less noisy, caused a decline in the traffic on elevated railroads.

In 1938, the municipal government of New York City, which purchased both the elevated and subway lines, proceeded to demolish all elevated railroads in Manhattan, and four main lines were eliminated in 1955. Some sections of the New York City subway system, in the boroughs of the Bronx, Brooklyn, and Queens, still remain elevated, however.   F.La.

ELEVATOR, device for vertical transportation of passengers or freight to different floors or levels, as in a building or a mine. The term "elevator" generally denotes a unit with automatic safety devices; the very earliest units were called hoists. Elevators consist of a platform or car traveling in vertical guides in a shaft or hoistway, with related hoisting and lowering mechanisms and a source of power. The development of the modern elevator profoundly affected both architecture and the mode of development of cities by making practical the use of many-storied buildings.

Early History. Primitive elevators, operated by human and animal power, or by water wheels, were in use as early as the 3rd century B.C. The palaces of some Roman emperors had elevators. In the Middle Ages, as a precaution against robbers, certain monasteries were built with entrances that could be reached only by hoists operated by windlasses or capstans. A tiny elevator

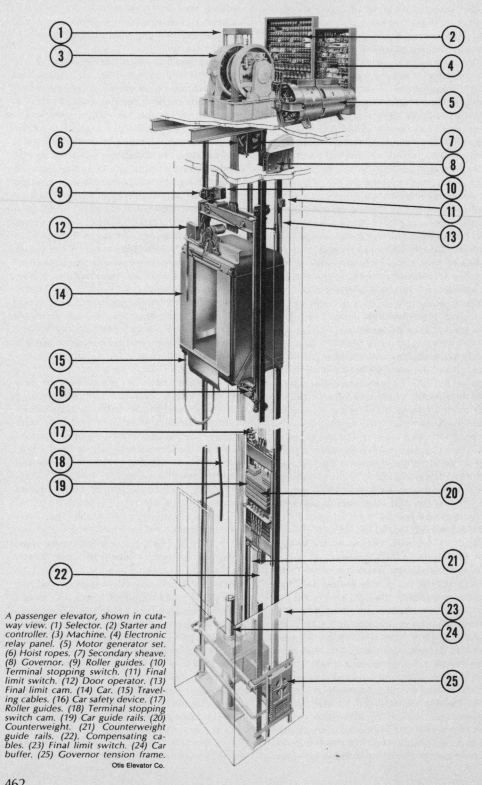

A passenger elevator, shown in cutaway view. (1) Selector. (2) Starter and controller. (3) Machine. (4) Electronic relay panel. (5) Motor generator set. (6) Hoist ropes. (7) Secondary sheave. (8) Governor. (9) Roller guides. (10) Terminal stopping switch. (11) Final limit switch. (12) Door operator. (13) Final limit cam. (14) Car. (15) Traveling cables. (16) Car safety device. (17) Roller guides. (18) Terminal stopping switch cam. (19) Car guide rails. (20) Counterweight. (21) Counterweight guide rails. (22). Compensating cables. (23) Final limit switch. (24) Car buffer. (25) Governor tension frame.

Otis Elevator Co.

balanced by a counterweight was developed in France in the 17th century, and was called a flying chair. The modern power elevator, however, is largely a product of the 19th century. Most elevators of the 19th century were powered by steam engines, either directly or through some form of hydraulic drive.

In the early 19th century, hydraulic plunger elevators were used in some European factories. In this type, later used to some extent in the United States and more extensively elsewhere, the car is mounted on a hollow steel plunger which drops into a cylinder sunk into the ground. The plunger must be slightly longer than the distance which the car is to travel. Water forced into the cylinder under pressure raises the plunger and car, which fall by gravity when water is released. In early installations the main valve controlling the flow of water was operated by hand by means of ropes running vertically through the car; lever control and pilot valves regulating acceleration and deceleration were later improvements.

A forerunner of the modern traction elevator was in use in Great Britain in 1835. In this case the hoisting rope passed over a belt-driven sheave, or pulley, to a counterweight traveling in guides. The downward pull of the two weights held the rope tight against its sheave, creating sufficient adhesive friction, or traction, between the two so that the turning sheave pulled the rope along.

Power Elevators. The history of power elevators in the U.S. began in 1850, when a crude freight hoist operating between two adjacent floors was installed in a New York City building. In 1853, at the New York Crystal Palace exposition, the American inventor and manufacturer Elisha Graves Otis (q.v.) exhibited an elevator equipped with a device called a safety to stop the fall of the car if the hoisting rope broke. In this event a spring would operate two pawls on the car, forcing them into engagement with racks at the sides of the shafts so as to support the car. This invention gave impetus to elevator construction. Three years later the first passenger elevator in the U.S., designed by Otis, was installed in a New York City store.

In these early elevators, a steam engine was connected by belt and gears to a revolving drum on which the hoisting rope was wound. In 1859 an elevator raised and lowered by a vertical screw was installed in the Fifth Avenue Hotel in New York City. In the 1870's the rope-geared hydraulic elevator was introduced. The plunger was replaced in this type by a relatively short piston moving in a cylinder which was mounted, either vertically or horizontally, within the building; the effective length of the stroke of the piston was multiplied by a system of ropes and sheaves. Because of its smoother operation and greater efficiency, the hydraulic elevator generally replaced the type with a rope wound on a revolving drum.

Electric Elevators. The electric motor (see DYNAMOELECTRIC MACHINERY) was introduced in elevator construction in 1880 by the German inventor Werner von Siemens; see under SIEMENS. His car, carrying the motor below, climbed its shaft by means of revolving pinion gears which engaged racks at the sides of the shaft. An electric elevator was constructed in Baltimore, Md., in 1887, operated by an electric motor turning a revolving drum on which the hoisting rope was wound. Within the next twelve years, electric elevators with worm gearing connecting the motor and drum came into general use except in tall buildings. In the drum elevator the length of the hoisting rope, and therefore the height to which the car can rise, are limited by the size of the drum; space limitations and manufacturing difficulties prevented the use of the drum mechanism in skyscrapers. The advantages of the electric elevator, however, including efficiency, relatively low installation costs, and virtually constant speed regardless of the load, spurred inventors to search for a way of using electric motive power in skyscrapers. Counterweights creating traction on electrically driven sheaves proved the solution to the problem.

Since the introduction of electric motive power for elevators, various improvements have been made in motors and methods of control. At first, single-speed motors only were used. Because a second, lower speed was desirable to facilitate leveling the car with landings, low-speed auxiliary motors were introduced, but, later, several systems were devised for varying speed by varying the voltage supplied to the hoisting motor. In recent years devices for automatic leveling of cars at landings are commonly used.

Originally the motor switch and the brakes were operated mechanically from the car by means of hand ropes. Soon electromagnets, controlled by operating switches in the car, were introduced to throw the motor switch and to release a spring brake. Push-button control was an early development, later supplemented by elaborate signal systems.

Safety devices have been highly developed. In 1878 Charles Rollin Otis (1835–1927), a son of the inventor of the original car safety, introduced a similar mechanism connected to a speed governor which applied the safety if the car was traveling at a dangerous speed, whether or not the rope broke. In later car safeties, clamps were used to grip the guide rails so as to bring the car to a stop gradually. Today so-called governors control a series of devices to slow down the car if it is speeding only slightly, to shut off the motor and apply an electromagnetic brake if the car continues to accelerate, and then to apply the mechanical safety if the speed becomes dangerous. Terminal switches independent of other controlling mechanisms stop the car at the upper and lower limits of travel. For low-speed cars, spring bumpers are provided at the bottom of the hoistway; high-speed cars are buffered by pistons fitting into oil-filled cylinders. Electric circuits, completed by contact points in the hoistway doors on the various floors and in the car gates, permit operation only when the gates and all doors are closed.

The great advances in electronic systems during World War II resulted in many changes in elevator design and installation; see ELECTRONICS. Computing equipment was developed for compiling automatically information which vastly improved the operational efficiency of elevators in large buildings; see COMPUTER. The equipment, which became available in 1948, made possible the solution of such scheduling problems as morning and evening peak loads and traffic balance and the elimination of operators.

The use of automatic programming equipment eventually eliminated the need for starters at the ground level of large commercial buildings, and thus the operation of elevators became completely automatic. Automatic elevators are now generally employed in all types of buildings. The World Trade Center in New York City, with its two 110-story towers, has 244 elevators with carrying capacities of up to 10,000 lb. and speeds of up to 1600 ft. per min. The 110-story Sears-Roebuck Building in Chicago has 109 elevators with speeds of up to 1800 ft. per min.

Observation and Double-Deck Elevators. A recent innovation is the so-called bubble elevator, with a car of transparent structural glass that operates in the open to let passengers observe the view. It first gained popularity on observation towers such as the Space Needle in Seattle, Wash., and is now installed in a number of hotels.

Double-deck elevators carry more passengers without taking proportionally more space in a building. Such elevators are in service in the Time-Life Building in Chicago, among other locations.

NATIONAL ELEVATOR MANUFACTURING INDUSTRY, INC.

464

EL FERROL, officially EL FERROL DEL CAUDILLO, city and seaport of Spain, in La Coruña Province, on the Bay of Ferrol, an arm of the Atlantic Ocean, about 15 miles N.E. of the city of La Coruña. It is an important naval station, with one of the largest natural harbors in Spain. The entrance to the harbor is a narrow, fortified strait, through which only one ship at a time can pass. The city is the site of a naval wireless telegraphic station and a large naval arsenal, with a basin containing two dry docks, foundries, and workshops. Nearby is the La Graña submarine base. The industries in the city center around the construction and repair of the ships and docks. Originally a fishing village, El Ferrol was selected by Charles IV, King of Spain (*see under* CHARLES), in 1726 as a suitable site for a naval station, and a few years later the shipbuilding yards were constructed. El Ferrol is the birthplace of the Spanish dictator Francisco Franco (q.v.). It was captured by Franco's army in 1936, soon after the outbreak of the Spanish Civil War. Pop. (1970) 87,351.

ELGAR, Sir Edward (1857–1934), British composer born near Worcester, England. He was educated at the Littleton House school near Worcester and as a boy studied the violin, organ, and other musical instruments. As a young man he filled several musical posts before succeeding his father as organist at Saint George's Roman Catholic Church, Worcester, in 1885. In 1889 he married and resigned his position to devote himself to composing music. After his marriage Elgar lived alternately in London and near Worcester. The performance of his overture *Froissart* in 1890 brought Elgar some recognition as a composer, but he did not become well known until 1899, when the Hungarian conductor Hans Richter (1843–1916) performed Elgar's *Variations on an Original Theme* in London. That composition, better known as the *Enigma Variations* because the central theme is suggested but never overtly stated, is one of his most highly regarded and popular works. *The Dream of Gerontius*, an oratorio based on a poem by the British churchman Cardinal John Henry Newman (q.v.), is generally considered Elgar's masterpiece. It was badly performed at the English premiere in 1900, but a successful performance the following year at Düsseldorf, Germany, firmly established the reputation of the composer. Elgar was knighted in 1904; in 1924 he was appointed Master of the King's Musick; and in 1931 he was created a baronet. Elgar was the first modern British composer to write important choral and orchestral music. His work, which is a late example of Romanticism (*see* Music: *History: The Romantic Era*), is notable for its wit, lyrical beauty, and distinctive form.

In addition to the works mentioned above, Elgar wrote the cantatas *The Black Knight* (1893) and *Caractacus* (1898); the oratorios *The Apostles* (1903) and *The Kingdom* (1906); two concertos, one for the violin (1910) and one for the cello (1919); and the five popular *Pomp and Circumstance* marches, of which four were written between 1901 and 1907 and the last in 1930. His major orchestral works include the overtures *Cockaigne* (1902) and *In the South* (1904); the symphonic study *Falstaff* (1913); and two symphonies, in A flat (1908) and in E flat (1911). He was at work on a third symphony at the time of his death, and he composed many smaller works.

ELGIN, city of Illinois, in Cook and Kane counties, on the Fox R., 36 miles N.W. of Chicago. The city, surrounded by a dairying region, is served by several railroads, and contains precision industries including factories producing watches and watchcases, as well as industries producing tools, belting, and electrical products. The city is the site of Elgin Academy, opened in 1856, and of the Northern State Hospital for the Insane. The Audubon Museum contains a large collection of natural-history specimens, and historical and Indian material, and the Laura Davidson Sears Academy of Fine Arts displays a collection of early American portraits. Elgin was first settled in 1835. It was incorporated as a village in 1847 and chartered as a city in 1854. Pop. (1960) 49,447; (1970) 55,691.

ELGIN. See Moray (county of Scotland).

ELGIN MARBLES, collection of Greek marble sculptures brought from Athens to Great Britain, in 1806 by the British diplomat Thomas Bruce, 7th Earl of Elgin (1766–1841), and acquired in 1816 by the British Museum in London. The chief pieces of the Elgin collection are the works from the Parthenon (q.v.) of Phidias (q.v.), the most important sculptor of ancient Greece. Other specimens are from the Erechtheum (q.v.), a temple on the Athenian Acropolis, and from the temple of Pandrosus, also in Athens.

The marbles came to Lord Elgin's attention while he was ambassador (1799–1802) to Ottoman Turkey, which at that time ruled Greece. He had them removed at his own expense to prevent the destruction which, under Turkish rule, had befallen other Greek monuments. Lord Elgin's action was praised by some, but others criticized him for having taken the sculptures from their original sites. The British poet George Gordon Byron, 6th Baron Byron (q.v.), in his poem "Childe Harold's Pilgrimage", lamented, "The walls defaced, the moldering shrines removed by British hands". In his own defense, Lord Elgin wrote a pamphlet, *Memorandum on the Subject of the Earl of Elgin's Pursuits in Greece* (1820). Further destruction by the Turks of Athenian monuments in 1826–27, during the Greek war for independence, put an end to criticism of Lord Elgin's action. The marbles helped to stimulate among the English Romantic poets a strong interest in the art of ancient Greece. They are the subject of a notable poem "On Seeing the Elgin Marbles", by the British poet John Keats (q.v.). Casts of the Elgin marbles can be found in the Metropolitan Museum of Art, New York City, and in other museums.

EL GRECO. See Greco, El.

ELIJAH, in the New Testament, ELIAS (fl. 9th cent. B.C.), the most popular Hebrew prophet. The period of his lifetime (1 Kings 17–19:21, 2 Kings 1, 2) was one of social and religious change. Elijah led the struggle against the idolatrous worship of the Phoenician god Baal (q.v.), whom Ahab, King of Israel (r. 875–853 B.C.), had worshiped. During Elijah's struggle against the Baalites he engaged in a contest of "miracles" with the prophets of Baal and stated that there would be no rain or dew except at his command. After three years of drought Elijah assembled the people of Israel on Mt. Carmel, where he demonstrated the supremacy of God over Baal. Then Elijah had the prophets of Baal put to death, whereupon the rains came. Elijah reprimanded King Ahab for the murder of Naboth, the vineyard owner described in 1 Kings 21. The anticipation of Elijah's return to earth, after his death, as the precursor of the Messiah (q.v.) is based on the account of his removal from earth in a chariot of fire (2 Kings 2:11) and finds support also in the words of Malachi, the last prophet (Mal. 4:5–6). Christ declared John the Baptist (q.v.) to be the spiritual fulfillment of this anticipation, John being said to have come "in the spirit and power of Elias" (Matt. 11:14, 17:11–13, Mark 9:13, Luke 1:17). In post-Biblical Judaism, Elijah is thought of as an invisible participant in the home celebration of Passover (*see* Pesach) and in the rites of circumcision (q.v.). *See also* Elisha. N.N.G.

ELIOT, Charles William (1834–1926), American educator, born in Boston, Mass., and educated at Harvard University. From 1858 to 1863 he was assistant professor of chemistry at Harvard. He spent the next few years in Europe studying chemistry and foreign educational methods. He returned to the United States in

1865 to become professor of analytical chemistry at the newly formed Massachusetts Institute of Technology, remaining there until 1869, when he became the twenty-second president of Harvard University. Influenced by what he had seen abroad, Eliot remodeled the university curriculum on a liberal basis. Although he did not originate the elective system, he established it so thoroughly that it spread to other colleges. By raising the requirements for university admission, he raised the standards of secondary schools. In 1894 he suggested cooperation among the colleges to establish a common entrance test and equalize standards, preparing the way for the College Entrance Examinations Board. In 1908 he was chosen president of the National Civil Service Reform League. After his retirement in 1909 from the presidency of Harvard, he devoted himself to various cultural and social movements. Eliot is credited with the statement that a five-foot shelf of books, if diligently studied, might supply a liberal education. He selected the contents of *The Harvard Classics* (1910), a set of books consisting of fifty volumes and commonly known as "Dr. Eliot's Five-Foot Shelf of Books". The books were specifically designed to supply a broad literary background to those who were not college-trained. In his lectures and writings he condemned the standardization of education and industry. He wrote *A Manual of Inorganic Chemistry* (1868), *Educational Reform* (1898), *More Money for Public Schools* (1903), *University Administration* (1908), *The Durable Satisfactions of Life* (1910), and *Late Harvest* (1924).

ELIOT, George (1819–80), pen name of MARY ANN EVANS *or* MARIAN EVANS, British novelist, born in Chilvers Coton, Warwickshire, England and educated at a local school in Nuneaton, and later at a boarding school in Coventry. At the age of seventeen, after the death of her mother and the marriage of her elder sister, she was called home to care for her father. From that time on she was self-taught.

A strict religious training, received at the insistence of her father, dominated her youth. In 1841 she began to read works concerning rationalism (q.v.), which influenced her to rebel against dogmatic religion, and she remained a rationalist throughout her life. Her first literary attempt, at which she worked for two years (1844–46), was a translation of *Das Leben Jesu* ("The Living Jesus", 1835–36) by the German theologian and philosophical writer David Friedrich Strauss (q.v.). In 1851, after traveling for two years in Europe, she returned to England and wrote a book review for the *Westminster*

Review. She subsequently became assistant editor of that publication. Through her work on the *Review* she met many of the leading British literary figures of the period, including Harriet Martineau, John Stuart Mill, James Anthony Froude, Herbert Spencer, and George Henry Lewes (qq.v.). Her meeting with Lewes, a philosopher, scientist, and critic, was one of the most significant events in her life. They fell in love and decided to live together, although Lewes was married and a divorce was not possible. Nevertheless, Mary Ann Evans looked upon her subsequent long and happy relationship with Lewes as a marriage.

George Eliot   British Information Services

She continued to write reviews, articles for periodicals, and translations from the German. Then, with encouragement from Lewes, she began to write fiction in 1856. Her first story, "The Sad Fortunes of the Reverend Amos Barton", appeared in *Blackwood's Magazine* in January, 1857. It was followed by two other stories in the same year and all three were collected in book form as *Scenes from Clerical Life* (1858). The author signed herself as George Eliot and kept her true identity secret for many years.

Her most popular works, and the ones that made George Eliot famous, are *Adam Bede* (1859), *The Mill on the Floss* (1860), and *Silas Marner* (1861). These novels dealt with the Warwickshire countryside and were based, to a great extent, on her own life. Her next novel, *Romola,* was a historical romance about the Italian preacher and reformer Girolamo Savonarola (q.v.) and 15th-century Florence. She began writing the book in 1861, and it appeared in 1863, after being serialized in *The Cornhill Magazine*. Following the completion of *Romola,* she wrote *Felix Holt, the Radical* (1866), a novel of English politics; *Middlemarch* (1862), dealing with English middle-class life in a provincial town; *Daniel Deronda* (1876), an attack on anti-Semitism; and *The Impressions of Theophrastus Such* (1879), a collection of essays. Her poetry, which is considered to have much less merit than her prose, includes *The Spanish Gypsy* (1868), a drama in blank verse; *Agatha* (1869); and *The Legend of Jubal and Other Poems* (1874).

During the period in which she wrote her major works, George Eliot was always encouraged and protected by Lewes. He prevented her even from seeing unfavorable reviews of her books. After his death in 1878, she became a recluse and stopped writing. In May, 1880, she married John Walter Cross (1840–1924), an American banker, who had long been a friend of both Lewes and herself, but she died in December of the same year.

George Eliot's novels, with their profound feeling and accurate portrayals of simple lives, gave her a place in the first rank of 19th-century English writers. Her fame was international, and her books greatly influenced the development of French naturalism exemplified by the work of such men as the French critic, poet, and novelist Charles Joseph Paul Bourget (1852–1935) and the French novelist Emile Zola (q.v.).

ELIOT, Sir John (1592–1632), English political leader, born in Port Eliot, Cornwall, and educated at Exeter College, University of Oxford. He was elected to Parliament in 1614, and was knighted four years later. In 1619 his friend and patron George Villiers. 1st Duke of Buckingham (*see under* VILLIERS), obtained for him an appointment as vice-admiral of Devon. Eliot returned to Parliament in 1624 where he distinguished himself by his eloquent fight against the encroachments of James I (q.v.), King of England, on the powers of Parliament. In the following year Buckingham's support of attempts to extend the power of the new monarch, Charles I (q.v.), King of England, caused Eliot to sever their friendly relations. In 1626 Eliot demanded an inquiry into the disastrous expedition which Buckingham had sent against Cádiz, Spain. Soon afterward he brought the case for the impeachment of the duke before the House of Lords. Eliot was jailed on the day following his statement of the charges, but the House of Commons quickly obtained his release by refusing to proceed while he remained in prison. Nevertheless, he was deprived of his office as vice-admiral. In 1627 when Eliot refused to pay a tax levy in the form of a forced loan, he was again put into prison. Released in 1628, he was reelected to Parliament, where he led the forces which presented the Petition of Right (q.v.). Early in 1629 Eliot was once again imprisoned as a result of his introduction in the House of Commons of a series of resolutions opposing arbitrary taxation and religious innovations. He steadfastly refused to submit to the king as the condition of his release, and he died in prison. Among his works, all of which were written in prison and published long after his death, are *The Monarchie of Man* (1879) and *An Apology for Socrates* (1881).

ELIOT, John, known as the APOSTLE OF THE INDIANS (1604–90), American clergyman, born in Widford, Hertfordshire, England, and educated at the University of Cambridge. Influenced by the American Congregationalist clergyman Thomas Hooker (q.v.), Eliot became a nonconformist (*see* NONCONFORMISTS), and in 1631 went to the New World, where for a time he assisted at the First Church, Boston. In 1632 he became "teacher" of the church in Roxbury, Mass. After learning the Indian dialect he first preached without an interpreter before the Indians at Nonantum, now Newton, Mass., in 1646. Thereafter he devoted most of his time to instructing the Indians. He gathered them into sixteen different settlements of which Natick, Mass. was the first to be established in 1651. The communities were supported by the Society for the Propagation of the Gospel Among the Indians created in 1649 by Parliament, and flourished until they were broken up in 1675 by King Philip's War; *see* PHILIP OR METACOMET. Eliot's works include *Primer or Catechism, in the Massachusetts Indian Language* (1654), the first book printed in the Indian language; *Christian Commonwealth, or the Civil Polity of the Rising Kingdom of Jesus Christ* (1659); an Indian translation of the New and Old Testaments (1661–63); *Indian Grammar Begun* (1666) and *Indian Primer* (1669).

ELIOT, T(homas) S(tearns) (1888–1965), American-born British poet, literary critic, and dramatist, born in Saint Louis, Mo., and educated at Harvard University, the Sorbonne, the University of Paris, and Merton College, University of Oxford. He became a resident of London in 1915 and a naturalized British citizen in 1927. His first important poem, "The Love Song of J. Alfred Prufrock", was published in 1915. He was

The Nobel Prize for literature in 1948 is awarded by Crown Prince Gustaf Adolf, now King Gustavus VI (center), to T. S. Eliot (right) in Stockholm, Sweden.

UPI

a teacher from 1915 to 1917 at Highgate School, London. In his first volume of verse, *Prufrock and Other Observations* (1917), he uses the imagery of urban life in a context of poetic intensity. The poems have no fixed verse form or regular pattern, and rhyme is used only occasionally. Eliot worked as a bank clerk from 1917 to 1925 and served (1917–19) as assistant editor of the literary magazine *Egoist*.

His long poem in five parts, *The Waste Land* (1922), is an erudite work that expresses vividly his conception of the sterility of modern society in contrast with societies of the past. Because of the symbolism, emotional power, and use of allusions, *The Waste Land* became one of the most widely discussed poems of the early-20th century.

During the 1920's Eliot developed pronounced views on literary, religious, and social subjects. In essays on such subjects as the Elizabethan dramatists, the English metaphysical poets, and the Italian poet Dante Alighieri (q.v.), he profoundly influenced the tenets of literary criticism. He contended in the collection *The Sacred Wood* (1920) that the critic must develop a strong historical sense in order to judge literature from a proper perspective and that the poet must be impersonal in the creative exercise of his craft. As founder and editor (1922–39) of *The*

Criterion he provided a literary forum for many prominent contemporary writers. In the collection of essays *For Lancelot Andrewes* (1928) Eliot describes his critical position as that of a classicist in literature, a royalist in politics, and an Anglo-Catholic in religion.

Beginning in the 1930's the qualities of serenity and religious humility became paramount in Eliot's poetry, notably in *Ash Wednesday* (1930), *The Rock* (1934), and his first long verse play, *Murder in the Cathedral* (1935), based on the martyrdom of Saint Thomas à Becket (q.v.). *Four Quartets* (1943) expresses in moving verse a transcendental sense of time. He received the Nobel Prize in literature in 1948 and was awarded the United States Presidential Medal of Freedom in 1964.

Eliot's fame as a playwright dates from the successful production of *The Cocktail Party* (1949), which explored the theme of salvation in a context of modern drawing-room comedy. Other dramatic presentations of religious and moral themes are *The Confidential Clerk* (1954), and *The Elder Statesman* (1958).

Among his other works are the plays *Sweeney Agonistes* (1932), and *The Family Reunion* (1939); and the prose works *The Idea of a Christian Society* (1940), and *Notes Toward a Definition of Culture* (1948).

Eliot is one of the most influential poets of the 20th century. Borrowing from the French Symbolists, he adapted to English verse a type of suggestive statement that helped shape one of the foremost styles of modern poetry. His plays, which rely upon a colloquial use of unrhymed verse, gave impetus to poetic drama in English. Eliot's methods of literary analysis have been a major influence on British and American critical writing.

ELISABETH, Saint (about 1st cent. B.C.), in the New Testament, mother of John the Baptist (q.v.). She was the wife of Zacharias, a priest, and a kinswoman of Saint Mary (q.v.). When the childless Elisabeth was well advanced in years, the angel Gabriel (q.v.) appeared to her husband and prophesied a son (Luke 1:5–20). Six months later, the angel appeared to Mary to announce the conception of Jesus. During the pregnancy of both women they met, and Elisabeth greeted Mary saying "Blessed art thou among women," and called her "mother of my Lord" (Luke 1:42, 43). In the Roman Catholic Church, the traditional feast day of St. Elisabeth is Nov. 5.

ELISABETHVILLE. *See* LUBUMBASHI.

ELISHA (d. 8th cent. B.C.), in the Old Testament (2 Kings 2–13), Hebrew prophet, the disciple and successor of Elijah (q.v.). The name Elisha means "God is deliverance" in Hebrew. Elisha was a farmer until chosen by Elijah to be his disciple. When Elijah ascended to heaven he cast his mantle upon Elisha as a symbol of the responsibility now placed upon the latter. Elisha continued Elijah's struggle against the idolatrous Baal (q.v.) cult. Although less fiery than his predecessor, he attained greater political influence through his power to work miracles. Having served Israel unstintingly during the reign of four kings, Elisha was regarded as a savior of Israel, and was deeply mourned on his death.

ELIZABETH, city in New Jersey, and county seat of Union Co., on Newark Bay, Staten Island Sound, and the Elizabeth R., adjacent to Newark, and 12 miles S.W. of New York City. Goethals Bridge, opened in 1928, connects Elizabeth with Staten Island. Port Elizabeth, the harbor of the city, accommodates oceangoing ships and has extensive railroad docks. The city is served by two railroads. Elizabeth is the site of the main plant of the Singer Sewing Machine Company; the city also contains automobile factories and an oil refinery. Cookies, toys, electronic equipment, pharmaceutical products, chemicals, and machine and foundry products are manufactured in the city.

Buildings of historical interest in Elizabeth include several colonial houses and the First Presbyterian Church, built in 1786 on the site of the convention of the first colonial assembly of New Jersey, held in 1688; the American statesmen Alexander Hamilton and Aaron Burr (qq.v.) attended grammar school on the site now occupied by the parish house of the church. The College of New Jersey, now Princeton University, was originally founded in Elizabeth in 1746. The oldest newspaper in the State, the Elizabeth *Daily Journal,* founded in nearby Chatham in 1779, was moved to Elizabeth in 1785. The first successful submarine was built in the city in 1898; *see* HOLLAND, JOHN PHILIP.

Elizabeth was settled as Elizabethtown in 1665 by colonists from Jamaica, Long Island. From 1665 to 1686 it was the capital of the colony. Elizabeth was incorporated as a borough in 1789 and was chartered as a city in 1855. It became the seat of Union County in 1857. Pop. (1960) 107,698; (1970) 112,654.

ELIZABETH, Saint (1207–31), daughter of Andrew II, King of Hungary (r. 1205–35), born in Bratislava. At the age of fourteen she married Louis IV, Landgrave of Thuringia (d. 1227), and became devoted to ascetic practices and to charitable works. After the death of her husband, she was driven from Thuringia by her brother-in-law, who claimed that she was exhausting the revenues from her estates by giving alms. She found refuge for herself and her three children with her maternal uncle, the bishop of Bamberg. When the regency of Thuringia was restored to her, she accepted the inheritance of the landgraviate for her son, but relinquished her own power as regent. Leaving her children, she joined the third order of Saint Francis (*see* FRANCISCANS). She passed the rest of her life undergoing austerities and ministering to the sick. Credited with having performed miracles, she was canonized in 1235 by Pope Gregory IX (1147?–1241). Her feast day is Nov. 17.

ELIZABETH *or* **ELIZABETH STUART** (1596–1662), Queen Consort of Bohemia (1619–20), born in Fife, Scotland, daughter of James VI, King of Scotland, later James I (q.v.), King of Great Britain. At the age of seventeen she was married to Frederick V, Elector of the Palatinate, (1596–1632). Their marriage was celebrated by the English poet John Donne (q.v.) in his poem *Epithalamium* (1613). Frederick was chosen king of Bohemia in 1619. In the following year the armies of Frederick and Elizabeth were defeated by the forces of the Catholic League (*see* THIRTY YEARS' WAR) and the two were forced to seek asylum abroad, eventually settling in The Hague. Frederick died in 1632; a year later Elizabeth managed to raise a small army to support the claim of her son Charles Louis (1617–80) to the Palatinate. Under the Peace of Westphalia in

1648, Charles Louis was awarded a part of the Rhine Palatinate. Because of Elizabeth's continued political activity, however, he refused to allow her to join him there. In 1661 her nephew, Charles II (q.v.), King of England, gave her refuge and settled a pension on her. Elizabeth's recurrent ill fortune, caused chiefly by her espousal of the Protestant cause, attracted the sympathy of many of her contemporaries, and at death she was honored with burial in Westminster Abbey. Her thirteen children included Sophia, Electress of Hannover and the mother of George I (q.v.), first of the Hanoverian kings of England; and Prince Rupert (q.v.), a noted soldier and scientist.

ELIZABETH I (1533–1603), Queen of England and Ireland (1558–1603), daughter of Henry VIII, King of England, and of his second wife, Anne Boleyn (qq.v.), and last of the Tudor rulers of England. Elizabeth's legitimacy was questioned and never settled, because an act of Parliament (1536) invalidated the marriage of her parents and enabled Henry to marry his third wife, Jane Seymour (*see under* SEYMOUR). Nevertheless, both Parliament and the king named Henry's children, Edward (*see* EDWARD VI), Mary (*see* MARY I), and Elizabeth, in that order, heirs to the throne of their father.

Childhood and Accession as Queen. Elizabeth spent her childhood away from the court, and received an excellent classical education under such scholars as Roger Ascham (q.v.),

Elizabeth I   British Information Services

who influenced her greatly. Henry's sixth wife, Catherine Parr (q.v.), later became fond of the young princess and brought her back to court. Elizabeth remained in Catherine's charge after Henry's death and took no part in the political intrigues following the coronation of her brother as King Edward VI. When Edward died, the princess became a partisan of her sister Mary, refusing to support the revolt led by the English poet and diplomat Sir Thomas Wyatt (q.v.) against Mary who became queen in 1553. Nevertheless, Mary, a devout Roman Catholic, was made uneasy by the Protestantism of her sister and her potential menace as an heir to the throne. In 1554 the princess was imprisoned on the false charge of having been implicated in Wyatt's rebellion. She was later released, having outwardly professed Catholicism, and regained Mary's favor.

At the death of Mary in 1558, Elizabeth became queen, beginning a reign that was one of the greatest in English history. At the time of Elizabeth's accession, England was torn by religious strife, was economically insecure, and was involved in a disastrous war with France. To these problems Elizabeth brought a thorough education, innate shrewdness, and a skill in diplomacy that she had constantly exercised during the reigns of Edward and Mary, when one mistake might have meant her death. Although she was excessively vain and capricious, her position as queen always took precedence over her position as a woman. Her policies and her colorful personality made her extremely popular with her subjects. Elizabeth's statecraft was due, to a great extent, to her choice of able and wise advisers, most notably Sir Francis Walsingham (q.v.) and William Cecil, 1st Baron Burghley (*see under* CECIL).

Religion was the queen's initial problem. She reverted to Protestantism immediately after Mary's death, and her first Parliament, in 1559, had a Protestant majority. Between 1559 and 1563, this Parliament passed religious legislation that became the doctrinal basis of the Church of England (q.v.). In the Elizabethan Compromise (1559), the Church of England became the established Church, and throughout Elizabeth's reign English Catholics and Puritans (q.v.) were persecuted.

A Popular Queen. Elizabeth's domination of the period to which she gave her name was due, in part, to the exuberant national spirit that she inspired and that characterized all of England during the second half of the 16th century. She restored popular confidence in the monarchy and a wave of prosperity swept every field of endeavor. With the religious question settled and the war with France concluded by the Treaty of Cateau-Cambrésis (1559), England was able to develop industrially and economically. Under the direction of the queen, the government began to regulate commerce and industry on a national scale. England grew to be a great maritime power with the exploits of such mariners as Sir Francis Drake and Sir Martin Frobisher (qq.v.). A new system of standard coinage was introduced in 1560 to replace the silver coins that had been considerably debased during the preceding three reigns. As a result, prices fell to normal levels and confidence in English money was restored. Foreign trade, encouraged by the government, became a great capitalistic enterprise. The Royal Exchange of London was opened in 1566 and the company of merchants that later became the English East India Company was chartered in 1600; see EAST INDIA COMPANY. Above all this activity stood the figure of the queen. Elizabeth, to Englishmen, was England. See ENGLAND: *History: The Elizabethan Age.*

From the very beginning of her reign, Elizabeth's marital status was a political concern because there was no English heir to the throne. Parliament insistently petitioned her to marry, but she replied with the statement that she intended to live and die a virgin, and she became known as the virgin queen. Her statement did not prevent her from toying constantly with the idea of marriage. She was besieged by royal suitors, each of whom she favored when it was in her political interest to do so. Her affections, however, were bestowed upon a succession of favorites, notably Sir Walter Raleigh, Robert Dudley, 1st Earl of Leicester (qq.v.), and Robert Devereux, 2nd Earl of Essex (*see under* DEVEREUX).

Elizabeth's greatest political blunder was her treatment of her Catholic cousin, Mary, Queen of Scots (q.v.). Mary sought refuge in England after being defeated in battle by her half brother, James Stewart, Earl of Moray (1531?–70). The English queen immediately imprisoned her because the Catholic monarchs of Europe, and her own Catholic subjects as well, considered Elizabeth illegitimate. By their reasoning, Mary was the lawful queen of England. Thus, to Elizabeth, Mary was the potential center of conspiracy. Queen Mary was kept captive for years, giving rise to many plots by English Catholics for her release. When, in 1586, Sir Francis Walsingham, then secretary of state, discovered a plot to assassinate Elizabeth and place Mary on the throne of England, Elizabeth was reluctantly persuaded to have Mary executed in 1587. The execution had serious results. Philip II (q.v.), King of Spain had, for years, been troubled by the raids of English mariners on his colonial possessions. Since both Mary and Philip were Catholic, her death provided him with a pretext to declare war on England, and he sent a fleet to invade the country in 1588. The Armada (q.v.), however, suffered an inglorious defeat, and England took the place of Spain as the great colonizer of the New World and the reigning power on the seas. Moreover, by defeating Catholic Spain, England established Protestantism as a force in international politics.

End of an Era. Elizabeth's popularity waned toward the end of her reign because of her heavy expenditures and abuse of royal power. Moreover, her policies became weaker, her later ministers being less able than Cecil or Walsingham. The close of Elizabeth's reign was disturbed by a revolt in Ireland that was led by Hugh O'Neill (q.v.), Earl of Tyrone. The favorite of the queen, the 2nd Earl of Essex unsuccessfully led an army against the Irish. When he returned to England he led a revolt against the queen and was executed in 1601. Following his death, Elizabeth was desolate. She spent the last years of her life unhappy and alone, having outlived a glorious age that witnessed the beginning of the history of what would become modern England.

In addition to political triumphs, the Elizabethan era was notable as one of the greatest periods of English literature. Edmund Spenser, William Shakespeare, and Christopher Marlowe (qq.v.) were only a few of the host of writers who created their great works under Elizabeth. The dramatic personality of the queen herself became the subject of a voluminous literature; see ENGLISH LITERATURE: *The Renaissance.*

ELIZABETH II, in full ELIZABETH ALEXANDRA MARY (1926–), Queen of Great Britain and Northern Ireland (1952–), daughter of King George VI (q.v.), born in London, England. In 1944 Princess Elizabeth served as a councillor of state while her father was on the war front in Italy. She married Prince Philip (q.v.), Duke of Edinburgh, in 1947, and a year later bore him a son, Charles Philip Arthur George (q.v.). In 1950 she bore him a daughter, Anne Elizabeth Alice Louise. Elizabeth succeeded to the throne on the death of her father in February, 1952. A second son, Andrew Albert Christian Edward, was born to Elizabeth in 1960, and another son, Edward Antony Richard Louis, in 1964.

The reign of Elizabeth II was marked by vast changes in the lives of her people and in the

Queen Elizabeth II and her husband, Prince Philip, reviewing an honor guard at Westminster Abbey.
UPI

power and prestige of her nation. By the mid-1970's more than thirty former British colonies, protectorates, and mandate territories had been granted their independence. Beginning in the mid-1950's there was constant turmoil in Northern Ireland. On the home front, the nation suffered economic difficulties after World War II. Many industries were nationalized, and in 1973 Great Britain became a member of the European Economic Community (q.v.). The primary role of the queen throughout this period was that of an ambassador. Elizabeth II made state visits all over the world. She and Prince Philip frequently toured the Commonwealth nations, visiting Canada in 1973 and Australia in 1974.

ELIZABETHAN AGE. See DRAMA: *National Drama: England*; ELIZABETH I; ENGLAND: *History*; ENGLISH LITERATURE: *The Renaissance*; ENGLISH

MUSIC: *The Fifteenth Century*; MUSIC: *History: The Renaissance.*

ELIZABETHAN ARCHITECTURE, in architecture, transitional style in building, characteristic of the early Renaissance in England. It represents the blending of the classical forms of the Renaissance with English Gothic modes. Curved and arched gables, bay windows, long galleries, large bedrooms, broad staircases, octagonal turrets, numerous fireplaces and chimneys, and classic orders are characteristic of the Elizabethan period. The term Tudor is often applied to the earlier, or predominantly Gothic, architecture of the Elizabethan period; the term Jacobean refers to the latter part of the period, in which the classical predominated over the Gothic. Among noteworthy examples of Elizabethan architecture are Hampton Court (q.v.), near Hampton, Middlesex, the royal residence until the reign of George II, and Hatfield House, in Hatfield, Hertfordshire.

ELIZABETH CITY, city and port of entry in North Carolina, and of Pasquotank Co., at the head of navigation on the Pasquotank R., near Albemarle Sound, about 140 miles N.E. of Raleigh, and 45 miles S. of Norfolk, Va. It has railroad and airline service and is also served by boats on the Dismal Swamp Canal, a link of the Intracoastal Waterway (q.v.). Elizabeth City is the trading and shipping center of a large agricultural region. The city has lumber mills, hosiery mills, textile plants, shipyards, and factories manufacturing furniture, candy, plastics, electronic equipment, bricks, plywood, baskets, and barrels. Elizabeth City has abundant recreational facilities, including one of the largest yacht basins between New York and Florida. A regatta for hydroplanes is an annual event. Nearby is the Great Dismal Swamp, an excellent fishing and hunting area. The city is the site of U.S. Coast Guard air and repair stations and of Elizabeth City State University (1891). It is less than 60 mi. from Cape Hatteras National Seashore, on Hatteras Island, a vacation area administered by the National Park Service (q.v.). The first general assembly of North Carolina met in 1665, on the banks of Halls Creek near the city. Elizabeth City was incorporated in 1793. Pop. (1960) 14,062; (1970) 14,381.

ELIZABETH PETROVNA (1709–62), Empress of Russia (1741–62), born near Moscow, the youngest daughter of Peter I and Catherine I (qq.v.). She became empress in 1741 by effectively staging a palace revolution which deposed the infant emperor Ivan VI (*see under* IVAN) and the regent, his mother Anna Leopoldovna (1718–46). In 1743 Elizabeth won an historic diplomatic victory by bringing to a successful conclusion the negotiations ending hostile relations between Sweden and Russia. She was chiefly responsible for establishing and maintaining the alliance of Austria, France, and Russia that almost defeated Prussia in the Seven Years' War (q.v.). Until her death, a year before the end of the war, the armies of the alliance had been successful, but soon afterward the alliance disintegrated and Prussia was able to gain the final victory. She named her nephew Peter III as her successor (*see under* PETER). Elizabeth's nonpolitical achievements include the establishment of the University of Moscow in 1755 and the Academy of Arts at Saint Petersburg (now Leningrad) in 1757.

ELIZABETHTON, city in Tennessee, and county seat of Carter Co., about 8 miles E. of Johnson City. Surrounded by an agricultural and timber region, the city manufactures wood

Staple Inn, one of the few remaining examples of Elizabethan architecture in London.

Thomas Hollyman — Photo Researchers

American elk or wapiti, Cervus canadensis

products and synthetic fibers. The Watauga Association was formed here in 1772. Nearby are the Cherokee National Forest and the Watauga Dam. Pop. (1960) 10,896; (1970) 12,269.

ELK, common name for certain members of the deer family, Cervidae, applied in America to the wapiti, *Cervus canadensis,* and in Europe to deer of the genus *Alces.* The American species of *Alces* is known as the moose. *See* DEER.

American Elk. The so-called American elk, or wapiti, is the only American species of the genus *Cervus,* which includes also the red deer (q.v.) of Europe and Asia. It is found in the mountainous regions of the western United States and Canada, from Alaska to northern New Mexico and Colorado. The American elk has dark-brown fur on the head and neck, and creamy-gray fur on the back and rump. The color of the back fur caused the Shawnee Indians to name the animal wapiti (q.v.), meaning "pale" or "white", but the colonists called it "elk" and this name continues to be in common usage. The wapiti is smaller than the European elk. The male stands about 5 ft. high at the shoulder, weighs about 700 lb., and has antlers that may grow to more than 4 ft. in length. The

antlers are shed in March, begin to grow again in late spring, and are fully grown by fall. The bulls live apart from the main herd during most of the year, joining the herd only during the mating season. At this time the bulls fight furiously over the right to the females, accompanying these fights with a braying call that has earned the animals the name "jackass deer" in certain sections of the Rocky Mountains. The cows are somewhat smaller than the bulls and have no antlers. Wapitis feed early in the morning and late in the afternoon, but never at night as do most deer. They eat a wide variety of plants and are both browsers and grazers.

European Elk. This animal, *Alces alces,* is the largest member of the deer family in the world. In Europe it inhabits forests in Siberia, Norway, Sweden, and the Baltic region; in North America it is found in wooded areas of Canada and the northern U.S. It reaches maximum size in Alaska, where a bull may stand well over 6 ft. at the shoulder, and weigh more than 1400 lb. The males bear enormous palmate antlers with marginal prongs or tines. As with most other members of the deer family, the antlers are shed each year after the mating season, by which time they have attained a spread of 5 ft. or more. The body color of the moose varies from almost black to light brown, becoming grayish in winter. The legs are lighter in color than the body. The protruding muzzle and the long legs adapt the animal to browsing on brush and to wading into lakes and ponds to feed on aquatic plants. The shoulders of the moose are higher than the hindquarters, giving him a strangely humpbacked appearance that is accentuated by the short neck. In order to reach low-growing plants, or drink from a shallow pool, the moose is forced to kneel. An excellent swimmer, it does not hesitate to swim across lakes and rivers.

Moose generally prefer a solitary existence, although they may form into small bands, especially in summer. During the mating season, bulls battle vigorously for the cows and their roars may be heard for great distances. Although normally timid animals, they are dangerous if approached during this period.

The moose is normally quite capable of protecting itself from its natural enemies, but in heavy snow, or if old and disabled, it falls prey to wolves and cougars. Although bears occasionally take straying calves in the spring, man is the primary enemy of the moose. For a time the species was threatened with extinction, both in Europe and North America, because of indis-criminate hunting. Modern game laws and areas set aside for the protection of these animals have helped save the species.

EL KARNAK (anc. *Hermonthis*), village of the Arab Republic of Egypt, on the E. bank of the Nile R., about 300 miles S.E. of Cairo. El Karnak occupies the N. half of the site of ancient Thebes (q.v.), the S. half being occupied by the present village of Luxor (q.v.). The fame of El Karnak rests upon the ruins of a group of temples built there when Thebes was a center of the Egyptian religion, beginning about the XI Dynasty in 2160 B.C. The temples, with their walled enclosures of rude brick and connecting avenues of sphinxes, extend over nearly 1 sq.mi. Two small enclosures surround temples built in honor of the god Mentu and the goddess Mut by Amenhotep III (1411–1375 B.C.). The greatest and most important temple, that of the god Amon, was begun by Sesostris I (1980–35 B.C.) and was completed by Ramses II (*see under* RAMSES), though additions continued to be made until the 1st century B.C. The temple of Amon stands in an enclosure measuring about 1500 sq.ft. Its most outstanding feature is a hypostyle hall, the roof of which rests on 122 columns that are more than 70 ft. high and built in 9 rows. Reliefs and inscriptions cover the walls, and obelisks, statues, and pylon

Columns in the Temple of Amon, largest of the group of temples at El Karnak.
Trans World Airlines

gates are found throughout the enclosure. Systematic restoration of the temple was started late in the 19th century.

ELKHART, city of Indiana, in Elkhart Co., at the confluence of the Saint Joseph and Elkhart rivers, 16 miles E. of South Bend, Ind. Power for extensive manufacturing industries is supplied by a large dam and power plant a few miles W. Plants in Elkhart produce more than half of the world output of band instruments and the city is noted also for the manufacture of mobile homes. Other industries include the manufacture of chemicals, electrical and nonelectrical machinery, transportation equipment, and rubber and plastic products. Elkhart was founded in 1832; it was incorporated as a town in 1858 and as a city in 1877. Pop. (1960) 40,274; (1970) 43,152.

ELKHOUND, NORWEGIAN. See NORWEGIAN ELKHOUND.

ELKS, BENEVOLENT AND PROTECTIVE ORDER OF. See BENEVOLENT AND PROTECTIVE ORDER OF ELKS.

ELLESMERE ISLAND, an island of Franklin District, Northwest Territories, Canada, in the Arctic Ocean approximately 480 miles S. of the North Pole. Located off the N.W. coast of Greenland, it forms part of the Arctic Archipelago. Its northern tip, Cape Columbia, is the most northerly point of the North American continent. The island, about 460 mi. long and 300 mi. wide, is mountainous, with some peaks in the United States Range reaching more than 9000 ft. Many fjords indent its E. and W. coasts.

Ellesmere Island has little vegetation, and much of its surface lies under glacial icecap. Herds of caribou and musk-oxen roam some of the ice-free regions of the island. Human habitation is very sparse, with only a few scattered communities; one of these, Alert, a radio and weather station maintained by the United States and Canada, is reputedly the northernmost permanent settlement in the world. Ellesmere Island was discovered by the English navigator William Baffin (q.v.) in 1616. Area, 82,119 sq.mi.

ELLICE ISLANDS. See TUVALU.

ELLINGTON, Edward Kennedy, popularly known as DUKE ELLINGTON (1899-1974), American composer, conductor, and pianist, born in Washington, D.C., and educated in the public schools there. Ellington made his professional debut as a pianist in Washington in 1916. Shortly thereafter he formed his first small jazz band. In 1923 he moved to New York City, where from 1927 to 1932 he appeared at the Cotton Club cabaret. Through the 1930's and 1940's Ellington and his band, greatly enlarged, ap-

Duke Ellington in 1969   UPI

peared in theaters, nightclubs, and on the radio. Ellington and his orchestra made the first of seven European tours in 1933. They also performed frequently in the Middle East and in Asia. In 1943 he conducted an evening of jazz at Carnegie Hall, New York City, the first of nine annual concerts. Among his most famous songs are "Mood Indigo" (1931), "Sophisticated Lady" (1933), and "Solitude" (1934). His extended orchestral works include *Black, Brown and Beige* (1943), *Liberian Suite* (1948), *A Concert of Sacred Music* (1965), and *Far East Suite* (1967). Ellington composed scores for the motion pictures *Anatomy of a Murder* (1959), *Paris Blues* (1961), and *Assault on a Queen* (1966), and for the musical comedies *Beggar's Opera* (1947) and *Pousse-Café* (1966). The theme song of Ellington's band after 1941 was "Take the 'A' Train", written by his longtime associate, the lyric writer, arranger, and pianist Billy Strayhorn (in full, William Thomas Strayhorn, 1915-67).

The compositions of Ellington emphasize a kind of modified concerto form, being constructed around solo instrumental performances. They also frequently introduce vocal passages without words. Ellington, who helped to bring jazz into the concert halls of the world, achieved an eclectic style combining blues, various forms of jazz, and the big-band sound of swing music. He also brought jazz into the church and cathedral, creating sacred music that is widely performed in various worship services. He wrote an autobiography, *Music Is My Business* (1974). *See* BLUES; JAZZ.

ELLIPSE, in geometry (q.v.), closed plane curve, one of the conic sections (q.v.), formed by a plane that cuts all the elements of a right circular cone. A circle (q.v.), which is formed by a plane perpendicular to the axis of the cone, is a specialized form of ellipse.

An ellipse may be defined as the locus of all points, P, the sum of whose distances, d_1 and d_2, from two fixed points is a constant; see Fig. 1.

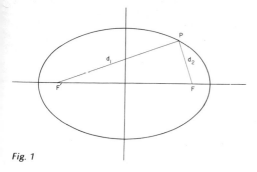

Fig. 1

The two fixed points that define an ellipse are known as its foci and are labeled F and F' in Fig. 1. This property of an ellipse is often used for drawing the figure. If pins are placed in the drawing surface at the two foci and a length of string is tied loosely between them, a point holding the string taut will trace an ellipse as it moves.

Any ellipse is symmetrical with respect to its major axis, which is a straight line passing through the two foci and extended to meet the curve at each end. It is also symmetrical with respect to its minor axis, a line perpendicular to the major axis at the midpoint between the two foci. In a circle the two foci of the ellipse coincide, and the major and minor axes are equal.

The eccentricity of an ellipse, that is, the ratio of the distance between the foci to the length of the major axis, is always less than 1. The eccentricity of a circle is 0.

The ellipse is one of the most important curves in physical science. In astronomy (q.v.), the orbits of the earth and the other planets around the sun are ellipses. It is used in engineering (q.v.) in the arches of some bridges and the design of gears for certain types of machinery such as punch presses.   J.Si. & J.McP.

ELLIS, (Henry) Havelock (1859–1939), British psychologist and author, born in Croydon, En-

gland, and educated for a medical career at Saint Thomas Hospital, London. While pursuing his studies he wrote and edited articles and pamphlets on literary and scientific subjects. After completing his medical education he devoted himself mainly to research and writing. From 1887 to 1889 he was general editor of the "Mermaid Series", a compilation of the works of old English dramatists, and from 1889 to 1914 he edited the "Contemporary Science" series. Ellis was an early advocate of birth control and a pioneer researcher into the psychology and sociology of sex, writing extensively on the latter subject. He is best known for his six-volume *Studies in the Psychology of Sex*, which influenced all writing on the subject thereafter. When his first volume, *Sexual Inversion*, was published in London in 1897, however, it occasioned a lawsuit and was banned as a "wicked, bawdy, scandalous, and obscene book". Subsequent volumes were first published in the United States, comprising *The Evolution of Modesty* (1899), *Analysis of the Sexual Impulse* (1903), *Sexual Selection of Man* (1905), *Erotic Symbolism* (1906), and *Sex in Relation to Society* (1910). His autobiography, *My Life*, deals primarily with his marriage to Edith Lees from their wedding in 1891 until her death in 1916. It was published posthumously in 1940.

ELLIS ISLAND, complex of one natural and two artificial islands, joined by causeways, belonging to the United States government, in Upper Bay of New York harbor, about 1 mile s.w. of Manhattan. It was the headquarters of an im-

Havelock Ellis

migration and naturalization district of the U.S. from 1892 until November, 1954. The original island was called Oyster Island by the early Dutch colonists, and was later known as Gibbet Island, after a pirate was hanged there in 1765. Samuel Ellis, a merchant of New York City, bought the island in the 18th century and gave it his name. From Ellis it passed to New York State; it was bought from the State by the Federal government in 1808, and for a time it served as the site of a Federal arsenal. In 1892, when Castle Garden, the immigrant station at the Battery in lower Manhattan (see BATTERY PARK), was no longer able to accommodate the flow of immigrants, the reception and care of them was transferred to Ellis Island. In 1947 it was estimated that almost 20,000,000 immigrants had entered the country through the station. As a result of declining immigration the Immigration Service closed the station in 1954, and transferred its activities to Manhattan. In 1898 and 1905, the two additional islands were created by the dumping of earth and rock, increasing the area of the island from 3 to the present 27½ acres. In May, 1965, Ellis Island was designated as part of the Statue of Liberty National Monument, and plans have been made to preserve the main buildings on the island.

ELLISON, Ralph (Waldo) (1914–), Negro American novelist, born in Oklahoma City, Okla., and educated at Tuskegee Institute. His best-known work, *Invisible Man* (1952), expounds the theme that American society willfully ignores the Negro. The novel, one of the first works to describe modern racial problems in America from the point of the Negro, received the National Book Award (q.v.) for fiction in 1953. *Shadow and Act,* a collection of his essays, was published in 1964. Ellison is noted for many magazine articles and short stories and has frequently lectured at colleges and universities on the subject of the Negro American.

ELLORA, village of the Republic of India, in Maharashtra State, about 15 miles N.W. of Aurangabad. Ellora is noted for its cave temples cut out of solid rock between the 5th and 13th centuries A.D. Of the nineteen large temples, some are Brahman and others Buddhist and Jain in origin. The Brahman Dumnar Lena temple is the largest, measuring 150 ft. each way; the most spectacular is the Brahman Kailasa temple, 138 ft. wide by 88 ft. deep. Melon-capitaled columns, called *amalaka,* are a feature of the temples.

ELLSWORTH, Lincoln (1880–1951), American explorer and engineer, born in Chicago, Ill., and educated at Columbia and Yale universities. In 1902 he joined the expedition exploring the route to be taken across Canada by the Canadian Pacific Railway. Later he worked as a surveyor and civil engineer in Canada, spending part of one year prospecting for gold. In 1924 he organized and led an expedition, sponsored by Johns Hopkins University, which made a geological survey of the Andes Mts. from the Pacific Ocean to the headwaters of the Amazon R. In 1925, using the fortune he had inherited from his father, he became an associate and financial supporter of the Norwegian explorer Roald Amundsen (q.v.). They formed the Amundsen-Ellsworth Polar Flying Expedition to attempt to fly over the North Pole. With four companions they left Svalbard (Spitsbergen) in two amphibian airplanes in May, 1925, but were forced to land about 135 mi. short of their goal. Out of radio contact and given up for lost, they spent thirty days carving an airstrip out of the rough ice and eventually returned to Svalbard in one plane without loss of life. The following year, with Italian explorer Umberto Nobile (1885–), they successfully carried out a 3390–mile flight in the dirigible *Norge,* from Kongsfjord, Svalbard, across the North Pole to Teller, Alaska. In 1931 Ellsworth, with the Australian explorer Sir George Hubert Wilkins (q.v.), made a transarctic submarine survey of the N. Arctic region. In November, 1935, Ellsworth made the first airplane flight across the Antarctic from the Weddel Sea to the Ross Sea, and claimed an Antarctic area of 300,000 sq.mi. for the United States. Again in 1939 Ellsworth made an airplane flight across the Antarctic, claiming an additional 77,000 sq.mi. of territory (called American Highland) for the U.S. Foremost among the many honors bestowed upon Ellsworth was a special Congressional medal (1931). He collaborated with Amundsen in writing *Our Polar Flight* (1925) and *First Crossing of the Polar Sea* (1927). In addition Ellsworth wrote *Search* (1932) and *Beyond Horizons* (1938).

See ANTARCTICA: *Exploration.*

ELLSWORTH, Oliver (1745–1807), American statesman and jurist, born in Windsor, Conn., and educated at Yale College (now Yale University). In 1775 he went to Hartford, Conn., where he practiced law and took a leading part in the State's activities during the American Revolution. He was a member of the Continental Congress from 1778 to 1783, and a judge of the State Superior Court from 1785 to 1789. In 1787 he was a representative in the Constitutional Convention at Philadelphia, and, with Roger Sherman (q.v.), proposed what became the basis of the national legislative system. The measure, known

American elm, Ulmus
americana
U.S. Forest Service

as the Connecticut Compromise, ended the conflict between large and small States over representation and provided for the establishment of the United States Senate and the United States House of Representatives. He was also responsible for the term "United States" appearing in the Constitution. From 1789 to 1796 he was U.S. Senator from Connecticut and was looked upon as the personal spokesman for President George Washington (q.v.). He was chairman of the committee which drew up the bill organizing the system of Federal courts, substantially as they exist today; *see* COURTS IN THE UNITED STATES: *Federal Courts.* At his suggestion John Jay (q.v.) was sent to England in 1794 to negotiate a new treaty with Great Britain. In 1796 Washington appointed Ellsworth chief justice of the United States Supreme Court, and he served until 1799, when President John Adams (q.v.) sent him as a commissioner to France to negotiate a trade agreement with Napoleon I (q.v.), Emperor of France. In 1807 Ellsworth was ap-

pointed chief justice of Connecticut, but died before taking office.

ELM, common name for various tall, deciduous trees comprising the genus *Ulmus* in the family Ulmaceae, widespread throughout the North Temperate Zone. The short leafstalks bear straight-veined leaves that are elliptic. The purple or sometimes yellowish flowers bloom in clusters and appear before the leaves unfold.

The most common and most popular of the North American elms is *U. americana,* a tree valued for its ornamental shade qualities, which often grows to 120 ft. in height. Five other species are native to the United States, from which numerous horticultural varieties have been developed. The Chinese elm, *U. parvifolia,* is a half-evergreen small tree, frequently planted in the South and in California. The red or slippery elm, *U. fulva,* is a common species of medium height (60 to 70 ft.). The rock or cork elm, *U. racemosa,* valued for its corky, winged twigs, is hardy in the New England area and northern portions of the U.S. The wahoo or winged elm, *U. alata,* is a small tree found primarily in Florida, Louisiana, and Arkansas.

Another important species of elm is the English elm, *U. procera,* ranging in height from 70 to 100 ft., although occasional specimens grow much taller. Found throughout western Asia, Europe, and northern Africa, it has been introduced into the U.S. and planted along the streets of many cities. The wood obtained from its trunk is compact, durable, and water resistant, and is used for the manufacture of numerous items, including furniture. The outer bark is used medicinally, both externally and internally; dyes are also made from it.

Within recent years the elm population in the U.S. has been markedly decreased by Dutch elm disease (q.v.). The disease was introduced into the U.S. accidentally from the Netherlands; no effective control has been discovered for it, although several varieties of elm have been developed, particularly *U. carpinifolia,* which are resistant to the disease.

Elm trees are also frequently destroyed by insects which feed on their foliage. Examples of these insects include the gypsy moth, the tussock moth, and the bagworm. The elm-leaf beetle, *Galerucella xanthomelaena,* is perhaps the most destructive to the foliage of the elm. It is a small yellowish-brown beetle, which begins to feed while the leaves are still young, eating large, round holes in them. The adult elm-leaf beetle deposits clusters of eggs on the undersides of the leaves and dies soon thereafter. The larvae feed voraciously on the leaves, rapidly skeletonizing them. *Phloem necrosis* is another serious disease of elms. It is caused by a virus and carried from tree to tree by an insect called the leaf hopper.

Zelkova serrata, a species related to the elm in the same family, has replaced the American elm as an ornamental tree in many areas of the U.S., as it is resistant to Dutch elm disease. The name elm is also applied in Australia to two timber trees, *Aphananthe philippinensis,* closely related to the true elms, and *Duboisia myoporoides,* in the family Solanaceae.

EL MAHALLA EL KUBRA, city of the Arab Republic of Egypt, in the Nile delta, about 65 miles N. of Cairo. Cotton is a major crop of the surrounding region; one of the leading textile-manufacturing centers of the country, the city has cotton-processing plants and spinning mills. Pop. (1970 est.) 255,800.

ELMAN, Mischa (1891–1967), Russian-American violinist, born in Talnoye. He first studied the violin at the Royal Music School, Odessa,

making his first public appearance at a school concert in 1899. In 1902, at the urging of the noted violin teacher Leopold Auer (q.v.), he entered the Conservatory of Saint Petersburg (now Leningrad), at which he studied the violin under Auer and harmony with the Russian composer César Cui (1835–1918). Elman made his debut in St. Petersburg in 1904 with great success. A triumphant tour of Germany followed in the same year. In 1905 he made his British debut in London as soloist with the London Symphony Orchestra, and in 1908 he made his American debut, in New York City, playing the Tchaikovsky Violin Concerto with the Russian Symphony Orchestra. He subsequently made many tours of the United States, and also of Europe and the Orient. He became a U.S. citizen in 1923. Elman was considered one of the foremost violinists of his time. A masterly interpreter of music, he had a thorough command of violin technique, and his playing was noted for its great feeling and beauty of tone.

ELMHURST, city of Illinois, in Du Page Co., 16 miles W. of Chicago. It is served by railroad and has an airport. A residential suburb of Chicago, Elmhurst has little industry except the making of stone and cement blocks from limestone quarried nearby. Elmhurst College (1865) is affiliated with the United Church of Christ. Settled in the mid-19th century by immigrants from Germany, Elmhurst was incorporated as a city in 1910. Pop. (1960) 36,991; (1970) 50,547.

EL MINYA or MINYA, city in the Arab Republic of Egypt, and capital of El Minya Governorate, in Upper Egypt between the western bank of the Nile R. and the Ibrahimiya Canal, 140 miles S. of Cairo. The city is on a railroad and is an important river port and trade center for cotton, sugarcane, and grain. Industries include cotton ginning, woolen and sugar milling, and dairying. A museum of antiquities is situated here. Founded possibly as a principality during the XII Dynasty, El Minya underwent reconstruction during the period of the Baghdad caliphs. El Minya has several other names; it is also known as Al-Minya, Minya ibn Khasib, Minia, and Minieh. Pop. (1970 est.) 122,100.

ELMIRA, city in New York, and county seat of Chemung Co., on the Chemung R., 147 miles S.E. of Buffalo and 5 miles N. of the New York border with Pennsylvania. A railroad center and airline terminus, Elmira is also an important manufacturing center, and contains factories producing fire engines and trucks, valves and hydrants, glass bottles, automobile transmissions, television tubes, radios, and foundry products. The city is the site of Elmira College for women, founded in 1855; the New York State Reformatory established in 1876, the oldest in the State; and an annual National Soaring and Gliding Contest. The city contains the grave of the American writer Samuel L. Clemens (q.v.), whose summer home, Quarry Farm, is situated just outside the city. Near the city is a monument to the Revolutionary War general John Sullivan (q.v.), marking the site of the Battle of Newtown in 1779. In this battle, Sullivan led his Continental army of 5000 men to victory over a force of 1500 Tory and Indian troops under the command of the American loyalist colonel Sir John Johnson (1742–1830) and the Mohawk Indian chief Joseph Brant (q.v.). In 1788 the first permanent settlers of the area built their cabins on the location of three former Indian villages. Elmira was incorporated as the village of Newtown in 1815, and was reincorporated as Elmira in 1828. It became the county seat in 1836 and was chartered as a city in 1864. In 1864–65, during the American Civil War, Elmira was the site of a camp for Confederate prisoners. Pop. (1960) 46,517; (1970) 39,945.

ELMONT, unincorporated community of New York, in Nassau Co., on Long Island, a part of the town of Hempstead, adjoining the borough of Queens, New York City, and about 15 miles E. of the borough of Manhattan. Belmont Park race track lies partly within the community. Industrial equipment, electrical and plastic products, and clothing are manufactured in Elmont. Pop. (1960) 30,138; (1970) 29,363.

EL MONTE, city of California, in Los Angeles Co., about 12 miles E. of central Los Angeles. The varied manufactures of the city include metal products and electronic equipment. Founded in the 1850's as Lexington, the city of El Monte was incorporated in 1912. Pop. (1960) 13,163; (1970) 69,837.

EL MORRO NATIONAL MONUMENT, area of natural interest in New Mexico. The outstanding feature of the monument is a sandstone rock about 200 ft. high, known as the "Inscription Rock" because it bears the carved names of Spanish explorers and early American emigrants and settlers. The earliest of such inscriptions in the soft sandstone is that made in 1605 by Don Juan de Oñate (1549?–1624), Spanish governor and colonizer of New Mexico. Indian symbols and pictures are also carved in the rock, and on its top are prehistoric pueblo ruins. It is administered by the National Park Service (q.v.).

ELMWOOD PARK, suburban residential village of Illinois, in Cook Co., adjoining Chicago and 9 miles N.W. of the downtown area. The village was incorporated in 1914. Pop. (1960) 23,866; (1970) 26,160.

ELOHIM, plural of the Hebrew *Eloah*, "God". In the Old Testament it is used occasionally as a general term for any divine being, but more frequently in reference to the God of the Israelites. The plural has been explained as signifying greatness and majesty. The frequent use of the term in certain passages of the Pentateuch (q.v.) has been regarded by Biblical scholars as the key identifying feature of the second oldest Pentateuchal source, known therefore as "E". Accordingly, the author of "E" is sometimes referred to as "the Elohist". *See* BIBLE: *The Growth of the Bible. See also* JEHOVAH.   S.L.

ELOI, Saint. *See under* DAGOBERT.

EL PASO, city and port of entry in Texas, and county seat of El Paso Co., in the extreme W. of the State, at the foot of Mt. Franklin (7100 ft.), on the Rio Grande R., opposite Ciudad Juárez, Mexico. El Paso, one of the largest cities of Texas and the largest on the international boundary, is served by several American railroads and airlines.

Because of its warm, dry climate, its position as the gateway to the Carlsbad Caverns National Park (q.v.) and the dude-ranch area of the Southwest, and its proximity to Ciudad Juárez, El Paso is a winter health and recreational resort, and has a large tourist trade. Public and private buildings of El Paso are predominantly Spanish colonial in design, and a picturesque Mexican section contains old adobe houses. Interesting structures in the city and vicinity include the Scottish Rite Cathedral, which is a reproduction of the Pan-American Building in Washington, D.C., and a 40-ft.-high statue of Christ on a mountaintop a few feet from the international boundary. Ysleta, 10 miles S.E., the oldest community in Texas, is the home of the last survivors of an ancient tribe of Pueblo Indians, and contains one of the oldest Spanish missions of the section, Nuestra Señora del Carmen, built in 1682. El Paso has a park area of 679 acres. A scenic drive, built in 1919 around Mt. Franklin, offers a panoramic view. El Paso is the site of the Texas Western College branch of the University of Texas, Texas Wesleyan College, Texas Christian University, and several private academies. Fort Bliss, on the N. outskirts of the city, is a major antiaircraft and guided-missile center; it includes Biggs Field Air Force Base and the William Beaumont General Hospital.

El Paso is the center of a vast mining and cattle-grazing area, which extends nearly 600 mi. in all directions and includes W. Texas, parts of New Mexico and Arizona, and N. Mexico. The region surrounding the city is made agriculturally productive by waters from the Elephant Butte Dam in Sierra Co., N. Mex., a large government irrigation project of the Rio Grande valley. The principal crop is a long-staple cotton; alfalfa, onions, beets, tomatoes, lettuce, cabbages, and cantaloupes are also cultivated. Copper, lead, and oil are the leading mineral products of the area. As the financial and commercial center of the region, El Paso is the site of a branch of the Federal Reserve Bank of Dallas, and has an international wholesale and retail trade in copper, lead, wool, mohair, hides, and fertilizers. It contains one of the largest copper refineries in the United States, and one of the largest custom smelters in the world. Other important industrial establishments in the city are oil refineries, railroad-repair shops, stockyards, cement plants, meat-packing plants, cotton gins and compresses, cottonseed-oil mills, planting mills, beverage plants, creameries, and factories manufacturing textiles, clothing, and wooden boxes.

The site of **El Paso** was first permanently settled in 1827. In 1858 the present town was laid out and named El Paso from the pass, El Paso del Norte, at the point at which the Rio Grande cuts through the mountains. In 1873 El Paso was incorporated as a city, growing from a population of 736 in 1880 to 10,338 in 1890. Pop. (1960) 276,687; (1970) 322,261.

EL RENO, city in Oklahoma, and county seat of Canadian Co., about 20 miles N.W. of Oklahoma City. The city has varied manufacturing and is a trading and shipping center for the area. El Reno has railroad shops, poultry hatcheries, and a livestock experimental station. It is the site of El Reno College, founded in 1938. Pop. (1960) 11,015; (1970) 14,510.

EL SALVADOR, smallest in area and most densely populated of the republics in Central America, bounded on the N. and E. by Honduras, on the extreme S.E. by the Gulf of Fonseca, on the S. by the Pacific Ocean, and on the W. and N.W. by Guatemala. It lies between about lat. 13°15′ N. and lat. 14°30′ N. and long. 87°40′ W. and long. 90°15′ W. El Salvador is the only Central American state that does not possess an Atlantic coastline. The country is about 60 mi. wide and 140 mi. long, with a total area of 8236 sq.mi.

THE LAND

Most of El Salvador consists of a plateau, lying between two mountain ranges crossing E. to W., with a general elevation 2000 ft. above sea level. The Pacific coastal belt is 160 mi. long and 10 to 15 mi. wide. The northern lowlands are bounded by high, rugged mountains. The high-

est point in the republic is the Santa Ana volcano, 7825 ft. above sea level. Earthquakes and volcanic eruptions are common; 90 percent of the land is of volcanic origin. None of the 150 rivers and streams is navigable.

Climate. El Salvador is in the tropical zone; the climate varies with the elevation. The climate of the coastal strip is tropical; that of the plateau and highlands is semitropical and temperate; the mountain regions have a temperate climate. The average annual rainfall is 72 in., and the rainy season lasts from May to October. The average annual temperature at San Salvador (q.v.), the capital, is 75° F.

Natural Resources. El Salvador has good natural resources, primarily agricultural. The mineral deposits include gold, silver, limestone, and gypsum. Such trees as oak, cedar, mahogany, balsam, and rubber are found.

Plants and Animals. The mountains have temperate grasslands and sparse forests of oak and pine. The natural vegetation of the remainder of the country consists of deciduous trees and subtropical grasslands. Tropical fruit and medicinal plants are abundant.

The animal life of El Salvador, less varied and rich than that of other Central American countries, includes monkeys, coyotes, jaguars, pumas, and ocelots. Among the reptiles are the iguana and the boa constrictor.

Waterpower. The capacity of hydroelectric power plants increased from 50,800 kw in 1956 to about 108,000 kw in 1970. Production in 1970 was 473,000,000 kw hours, out of a total electricity production of 645,000,000 kw hours.

THE PEOPLE

About 92 percent of the total population is mestizo; that is, of Spanish and Indian parentage. The remainder is composed of white and Indian groups.

Population. The population of El Salvador (census 1971) was 3,541,010. The overall population density is about 429 per sq.mi. (U.N. est. 1967). The population density is more than three times higher than that of any other country in Central America. The society is primarily rural.

About one third of the population lives in urban areas.

Spanish is the official language. Some Indians speak Nahuatl. The principal religion is Roman Catholicism.

Political Divisions. The nation is divided into fourteen departments: Ahuachapán, Cabañas, Chalatenango, Cuscatlán, La Libertad, La Paz, La Unión, Morazán, San Miguel, San Salvador, Santa Ana, San Vicente, Sonsonate, and Usulután. Eight have access to the Pacific; the others are landlocked.

San Salvador, the capital and largest city of El Salvador, has a population (1971 prelim.) of about 337,170. The second largest city, Santa Ana, with a population of about 96,300, is the center of a rich coffee, sugar, and cattle region. San Miguel, at the foot of San Miguel volcano, has a population of about 59,300.

Education. Children in the elementary grades are provided with free compulsory schooling. El Salvador had about 3750 primary and secondary

San Vicente, an active volcano, provides a dramatic background for the National Palace in the capital city of San Salvador. United Nations

Coffee is the staple of the economy of El Salvador. Most work is done by hand, as in this coffee-bagging room. *United Nations*

schools with a total enrollment of about 618,000 in 1971. The National University of El Salvador in San Salvador registered more than 7700 students in 1971.

Culture. The people of El Salvador are predominantly a blend of Indian and Spanish, and the culture of El Salvador reflects this dual heritage. In addition to a genuine and highly developed interest in the classical art forms, Salvadorans have preserved the folk heritage of their Indian and Spanish ancestors. Colonial festivals from both traditions, such as the Day of the Moors and Christians, and the Day of the Indian, are still celebrated.

Folk music of El Salvador resembles that of other Central American countries, but some popular dances uniquely combine elements from various European countries. The *danza,* for instance, is an offspring of the English country dance and the Spanish *contradanza.*

THE ECONOMY

The economy of El Salvador is underdeveloped and has been heavily dependent on coffee. The economic substructure, such as roads, electric power, and commercial banking facilities, is fairly well developed. The favorable investment climate of the mid-1960's contributed to the development of light consumer goods manufacturing. In a recent year, budget figures showed about $103,000,000 in revenue with slightly higher expenditures.

Agriculture. The principal economic activity of the country is agriculture. About 75 percent of the arable land is cultivated. Coffee, the major crop, accounted for one half of the total annual value of exports in 1970, and cotton, the second principal crop, accounted for about 20 percent. Corn, sugarcane, rice, and beans are the principal food crops. Fruits grown include bananas, mangoes, pineapples, apples, avocados, coconuts, and papayas.

Forest and Fishing Industries. The forest resources of El Salvador have been reduced to about 13 percent of the total area of the country and offer little actual or potential lumber production. Some 90 percent of the building wood must be imported. Balsam trees are abundant. El Salvador is the world's largest supplier of the medicinal gum, balsam.

Shrimp is the leading commercial fishing catch. Tuna, mullet, mackerel, and swordfish are also caught.

Mining, Manufacturing, and Commerce. The country has no significant mineral resources, but gold, silver, coal, copper, and lead are mined. Since the early 1950's the government has assisted in developing industry. The principal items produced are textiles and apparel, food and beverages, footwear, cement, and fertilizers. The first steel-rolling mill in the country was opened in 1966.

Chief exports are coffee, cotton, and sugar. Exports were valued at about $228,000,000 in 1970. Imports, valued at $214,000,000, include wheat (of which 90 percent used by El Salvador is imported), flour, fuel oil, cement, fertilizers, machinery, and iron and steel products. El Salvador trades principally with West Germany and the United States and is a member of the Central American Common Market (*see* INTER-AMERICAN COOPERATION).

The colón is the basic monetary unit (valued at U.S.$0.40; 1972). The Banco Central de Reserva de El Salvador (Central Reserve Bank of El Salvador) is the sole bank of issue.

Transportation and Communications. In 1970 El Salvador had some 5390 mi. of roads and 465 mi. of railroads. Although the country has almost no domestic air service, it is served by several foreign airlines. In 1970 the country had some 405,000 radios in use, and about 92,000 television receivers.

Labor. Some 60 percent of the labor force is engaged in agricultural work, 13 percent in industry, and 20 percent in commerce and other activities. Labor was permitted to organize in 1950 with the exception of the agricultural workers. By the late 1960's the country had some sixty-eight unions with a membership of about 5 percent of the total labor force.

GOVERNMENT

The constitution of January, 1962, provided for a republican, democratic, and representative government. The right to vote is guaranteed to all citizens over the age of eighteen.

Central Government. Executive power is exercised by the president and eleven cabinet ministers. The president is elected by direct popular vote for a term of five years; he may not succeed himself.

HEALTH AND WELFARE. The Salvadoran Social Security Institute was created in 1949 to provide national health, accident, unemployment, old-age, and death insurance. The program, covering industrial workers and employees earning up to $200 a month, is supported by compulsory contributions from workers, employers, and government and is expected eventually to cover all workers. The government supervises institutions and hospitals for the sick and aged, and provides child-welfare and maternity services.

Legislature. The cabinet is responsible to a unicameral legislature, the Legislative Assembly. Fifty-two deputies are elected by popular vote for terms of two years.

Political Parties. The country has three principal parties. The major political party is the Partido de Conciliación Nacional (National Conciliation Party). The principal minority party is the Partido Demócrata Cristiano (Christian Democratic Party).

Local Government. The country is divided into fourteen departments, each administered by a governor appointed by the central government for a term of four years. The mayors of the 261 municipalities are elected by popular vote every two years.

A port worker in El Salvador. *United Nations*

Judiciary. The independent judiciary is headed by the president of the Supreme Court, who is elected for a term of three years. The members of the Supreme Court are selected by the National Assembly.

Defense. The country maintains an army, navy and air force; the total strength is about 4500. Service is compulsory for men between the ages of eighteen and thirty for a period of at least one year.

HISTORY

After the conquest of Central America in 1524–25 by Pedro de Alvarado, the lieutenant of Hernando Cortes (qq.v.), El Salvador formed part of the captaincy-general of Guatemala, which successfully revolted against Spain in 1821. For a short time El Salvador was under the domination of the Mexican empire established by Agustín de Iturbide (q.v.). In 1823, when that empire was dissolved, El Salvador became one of the component states of the Central American Federation (which included Guatemala, Honduras, Nicaragua, and Costa Rica as well). El Salvador gained independence on Jan. 1, 1841, when the Federation broke up; the republic was formally proclaimed on Jan. 25, 1859. During the remainder of the 19th century the history of El Salvador was a turbulent one. Periods of domestic turmoil alternated with armed conflicts with the neighboring states of Guatemala, Honduras, and Nicaragua. The early part of the 20th century was a rare period of relative stability, and the economy of the country made considerable progress. The production and export of coffee became the leading industry. A railroad network was built and extensive port facilities were developed at La Unión. But the progress benefited only a small number of landowners, while vast numbers of the people remained poor.

485

From 1931 to 1944 the country was under the dictatorial rule of General Maximiliano Hernández Martinez (1882–1969). Although his regime had friendly relations with the German and Italian dictators in the late 1930's, El Salvador cooperated with the U.S. and its allies during World War II and became a charter member of the United Nations in 1945. The country joined the Organization of American States (O.A.S.) when it was formed in Bogotá, Colombia, in 1948.

The old dream of a Central American federation was revived in the postwar years, and in October, 1951, representatives of Costa Rica, El Salvador, Guatemala, Honduras, and Nicaragua met in San Salvador and signed the Charter of the Organization of Central American States (O.C.A.S.). This was followed in 1958 by the formation of the Central American Common Market. See INTER-AMERICAN COOPERATION.

Beginning in the late 1940's, the demands of the submerged classes for economic and social reforms became more urgent. They met with little response, however, from the series of military and civilian juntas which came to power. But in January, 1961, a directorate took over the country and soon began to institute major economic reforms while retaining a system of private ownership.

In elections to a constituent assembly, held in December, 1961, the government-supported National Conciliation Party (P.C.N.) won all the seats. In April, 1962, under a new constitution, Lieutenant Colonel Julio Adalberto Rivera (1921–73) of the P.C.N. was unopposed in the presidential election. During his term and that of his successor, Colonel Fidel Sánchez Hernández (1917–   ), reforms continued, greatly aided by increased foreign investment and Alliance for Progress (q.v.) funds.

In 1969 a brief war with Honduras, resulting from migration of Salvadorans to Honduras, disrupted the economies of both countries.

The political situation was tense as El Salvador prepared for elections in 1972. The main candidates were Colonel Arturo Armando Molina (1927–   ) of the P.C.N. and José Napoleon Duarte, candidate of a Christian Democrat coalition. In the absence of a majority for any candidate, Molina was declared president. Violence erupted as opposition leaders charged electoral fraud. The government put down an attempted army coup; and Duarte went into exile. Molina was inaugurated on July 1. Protests against national sponsorship of a Miss Universe contest were bloodily suppressed in July, 1975, and after a further wave of violence Molina declared a state of siege in September.

EL SEGUNDO, city of California, in Los Angeles Co., about 14 miles s.w. of central Los Angeles, on the Santa Monica Bay. The city has oil refineries and manufactures chemicals, electronic equipment, and metal products. Pop. (1960) 14,219; (1970) 15,620.

ELSINORE. See HELSINGØR.

ELWOOD, city of Indiana, in Madison Co., about 33 miles N.E. of Indianapolis. Elwood is a processing and shipping center for the surrounding agricultural region. Manufactures include aircraft parts and wire goods. The political leader Wendell Lewis Willkie (q.v.) was born there. Pop. (1960) 11,793; (1970) 11,196.

ELY, Great Britain, city and urban district in Cambridgeshire and Isle of Ely, England, on the w. bank of the Ouse R., about 15 miles N.E. of Cambridge. The city has manufactures of shoes, farm machinery, and refined beet sugar. Ely derives its importance from its ecclesiastical buildings. These are Ely Cathedral, one of the largest in England; the adjoining Lady Chapel of the cathedral; the 13th-century parish church of Saint Mary; the towered bishop's palace, dating from the 15th and 16th centuries; and surviving monastery buildings still used as clerical dwellings. The cathedral, begun in 1083 and completed in 1534, is a cruciform structure in a mixture of Saxon, Norman, and Early English architectural styles. Its principal feature is the decorated octagonal tower and surmounting lantern, 170 ft. high. The carvings and sculpture of the choir and the Early English galilee, or west porch, are also notable. An Anglican theological college (1881) and the King's grammar school (1541) are within the cathedral grounds.

History. Saint Etheldreda, Queen of Northumbria (630?–79), founded a monastery at Ely about 673 A.D. In 870 the Danes ravaged the Isle of Ely and destroyed the monastery, which was rebuilt in 970 by Saint Ethelwold, bishop of Winchester (908?–84). This remained until 1083, when the new church was begun, which in turn was converted into a cathedral in 1109, the year after Ely was made a see. Ely was one of the last strongholds of the Saxons after the Norman Conquest, and in 1070 was the site of the rebellion against William I (q.v.), King of England, headed by the Saxon yeoman Hereward the Wake. Pop. (1971) 9966.

ELY, Richard Theodore (1854–1943), American economist, born in Ripley, N.Y., and educated at Columbia College (now Columbia University) and the University of Heidelberg. He was head of the department of political economy at Johns Hopkins University from 1881 to 1892, professor of political economy at the University of Wisconsin from 1892 to 1925, and research professor of economics at Northwestern University from 1925 to 1933. He was a founder of the American Economic Association, which he served as president from 1899 to 1902. Ely was among the first American economists to discard the theory that government interference in order to regulate the economy is an evil. He wrote *Studies in the Evolution of Industrial Society* (1903) and *Ground under Our Feet* (1938).

ELY, ISLE OF. See CAMBRIDGESHIRE AND THE ISLE OF ELY.

ELYRIA, city in Ohio, and county seat of Lorain Co., on the Black R., 9 miles S. of Lake Erie, and about 25 miles S.W. of Cleveland. It is served by two railroads, and is an important manufacturing city. The leading products are furnaces, automotive equipment, screw-machine products, plastics, and chemicals. Cascade Park in the heart of the city, is noted for its caves and waterfalls. Elyria was settled in 1817 by Heman Ely, member of a pioneer Connecticut family, who gave it his name. It became the county seat in 1823, and was chartered as a city in 1892. Pop. (1960) 43,782; (1970) 53,427.

ELYSEE, PALAIS DE L', palace in Paris, on the Rue du Faubourg Saint-Honoré and the Champs Elysées, since 1873 the official residence of the presidents of France. It was built in 1718 for Louis d'Auvergne, Comte d'Evreux, and later was acquired by Madame de Pompadour (q.v.). From 1848 to 1852, during the Second Republic, the palace was occupied by Louis Napoleon, later Napoleon III (q.v.), Emperor of France.

ELYSIUM, also known as the ELYSIAN FIELDS, in Greek mythology, a pre-Hellenic paradise, a land of perfect peace and happiness. In the works of the early Greek epic poet Homer (q.v.) Elysium was a land at the farthest and western edge of the world to which the great heroes were carried, body and soul, and made immortal. There each was free to pursue his favorite activities, and worries and illness were unknown. Soon, however, Elysium was regarded as the abode of the blessed dead, where the souls of dead heroes, poets, priests, and other virtuous men, lived in perfect happiness, surrounded by grass, trees, and gentle winds, and enveloped in rose-tinted, perpetual light.

In Roman mythology, Elysium was a part of the underworld and a place of reward for the virtuous dead. For some it was only a temporary paradise, and at the edge of its soft, green meadows flowed the Lethe (q.v.), river of forgetfulness, from which all souls returning to life in the world above had to drink.

ELYTRA. See BEETLE.

ELZEVIR *or* ELZEVIER, Dutch family engaged in printing and publishing. See BOOK TRADE: *The Modern Book Trade.*

EMANCIPATION PROCLAMATION, in United States history, name given to the Presidential proclamation issued by Abraham Lincoln on Jan. 1, 1863, during the Civil War (*see* CIVIL WAR, THE AMERICAN) declaring all "slaves within any State, or designated part of a State, . . . then . . . in rebellion . . . shall be then, thence forward, and forever free". The States affected were enumerated in the proclamation; specifically exempted were slaves in parts of the southern States then held by Union armies.

Issuance of the Emancipation Proclamation marked a radical change in Lincoln's policy; historians regard it as one of the great state documents of the United States.

After the outbreak of the Civil War, the slavery issue was made acute by the flight to Union lines of large numbers of slaves who volunteered to fight for their freedom and that of their fellow slaves. In these circumstances, a strict application of established policy would have required return of fugitive slaves to their Confederate masters, and would have alienated the staunchest supporters of the Union cause in the North and abroad.

Abolitionists (q.v.) had long been urging the President to free all slaves, and public opinion seemed to support this view. Lincoln moved slowly and cautiously nonetheless; on March 13, 1862, the Federal government forbade all Union army officers to return fugitive slaves, thus annulling in effect the Fugitive Slave Laws (q.v.). On April 10, on Lincoln's initiative, Congress declared the Federal government would compensate slave owners who freed their slaves. All slaves in the District of Columbia were freed in this way on April 16, 1862. On June 19, 1862, Congress enacted a measure prohibiting slavery in the territories of the United States, thus defying an earlier Supreme Court decision in the Dred Scott Case (q.v.) that Congress was powerless to regulate slavery in the territories.

Finally, after the Union victory in the battle of Antietam (Sept. 17, 1862), Lincoln issued a proclamation on Sept. 22, declaring his intention of promulgating another proclamation in 100 days, freeing the slaves in the States deemed in rebellion at that time. On Jan. 1, 1863, he issued the Emancipation Proclamation, conferring liberty on about 3,120,000 slaves. With the enactment of the Thirteenth Amendment to the Constitution of the United States (q.v.), in effect in 1865, slavery was completely abolished in the U.S.

The results of the Emancipation Proclamation

President Abraham Lincoln meets with his Cabinet in a discussion of the Emancipation Proclamation.

were far reaching. From then on, sympathy with the Confederacy was identified with support of slavery. Antislavery sentiment in France and Great Britain, whose governments were friendly to the Confederacy, became so strong that it precluded the possibility of intervention by those governments in behalf of the Confederacy.

As a further result of the proclamation, the Republican Party became unified in principle and in organization, and the prestige it attained enabled it to hold power until 1884. *See* LINCOLN, ABRAHAM; NEGROES IN THE UNITED STATES; RECONSTRUCTION; REPUBLICAN PARTY; UNITED STATES: *History.*

The Proclamation. The text of the Emancipation Proclamation follows.

BY THE PRESIDENT OF THE UNITED STATES OF AMERICA:
A PROCLAMATION.

Whereas on the 22nd day of September, in the year of our Lord one thousand eight hundred sixty-two, a proclamation was issued by the President of the United States, containing, among other things, the following, to wit:

"That on the 1st day of January, in the year of our Lord one thousand eight hundred sixty-three, all persons held as slaves within any State, or designated part of a State the people whereof shall then be in rebellion against the United States, shall be then, thenceforward, and forever free; and the executive government of the United States, including the military and naval authority thereof, will recognize and maintain the freedom of such persons and will do no act or acts to repress such persons, or any of them, in any efforts they may make for their actual freedom.

"That the executive will on the 1st day of January aforesaid, by proclamation, designate the States and parts of States, if any, in which the people thereof, respectively, shall then be in rebellion against the United States; and the fact that any State or the people thereof shall on that day be in good faith represented in the Congress of the United States by members chosen thereto at elections·wherein a majority of the qualified voters of such State shall have participated, shall in the absence of strong countervailing testimony, be deemed conclusive evidence that such State and the people thereof are not then in rebellion against the United States."

Now, therefore, I, Abraham Lincoln, President of the United States, by virtue of the power in me vested as Commander-in-Chief of the Army and Navy of the United States in time of actual armed rebellion against the authority and government of the United States, and as a fit and necessary war measure for repressing said rebellion, do, on this first day of January, in the year of our Lord one thousand eight hundred sixty-three, and in accordance with my purpose so to do, publicly proclaimed for the full period of one hundred days from the first day above mentioned, order and designate as the States and parts of States wherein the people thereof, respectively, are this day in rebellion against the United States, the following, to wit:

Arkansas, Texas, Louisiana (except the parishes of St. Bernard, Plaquemines, Jefferson, St. John, St. Charles, St. James, Ascension, Assumption, Terre Bonne, Lafourche, St. Mary, St. Martin, and Orleans, including the city of New Orleans), Mississippi, Alabama, Florida, Georgia, South Carolina, North Carolina, and Virginia (except the forty-eight counties designated as West Virginia, and also the counties of Berkeley, Accomac, Northhampton, Elizabeth City, York, Princess Ann, and Norfolk, including the cities of Norfolk and Portsmouth), and which excepted parts are for the present left precisely as if this proclamation were not issued.

And by virtue of the power and for the purpose aforesaid, I do order and declare that all persons held as slaves within said designated States and parts of States are, and henceforward shall be, free; and that the executive government of the United States, including the military and naval authorities thereof, will recognize and maintain the freedom of said persons.

And I hereby enjoin upon the people so declared to be free to abstain from all violence, unless in necessary self-defense; and I recommend to them that, in all cases when allowed, they labor faithfully for reasonable wages.

And I further declare and make known that such persons of suitable condition will be received into the armed service of the United States to garrison forts, positions, stations, and other places, and to man vessels of all sorts in said service.

And upon this act, sincerely believed to be an act of justice, warranted by the Constitution upon military necessity, I invoke the considerate judgment of mankind and the gracious favor of Almighty God.

In witness whereof, I have hereunto set my hand, and caused the seal of the United States to be affixed.

Done at the city of Washington, this first day of January, in the year of our Lord one thousand eight hundred [L.S.] sixty-three, and of the independence of the United States of America the eighty-seventh.

By the President:

ABRAHAM LINCOLN.

WILLIAM H. SEWARD, Secretary of State.

EMANUEL, or MANUEL I, called EMANUEL THE GREAT and EMANUEL THE FORTUNATE, (1469–1521), King of Portugal (1495–1521), great-grandson of John I (1357?–1433). During his reign, called the golden era of Portuguese history, great explorations and discoveries took place. He sponsored the epoch-making expedition of the Portuguese navigator Vasco da Gama (q.v.), which resulted in the opening of a sea route to India by way of the Cape of Good Hope; the voyage of Pedro Álvares Cabral (q.v.), on which Cabral reached Brazil, claimed it for Portugal, and then sailed westward to India, where he established a trading post on the site of Calicut (now Kozhikode); the exploration of Gaspar Corte-Real (q.v.) of the coasts of Labrador and Newfoundland; and the expedition of Affonso de Albuquerque (q.v.), who established the Portuguese empire in the Far East. During Emanuel's reign, commercial relations were established with Persia and China, and great wealth was also acquired from New World possessions. Emanuel made his court a center of the arts and sciences. He issued a code of laws which bears his name, and exhibited great religious zeal, sponsoring missionary enterprises in his overseas possessions and endeavoring to promote a crusade against the Turks. Emanuel persecuted the Jews in Portugal, and expelled them from the country in 1497–98, an act that deprived Portugal of many people of brilliant mind and great wealth.

EMBALMING, mortuary custom, the art of preserving bodies after death, generally by the use of chemical substances. It is believed to have originated among the Egyptians, probably before 4000 B.C., and was used by them for more than thirty centuries. Much evidence demonstrates that embalming is religious in origin, conceived as a means of preparing the dead for the life after death; see EGYPTIAN RELIGION.

From the Egyptians, the practice of embalming spread to other ancient peoples, including the Assyrians, Jews, Persians, and Scythians. Ancient embalming methods consisted of removal of the brains and viscera, and the filling of bodily cavities with a mixture of balsamic herbs and other substances. The Egyptians immersed the body in carbonate of soda; injected the arteries and veins with balsams; filled the cavities of the torso with bituminous and aromatic substances and salt; and wound around the body cloths saturated with similar materials. The Assyrians used honey in embalming, the Persians used wax, and the Jews used spices and aloes. Alexander III (q.v.), King of Macedonia, known as the Great, was emblamed with honey and wax.

The Egyptians were particularly adept at embalming; the soles of the feet of mummies, when unwrapped after as much as 3000 years, are often still soft and elastic. Historians estimate that by 700 A.D., when the practice had died out among them, the Egyptians had embalmed approximately 730,000,000 bodies. Although many were destroyed, or disintegrated in the tropical heat of northern Africa, a large

489

number of mummies were preserved; archeologists estimate that several million are still preserved in undiscovered tombs and burial places.

From the ancient peoples of Africa and Asia, embalming spread to Europe, where, in time, it became a widespread practice. Descriptions of methods used in Europe for almost 1200 years, from about 500 A.D., have been preserved in the writings of contemporary physicians. Embalming during the Middle Ages included evisceration, immersion of the body in alcohol, insertion of preservative herbs into incisions previously made in the fleshy parts of the body, and wrapping the body in tarred or waxed sheets. The Danish king of England, Canute II, was embalmed by the above, or similar, methods, as were the English monarchs William I the Conqueror and Edward I (qq.v.). William's body was found well preserved in the French city of Caen in the 16th century; Edward's was also found to be well preserved when it was disinterred in Westminster Abbey in 1700; and Canute's body was still in a state of good preservation when it was discovered in Winchester Cathedral in 1776.

The first man to embalm by injecting a prepared preservative chemical solution into the blood vessels is believed to be the Dutch anatomist Fredrik Ruysch (1638–1731), but his technique is unknown. During the 19th century, French and Italian scientists perfected techniques of embalming by injection of preservative chemical solutions into the blood vessels, thereby reaching every part of the cadaver. Modern embalming is believed to have begun in the United States during the American Civil War.

The essential purposes of modern embalming are preservation of the body to permit burial without unseemly haste, and prevention of the spread of infection both before and after burial. Cosmetic work is used to restore injured facial features or for esthetic reasons. Embalming methods now consist essentially of the removal of all blood and gases from the body and the insertion of a disinfecting fluid; the viscera are removed and are immersed in an embalming fluid and are then replaced in the body, in which they are surrounded with a preservative powder. Most corpses in the U.S. and Canada are embalmed, and the practice is widespread in other countries.

See also MORTUARY CUSTOMS.

EMBARGO, edict, decree, or order, usually issued by a government, prohibiting the departure of merchant ships from ports under its control, or prohibiting them from carrying certain

The ancient Egyptians placed embalmed bodies in cases painted to represent the deceased and various aspects of their earthly lives.   Brooklyn Museum

types of goods out of the country. An embargo may be levied both on domestic and foreign vessels. Embargoes on foreign ships were formerly levied principally to prevent the spread of information about developments in the country declaring the embargo, or in reprisal for an injury committed by another government and as a means of securing redress for it. Both reasons lost their force, and embargoes on foreign ships declined in importance, chiefly as a result of extraordinary developments in communications in the 19th and 20th centuries. Rapid transmission of news by electronic means made obsolete the spread of information by ship, and also facilitated the settlement of disputes through diplomatic channels. Changing juridical views, which condemned such means of coercion, contributed to the decline in the importance of embargoes on foreign vessels. Embargoes on domestic ships, sometimes called civil embargoes, have been levied because of an existing or anticipated shortage in a vital commodity within a country and for reasons of international policy. An example of an embargo levied for reasons of international policy is the prohibition by the United States against most shipments to Cuba (q.v.). This policy began in 1960.

In late 1973 certain oil-producing states in the Middle East placed an embargo against shipment of oil to countries they regarded as favoring Israel in the ongoing political struggle between these neighboring states. Although the embargo was short-lived, ending in early 1974, it did establish that such group action could be disruptive to world trade and injurious to particular states' economies. Essential traded commodities, such as oil, are in a unique position to be used as political tools, as they have a small number of primary producers. The success of the embargo, though not total, did suggest that such producing cartels may again try to use their natural resources to attain specific goals. See also BLOCKADE.

EMBARGO ACT, in United States history, measure placing a ban on all foreign commerce, recommended by President Thomas Jefferson (q.v.), and enacted by Congress on Dec. 22, 1807. Under the terms of the Embargo Act, American vessels were forbidden to sail for foreign ports, but were allowed to engage in coastwise trade after posting bonds equal to twice the value of ship and cargo, as a guarantee of their compliance with the embargo. Foreign vessels were allowed to depart from United States ports carrying only ballast.

The principal intent of the act was to compel Great Britain and France, chief protagonists in the Napoleonic Wars (q.v.), to stop interfering with the trade of the U.S. As the U.S. was the main source of foodstuffs for both belligerents, each tried to destroy the commerce between the other and the American republic. Great Britain, also alarmed at the rapid development of American commerce, was determined to protect its position as the world's leading maritime nation.

By a series of acts, called Orders in Council, issued between 1804 and 1807, Great Britain declared much of the west coast of Europe, all French colonial ports, and all the ports of France's allies to be in a state of blockade, and proclaimed all vessels violating the blockade to be subject to capture. Great Britain also refused to recognize the right of neutral ships to carry enemy property, and the British navy stopped, searched, and seized American vessels on the high seas in an effort to suppress trade between the West Indies and France by U.S. ships. Napoleon I (q.v.), Emperor of France, in a number of decrees issued in 1806–07, proclaimed a blockade of the British Isles, barred from France any vessel that had entered British port, and finally declared subject to seizure any ship that submitted to British wartime maritime regulations. Neither power was able to enforce its embargo, and American vessels defied both proclamations in pursuit of the large profits to be made. The British and French, however, licensed privateers to prey on neutral, chiefly American, shipping; approximately 1600 U.S. ships and about $60,000,000 in cargo were lost to these privateers. Fearing that all American foreign trade was in danger of destruction, a number of influential leaders, including President Jefferson, persuaded Congress to enact the Embargo Act.

Effects on United States Commerce. The Embargo Act had a disastrous effect on the economy of the U.S. At the time the embargo was instituted, the U.S., despite the depredations of the British and French on American commerce, was in a flourishing economic position, chiefly as a result of the French Revolution and the Napoleonic Wars and of a consequent, if temporary, decline in the British merchant marine. United States foreign trade had increased from about $48,000,000 in 1792 to $247,000,000 in 1807. That part of the merchant marine engaged in foreign trade had increased from about 125,000 tons in 1789 to approximately 810,000 tons, and much shipping was also being constructed for foreign accounts. American foodstuffs and other agricultural products were selling for high prices, bringing prosperity to farmers.

The Embargo Act, rather than inducing Great Britain and France to agree to cease interfering with American trade, brought U.S. prosperity to a precipitate end. New England and New York

State, the leading centers of foreign trade, suffered most, but all areas were affected. One year after the act was passed, export trade had fallen from $108,300,000 to $22,400,000; agricultural prices had declined sharply, bankrupting farmers who had brought land on credit and had expanded production. Great stores of products accumulated in the hands of merchants, who could not dispose of the goods and went bankrupt. The shipbuilding industry was at a standstill, with consequent disastrous effects on the lumbering and sailmaking trades. About 55,000 seamen and 100,000 other workmen were unemployed and jails were overcrowded with debtors.

The Embargo Act had its beneficial results, however, for when imports from Europe ended, Americans began to develop household manufactures. Clothing, hosiery, and personal and table linen were made in homes, and by 1809, about two thirds of all these articles used in rural areas were produced in the U.S. A number of manufacturing industries, established along the Atlantic coast, attained a solid business basis.

Opposition to the Embargo Act was generally widespread and intense. Blockade-running to Canada became such a profitable enterprise that to stamp it out, Congress enacted measures giving the President almost dictatorial control over commerce. Still the opposition to the embargo continued. In New England, judges refused to sentence smugglers, and John Quincy Adams (q.v.) threatened secession of Massachusetts from the Union if the embargo were not lifted.

The Federal government was finally forced to reverse its policy. In 1809, Congress replaced the Embargo Act with the Non-Intercourse Act, which forbade commerce with Great Britain and France but allowed trade with other foreign countries and also unrestricted coasting trade. Like the Embargo Act, which has been regarded by most historians as a serious mistake, the Non-Intercourse Act was unsuccessful in freeing American trade from interference by France and England. Freedom of the seas for American ships and cargoes was achieved only after the downfall of Napoleon and victory by the United States over Great Britain in the War of 1812 (q.v.).

EMBER DAYS, in the Roman Catholic Church and the Church of England (qq.v.) and other churches of the Anglican Communion, three penitential days at the beginning of each church season. These days are Wednesday, Friday, and Saturday of the weeks occurring after the third Sunday of Advent (q.v.), the first Sunday of Lent (q.v.), the feast of Pentecost (q.v.), and the feast of the Exaltation of the Holy Cross (Sept. 14). Conferring of Holy Orders (see ORDERS, HOLY) usually takes place on ember days. When the penitential discipline of the church was updated by Pope Paul VI (see under PAUL) in 1966, fasting and abstinence from meat were dropped as requirements on ember days.

EMBEZZLEMENT, the wrongful taking and using of property by a person who has been entrusted with it. Embezzlement differs from larceny (q.v.) in that the property wrongfully appropriated has been in the lawful care of the embezzler, as for example in the case of a legal guardian who takes for his own use money that has been entrusted to him. Today embezzlement is classified as a felony (q.v.) under Federal law and under the laws of most States of the U.S.

EMBOLISM, obstruction of a blood vessel by an embolus, or foreign substance, that has been transported by the circulatory system. The embolus may be a blood clot, an air bubble, a fat globule, a clump of bacteria, a tumor cell, a piece of foreign matter such as a bullet fragment, or a portion of a parasite such as a tapeworm. Embolism in the lymph system is rare. Emboli are usually carried along by the flow of the bloodstream until they lodge in blood vessels too small to permit their passage. The result is an infarct, an area of dead tissue caused by obstruction of the flow of blood to the body cells in an area fed by no collateral system. The area in which this process, called infarction, occurs determines the pathological conditions that follow. Infarcation may damage the heart or brain, causing heart failure or paralysis.

Thrombosis differs from embolism in that a thrombus consisting of a blood clot or clump of blood cells forms inside the affected blood vessel; a fragment of a thrombus becomes an embolus if it is dislodged and moves through the bloodstream to create an obstruction or embolism. Thrombosis may be obviated and thrombi prevented from growing by the use of anticlotting drugs, such as coumarin or heparin (q.v.). Although these drugs do not dissolve clots already formed, experimental drugs called thrombolytic and fibrinolytic agents have been shown to dissolve those that have existed for three days or less.

See ARTERY: *Diseases of the Arteries;* AVIATION MEDICINE: *Aeroembolism;* DICUMAROL. D.A.C.

EMBROIDERY, art of ornamenting textiles and other fabrics with needlework. The art is closely related to tapestry work which is, in fact, an intermediate craft between embroidery and weaving. The essential distinction is that whereas embroidery is always worked upon an already woven texture, tapestry is worked directly into the warp, and becomes part of the weaving of the texture. In its crudest form, embroidery is one of the oldest of the decorative arts. It was probably applied to skins before the development of spinning and weaving, and would seem to date from the early use of the needle and thong for the joining together of skin garments. Needlework is mentioned in the book of Exodus (q.v.), and has been discovered on mummy wrappings dating back to the 15th century B.C. The knowledge of artistic embroidery came to Europe from the East. It reached Greece and Rome by way of Phrygia; in Rome the embroiderer was called a *phrygio,* and gold embroidery, *auriphrygium,* from which is derived the English ecclesiastical term orphrey. The embroiderer's art achieved its greatest perfection in Europe in medieval times, and the finest examples of this work were of English origin. One beautiful specimen of medieval embroidery, the Syon Cope, is English work of the 13th century. A work of far greater historical importance, is the famous Bayeux Tapestry (q.v.) which is not a tapestry at all, but embroidery depicting the history of the Norman Conquest of England in 1066.

In embroidery the materials employed are colored worsted yarns called crewels, tapestry wools, embroidery silks, gold and silver threads, spangles, and plates or disks of metal. Portions of feathers, the elytra of beetles, pearls, and precious stones may also be used, but these find their place principally in Oriental embroideries. The fabrics chiefly used are durable types of linen, silks, satins, velvets, and flannels. Small work is done without any special mounting, but for elaborate designs the fabric is fitted and tightly stretched on a frame. The variety of embroidery stitches is considerable. The principal stitches are the stem stitch, the satin stitch, the knotted stitch, the buttonhole or blanket stitch, the chain or tambour stitch, the feather stitch, the cushion or Berlin-work stitch, cross stitch, and needlepoint, all of which may be learned from practical manuals. In framework, "couching" is largely employed; this consists in laying lengths of thread on the surface, and securing them by stitches through the cloth at various points. A distinct type of embroidery consists of appliqué or cut work, in which designs of different materials and colors are cut out and sewed to the surface of the cloth to be ornamented. Inlaid appliqué consists of cutting precisely the same pattern out of two different fab-

Top: Finely embroidered woman's jacket made in England at the turn of the 16th century. Bottom: Intricate and colorful embroidery greatly enhances this 19th-century Austrian peasant dress.

Metropolitan Museum of Art — Rogers Fund

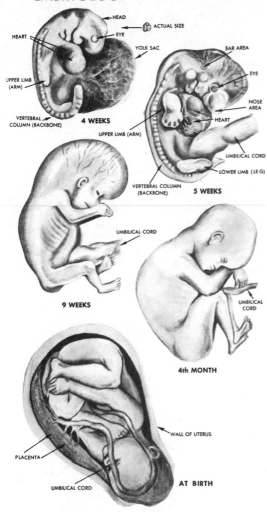

Stages in the development of the human embryo.
TODAY'S HEALTH, published by the
AMERICAN MEDICAL ASSOCIATION

rics, and inserting the one into the cut space in the other.

EMBRYOLOGY, branch of biology dealing with the development of the animal from the fertilized ovum; for the embryology of plants, *see* FERTILIZATION; PLANT MORPHOLOGY; SEED. Embryology includes within its province the development of the egg and embryo and the growth of the larva or fetus (qq.v.). The terms "larva" and "fetus" refer to later stages of development of the embryo.

History. Until the second half of the 18th century, embryology was a matter of speculation rather than of knowledge. One generally accepted theory was that of preformation: the complete animal with all its organs was believed to exist in the germ in miniature, needing only to unfold like a flower. It followed that each germ must contain within itself the germs of all its future descendants, one within another, as in a nest of boxes. Many naturalists believed the germ to be contained in the ovum, the female germ cell, but after the microscope had revealed spermatozoa, the male germ cells, in 1677, a school of so-called spermists advanced the hypothesis that the germ was contained in the spermatozoon. Their drawings show the spermatozoon encasing a minute human figure, called the homunculus.

Little attention was given to the theory, called the theory of epigenesis, that the English physician and anatomist William Harvey (q.v.), discoverer of the circulation of the blood, had stated in 1651. This theory, which had been vaguely expressed much earlier by the Greek philosopher Aristotle (q.v.), held that the specialized structures of the individual develop step by step from unspecialized antecedents in the egg. Proof of this theory was not forthcoming, however, until 1759, when the German anatomist Kaspar Friedrich Wolff (1733–94) reported on his study of the development of the chick in the egg and showed that the organs arise from undifferentiated material. The basic potential nature and organization of the structures of the organism are determined by the genetic constitution of the fertilized egg; *see* HEREDITY. Wolff is called the founder of modern embryology, a title also sometimes given to the Russian naturalist Karl Ernst von Baer (q.v.), who in the 19th century described the principal phases in the development of the chick and pioneered in comparative embryology. A firm basis for the new science was established by the cell theory formulated in 1838 by the German botanist Matthias Jakob Schleiden (q.v.) who stated that all plants and animals are made up of cells. A year later his compatriot, the anatomist and physiologist Theodor Schwann (q.v.), confirmed this theory. In later work these men demonstrated that tissues and organs develop by cell division. *See* CELL.

Much work was done in experimental embryology after the late 19th century in an effort to disclose the factors involved in development. Experimental studies have shown that, although the fertilized egg is only a single cell with no apparent differentiation, it nevertheless has a fundamental organization, so that particular regions of the egg give rise to specific structures. There exist two groups of eggs, known as mosaic and regulative eggs, which differ from one another in the time at which the developmental pattern of the egg becomes fixed. In mosaic eggs, the pattern for future development is firmly established in the cytoplasm either before or at fertilization. Therefore, destroying a given part of a mosaic egg results in the failure of a particular structure or organ to develop. In regulative eggs, the pattern is fixed later at some multicellular stage of development. Such eggs can produce normal embryos despite damage or loss of material before the pattern of organization is irreversibly fixed. Even a single cell derived from a two-, four-, or eight-cell embryo may, in some cases, bring forth an entire organism. Experiments with the regulative eggs of amphibians (see AMPHIBIA), such as the newt or the salamander (qq.v.), have involved grafting or transplanting a portion of one larva to an abnormal location on another larva. When such grafting is done at an early stage of development, cells that ordinarily would give rise to brain tissue may instead differentiate into normal gill tissue. At a later stage, however, grafted tissues follow their normal developmental fate, and bizarre results can be produced. Thus, an eye will develop in the abdominal wall or a leg will appear where a tail ought to be.

Normal Development. Development consists of a series of events beginning with fertilization of the egg. For a description of male and female germ cells, called gametes, and the process of nuclear fusion of these germ cells to produce a zygote, see EGG; FERTILIZATION.

After fertilization, the egg undergoes cell division, or cleavage. Thus, one cell divides into two; the daughter cells, called *blastomeres,* then cleave into four; these cleave into eight, and so on. When the embryo consists of a hundred or more cells it may form a solid mass called a *morula* from its resemblance to a mulberry. In most species the mass then resolves itself into a single layer of cells forming a hollow sphere, the *blastula.* The next step is the formation of a double-walled sac or cup, the *gastrula.* The outer wall is called the *ectoderm,* and the inner wall is the *endoderm.* The endoderm surrounds a new cavity known as the primitive gut. In some cases these two layers are formed by delamination, or splitting, of a mass of cells, but more commonly they are formed by invagination, that is, the pushing in of a portion of the wall of the blastula. In all animals except the simplest, a third layer, the *mesoderm,* develops between the other two layers.

These three layers, known as the primary germ layers, differentiate into analogous organs in all species of animals. The endoderm produces specialized cells in the principal digestive glands and forms the lining of the air passages and of most of the alimentary canal. The mesoderm gives rise to the blood and blood vessels, the connective tissues, the muscles, and usually the reproductive glands and the kidneys. The ectoderm gives rise to the epidermis and derivative structures such as the hair and nails, to the mucous membranes lining the mouth and anus, to the enamel of the teeth, and to the central nervous system.

Embryonic Induction. One of the outstanding achievements in embryology during the 20th century has been the elucidation of some of the factors responsible for morphogenesis, that is, the development of pattern and form, and for differentiation, that is, the development of diversity of cell and tissue types. Through observation and experiment, especially on amphibian embryos, it has been shown that a stimulus emanates from some of the material that invaginates during the process of gastrulation. Those cells that invaginate on what will be the future dorsal side of the embryo have the capacity to induce overlying cells to differentiate into the primary axial organs and associated structures, such as the nervous system, notochord, and muscle segments. If the potentially inducing cells comprising the so-called dorsal lip of the blastopore, which is the opening of the cavity of the gastrula, are prevented from invaginating, the embryo remains alive but will not undergo further differentiation. Conversely, grafting a second dorsal lip to the flank of an embryo induces the formation of a secondary embryo out of tissues that normally would have formed something altogether different. In recent years it has been demonstrated that various chemical substances can imitate in part the stimulus or stimuli that derive from the inducing embryonic tissue.

The importance of environmental factors for normal embryonic development also has been demonstrated in laboratory experiments. It has been found that temperature, radiations, oxygen, inorganic salts, and various organic compounds can affect development, in some cases by interfering with or blocking specific chemical reactions.

Nutrition and Respiration. A large ovum such as that of a bird or reptile (qq.v.) contains abundant yolk, which, with the albuminous white, is sufficient to nourish the embryo until birth. The nutrients in a small ovum, however, are soon used up, and therefore the embryo must be nourished by other means. In many species the embryo is hatched at this point as a larva, a form capable of feeding itself though still lacking some of the organs of the adult form. In viviparous animals, including all mammals except the monotremes (qq.v.), the embryo receives nourishment from the mother by diffusion through specially developed extraembryonic membranes. Marsupial females secrete a nutrient fluid for this purpose from uterine glands; see MARSUPIALS. In most mammals soluble nutrients are supplied to the embryo from the bloodstream of the mother.

Extraembryonic Membranes. In reptiles, birds, and mammals, several types of extraembryonic membrane develop. These membranes serve to protect and to nourish the embryo and to aid in respiratory exchange and excretion. Early in development a sac known as the *amnion* forms around the embryo and becomes filled with the so-called amniotic fluid. Thus, the embryo develops in an aquatic medium that serves to keep it moist, to provide a proper osmotic environment, and to protect it from mechanical shock or injury. Another membrane, the *chorion,* develops around the amnion. In reptiles and birds the chorion underlies the shell membrane; in mammals it lines the uterine wall (*see* UTERUS). The *allantois* develops as a saclike protrusion from the hind gut of the embryo and insinuates itself between the amnion and chorion. In reptiles and birds, the allantois and chorion fuse to form the *chorio-allantoic* membrane. This membrane, which adheres closely to the shell membrane, becomes richly supplied with blood vessels and functions as a respiratory surface for the embryo. The allantois also serves as a repository for nitrogenous wastes.

In mammals the allantois and chorion make intimate connection with the uterine wall at one or more points. Fingerlike projections, known as the *chorionic villi,* protrude into pockets or depressions in the tissue of the uterine wall. Blood vessels from the embryo, which at this stage is called a fetus, develop along the allantoic stalk and become the veins and arteries of the umbilical cord, which suspends the fetus in the amniotic fluid. Branches of the umbilical vessels make their way into the chorionic villi, where they open into elaborate capillary networks. Rich vascular beds develop similarly in the maternal uterine tissue. Thus, the chorion, allantois, and maternal tissues conjoin to form the *placenta,* found in all mammals except the monotremes and most of the marsupials. The uterine tissue involved is called the *decidua,* because it is discarded by the maternal body or torn from it at the birth of the fetus.

In reptiles and birds a yolk sac filled with stored raw material for development is a promi-nent structure in the egg. A yolk sac develops also in mammals, but it is devoid of nutritive material and is present only as a rudimentary structure.

Human Embryology. The human ovum, fertilized high in one of the Fallopian tubes (q.v.), is brushed by the hairlike cilia in the tube toward the uterus, where it becomes implanted, that is, attached to and enclosed by decidual tissue of the uterine lining. Studies of primate embryos indicate that in man as well as in apes, cell multiplication begins during the journey of the ovum through the tube. The age of the youngest human embryos yet studied is estimated at a few days, and at this stage the implanted embryo consists of a hollow sphere, the *blastocyst,* containing a mass of cells, called the *embryonic mass,* attached by a stalk to one side of the encircling membrane. In a blastocyst less than two weeks old and measuring 1 mm in diameter, the microscope revealed chorion, amnion, yolk sac, and distinct germ layers.

In the third week there appears a closed tube in which the brain and spinal cord are to develop. Another tube, folding on itself, is developing into the heart, and at about this stage a portion of the minute yolk sac is enclosed in the body of the embryo to form a part of the embryonic alimentary canal. At the beginning of its fourth week the embryo, now about 4 to 5 mm long, has the rudiments of eyes and ears, and each side of the neck shows four gill clefts. A tail is also present.

Early in the second month the buds of the arms and legs appear. The major internal organs begin to take shape, and in about the sixth week bones and muscles begin to form. By the third month the embryo is recognizable as that of a primate. It has a definite face, with the mouth and nostrils distinct, and the external ears are forming. By the end of the eighth week the tail has usually been incorporated in the body, and in the eleventh or twelfth week the external genitals become evident. The human embryo is especially vulnerable to the damaging effects of X rays, of disease viruses such as measles, and of drugs such as thalidomide, during the fourth to the eighth week of gestation. The damage from these agents can result in the death of the embryo or in the birth of a child with deformed limbs or other abnormalities. By the fourth month an embryo is called a fetus and is clearly recognizable as a human being. For development in the fetal stage, *see* FETUS. For abnormalities due to anomalous development of the embryo, *see* BIRTH DEFECTS; CLEFT PALATE; CLUBFOOT. *See also* MULTIPLE BIRTH; OBSTETRICS.   E.J.B. & J.R.